WORLD POLITICS

TREND AND TRANSFORMATION

Fourth Edition

Charles W. Kegley, Jr. & Eugene R. Wittkopf

University of South Carolina   Louisiana State University

WORLD POLITICS

TREND AND TRANSFORMATION

Fourth Edition

St. Martin's Press
New York

To Suzanne, Debra, and Jonathan

Senior editor: Don Reisman
Managing editor: Patricia Mansfield-Phelan
Project editor: Suzanne Holt
Production supervisor: Katherine Battiste
Art director: Sheree Goodman
Text design: Patrice Fodero
Graphics: TCSystems
Maps: Maryland CartoGraphics, Inc.
Cover design: Patrice Fodero
Cover art: Hothouse Designs, Inc.

Published and distributed outside North America by
THE MACMILLAN PRESS LTD
Houndmills, Basingstoke, Hampshire RG21 2XS and London Companies and representatives
throughout the world.

ISBN 0-333-58891-6

A catalog record for this book is available from the British Library.

ACKNOWLEDGMENTS

Acknowledgments and copyrights are on page 589, which constitutes an extension of the copyright
page. Acknowledgments for figures and maps are cited below art.

PREFACE

. . .

Since 1989 the world has witnessed changes so dramatic as to be virtually unimaginable to even the most prescient observers of world politics. The end of the Cold War, the third great-power conflict of the twentieth century, is propelling a transformation of world politics whose scope and dimensions continue to unfold daily. The end of Soviet-American competition has marked the end of bipolarity, the disintegration of the Soviet external empire and the Soviet Union itself, the emergence of the United States as the world's only superpower, and the triumph of liberalism and democratic capitalism over competing ideologies. In this new world order, nuclear weapons—so dominant a part of world politics since World War II—have assumed a diminished role; economic power increasingly challenges military power as an instrument of statecraft; and new centers of power in Europe and Asia portend the emergence of a multipolar world. War and other forms of violence inspired by ethnic and nationalist animosities long suppressed by the Cold War have also erupted with increasing frequency and ferocity.

Understanding the dramatic changes unleashed by the end of the Cold War poses an enormous challenge to scholarship. It requires that we confront not only the evidence of change but also of continuity in world politics, and it demands that we probe seriously the theoretical underpinnings of our knowledge, asking not only what is new in world politics but also how we know what we know about the forces of change and continuity in the world around us.

World Politics: Trend and Transformation is a comprehensive treatment of the theory and evidence that inform our understanding of the pattern of relations among global actors, the historical developments that underlie them, and how they have been affected by the pace of change in today's world.

The book is divided into five parts. Part I explains the macro, or holistic, view of world politics that frames the book's analyses and focuses on the contending analytic perspectives that scholars and policymakers have developed to comprehend the kaleidoscopic trends and transformations occurring in world politics. We draw on these perspectives throughout the remainder of the book, using them to enhance an understanding of contemporary world politics.

Part II examines the principal actors on the world stage. Nation-states necessarily command particular attention, and we examine the nature of their decision-making processes, world views, national capabilities, and position in the international hierarchy, all of which propel conflict in world politics. Great-power rivalries, as played out in the three global conflicts of the twentieth century and the North-South conflict between the world's rich and poor nations since World War II, are given particular attention. We also examine the role of international institutions and other nonstate actors in world politics, inquiring into their capacity not only to *be shaped* but also *to shape t*he contours of contemporary world politics.

Parts III and IV probe the nature of transnational policy issues. Issues comprising the *low politics* of material well-being are examined in Part III. Here we direct attention to the nature of the world political economy, the forces promoting conflict and cooperation within it, and developments in demography, the environment, and resources as they relate to contemporary world politics. Although matters of low politics have long animated the global agenda, many analysts now believe that increasingly they will be the dominant issues underlying power and contention in world politics.

In Part IV we examine the *high politics* of peace and security: the nature of power and influence, the role of military force in world politics, and the causes and control of war and other forms of violence. These, of course, are the traditional issues in world politics, and while the end of the Cold War may have changed their character, it has not diminished the compelling need to understand them.

We conclude *World Politics: Trend and Transformation* in Part V, where we ask how the underlying tendencies in contemporary world politics enable us to anticipate future trends. Our concern is how today's world will affect tomorrow's world, and with the questions that prevailing developments raise about the human prospect on the threshold of the twenty-first century.

Readers familiar with the previous edition of the book, published in 1989, will quickly recognize that its structure and organization remain intact, but the end of the Cold War and the disintegration of the Soviet Union caused us to revisit and rethink every chapter, every paragraph, indeed, every sentence in the book. We also seized this opportunity simultaneously to elaborate the book's theoretical content and to enhance its pedagogical effectiveness. The result is a text completely revised in every way from beginning to end.

Several examples illustrate how thoroughly this edition has been revised:

- The causes and consequences of World Wars I and II are given detailed treatment for the first time. This permits the Cold War to be examined not as an isolated historical period but as the most recent instance of great-power conflict in the twentieth century.

- The institutional characteristics of the European Community (EC) and its growing importance as a nonstate actor are fully developed for the first time.

- The regionalization of the world political economy, as manifested in transnational capital flows and the emergence of regional monetary and trade blocs, is given greatly expanded coverage.

- Neoliberal institutionalism is elaborated as the theoretical umbrella that gives meaning to the European Community and related developments in the world political economy.

- Hegemonic stability theory and the contribution of classical and structural realism to the forces that inhibit international cooperation are given new treatment. Both theoretical thrusts are used to explain the importance of the relative decline of U.S. power and how it relates to the regionalization of the world political economy and the emergent multipolar international political system.

- Just war theory is treated for the first time, and recent developments in the international law of war are emphasized.

- Global warming and related environmental issues are treated more completely than before.

- The Persian Gulf War and its "lessons" as applied to both high and low politics are examined.

- Trends toward democratization of the world and their implications are examined.

- The rise of ethnic nationalism as a disintegrative force and potential source of international conflict is treated systematically.

- Nearly two dozen maps and cartograms have been added, all designed to enhance the clarity of the text and contribute to readers' geographic literacy.

The list of those to whom we are indebted for their contributions of time and insight to this book continues to grow. In addition to those who have helped so generously in the past, we are especially pleased to acknowledge the contributions to this edition: Mark N. Crislip, Donald L. Hafner, Cynthia D. Hall, Steven W. Hook, Jeffrey Morton, Michael Murdoch, Christina Payne, Clayton Turner, Gregory A. Raymond, Philip Rogers, Philip A. Schrodt, Linda S. Schwartz, and Randolph M. Siverson. The many professional staff members at St. Martin's Press contributed importantly to the final production of the book. Suzanne Holt, our always pleasant project editor, eased the strains of final production measurably, and Don Reisman, our editor and friend, was unfailing in his support and encouragement throughout a project that proved much longer and more arduous than any of us anticipated when we began.

Charles W. Kegley, Jr.
Eugene R. Wittkopf

About the Authors

CHARLES W. KEGLEY, JR., received his doctorate from Syracuse University. Currently, he is Pearce Professor of international relations at the University of South Carolina and president of the International Studies Association. Kegley has held visiting professorships at Georgetown University, the University of Texas, and Rutgers University. He is the editor of *International Terrorism: Characteristics, Causes, Controls* (St. Martin's Press, 1990) and *The Long Postwar Peace* (HarperCollins, 1991). With Gregory A. Raymond, Kegley is the coauthor of *When Trust Breaks Down: Questioning the Morality of Nuclear Deterrence* (University of South Carolina, 1990).

EUGENE R. WITTKOPF received his doctorate from Syracuse University. He is professor of political science at Louisiana State University. Wittkopf is a past president of the Florida Political Science Association and of the International Studies Association/South. He has also held appointments at the University of Florida and the University of North Carolina at Chapel Hill. Wittkopf is the author of *Faces of Internationalism: Public Opinion and American Foreign Policy* (Duke University, 1990).

Together, Kegley and Wittkopf have coauthored and edited several texts and readers for St. Martin's Press, including *The Future of American Foreign Policy* (1992); *American Foreign Policy: Pattern and Process*, fourth edition (1991); *The Nuclear Reader: Strategy, Weapons, War*, second edition (1989); and *Domestic Sources of American Foreign Policy* (1988). They are also the coeditors of *The Global Agenda: Issues and Perspectives*, third edition (McGraw-Hill, 1992).

SUMMARY TABLE OF CONTENTS

• • •

PREFACE   v

MAPS   xxv

PART I   CHANGE AND TRANSFORMATION IN WORLD POLITICS   1

CHAPTER 1   TREND AND TRANSFORMATION IN WORLD POLITICS:
A THEMATIC INTRODUCTION   3

CHAPTER 2   THE STUDY OF WORLD POLITICS: RIVAL PERSPECTIVES
IN CHANGING CONTEXTS   10

PART II   RELATIONS AMONG GLOBAL ACTORS   41

CHAPTER 3   FOREIGN POLICY DECISION MAKING: COPING
WITH INTERNATIONAL CIRCUMSTANCES   43

CHAPTER 4   GREAT-POWER RIVALRY IN CONTEMPORARY WORLD POLITICS   71

CHAPTER 5   THE NORTH-SOUTH CONFLICT: ROOTS AND CONSEQUENCES
OF GLOBAL INEQUALITIES   115

CHAPTER 6   NONSTATE ACTORS IN WORLD POLITICS: THE ROLE
OF INTERNATIONAL ORGANIZATIONS AND MULTINATIONAL
CORPORATIONS   154

PART III   LOW POLITICS: TRANSNATIONAL POLICY ISSUES   207

CHAPTER 7   THE TRANSFORMATION OF THE WORLD POLITICAL ECONOMY:
PERSPECTIVES FROM THE FIRST WORLD   209

CHAPTER 8   THE TRANSFORMATION OF THE WORLD POLITICAL ECONOMY:
PERSPECTIVES FROM THE THIRD WORLD   262

CHAPTER 9   THE GLOBAL COMMONS: DEMOGRAPHY AND THE
ENVIRONMENT IN WORLD POLITICS   297

CHAPTER 10 OIL, ENERGY, AND RESOURCE POWER   341

PART IV   HIGH POLITICS: NATIONAL SECURITY, ARMS,
AND WAR   387

CHAPTER 11 THE QUEST FOR NATIONAL SECURITY: TRENDS
IN MILITARY CAPABILITIES   389

CHAPTER 12 RESORT TO FORCE: ARMED CONFLICT AND VIOLENCE
IN WORLD POLITICS   436

CHAPTER 13 MILITARY PATHS TO PEACE: ALLIANCES, THE BALANCE
OF POWER, AND ARMS CONTROL   466

CHAPTER 14 POLITICAL PATHS TO PEACE: INTERNATIONAL LAW,
ORGANIZATION, AND INTEGRATION   498

PART V   TOWARD THE TWENTY-FIRST CENTURY   533

CHAPTER 15 THE GLOBAL PREDICAMENT: TWELVE QUESTIONS FOR A
TRANSFORMING WORLD   535

REFERENCES   546

GLOSSARY   575

INDEX   591

CONTENTS

. . .

PREFACE   v

ABOUT THE AUTHORS   viii

MAPS   xxv

PART I   CHANGE AND TRANSFORMATION IN WORLD POLITICS   1

CHAPTER 1   TREND AND TRANSFORMATION IN WORLD POLITICS:
A THEMATIC INTRODUCTION   3

Continuity and Change in World Politics   4
Predicting the Problematic Future   7
Organizing Inquiry: A Framework for Analysis   7
Suggested Readings   8

CHAPTER 2   THE STUDY OF WORLD POLITICS: RIVAL PERSPECTIVES IN
CHANGING CONTEXTS   10

Image and Reality in World Politics   11
    Images of Reality   16
        THE SOURCES OF IMAGES   16
        THE NATURE OF IMAGES   16
        THE ROLE OF IMAGES IN INTERNATIONAL POLITICS   17
    Sources of Image Change   18

Understanding World Politics: The Elusive Quest for Theory   18

  Current History   19

  Political Idealism   20

    THE IDEALIST WORLD VIEW   20
    THE IDEALIST REFORM PROGRAM   21

  Political Realism   22

    THE REALIST WORLD VIEW   22
    REALISM'S CONTINUING RELEVANCE   25

  The Behavioral Approach   25

    SCIENCE VERSUS TRADITIONALISM   25
    A SCIENCE OF INTERNATIONAL POLITICS?   26
    POSTBEHAVIORALISM   27

  Extending Realism: The Neorealist Structural Approach   28

    A SYSTEMS THEORY OF INTERNATIONAL POLITICS   28
    IMPLICATIONS OF SYSTEMIC CONSTRAINTS   29

  Neoliberal Institutionalism   30

    COMPLEX INTERDEPENDENCE AS A WORLD VIEW   31
    INTERNATIONAL REGIMES   32
    HEGEMONIC STABILITY THEORY   33

International Politics in a World of Change   34

  Rival Theories and Evidence   36

    LONG-CYCLE THEORY   36
    WORLD SYSTEM THEORY   36
    DEPENDENCY THEORY   36
    COMPARATIVE FOREIGN POLICY   36

  Levels of Analysis   37

World Politics: The Analytical Challenge   38

Suggested Readings   38

PART II   RELATIONS AMONG GLOBAL ACTORS   **41**

  CHAPTER 3 FOREIGN POLICY DECISION MAKING: COPING WITH
           INTERNATIONAL CIRCUMSTANCES   43

    The Unitary Actor and Rational Decision Making   44

      States as Unitary Actors   44
      Policy Making as Rational Choice   45
      Impediments to Rational Choice   47

The Bureaucratic Politics of Foreign Policy Decision Making   49

Foreign Policy–making Organizations   50
Bureaucracy, Efficiency, and Rationality   50

    THE LIMITS OF BUREAUCRATIC ORGANIZATION   50
    ATTRIBUTES OF BUREAUCRATIC BEHAVIOR   53
    THE CONSEQUENCES OF BUREAUCRATIC POLICY MAKING   54

The Role of Leaders in Foreign Policy Decision Making   56

Leaders as Makers and Movers of World History   56
Factors Affecting Leaders' Capacity to Lead   57
Limits to the Hero-in-History Model   59

Other Determinants of Foreign Policy Behavior   60

Geopolitics   61
Military Capabilities   62
Economic Development   63
Type of Government   64

    DEMOCRACIES' FOREIGN POLICY PERFORMANCE   65
    CONSEQUENCES OF THE SPREAD OF DEMOCRACY   66

Constraints on Foreign Policy Making in a Transforming World:
Problems and Prospects   69
Suggested Readings   70

CHAPTER 4   GREAT-POWER RIVALRY IN CONTEMPORARY WORLD POLITICS   71

The Quest for Great-Power Hegemony   72
The First World War   73

The Causes of World War I   74

    STRUCTURALISM   74
    RATIONAL CHOICE   75
    OTHER EXPLANATIONS   76

The Consequences of World War I   77

The Second World War   79

The Causes of World War II   79

    PROXIMATE CAUSES   80
    UNDERLYING CAUSES   81

The Consequences of World War II   83

The Cold War   85

The Causes of the Cold War   86

    A CONFLICT OF INTERESTS   86
    IDEOLOGICAL INCOMPATIBILITIES   86

MISPERCEPTIONS   88
OTHER CONTRIBUTING FACTORS   90

The Cold War's Phases and Character   90

WARY FRIENDSHIP, BELLIGERENCE, AND ACCOMMODATION,
1945–1962   93
PEACEFUL COEXISTENCE AND DÉTENTE, 1963–1978   96
RENEWED CONFRONTATION, RENEWED DIALOGUE, 1979–1991   101
THE END OF THE COLD WAR   103
CAUSES OF THE "LONG PEACE"   108

Great-Power Rivalry in the Post–Cold War World   111
Suggested Readings   114

CHAPTER 5   THE NORTH-SOUTH CONFLICT: ROOTS AND CONSEQUENCES
             OF GLOBAL INEQUALITIES   115

The Rise and Fall of European Empires   117

The Emergence of the Modern State System   117
The First Wave of European Imperialism   120
The Second Wave of European Imperialism   121

ECONOMIC EXPLANATIONS OF THE NEW IMPERIALISM   123
POLITICAL EXPLANATIONS OF THE NEW IMPERIALISM   124

Colonialism and Self-Determination in the
Interwar Period   125
The End of Empire   126

Profiles and Projections: Global Disparities in Income and Wealth 127

Third World Diversity   127

LEAST DEVELOPED COUNTRIES   130
OIL-EXPORTING COUNTRIES   130
NEWLY INDUSTRIALIZED COUNTRIES   131

Measuring Economic Development and Standards
of Living   132
Impediments to Growth in a Typical Developing
Country   138
HIGH POPULATION GROWTH   138
LOW LEVELS OF INCOME   139
TECHNOLOGICAL DEPENDENCE   139
DUALISM IN DEVELOPING SOCIETIES   140

Dominance and Dependence in International
Economic Relations   141
CONVENTIONAL THEORY   142

DEPENDENCY THEORY 142
WORLD-SYSTEM THEORY 144

*Beyond Dependence: The Foreign Policy Goals of Third
World Nations* 145

A New International Economic Order 145
Political Autonomy 147
Nonalignment 148
Military Might 149

The End of Third Worldism? 152
Suggested Readings 153

CHAPTER 6 NONSTATE ACTORS IN WORLD POLITICS: THE ROLE OF
INTERNATIONAL ORGANIZATIONS AND
MULTINATIONAL CORPORATIONS 154

The Growth of International Organizations 155

International Intergovernmental Organizations 156
International Nongovernmental Organizations 158
International Organizations and the Politics
of Peace and Security 158

The United Nations: Between East and West, North and South 159

Evolving Political Strategies in the Security Council and
the General Assembly 160

THE SECURITY COUNCIL AND THE UNANIMITY RULE 161
THE GENERAL ASSEMBLY AND MAJORITY RULE 162

Changing Superpower Fortunes: The Special Case
of the United States 166

CONTROL OF UN PEACEKEEPING OPERATIONS 166
CONTROL OF UN PURSE STRINGS 168
MEMBERSHIP IN AFFILIATED UN AGENCIES 172

The Third World: From Background to Center Stage 174
The United Nations beyond the Cold War 176

The European Community and Other Regional Organizations 176

The European Community 177

ORGANIZATIONAL COMPONENTS AND DECISION-MAKING
PROCEDURES 177
SUPRANATIONALISM OR POOLED SOVEREIGNTY? 179
EUROPE: AN ECONOMIC GIANT 183
EUROPE: A POLITICAL DWARF AND MILITARY WORM? 185

Other Regional Organizations 187

The Role of Multinational Corporations   189

The Global Reach and Economic Power of
Multinational Corporations   191

    PATTERNS OF FOREIGN DIRECT INVESTMENT   193

Impact on Home and Host Nations   198
Politics and Multinational Corporations   200
Controlling Multinational Corporations   201

*Nonstate Actors, International Regimes, and the Transformation
of World Politics*   203
Suggested Readings   204

PART III   LOW POLITICS: TRANSNATIONAL POLICY ISSUES   **207**

CHAPTER 7   THE TRANSFORMATION OF THE WORLD POLITICAL ECONOMY:
PERSPECTIVES FROM THE FIRST WORLD   209

National Economies in the World Political Economy   210

Open versus Closed Economies   211
Realism, Relative Gains, and International Cooperation   213
Hegemony and Hegemonic Stability   214

    HEGEMONS' ROLES, RESPONSIBILITIES, AND BENEFITS   214
    INTERNATIONAL STABILITY AND HEGEMONIC DECLINE   216

The Transformation of the International Monetary Regime   218

The U.S. Role in the Bretton Woods Regime   219

    UNCHALLENGED HEGEMONY   219
    HEGEMONY UNDER STRESS   222
    HEGEMONY IN DECLINE   224

From Hegemony toward Multilateral Management   225

    THE OPEC DECADE   225
    THE AFTERMATH OF THE OPEC DECADE   227
    MACROECONOMIC POLICY COORDINATION   229

Toward a Regionalized Monetary Arrangement   230

Trade Strategies in an Interdependent World   231

Free Trade and Protectionism   232

    COMPARATIVE ADVANTAGE   232
    NEOMERCANTILISM   233
    STRATEGIC TRADE   238

Free Trade and Hegemonic Decline   239

The Transformation of the International Trade Regime   241

Creating the Liberal Trade Regime: America's
Leadership Role   241

    THE U.S. ROLE IN THE BRETTON WOODS PERIOD   243
    THE REGIME UNDER STRESS   245

Challenges to American Leadership and the Liberal
Trade Regime   245

    *THE TOKYO ROUND OF MULTILATERAL
    TRADE NEGOTIATIONS*   245
    *THE URUGUAY ROUND OF MULTILATERAL
    TRADE NEGOTIATIONS*   246

From Multilateralism to Regionalism   250

From Socialism to Capitalism   251

The End of Empire   253
East-West Commercial Ties in
Historical Perspective   256

    THE ISOLATION OF EAST FROM WEST   256
    FROM DÉTENTE TO RENEWED HOSTILITY   256

Integrating the Socialist Economies into
the World Political Economy   258

The Turbulent 1990s: Triumph and Trouble   260
Suggested Readings   261

CHAPTER 8   THE TRANSFORMATION OF THE WORLD POLITICAL ECONOMY:
PERSPECTIVES FROM THE THIRD WORLD   262

The New Climate for Economic Development   263
The North-South Dialogue: A Historical Overview   264

The New International Economic Order   264
The Demise of the NIEO   267

The Political Economy of North-South Relations   270

Exporters of Primary Products and
Manufactured Goods   271

    A NEW INTERNATIONAL DIVISION OF LABOR?   271
    GROWTH STRATEGIES   273
    PREFERENTIAL TRADE   273

Commodity Exports and the Terms of Trade   275

    THE TERMS OF TRADE   276
    PRICE STABILIZATION   277

Development Finance 279
    THE FORM AND PURPOSES OF FOREIGN AID 280
    THE VOLUME AND VALUE OF FOREIGN AID 280
    CONDITIONALITY 284
Engines of Growth 286
    THE BENEFITS OF MULTINATIONAL
    CORPORATIONS 286
    THE COSTS OF MULTINATIONAL CORPORATIONS 287
Third World Debt and the Management of Interdependence 289
Averting Disaster 290
The Search for Long-term Solutions 291
The Debt Decade in Retrospect 293
North-South Relations in the 1990s 295
Suggested Readings 295

CHAPTER 9   THE GLOBAL COMMONS: DEMOGRAPHY AND THE
    ENVIRONMENT IN WORLD POLITICS 297

Global Demographic Patterns and Trends 299
Factors Affecting National and Regional
Variations in Population Growth 301
    FERTILITY RATES 303
    POPULATION MOMENTUM 304
    THE DEMOGRAPHIC TRANSITION THEORY 307
Population Projections 309
    UNCERTAIN DEATHRATES 309
    UNCERTAIN BIRTHRATES 310
Global Patterns of Emigration and Immigration 311
    CAUSES OF MIGRATION 312
    CONSEQUENCES OF MIGRATION 312
Optimists, Pessimists, and Public Policy 315
Correlates of Demographic Changes 317
The Impact of Demographic Trends on
National Security 317
The Impact of Demographic Trends on
Economic Development 318
    THE THIRD WORLD 319
    THE FIRST WORLD 321

The Impact of Demographic Trends on Global
Food Security   323
   TRENDS IN AGRICULTURAL PRODUCTIVITY   323
   FOOD SECURITY   324

The Impact of Demographic Trends on the
Global Commons   328
   THE THIRD WORLD   328
   THE FIRST WORLD   329
   MILITARY PREPAREDNESS AND WAR   330
   GLOBAL WARMING   330

Toward a Managed Commons Arrangement   334

The Prospects for International Cooperation   334
   COPING WITH OZONE DEPLETION   335
   COPING WITH GLOBAL WARMING   337

The Freedom of the Commons   339
Suggested Readings   339

Chapter 10 Oil, Energy, and Resource Power   341

The Political Economy of Oil: The Making of the OPEC Decade 342

Global Patterns of Energy Consumption   342

The Development of Fossil Fuel Dependence   344
   THE DEVELOPMENT AND IMPACT OF INEXPENSIVE OIL 344
   THE ROLE OF THE MAJORS   347

The Rise of OPEC   347
The U.S. Role in Shaping the OPEC Decade   349

The Political Economy of Oil: The Unmaking of the OPEC Decade 350

Consumption: The Changing Demand Picture   351
Production: The Changing Supply Picture   353

The Political Economy of Oil: The Shape of the Future   354

OPEC's Changing Fortunes   354
Oil Supply and Demand   355
   OIL RESERVES   355
   THIRD WORLD DEMAND   355
   NON-OPEC PRODUCTION   357
   SOVIET ENERGY PRODUCTION   358

U.S. Oil Import Vulnerability and Dependence   359

Oil and National Security   360

   Oil and the Persian Gulf War   360
   The Emerging Security Threat   362
   Ensuring Energy Security   364
   Oil and the Middle East in the New World Order   366

Alternative Energy Sources   367

   Coal   369
   Natural Gas   369
   Hydropower   370
   Nuclear Energy   370

On the (Dis)utility of Resource Power   373

   Resource Dependence and Commodity Power   373

      ECONOMIC FACTORS   375
      POLITICAL FACTORS   376

Economic Sanctions as Instruments of Foreign Policy   378

   Cold War Competition   378

      CUBA   378
      THE SOVIET UNION AND AFGHANISTAN   379
      THE SOVIET UNION AND POLAND   379

   South Africa and *Apartheid*   380
   Iraq and the Crisis over Kuwait   381
   Why Sanction?   382

Toward the Future   384
Suggested Readings   385

PART IV   HIGH POLITICS: NATIONAL SECURITY, ARMS,
                AND WAR   **387**

CHAPTER 11 THE QUEST FOR NATIONAL SECURITY: TRENDS IN MILITARY
                CAPABILITIES   389

The Security Dilemma   390
Power in International Politics   391

   The Elements of National Power   392
   Inferring Power from Capabilities   393
   The Changing Nature of World Power   394

The Quest for Military Capabilities   395

   Trends in Military Spending   395

Trends in Military Capabilities 396
    TRENDS IN THE ARMS TRADE 397
    TRENDS IN WEAPONS TECHNOLOGY 402

The Proliferation Problem 406
    BALLISTIC MISSILES AND UNCONVENTIONAL WEAPONS 406
    NUCLEAR WEAPONS 407

The Social and Economic Consequences of Military Spending 411
    MILITARY SPENDING AND SOCIAL PRIORITIES 411
    MILITARY SPENDING AND ECONOMIC GROWTH 415

Strategic Doctrine during the Cold War and Beyond 419
    Coercive Diplomacy, 1945–1962 419
    Mutual Deterrence, 1962–1983 420
        MUTUAL ASSURED DESTRUCTION 421
        NUCLEAR UTILIZATION THEORY 422

    From Offense to Defense, 1983–? 423
    The New Strategic Balance 424
    U.S.-Soviet Strategic Competition: Retrospect
    and Prospect 425

Deterrence after the Cold War 428
    U.S. Strategy in the New World Order 430
    Russian Strategy in the New World Order 431

Escaping the Security Dilemma? 433
Suggested Readings 435

CHAPTER 12 RESORT TO FORCE: ARMED CONFLICT AND VIOLENCE
    IN WORLD POLITICS 436

The Frequency of War 436
The Nature of War 438
    The Destructiveness of War 439
    Weapons and the Obsolescence of Great-Power War? 440

The Causes of War: Contending Perspectives 442
    War and Human Nature 442
    Internal Characteristics and War Involvement 443
        DURATION OF INDEPENDENCE 444
        NATIONAL POVERTY 444
        POWER TRANSITIONS 444
        MILITARIZATION 445

ECONOMIC SYSTEM	446
TYPE OF GOVERNMENT	447
NATIONALISM	449
Cycles of War and Peace	451
DOES VIOLENCE BREED VIOLENCE?	451
CYCLICAL THEORIES	451
Other Modes of Violence in World Politics	453
Crisis, Coercive Diplomacy, and Intervention	453
Low-Intensity Conflict	456
Civil War	457
CAUSES OF CIVIL WAR	459
CIVIL WAR AND INTERVENTION	460
CIVIL STRIFE AND EXTERNAL AGGRESSION	460
Terrorism	462
The Human Tragedy of Violent Conflict	464
Suggested Readings	465
CHAPTER 13 MILITARY PATHS TO PEACE: ALLIANCES, THE BALANCE OF POWER, AND ARMS CONTROL	466
Alliances	466
Alliances in World Politics: Rival Theories	467
THE ADVANTAGES OF ALLIANCE	467
THE DISADVANTAGES OF ALLIANCE	468
THE DANGERS OF ALLIANCE	468
Alliances in the Realist and Idealist Images	470
The Balance of Power	470
Assumptions of Balance-of-Power Theory	470
THE BALANCE PROCESS	471
THE BREAKDOWN OF POWER BALANCES	473
COLLECTIVE SECURITY VERSUS POWER BALANCES	474
THE REVIVAL OF BALANCE-OF-POWER POLITICS	474
Post–World War II Models of the Balance of Power	475
UNIPOLARITY	475
BIPOLARITY	475
BIPOLYCENTRISM	476
MULTIPOLARITY	479
Polarity and Peace?	479
UNIPOLARITY AND PEACE	480
BIPOLARITY AND PEACE	480
MULTIPOLARITY AND PEACE	481

A Multipolar Future   482

Disarmament and Arms Control   482

Controlling Weapons Proliferation   482
The Disarmament and Arms Control Record   484
Controlling Nuclear Arms: Superpower Agreements   487

SALT   490
START   490
THE POST–COLD WAR DISARMAMENT RACE   491

The Problematic Future of Arms Control   493

In Search of Peace   496
Suggested Readings   497

CHAPTER 14 POLITICAL PATHS TO PEACE: INTERNATIONAL
LAW, ORGANIZATION, AND INTEGRATION   498

International Law and World Order   498

Law at the International Level: Concepts and Principles   499
PRINCIPLES OF INTERNATIONAL LAW   499
PROCEDURES FOR DISPUTE SETTLEMENT   501

The Structural Limitations of the International
Legal System   501
The Relevance of International Law   503
The Legal Control of Warfare   505

THE JUST WAR DOCTRINE   506
THE EVOLVING LAWS OF WARFARE   507

Law's Contribution to Peace   510

THE WORLD COURT   511
INTERNATIONAL LAW AFTER THE COLD WAR   512

International Organization and World Order   512

The United Nations and the Preservation of Peace   513

COLLECTIVE SECURITY   513
FROM COLLECTIVE SECURITY TO PEACEKEEPING   514
THE CHANGING ROLE OF THE SECRETARY GENERAL   515
COLD WAR OBSTACLES TO CONFLICT PREVENTION   520
THE UNITED NATIONS AFTER THE COLD WAR   521

Regional Security Organizations and
Conflict Management   523

*Political Integration: The Functional and Neofunctional Paths
to Peace*   524

World Federalism   525
Functionalism   525

Neofunctionalism   527
    THE EUROPEAN EXPERIENCE   528
    THE PRECONDITIONS FOR REGIONAL INTEGRATION   529
Political Disintegration   529
Law, Organization, and World Order   530
Suggested Readings   531

PART V   TOWARD THE TWENTY-FIRST CENTURY   **533**

CHAPTER 15 THE GLOBAL PREDICAMENT: TWELVE QUESTIONS FOR A
TRANSFORMING WORLD   535

  1. *Are Nation-States Obsolete?*   535
  2. *Is Interdependence a Cure or a Curse?*   536
  3. *What Is the "National Interest"?*   537
  4. *Are Technological Innovations a Blessing or a Burden?*   537
  5. *Of What Value Is Military Power?*   538
  6. *Is War Obsolete?*   539
  7. *The End of Empire?*   539
  8. *What Price Preeminence?*   540
  9. *Is the World Preparing for the Wrong War?*   540
10. *What Is Human Well-Being?*   541
11. *The End of History?*   542
12. *A Reordered Global Agenda?*   543

A New World Order?   544
Suggested Readings   545

  REFERENCES   546

  GLOSSARY   575

  INDEX   590

MAPS

. . .

Political Map of the World   xxvi

Map 2.1   World Political Map: Robinson Projection   12

Map 2.2   World Political Map: Mercator Projection   13

Map 2.3   World Political Map: Peters Projection   14

Map 2.4   World Political Relations, 1991: Polar Projection   15

Map 4.1   Territorial Changes in Europe Following World War I   78

Map 4.2   Territorial Changes in Europe Following World War II   84

Map 4.3   The West's Perception of Soviet and Communist Expansionism Worldwide at the Beginning of the Cold War (1948–1952)   91

Map 4.4   The New Eurasian Landscape, 1992   107

Map 5.1   The Imperial Powers, circa 1914   122

Map 5.2   Physical Quality of Life Index (PQLI) Map of the World   137

Map 6.1   Europe and the European Community   184

Map 9.1   Patterns of Emigration and Immigration, 1985–2000   313

Map 10.1   Major Middle East Oil Fields and Pipelines, circa 1987   363

Map 10.2   Soviet and American Military Presence in the Middle East, circa 1989   365

Map 10.3   Main Oil Trade Movements, 1990   366

Map 11.1   The Spread of Nuclear Weapons   408

Map 12.1   Freedom Spreads: The Diffusion of Democratic Governance, December 31, 1991   448

Map 12.2   The Locus of War, 1990   461

Map 14.1   UN Peacekeeping Forces and Observer Missions, 1948–1992   519

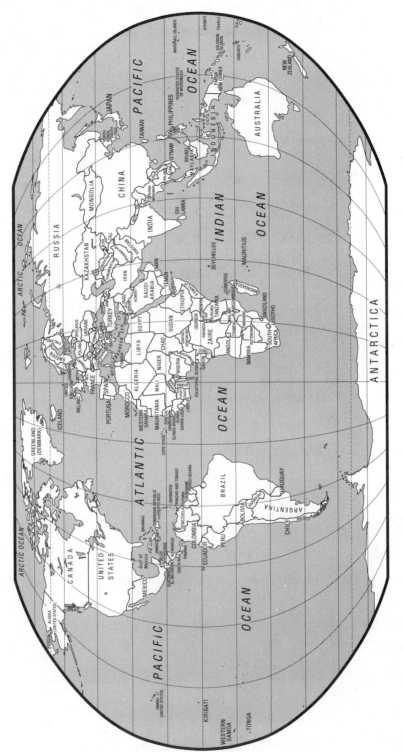

Political Map of the World

Part I

Change and Transformation in World Politics

. . .

1.
Trend and Transformation in World Politics:
A Thematic Introduction

2.
The Study of World Politics: Rival Perspectives in
Changing Contexts

CHAPTER 1

· · ·

TREND AND TRANSFORMATION IN WORLD POLITICS: A THEMATIC INTRODUCTION

· · ·

Revolutionary and astounding, the great events of 1991 changed the world. . . . The year 1991 will now enter the political vocabulary—like 1917 and 1918, those other years of revolution and the fall of empires. But the transformation of the past year took place—blessedly—in a time of peace among the leading powers. Never before has an empire dissolved as quickly or with as little violence.

The Washington Post, January 1, 1992

We [are] at a dramatic and deeply promising time in our history, and in the history of man on earth. For the past twelve months, the world has known changes of almost biblical proportions.

George Bush,
U.S. President, 1992

The spinning sphere we call earth is a planet in space approximately 8,000 miles in diameter and 25,000 miles in circumference. It is at least 4.5 billion years old. In the course of its evolution, it has constantly changed. Only in the last 3 billion years of its existence, for instance, can we speak of the earth as possessing a biosphere—a system of life and living organisms. And a sociosphere—a system of interacting human beings—is, since the planet's origins, a relatively recent development. A cosmic calendar would tell us that the drama of human history commenced only in the last 340,000 years (Childe, 1962). Humankind has inhabited the earth's biosphere for merely $^1/_{1,000}$th of its existence, and only for the past 5,000 years or so can we speak of a record of human history.

Ever since Homo sapiens first began to roam the some 200 million square miles of the earth's surface, human behavior has transformed the earth's terrestrial habitat. In the earth's ecosphere, the natural environment in which humans live, the quality of life has been influenced by the ways that humans have organized themselves politically for making decisions and managing disputes, how they have extracted resources from the earth to sustain and enhance life, and how they have exchanged and transferred

· · ·

those resources. And the technologies they have developed to make weapons have affected their capacity to defend themselves from attack and to destroy others.

Although the modes of human behavior that change global conditions are relentlessly varied, they are not random. Since antiquity, *patterns* of political, economic, and social behaviors are discernible. These regularities make it meaningful to talk about characteristic ways in which people act toward one another. To understand contemporary world politics, therefore, we must look for commonalities in past patterns of human and national interaction.

Today the world stands on the threshold of a new era. It has witnessed in the space of a few short years an enormous tide of change—so enormous, in fact, that historical continuities are sometimes obscured. The end of the Cold War signals the dawning of a new day. For nearly fifty years the Cold War, a conflict between the United States and the Soviet Union coloring virtually every dimension of political, economic, and social life, was the dominant force in world politics. Now the Cold War is over. Its end began in 1989 with the destruction of the Berlin Wall, a barricade to the free movement of people and ideas that symbolized the division of the world between East and West. Today the Berlin Wall is history, the Soviet Union has disintegrated, Germany is united, communism is in retreat, and the forces of peace and democracy are on the march throughout the world.

How can we best understand these political convulsions and others in the world that engulf us almost daily? How can we anticipate their significance for the future? To begin, we must heed philosopher George Santayana's warning that "Those who cannot remember the past are condemned to repeat it." As Winston Churchill once remarked, "The farther backward you look, the farther forward you are likely to see." We must judge today's dramatic changes from a long-term perspective that brings into view both the extent of change and the force of continuity, both the hopes for lasting order and the entrenched pressures that threaten to disrupt it.

To explore world politics, then, we must examine the ways in which the contemporary international system has changed and the ways in which its fundamental characteristics have resisted change. What do recurrent historical practices, and deviations from them, tell us about the current state of world politics? What are the implications of the dramatic recent changes in world politics that have sent shock waves throughout the world? Are these revolutionary changes symbolic of an earthquake in world affairs, setting the stage for a truly new world order? Or will these dramatic developments prove temporary, mere spikes on the seismograph of history without lasting impact? These are among the principal questions we address in *World Politics: Trend and Transformation*.

CONTINUITY AND CHANGE IN WORLD POLITICS . . . .

Every historical period is marked to some extent by change, but the period we are in now is different. The pace of change has seemingly been more rapid and the consequences more profound than ever before. Numerous signs point to a revolutionary restructuring of world politics. Indeed, the cascade of recent events suggests that a restructuring has occurred. So, too, does the disorder caused by the force of many disintegrative trends, such as environmental deterioration, weapons proliferation, the end of bipolarity, and the resurgence of nationalism and ethnic conflict. Restructuring is also suggested by integrative trends. The nations of the world are drawing more closely together in communications, ideas, economics, and even peace and security. Together, the countervailing forces of integration and disintegration (see Gaddis, 1991b) point toward a transformation in world politics that matches in extensiveness and importance the system-disrupting convulsions that swept the world following World War II. The Camp David Declaration on New Relations, issued by the presidents of the United States and the Russian Federation during an early 1992 summit, is a striking symbol of the new era in world politics. The declaration boldly proclaims that "Russia and the United States do not regard each other as potential adversaries."

In the past several decades, scholars energetically examined the nature of transformation in history in order to isolate the "turning points in international politics" (Oren, 1984). Differentiating meaningful transformations in world politics, true historical watersheds, from ephemeral changes or those that occur with the passage of time is difficult, as turning points do not fall neatly into easily defined periods, signaling that one system has truly ended and a new one has commenced.[1]

Throughout history, major wars have symbolized the most important turning points. They disrupt or destroy preexisting international arrangements. World Wars I and II symbolize fundamental breaks with the past because each set in motion major transformations in world politics. Similarly, the end of the Cold War is a historical breakpoint of no less epic proportions. The conclusion of the ideological conflict between communism and capitalism at the root of the so-called East-West dispute gives states "the luxury of some genuine choices for the first time since 1945" (Hyland, 1990). We are now at the threshold of an entirely new era in world politics, having just experienced, as George Bush put it, changes "of almost biblical proportions."

Yet, despite all in world politics that is radically different, there is much that remains the same. Indeed, "history usually makes a mockery of our hopes and expectations. . . . We are entering a new world and . . . many well-established generalizations about world politics may no longer hold." Thus we must "question . . . the ways and areas in which the future is likely to resemble the past" (Jervis, 1991–1992). Some continuities doubtless will persist.

How, then, can we recognize the beginning of a new international system? Political scientist Stanley Hoffmann (1961) argues that we have a new international system when we have a new answer to any of three questions (see also Zinnes, 1980; Thompson, 1988). First, what are the system's basic units (for example, nation-states instead of city-states)? Second, what are the predominant foreign policy goals that the units seek with respect to each other (for example, deterrence rather than the conquest of

---

[1] The disagreement among analysts about the dates of previous transformations in world politics testifies to the problems. See Kaplan (1957), Oren (1984), and Rosecrance (1963) for alternative ways to distinguish periods in world politics and discussions of the analytic principles on which distinctions are made.

others)? And third, what can the units do to each other with their military and economic capabilities?

By these criteria, it looks as though a new system *has* today emerged. First, European national units are amalgamating into a new economic union of unprecedented size and scope. A similar quest is underway in North America. Moreover, some international organizations, like the United Nations, whose power has long remained latent, are now flexing their political muscles. The Soviet Union, however, once the largest territorial unit in the world and a powerful actor on the world stage for more than seventy years, has fragmented into smaller, often fractious political entities searching for national identity.

Second, territorial conquest is no longer the predominant goal of nations' foreign policies. There is evidence, furthermore, that nations have shifted their emphasis from traditional military methods of exercising influence to economic means (Luttwak, 1990). At the same time, ideological contests, like that between democratic capitalism and Marxism-Leninism, which animated the Cold War contest between the United States and the Soviet Union, no longer provide the base on which threats to national security rest.

Third, advances in weapons technology and its proliferation represent a sea change in the boundaries of what states can do to each other. Great powers alone no longer control the world's most lethal weapons. Their economic well-being, however, is sometimes dependent on those with an increasing capacity to destroy.

The profound changes in units, goals, and capabilities witnessed in recent years have dramatically altered the rank of particular nations in the pecking orders that define the structure of international politics. Still, the hierarchies themselves endure. The *economic* hierarchy that divides the rich from the poor, the *political* hierarchy that separates the rulers from the ruled, the *resource* hierarchy that makes some suppliers and others dependents, and the *military* asymmetries that pit the strong against the weak—all still shape the relations among nations, as they have in the past. Similarly, the perpetuation of international anarchy and insecurity continue to encourage preparations for war and the use of force without international mandate. Thus change and continuity coexist to define the shape of contemporary world politics.

The interaction of constancy and change makes it difficult to determine unambiguously that the post-Cold War era is an altogether new international system. What is clear is that constancy and change will determine the structure of relations among global actors in the 1990s. Their interactions prevent extreme deviations from the general course of world politics and can pull conditions back to the patterns characteristic of an earlier period. This is why the impression is sometimes conveyed that in world politics "the more things change the more they stay the same." Trends in world politics rarely unfold in a constant, linear direction. Historical trends sometimes exhaust themselves. Others stabilize or even reverse themselves as natural barriers interrupt their evolutionary progression. Indeed, persistence forecasting (pointing to automatic eventual transformation) usually fails because the conditions that coalesce to produce a development almost never continue indefinitely. As conditions change, they breed obstacles to their continuation. Thus the historically minded observer may encounter a sense of *déjà vu*, because the new international system that has just emerged shares many characteristics with those that existed in earlier periods.

PREDICTING THE PROBLEMATIC FUTURE . . . .

Change and continuity in world politics do not allow us confidently to know what is in store for the world's political future. As we will elaborate throughout *World Politics: Trend and Transformation*, some analysts see political authority fragmenting into even smaller parcels. Others see authority consolidating into large, competitive military or trade blocs, which will expand the number of great-power rivals. Some perceive science and technology propelling the world into abundance and affluence. Others see it breeding chaos and environmental destruction. And some project the spread of democracy worldwide, whereas others foresee a resurgence of hypernationalism and a rekindling of support for strong (and, potentially, war-waging) autocratic rulers.

To predict which forces will dominate the future, we must think in multicausal terms. No trend or trouble stands alone; all interact simultaneously. The path toward the future is influenced by multiple determinants. Each causal force is connected to the rest in a complex set of linkages. Collectively, these may produce stability by inhibiting the impact of any single disruptive force. On the other hand, if interacting forces converge, their combined effects could accelerate the pace of change in world politics, moving it in directions not possible without such a symbiosis.

In *World Politics: Trend and Transformation* we look at world politics as a system, with patterns of interaction among parts. We direct attention to underlying causes and the ways they interact to shape the system. We assume the need to be sensitive to the impact of the past on the present. And we picture the world as it might appear if it were viewed from outer space. Such a macroscopic perspective provides a bird's-eye view and sacrifices detail (in contrast to a microperspective that yields a worm's-eye view of the world). A macro approach prevents dwelling on particular events, particular nations' foreign policies, particular individuals, or other transitory phenomena whose long-term significance is likely to diminish. It helps identify behaviors that cohere into general global patterns—trends and transformations that will measurably affect the human political habitat as we enter the twenty-first century.

The macropolitical orientation of *World Politics: Trend and Transformation* is not meant to denigrate the importance of examining political processes peculiar to individual nations and their impact on the larger context of world politics.[2] However, a concern for the larger picture necessarily implies a greater focus on the general than on the particular, on the recurrent rather than the ephemeral. Thus we explore the nature of international relations from a perspective that places general patterns into a larger, lasting theoretical context, providing the conceptual tools and theories that will enable us to interpret subsequent developments.

ORGANIZING INQUIRY: A FRAMEWORK FOR ANALYSIS . . . .

The chapters that follow provide a framework for investigating the forces driving contemporary world politics. We begin in Chapter 2 with a review of contending

---

[2] Our previous work on U.S. foreign policy and policy-making processes (Kegley and Wittkopf, 1991) demonstrates our commitment to understanding international politics from the viewpoint of individual actors as well as from the macropolitical perspective that underlies this book.

theories used by scholars and policymakers to make sense of world politics. This theoretical overview shows, among other things, how events in the world shape our views of the world and how prevailing theories of international politics change in accordance with changes in the real world of diplomatic practices and dramatic events that disrupt those practices.

The next thirteen chapters are divided into four parts. In Part II we focus on the actors in world politics. Nation-states are a primary concern here, with attention given to the way in which they make decisions to cope with the international environment (Chapter 3) and to the conflicts that characterize rivalries among great powers (Chapter 4) and between them and the less economically developed states in the Third World (Chapter 5). This part concludes (Chapter 6) with an examination of the nonstate actors that play important roles in world politics and sometimes challenge nation-states' preeminence.

Parts III and IV focus on transnational policy issues. Part III addresses the increasingly important *low politics* of material well-being. Here questions relating to the world political economy and the impact of national and international behavior on the global commons are examined. In Part IV the emphasis shifts to issues of war and peace, those geostrategic matters of *high politics* that are the essence of the traditional concerns of scholars and diplomats seeking to grapple with the politics of peace and security.

We conclude in Part V by returning briefly to themes examined in greater detail in previous chapters. Here we ask how the underlying tendencies in contemporary world politics enable us to anticipate future trends. Our concerns are how today's world will affect tomorrow's and the questions that prevailing developments raise about the human prospect on the eve of the twenty-first century.

Understanding today's complex world requires a willingness to understand complexity. The challenge is difficult. A true but complicated idea always has less chance of succeeding than does a simple but false one, the French political sociologist Alexis de Tocqueville (1969 [1835]) warned over 150 years ago. But the rewards warrant the effort. Humankind's ability to free the future from the paralyzing grip of the past is contingent on its ability to entertain complex ideas for a complicated world and to develop a questioning attitude about rival perspectives on international realities.

SUGGESTED READINGS

Brecher, Michael, and Patrick James. *Crisis and Change in World Politics*. Boulder, Colo.: Westview Press, 1986.

Czempiel, Ernst-Otto, and James N. Rosenau, eds. *Global Changes and Theoretical Challenges: Approaches to World Politics for the 1990s*. Lexington, Mass.: Lexington Books, 1989.

Doran, Charles F. *Systems in Crisis: New Imperatives of High Politics at Century's End*. Cambridge: Cambridge University Press, 1991.

Holsti, Ole R., Randolph M. Siverson, and Alexander L. George, eds. *Change in the International System*. Boulder, Colo.: Westview Press, 1980.

Jervis, Robert. "The Future of World Politics: Will It Resemble the Past?," *International Security* 16 (Winter 1991–1992): 39–73.

Kegley, Charles W., Jr., and Eugene R. Wittkopf, eds. *The Global Agenda: Issues and Perspectives*, 3rd ed. New York: McGraw-Hill, 1992.

Morse, Edward L. *Modernization and the Transformation of International Relations*. New York: Free Press, 1976.

Rosenau, James N. *Turbulence in World Politics: A Theory of Change and Continuity*. Princeton, N.J.: Princeton University Press, 1990.

Ruggie, John Gerard. "Continuity and Transformation in the World Polity: Toward a Neorealist Synthesis," *World Politics* 35 (January 1983): 261–285.

Szulc, Tad. *Then and Now: How the World Has Changed Since World War II*. New York: Morrow, 1990.

Vasquez, John A., and Richard W. Mansbach. "The Issue Cycle: Conceptualizing Long-Term Global Change," *International Organization* 37 (Spring 1983): 257–280.

CHAPTER 2

· · ·

THE STUDY OF WORLD POLITICS: RIVAL PERSPECTIVES IN CHANGING CONTEXTS

· · ·

It's important that we take a hard, clear look . . . not at some simple world, either of universal goodwill or of universal hostility, but the complex, changing and sometimes dangerous world that really exists.

Jimmy Carter,
U.S. President, 1980

We are stranded between old conceptions of political conduct and a wholly new conception, between the inadequacy of the nation-state and the emerging imperative of global community.

Henry A. Kissinger,
U.S. Secretary of State, 1975

We live in a world defined by our expectations and images. No one really "knows" what that world is like; we infer its nature from how we perceive it. Because we cannot "see" international relations directly, many of our images of the world's political realities may be built on illusions and misconceptions. Even if our images are not inaccurate, they are likely to become obsolete, as adjustments in the way we think about world politics often follow changes in international conditions.

The shape of the world's future will be determined not only by changes in the "objective" facts of world politics but also by the meanings that people ascribe to those facts, the assumptions on which their interpretations are based, and the actions that flow from these assumptions and interpretations. Because the way we act is shaped by what we perceive, we must continually question the validity of our images of world politics and ask if they are accurate views of reality or misperceptions.

Our purpose in this chapter is to describe the major analytical perspectives through which scholars and policymakers have interpreted international relations. The perceived "realities" of the international phenomena these perspectives seek to describe and explain understandably influence their content. We will therefore relate the perspectives to the underlying political climate in which they emerged. We will also use them to identify the intellectual heritage informing *World Politics: Trend and Transformation*. In particular, the conceptual distinction between the "low politics" of material well-being and the "high politics" of peace and security used to categorize the analyses in Parts III and IV is based on these perspectives or analytical traditions.[1]

We begin with a discussion of individuals' perceptions of their social and political environments, the factors that shape them, and their importance for understanding world politics.

IMAGE AND REALITY IN WORLD POLITICS

We all have some kind of "mental model" of world politics. It may be explicit or implicit, conscious or subconscious. But whatever our level of awareness, the mental models we carry with us simplify "reality" by exaggerating some features of the real world and ignoring others.

Consider the four world maps, Maps 2.1 to 2.4. All depict the distribution of political and territorial boundaries on the earth's land surfaces, but the image portrayed by each is unique. Moreover, all are poor replications of reality in that the earth is round, but the maps are flat. (The difficulty cartographers face can be appreciated by trying to flatten the peel of an orange.)

Map 2.1 on page 12 is the widely adopted Robinson projection of the world, named after the cartographer Arthur Robinson, who created it. The map centers on Europe so as to avoid splitting the Asian landmass, and it conveys some sense of the curvature of the earth by using rounded edges. The relationships among sizes and shapes are inevitably inaccurate in some places, but the distortions caused by depicting a sphere on a flat surface are less than in many other configurations.

Map 2.2 on page 13 is a Mercator projection, created in the sixteenth century by the Flemish cartographer Gerardus Mercator. Here the distortions in sizes and shapes are egregious. Greenland looks as though it is larger than China, even though China covers nearly four times as much land surface, and Europe appears larger than South America, which is twice Europe's size. Moreover, two-thirds of the map is used to represent the northern half of the world, and only one-third the southern half. The Mercator projection is a classic Eurocentric view of the world.

Map 2.3 on page 14 illustrates a quite different geographic world view. Here each country appears in correct proportion and in its correct position in relation to all others. The map, known as a Peters projection, is the work of the German historian Arno Peters. In contrast with most geographic representations, it draws attention to those parts of the world that are today the home of more than three-quarters of the world's population. We will later describe these areas collectively as the South, most of which are in Asia, Africa, and Latin America.

---

[1] The distinction between high and low politics can be traced to the experience of the United States in the years following World War II. With the onset of the Cold War, top-level elected and career officials found that national security issues relating to the East-West struggle dominated their time and attention. In such an environment, nonsecurity issues, especially those pertaining to economic matters, were left to lower-level career bureaucrats. For a variety of reasons (discussed in Chapters 4, 5, 7, and 8), since the 1970s low politics has come to compete with high politics for the attention of key policymakers.

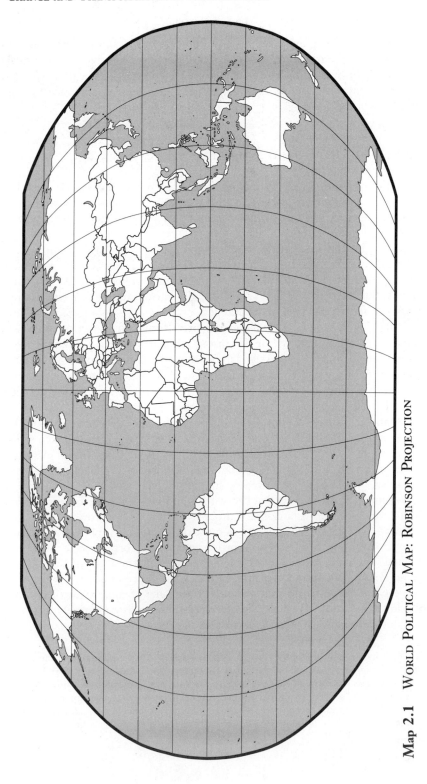

Map 2.1 WORLD POLITICAL MAP: ROBINSON PROJECTION

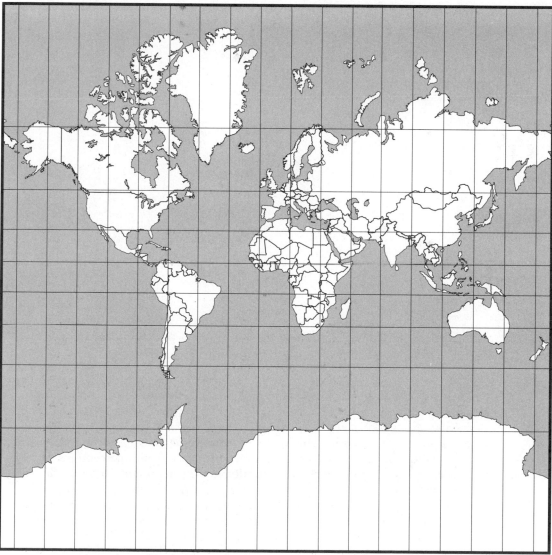

Map 2.2 WORLD POLITICAL MAP: MERCATOR PROJECTION

Finally, Map 2.4 on page 15 uses a polar projection of the world to depict the principal political relationships and military alignments as they existed shortly before the breakup of the Soviet Union. The perspective highlights military planners' view of the world during the height of the Cold War. If intercontinental war between the United States and the Soviet Union had broken out, and if the antagonists had resorted to ballistic missiles to fight it, the polar icecap that here is the center of the world would have become a major pathway to destruction.

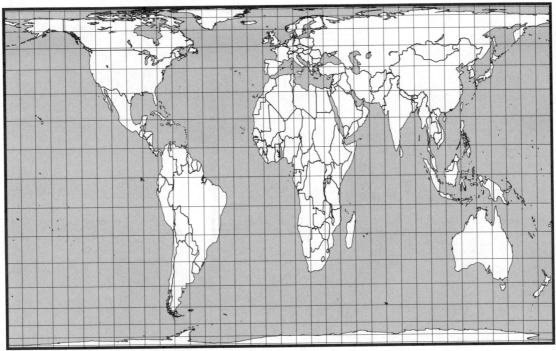

Map 2.3   WORLD POLITICAL MAP: PETERS PROJECTION

There is nothing pernicious about simplifying our views of the world. Just as cartographers create simplifications of a complex geophysical space so we can better understand the world around us, each of us creates mental maps of the world to make sense out of a confusing abundance of information. Mental maps are actually conceptual models, since concepts are abstractions that organize perceptions.[2] They are neither inherently right nor wrong but derive their importance from our human tendency to "respond [not] to the 'objective' facts of the situation . . . but to [our] image of the situation. It is what we think the world is like, not what it is really like, that determines our behavior. . . . We act according to the way the world appears to us, not necessarily according to the way it 'is'" (Boulding, 1959). Even political leaders are captives of this tendency. As political scientist Richard Ned Lebow (1981) warns, "Policy-makers are prone to distort reality in accord with their needs even in situations that appear . . . relatively unambiguous."

---

[2] We use the word *map* to indicate the extent to which mental models are necessarily imperfect replicas of the global realities they are intended to portray. We are referring not only to the kind of world geography that people carry in their heads regarding distance, size, and topography but also to how resources, military capabilities, power, diplomatic influence, and populations, as well as their political meaning, are distributed. Having described mental models in these terms, it is perhaps axiomatic that many such maps may bear little relationship to the realities of a fast-changing, interdependent planet (see Sprout and Sprout, 1971).

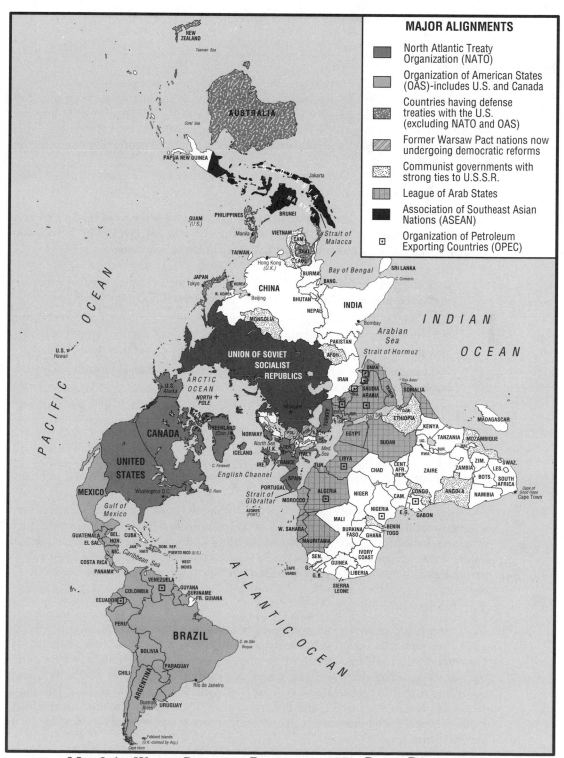

MAJOR ALIGNMENTS

- North Atlantic Treaty Organization (NATO)
- Organization of American States (OAS)-includes U.S. and Canada
- Countries having defense treaties with the U.S. (excluding NATO and OAS)
- Former Warsaw Pact nations now undergoing democratic reforms
- Communist governments with strong ties to U.S.S.R.
- League of Arab States
- Association of Southeast Asian Nations (ASEAN)
- ⊡ Organization of Petroleum Exporting Countries (OPEC)

Map 2.4 WORLD POLITICAL RELATIONS, 1991: POLAR PROJECTION
Source: Comparative World Atlas (Maplewood, N.J.: Hammond Corporation, 1992), p. 12.

Images of Reality

Scholars interested in the psychological dimensions of international relations stress the importance of understanding the sources of individuals' images of reality. Political psychology is important to the study of international relations because (among other reasons) people differ in their perceptions of and reactions to conflicting or discrepant information.

The Sources of Images

Social cognition theory demonstrates that one's perception of the world is not a passive act. The mind learns to select, screen, and filter what it perceives. The factors that influence individuals' perceptions of politics include the following:

- psychological needs, drives, and dispositions (for example, trust or mistrust) ingrained in personalities as a result of early childhood experiences
- what we are socialized into thinking about international relations as children (for example, tolerance of cultural diversity or the fear of it) by parents, teachers, and peer groups and the values embedded in our cultural system
- our images of world history as shaped by our teachers and the kinds of history books to which we are exposed
- opinions about world affairs articulated by those with whom we routinely associate, such as our close friends
- attitudes expressed by policymakers and others respected as experts
- the positions we occupy and the roles we perform (What we see depends on where we sit: child, student, bureaucrat, policymaker, diplomat, and so forth.)

Tolerance of ambiguity and receptivity to new ways of organizing thinking vary among individuals and personality types. Some are more "open" and less rigid than others and therefore more accepting of diversity and more able to revise perceptual habits to accommodate new realities. Nevertheless, all of us are to some extent prisoners of the perceptual predispositions to which we are conditioned.

The Nature of Images

Most people are prone to look for information that reinforces preexisting beliefs, to assimilate new data into familiar images, and to distort cognitions (facts) that deny information that fails to conform to previous expectations. Individuals process information using schematic reasoning, which causes them to interpret new information according to existing schema (a kind of psychological diagram) (Conover and Feldman, 1984; also Kuklinski, Luskin, and Bolland, 1991). They use information short cuts to make political judgments and to relate preferences toward specific policy issues to general attitudes or postures.

Individuals organize information about the world because it helps them to simplify the world. The process applies to international politics, as individuals attempt "to cope with an extraordinarily confusing world by structuring views about specific foreign policies according to their more general and abstract beliefs" (Hurwitz and Peffley, 1987). Preexisting values and beliefs encourage individuals to accept some cognitions but to exclude others from their consciousness that may be discrepant or "dissonant" (Festinger, 1957). This means that what we "see" about world politics depends not just on what happens in the world but also on how we interpret and internalize those events. Thus mental maps inescapably play a central role in shaping individuals' dispositions toward world politics.

The Role of Images in International Politics

We must be careful not to assume automatically that what applies to individuals applies to entire nations. Still, leaders' images of historical circumstances often predispose them to behave in particular ways toward others, regardless of the "objective" facts of the situation. For example, the loss of 26 million Soviet soldiers and citizens in the "Great Patriotic War" (as the Russians refer to World War II) created an exaggerated fear of foreign invasion. This caused a generation of Soviet policymakers to perceive moves made by the United States for defense with considerable suspicion and, often, alarm. Similarly, the U.S. image of European power politics as "dirty" reinforced its isolationist impulse—its disposition to withdraw from world affairs—and also its counter impulse—a determination to reform the world in its own image. The latter gave rise to the globalist foreign policy the United States pursued following World War II. That others might regard that policy orientation as ill advised and sometimes threatening is not easily understood by Americans. (As former U.S. President Jimmy Carter once lamented, "The hardest thing for Americans to understand is that they are not better than other people.")

Because individuals (and, by inference, nations) are prone either to ignore or reinterpret information that runs counter to their beliefs and values, mutual misperceptions often fuel discord in world politics, especially when relations between nations are hostile. For example, distrust and suspicion between conflicting parties may arise because each sees the other as the other sees it. That is, *mirror images* emerge. This syndrome is especially clear in the images the leaders in Moscow and Washington held of each other during the Cold War conflict. It applies to many other antagonistic relationships as well. When mirror images develop, self-righteousness often leads parties entrapped in conflict to view their own actions as constructive but to view their adversary's responses as negative and hostile. When this occurs, resolution of the conflict is extraordinarily difficult, as the seemingly endless wars in the Middle East illustrate. Thus peace is not simply a matter of expanding trade and other forms of transnational contact, or even of bringing political leaders together in international summits. Rather, it is a matter of changing deeply entrenched beliefs.[3]

---

[3] The classic empirical examination of the impact of images on foreign policy making is Ole R. Holsti's (1962) study of John Foster Dulles, U.S. secretary of state in the Eisenhower administration. Demonstrating that Dulles operated within the framework of an "inherent bad faith" model of the Soviet Union, Holsti's findings "suggest the fallacy of thinking that peaceful settlement of outstanding international issues is simply a problem of devising 'good plans.' Clearly as long as decision-makers on either side of the Cold War [adhered] to rigid images of the other party, there [was] little likelihood that even genuine 'bids' to decrease tensions [would] have the desired effect."

Sources of Image Change

Although individuals' mental maps of world politics are resistant to change, change is possible. It occurs when people experience punishment or discomfort as a result of clinging to false assumptions. (As Benjamin Franklin once observed, "The things that hurt, instruct.") Dramatic events also can alter international images, sometimes drastically (see Deutsch and Merritt, 1965; also Wittkopf, 1990). The use of atomic bombs against Japan in 1945, the Korean and Vietnam conflicts, and the Cuban missile crisis in 1962 were learning experiences for many people, causing them to adjust their previous images of international politics.

Similarly, the surprising collapse of communist rule in the Soviet Union and Eastern Europe exerted pressure on the world views of policymakers and political commentators alike, provoking them to reexamine their assumptions about foreign policy priorities in a new world order. Often such jolting experiences encourage the creation of new mental maps, new perceptual filters, and new criteria through which later events may be interpreted and situations defined.

UNDERSTANDING WORLD POLITICS: THE ELUSIVE QUEST FOR THEORY ·

Like the mental maps individuals use to make sense of a complex and often confusing world, social scientists devise different models to think about world politics and help make it more comprehensible. Like cartographers, they develop analytical models that highlight some features of reality but distort others. And, like the geographic world views maps with different purposes convey in different times, the models (sometimes called theories or paradigms[4]) scholars fashion change as new problems cry out for new understanding and solution. Thus the analytical perspectives dominant in the thinking of both scholars and policymakers in different historical circumstances tell us much about world politics itself. They flourish in international climates with often distinctive normative or value orientations not only because of the persuasiveness of their proponents' message but also because of their ability to explain developments then unfolding in world affairs (Ferguson and Mansbach, 1988).[5]

---

[4] The word *paradigm* is commonly used to describe the dominant way of looking at a subject of inquiry, such as international relations. It was popularized by Thomas Kuhn's (1970) influential book *The Structure of Scientific Revolutions*. Unfortunately, the term has been used in a variety of overlapping ways, but the general idea underlying the term is that thoughts about an area of inquiry tend to be structured by the acceptance of particular aspects of the subject's characteristics as more important than others and by agreement about the puzzles to be solved and the criteria that should govern their investigation. The concept is helpful to understanding how images of world politics are shaped by sociological forces operating within the intellectual community of scholars as it seeks to assess the nature and meaning of global political developments.

[5] To be sure, there have always been scholars outside the intellectual paradigm dominant during any particular time, challenging it, questioning its relevance to world politics, and proposing alternative conceptions of reality and what knowledge about it should entail. Often those outside the paradigm have come from countries other than those dominant in world politics itself. Marxist thinking clearly was dominant

Major wars involving the preponderant (hegemonic) powers in particular historical epochs have been major turning points in world history.

> These periodic conflicts have reordered the international system and propelled history in new and uncharted directions. They resolve the question of which state will govern the system, as well as what ideas and values will predominate, thereby determining the ethos of succeeding ages. The outcomes of these wars affect the economic, social, and ideological structures of individual societies as well as the structure of the larger international system. (Gilpin, 1981: 203)

The twentieth century has been dominated by three such conflicts: World War I, World War II, and the Cold War. Each stimulated a search for the causes of war and the foundations of peace; each reshaped policymakers' images about the principles that organize world politics and the policy programs that can best preserve world order; each caused the dominant world view to be jettisoned and encouraged the search for new theoretical orientations. As the historian Arthur Schlesinger (1986) mused, "Every war in American history has been followed in due course by skeptical reassessments of supposedly sacred assumptions."

The theoretical perspectives fashioned during this century demonstrate the impact of these wars on the study of world politics. We will discuss six of them: (1) current history, (2) political idealism, (3) political realism, (4) behavioralism, (5) neorealism, and (6) neoliberal institutionalism. We will conclude by identifying four additional schools of thought believed by their proponents to better address particular aspects of world politics and foreign policy.

Current History

International relations as a distinct field of intellectual inquiry is largely a phenomenon of the twentieth century. The historical roots of the discipline lie in diplomatic history, an approach to understanding international relations that focuses on the description of historical events, not theoretical explanation. For convenience, we call this the *current history* approach to the study of international relations.

The environment at the dawn of the century when the formal study of international relations began was filled with optimism. Many believed that peace and prosperity had taken root and would persist. International law had recently been strengthened, and The Hague peace conferences in 1899 and 1907 inspired hope that arms would be controlled and Europe would be spared another series of wars, like those experienced between 1848 and 1870. Moreover, many people, including, for example, the American industrialist and philanthropist Andrew Carnegie, who gave much of his fortune to the cause of world peace, assumed that as industrialization progressed and the costs

---

in the scholarly work of those living in socialist societies during the Cold War, for example. However, the ability of Marxist interpretations of reality to attain dominance worldwide was constrained by the inability of communism as defined by Karl Marx (that is, a classless, stateless society) to become the world's preferred form of political and social organization.

and risks of war increased, the chance of protracted war among the great powers would decline dramatically (see also Angell, 1910).

In these halcyon times, students of international relations studied history to provide insightful commentary on the events of the day. Thus the study of international relations was largely the study of personalities and events, past and present. Rarely did scholars seek to generalize theoretically about the "lessons" of history or about the principles or "laws" that could account for the characteristic responses of states to similar stimuli or influences.[6]

The large-scale death and destruction World War I exacted destroyed the security that had made current history a comfortable approach to international politics. That catastrophic global war, begun in 1914, was a painful learning experience that stimulated the search for knowledge that could address contemporary policy problems—notably war—in a theoretical context. However interesting descriptions of past wars and the individuals who waged them might be, they were of dubious utility to a world in search of peace and ways to prevent wars of mass destruction. For those purposes, policymakers and scholars needed a *theory* that could reliably predict the outbreak of war and instruct leaders on the policies that could best prevent it.

Political Idealism

World War I opened the door to a paradigmatic revolution in the study of world politics. Several perspectives on international relations competed for attention in the period of intellectual ferment that followed. Current history as an approach continued to claim some adherents, and Marxist-Leninist thought became an increasingly influential paradigm following the Bolshevik Revolution in Russia in the waning days of World War I. Later, with the rise of Adolf Hitler and the Nazis in Germany, national socialism (that is, fascism) also challenged conventional European thinking about international politics. Nazism, the German variant of national socialism, was particularly provocative. Not only did Nazism glorify the role of the state (as opposed to the individual) in political life. It also advanced a political philosophy that rationalized war as an instrument of national policy. Emerging as dominant, however, was a perspective known as *political idealism*.

The Idealist World View

Idealists held divergent views of world politics. What joined them were their shared assumptions about reality and the homogeneity of their conclusions. Collectively, idealists embraced a world view based on the beliefs that (1) human nature is essentially "good" or altruistic and people are therefore capable of mutual aid and collaboration;[7]

---

[6] Sir Halford Mackinder (1919) and Alfred Thayer Mahan (1890) are exceptions to this broad generalization. Both sought to generate theoretical propositions pertaining to the influence of geographic factors on national power and international politics. Their efforts laid the foundations for the study of political geography that survives today as an important approach to world politics.

[7] The role of human nature in theories of politics is controversial. See Nelson (1974), Lewontin, Rose, and Kamin (1984), and Somit (1990) for critical reviews.

(2) the fundamental human concern for the welfare of others makes progress possible (that is, the Enlightenment's faith in the possibility of improving civilization was reaffirmed); (3) bad human behavior is the product not of evil people but of evil institutions and structural arrangements that motivate people to act selfishly and to harm others—including making war; (4) war is not inevitable and its frequency can be reduced by eradicating the institutional arrangements that encourage it; (5) war is an international problem that requires collective or multilateral rather than national efforts to eliminate it; and therefore, (6) international society must reorganize itself to eliminate the institutions that make war likely.

To be sure, not all advocates of political idealism subscribed to each of these tenets with equal conviction. Many political idealists would probably disagree with some of them or be uncomfortable with their simplistic wording. Nevertheless, these tenets describe the basic assumptions articulated in one way or another by the leaders and theorists whose orientation toward international relations captivated the discussion of world politics in the period between the two world wars. Overtones of moralism, optimism, and universalism laced the discussion.

The Idealist Reform Program

Although important differences existed in the idealists' prescriptions for dealing with international problems (see Herz, 1951), the prescriptions tended to fall into three groups. One group called for the creation of international institutions to replace the anarchical and war-prone balance-of-power system that had precipitated World War I. That system was characterized by independent states who formed coalitions (in the form of shifting alliances) to wage war or defend a weaker coalition partner from attack. Idealists sought to create in its place a new system based on the principle of collective security. It would deal with the problem of war by making aggression by any one state an aggression against all who, acting in concert, would thwart the ambitions of the dominance-seeking actor. The League of Nations was the embodiment of the collective security principle. It reflected simultaneously the emphasis that idealists placed on international institutions as a mechanism for coping with the problem of war (and, secondarily, social injustice) and the possibility of international cooperation as a mechanism of global problem-solving.

A second group of idealist prescriptions emphasized the legal control of war. It called for the use of legal processes, such as mediation and arbitration, to settle disputes and inhibit recourse to war. Creation of the Permanent Court of International Justice to litigate interstate conflicts and ratification of the Kellogg-Briand Pact of 1928, which "outlawed" war as an instrument of national policy, illustrated this face of the idealists' policy prescriptions.

A third group of prescriptions followed the biblical injunction that nations should beat their swords into plowshares. The efforts during the 1920s (the Washington and London naval conferences, for instance) to secure arms control and disarmament agreements exemplified this orientation.

Several corollary ideas gave definition to the emphasis that idealists placed on international organization, law, and disarmament. Among them were the need to substitute attitudes that stressed the unity of humankind for those that stressed parochial national loyalties; the promotion of free international trade in place of economic nationalism; the replacement of secret diplomacy by a system of "open covenants, openly arrived at"; and, above all, the termination of interlocking bilateral alliances and the power balances they sought to achieve. Some idealists saw in the principle of self-determination a chance to redraw the world's political geography to make national borders conform to ethnic groupings, under the conviction that a world so arranged would be a more peaceful world. Related to this was the call for democratic domestic institutions. "Making the world safe for democracy," idealists believed, would also make it secure and free from war. Woodrow Wilson's celebrated Fourteen Points speech (delivered by the U.S. president before Congress in 1918), which proposed the creation of the League of Nations and, with it, the pursuit of other idealists' aims, expressed the sentiments of the idealist world view and program perhaps better than did any other statement.

Although idealism dominated policy rhetoric and academic discussions during the interwar period, much of the idealist program for reform was never tried, and even less of it was ever achieved. When the winds of international change again shifted and the world confronted the German, Italian, and Japanese pursuit of hegemony and world conquest, idealism as a world view receded.

Political Realism

The drive for world conquest that led to World War II provoked strong criticism of the idealist paradigm. Critics blamed the outbreak of war on what they believed to be the idealists' naive legalistic and moralistic assumptions and their alleged neglect of the "realities" of power politics (see Carr, 1939). The "lessons" the critics drew from the interwar period gave shape to a new set of perceptions and beliefs.

Advocates of the new, ascendant paradigm, known as *political realism*, coalesced to frame an intellectual movement. Their message reads like the antithesis of idealism.[8] Because it was compelling—and because it remains so today—it deserves careful scrutiny.

The Realist World View

As a political theory, realism's intellectual roots can be traced to the ancient Greek historian Thucydides and his account of the Peleponnesian War between Athens and Sparta (431–404 B.C.).[9] It is also linked to the political philosophy of the sixteenth-century Italian theorist Niccolò Machiavelli, who emphasized in his treatise *The Prince*

---

[8] Among the principal prophets of this new world view were E. H. Carr (1939), Hans J. Morgenthau (1948), Kenneth W. Thompson (1958, 1960), Reinhold Niebuhr (1947), George F. Kennan (1954, 1967), and, later, Henry A. Kissinger (1964). Readers familiar with the Western intellectual tradition will note that realism drew its inspiration from the classic political philosophies of such theorists as Niccolò Machiavelli, Thomas Hobbes, and Friedrich Nietzsche, although in ways that bent them to the needs of the time. For critical reviews of the realist paradigm, see Smith (1986) and Rosenthal (1991).

[9] Elements of realist thought can also be found in the writings of Kautilya, minister to the Maurya emperor of India more than two thousand years ago.

a political calculus based on interest, prudence, and expediency above all else, notably morality. Thus political realism is synonymous with *realpolitik*, as moral crusades are anathema to realist thinking.

As applied to twentieth-century world politics, realism views nation-states as the principal actors in world politics, for they answer to no higher political authority. Moreover, conflicts of interests among them are assumed to be inevitable. Realism also emphasizes the way the (perceived) realities of international politics dictate the choices that foreign policymakers, as rational problem solvers, must make. States are the superordinate actors on the world's stage. The purpose of statecraft is national survival in a hostile environment. No means is more important to that end than the acquisition of *power*, and no principle is more important than *self-help*. State *sovereignty*, a cornerstone of international law, enshrines this perspective, giving heads of state the freedom—and responsibility—to do whatever is necessary to serve the state's interests and survival. Moralism is a wasteful and dangerous interference in the rational pursuit of national power. To the realist, therefore, questions about the relative virtues of this or that *ism* (ideological system) are irrelevant to sound policy making. The ideological preferences of states are immaterial, neither good nor bad—what matters is whether one's self-interest is served. Accordingly, the game of international politics revolves around the pursuit of power: acquiring it, increasing it, projecting it, and using it to bend others to one's will.

At the risk of oversimplification, realism's message can be summarized in the form of nine assumptions and related propositions: (1) a reading of history teaches that people are by nature sinful and wicked; (2) of all of people's evil ways, no sins are more prevalent, inexorable, or dangerous than are their instinctive lust for power and their desire to dominate others; (3) the possibility of eradicating the instinct for power is a utopian aspiration; (4) under such conditions international politics is, as the English philosopher Thomas Hobbes put it, a struggle for power, "a war of all against all"; (5) the primary obligation of every state in this environment—the goal to which all other national objectives should be subordinated—is to promote the "national interest," defined as the acquisition of power; (6) the nature of the international system necessitates the acquisition of military capabilities sufficient to deter attack by potential enemies; (7) allies might increase the ability of a state to defend itself, but their loyalty and reliability should not be assumed; (8) never entrust the task of self-protection to international organizations or to international law; and, finally, (9) if all states seek to maximize power, stability will result from maintaining a *balance of power*, lubricated by fluid alliance systems.

REALISM IN THE NUCLEAR AGE The realist thinking that came to dominate actual policy making as well as academic discourse in the 1940s and 1950s (often described as *classical realism*) fit the needs of a pessimistic age. World War II, the onset of rivalry between the United States and the Soviet Union, the expansion of the Cold War confrontation between the emergent superpowers into a global struggle between East and West, the stockpiling of nuclear weapons, the periodic crises that threatened to erupt into global violence—all confirmed the realists' image of world politics.

The realists' belief that the structure of the international system and humankind's lust for power determined the behavior of all nations appeared particularly persuasive considering these developments. States and their incessant competition were the defining elements of global reality. All other aspects of world politics became secondary. Simultaneously, the view that a threatening international environment demanded that foreign policy take precedence over domestic problems and policies also appeared cogent. As the historical imperatives of "power politics" required unceasing attention to the politics of peace and security in the global arena, the logic of *realpolitik* asserted that high politics *was* world politics.

THE LIMITATIONS OF REALISM   Persuasive though the realists' arguments about the essential properties of international politics may have been, their arguments and the conclusions they drew were frequently at odds and even contradictory.

> Critics . . . noted a lack of precision and even contradiction in the way classical realists use such concepts as "power," "national interest," and "balance of power." They also see possible contradictions between the central descriptive and prescriptive elements of classical realism. On the one hand, nations and their leaders "think and act in terms of interests defined as power," but, on the other, statesmen are urged to exercise prudence and restraint, as well as to recognize the legitimate national interests of other nations. Power plays a central role in classical realism, but the correlation between the relative power balance and political outcomes is often less than compelling, suggesting the need to enrich analyses with other variables. (Holsti, 1989b: 19)

Thus, once analysis moved beyond the pithy notion that people are wicked and beyond the rhetoric requiring that foreign policy serve the national interest, important questions remained. What policies best serve the national interest? Do alliances encourage peace or instability? Do arms promote national security or provoke costly arms races and war? Are states more prone to act aggressively when they are strong or weak? Are the interests of nations served only through competition with one another, never through cooperation?

Such questions are empirical and need real-world evidence and corresponding means of analyzing them to find satisfactory answers. In these respects, political realism failed. Realism posed a distinctive perspective on international affairs, but it lacked a methodology for resolving competing claims. It had no criteria to determine what data were significant and what rules to follow to interpret the information perceived to be relevant. Even the policy recommendations that purportedly flowed from the logic of *realpolitik* was often divergent. Realists themselves, for example, were sharply divided about whether the intervention of the United States in Vietnam served U.S. national interests.

A growing number of critics also pointed out that political realism did not account for significant new developments in world politics. It could not explain the forces behind the new institutions that began to be constructed in Western Europe in the 1950s and 1960s, for example, where the cooperative pursuit of mutual advantage rather than narrow self-interest seemed to dominate (at least in economic if not always in military affairs). Other critics began to worry about realism's disregard for ethical principles and the material and social costs that some of its policy prescriptions seemed to impose, such as retarded economic growth as a result of unrestrained military expenditures.

Thus, by the end of the 1960s, (classical) realism, which had emerged as the dominant paradigm in international relations following World War II, found itself bombarded by criticism. Some found its logical consistency flawed, others found its empirical content dubious, and still others found its policy recommendations confusing and its neglect of ethical norms disquieting.

Realism's Continuing Relevance

Despite the shortcomings of classical realism, its shadow is still visible. Much of the world continues to think about international politics in its terms. Indeed, realism enjoyed a resurgence in the early 1980s, as the embittered Cold War competition between the United States and the Soviet Union entered a new phase and the role of military power in world politics received renewed emphasis. Even without that resurgent emphasis, however, realism provides important insight into the drive for national security that continues to motivate states' foreign policy behavior. Thus it provides the intellectual foundations underlying our discussion of high politics in Part IV of *World Politics: Trend and Transformation*.

The continuing relevance of classical realism also finds expression in its recent reformulation, known as *neorealism* or *structural realism*. This variant of classical realism continues to recognize the anarchical nature of world politics and the dominance of the nation-state in world politics, but it severs the link classical realists postulated between human nature and the behavior of states in world politics. Instead, the structure of the system, rather than the unceasing lust for power, dictates exclusively the foreign policy choices of national leaders. Thus neorealism speaks directly to the importance of the recent transformation in the structure of world power, which has moved away from a bipolar configuration of power to one variously described as unipolar or multipolar. We will therefore return below to a consideration of neorealist theory. First, however, we will briefly address the methodological debate that dissatisfaction with classical realism provoked.

The Behavioral Approach

Among its other contributions, classical realism prepared the way for serious theoretical thinking about global conditions and empirical (verifiable) linkages among them. Nonetheless, as dissatisfaction with its shortcomings mounted, a counterreaction, cast largely in terms of language and method, gained momentum in the 1960s and early 1970s. Because the *behavioral* approach to the study of international relations, as it came to be known, was defined largely by its approach to theory and the logic and method of its inquiry, it is better described as a methodology than as a theoretical perspective.

Science Versus Traditionalism

Behavioralism in international relations was part of a larger movement spreading across the social sciences in general. Often called the *scientific* approach, behavioralism challenged preexisting modes of studying human behavior and the basis on which previous theorists, now called *traditionalists*, derived their truth-claims. An often heated debate among scholars about the principles and procedures most appropriate for investigating international phenomena resulted. The debate centered on the meaning of theory, on the requirements for adequate theory, and on the methods best suited to testing theoretical propositions.

Much of the debate between the behavioralists and traditionalists was strident. Indeed, "theorizing about theory" (Singer, 1960) rather than theorizing about international relations often typified the debate. The literature of this period attests to the extent to which methodological issues, and not substantive ones, commanded the attention of professional analysts. This perhaps reflected the uncertainty and immaturity of a "new" science in its incipient stages of development, one unsure about itself and its goals.[10]

A Science of International Politics?

A number of shared assumptions and analytic prescriptions were at the core of the behavioral movement. Behavioralism sought *nomothetic* or lawlike generalizations about international phenomena, that is, statements about patterns and regularities presumed to hold across time and place. Science, the behavioralists claimed, is foremost a generalizing activity. The purpose of scientific inquiry, therefore, is to discover recurrent patterns of interstate behavior and their causes. From this perspective (a view incidentally consistent with that of many "traditional" realists and idealists), a *theory* of international relations should contain a statement of the relationship between two or more variables, specify the conditions under which the relationship(s) holds, and explain why the relationship(s) should hold. To uncover such theories, behavioralists leaned to comparative cross-national analyses rather than to case studies of particular countries at particular times (as is characteristic of the current history approach). Behavioralists also stressed the need to gather data about the characteristics of nations and how they behaved toward one another. Hence, the behavioral movement spawned and encouraged the quantitative study of international relations (see, for example, Singer, 1968).

What made behavioralism innovative was not so much its reliance on controlled comparative techniques and quantitative analyses as its temperament toward inquiry. Behavioralists sought greater rigor and precision in analysis. They tried to replace subjective belief with verifiable knowledge, to supplant impressionism and intuition with testable evidence, and to substitute data and reproducible information for appeals to the allegedly "expert" opinion of authorities in order to acquire knowledge and build on it cumulatively. They aspired to conduct objective or value-free research (while recognizing the obstacles to that goal). They sought to replace ambiguous verbal definitions of concepts (such as *power*) with so-called "operational" ones built on

---

[10] For examples of the debate and illustrations of the tone of dialogue, see Hoffmann (1960), Kaplan (1968), Knorr and Rosenau (1969), Knorr and Verba (1961), Tanter and Ullman (1972), and Wright (1955). See also Lijphart (1974) for a review of the issues the debate encompassed.

indicators on which empirical tests could be conducted and whose meaning was easily communicated from one analyst to the next. They also sought to avoid the tendency of previous scholarship to select facts and cases to make them fit preexisting hunches. Instead, *all* available data, those not supportive of as well as those consistent with existing theoretical hypotheses, were to be examined. Knowledge, they argued, would advance best if a cautious, skeptical attitude toward any empirical statement were assumed. "Let the data, not the armchair theorist, speak." "Seek evidence, but distrust it." These slogans represented the behavioral posture toward the acquisition of knowledge.

The advocates of behavioralism were understandably enthusiastic about their approach. They came armed with new tools for analyzing international relations, with newly generated data for testing competing hypotheses voiced over decades of traditional speculation, and with sometimes generous research support from governments and private foundations. An entire generation of scholars was trained to study international relations with powerful new conceptual and methodological tools. In the process, some behavioralists addressed empirical questions at the core of competing ideas about the social and political organization of national societies, including not just propositions grounded in realism but also Marxist and other ideas about the causes and consequences of the inequalities within and between states.

Postbehavioralism

Cumulating verifiable knowledge is a difficult, even tedious, task. It requires dedication and patience. The early enthusiasm and optimism of the effort thus began to wane, as the labors invested failed to produce prompt results. Voices even within the behavioral movement itself began to ask sometimes embarrassing questions about the approach and its suitability. One of the early proponents of behavioralism, David Easton (1969), asked if the field was not moving into a *postbehavioral* period.

At the heart of this self-scrutiny was a common set of criticisms: that some devotees of behavioralism had become preoccupied with method to the exclusion of real-world problems; that they had focused on testing interesting (and often the most accessible) hypotheses but ones that were largely trivial and meaningless to the policymakers responsible for protecting their nations and making the world a better place in which to live; and that the methodology of behavioralism, which sought to ground theories in hard data, relied on past patterns of human experience that sometimes did not relate to a rapidly changing world or the future. Hence the findings might be historically accurate but largely irrelevant to today's world or tomorrow's.

Although some behavioral research spoke directly to the moral issues central to the differences between realism and idealism, its relative neglect of many of the ethical questions raised in a world of poverty, hunger, violence, and other forms of malaise was also criticized. Hence the postbehavioral critique called for a new research agenda that would focus on new types of issues and reexamine their underlying philosophical implications from a multidisciplinary perspective. Interestingly, however, the advocates of new approaches to the study of international relations rarely recommended discarding scientific methods. More commonly they urged the application of such methods to new kinds of questions or to the reconstruction of theories grounded in the realist (and idealist) tradition (for example, Wayman and Diehl, 1993; Cusack and Stoll, 1990).

The most recent critique of behavioralism is broadly described as "postpositivist." Positivism is a philosophical tradition concerned with positive facts and phenomena, to the exclusion of speculation about ultimate causes or origins. Thus behavioralists and those committed to the scientific method as a way of understanding the social and political world are typically described as positivists. Postpositivism implies a reexamination of the philosophical foundations of international relations theory.

As with the earlier debate between traditionalists and behaviorists, the postpositivist debate is part of a broader inquiry in the social sciences and humanities variously known as *critical social theory, poststructuralism, postmodernism,* or *deconstructionism.* Critical theorists take the inherently subjective nature of images of world politics and the "social construction of reality" as its point of departure.[11] A common feature of poststructuralism is its critical introspection into the foundations of scientific methods of inquiry and its questioning posture toward the possibility of truly understanding reality. It is a position better suited to exposing the limits of others' analyses (deconstructing their logic) than to constructing theories that might identify ways of better explaining and improving world affairs.

Extending Realism: The Neorealist Structural Approach

As noted, political realism remains an important theoretical perspective underlying contemporary analyses of national security affairs, but it has also gained popularity in revised form as a general theory of international politics known as *neorealism* or *structural realism.*[12]

A Systems Theory of International Politics

Neorealism distinguishes between explanations of international politics cast at the national level of states, commonly known as foreign policy, from explanations cast at the level of the international system, which are systems or systemic theories. What neorealists have sought is "to systematize political realism into a rigorous, deductive systemic theory of international politics" (Keohane, 1986b).

> The new realism, in contrast to the old, begins by proposing a solution to the problem of distinguishing factors internal to international political systems from those that are external. Theory isolates one realm from others in order to deal with it intellectually. By depicting

---

[11] For a discussion as it applies to world politics, see the special issue of *International Studies Quarterly* on "Speaking the Language of Exile: Dissident Thought in International Studies," co-edited by Ashley and Walker (1990), and Der Derian and Shapiro (1989); for a critique of the postmodern critique, see Rosenau (1992).

[12] For a discussion, see the "Symposium on the New Realism" in *International Organization* 38 (Spring 1984), with special attention to the essays by Ashley (1984) and by Gilpin (1984). In addition, Keohane (1986a) and Walker (1987) provide overviews.

an international-political system as a whole, with structural and unit levels at once distinct and connected, neorealism establishes the autonomy of international politics. . . . Neorealism develops the concept of a system's structure which at once bounds the domain that students of international politics deal with and enables them to see how the structure of the system, and variations in it, affect the interacting units and the outcomes they produce. (Waltz, 1991: 29)

As argued by Kenneth N. Waltz, whose influential book *Theory of International Politics* (1979) is a centerpiece of neorealist thinking, "international structure emerges from the interaction of states and then constrains them from taking certain actions while propelling them toward others" (Waltz, 1991). As in classical realism, anarchy and the absence of central institutions (a government) characterize the structure of the system. States remain the primary actors. They act according to the principle of self-help, and all seek to ensure their own survival. Thus, according to structural realism, states do not differ in the tasks they face, only in their capabilities. Capabilities define the position of states in the system, and the distribution of capabilities defines the structure of the system. Similarly, changes in the distribution of capabilities stimulate changes in the structure of the system, as from a multipolar to a bipolar power configuration, or from a bipolar to a unipolar one.

Power also remains a central concept in structural realism. However, the quest for power is no longer considered an end in itself, as in classical realism; nor does it derive from human nature. Instead, states pursue power as an instrument of survival. As Waltz (1979) explains, "states . . . try in more or less sensible ways to use the means available in order to achieve the ends in view. Those means fall into two categories: internal efforts (moves to increase economic capability, to increase military strength, to develop clever strategies) and external efforts (moves to strengthen and enlarge one's own alliance or to weaken and shrink an opposing one)." A *balance of power* emerges more or less automatically from the instinct for survival. "Balances of power tend to form whether some or all states consciously aim to establish and maintain a balance, or whether some or all states aim for universal domination" (Waltz, 1979). Once the international system is formed, it "becomes a force that the units may not be able to control; it constrains their behavior and interposes itself between their intentions and the outcomes of their actions" (Ruggie, 1983).

Implications of Systemic Constraints

The deduction that balances of power must form is a central element in neorealism. It reinforces the notion the structure of the system determines outcomes, not the characteristics of the units that make up the system. Neorealists recognize that states pursue many goals that sometimes "fluctuate with the changing currents of domestic politics, are prey to the vagaries of a shifting cast of political leaders, and are influenced by the outcomes of bureaucratic struggles," but they contend that such factors tell little about the process whereby states come to pursue the goal of balancing power with power. Instead, "structural constraints explain why the [same] methods are repeatedly used despite differences in the persons and states who use them" (Waltz, 1979).

Neorealist theory also provides insight into the limited possibility of international cooperation. Fear is endemic to the international system. As long as states wish to survive, they must be wary of the threat posed by others and protect themselves against others. Hence, they must be sensitive to their *relative position* in the distribution of power.

> When faced with the possibility of cooperating for mutual gain, states that feel insecure must ask how the gain will be divided. They are compelled to ask not "Will both of us gain?" but "Who will gain more?" If an expected gain is to be divided, say, in the ratio of two to one, one state may use its disproportionate gain to implement a policy intended to damage or destroy the other. Even the prospect of large absolute gains for both parties does not elicit their cooperation so long as each fears how the other will use its increased capabilities. (Waltz, 1979: 105)

The impediments to cooperation thus inhere not in the intentions of the parties to potential collaborative endeavors. Instead, they result from the insecurity bred by the anarchical system. "The condition of insecurity—at the least, the uncertainty of each about the other's future intentions and actions—works against their cooperation" (Waltz, 1979).

Waltz claims there is a second reason why states shy away from international cooperation, namely, fear that they may become too dependent on others for their own well-being. Dependence can take the form of a superior-subordinate relation, a one-way street, or it can take the form of interdependence, a two-way street. Both kinds of relationships exist in world politics, and, according to the logic of structural realism, both may be perceived as threatening. "Like other organizations, states seek to control what they depend on or to lessen the extent of their dependency. This simple thought explains quite a bit of the behavior of states: their imperial thrusts to widen the scope of their control and their autarchic strivings toward greater self-sufficiency" (Waltz, 1979).

Not everyone agrees that increased interdependence will diminish the prospects for international cooperation. Conflict among states is endemic in today's world, but there are also compelling reasons to expect that increased interdependence may be a source of increased cooperation. Three theoretical perspectives subsumed by the general label *neoliberal institutionalism* (Grieco, 1988a; Nye, 1988) encapsulate that viewpoint. All derive from the heritage of classic political idealism but move beyond it. The three perspectives that make up neoliberal institutionalism are complex interdependence, international regimes, and hegemonic stability theory.

Neoliberal Institutionalism

Like neorealists, neoliberal institutionalists embrace a structural theory of international politics. They concentrate primarily on the international system (rather than on the characteristics of the units and subunits that comprise it), but they give relatively more attention to the ways international institutions and other nonstate actors promote international cooperation. Instead of picturing a world in which states are reluctant to cooperate because each feels insecure and threatened by all others, neoliberal institutionalists probe the conditions under which cooperation may still be possible as a result of the convergent and ovelapping interests among otherwise sovereign political entities.

In addition to classical idealism, the intellectual roots of neoliberal institutionalism (sometimes called neoliberalism) can be traced to studies of regional integration that began to flourish in the 1950s and 1960s as scholars sought to understand the processes whereby the political unification of sovereign states might be achieved. Efforts to create new institutions in Western Europe, historically one of the most war-prone of all world regions, commanded the most attention, as expanding transaction flows propelled Europeans to sacrifice portions of their sovereign independence in an effort to create new political units out of previously separate ones. The integrative achievements unfolding in Europe also inspired interest in their applicability to other world regions (see Nye, 1971).

The rapid growth of international economic transactions during the 1960s and 1970s further undermined the cogency of the state-centric perspective of political realism and made greater attention to transnational collaboration imperative. A growing number of economically powerful transnational actors, particularly multinational corporations, pushed theoretical inquiry away from its conventional focus on nation-states and toward the threats nonstate actors posed to state sovereignty. As the costs and benefits of growing interdependence affected politics within states, not just between them, the importance of issues of low politics on national political agendas, previously dominated by the high politics of peace and security, increased sharply.

As the density of interdependent transnational linkages multiplied in the 1970s and 1980s, the perceived utility of military power as an instrument of political influence, so central in realist theory, also began to lose its cogency. The balance of military power seemed to lose instrumental value compared with the balance of economic power, as the United States and the other industrial nations of the Western world found when the world's oil-producing nations restricted oil supplies and drove up prices during the 1970s and early 1980s.

To elaborate the tenets underlying neoliberal thinking, let us examine the three perspectives most closely associated with it.

Complex Interdependence as a World View

As an explicit analytical perspective, *complex interdependence* arose in the 1970s to challenge the key assumptions of its rival theoretical frameworks, particularly classical realism. First, it challenged the prevailing assumption that nation-states are the only important actors in world politics by treating other actors, such as multinational corporations and transnational banks, as "important not only because of their activities in pursuit of their own interests, but also because they act as transmission belts, making government policies in various countries more sensitive to one another" (Keohane and Nye, 1988). In this sense complex interdependence is a "holistic," systemic conception that pictures world politics as the sum of its many interacting parts in a "global society" (see Holsti, 1989b).

Second, complex interdependence questioned whether national security issues dominate nation-states' decision-making agendas. Under conditions of interdependence, foreign policy agendas become "larger and more diverse" because a broader range of "governments' policies, even those previously considered merely domestic, impinge on one another" (Keohane and Nye, 1988).

Third, the perspective disputed the popular notion that military force is the only, even dominant, means of exercising influence in international politics, particularly among the industrial and democratic societies in Europe and North America. "Intense relationships of mutual influence exist between these countries, but in most of them force is irrelevant or unimportant as an instrument of policy" (Keohane and Nye, 1988).

Advocates of the complex interdependence perspective extended many of these insights to the range of issues relating to international economic interdependence that came to the fore in the 1970s (Puchala, 1988). International institutions commanded a central place in many of these analyses, as demonstrated in Robert O. Keohane and Joseph S. Nye's (1977, 1989) *Power and Interdependence*, which remains the classic statement on the complex interdependence perspective. In this sense the perspective embraces classical idealism.

However, a careful reading of *Power and Interdependence* shows that complex interdependence does not reject realism. Instead, the initial concern of many of those dedicated to the perspective was "the conditions under which assumptions of Realism were sufficient or needed to be supplemented by a more complex model of change" (Nye, 1987; see also Keohane, 1983). Keohane and Nye in particular sought to devise structural models of international *regime* change. The regime concept derived from and extended international legal studies. It eventually became a central component of the neoliberal institutionalist perspective and has been widely used in analyses of international politics that seek to understand cooperation under conditions of anarchy.

International Regimes

Although the international system continues to be characterized by anarchy, its nature is more properly conceptualized as an ordered anarchy, and the system as a whole as an "anarchical society" (Bull, 1977), because cooperation, not conflict, is often the observable outcome of relations among states.

Given this reality, the question arises: How can institutionalized procedures and rules for the collective management of global policy problems—*international regimes* based on coordinated cooperation—be established and preserved? Interest in that question derives from two goals that motivate many neoliberal analysts. One is "a desire to understand the extent to which mutually accepted constraints affect states' behaviors" (Zacher, 1987). The other is an interest in devising strategies for creating a less disorderly "world order."

As the study of regimes or rules for the management of global problems developed in the 1980s, Stephen Krasner's definition of a regime emerged dominant:

> Regimes can be defined as sets of implicit or explicit principles, norms, rules, and decision-making procedures around which actors' expectations converge in a given area of international relations. Principles are beliefs or fact, causation, and rectitude. Norms are standards

of behavior defined in terms of rights and obligations. Rules are specific prescriptions or proscriptions for action. Decision-making procedures are prevailing practices for making and implementing collective choice.[13] (Krasner, 1982: 186)

According to this definition, regimes are institutionalized systems of cooperation in a given issue-area. As Krasner (1982) explains, "It is the infusion of behavior with principles and norms that distinguishes regime-governed activity in the international system from more conventional activity, guided exclusively by narrow calculations of interest." Thus an essential property of a regime is that it constitutes "a system of injunctions about international behavior" (Smith, 1987). Because the international regime perspective directs attention to institutions and to the influence of norms on patterns of state behavior,[14] as opposed simply to the pursuit of national interests, it is in some ways best viewed as an attempt to reconcile the idealist and realist perspectives on world politics (Haggard and Simmons, 1987).

The global monetary and trade systems created during and after World War II are vivid expressions of international regimes. And both, as well as particular sectors within the trade system, have been the focus of considerable inquiry from the regime perspective.[15] Together the monetary and trade regimes defined a Liberal International Economic Order (LIEO) that limited government intervention in the world political economy and otherwise facilitated the free flow of capital and goods across national boundaries. The International Monetary Fund (IMF) and the General Agreement on Tariffs and Trade (GATT) played important institutional roles in the LIEO and reconfirmed the importance of international institutions in fostering transnational cooperation (see Chapter 7 for elaboration).

Most illustrations of the regime perspective appear in the world political economy arena. Few "security regimes" (Jervis, 1982) have emerged in the defense issue-area to provoke examination. Exceptions are the nuclear nonproliferation regime and the regime used by the former superpowers to manage crises (see George, 1986; Tarr, 1991). With the end of the Cold War, the pressures of interdependence may propel creation of regimes in widening areas of international conduct to facilitate states' control over their common fates (Zacher, 1991).

Hegemonic Stability Theory

As stressed by the neoliberal institutionalist perspective, nonstate actors play key roles in the patterns of transnational cooperation that characterize the LIEO. The

---

[13] For reviews of the regime concept and this and other definitions that have been offered, see Haggard and Simmons (1987), Kratochwil and Ruggie (1986), Strange (1982), and Young (1986).

[14] International institutions figure prominently as the bridge linking these orientations, although it should be understood that the term *regime* was construed to cover more than just organizations. As Oran Young (1986) explains, "Institutions are practices composed of recognized roles coupled with sets of rules or conventions governing relations among the occupants of these roles. Organizations are physical entities possessing offices, personnel, equipment, budgets, and so forth."

[15] The literature on international regimes is large and growing. The best single introduction remains the special issue of *International Organization* edited by Stephen D. Krasner (1983), which was published in book form by Cornell University Press in 1983. The journal *International Organization* publishes many analyses of issues related to regime dynamics.

perspective also draws attention to the decisive role that the overriding power of the United States exerted in promoting stability and the effective operation of the post–World War II monetary and trade regimes. That being so, the question arises: What impact will the decline of U.S. power perceived by so many (but disputed by others)[16] have on institutions designed to foster international cooperation? Does that alleged decline explain the global economic disorders so prevalent since the 1970s? The questions are of special concern to analysts whose interests center on *hegemonic stability*.

Hegemonic stability theorists differ in their definitions of hegemony, with some (for example, Gilpin, 1981) emphasizing the capacity of a leading military power to manage world order, and others (for example, Keohane and Nye, 1989) the capacity of a leading economic power to set and enforce the rules governing international trade, finance, and investment (see Levy, 1991). In the context of neoliberal institutionalism, hegemonic stability theory is dedicated primarily to the task of explaining not the incidence of peace and war but why preeminent states (hegemons) at the top of the international hierarchy (such as the United States in the decades following World War II) are motivated to promote international regimes that benefit not only themselves but also others. This stability-seeking behavior runs counter to the widespread belief among political realists that hegemonic power, once acquired, will be abused and used to exploit others, thereby provoking threats to international stability.

Whether the theory of hegemonic stability explains the basis of cooperation in post–World War II international politics is unclear (see Haggard and Simmons, 1987; Snidal, 1985). Indeed, the question has stimulated considerable scholarly controversy. By drawing attention to the impact that the acquisition of preponderant economic power can exert on international cooperation, hegemonic stability theory nonetheless promises to continue to command interest in the post–Cold War era where, at least on some issues, the ability of the United States to exercise decisive leadership will influence the prospects for global order and stability.

INTERNATIONAL POLITICS IN A WORLD OF CHANGE . . . .

To understand today's changing world and make reasonable prognoses about tomorrow's, we must first arm ourselves with an array of knowledge and conceptual tools, entertain rival interpretations of the alternative ways to map world politics, and question the assumptions on which these contending world views rest. As we have demonstrated (see Table 2.1 for a brief summary), there are several alternative, sometimes incompatible ways of organizing theoretical perspectives about world politics. The reason is clear. The *global problématique* is one of vast proportions and complexity—a challenge to insight and understanding—that cannot be reduced to a single, simple, yet compelling account.

---

[16] For discussions of this thesis, see Kennedy (1987) and Dietrich (1992); for rebuttals, see Nau (1990) and Nye (1990).

TABLE 2.1 THE QUEST FOR THEORY: FOUR PERSPECTIVES

Model	Idealism	Realism	Behavioralism	Neoliberal Institutionalism
Core Concern	Institutionalizing peace	War and security	Discovering through science "laws" about the causes and consequences of interstate interaction	Fostering interstate cooperation on the globe's shared economic, social, and ecological problems
Submodel(s)	International law; international organization; neo-idealism	Neorealism; structural realism	Comparative study of foreign policy, quantitative analysis	Complex interdependence; regimes; hegemonic stability theory
Outlook on Global Prospects	Optimistic/ Progress	Pessimistic/ Stability	Progress through reason	Expectation of cooperation and creation of a global community
Key Units	Institutions transcending nations	Independent nation-states	Individuals, states, and the international system	"Penetrated" nations and nonstate transnational actors
Motives of Actors	Collaboration; mutual aid; meeting human needs	National interests; zero-sum competition; security; power	Rational choice, as modified by environmental opportunities and constraints	National interests; international peace and prosperity
Central Concepts	Collective security; world order; law; integration; international organization	Structural anarchy; power; national interests; balance of power; polarity	Theory building and hypothesis testing against reproducible evidence and deductive modeling	Transnational relations; regimes; hegemonic stability; interdependence; political economy; integration
Prescriptions	Institutional reform	Increase national power; resist reduction of national autonomy	Ground policy advice on verifiable knowledge	Develop regimes to coordinate collective responses to diverse national and global problems

Rival Theories and Evidence

Although the theoretical perspectives discussed in this chapter begin to equip us for the challenge of understanding the changing world, from time to time we will also find it useful to draw on still other theoretical focuses. Four that are elaborated in greater detail in later chapters are briefly identified here: long-cycle theory, world system theory, dependency theory, and comparative foreign policy.

Long-cycle Theory

Long-cycle theory seeks to explain the historical ebb and flow of world politics, global leadership, and system-wide war. The rise and fall of the great powers is a central concern. An important assumption is the belief that many features of international politics—especially the patterns of great-power rivalry—cannot be understood adequately without a long-term historical perspective focused on recurrent patterns.

World System Theory

World system theory also looks at system dynamics from a long-term perspective. It arose in part in response to the theories of political development and nation building prevalent in comparative politics in the 1950s and 1960s and seeks to explain the rise to dominance of the capitalist societies of the Western world and the lack of economic development in many other geographic areas. There are several contending variants of world system theory that stress different factors. The best known is Immanuel Wallerstein's macrosociological theory of economic change in the world capitalist system, which examines the forces driving the formation and disintegration of world empires (see Chapter 5).

Dependency Theory

The primary concern of *dependency theory* is the pattern of dominance and dependence that characterizes the relationship between the world's rich and poor nations. Its intellectual father is Dr. Raúl Prebisch, an Argentinean economist who directed the United Nations Economic Commission for Latin America in the 1950s. Initially looking at the unfavorable terms of trade alleged to have led to economic stagnation and foreign control of Third World economies, dependency theorists have expanded their analysis to account for other phenomena, such as "dependent development," that is, economic growth where previously it was thought impossible. They are also concerned with such paradoxes as the tendency of Third World economic growth to exacerbate social inequalities and class cleavages.

Comparative Foreign Policy

Most of the perspectives described in this chapter focus on the so-called international system level of analysis. Structural realism does so unabashedly. It argues that differences in the characteristics of the international actors and their decision processes are irrelevant to an understanding of recurrent behavior in international politics. As explained by Robert O. Keohane (1983), "The key distinguishing characteristic of a systemic theory is that *the internal attributes of actors are given by assumption rather than treated as variables*. Changes in actor behavior, and system outcomes, are explained not on the basis of variation in these actor characteristics, but on the basis of changes in attributes of the system itself."

Other scholars are critical of this perspective. Those working in the neoliberal tradition, for example, place considerable emphasis on the potential role that domestic politics and politics within national bureaucratic organizations may play in shaping the responses of different foreign policymakers to the challenge of interdependence. Still, no one has yet articulated a coherent theory of international politics that adequately links explanations of international politics derived from the level of state actors (domestic politics) to that of the global system (systemic constraints and opportunities). Thus the quest for theory continues.

Advocates of the comparative study of foreign policy pursue that goal by probing patterns in the similarities and differences in states' national attributes and capabilities, foreign policy decision-making processes, and individual policymakers. The Soviet Union's peaceful retreat from the world stage that marked the end of the Cold War highlights the cogency of their focus. Soviet domestic conditions, both economic and political, and Mikhail Gorbachev's personal preferences stimulated that remarkable and unexpected development. The subsequent disintegration of the Soviet Union alters the opportunities and constraints that global actors now face. But the configuration of world power prior to the onset of the Soviets' disintegrative domestic tendencies would not have predicted them. Thus the comparative study of foreign policy commands considerable analytical attention. We will therefore devote an entire chapter (Chapter 3) to that single perspective.

Levels of Analysis

The comparative study of foreign policy focuses analytical attention primarily on the nation-state. Other theories and perspectives discussed in this chapter direct attention to other levels of analysis. Thus the psychological approach emphasizes the role of individuals in world politics, while the neorealist perspective directs attention exclusively to the international system as a whole. What we learn about world politics, then, depends in part on the analytical perspective we choose and on the analytical level it emphasizes.

The levels-of-analysis issue in the study of world politics (see Singer, 1961; also Waltz, 1954) underscores the need to trace changes in world politics to different groups of actors, their attributes, and their activities and interactions. Levels are commonly determined by the relative size and scope of their composition. Three are distinctly identifiable and theoretically important.

At the smallest (narrowest) level is the so-called idiosyncratic or *individual level* of analysis. It refers to the personal characteristics of those who make the important decisions on behalf of both state and nonstate actors in world politics. At the second or *national level* are the authoritative decision-making units that govern nation-states' foreign policy processes and the attributes of those states, such as their size, location, and power, that shape and constrain the foreign policy choices of those who govern. And at a third level are the conditions that result from the interactions of nations and nonstate actors with one another around the globe. This international or *system level* of analysis is also used to refer to those macro properties that simultaneously influence the entire global environment, such as its international legal rules, distribution of power, or the number of cross-cutting alliances in existence and amount of war under way.

The differentiation of levels of analysis is important because it highlights the fact that transformations in world politics cannot be attributed to a single source but must be traced to the influence of many causes. Common sense suggests there are interrelationships across all levels and that trends and transformations in world politics are linked simultaneously to forces operating at each level. The behavior of any one nation, for instance, will likely be affected by the dispositions of its leaders, its domestic political and economic circumstances and type of government, and changes in the conditions beyond its borders. Similarly, changes in international tension tomorrow will be governed in part by how actors at each level choose to act toward one another today. For this reason, we must examine trends and transformations in world politics by reference to a variety of causal factors operating at all three levels of analysis. It is an analytical task that permeates the remaining chapters of this book.

WORLD POLITICS: THE ANALYTICAL CHALLENGE . . . .

Armed with the tools and theories described in preceding sections, and being sensitive to which each highlights or obscures, we can begin to address difficult and often disturbing questions. Will the world's complex metamorphoses outrun its ability to devise new mechanisms of political and social control? Will the world be flexible enough to adjust its perceptions to changing global realities? Indeed, have some theories that were once popular but later fell out of favor again become relevant to an understanding of the continuing transformation of world politics? For example, because the end of the Cold War has seemingly put to rest the ideological conflict between communism and capitalism, is now the time to give Woodrow Wilson's idealist vision of collective international collaboration "the fair test it has never received" (Gaddis, 1990)?[17] Can we adapt conventional mental habits to comprehend unconventional circumstances? The challenge is ours to meet.

SUGGESTED READINGS

Dougherty, James E., and Robert L. Pfaltzgraff, Jr. *Contending Theories of International Relations*, 3rd ed. New York: Harper & Row, 1990.

---

[17] For discussions of the possible revival of theories grounded in the idealist tradition, see Kegley (1988, 1992) and Kober (1990).

Dyer, Hugh C., and Leon Manganian, eds. *The Study of International Relations: The State of the Art*. New York: St. Martin's Press, 1989.

Ferguson, Yale H., and Richard W. Mansbach. *The Elusive Quest: Theory and International Politics*. Columbia: University of South Carolina Press, 1988.

Holsti, K. J. *The Dividing Discipline: Hegemony and Diversity in International Theory*. Boston: Allen & Unwin, 1985.

Holsti, Ole R. "Models of International Relations and Foreign Policy," *Diplomatic History* 13 (Winter 1989): 15–43.

Keohane, Robert O., ed. *Neorealism and Its Critics*. New York: Columbia University Press, 1986.

Keohane, Robert O., and Joseph S. Nye, Jr. *Power and Interdependence: World Politics in Transition*, 2nd ed. Glenview, Ill.: Scott, Foresman/Little, Brown, 1989.

Knorr, Klaus, and James N. Rosenau, eds. *Contending Approaches to International Politics*. Princeton, N.J.: Princeton University Press, 1969.

Rothstein, Robert L., ed. *The Evolution of Theory in International Relations*. Columbia: University of South Carolina Press, 1991.

Viotti, Paul, and Mark V. Kauppi. *International Relations Theory*. New York: Macmillan, 1987.

Part II

Relations Among Global Actors

• • •

3.
Foreign Policy Decision Making: Coping with
International Circumstances

4.
Great-Power Rivalry in Contemporary World Politics

5.
The North-South Conflict: Roots and
Consequences of Global Inequalities

6.
Nonstate Actors in World Politics: The
Role of International Organizations and
Multinational Corporations

CHAPTER 3

* * *

FOREIGN POLICY DECISION MAKING: COPING WITH INTERNATIONAL CIRCUMSTANCES

* * *

Foreign policy is the system of activities evolved by communities for changing the behavior of other states and for adjusting their own activities to the international environment.

George Modelski,
Political Scientist, 1962

One of the most unsettling things for foreigners is the impression that [U.S.] foreign policy can be changed by any president on the basis of the president's personal preference.

Henry A. Kissinger,
Political Consultant, 1979

People who study world politics typically use the term *actor* to refer to entities that are its primary performers. The image portrayed is that of a stage on which those most capable of capturing the drama of world politics act out the roles assigned to them. The leading actors dominate the center of the stage, and others cast in supporting roles are less in evidence as they move along the periphery. Moreover, they play their roles under constraints not readily visible to the casual observer, much as the actors in a community playhouse production follow their scripts under the guiding hand of the director.

Today the actors on the world stage are many and varied. They include countries, properly called nation-states (like the United States and Japan), international organizations (the United Nations), multinational corporations (Ford Motor Company), non-state nations (the Palestine Liberation Organization), and terrorist groups (the Irish Republican Army). We will discuss each of these types of actors in later chapters. Here we focus on nation-states, and in particular on the processes they use to make foreign policy decisions designed to cope with challenges from abroad. Nation-states demand attention because they remain the principal repositories of economic and military capabilities in world affairs, and they alone assert the legal right to use force.

The term nation-state is often used interchangeably with *state* and *nation*, but technically the three are different. A *state* is a legal entity that enjoys a permanent population, a well-defined territory, and a government capable of exercising sovereignty (that is, supreme authority over its inhabitants and freedom from interference by others). A *nation* is a collection of people who, on the basis of ethnic, linguistic, or cultural affinity, perceive themselves to be members of the same group. Thus *nation-state* refers to a polity controlled by members of some nationality recognizing no authority higher. It implies a convergence between territorial states and the psychological identification of people with them.[1]

When we speak generically about *foreign policy* and the decision-making processes that produce it, we refer to the goals that the officials representing nation-states seek abroad, the values that underlie those goals, and the means or instruments used to pursue them. We begin our inquiry of how nations make foreign policy choices by studying the model of rational decision making. Following this, we will consider two alternative frameworks: the bureaucratic politics and the hero-in-history models. We conclude by examining how states' national attributes influence their foreign policy behavior.

THE UNITARY ACTOR AND RATIONAL DECISION MAKING . . . .

According to the theory of political realism, discussed in Chapter 2, the primary goal of nation-states' foreign policies is to ensure their survival. That is, states seek to preserve their independence or sovereignty in a hostile environment. From this viewpoint, strategic calculations in the arena of high politics are the primary determinants of policymakers' choices. Domestic politics and the process of policy making itself are of secondary concern.

States as Unitary Actors

Political realism in both its classical and neorealist forms emphasizes that the international environment determines state action. It assumes that foreign policy making consists primarily of adjusting the nation-state to the pressures of an anarchical world system whose essential properties remain invariant. Accordingly, it assumes that all states and the individuals responsible for their foreign policies confront the problem of national survival in similar ways. Thus all decision makers are essentially alike insofar as they approach foreign policy making and world politics.

If they follow the [decision] rules, we need know nothing more about them. In essence, if

---

[1] Many states are made up of many nations, not just one, and some nations are not states. These nonstate nations are ethnic groups, such as native American tribes in the United States or Palestinians residing in the Middle East, composed of people without sovereign power over the territory they occupy, some of whom seek national (ethnic) independence and/or merger with another state with which they feel greater solidarity. See Bertelsen (1977) for a discussion of nonstate nations and Nietschmann (1991) for a discussion of national independence movements.

the decision-maker behaves rationally, the observer, knowing the rules of rationality, can rehearse the decisional process in his own mind, and, if he knows the decision-maker's goals, can both predict the decision and understand why that particular decision was made. (Verba, 1969: 225)

Because the goals and corresponding decision calculus of states are the same, the foreign policy decision-making processes of each can be studied as though it were a *unitary actor*. One way to picture this assumption is to think of states as billiard balls and the table on which they interact as the state system. The metaphor compares world politics to a game in which the billiard balls (states) continuously clash and collide with one another. The actions of each are determined by their interactions with the others, not by what occurs within them. According to this mental map, the leaders who make foreign policy, the types of governments they head, the characteristics of their societies, and the internal economic and political conditions of the states they lead are unimportant.

Policy Making as Rational Choice

The decision processes of unitary actors designed to determine their national interests are typically described as *rational*. What is rationality? And how do decision makers go about making foreign policy rationally?

For our purposes, we can define rationality as purposeful, goal-directed behavior exhibited when "the individual responding to an international event . . . uses the best information available and chooses from the universe of possible responses that alternative most likely to maximize his goals" (Verba, 1969). By way of elaboration, scholars who study decision making and advise policymakers on ways to improve their policy-making skills describe rationality as a sequence of decision-making activities involving the following intellectual steps:

1. *Problem recognition and definition.* The need to decide begins when policymakers perceive an external problem with which they must deal and attempt to define its distinguishing characteristics objectively. Objectivity requires full information about the actions, motivations, and capabilities of other actors as well as the state of the international environment and trends within it. The search for information must be exhaustive, and all the facts relevant to the problem must be gathered.

2. *Goal selection.* Next, those responsible for making foreign policy choices must determine what they want to accomplish. This disarmingly simple requirement is often difficult. It requires the identification and ranking of *all* values (such as security, democracy, freedon, economic well-being) in a hierarchy from most to least preferred.

3. *Identification of alternatives.* Rationality also requires the compilation of an exhaustive list of *all* available policy options and an estimation of the costs associated with each alternative course of action.

4. *Choice.* Finally, rationality requires selecting from competing options the single alternative with the best chance of achieving the desired goal(s). For this purpose, policymakers must conduct a rigorous means-ends, cost-benefit analysis, one guided by an accurate prediction of the probable success of each option.[2]

The requirements of perfect rationality are stringent. Nonetheless, policymakers often describe their own behavior as resulting from a rational decision-making process designed to reach the "best" decision possible. Moreover, some past foreign policy decisions reveal elements of this idealized process.

The 1962 Cuban missile crisis, for example, illustrates several ways the deliberations of the key U.S. policymakers conformed to a rational process (Allison, 1971; for reassessments by U.S. and Soviet participants, see Blight and Welch, 1989). Once Washington discovered the presence of Soviet missiles in Cuba, President John F. Kennedy charged the crisis decision-making group he formed to "set aside all other tasks to make a prompt and intensive survey of the dangers and all possible courses of action." Six options were ultimately identified: do nothing; exert diplomatic pressure; make a secret approach to the Cuban leader Fidel Castro; invade Cuba; launch a surgical air strike against the missiles; and blockade Cuba. Goals had to be prioritized before a choice could be made among these six. Was removal of the Soviet missiles, retaliation against Castro, or maintenance of the balance of power the objective? Or did the missiles pose little threat to the vital interests of the United States? "Do nothing" could not be eliminated as an option until the missiles were determined to pose a serious threat to U.S. security.

Once the advisers agreed that the elimination of the missiles was the goal, their discussion turned to evaluating the surgical air strike and blockade options. The latter was eventually chosen because of its presumed advantages. Among them was the demonstration of firmness it permitted the United States and the flexibility about further choices it allowed both parties.

The decision of U.S. President George Bush to send a military force to the Middle East following Iraq's invasion of Kuwait on August 2, 1990, is another example of crisis decision making that conforms in part to the model of rational choice. As in the Cuban case, the "do nothing" option was quickly dismissed by the president and his advisers. Instead, "much of the initial debate among senior government officials on August 2 and 3 focused on diplomatic and economic retaliation against Iraq, and possible covert action to destabilize and topple Saddam Hussein" (Woodward and Atkinson, 1990). By August 4 Bush decided to mount a military response. Two days later, after vowing that Iraq's invasion of Kuwait "will not stand," he ordered the dispatch of U.S. troops in pursuit of three missions: to deter further Iraqi aggression,

---

[2] As we will note in more detail below, the concept of "rationality" has been defined in different ways. For our purposes, we at this point employ a "procedural" definition of rationality but will later contrast it to an "instrumentalist" definition that is more suited to individuals than to the policy-making process whereby organizations make foreign policy choices (see also Bueno de Mesquita, 1981; Levi 1990–1991; Moser, 1990; and Zagare, 1990).

to defend Saudi Arabia, and to "improve the overall defense capabilities of the Saudi peninsula" (Woodward and Atkinson, 1990). Eventually, those defensive missions gave way to an offensive one designed to force Iraq out of Kuwait.

Impediments to Rational Choice

Despite the apparent application of rationality in these important crises, the rational decision-making model is often more an idealized standard by which to evaluate preferences than an accurate description of real-world behavior. Theodore Sorensen, himself a participant in the Cuban missile deliberations, has written about the steps policymakers in the Kennedy administration followed as they sought to emulate the process of rational choice[3] but also of how actual decision making often departed from it:

> Each step cannot be taken in order. The facts may be in doubt or dispute. Several policies, all good, may conflict. Several means, all bad, may be all that are open. Value judgments may differ. Stated goals may be imprecise. There may be many interpretations of what is right, what is possible, and what is in the national interest. (Sorensen, 1963: 19–20)

Despite the virtues promised by rational choice, then, the impediments to its realization are substantial. Some are human. They derive from deficiencies in the intelligence, capability, and psychological needs and aspirations of those who make foreign policy decisions under conditions of uncertainty. Others are organizational. Individuals meeting in groups make most policy decisions. As a result, most decisions require group agreement about the national interest and the wisest course of action to pursue. Reaching agreement is not easy, however, as reasonable people with different human characteristics and values understandably often disagree about goals or preferences and the probable results of alternative options. Thus the impediments to sound (rational) policy making are substantial.

Scrutiny of the actual process of decision making reveals these impediments. Problem recognition is often delayed, for example. Information sufficient to define emergent problems accurately is frequently lacking, resulting in decisions that are made on the basis of incomplete information. In fact, rationality is usually "bounded" (Simon, 1985), not "comprehensive," as policymakers must deal not with perfect information but only with approximations of it. Moreover, the available information is often inaccurate because the bureaucratic organizations on which political leaders depend for information and advice screen, sort, and rearrange it.

In addition, goal selection is difficult because of the inherent ambiguities that surround the national interest. The constraints on information processing that decision

---

[3] Sorensen (1963) described an eight-step process for policy making that the Kennedy administration sought to follow that is consistent with the model we have described: (1) agreement on the facts; (2) agreement on the overall policy objective; (3) precise definition of the problems; (4) canvassing of all possible solutions; (5) listing of the possible consequences flowing from each solution; (6) recommendation of one option; (7) communication of the option selected; (8) provisions for its execution.

makers face limit their capacity for rational choice. "Decision making often takes place within an atmosphere marked by value-complexity and uncertainty. The existence of competing values about a single issue forces value trade-offs; uncertainty refers to the absence of complete and well-organized information on which to base a confident policy choice" (Walker, 1991).

Furthermore, because policymakers work constantly with overloaded agendas and short deadlines, the search for policy options is seldom exhaustive. "There is little time for leaders to reflect," observes former U.S. Secretary of State Henry Kissinger (1979). "They are locked in an endless battle in which the urgent constantly gains on the important. The public life of every political figure is a continual struggle to rescue an element of choice from the pressure of circumstance." In the choice phase, then, decision makers rarely make value-maximizing choices. Instead of selecting the one option or set of options with the best chance of success, they typically terminate their evaluation as soon as an alternative appears that seems superior to those already considered. Herbert Simon (1957) describes this as *satisficing* behavior. Rather than seeking optimal alternatives, decision makers are routinely content to select the choice that meets minimally acceptable standards. For this reason they frequently face "unresolvable" choices that preclude satisfaction across competing preferences; instead of "optional" choices, often only "admissible" ones are available (see Levi, 1990).

The assumption that states are unitary actors explains in part the discrepancy between the theory and practice of rational decision making. As suggested above, states consist of individuals with different beliefs, values, preferences, and psychological needs. These differences generate disagreements about goals and alternatives that are seldom resolved through tidy, orderly, rational processes. As one former U.S. policymaker put it, "Rather than through grand decisions or grand alternatives, policy changes seem to come through a series of slight modifications of existing policy, with new policy emerging slowly and haltingly by small and usually tentative steps, a process of trial and error in which policy zigs and zags, reverses itself, and then moves forward" (Hilsman, 1967).

Thus, despite the image that policymakers seek to project, the actual practice of foreign policy decision making is an exercise that lends itself to miscalculations, errors, and fiascoes. Policymakers themselves frequently absorb new information under great pressure quickly and take calculated risks through deliberate planning, but the degree of rationality in foreign policy decision making often "bears little relationship to the world in which officials conduct their deliberations" (Rosenau, 1980). Instead of acting rationally, then, policymakers tend "to avoid new interpretations of the environment, to select and act upon traditional goals, to limit the search for alternatives to a small number of moderate ones, and finally to take risks which involve low costs if they prove unsuccessful" (Coplin, 1971). (See Table 3.1.)

Although rational foreign policy making is more an ideal than a description of reality, we can still profit from the assumption that policymakers aspire to rational decision-making behavior, which they may occasionally approximate. Indeed, as a working proposition, it is useful to accept rationality as a picture of how the decision process should work and as a description of key elements of how it does work:

TABLE 3.1 FOREIGN POLICY DECISION MAKING IN THEORY AND PRACTICE

Ideal Rational Process	Common Actual Practice
Accurate, comprehensive information	Distorted, incomplete information
Clear definition of national interests and goals	Personal motivations and organizational interests bias national goals
Exhaustive analysis of all options	Limited number of options considered, none thoroughly analyzed
Selection of optimal course of action most capable of producing desired results	Selection of course of action by political bargaining and compromise
Effective statement of decision and its rationale to mobilize domestic support	Confusing and contradictory statements of decision often framed for media consumption
Careful monitoring of implementation of decision by foreign affairs bureaucracies	Neglect of tedious task of managing implementation of decision by foreign affairs bureaucracies
Instantaneous evaluation of consequences followed by correction of errors	Superficial policy evaluation, uncertain responsibility, poor follow-through, and delayed correction

Officials have some notion, conscious or unconscious, of a priority of values; . . . they possess some conceptions, elegant or crude, of the means available and their potential effectiveness; they engage in some effort, extensive or brief, to relate means to ends; and . . . therefore, at some point they select some alternative, clear-cut or confused, as the course of action that seems most likely to cope with the immediate situation. (Rosenau, 1980: 304–305)

THE BUREAUCRATIC POLITICS OF FOREIGN POLICY DECISION MAKING . . . . .

Picture yourself as a head of state charged with managing your nation's relations with the rest of the world. To make the right choices, you must seek information and advice, and you must see that the actions generated by your decisions are carried out properly. To whom can you turn to aid you in these tasks? Out of necessity, you must turn to those with the time and expertise you lack.

In today's world, the extensive political, military, and economic relations of states require dependence on large-scale organizations. Leaders turn to them for aid as they face critical foreign policy choices. This is more true of major powers than of small states. But even those without large budgets and complex foreign policy bureaucracies make most of their decisions in an organizational context (Korany, 1986). The reasons are found in the vital services organizations perform, services that enhance the state's capacity to cope with changing global circumstances.

Foreign Policy–making Organizations

Not only has bureaucracy become a necessary component of modern government but making and executing a nation's foreign policy also usually involves many different organizations. In the United States, for example, the State Department, the Defense Department, and the Central Intelligence Agency are key elements in the nation's foreign policy machinery. They are joined by other agencies that bear responsibility for specialized aspects of U.S. foreign relations, such as the Treasury, Commerce, and Agriculture departments. Multiple agencies with similar responsibilities characterize the foreign affairs machinery of most other major powers, whose governments face many of the same foreign policy management problems as the United States.

Bureaucracy, Efficiency, and Rationality

Bureaucratic management of foreign relations is not new. It was in evidence long ago in Confucian China, but it is a peculiarly modern phenomenon. Bureaucratic procedures are commonplace throughout the world, in large measure because of the perception that they enhance rational decision making and efficient administration. The source of those ideas is the theoretical work on bureaucracies by the German social scientist Max Weber, who argued nearly a century ago that bureaucratic organizations could produce effective administration and enhance rational choice.

Bureaucracies increase efficiency and rationality by assigning responsibility for different tasks to different people, defining rules and standard operating procedures that specify how tasks are to be performed, relying on systems of records to gather and store information, and dividing authority among different organizations to avoid duplication of effort. They also permit some specialists the luxury of engaging in forward planning, designed to determine long-term needs and the means to attain them. Unlike heads of state, whose roles require attention to the crisis of the moment, bureaucracies can consider the future as well as the present.

Even the existence of many organizations may be a virtue. Ideally, when foreign policy choices and alternatives to meet them are required, the presence of several organizations may result in "multiple advocacy" (George, 1972) and, with it, improve the chance that all possible policy options are considered.

The Limits of Bureaucratic Organization

What emerges from this description of bureaucracy is another idealized picture of the policy-making process. Before jumping to the conclusion that bureaucratic decision making is a modern blessing, we should emphasize that these propositions tell us how, according to organization theory, bureaucratic decision making *should* occur. They do not tell us how it *does* occur. The actual practice and the foreign policy choices that result depict a reality of burdens and not just benefits.

THE CUBAN MISSILE CRISIS   Consider again the 1962 Cuban missile crisis, probably the single most threatening crisis in the post–World War II era. The way U.S. policymakers went about orchestrating a response to the surreptitious deployment of offensive Soviet missiles to Cuba is often viewed as having nearly approximated the ideal of rational choice. From another decision-making perspective, however, often described as the *bureaucratic politics* model,[4] the missile crisis reveals how decision making by and within organizational contexts sometimes compromises rather than facilitates rational choice.

As described by Graham Allison (1971) in his well-known book on the missile crisis, *Essence of Decision*, there are really two elements in the bureaucratic politics model. One, which Allison calls *organizational process*, reflects the constraints that organizations place on decision makers' choices. The other, which he calls *governmental politics*, draws attention to the "pulling and hauling" that occurs among the key participants in the decision process.

How do large-scale bureaucratic organizations contribute to the policy-making process? As noted, one way is by devising *standard operating procedures* (SOPs) for coping with policy problems when they arise. For example, once the Kennedy administration opted for a naval quarantine of Cuba during the 1962 missile crisis to prevent further shipments of Soviet missiles, the U.S. Navy could carry out the president's decision according to previously devised routines. Curiously, however, these routines or SOPs effectively limit the range of viable policy choices from which policymakers might select options. That is, rather than expanding the number of policy alternatives in a manner consistent with the logic of rational decision making, what organizations can and cannot do shapes what is possible and what is not. In the Cuban crisis, a surgical air strike designed to destroy the Soviet missiles then under construction was a leading alternative to the blockade, but when it was discovered that the U.S. Air Force could not guarantee 100 percent success in taking out the missiles, the alternative was dropped. Thus organizational capabilities profoundly shaped the means from which the Kennedy administration could choose to realize its goal of removing all Soviet missiles from Cuban soil.

Governmental politics, the second element in the bureaucratic politics model, is related to the organizational character of foreign policy making in complex societies. Not surprisingly, the many participants in the deliberations that lead to policy choices often define issues and favor policy alternatives that reflect their organizational affiliations. "Where you stand depends on where you sit" is a favorite aphorism reflecting these bureaucratic imperatives. Thus professional diplomats typically favor diplomatic approaches to policy problems, while military officers routinely favor military solutions.

Because the players in the game of governmental politics are responsible for protecting the nation's security, they are "obliged to fight for what they are convinced is right." The consequence is that "different groups pulling in different directions

---

[4] The characteristics of the bureaucratic politics model are elaborated in Allison (1971), Caldwell (1977), C. Hermann (1988), Kissinger (1973), and Townsend (1982); for critiques, see Art (1973) and Krasner (1972).

produce a result, or better a resultant—a mixture of conflicting preferences and unequal power of various individuals—distinct from what any person or group intended" (Allison, 1971). Rather than being a value-maximizing choice, then, the process of policy making is itself intensely political. Thus, one explanation of why nations make the choices they do lies not in their behavior vis-à-vis one another but within their own governments. And rather than presupposing the existence of a unitary actor, "it is necessary to identify the games and players, to display the coalitions, bargains, and compromises, and to convey some feel for the confusion" (Allison, 1971). From this perspective, the decision to blockade Cuba was as much a product of *who* favored the choice as of any inherent logic that may have commended it. Once Robert Kennedy, the president's brother and the attorney general, Theodore Sorensen, the president's special counsel and "alter ego," and Robert McNamara, his secretary of defense, united behind the blockade, a coalition of the president's most trusted advisers and those with whom he was personally most compatible had formed (Allison, 1971). How could the president have chosen otherwise?

THE CRISIS OVER KUWAIT Who favored what also colored President Bush's decision to dispatch U.S. troops to Saudi Arabia? Key Pentagon officials might have been expected to be hawkish. But some—specifically Dick Cheney, secretary of defense, and Colin Powell, the four-star general who was chairman of the Joint Chiefs of Staff—were reluctant supporters of the military option. Instead, members of the president's White House staff, notably Brent Scowcroft, the president's national security adviser (and a retired air force lieutenant general), and the president himself were the principal advocates of a military response (Woodward, 1991). Scowcroft continued to push a reluctant military as the crisis evolved into the fall, when the strategic plan changed from defense to offense.

The disastrous Vietnam War, which the professional military regarded as a debacle in part because it lacked public support at home and a clear political objective abroad, helps to explain the nonaggressiveness of the Pentagon on the military option. General Powell, who had himself served President Reagan as national security adviser, believed in the axiom "There is no legitimate use of military force without a political objective." And he apparently gave so much political advice during the early days of the crisis over Kuwait that "Cheney firmly suggested that the president would be better served if Powell offered more military advice" (Woodward and Atkinson, 1990).

Beyond the pulling and hauling at the top levels of government, what the military could offer in some sense presented the Bush administration with constraints similar to those Kennedy faced in Cuba. For many years the Pentagon had been preparing for "low-intensity" conflicts in jungle or forested terrain. Thus the standard operating procedures it had devised were ill-suited to mechanized warfare in flat, open, and featureless desert terrain. True, the United States had planned since the late 1970s for the possibility of desert warfare in the Middle East, but those plans assumed that either the Soviet Union or Iran would be the enemy. They did not anticipate Iraq as the aggressor or Kuwait as the victim.

The logistical obstacles the Pentagon faced as it contemplated fulfilling a mission in a distant region where the United States had no military bases were so daunting that the gut response of Powell and others during the early hours of the crisis was that no viable military options existed (Woodward and Atkinson, 1990). The specific plan that did exist, known as Operations Plan 90-1002, was first devised in the early 1980s. It called for a massive air and sea lift of U.S. military personnel and equipment and ground deployment of heavy armor and antitank weapons (Woodward and Atkinson, 1990). It became the basis for Operation Desert Shield. Once the president ordered troops to the Persian Gulf region, it was an alternative the professional military could support and execute. It became their standard for operations.

Attributes of Bureaucratic Behavior

Besides the influence that bureaucratic organizations exert on the policy choices of political leaders, several other characteristics associated with the way they affect the decision-making environment warrant scrutiny.

One characteristic derives from the proposition that bureaucratic agencies are parochial. According to this argument, every administrative unit within a state's foreign policy–making bureaucracy seeks to promote its own purposes and power. Organizational needs come before the state's needs, a practice that sometimes encourages the sacrifice of national interests to bureaucratic interests.

As a corollary, bureaucratic parochialism breeds competition among the agencies charged with foreign policy responsibilities. Far from being neutral or impartial managers desiring only to carry out orders from the head of state, bureaucratic organizations frequently take policy positions designed to increase their own influence relative to that of other agencies. Characteristically they are driven to enlarge their prerogatives and expand the conception of their mission; they seek to take on the responsibilities of other units and to gain the powers that go with those responsibilities. Thus organizations driven by the need to enhance their own importance—not always the national interest—determine nations' foreign policies.

To protect their interests, bureaucratic organizations attempt to reduce interference from and penetration by political leaders to whom they report as well as other agencies within governments. Because knowledge is power, a common device for promoting organizational exclusivity is to hide inner workings and policy activities from others. The "invisible government" operating within the U.S. National Security Council during the Reagan administration illustrates this syndrome. Lieutenant Colonel Oliver North used his authority as a staff member of the council to orchestrate a secret arms-for-hostages deal with the Iranian government, part of what became popularly known as the Iran-*contra* affair.

The natural proclivity of professionals who work in large organizations is to adapt their outlook and beliefs to those prevailing where they work. This reinforces the tendency of bureaucracies to act as entities unto themselves. Every bureaucracy develops a shared "mind set" or dominant way of looking at reality akin to the "groupthink" characteristic of the cohesiveness and solidarity that small groups often develop (Janis, 1982). An institutional mind-set discourages creativity, dissent, and independent thinking; it encourages reliance on standard operating procedures and deference to precedent rather than the exploration of new options to meet new challenges.

The Consequences of Bureaucratic Policy Making

A corollary of the notion that bureaucracies are often self-serving and guardians of the status quo finds expression in their willingness to defy directives by the political authorities they are supposed to serve. Bureaucratic unresponsiveness and inaction sometimes manifest themselves as lethargy. At other times bureaucratic sabotage is direct and immediate, as vividly illustrated again by the U.S. experience in the 1962 Cuban missile crisis. While President Kennedy sought to orchestrate U.S. action and bargaining, his bureaucracy in general, and the navy in particular, were in fact controlling events by doing as they wished.

> [The bureaucracy chose] to obey the orders it liked and ignore or stretch others. Thus, after a tense argument with the Navy, Kennedy ordered the blockade line moved closer to Cuba so that the Russians might have more time to draw back. Having lost the argument with the President, the Navy simply ignored his order. Unbeknownst to Kennedy, the Navy was also at work forcing Soviet submarines to surface long before Kennedy authorized any contact with Soviet ships. And despite the President's order to halt all provocative intelligence, an American U-2 plane entered Soviet airspace at the height of the crisis. When Kennedy began to realize that he was not in full control, he asked his Secretary of Defense to see if he could find out just what the Navy was doing. McNamara then made his first visit to the Navy command post in the Pentagon. In a heated exchange, the Chief of Naval Operations suggested that McNamara return to his office and let the Navy run the blockade. (Gelb and Halperin, 1973: 256)[5]

Bureaucratic recalcitrance is a recurrent annoyance that leaders throughout the world experience, in authoritarian and democratic political systems alike. Bureaucratic resistance to change is one of the major problems reformers in the Soviet Union and the other centralized communist countries of Eastern Europe encountered, which impaired their efforts to chart new policy directions and to remain in power. The foreign policy process in China, also a centralized communist regime, operates similarly. It is "subject to the same vicissitudes of subjective perception, organizational conflict, bureaucratic politics, and factional infighting that bedevil other governments, perhaps more so given its size" (Whiting, 1985). And in the United States nearly every president has complained at one time or another about how the bureaucracy ostensibly designed to serve him has undercut his policies (see Box 3.1). The implementation of foreign policy innovations thus poses a major challenge to most leaders (see Smith and Clarke, 1985).

Bureaucratic recalcitrance is not the only force promoting status quo foreign policies and preventing change. The dynamics of governmental politics, which reduce policy choices to the outcome of a political tug of war, also retard the prospects for change. From the perspective of the participants, decision making is a political game with high stakes, in which differences are often settled at the minimum common denominator instead of by rational, cost-benefit calculations. As former U.S. Secretary of State Henry A. Kissinger described the process:

---

[5] Although this anecdote illustrates graphically the potential ability of bureaucratic agencies to defy political leaders, its historical accuracy has been questioned. For an examination of the events surrounding the account, see Caldwell (1978).

Box 3.1

BUREAUCRATIC OBSTACLES TO DECISIVE FOREIGN POLICY MAKING:
ACCOUNTS BY U.S. PRESIDENTS

• • •

You should go through the experience of trying to get any changes in the thinking, policy, and action of the career diplomats and then you'd know what a real problem was. But the Treasury and the State Department put together are nothing as compared with the Navy. . . . To change anything in the Navy is like punching a feather bed. You punch it with your right and you punch it with your left until you are exhausted, and then you find the damn bed as it was before you started punching.

Franklin D. Roosevelt

I sit here all day trying to persuade people to do the things they ought to have sense enough to do without me persuading them.

Harry S Truman

There is nothing more frustrating for a President than to issue an order to a Cabinet officer, and then find that, when the order gets out in the field, it is totally mutilated. I have had that happen to me, and I am sure every other President has had it happen.

Gerald Ford

You know, one of the hardest things in a government this size is to know that down there, underneath, is the permanent structure that's resisting everything you're doing.

Ronald Reagan

Each of the contending factions within the bureaucracy has a maximum incentive to state its case in its most extreme form because the ultimate outcome depends, to a considerable extent, on a bargaining process. The premium placed on advocacy turns decision making into a series of adjustments among special interests—a process more suited to domestic than to foreign policy. This procedure neglects the long-range because the future has no administrative constituency and is, therefore, without representation in the adversary proceedings. Problems tend to be slighted until some agency or department is made responsible for them. . . . The outcome usually depends more on the pressure or the persuasiveness of the contending advocates than on a concept of over-all purpose. (Kissinger, 1969: 268)

Thus it is not surprising that bureaucracies throughout the world are frequently the object of criticism by both the political leaders they ostensibly serve and the citizens whose lives they so often touch.

The Role of Leaders in Foreign Policy Decision Making . . . .

The decisions of political elites determine the course of history. Leaders—and the kind of leadership they exert—shape the way foreign policies are made and the consequent behavior of nation-states in world politics. These simple propositions describe a popular image: that the world's political elites control their nations' foreign policies. "There is properly no history, only biography," is the way Ralph Waldo Emerson encapsulated the view that individual leaders move history.

Leaders as Makers and Movers of World History

This *hero-in-history* model equates national action with the preferences and initiatives of the highest officials in national governments. Leaders are expected to lead, and new leaders are assumed to make a difference. We reinforce this image when we routinely attach the names of leaders to policies, as though the leaders were synonymous with the nation itself, and when we attribute most successes and failures in foreign affairs to the leaders in charge at the time they occur.

Citizens are not alone in thinking that leaders are the decisive determinants of states' foreign policies and, by extension, world history. Leaders themselves seek to inculcate impressions of their own self-importance while attributing extraordinary powers to other leaders. The assumptions they make about the personalities of their counterparts, consciously or unconsciously, in turn influence their own behavior toward them (Wendzel, 1980).[6]

One of the dilemmas leader-driven explanations of foreign policy behavior pose is that the movers and shakers of history often pursue decidedly irrational policies. The classic example is Adolf Hitler, whose determination to seek military conquest of the entire European continent proved disastrous for Germany. How do we square this kind of behavior with the logic of political realism, which says that survival is the paramount goal of all states and that all leaders engage in rational decision making designed to maximize the benefits to their nation and minimize the costs? If the realists are indeed correct, even defects in states' foreign policy processes cannot easily explain such wide divergences between what leaders sometimes do and what is expected of them.

We can explain this divergence in part by distinguishing between *procedural* rationality and *instrumental* rationality (Zagare, 1990). Procedural rationality underlies the

---

[6] This interpretation stresses that leaders' images shape their actions (see Kelman, 1965, 1970). It is because perceptions indisputably shape foreign policy decisions that political psychology is so important to an understanding of international relations.

billiard ball view of world politics. That view sees all states acting similarly because all decision makers engage in the same "cool and clearheaded ends-means calculation" (Verba, 1969) based on perfect information and a careful weighing of all possible alternative courses of action. Instrumental rationality, on the other hand, is a more limited view of rationality. It says simply that individuals have preferences and, when faced with two (or more) alternatives, that they will choose the one that yields the preferred outcome.

> In contrast to the proceduralist [definition of rationality], the instrumentalist [definition] does not presume to offer normative evaluations of an actor's preferences, however bizarre, reprehensible, or ill-founded they may be. For instance, consider a leader who prefers systematic genocide to the benign neglect of a minority population. If his actions are consistent (or are perceived by the actor to be consistent) with this obviously repugnant order [of preferences], he is rational by [the instrumentalist definition of rationality]. . . . How best to understand Hitler's behavior? Simply by understanding his goals. (Zagare, 1990: 242)

The implications of these seemingly semantic differences are important. They demonstrate that rationality does not "connote superhuman calculating ability, omniscience, or an Olympian view of the world," as is often assumed when the rational actor model described above is applied to real world situations. They also suggest that individuals may act rationally (in the instrumentalist sense) at the same time that the process of decision making and its product appear decidedly irrational (Zagare, 1990). Why did Libya's leader, the mercurial Muammar Qaddafi, repeatedly challenge the United States, almost goading President Ronald Reagan into striking the North African desert country militarily? Because, we can postulate, Qaddafi's actions were consistent with his preferences, regardless of how "irrational" it was for a fourth-rate military power to take on the world's preeminent superpower.

Factors Affecting Leaders' Capacity to Lead

Despite the popularity of the hero-in-history model, we must be wary of ascribing too much importance to individual leaders. Their influence is likely to be much more subtle than popular impressions would have us believe. Henry Kissinger, himself a highly successful U.S. diplomatic negotiator once described as "the most powerful individual in the world in the 1970s" (Isaak, 1975), warned against placing too much reliance on personalities. Discussing Soviet-American relations in 1985, when the Cold War was still in full swing, he noted:

> [There is] a profound American temptation to believe that foreign policy is a subdivision of psychiatry and that relations among nations are like relations among people. But the problem [of reducing tension with the Soviet Union] is not so simple. Tensions that have persisted for forty years must have some objective causes, and unless we can remove these causes, no personal relationship can possibly deal with them. We are doing neither ourselves nor the Soviets a favor by reducing the issues to a contest of personalities.

Most leaders operate under a variety of political, psychological, and circumstantial constraints that limit what they can accomplish and reduce their control over events. In this context, Emmet John Hughes, an adviser to President Dwight D. Eisenhower, concluded that "all of [America's past presidents] from the most venturesome to the most reticent have shared one disconcerting experience: the discovery of the limits and restraints—decreed by law, by history, and by circumstances—that sometimes can blur their clearest designs or dull their sharpest purposes." "I have not controlled events, events have controlled me" was the way Abraham Lincoln summarized his presidential experience.

The question at issue is not whether political elites lead. Nor is it whether they can make a difference. They clearly do both. But leaders are not in complete control, and their influence is severely circumscribed. Thus personality and personal political preferences do not determine foreign policy directly. The relevant question, then, is not whether leaders' personal characteristics make a difference but, instead, under what conditions their characteristics are influential.[7]

In general, the impact of a leader's personal characteristics on his or her nation's foreign policy increases when the leader's authority and legitimacy are widely accepted by citizens or, in authoritarian or totalitarian regimes, when leaders are protected from broad public criticism. Moreover, certain kinds of circumstances enhance individuals' potential impact. Among them are new situations that free leaders from conventional approaches to defining the situation; complex situations involving a large number of different factors; and situations devoid of social sanctions that permit freedom of choice because norms delineating the range of permissible options are unclear (Di-Renzo, 1974).

A leader's self-image—that person's belief in his or her own ability to control events politically (known as political efficacy)—will also influence the degree to which personal values and psychological needs govern decision making (DeRivera, 1968). Conversely, when a sense of self-importance or efficacy is absent, self-doubt will undermine a leader's capacity to lead and to initiate policy changes. This linkage is not direct, however. The citizenry's desire for strong leadership will also affect it. When public opinion coalesces to produce a strong preference for a powerful leader and when the head of state has an exceptional need for admiration, for example, foreign policy will more likely reflect that leader's inner needs. Thus Kaiser Wilhelm II's narcissistic personality allegedly met the German people's desire for a symbolically powerful leader, and German public preferences in turn influenced the foreign policy that Germany pursued during Wilhelm's reign, which ended with the disaster of World War I (see Baron and Pletsch, 1985).

Other factors undoubtedly also influence how much leaders can shape their nation's

---

[7] As Margaret G. Hermann has observed, the impact of leaders is modified by at least six factors:

(1) what their world view is, (2) what their political style is like, (3) what motivates them to have the position they do, (4) whether they are interested in and have any training in foreign affairs, (5) what the foreign policy climate was like when the leader was starting out his or her political career, and (6) how the leader was socialized into his or her present position. World view, political style, and motivation tell us something about the leader's personality; the other characteristics give information about the leader's previous experiences and background. (Hermann, 1988: 268)

choices. For instance, when leaders believe that their own interests and welfare are at stake in a situation, they tend to respond in terms of their private needs and psychological drives, as suggested by the highly personalized policy reactions of the shah of Iran and Ferdinand Marcos of the Philippines when they felt themselves personally threatened by internal insurrections that led to their regimes' overthrow. However, when circumstances are stable and when leaders' egos are not entangled with policy outcomes, the impact of their personal characteristics is less obtrusive.

The amount of information available about particular situations is also important. Without pertinent information, policy is likely to be based on leaders' gut likes or dislikes. Conversely, "the more information an individual has about international affairs, the less likely is it that his behavior will be based upon non-logical influences" (Verba, 1969).

Similarly, the timing of a leader's assumption of power is important. When an individual first assumes a leadership position, the formal requirements of that role are least likely to circumscribe what he or she can do. That is especially true during the "honeymoon" period routinely given to new heads of state, during which time they are relatively free of criticism and excessive pressure. Moreover, when a leader assumes office following a dramatic event (a landslide election, for example, or the assassination of a predecessor), he or she can institute policies almost with a free hand, as "constituency criticism is held in abeyance during this time" (Hermann, 1976).

A national crisis is an especially critical circumstance that affects a leader's control over foreign policy making. Decision making during crises, which are ambiguous but threatening situations, is typically centralized and handled exclusively by the top leadership. Crucial information is often unavailable, and leaders see themselves as responsible for outcomes. Not surprisingly, therefore, great leaders in history, like Napoleon Bonaparte, Winston Churchill, and Franklin D. Roosevelt, customarily arise during periods of extreme challenge. Leaders are heroes capable of determining events. The moment may make the person, rather than the person the moment, in the sense that a crisis can liberate a leader from the constraints that normally would inhibit his or her capacity to control events or engineer foreign policy change.

History abounds with examples of the seminal importance of political leaders who arise in different times and places and under different circumstances to play critical roles in shaping the contours of world history. Mikhail Gorbachev is a dramatic recent illustration of an individual's capacity to change the course of history. Many experts believe that the Cold War could not have been brought to an end, nor Communist party rule in Moscow terminated and the Soviet state set on a path toward democracy and free enterprise, had it not been for Gorbachev's vision, courage, and commitment to engineering these revolutionary, system-transforming changes (see Bundy, 1990). Ironically, those reforms led to his loss of power when the Soviet Union imploded in 1991.

Limits to the Hero-in-History Model

Having said that the hero-in-history model may be compelling, we must be cautious and remember that leaders are not all-powerful determinants of states' foreign policy behavior. Rather, they shape decision making more completely in some circumstances than in others. The impact of personal factors varies with the context, and often the context is more influential than the leader.

Thus, the utility of the hero-in-history model of foreign policy is questionable. The "great man" versus "zeitgeist" debate is pertinent here. At the core of this timeless controversy is the perhaps unanswerable question of whether the times must be conducive to the emergence of great leaders or whether, instead, great people would have become famous leaders regardless of when and where they lived (see Greenstein, 1987). At the very least, the hero-in-history model appears much too simple an explanation of how states react to challenges from abroad. Most world leaders follow the rules of the "game" of international politics, which suggests that how states cope with their external environments is often influenced less strongly by the types of people heading them than by other factors. Put differently, states respond to international circumstances in often similar ways, regardless of the predispositions of those who lead them. This may account for the striking uniformities in state practices in a world of diverse leaders, different political systems, and turbulent change. In this sense, political realists' postulates about nations' foreign policy goals, which are hypothesized to derive from the rational calculation of opportunities and constraints and stress survival above all else, are not without foundation.

OTHER DETERMINANTS OF FOREIGN POLICY BEHAVIOR . . . .

The three models described above of how nations make foreign policy decisions—the rational actor model, the bureaucratic politics model, and the hero-in-history model—apply to all countries to some degree, but none applies to every country under every circumstance. It is useful, therefore, to consider other factors in the international system and within states themselves that may enhance or impede the foreign policy choices that different countries make.

History, culture, geostrategic location, military might, economic prowess, resource endowments, system of government, and position in the international pecking order—all are mediating variables that affect foreign policy choice. Still, it is difficult to generalize about these factors because of the diversity that characterizes the actors that make up the contemporary state system.

To help determine the relative impact of these factors under different circumstances, we can first distinguish usefully between the international and domestic sources of, or influences on, national choice. The international or *external* influences on foreign policy refer to all activities occurring beyond a country's borders that structure the choices made by its officials (that is, the conditioning impact of the international system).[8] Here, ideological challenges, the content of international law,

---

[8] In classifying the determinants not only of the foreign policies of states but also of trends in world politics generally, it is important to recall the *level of analysis* distinction introduced in Chapter 2. Nation-states and the international system comprise two distinct levels, the "national" level encompassing domestic characteristics and the "systemic" or international level encompassing interstate relations and temporal changes in them.

the cohesiveness of military alliances, and the levels of trade ties with others illustrate factors that sometimes profoundly affect the choices of decision makers.

Domestic influences, on the other hand, are those that exist at the level of the state, not the system. Here attention focuses on variations in *national attributes*—such as military capabilities, level of economic development, and type of government—insofar as they may influence different nations' foreign policy behavior. Examples of both orientations follow.

Geopolitics

One of the most important influences on states' foreign policy behavior is their location on the global terrain. The presence of natural frontiers, for example, may profoundly shape the mental maps that guide policymakers' choices. Consider the United States, which has prospered under a fortuitous set of circumstances because vast oceans separate it from Europe and Asia. This, combined with the absence of militarily powerful neighbors, permitted the United States to develop into an industrial giant and to practice safely an isolationist foreign policy without any immediate security threat for more than 150 years. Or consider Switzerland. Its topography and geostrategic position have made the practice of neutrality a compelling foreign policy posture.

In much the same vein, maintaining autonomy from continental politics has been an enduring theme in the foreign policy of Great Britain, an island nation whose physical separation from continental Europe served historically as a buffer separating it from major-power machinations on the continent itself. Preserving this protective shield has been a priority for Britain and helps explain why the British government has resisted greater integration of the British economy into the European Community.

Most countries are not insular, however; they have many states on their borders, and this situation denies them the option of noninvolvement in world affairs. Germany, which sits in the very heartland of Europe, historically has found its domestic political system and foreign policy preferences profoundly affected by its geostrategic position. Even before the unification of East and West Germany, in this century alone Germany has "undergone five radical changes in political personality—from Wilhelm II's empire to the Weimar Republic, from Hitler's *Reich* of the Thousand Years to its two postwar successors, the Federal Republic of Germany . . . and the German Democratic Republic" (Joffe, 1985). Significantly, these changes have been tied directly to the geopolitical aspects of war, the five noted above by lethal wars, and the sixth, unification, by a Cold War whose conclusion made possible the peaceful absorption of communist East Germany into West Germany's capitalistic democracy.

Similar to Germany, extended frontiers with the Soviet Union shaped the foreign policies of China and Finland. For Finland, neutrality in the Cold War contest between the United States and the Soviet Union helped ensure Finnish survival in the face of a powerful and threatening neighbor. China, on the other hand, has long regarded its relationship with the (now defunct) Soviet Union and its Czarist predecessor as unequal, and in the late 1960s the two communist giants clashed militarily as the Chinese sought to rectify past injustices. The "unequal treaties" between China and outside powers, in part a product of China's location, which seemed to fate its penetration by the great powers who carved China into spheres of influence with relative ease in previous centuries, encapsulate these perceived injustices.

China's fate is similar to that of Latin American nations in the sense that they have found themselves geographically proximate to a much stronger power (whose capabilities are in part a function of geophysical resource endowments). Latin America has long been the object of studied interest and frequent intervention by the giant to the north. Given their economic dependence on the United States, it is understandable that concern for Yankee imperialism has been a continuing theme in many Latin American nations' foreign policies. In this sense the countries of Latin America share a concern with other states in world politics that find themselves unable to compete on an equal footing with the world's more advantaged nations.

History is replete with many other examples of the influence of geography on states' foreign policy goals. The underlying principle is axiomatic: Leaders' perceptions of available foreign policy options are influenced by the geopolitical circumstances that define their countries' place on the world stage.[9]

Geopolitics is only one aspect of the external environment that may influence states' foreign policies. In the chapters that follow we will examine more thoroughly other external factors and how they intertwine to shape states' foreign policy behavior.[10] We also will examine in greater detail how characteristics of nations themselves and their relative position in the structure of the international system affect their behavior abroad. Here, by way of illustration, we will comment briefly on three national attributes: military capabilities, economic development, and type of government.

Military Capabilities

The proposition that states' internal capabilities shape their foreign policy priorities is captured by the demonstrable fact that countries' preparations for war strongly influence their later use of force (see Levy, 1989a; Vasquez, 1993). Thus all states may seek similar goals, but their ability to realize them will vary depending on their military capabilities.

---

[9]. The "geopolitics" school of realist thought and political geography generally direct attention to the influence of geographic factors on national power and international conduct. Illustrative of the early geopolitical thinking is Alfred Thayer Mahan's (1890) *The Influence of Seapower on History*, which maintained that national power was shaped by control of the seas. Thus states with extensive coastlines and ports purportedly enjoyed a competitive advantage in the race for hegemony. Later geopoliticians, such as Sir Halford Mackinder (1919) and Nicholas Spykman (1944), stressed that not only location but also topography, size (territory and population), climate, and distance between states are powerful determinants of the foreign policies of individual countries.

[10] See Macridis (1989) for essays that explore ideas related to the historical, strategic, and cultural conditions that affect nations' foreign policy behavior.

Because military capabilities limit a state's range of prudent policy choices, they act as a mediating factor on leaders' national security decisions. Consider two recent examples. Libyan leader Muammar Qaddafi, as noted earlier, repeatedly provoked the United States through anti-American and anti-Israeli rhetoric and by supporting various terrorist activities. Qaddafi played out the "hero-in-history" model because of the failure of bureaucratic organizations or a mobilized public to constrain his personal whims and militaristic foreign policy preferences. However, Qaddafi was doubtless more highly constrained by the outside world than were the leaders in the more militarily capable countries toward whom his anger was directed. Limited military muscle, compared with the United States, precluded the kinds of bellicose behaviors he threatened to practice. Conversely, Saddam Hussein, the Iraqi dictator, made strenuous efforts to build Iraq's military might, which, by 1990, made his army the fourth largest in the world. The invasion of Kuwait became a feasible foreign policy option as a result. In the end, however, even Iraq's impressive military power proved ineffective against a vastly superior coalition of military forces, headed by the United States, which forced Saddam Hussein's capitulation and withdrawal from his conquered territory.

Economic Development

The level of economic and industrial development enjoyed by a state affects the foreign policy goals it can pursue. As a general proposition, the more developed a state is economically, the more likely it is that it will play an activist role in the world political economy. Rich nations have interests that extend far beyond their borders and typically command the means necessary to pursue and protect them. Not coincidentally, countries that enjoy industrial capabilities and extensive involvement in international trade also tend to be militarily powerful, in part because military might is a function of economic capabilities. Historically, only the world's most scientifically sophisticated industrial economies have produced nuclear weapons, for example, which many regard as the ultimate expression of military prowess. In this sense nuclear weapons are the *result* of being powerful, not its cause.

For four decades after World War II, the United States and the Soviet Union stood out as superpowers precisely because they benefited from that combination of economic and military capabilities, including extensive arsenals of nuclear weapons and the means to deliver them anywhere, that enabled both to practice unrestrained globalism. Their "imperial reach" and interventionist behavior were seemingly unconstrained by limited wealth or resources. In fact, major powers (rich states) have been involved in foreign conflict more frequently than minor powers (poor states). For this reason gross national product (GNP) is often used in combination with other factors to distinguish great powers from middle-ranked or minor powers, and by itself is an important national attribute predicting the extensiveness of states' global interests and involvements.

Although economically advanced nations are more active globally, this does not mean that their privileged circumstances dictate adventuresome policies. Rich nations are usually "satisfied" ones that have much to lose from the onset of revolutionary change or global instability. For this reason, they usually perceive preservation of the status quo as serving their interests best (see Wolfers, 1962), and they often practice international economic policies designed to protect and expand their envied position at the pinnacle of the global hierarchy.

Levels of productivity and prosperity also affect the foreign policies of the poor states at the bottom of the hierarchy. Some respond to their economic weakness by complying subserviently with the wishes of the rich on whom they depend. Others rebel defiantly, and they sometimes succeed (despite their disadvantaged bargaining position) in resisting major power efforts to control their international behavior.

Hence efforts to generalize about the economic foundations of states' international political behavior often prove unrewarding. Levels of economic development vary widely among states in the international system, but they do not by themselves determine foreign policies. Instead the opportunities and constraints that leaders perceive in their nations' attributes, rather than the actual level of development, may be the determining source of states' international conduct.

Type of Government

Besides levels of military capability and economic development, a third important national attribute that affects states' international behavior is the nature of their political system. Type of government demonstrably constrains important choices, including whether the use of force is threatened and whether the threat is carried out. Here the important distinction is between liberal democracy (representative government), on one end of the spectrum, and autocratic (authoritarian or totalitarian) rule, on the other.

In neither democratic (sometimes called "open") nor autocratic ("closed") political systems can political leaders long survive without the support of organized domestic political interests (and sometimes the mass citizenry), but in the former those interests are likely to be potent politically, dispersed beyond the government itself, and active in their pressure on the government to make policy choices from which they benefit. Public opinion, interest groups, and the mass media are a more visible part of the political process in democratic systems, and the public participates openly in an effort to penetrate government structures and influence their policies in ways actively prevented in closed political systems. Similarly, the electoral process in democratic societies typically frames choices and produces results about who will lead more meaningfully than in authoritarian regimes, where the real choices are made by a few elites behind closed doors. In short, in a democracy public beliefs and preferences matter, and therefore differences in who is allowed to participate and how much they exercise their right to participate are critical determinants of foreign policy choice (see Hermann and Hermann, 1989).

Contrast, for example, the foreign policy of Saudi Arabia, which is controlled by a king and royal family, with that of Switzerland, which is governed by a multiparty democratic process. In the former, foreign policy decisions have sometimes been bold and unexpected, as illustrated by the revolutionary policies of the Saudi family when it authorized the dispatch of U.S. military forces to its territory in contravention of long-standing Arab policies designed to prevent Western encroachments against Muslim lands. In the latter, the policy of neutrality has been pursued without deviation since Switzerland's last war in 1815, to the point that Swiss leaders have found it difficult to reverse the traditional policy to permit Swiss entry into the European Community.

Public preferences help shape democratic societies' foreign policies. However, this does not deny that *elitism* operates in them, too, for it clearly does (Mills, 1956). Often, but especially when international crises erupt, decisions are made even in democratic governments by a small ruling elite, and opposition is usually silenced. The military-industrial complexes obtrusively evident in many countries are examples of elite groups sometimes believed to exercise disproportionate control over defense policy making, in both turbulent and calm times (see Hooks, 1991). But the rival model, known as *pluralism*, which sees policy making as an upward-flowing process in which competitive domestic groups pressure the government for policies responsive to their interests and needs, is a peculiarly democratic phenomenon whose pervasiveness is widespread even if its effects are sometimes difficult to pinpoint.

Democracies' Foreign Policy Performance

The proposition that domestic stimuli and not simply international events are a source of foreign policy is not novel. In ancient Greece, for instance, Thucydides observed that what happened within the Greek city-states often did more to shape their external behavior than what each did toward the others. He added that Greek leaders frequently behaved in ways designed not to influence relations with the targets of their action but, instead, the political climate within their own polities. Similarly, leaders today sometimes make foreign policy decisions for domestic political purposes, as, for example, when bold or aggressive acts abroad are intended to influence election outcomes or to divert public attention from economic woes.[11]

In the eyes of some observers, the intrusion of domestic politics into foreign policy making in democratic political systems is a disadvantage that undermines their ability to deal decisively with foreign policy crises or to bargain effectively with less democratic adversaries and allies. As the French political sociologist Alexis de Tocqueville put it more than a century ago, in the management of foreign relations democracies are "decidedly inferior" to centralized governments because they are prone to "impulse rather than prudence." Democracies, so this reasoning goes, are slow to respond to external dangers but, once they are recognized, to overreact to them (see Box 3.2 on page 66). "There are two things that a democratic people will always find difficult,"

---

[11] Of interest here is the "scapegoat" phenomenon, according to which even democratic leaders provoke war and crises abroad to distract their populations from economic and political problems at home. For an examination of the scapegoat phenomenon and "the diversionary theory of war," see Levy (1989).

Box 3.2
DEMOCRACIES IN FOREIGN AFFAIRS:
A U.S. POLICYMAKER'S CHARACTERIZATION

• • •

I sometimes wonder whether . . . a democracy is not uncomfortably similar to one of those prehistoric monsters with a body as long as this room and a brain the size of a pin: he lies there in his comfortable primeval mud and pays little attention to his environment; he is slow to wrath—in fact, you practically have to whack his tail off to make him aware that his interests are being disturbed; but, once he grasps this, he lays about him with such blind determination that he not only destroys his adversary but largely wrecks his native habitat. You wonder whether it would not have been wiser for him to have taken a little more interest in what was going on at an earlier date and to have seen whether he could not have prevented some of these situations from arising instead of proceeding from an undiscriminating indifference to a holy wrath equally undiscriminating.

Source: George F. Kennan, *American Diplomacy, 1900–1950* (New York: Mentor, 1951), p. 59.

de Tocqueville mused, "to start a war and to end it." In contrast, authoritarian regimes can "make decisions more rapidly, ensure domestic compliance with their decisions, and perhaps be more consistent in their foreign policy" (Jensen, 1982). But there is a cost: "Authoritarian regimes often are less effective in developing an innovative foreign policy because of subordinates' pervasive fear of raising questions." In short, the concentration of power and the suppression of public opposition can be dangerous as well as advantageous.

Consequences of the Spread of Democracy

The impact of regime type on foreign policy is not a mere abstract theoretical question. It has real-world consequences whose effects are likely to take on added significance in the post–Cold War world as Eastern Europe and the political units that formerly made up the constituent republics of the Soviet Union attempt to institutionalize the transition from centralized communist control to new forms of political organization.

The diffusion of democratic governance had already begun elsewhere during the 1980s (see Box 3.3 on page 68). By 1992, the number of countries that were democratic reached unprecedented proportions. As democracy spread, speculation arose as to its long-term impact. Francis Fukuyama (1989), a high-level official in the U.S. State

Department, predicted that "we may be witnessing . . . the end of mankind's ideological evolution and the universalization of Western liberal democracy as the final form of government." The contagious proliferation of democratic states could end, of course, because many of these fledgling new democracies are fragile. If they survive, however, and if democratic governments take root elsewhere, new types of foreign policies could propel transformations in the international system of the twenty-first century.

Because changes in domestic political regimes often precede changes in foreign policy behavior (see Hagan, 1992), the recent growth of democracy has caused people to ask whether a world increasingly dominated by democratic governments will be a more peaceful world. Immanuel Kant addressed this question centuries ago in his treatise *Perpetual Peace*. He maintained that democracies are inherently less warlike than autocracies because democratic leaders are accountable to the public, which restrains them from waging war. Because ordinary citizens would have to supply the soldiers and bear the human and financial costs of imperial policies, he contended, liberal democracies are "natural" forces for peace.

The tradition of political idealism provides theoretical support for this prediction, and empirical evidence buttresses it. Whereas democracies experience just as many wars as nondemocratic polities because they may be the targets of dictatorships' aggression (Small and Singer, 1976), they almost never initiate wars against one another (Chan, 1984; Doyle, 1986b). In addition, democracies are prone to seek each other as alliance partners (Siverson and Emmons, 1991)—a communitarian effect evident since World War II that arguably has contributed to the obsolescence of large-scale war, especially in Europe.[12]

These observations about the ways states' attributes relate to their foreign policy–making processes highlight the extent to which internal conditions, not just those external ones captured in the billiard ball model, influence foreign policy choices. Contrary to political realism's structural model, which presumes only the existence of unitary actors, it is apparent that type of government, domestic pressures on politicians, grass-roots movements, and whether leaders are answerable to the public can make a decisive difference in the goals states pursue abroad. Thus the degree of freedom citizens enjoy constrains their leaders' choices, shapes the manner in which policy decisions are implemented by their governments, and influences the pattern of international interactions (see Russett, 1990). Many developments in world politics examined in later chapters will draw further attention to the internal roots of external behavior.

---

[12] We must be careful not to assume that the historically tight linkage between democracy and peace will necessarily hold in the future. As Samuel Huntington (1989) warns, "The 'democratic zone of peace' argument is valid as far as it goes, but may not go all that far." Democracies are prone to aggression during times of economic and domestic crisis (Morgan and Campbell, 1991), and important exceptions to the propensity of democratic regimes to be less bellicose exist (Wright, 1942). Indeed, critics note that the longest-surviving democracy, the United States, initiated or supported military or paramilitary actions against elected governments in Vietnam, Grenada, and Nicaragua, and that Hitler came to power through the ballot, only to wage the most destructive war in history. Hence we must suspend judgment on the question of whether a world of democracies will necessarily be a more peaceful world.

Box 3.3
THE TIDE OF FREEDOM

• • •

Transitions from autocratic to democratically elected political systems have come in waves over the past decade.

The first wave swept through Latin America. It began in Peru in 1980 with the completion of a transition to an elected government after twelve years of military rule. In the following years, South America's military regimes fell one by one: Argentina in 1983, Brazil and Uruguay in 1985, Chile in 1988, and Paraguay in 1989. There have been more than 180 coups in 157 years in Bolivia, but democratic, civilian rule was restored in 1982.

Haiti is undergoing the region's most painful transition. Violence and coups have plagued the country since the Duvalier regime was ousted in a 1986 military coup. The latest setback occurred in December when Jean-Bertrand Aristide, Haiti's first democratically elected president, was overthrown and forced into exile.

The fall of the Berlin Wall in 1989 heralded a wave of transitions in the Eastern European countries and what was the Soviet Union. Radical political changes begun in Poland in 1988 were consolidated. Other countries followed: Bulgaria, Czechoslovakia, German Democratic Republic, Hungary, and Romania either began or completed transitions to democratic rule in 1990. In 1991, Albania held its first multiparty elections in sixty-eight years. That same year, the republics of the former Soviet Union experienced rapid political change toward democracy.

There was little political change in post-independence Africa until the late 1980s, but since then the transformations have been dramatic. Elections were held in Namibia in 1989 and the new government guided the country into independence in 1990. In 1991, multiparty elections were held in Benin, Cape Verde, São Tomé and Príncipe, and Zambia. The military government in Nigeria has committed itself to transfer rule to civilians through elections in 1992.

Many other African countries also moved toward ending single-party systems: Angola, Burkina Faso, Congo, Côte d'Ivoire, Ghana, Kenya, Niger, and Tanzania. And opposition forces in such other countries as Cameroon, Madagascar, and Zaire are pressing for political change.

Political change has transformed many countries in Asia over the past several years as well. In 1985, Filipinos poured into the streets to overthrow the Marcos government and, shortly thereafter, held a democratic presidential election. In 1990, Mongolians ratified a new constitution that established a multiparty system.

During 1991, Nepal held its first democratic elections in thirty years. Hong Kong took its first steps toward democracy with direct elections to its legislature, and Samoa held its first elections with universal adult suffrage. Pakistan and Bangladesh switched from martial law regimes to elected parliamentary systems. Warring factions in Cambodia signed a peace accord, and an international effort is under way to help smooth the transition to a multiparty system.

In the Middle East, election fever gripped Jordan at the end of the decade, and in 1991 a national charter legalized a multiparty system. Algeria's democratic transition is still incomplete. Multiparty elections are scheduled for November 1992 in Yemen.

Close to a third of humankind still lives in countries that place restrictions on political freedom and participation. But the world today is a much freer place than it was three decades ago.

Source: Human Development Report 1992 (New York: Oxford University Press, 1992), p. 28.

CONSTRAINTS ON FOREIGN POLICY MAKING IN A TRANSFORMING WORLD: PROBLEMS AND PROSPECTS . . . .

Can states respond to the demands that external challenges and internal politics simultaneously place on their leaders? For many reasons, that capability is increasingly strained.

Foreign policy choice occurs in an environment of uncertainty and multiple, competing interests. On occasion, it is also made in situations that threaten national values, when policymakers are caught by surprise and a quick decision is needed. The stress these conditions produce impairs leaders' cognitive abilities and may cause them, preoccupied with sunk costs, short-run results, and postdecisional rationalization, to react emotively rather than as analytical thinkers.

Although a variety of impediments stand in the way of wise foreign policy choice, it fortunately is possible to design and manage policy-making machinery to reduce their impact. Multiple advocacy, subgrouping, formal options systems, second-chance meetings, and the use of devil's advocates are among the procedural tools often recommended for this purpose (Janis, 1982). None, however, can transform foreign policy making into a neat, orderly system. Policy making is a turbulent political process, one that involves complex problems, a chronic lack of information, and a multiplicity of conflicting actors. As President Kennedy summarized it, there will always be "the dark and tangled stretches in the . . . process—mysterious even to those who may be most intimately involved."

The trends and transformations currently unfolding in world politics are the product of countless decisions taken daily in diverse national settings throughout the world. Some decisions are more consequential than others, and some actors making them are more important than others. Throughout history, great powers like the United States and Russia have at times stood at the center of the world political stage, possessing the combination of natural resources, military might, and the means to project power abroad that earned them great-power status. How such powers have responded to one another has had profound consequences for the entire drama of world politics. To better understand that, we turn our attention in the next chapter to the dynamics of great-power rivalry on the world stage.

SUGGESTED READINGS

Allison, Graham. *Essence of Decision.* Boston: Little, Brown, 1971.

DeRivera, Joseph H. *The Psychological Dimension of Foreign Policy.* Columbus, Ohio: Merrill, 1968.

Hermann, Charles F., Charles W. Kegley, Jr., and James N. Rosenau, eds. *New Directions in the Study of Foreign Policy.* Boston: Allen & Unwin, 1987.

Hermann, Margaret G., and Charles F. Hermann. "Who Makes Foreign Policy Decisions and How: An Empirical Inquiry," *International Studies Quarterly* 33 (December 1989): 316–388.

Hilsman, Roger. *The Politics of Policy Making in Defense and Foreign Affairs: Conceptual Models and Bureaucratic Politics,* 2nd ed. Englewood Cliffs, N.J.: Prentice-Hall, 1990.

Janis, Irving L. *Crucial Decisions: Leadership in Policymaking and Crisis Management.* New York: Free Press, 1989.

Jensen, Lloyd. *Explaining Foreign Policy.* Englewood Cliffs, N.J.: Prentice-Hall, 1982.

Korany, Bahgat. *How Foreign Policy Decisions Are Made in the Third World.* Boulder, Colo.: Westview Press, 1986.

Roberts, Jonathan M. *Decision-Making During International Crises.* New York: St. Martin's Press, 1988.

Snyder, Richard C., and James A. Robinson. *National and International Decision-Making.* New York: Institute for International Order, 1961.

• • •

CHAPTER 4

GREAT-POWER RIVALRY IN CONTEMPORARY WORLD POLITICS

• • •

Time and again in this century, the political map of the world was transformed. And in each instance, a new world order came about through the advent of a new tyrant or the outbreak of a bloody global war, or its end. Now the world has undergone another upheaval, but this time, there's no war.

George Bush, U.S. President, 1990

One day the Iron Curtain will lift and the captive nations of the East will become part of a United Europe. Even Russia, purged by future events of its desire to bully and subdue its neighbors, will be a member, and given the innate genius of the Russian people, a highly respected and valued member.

General "Wild Bill" Donovan, Head,
U.S. Office of Strategic Services, 1951

Change is endemic to world politics, but one constant stands out: great-power rivalry for position in the hierarchy of nations. British historian Arnold J. Toynbee (1954) underscores the centrality of this fact in his famous theory on the cycles of history. "The most emphatic punctuation in a uniform series of events recurring in one repetitive cycle after another," he writes, "is the outbreak of a great war in which one Power that has forged ahead of all its rivals makes so formidable a bid for world domination that it evokes an opposing coalition of all the other powers." That conclusion is also a central element in the theory of political realism. "All history shows that nations active in international politics are continuously preparing for, actively involved in, or recovering from organized violence in the form of war," argues Hans Morgenthau (1985), who, like Toynbee, is a well-known realist.

Cycles of war and peace have dominated twentieth-century world politics. As U.S. Secretary of State James Baker observed in late 1991, "For the third time this century, we have ended a war—this time a cold one—between the Great Powers." In this chapter we explore the causes and consequences of these great-power rivalries that led to total war. Two of them, World Wars I and II, which began in Europe and then spread to engulf the entire world, were fought by fire and blood. The third, the

• • •

Cold War, which pitted the United States against the Soviet Union, was fought by different means but was no less intensive for that reason. Moreover, the transformations in world politics set in motion by the end of the Cold War are only now becoming apparent and will continue to manifest themselves for many years into the future.

THE QUEST FOR GREAT-POWER HEGEMONY . . . .

Great-power war is not unique to this century. Indeed, the thrust of Toynbee's cyclical theory of history is that great-power war is endemic to world politics. Others reinforce that conclusion, noting the long progression of war and leadership change over the past five hundred years. It is not surprising, therefore, that a popular mental map of international affairs is one that equates world politics with great-power war.

Long-cycle theory seeks to explain the rhythmic pattern of war and peace underlying "the rise and fall of the great powers" (Kennedy, 1987; also Goldstein, 1988; Levy, 1992; Modelski and Thompson, 1989; Rapkin, 1990). Each global war witnesses the emergence of a victorious *hegemon*, a dominant military and economic leader. With its acquisition of unrivaled power, the hegemon reshapes the existing system by creating and enforcing rules to preserve not only the existing world order but also its own power.

Hegemony characteristically imposes an extraordinary tax on the world leader. The costs of maintaining economic and political order and preserving an empire eventually weaken the hegemon. In time, as the weight of global responsibilities take their toll, new rivals ascend to challenge the increasingly vulnerable world leader. Historically, this deconcentration of power has set the stage for another global war, the demise of one hegemon, and the rise of another.

Long-cycle theory also draws attention to the fact that "world politics has rarely been reordered without a major war" (Jervis, 1991–1992). Often such attempts to reorganize international society have centered on the task of war prevention, as in the case of the Peace of Westphalia (1648) following the Thirty Years' War, the Congress of Vienna (1815) following the Napoleonic wars, the League of Nations (1919) following World War I, and the United Nations (1945) following World War II. "Only after such a total breakdown has the international situation been sufficiently fluid to induce leaders and supporting publics of dominant nations to join seriously in the task of reorganizing international society to avoid a repetition of the terrible events just experienced" (Falk, 1970). Table 4.1 summarizes the cyclical rise and fall of great powers, and the political transitions associated with them, over the past five hundred years.

Long-cycle theory is disarmingly simple, and for this reason it is not without critics. Must great powers rise and fall in conformity with the law of gravity—that what goes up must come down?[1] There is something disturbingly deterministic in that question, which implies that global destiny is beyond the control of humankind. Still, long-cycle theory provides important insight into the fundamental continuities

---

[1] Fundamental hypotheses drawn from long-cycle theory are difficult to confirm, for example. Long-cycle theorists differ about whether economic, military, or domestic factors produce these cycles, and about their comparative influence. They also fall short in accounting for differences in processes in different historical epochs.

TABLE 4.1 THE EVOLUTION OF GREAT-POWER RIVALRY FOR WORLD LEADERSHIP SINCE 1495

State(s) Seeking Military Hegemony	Other Powers Resisting Domination	Global War	New Order After Global War
Portugal	Spain, Valois France, Burgundy, England	Wars of Italy and the Indian Ocean, 1494–1517	Treaty of Tordesillas, 1517
The Netherlands	Spain, France, England	Spanish-Dutch Wars, 1580–1608	Truce of 1609; Evangelical Union; the Catholic League formed
Holy Roman Empire (Habsburg Spain and Austria-Hungary)	Shifting ad hoc coalitions of mostly Protestant states (Sweden, Holland) and German principalities as well as Catholic France against remnants of rule by the papacy	Thirty Years' War, 1618–1648	Peace of Westphalia, 1648
France (Louis XIV)	The United Provinces, England, the Habsburg Empire, Spain, major German states, Russia	Wars of the Grand Alliance, 1688–1713	Treaty of Utrecht, 1713
France (Napoleon)	Great Britain, Prussia, Austria, Russia	Napoleonic Wars, 1792–1815	Congress of Vienna and Concert of Europe, 1815
Germany, Austria-Hungary, Turkey	England, France, Russia, United States	World War I, 1914–1918	Versailles, creating League of Nations, 1919
Germany, Japan, Italy	Great Britain, France, Soviet Union, United States	World War II, 1939–1945	Bretton Woods, 1944; United Nations, 1945

of world politics. Thus it usefully orients us to a consideration of the three great-power conflicts of the twentieth century, to which we now turn.

THE FIRST WORLD WAR . . . .

The First World War tumbled onto the world stage when a Serbian nationalist seeking to free Slavs from Austrian rule assassinated Archduke Ferdinand, heir to the throne of Austria-Hungary, at Sarajevo in June 1914. In the two months that followed, this singular event sparked a series of moves and countermoves by nations and empires uncertain about each other's intentions.

Two hostile alliances had formed before Sarajevo. They pitted Germany and Austria-Hungary, on the one hand, against France, Britain, and Russia, on the other. The strategic choices of the two alliances culminated in the cataclysm that involved all of the most powerful nations in the world in what became the longest European war in a century. By the time it ended, nearly ten million people had died, empires had crumbled, new regimes were born, and the face of the world's geopolitical map took on a profoundly new shape.

The Causes of World War I

How is such a catastrophic war explained? The answers are numerous, but many converge around *structural* explanations. A prominent element of this theme is that World War I was an *inadvertent war*, not the result of anyone's master plan. Instead, it was a war influenced by uncertainty and circumstances beyond the control of those involved, but one that none either wanted or expected.

Structuralism

Many historians find the structural interpretation convincing, as the European great powers were aligned against one another on the eve of World War I in a way that made a military struggle to resolve their rivalry irresistible. The viewpoint takes for granted that "the sort of military system that existed in Europe at the time—a system of interlocking mobilizations and of war plans that placed a great emphasis on rapid offensive action—directly led to a conflict that might otherwise have been avoided" (Trachtenberg, 1990–1991). Thus, historians see the anarchical international system creating a climate conducive to a great-power struggle.

Proponents of this interpretation draw attention to the great powers' prior rearmament efforts and their alliances and counteralliances. The Triple Alliance of Germany, Austria-Hungary, and Italy, initiated in 1882 and renewed in 1902, and the Entente Cordiale between Britain and France, forged in 1904, were among them. These, they argue, created a momentum that, along with "the pull of military schedules," dragged European statesmen toward war (Tuchman, 1962). In short, the mutually reinforcing alliances in what had become a polarized balance-of-power system dictated the great powers' reactions to the 1914 Austrian succession crisis.

A related element in the structuralist explanation directs attention to the period prior to the outbreak of hostilities. Britain dominated world politics in the nineteenth century. An island nation isolated by temperament, tradition, and geography from European affairs, Britain's sea power gave it command of the world's shipping lanes and control of a vast empire stretching from the Mediterranean to Southeast Asia. It was a world leader without rival. A challenger was emerging, however. The challenger was Germany.

Although Germany did not become a unified country until 1871, it prospered and used its growing wealth to create a formidable army and navy. With strength came ambition and resentment of British preeminence. As the predominant military and industrial power on the European continent, Germany sought to compete for international position and status. As Kaiser Wilhelm II put it in 1898, Germany had "great tasks . . . outside the narrow boundaries of old Europe." With Germany ascendant, the balance of power shifted, as its rising power and global aspirations altered the European geopolitical landscape.

Germany was not the only newly emergent power at the turn of the century. Russia was also expanding at the time, and therefore threatened Germany. The decline in power of the Austro-Hungarian Empire, Germany's only ally, heightened Germany's fear of Russia. Hence Germany reacted strongly to Archduke Ferdinand's assassination. It became convinced that a short, localized, and victorious war was possible. It feared an unfavorable shift in the balance of power in the event of a long war. Accordingly, Germany, while the advantages seemed clear-cut, gave Austria-Hungary a "blank check" to crush Serbia. Its unconditional support proved to be a serious miscalculation.

The risk involved in the blank check made sense from the viewpoint of preserving the Austro-Hungarian Empire. Its disintegration would have left Germany isolated without an ally. Unfortunately for Germany, however, its guarantee provoked an unexpected reaction. France and Russia, the two powers on Germany's eastern and western borders, combined forces to defend the Slavs. Britain then abandoned its traditional "splendid isolation" and joined France and Russia in opposing Germany. The immediate objective was to defend Belgian neutrality. The war later expanded across the ocean when, in April 1917, the United States, reacting to German submarine warfare, entered the conflict. War then, for the first time ever, became truly global in scope.

This chain reaction and the rapidity of escalation that led to World War I fit the interpretation that it was an "inadvertent war." Simply put, European leaders were not in full control of their own fate. Still, historians ask why they miscalculated so badly. Did they simply fail to recognize their primary interest in successfully managing the crisis? If so, was this because the alliances in which they were partners gave them a false sense of assurance, blinding them to the dangers and dragging them into a conflict that was not a part of anyone's design?

Rational Choice

There is an alternative interpretation of World War I that sees it as *rational choice*. From this perspective, its outbreak is properly viewed as a result of the enthusiasm of German elites for a war with France and Russia in order to preserve Germany's position on the continent, confirm its status as a world power, and deflect domestic attention from Germany's internal troubles (see Fischer, 1967; Kaiser, 1990).

If the rational choice interpretation is correct, then World War I is best seen as another instance of the quest for power that political realists believe is an "iron law of history." In this light, Germany's challenge to British dominance was driven by its desire to become a leading state and to prevent it from being surpassed by lesser challengers, who were also growing in strength (Gilpin, 1981). From this perspective, World War I can be interpreted as "an attempt by Germany to secure its position before an increasingly powerful Russia had achieved a position of equality with Germany (which the latter expected to happen by 1917)" (Levy, 1992).

As these alternative interpretations suggest, the causes of World War I remain in dispute. Questions about motives and causes—the decisive forces behind historic events—are difficult to resolve. Structural explanations that emphasize the distribution of power and others that direct attention to the (mis)perceptions and related behavior of individual leaders undoubtedly help us to understand the sequences that produced the world's first truly global war. We must, however, also consider other factors that, in association with these underlying causes, led to the guns of August.

Other Explanations

Some historians, for example, see the growth of nationalism, especially in southeastern Europe, and long-suppressed ethnic and national hatreds, as exerting a strong cultural influence on the inability of European statesmen to avoid war.[2] Domestic unrest inflamed these passions, as did the pressure for war fostered by munitions makers, who played on nationalistic sentiments (Blainey, 1988). The reaction of the Austro-Hungarian Empire to the assassination crisis, although based in part on misperceptions, suggests the potency of national passions. Nationalism and ethnic hatred fed Austria-Hungary's diabolic image of the enemy, its hypersensitivity about the preservation of the empire, and its overconfidence in its military capabilities.

Austria-Hungary was not the only player governed by nationalistic passions. The Germans and Russians were also driven by ethnocentrism, causing them to make serious miscalculations. In particular, Germany's lack of empathy prevented it from understanding "the strength of the Russians' pride, their fear of humiliation if they allowed the Germans and Austrians to destroy their little protégé, Serbia, and the intensity of Russian anger at the tricky, deceptive way the Germans and Austrians went about their aggression" (White, 1990).

Still, as powerful as these national passions may have been, the inertia produced by the evolving diplomatic relationships clearly structured the context in which such psychological forces became influential. World War I is unlikely to have unfolded without Anglo-German commercial rivalry, the Franco-Russian alliance, the blank check given to Austria-Hungary by Germany, and, most important perhaps, the presence of entangling alliances. "One cannot conceive of the onset of World War I without the presence of the Triple Entente [encompassing Britain, France, and Russia], which existed as an alliance of ideologically dissimilar governments" (Midlarsky, 1988). Hence, the multipolar balance-of-power system, composed of a growing number of great-power contenders without a hegemon to maintain order, may have made war inevitable.

---

[2] As discussed in Chapter 11, nationalism is widely regarded as a cause of war. Nationalism is "a state of mind, permeating the large majority of a people and claiming to permeate all its members," which "recognizes the nation-state as the ideal form of political organization and the nationality as the source of creative cultural energy and of economic well-being" (Kohn, 1944).

Thus a world war began, even though "political leaders in each of the great powers . . . preferred a peaceful settlement" of their differences.

The primary explanation for the outbreak of the world war, which none of the leading decision-makers of the European great powers wanted, expected, or deliberately sought, lies in the irreconcilable interests defined by state officials, the structure of international power and alliances that created intractable strategic dilemmas, the particular plans for mobilization and war that were generated by these strategic constraints, decision-makers' critical assumptions regarding the likely behavior of their adversaries and the consequences of their own actions, and domestic political constraints on their freedom of action. (Levy, 1990–1991: 184)

The Consequences of World War I

World War I was tragic in its human, social, economic, and political costs. It destroyed life and property, and it changed the face of Europe (see Map 4.1). Three empires, the Austro-Hungarian, Russian, and Ottoman (Turkish), crumbled. In their place emerged the independent nations of Poland, Czechoslovakia, and Yugoslavia. Finland, Estonia, Latvia, and Lithuania were also given birth. In addition, the war contributed to the overthrow of the Russian czar in 1917. The destruction of the monarchy by the Bolsheviks, under the leadership of Vladimir I. Lenin, produced a change in government and ideology that would have far-reaching consequences.

Despite its costs, the coalition consisting of Britain, France, Russia, and (later) the United States did succeed in meeting the threat of domination posed by the Central Powers (Germany, Austria-Hungary, and Turkey). Moreover, the war set the stage for a determined effort to build a new world order that would deal with the causes of war and prevent its recurrence.

For most Europeans, the Great War had been a source of disillusionment. . . . When it was all over, few remained to be convinced that such a war must never happen again. Among vast populations there was a strong conviction that this time the parties had to plan a peace that could not just terminate a war, but a peace that could change attitudes and build a new type of international order. . . .

For the first time in history, broad publics and the peacemakers shared a conviction that war was a central problem in international relations. Previously, hegemony, the aggressive activities of a particular state, or revolution had been the problem. In 1648, 1713, and 1815, the peacemakers had tried to resolve issues of the past and to construct orders that would preclude their reappearance. But in 1919 expectations ran higher. The sources of war were less important than the war itself. There was a necessity to look more to the future than to the past. The problem was not just to build a peace, but to construct a peaceful international order that would successfully manage all international conflicts of the future. (Holsti, 1991: 175–176; 208–209)

Thus World War I evoked revulsion of war and the logic of *realpolitik* that rationalized great-power rivalry, arms races, secret alliances, and balance-of-power politics. The experience led the policymakers gathered at the Paris peace talks at the Versailles

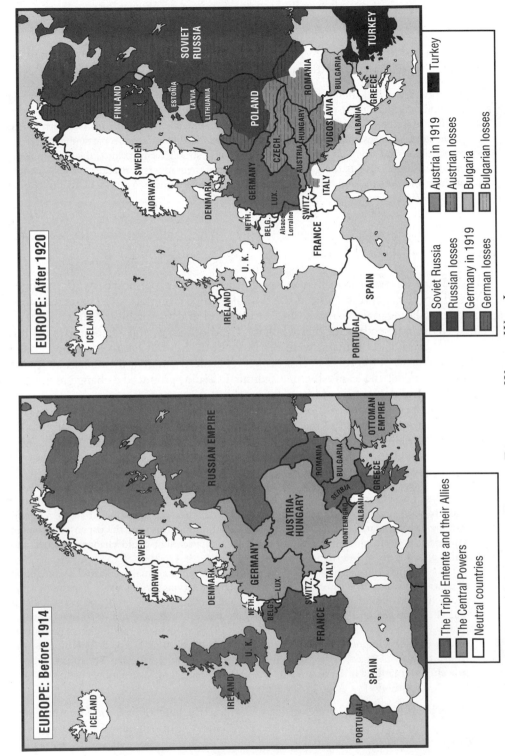

MAP 4.1 TERRITORIAL CHANGES IN EUROPE FOLLOWING WORLD WAR I
Source: Gerald Chaliand and Jean-Pierre Rageau, *A Strategic Atlas* (New York: Harper & Row, 1990), p. 34.

Palace to reevaluate assumptions about the rules of statecraft and to search out ways to replace them with a new world order.

The two decades following World War I were the high point of political idealism. Woodrow Wilson's ideas about world order, expressed in his "Fourteen Points" speech, gave voice to the tenets of idealism. As noted in Chapter 2, his reform program included a diplomacy of "open covenants, openly arrived at"; "making the world safe for democracy" by making leaders accountable to public opinion; creating the first universal international organization (the League of Nations) to mediate disputes and safeguard peace; and the substitution of collective security for interlocking alliances that came to be part of the European balance-of-power system.

Idealists also advocated bringing state sovereignty under the jurisdiction of international law; permitting national independence movements to determine their own fate according to the principle of self-determination (as seen in the creation of Poland, Czechoslovakia, and Yugoslavia); and promoting global prosperity through free trade. The Washington Naval Conference, which sought to maintain the arms balance, and the Kellogg-Briand Pact (or Pact of Paris) in 1928, which outlawed war as part of a design to substitute peaceful methods of dispute settlement for war, were symptomatic of the reforms the idealist vision inspired. But the idealists' proposals failed to deter the resumption of great-power rivalry. Another system-transforming global war was on the horizon.

THE SECOND WORLD WAR . . . .

Germany defeated Russia in World War I and was then itself defeated by a coalition of Western states. Germany's defeat did not extinguish its hopes for global status and influence, however. On the contrary, it intensified them. Thus conditions were ripe for the second great-power war of the twentieth century, as Germany again pursued an aggressive course.

World War II was a struggle for power cast in the image of realism. Global in scope, it pitted a coalition striving for world supremacy against an unlikely "grand alliance" of great powers who held incompatible beliefs—communism in the case of the Soviet Union, and democratic capitalism in the case of Britain, France, and the United States. The overriding interest in preventing their fascist rivals from establishing hegemony is what united the Grand Alliance.

The world's fate hinged on the outcome of this massive effort to meet the Axis threat of world conquest and restore the balance of power. Success was achieved but at a terrible cost over a six-year ordeal. Each day 23,000 lives were lost, as World War II resulted in the death of nearly 17 million soldiers and 34 million civilians.[3]

The Causes of World War II

Several factors propelled renewal of Germany's hegemonic ambitions. Domestically, German nationalism inflamed latent irredentism (forceful recovery of lost territory)

---

[3] For accounts of the campaigns that finally led to victory, see Churchill (1948–1953).

and rationalized the expansion of German borders to regain provinces ceded to others and to absorb Germans living in Austria, Czechoslovakia, and Poland. The rise of fascism animated this renewed imperialistic push. That ideology glorified the "collective will" of the nation and preached *machtpolitik* (power politics) to justify the forceful expansion of the German state.

German resentment was fueled further by the punitive terms imposed at the 1919 Paris peace conference by the victorious World War I powers (France, Great Britain, Italy, Japan, and the United States). Bending to French pressure, the Peace of Paris (the Versailles treaty) insisted on the destruction of Germany's armed forces, the loss of territory (such as Alsace-Lorraine, absorbed by Germany following the Franco-Prussian war of 1870–1871), and the imposition of heavy reparations to compensate the Allies for the damage that German militarism had exacted. The Austro-Hungarian Empire was also divided.

Not only was the Peace of Paris punitive; more significantly and painfully, it prevented Germany's reentry into the international system as a coequal member. (Symbolically, Germany was denied membership in the League of Nations until 1926.) As a result of its exclusion, Germany, propelled by nationalistic sentiments and the rise of fascism, sought to recover its rightful status as a great power by force of arms.

Proximate Causes

Why did the other great powers permit German rearmament? A key reason was the failure of the British hope for Anglo-American collaboration to maintain world order. That hope vanished when the United States, in a fit of anger, repudiated the Treaty of Versailles and retreated to isolationism. In this circumstance, Britain and France fought for advantage in the treatment of Germany. France wanted to deny Germany's reentry into the system and prevent its revival. Britain, in contrast, preferred to preserve the new balance of power by encouraging German rearmament and recovery as a counterweight against the chance that France or the Soviet Union might dominate continental Europe. Thus Britain's belief (and U.S. indifference) that a revitalized Germany would help preserve the balance of power led to British neglect of the threat posed by growing German power and the fascists' goals of aggrandizement.

Unfortunately, acquiescence to German rearmament and other militaristic maneuvers led to *appeasement*. Adolf Hitler, the German dictator who by this time controlled Germany's fate, pledged not to expand German territory by force. He betrayed that promise when, in March 1938, he forced Austria into union with Germany (the *Anschluss*). Shortly thereafter he demanded the annexation of the German-populated area of Sudetenland in Czechoslovakia. The fears German actions provoked led to the September 1938 Munich Conference between Hitler, British Prime Minister Neville Chamberlain, and leaders from France and Italy (Czechoslovakia was not invited). Under the erroneous conviction that appeasement would halt further German expansionism and lead to "peace in our time," Chamberlain and the others agreed to Hitler's demands.

Instead of satisfying Germany, appeasement whetted its appetite and that of the newly formed fascist coalition consisting of Germany, Italy, and Japan, whose goal was the overthrow of the international status quo.

Japan was disillusioned with Western liberalism and disgusted with the Paris settlements, and suffered economically from the effects of the Great Depression of the 1930s. To end dependency and subordination, and to create a Greater East Asian Co-Prosperity Sphere under its influence, Japan embraced militarism. In the might-makes-right climate that Germany's imperialistic quest for national aggrandizement helped to create, Japanese imperialism and colonialism seemed justifiable. Japan invaded Manchuria in 1931 and China proper in 1937. This accelerated the momentum for still other aggression. Italy absorbed Abyssinia in 1935 and Albania in 1939. Germany and Italy also intervened in the 1936–1939 Spanish civil war on the side of the fascists, headed by General Francisco Franco, while the Soviet Union supported antifascist forces.

Despite these aggressions elsewhere, appeasement of Germany was the catalyst that paved the way for the century's second global war. Germany occupied the rest of Czechoslovakia in March 1939. Belatedly, Britain and France reacted by joining in an alliance to protect the next likely victim, Poland. They also opened negotiations in Moscow in hopes of enticing the Soviet Union to join the alliance, but they failed. Then, on August 23, 1939, Hitler, a fascist, and Joseph Stalin, a communist and the Soviet dictator, stunned the world with the news that they had signed a nonaggression pact. Now certain that Britain and France would not intervene, Hitler promptly invaded Poland on September 1, 1939. Britain and France, honoring their pledge to defend the Poles, declared war on Germany two days later. World War II had begun.

The war expanded rapidly as Hitler turned his forces to the Balkans, to North Africa, and westward. The powerful, mechanized German troops invaded Norway and marched through Denmark, Belgium, Luxembourg, and the Netherlands. They broke through France's defensive barrier, the Maginot Line, and forced the British to evacuate a sizable expeditionary force from the French beaches at Dunkirk. Paris itself fell in June 1940. In the months that followed, the German air force (the Luftwaffe) pounded Britain in an attempt to force it into submission. Instead of invading Britain, however, the Nazi troops now turned against Hitler's former ally, attacking the Soviet Union in June 1941. Japan launched a surprise assault on the United States at Pearl Harbor on December 7. Almost immediately, Germany declared war on the United States. The unprovoked Japanese assault and the German challenge pushed U.S. aloofness and isolationism aside, enabling President Franklin Roosevelt to forge a coalition with Britain and the Soviet Union to oppose the fascists.

Underlying Causes

Many historians regard the reemergence of a multipolar distribution of power as a key factor in the onset and expansion of World War II. The post–World War I system was placed "at risk when the sovereign states, which were its components, became too numerous and unequal in power and resources, particularly when (as happened after 1919) the Great Powers were reduced in number and new, lesser states proliferated" (Calvocoressi, Wint, and Pritchard, 1989). "By 1921 the League of Nations had

41 members, whereas in 1914 the European central states had only 22 members." When combined with resentment over Versailles, the Russian revolution, and the rise of fascism, the growth in the number of national actors made "the interwar years the most violent period in international relations since the Thirty Years' War and the wars of the French Revolution and Napoleon" (Holsti, 1991).

The collapse of the international economic system during the 1930s was also a major contributor to the war. Great Britain found itself unable to perform the leadership and regulatory roles in the world political economy, as it had before World War I. The United States was the logical successor to Britain as world economic leader, but its refusal to exercise leadership hastened the war. "The Depression of 1929–31 was followed in 1933 by a world Monetary and Economic Conference whose failures—engineered by the United States—deepened the gloom, accelerated nationalist protectionism and promoted revolution" (Calvocoressi, Wint, and Pritchard, 1989). Faced with depression, German and Japanese imperialism abroad were motivated in part by their deteriorating economic circumstances at home.

The failure of the League of Nations to mount a collective response to the German, Japanese, and Italian acts of aggression symbolized the weak institutional barriers to war. So, too, did the preceding collapse of the Disarmament Conference in 1934. When Germany withdrew from the League of Nations in 1933, as did Italy in 1937, war clouds gathered that the League was powerless to dispel.

The Soviet Union's invasion of neutral Finland in 1939 provoked public indignation and united the League of Nations. In a final act of retaliation, it expelled the Soviet Union. Yet, characteristically, defense fell on the shoulders of the victim. Ninety thousand fiercely independent Finns gave their lives in the "Winter War" to defend their country while the rest of the astonished world watched and cheered but did little to help.

Other forces that led to World War II include "the domination of civilian discourse by military propaganda that primed the world for war," the "great wave of hypernationalism" that swept over Europe as "each state taught itself a mythical history of its own and others' national past, and glorified its own national character while denigrating that of others," and the demise of democratic governance (Van Evera, 1990–1991).

In the final analysis, however, the war would not have been possible without Adolf Hitler and his plans to conquer the world by force. Hence "German responsibility for the Second World War is in a class of its own" (Calvocoressi, Wint, and Pritchard, 1989). Under the mythical claim of German racial superiority as a "master race" and virulent anti-Semitism and anticommunism, Hitler waged war to create an empire that would settle the historic competition and precarious coexistence of the great powers in Europe by expunging Germany's rivals.

> The broad vision of the Thousand-Year Reich was . . . of a vastly expanded—and continually expanding—German core, extending deep into Russia, with a number of vassal states and regions, including France, the Low Countries, Scandinavia, central Europe and the Balkans, that would provide resources and labor for the core. There was to be no civilizing mission in German imperialism. On the contrary, the lesser peoples were to be taught only

to do menial labor or, as Hitler once joked, educated sufficiently to read the road signs so they wouldn't get run over by German automobile traffic. The lowest of the low, the Poles and Jews, were to be exterminated. . . .

To Hitler . . . the purpose of policy was to destroy the system and to reconstitute it on racial lines, with a vastly expanded Germany running a distinctly hierarchical and exploitative order. Vestiges of sovereignty might remain, but they would be fig leaves covering a monolithic order. German occupation policies during the war, whereby conquered nations were reduced to satellites, satrapies, and reservoirs of slave labor, were the practical application of Hitler's conception of the new world order. They were not improvised or planned for reasons of military necessity. (Holsti, 1991)

The Consequences of World War II

By May 1945 the Thousand-Year Reich lay in ruins. By August, Japan was devastated, as the atomic bombs the United States dropped on Hiroshima and Nagasaki destroyed Japan's receding hope of carrying on its war of conquest. The allied victory over the Axis redistributed power and reordered borders, as a new geopolitical terrain emerged. The Soviet Union absorbed the Baltic states of Estonia, Latvia, and Lithuania into the Soviet Union itself.[4] Elsewhere its borders were pushed far to the West. Poland, a victim of Soviet expansionism, was compensated with land taken from Germany. Germany itself was divided into occupation zones that eventually provided the basis for its partition into East and West Germany. And pro-Soviet regimes assumed power throughout Eastern Europe (see Map 4.2 on page 84). In the Far East, the Soviet Union also took over some Japanese islands, and Korea was divided into Soviet and U.S. occupation zones at the thirty-eighth parallel.

The end of the war also produced uncertainty and mistrust. The agreements governing goals, strategy, and obligations that guided the collective Allied effort to defeat the common enemy began to erode even as victory neared. Victory only magnified the growing distrust each great power harbored about the others' intentions in an environment of ill-defined borders, altered allegiances, power vacuums, and economic ruin.

The "Big Three" leaders—Winston Churchill, Franklin Roosevelt, and Joseph Stalin—met at Yalta in the Crimea in February 1945 to design a new world order, but the vague compromises reached concealed the differences percolating below the surface. Following the death of Franklin Roosevelt in April and Germany's unconditional surrender in May, the Big Three, with the United States now represented by Harry Truman, met again at Potsdam in July 1945. The meeting ended without agreement, and the façade of Allied unity began to fade.

Perhaps the most certain characteristic of this otherwise uncertain environment was the ascendancy of the United States and the Soviet Union as the dominant powers. The other major-power "victors," Great Britain and France, had themselves been

---

[4] These and other territorial adjustments the Soviet Union made were anticipated in the 1939 nonaggression pact signed by Hitler and Stalin.

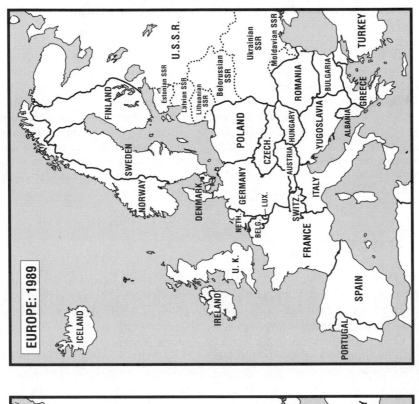

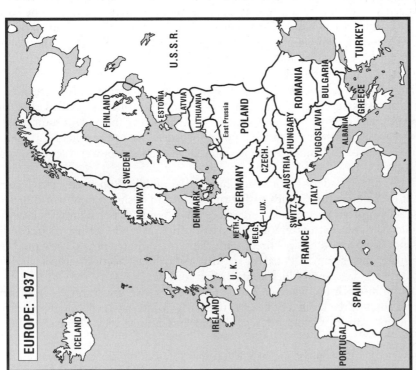

MAP 4.2 TERRITORIAL CHANGES IN EUROPE FOLLOWING WORLD WAR II

Source: U.S. Department of State

exhausted by the war and fell from the apex of the world power hierarchy. Germany and Japan, defeated in war, also fell from the ranks of the great powers.

As noted, Germany, which lay in ruins following the war, was partitioned into four occupation zones that the victorious powers later used as the basis for creating the Federal Republic of Germany (West Germany) and the German Democratic Republic (East Germany). This followed a simple principle of *realpolitik:* divide and rule (the victors loved Germany so much, some noted, that they created two of them). Japan, too, was removed from the game of great-power politics, having been devastated by atomic bombs and then occupied by the United States. Thus, as Alexis de Tocqueville had foreseen in 1835, the Americans and Russians now held in their hands the destinies of half of mankind. In comparison, all others were dwarfs.

Despite the emergent differences between the United States and the Soviet Union, World War II, like all previous great-power wars, paved the way for a new world order. Planning by the Allies for a new postwar structure of peace began even as the war raged. As early as 1943 the Four Power Declaration advanced principles for Allied collaboration in "the period following the end of hostilities." The Allies' determination to create a new international organization, the United Nations, to manage the postwar international order was born in this and other wartime agreements. Consistent with the expectation that the great powers would cooperate to manage world affairs, China was promised a seat on the United Nations Security Council along with France and the Big Three. The purpose was to guarantee that all of the dominant states would share responsibility for keeping the peace.

In practice, the United States and the Soviet Union mattered most. And they used the fledgling United Nations, not to keep the peace but to pursue their competition with one another (see Chapters 6 and 14). That competition eventually became known as the Cold War. As the most recent great-power war of the twentieth century, it deserves special attention.

THE COLD WAR . . . .

As World War II drew to a close in 1945, it became increasingly apparent that one era of international politics was coming to an end and a new one was commencing. Unparalleled in scope and unprecedented in destructiveness, the second great war of the twentieth century brought into being a transformed system dominated by two superstates, the United States and the Soviet Union, whose combined power and resources far surpassed those of all the rest of the world. It also speeded the disintegration of the great colonial empires assembled by imperialist nations in previous centuries, thereby hastening the emancipation of many peoples from foreign rule. Unlike earlier international systems, the emergent one consisted of a large number of sovereign states outside the European core area that were dominated by the two most powerful ones. The advent of nuclear weapons also contributed to a novel system of world politics, for they radically changed the role that threats of force and warfare would henceforth play in world politics. Out of these circumstances grew the conflict between East and West, that is, the Cold War.

The Causes of the Cold War

Determining the origins of the twentieth century's third great-power conflict is difficult because the historical evidence is amenable to different interpretations (see Gaddis, 1972; Schlesinger, 1986; Melanson, 1983). Despite this, an evaluation of its postulated causes is important if we are to understand the evolutionary course of a global rivalry that, unlike its other twentieth-century counterparts, ended without recourse to war.

A Conflict of Interests

According to the logic of political realism, rivalry between the emergent superpowers was inescapable. From this perspective, the preeminent status of the United States and the Soviet Union at the top of the international hierarchy made each suspicious of the other. And each had reasons to counter the other's potential global leadership.

> The principal cause of the Cold War was the essential duopoly of power left by World War II, a duopoly that quite naturally resulted in the filling of a vacuum (Europe) that had once been the center of the international system and the control of which would have conferred great, and perhaps decisive, power advantage to its possessor. . . . The root cause of the conflict was to be found in the structural circumstances that characterized the international system at the close of World War II. (Tucker, 1990: 94)

But was the competition necessary? The United States and the Soviet Union had both demonstrated during World War II an ability to subordinate their ideological differences and competition for power to larger purposes. Neither sought unilateral advantage relentlessly. Both practiced accommodation to protect their mutual interest in remaining alliance partners. Their success suggests that Cold War rivalry was not predetermined, that continued collaboration was possible.

In fact, U.S. and Soviet leaders both expressed in official discourse their hope that wartime collaboration would continue once the war ended (Gaddis, 1972). President Roosevelt, for example, argued that it was possible to preserve great-power accommodation if the United States and the Soviet Union both respected the other's national interests. He predicated his belief on an informal agreement that suggested that each superpower would enjoy dominant influence in its own *sphere of influence* or specified area of the globe, and not oppose the other in the other's areas of influence (Morgenthau, 1969; Schlesinger, 1967). As presidential policy adviser John Foster Dulles noted in January 1945, "The three great powers which at Moscow agreed upon the 'closest cooperation' about European questions have shifted to a practice of separate, regional responsibility." Rules written into the United Nations Charter that obligated the United States and the Soviet Union to share, through the United Nations Security Council, responsibility for preserving world peace further symbolized the expectation of continued cooperation.

If these were the superpowers' hopes and aspirations when World War II ended, why did they fail? To answer that question, we must go beyond the logic of *realpolitik* and probe other explanations of the origins of the Cold War.

Ideological Incompatibilities

Another interpretation holds that the Cold War was simply an extension of the superpowers' mutual disdain for the other's political system and way of life. U.S.

Secretary of State James F. Byrnes embraced this thesis at the conclusion of World War II, arguing that "there is too much difference in the ideologies of the U.S. and Russia to work out a long term program of cooperation." Later, in the 1950s, President Dwight D. Eisenhower declared that the United States faces "a hostile ideology—global in scope, atheistic in character, ruthless in purpose, and insidious in method." Not surprisingly, therefore, the United States responded combatively to what it perceived as an alien and threatening ideology. Thus the Cold War was a conflict "not only between two powerful states, but also between two different social systems" (Jervis, 1991).

U.S. animosity was stimulated by the 1917 Bolshevik revolution, which brought to power a government embracing Marxist philosophy in a country that Karl Marx himself felt was infertile soil for a communist experiment. Whether real or imagined, U.S. fears of Marxism generated a counterreaction, as U.S. foreign policy itself became ideological. Consistent with the proposition that every ideological movement breeds its antithesis, the counterideology was *anticommunism* (see Commager, 1983; Morgenthau, 1983). Accordingly, the United States embarked on a missionary crusade of its own, dedicated to meeting and expunging communism from the face of the earth (see Gardner, 1970; Parenti, 1969).

U.S. policymakers concluded that it was imperative that the United States mount successful opposition to the "export" of the communist revolution. As the leader of the "free world," they saw the United States as the only nation that could repel the spread of Soviet communism. And like their rivals in the Kremlin, they saw the world in *zero-sum* terms: when one side won converts, the other side lost them.

U.S. policymakers also feared that communism's appeal to the world's less fortunate nations and people made its continued spread likely. This conviction became known as the *domino theory*, a popular metaphor in the 1960s, which predicted that the fall to communism in one country would cause the fall of its neighbors, and in turn still others. Like a row of falling dominoes, a chain reaction would bring the entire world under communist domination. The metaphor suggested that the process would continue unabated unless checked by U.S. power.

The interpretation of the Cold War as a battle between diametrically opposed systems of belief contrasts sharply with the view that the superpowers' differences stemmed from discordant interests. Although the adversaries may have viewed "ideology more as a justification for action than as a guide to action," once the interests they shared disappeared, "ideology did become the chief means which differentiated friend from foe" (Gaddis, 1983).

Ideological incompatibilities also precluded compromise. Like religious wars in the past (for example, Christianity versus Islam during the crusades in the Middle Ages), the Cold War was a battle for people's hearts and minds. Its bitterness stemmed from the antagonists' perception that it was a struggle between right and wrong, good and evil. A conflict driven by ideology "excludes the idea of co-existence. How can [one] compromise or co-exist with evil? It holds out no prospect but opposition with all might, war to the death. It summons the true believer to a *jihad*, a crusade of extermination against the infidel" (Schlesinger, 1983).

There is irony here. The superpowers' ideologies and messianic world views were in many respects identical, in that both believed the adversary's beliefs were a threat to its own way of life (Jönsson, 1982). Nonetheless, ideological incompatibilities rule out compromise or coexistence. Lenin described the predicament—prophetically, it turned out—this way: "As long as capitalism and socialism exist, we cannot live in peace; in the end, either one or the other will triumph—a funeral dirge will be sung either over the Soviet Republic or over world capitalism."

Misperceptions

A third explanation sees the Cold War rooted in psychological factors, particularly the superpowers' *misperceptions* of each other's motives. Their conflicting interests and ideologies were secondary.

There is evidence on the tendency of mistrustful parties to see in their own actions only virtue and in those of their adversaries only malice. When such *mirror images* and "we-they," "we're OK, you're not" outlooks exist, hostility is inevitable (Bronfenbrenner, 1971). Moreover, as perceptions of the adversary's evil intentions become accepted as dogma, their prophecies also become self-fulfilling.[5] Mirror images and self-fulfilling prophecies contributed heavily to the onset of the Cold War.

A month before Roosevelt died, he expressed to Stalin his desire, above all, to prevent "mutual distrust." Yet, as noted, mistrust soon developed. Misunderstandings followed, as did exchanges of accusations and threats. In this climate of suspicion the Cold War grew. Consider the superpower's competing images.

THE SOVIET IMAGE To the Soviets, reasons for doubting American intentions were abundant. The Soviets lived with the memory of U.S. participation in the 1918–1919 Allied military intervention in Russia, which turned from its initial mission of keeping arms from falling into the hands of Germany into an anti-Bolshevik undertaking. They resented that the United States did not recognize the Soviet Union diplomatically until 1933 in the midst of a depression (perceived to be a sign of capitalism's weakness and the beginning of its ultimate collapse).

Moreover, the wartime experience heightened Soviet suspicions. The Soviets recalled U.S. procrastination before entering the war against the fascists; the U.S. refusal to inform the Soviets of the Manhattan Project to develop the atomic bomb; the delay in sending the Soviets promised Lend Lease supplies; the failure to open up the second front (leading Stalin to suspect that U.S. policy was to let the Russians and Germans destroy each other so that the United States could then pick up the pieces from among the rubble[6]); the U.S. failure to inform the Soviets of wartime

[5] Prophecies are sometimes self-fulfilling because the future can be affected by the way it is anticipated. The tendency is illustrated by arms races, often propelled when defensive moves by one party provoke others to act similarly out of fear, thus justifying the first state's initial decisions.
[6] Stalin's suspicions may not have been unfounded. While still a senator, for example, Harry Truman expressed the hope that, following Hitler's invasion of Russia, the Nazis and communists would destroy each other. He stated flatly, "Let's help the Russians when the Germans are winning and the Germans when the Russians are winning. So each may kill off as many as possible of the other" (*New York Times*, June 23, 1941).
Although Truman was not speaking for President Roosevelt or the U.S. government, when expressed publicly by a member of Congress such sentiments are unlikely to be ignored. They resurfaced again after World War II when, in a speech before the United Nations (April 26, 1945), Soviet Foreign Minister V. M. Molotov accused the Western powers of complicity with Hitler.

strategy to the extent that it informed Great Britain; and the use of the atomic bomb against Japan, perceived as an attempt to intimidate the Soviets and to prevent their involvement in the Pacific peace settlement (see Alperovitz and Messer, 1991–1992; also Shevardnadze, 1991; in contrast, see Bundy, 1988).

Those suspicions grew when the United States supported previous Nazi collaborators in U.S.-occupied countries, notably France and Italy, at the same time it pressured the Soviet Union to abide by its promise to allow free elections in areas vital to Soviet national security, notably Poland. The Soviets also resented the U.S. refusal to carry out its pledge to help finance the Soviet Union's economic recovery. Thus Soviet distrust of U.S. intentions stemmed in part from fears of U.S. encirclement that were exacerbated by past U.S. hostility.[7]

THE U.S. IMAGE The United States felt that it had legitimate reasons to distrust the Soviet Union. Soviet belligerence appeared obtrusive: Stalin's announcement in February 1946 that the USSR was not going to demilitarize its armed forces, at the very time that the United States was engaged in the largest demobilization by a victorious power in world history; Russian unwillingness to permit democratic elections in the territories they liberated from the Nazis; their refusal to assist in postwar reconstruction in regions outside Soviet control; their removal of supplies and infrastructure from Soviet-occupied areas; their selfish and often obstructive behavior in the fledgling new international organizations; their occasional opportunistic disregard for international law and violation of agreements and treaties; their infiltration of Western labor movements; and their anti-American propaganda and espousal of an alien ideology that promised to destroy the American way of life.

The implied threats provoked fears that greatly intensified as a result of the Soviet unwillingness to withdraw the Red Army from Eastern and Central Europe and Iran, and the Soviet Union's creation in 1947 of the Communist Information Bureau (Cominform) to manage communist governments and political parties in Europe (in reality a Soviet agent of the international communist revolution).

The two countries' leaders thus operated from very different images. They imposed on events different definitions of reality and became captives of those visions. Expectations shaped the way they interpreted developments: what they saw is what they got. George F. Kennan, the American ambassador to the Soviet Union in 1952, noted that misread signals were common to both sides:

> The Marshall Plan, the preparations for the setting up of a West German government, and the first moves toward the establishment of NATO were taken in Moscow as the beginnings of a campaign to deprive the Soviet Union of the fruits of its victory over Germany. The Soviet crackdown on Czechoslovakia (1948) and the mounting of the Berlin blockade, both essentially defensive . . . reactions to these Western moves, were then similarly misread

---

[7] In a 1946 memorandum to the president, Secretary of Commerce Henry A. Wallace asked how U.S. actions since V-J Day—especially U.S. weapons production—looked. Wallace warned that they "make it appear either (1) that we are preparing ourselves to win the war which we regard as inevitable or (2) that we are trying to build up a predominance of force to intimidate the rest of mankind. How would it look to us if Russia had the atomic bomb and we did not, if Russia had 10,000 mile bombers and air bases within 1,000 miles of our coastline, and we did not?"

on the Western side. Shortly thereafter there came the crisis of the Korean War, where the Soviet attempt to employ a satellite military force in civil combat to its own advantage, by way of reaction to the American decision to establish a permanent military presence in Japan, was read in Washington as the beginning of the final Soviet push for world conquest; whereas the active American military response, provoked by this move, appeared in Moscow . . . as a threat to the Soviet position in both Manchuria and in eastern Siberia. (Kennan, 1976: 683–684)

Hence, U.S. leaders and their allies in the West saw Soviet actions as part of a plan to take over the world (see Map 4.3). Of course, the Soviets saw these same crises that erupted between 1948 and 1952 in Europe and elsewhere in a far different light—as tests of their resolve and the West's effort to encircle and destroy their socialist experiment. Both states harbored the same images of the rival's intentions: one's image mirrored the other's. Thus they were the same. Because each power saw its adversary in remarkably similar terms, their misperceptions bred conflict.

If the Cold War originated in divergent images and each power's insensitivity to the impact of its actions on the other's fears, it is difficult to assign blame for the deterioration of U.S.-Soviet relations. Both superpowers were responsible because both were victims of their misperceptions. The Cold War was not simply a U.S. response to communist aggression, the orthodox American view. Nor was it simply a product of postwar U.S. assertiveness, as revisionist historians argue (see Schlesinger, 1986). Both of the great powers felt threatened. And each had legitimate reasons to regard the other with suspicion. Thus, we can view the Cold War as a conflict over reciprocal anxieties bred by the way policymakers on both sides interpreted each other's actions.

Other Contributing Factors

An accurate picture of the origins of the Cold War must consider other causes beyond those rooted in divergent interests, ideologies, and images. For example, an objective accounting must also cite the emergence of "power vacuums" that invited confrontation, the pressures exerted on foreign policies by interest groups and changes in the climate of domestic opinion within each society, innovations in weapons technology and the shifts in strategic balances they introduced, and the role that military planners played in fomenting the conflict (Sherry, 1977).

Regardless of the reasons for its eruption, the Cold War became *the* central issue in world affairs. Its shadow stretched across the entire spectrum of world politics from 1945 until its ultimate demise in 1991. To understand the actions that shaped this great-power conflict, we must go beyond the origins of the Cold War and chart the course of superpower relations across the entire Cold War era.

The Cold War's Phases and Character

Figure 4.1 on page 92 describes the history of the two most powerful states' behavior toward one another during the Cold War. The evidence shows at least three characteristics of U.S.-Soviet interactions since 1948. First, throughout most of its duration,

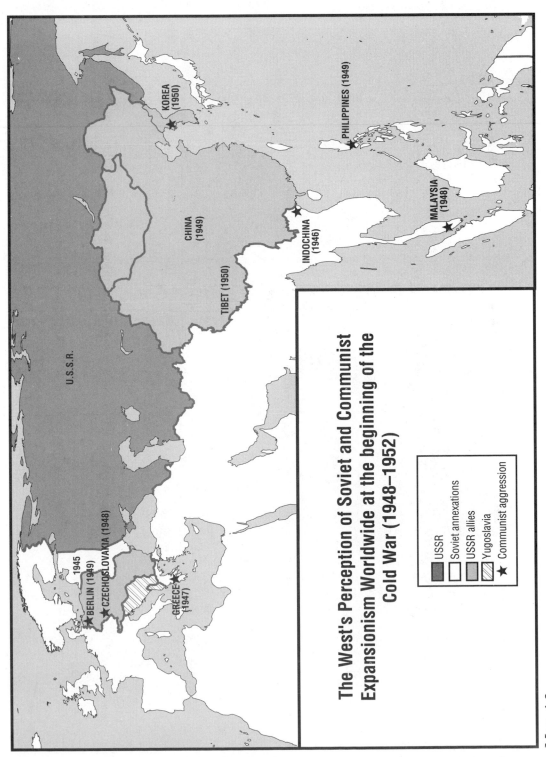

The West's Perception of Soviet and Communist Expansionism Worldwide at the beginning of the Cold War (1948–1952)

KOREA (1950)

PHILIPPINES (1949)

MALAYSIA (1948)

CHINA (1949)

INDOCHINA (1946)

TIBET (1950)

U.S.S.R.

1945

BERLIN (1949)

CZECHOSLOVAKIA (1948)

GREECE (1947)

USSR
Soviet annexations
USSR allies
Yugoslavia
★ Communist aggression

Map 4.3

91

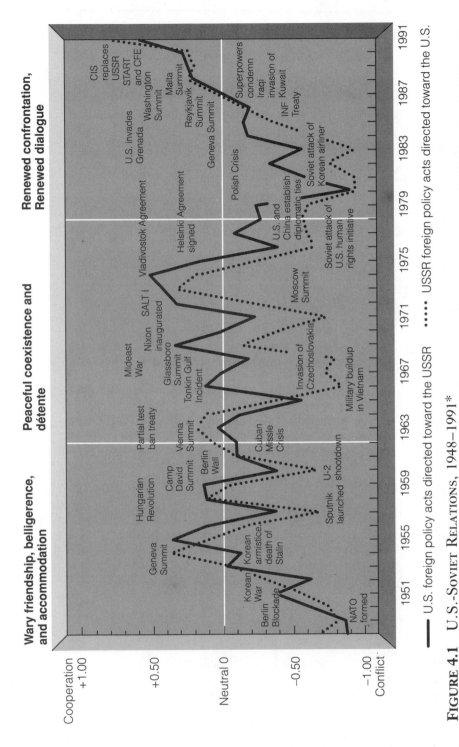

FIGURE 4.1 U.S.-Soviet Relations, 1948–1991*

Source: Adapted from Edward E. Azar and Thomas J. Sloan, *Dimensions of Interaction* (Pittsburgh: University Center for International Studies, University of Pittsburgh, 1973). Data for 1966–1991 are derived from the World Event Interaction Survey (WEIS), as compiled and scaled by Professor Rodney G. Tomlinson.

* The net conflict index is the sum of the proportion of cooperative acts and conflictual acts.

Cooperation +1.00

+0.50

Neutral 0

–0.50

–1.00 Conflict

1951 1955 1959 1963 1967 1971 1975 1979 1983 1987 1991

Wary friendship, belligerence, and accommodation

Peaceful coexistence and détente

Renewed confrontation, Renewed dialogue

——— U.S. foreign policy acts directed toward the USSR   ••••• USSR foreign policy acts directed toward the U.S.

NATO formed

Berlin Blockade

Korean War

Korean armistice death of Stalin

Geneva Summit

Hungarian Revolution

Camp David Summit

Sputnik launched

U-2 shootdown

Berlin Wall

Vienna Summit

Partial test ban treaty

Cuban Missile Crisis

Glassboro Summit

Tonkin Gulf Incident

Mideast War

Nixon inaugurated

SALT I

Vladivostok Agreement

Helsinki Agreement signed

Invasion of Czechoslovakia

Military buildup in Vietnam

Moscow Summit

U.S. and China establish diplomatic ties

Soviet attack of U.S. human rights initiative

Polish Crisis

Soviet attack of Korean airliner

U.S. invades Grenada

Geneva Summit

Reykjavik Summit

Malta Summit

Washington Summit

START and CFE

INF Treaty

Superpowers condemn Iraqi invasion of Kuwait

CIS replaces USSR

the Cold War was characterized by a high level of superpower conflict. Second, periods of intense conflict alternated rhythmically with periods of relative cooperation. Third, reciprocal, action-reaction relations occurred: periods when the United States directed friendly initiatives toward the Soviets were also periods when the Soviets acted with friendliness toward the United States; similarly, periods of U.S. belligerence were periods of Soviet belligerence.

For analytical purposes the Cold War can be divided into the three chronological phases depicted in Figure 4.1.

Wary Friendship, Belligerence, and Accommodation, 1945–1962

A brief period of wary friendship preceded the mutual antagonism that developed between the superpowers in 1947. Two characteristics mark this period. First, it was colored by mutual apprehension about the rivals' ambitions. Apprehension fed growing pessimism about continued amity and a diminished willingness by each great power to accept the (potential) rival as an ally. Second, the United States was unquestionably preeminent militarily. It alone possessed the capacity to devastate its adversary with the atomic bomb.

U.S. power constrained latent hostility during this brief *unipolar* period. Even though U.S. strategic dominance would continue until the end of the decade, by 1947 all pretense of superpower collaboration ceased, as their vital security interests collided over the issues surrounding the structure of post–World War II European politics. The Cold War had begun.

THE CONTAINMENT DOCTRINE In February 1946 Stalin gave a speech in which he spoke of "the inevitability of conflict with the capitalist powers. He urged the Soviet people not to be deluded that the end of the war meant that the nation could relax. Rather, intensified efforts were needed to strengthen and defend the homeland" (Lovell, 1970). Shortly thereafter, George F. Kennan, then a diplomat in the U.S. embassy in Moscow, sent to Washington his famous "long telegram" assessing the sources of Soviet conduct. Kennan's conclusions were ominous: "In summary, we have here a political force committed fanatically to the belief that with [the] U.S. there can be no permanent modus vivendi, that it is desirable and necessary that the internal harmony of our society be disrupted, our traditional way of life be destroyed, the international authority of our state be broken, if Soviet power is to be secure."

Kennan's ideas were circulated widely when, in 1947, the influential journal *Foreign Affairs* published his ideas in an article he signed "X" instead of disclosing himself as the author. In it, Kennan argued that Soviet leaders would forever feel insecure about their political ability to maintain power against forces both within Soviet society itself and in the outside world. Their insecurity would lead to an activist—and perhaps aggressive—Soviet foreign policy. Yet it was within the power of the United States to increase the strains under which the Soviet leadership would have to operate, which eventually could lead to a gradual mellowing or final end of Soviet power. Hence, Kennan concluded: "In these circumstances it is clear that the main element of any

United States policy toward the Soviet Union must be that of a long-term, patient but firm and vigilant containment of Russian expansive tendencies" (Kennan, 1947).

Not long thereafter, Harry S Truman made this prescription the cornerstone of American postwar policy. Provoked in part by domestic turmoil in Turkey and Greece, which he and others believed to be communist inspired, Truman declared, "I believe that it must be the policy of the United States to support free peoples who are resisting attempted subjugation by armed minorities or by outside pressures."

Truman's declaration, eventually known as the Truman Doctrine, outlined the U.S. foreign policy strategy of *containment* as a way to inhibit the Soviet Union's perceived expansionist ambitions and global designs. It also led the United States to recruit allies to support it in pursuit of this goal.

Whether the policy of containment was appropriate, even at the time of its initial promulgation, remains controversial. Kennan himself became alarmed at the way he felt U.S. leaders took his celebrated statement out of context and misinterpreted it. To him "containment" became an "indestructible myth," a doctrine "which was then identified with the foreign policy of the Truman administration."

> I . . . naturally went to great lengths to disclaim the view, imputed to me by implication, . . . that containment was a matter of stationing military forces around the Soviet borders and preventing any outbreak of Soviet military aggressiveness. I protested . . . against the implication that the Russians were aspiring to invade other areas and that the task of American policy was to prevent them from doing so. "The Russians don't want," I insisted, "to invade anyone. It is not in their tradition. They tried it once in Finland and got their fingers burned. They don't want war of any kind. Above all, they don't want the open responsibility that official invasion brings with it." (Kennan, 1967:361)

As Kennan later lamented, "the image of a Stalinist Russia poised and yearning to attack the West, and deterred only by [U.S.] possession of atomic weapons, was largely a creation of the Western imagination." Cautioning against "demonizing the adversary, overestimating enemy strength and overmilitarizing the Western response" (Talbott, 1990), Kennan recommended a political rather than military approach to the containment of Soviet expansionism outside its existing sphere of influence.

Kennan's advice notwithstanding, the view that defeating Soviet communism required a militantly confrontational approach became the guiding premise behind post–World War II U.S. foreign policy. The Soviets held similar views about the need for a militant approach to counter what they perceived as Western encirclement designed to reduce the Soviet Union's international influence.

SPHERES OF INFLUENCE AND THE FORMATION OF BLOCS   The inability of the superpowers to maintain the "sphere-of-influence" posture tacitly agreed to earlier contributed to their propensity to interpret crisis situations as the product of the other's program for global domination.

When the Soviets moved into portions of Eastern Europe, U.S. leaders interpreted this as confirmation that they sought world conquest. Yet the Soviet Union perhaps had reason to think that the Americans would readily accede to Soviet domination in Eastern Europe. In 1945, for example, Secretary of State James Byrnes stated that the "Soviet Union has a right to friendly governments along its borders." Under Secretary of State Dean Acheson spoke of "a Monroe Doctrine for Eastern Europe." These viewpoints and others implied in the Yalta agreements reinforced the Soviet belief that the Western powers would accept the Soviets' need for a buffer zone in Eastern Europe that had been the common invasion route into Russia for more than three centuries. Hence, when the U.S. government began to challenge Soviet supremacy in eastern Germany and elsewhere in East Europe, the Soviet Union felt that previous understandings had been violated and that the West harbored "imperialist designs."

A seemingly unending eruption of Cold War crises followed. They included the Soviet refusal to withdraw troops from Iran in 1946, the communist coup d'état in Czechoslovakia in 1948, the Soviet blockade of West Berlin in June of that year, the communist acquisition of power on the Chinese mainland in 1949, the outbreak of the Korean War in 1950, the Chinese invasion of Tibet in 1950, and the on-again, off-again Taiwan Straits crises that followed. Hence the "war" was not simply "cold"; it became an embittered worldwide quarrel that threatened to escalate into open warfare.

Nonetheless, superpower relations took on a more promising coloration in the 1950s as a result of shifts in the balance of power. The United States enjoyed clear military superiority at the strategic level until 1949, for it alone possessed the ultimate winning weapon and the means to deliver it. The Soviets finally broke the U.S. atomic monopoly that year. Thereafter, the Soviet quest for military equality and the superpowers' eventual relative strategic strengths influenced the entire range of their relations.

The global power configuration quickly became *bipolar*. The United States and its allies were one pole and the Soviet Union and its allies the other. Both superpowers recruited allies in an almost predatory fashion to strengthen them in their bilateral struggle.

Europe, where the Cold War first erupted, was the focal point of their jockeying for influence. The principal European allies of the superpowers divided into the North Atlantic Treaty Organization (NATO) and the Warsaw Treaty Organization (WTO). Both alliances became the cornerstones of the superpowers' external policies, as the European members of the Eastern and Western alliances willingly acceded to the leadership of their superpower patrons.

To a lesser extent, alliance formation outside of Europe also enveloped other states in the two giants' contest. The United States in particular sought to contain Soviet (and Chinese) influence on the Eurasian landmass by building a ring of pro-U.S. allies on the very borders of the communist world. In return, the United States promised to protect its growing number of clients from external attack. Thus the Cold War extended across the entire globe.

In the rigid two-bloc system of the 1950s the superpowers talked as if war was imminent.[8] But in deeds (especially after the Korean War) both acted cautiously.

---

[8] For example, in 1952 President Truman twice considered all-out war against the Soviet Union and China (*New York Times*, August 3, 1980). For assessments arguing that prospects of another general war were largely a figment of policymakers' imaginations and that nuclear deterrence was therefore unnecessary, see Mueller (1989, 1991) and Vasquez (1991).

President Eisenhower and his secretary of state, John Foster Dulles, promised a "rollback" of the iron curtain and the "liberation" of the "captive nations" of Eastern Europe. They pledged to respond to aggression with "massive retaliation." And they criticized the allegedly "soft" and "restrained" Truman Doctrine, claiming to reject containment in favor of an ambitious "winning" strategy that would finally end the confrontation with godless communism. But communism was not rolled back in Eastern Europe, and containment was not replaced by a more assertive strategy. In 1956, for example, the United States failed to respond to the call for assistance from the Hungarians who had revolted against Soviet control. Despite their threatening language, then, U.S. leaders promised more than they delivered.

For its part, the Soviet Union remained strategically inferior compared with the United States. For this reason, Nikita Khrushchev, who assumed the top Soviet leadership position following Stalin's death in 1953, claimed to accept "peaceful coexistence" with capitalism. (Communist China protested, accusing Khrushchev of "revisionism" and challenging the Soviet claim to leadership of the international communist movement.) But the Soviet Union also continued, however cautiously, to exploit opportunities for advancing Soviet power wherever it perceived them to exist, as in Cuba in the early 1960s.

The period following Stalin's death was punctuated by a continuation of the Cold War crises and confrontations that had marked the earlier Cold War years. Now Hungary, Cuba, Egypt, and Berlin became the flash points. In 1960 there was even a crisis resulting from the downing of a United States' U-2 spy plane deep over Soviet territory.

Despite the intensity and regularity of the superpowers' confrontations, none of these threats to peace resulted in open warfare. Indeed, both superpowers took halting but meaningful steps toward improving relations. For example, the Soviets dissolved the Cominform in 1956, and the 1955 Geneva summit established an important precedent for the antagonists' communication about world problems, which would later become commonplace (see Table 4.2 on page 98).

Peaceful Coexistence and Détente, 1963–1978

Despite the Geneva precedent, numerous events cast a dark shadow over the hope for superpower coexistence. These included the surreptitious placement of Soviet missiles in Cuba in 1962; escalation of U.S. military intervention in Vietnam; Khrushchev's overthrow and his replacement by a hardliner, Leonid Brezhnev, in 1964; the Soviet invasion of Czechoslovakia in 1968; the enunciation of the *Brezhnev Doctrine* defending the right of the Soviet Union to intervene to preserve Communist party rule in any state in the Soviet Bloc; and the acceleration of the arms race in the 1960s.

The 1962 Cuban missile crisis was the most serious challenge to peace. This "catalytic" event transformed thinking about how the Cold War could be waged and expanded awareness of the suicidal consequences of a nuclear war. The superpowers stood eyeball to eyeball. Fortunately, one blinked.

COEXISTENCE   Recurrent crises alongside the growing threat of mutual destruction intensified the superpowers' search for ways to manage their differences. The growing parity of U.S. and Soviet military capabilities made coexistence or nonexistence the alternatives. Given this equation, finding ways to coexist became compelling. This alleviated the danger posed by some issues and opened the door for new initiatives in other areas. For example, the Geneva and Camp David experiments in summit diplomacy set precedents for other tension-reduction activities. Installation of the "hot line" in 1963 linking the White House and the Kremlin with a direct communication system followed. So, too, did the 1967 Glassboro summit and several negotiated agreements, including the 1963 Partial Test Ban Treaty, the 1967 Outer Space Treaty, and the 1968 Nuclear Nonproliferation Treaty. In addition, the United States tacitly accepted a divided Germany and Soviet hegemony in Eastern Europe (as illustrated by its failure to respond forcefully to the Warsaw Pact invasion of Czechoslovakia in 1968).

At the American University commencement exercises in 1963, U.S. President John F. Kennedy explained why tension reduction had become imperative and war could not be risked.

> Among the many traits the people of [the United States and the Soviet Union] have in common, none is stronger than our mutual abhorrence of war. Almost unique among the major world powers, we have never been at war with each other. . . .
>
> Today, should total war ever break out again—no matter how—our two countries would become the primary targets. It is an ironical but accurate fact that the two strongest powers are the two in the most danger of devastation. . . . We are both caught up in a vicious and dangerous cycle in which suspicion on one side breeds suspicion on the other and new weapons beget counterweapons.
>
> In short, both the United States and its allies, and the Soviet Union and its allies, have a mutually deep interest in a just and genuine peace and in halting the arms race. . . .
>
> So let us not be blind to our differences, but let us also direct attention to our common interests and to the means by which those differences can be resolved. And if we cannot end now our differences, at least we can help make the world safe for diversity.

Kennedy signaled a shift in how the United States hoped to deal with its adversary. The Soviet Union by this time had also begun to temper its rhetoric. In particular, it began to revise the support for revolution that doctrinaire Marxism-Leninism advocated. Thus, in style and tone the superpowers began to depart from the confrontational tactics of the past. To be sure, competition for advantage and influence continued, but tacitly the superpowers seemed to accept the status quo. Neither was willing to give ground ("For us," Leonid Brezhnev declared in August 1968, "the results of World War II are inviolable and we will defend them even at the cost of risking a new war"), but neither was willing to launch a new war to secure new geostrategic gains. This laid the foundation for "détente."

DÉTENTE Soviet-American relations took a dramatic turn with Richard Nixon's election. Coached by his national security adviser, Henry A. Kissinger, Nixon tried a new approach to Soviet relations that, in 1969, he officially labeled *détente*. The Soviets also adopted the term to describe their policies toward the United States.

TABLE 4.2 U.S.-SOVIET SUMMIT MEETINGS SINCE 1955

Summit	Participants	Results
Geneva July 18–23, 1955	Eisenhower-Bulganin	Soviets pledge to return German prisoners of war to Germany
Camp David September 15–27, 1959	Eisenhower-Khrushchev	Settlement of issue of Germany is advanced
Vienna June 3–4, 1961	Kennedy-Khrushchev	Soviets assure U.S. it will not be the first to resume nuclear testing
Glassboro, N.J. June 23, 1967	Johnson-Kosygin	Kosygin rejects U.S. proposals for negotiations to ban ABMs
Moscow May 22–29, 1972	Nixon-Brezhnev	SALT I and ABM agreements concluded
Camp David June 17–25, 1973	Nixon-Brezhnev	Leaders agree to meet on a regular basis
Moscow June 27–July 3, 1974	Nixon-Brezhnev	Threshold Test Ban Treaty signed
Vladivostok November 23, 1974	Ford-Brezhnev	Superpowers establish guidelines for a SALT II agreement
Vienna June 14, 1979	Carter-Brezhnev	SALT II Treaty signed
Geneva November 19–21, 1985	Reagan-Gorbachev	Agreement reached to open consulates in New York and Kiev
Reykjavik October 10–12, 1986	Reagan-Gorbachev	Arms control issues discussed without substantive agreement
Washington December 7–10, 1987	Reagan-Gorbachev	INF Treaty signed
Moscow May 5–June 7, 1988	Reagan-Gorbachev	Joint Verification Experiment signed, INF Treaty instruments of ratification exchanged
Malta December 2–3, 1989	Bush-Gorbachev	Superpowers agree to push for strategic and conventional arms control agreements at a new summit scheduled for mid-1990
Washington May 31–June 3, 1990	Bush-Gorbachev	Accord on methods for verifying limits on nuclear testing and on cutting U.S. and Soviet stockpiles of chemical weapons signed
Helsinki September 9, 1990	Bush-Gorbachev	Joint communiqué condemning Iraq's invasion of Kuwait issued, along with agreement to coordinate policy on the Persian Gulf crisis
London July 15–17, 1991	Bush-Gorbachev and leaders of top industrialized states	Soviets offered economic assistance, contingent upon further reforms

TABLE 4.2 (*continued*)

Summit	Participants	Results
Moscow July 30–31, 1991	Bush-Gorbachev	First arms agreement (START) to reduce intercontinental nuclear weapons signed
Madrid October 29, 1991	Bush-Gorbachev	Ways to bridge differences and reduce stockpiles of long-range missiles beyond the START agreement discussed
Camp David January 31, 1992	Bush-Yeltsin	Confidence-building to "cement partnership" "in a new era" by working together "to remove any remnants of Cold War hostility," plans to exchange summits later in 1992 in each other's country
Washington June 16–17, 1992	Bush-Yeltsin	Deep cuts in strategic nuclear arsenals and plans to scrap all land-based, multiple warhead nuclear weapons announced

As a foreign policy strategy, détente, in Kissinger's words, sought to create "a vested interest in cooperation and restraint," "an environment in which competitors can regulate and restrain their differences and ultimately move from competition to cooperation."

To engineer the relaxation of superpower tensions, Nixon and Kissinger fashioned the *linkage theory*. Predicated on the expectation that the development of economic, political, and strategic ties between the nations would bind the two in a common fate, linkage would make superpower relations dependent on the continuation of mutually rewarding exchanges (such as trade concessions). In this way, linkage would lessen the superpowers' incentives for war.

Furthermore, Nixon and Kissinger designed linkage to make the entire range of U.S.-Soviet relations interdependent so that concessions in any one problem area would be compensated for by roughly equivalent concessions in others. For instance, they linked negotiated arms control agreements to the acceptance of rules prohibiting military intervention outside the regions defining the superpowers' traditional security interests. In short, linkage made cooperation in one policy area contingent on acceptable conduct in other areas.

As both a goal of and a strategy for expanding the superpowers' mutual interest in restraint, détente symbolized an important shift in the superpowers' global relationship. In diplomatic jargon, relations between the Soviets and Americans were "normalized," as the expectation of war receded. As shown in Figure 4.2 on page 100, cooperative interaction became more commonplace than hostile relations. Visits, cultural exchanges, trade agreements, and joint technological ventures replaced threats, warnings, and confrontations.

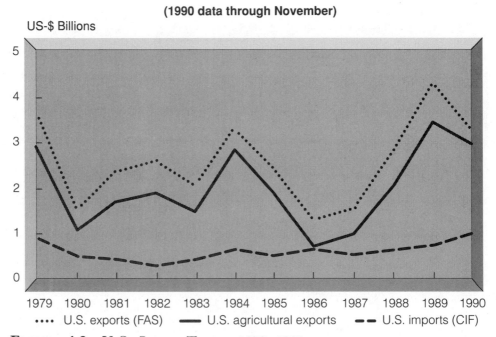

(1990 data through November)

US-$ Billions

•••• U.S. exports (FAS)   ——— U.S. agricultural exports   —— U.S. imports (CIF)

Figure 4.2 U.S. Soviet Trade, 1979–1990
Source: Soviet-American Relations: A Briefing Book (Washington, D.C.: Congressional Research Service, March 1991), p. 76.

Arms Negotiations and SALT Several factors account for the changes in superpower relations that occurred in this period. They included recognition of the probability that a nuclear attack by either side would be mutually suicidal, growing sensitivity to and empathy for the security needs of the other, and shared concern for an increasingly powerful and assertive China. In addition, the superpowers' tacit revival of the sphere-of-influence concept and their acceptance, in the Helsinki Accords of 1975, of the integrity of established borders in Europe, helped stabilize relations. The escalating costs of a continued arms race also induced restraint.

Especially important for the United States was recognition of the erosion of its hegemonic position and role of world policeman in the wake of the unpopular Vietnam War. The Nixon Doctrine symbolized the changes under way, as it effectively asked U.S. allies to bear a greater share of the burden for their own defense.

Arms control stood at the center of the dialogue surrounding détente. The Strategic Arms Limitation Talks (SALT) became the test of détente's viability. Initiated in 1969, the SALT negotiations sought to restrain the threatening, expensive, and spiraling arms race. They produced two agreements, the first in 1972 (SALT I) and the second in 1979 (SALT II). With their signing, each of the superpowers gained the principal objective it had sought in détente. The Soviet Union gained recognition of its status as a coequal of the United States. The United States gained a commitment from the Soviet Union to moderate its quest for preeminent power in the world.

But the SALT II agreement was not brought to fruition. It was signed but never ratified by the United States. The failure underscored the substantial differences that still separated the superpowers. By the end of the 1970s, détente had lost nearly all of its momentum and much of the hope it had symbolized only a few years earlier. During the SALT II treaty ratification hearings, the U.S. Senate expressed disapproval of an agreement with a rival that continued high levels of military spending, that sent arms to states outside its traditional sphere of influence (Algeria, Angola, Egypt, Ethiopia, Somalia, Syria, Vietnam, and elsewhere), and that stationed military forces in Cuba. All these complaints spoke to the persistence of the deep-seated U.S. distrust of the Soviet Union and its understandable concern about Soviet intentions.

Renewed Confrontation, Renewed Dialogue, 1979–1991

Despite the careful nurturing of détente, it did not endure. As events unfolded in the late 1970s, the spirit of détente gave way to a hardening of political relations. Commercial relations between the United States and the Soviet Union mirrored these changes in attitude (see Figure 4.2). Note in particular how sharply U.S. exports to the Soviet Union fell between 1979 and 1980.

The reassuring terminology of détente concealed the unpleasant reality of an enduring, fundamental rivalry between the superpowers, a dual compulsion to oppose each other around the globe tempered only by respect for tacit rules to avoid nuclear annihilation. The Cold War, it appeared, had never really disappeared.

THE DEMISE OF DÉTENTE   The decade-long effort to nurture détente proved ephemeral as a confrontational relationship reminiscent of the 1950s resumed. In many respects, the Soviet invasion of Afghanistan in 1979 was the catalyst to the demise of détente. As U.S. President Jimmy Carter viewed it, "Soviet aggression in Afghanistan—unless checked—confronts all the world with the most serious strategic challenge since the Cold War began."

The retaliatory response of the United States added to the atmosphere of renewed tension that followed. Its countermoves included enunciation of the *Carter Doctrine*, declaring U.S. willingness to use military force to protect its interests in the Persian Gulf, an effort to organize a worldwide boycott of the 1980 Moscow Olympics, and suspension of U.S. grain exports to the Soviet Union and other trade restrictions. Not surprisingly, hostility again dominated superpower relations.

The deterioration of relations accelerated thereafter. President Ronald Reagan and his Soviet counterparts (first Yuri Andropov and then Konstantin Chernenko) delivered a barrage of confrontational rhetoric redolent of that exchanged in the 1950s. As talk of war became endemic, so did preparations for it. The 1980 platform of the Republican party in the United States promised that a Republican administration would reestablish U.S. strategic superiority. Reagan asserted later that the Soviet Union "underlies all the unrest that is going on" and described the Soviet Union as "the focus of evil in the modern world." The atmosphere was punctuated by Reagan policy adviser Richard Pipe's bold challenge in 1981 that the Soviets would have to choose either "peacefully changing their Communist system . . . or going to war." Soviet rhetoric was no less restrained or alarmist.

In many respects the early 1980s were like the 1950s, in that tough talk was not matched by aggressive action. But the 1979–1984 phase did witness some match between words and deeds. Resumption of the arms race was the most visible result. The contestants put weapons above all other priorities, at the expense of addressing domestic economic problems. They also extended the confrontation to new territory, such as Central America, and renewed their public diplomacy (propaganda) efforts to extol the ascribed virtues of their respective systems throughout the world.

Events punctuated the renewal of conflict. The Soviets destroyed Korean Airlines flight 007 in 1983; the United States invaded Grenada soon thereafter. Arms control talks then ruptured, the Soviets boycotted the 1984 Olympic Games in Los Angeles, and the *Reagan Doctrine* pledged U.S. support of anticommunist insurgents in Afghanistan, Angola, and Nicaragua—euphemistically described as "freedom fighters"—who sought to overthrow Soviet-supported governments. In addition, U.S. leaders spoke loosely about the "winnability" of a nuclear war through a "prevailing" military strategy that included the threat of a "first use" of nuclear weapons in the event of the outbreak of a conventional war. Normal relations ceased as the compound impact of these moves and countermoves took their toll. The new Soviet leader, Mikhail Gorbachev, summarized the alarming state of superpower relations by fretting in the fall of 1985 that "The situation is very complex, very tense. I would even go so far as to say it is explosive."

But the situation did not explode. Instead, the superpowers resumed their dialogue and laid the basis for a new phase in their relations.

RENEWED DIALOGUE   Prospects for a more constructive phase improved greatly following Gorbachev's assumption of power in 1985. His goals were difficult to discern at first, but it soon became clear that Gorbachev felt it was imperative that the Soviet Union reconcile its differences with the capitalist West if his country was to have any chance of rectifying the deterioration of its economy and international position. In his words, these goals dictated "the need for a fundamental break with many customary approaches to foreign policy." Shortly thereafter, he embarked on a road to domestic reform marked by political democratization and transition to a market economy. And he proclaimed the need for "new thinking" in foreign and defense policy to relax superpower tensions.

Acknowledging that Soviet economic growth had ceased and its global power had eroded, Gorbachev proclaimed his desire to end the Cold War contest. "We realize that we are divided by profound historical, ideological, socioeconomic and cultural differences," Gorbachev noted during his first visit to the United States in 1987. "But the wisdom of politics today lies in not using those differences as a pretext for confrontation, enmity and the arms race." Soviet spokesperson Georgy Arbatov went as far as to tell the United States that "we are going to do a terrible thing to you—we are going to deprive you of an enemy."

To carry out "new thinking," Gorbachev in 1986 abrogated the long-standing Soviet ideological commitment to aid national liberation movements struggling to overthrow capitalism, declaring "it is inadmissible and futile to encourage revolution from abroad." He also for the first time embraced *mutual security*, proclaiming that a diminution of the national security of one's adversary reduces one's own security.

Gorbachev acknowledged that the Soviet Union could no longer afford guns *and* butter. To reduce the financial burdens of defense and the dangers of an escalating strategic arms race, he offered unilateral arms reductions. "We understand," Gorbachev lamented, "that the arms race . . . serves objectives whose essence is to exhaust the Soviet Union economically."

Fears that these reforms might fail, that Gorbachev was an evil genius conning the West, or that his promises could not be trusted were uppermost in the minds of both Presidents Ronald Reagan and, later, George Bush. "The Soviet Union," Bush warned in May 1989, had "promised a more cooperative relationship before—only to reverse course and return to militarism." Thus, although claiming in May 1989 its desire to move "beyond the Cold War," the Bush administration did not abandon containment. Instead, it resurrected the linkage strategy by making U.S. cooperation contingent on continuing Soviet concessions and constructive practices.

Surprisingly, these demands were soon met. In 1990 the United States sought and received support from the Soviets for Operation Desert Shield designed to reverse Iraqi dictator Saddam Hussein's military conquest of Kuwait. The Soviet Union also announced that it would liberalize its emigration policies and allow greater political and religious freedom.

The End of the Cold War

Gorbachev's reforms reduced or removed many of the sources of superpower tension. The Soviets' position abroad was constrained by domestic circumstances that prevented a reversal of both Gorbachev's domestic reforms and his accommodations abroad. Building on the momentum created by the Intermediate-range Nuclear Forces (INF) agreement signed in 1987, the withdrawal of Soviet troops and tanks from Afghanistan and Eastern Europe, and announced unilateral reductions in Soviet military spending, the prospects for improved relations accelerated with dizzying speed (see Table 4.3 on page 104).

The normalization of Soviet-American relations moved rapidly apace. The Cold War—which began in Europe and had centered on Europe for forty-five years—ended there. All the communist governments in the Soviet "bloc" in Eastern Europe, including even hardline Albania, permitted democratic elections, in which Communist party candidates routinely lost. Capitalist free market principles also replaced socialism. To the surprise of nearly everyone, the Soviet Union acquiesced in these revolutionary changes. Without resistance, the Berlin Wall was dismantled, the Germanies united, and the Warsaw Pact ended.

As these seismic changes shook the world, the Soviet Union itself sped its reforms to introduce democracy and a market economy, and eagerly sought cooperation with and economic assistance from the West.

TABLE 4.3 KEY EVENTS IN THE SOVIET UNION'S DISINTEGRATION AT HOME
AND RETREAT ABROAD, 1985–1991

1985

March   Mikhail S. Gorbachev, 54, named general secretary of the Communist party, following the death of Konstantin Chernenko.

July   Eduard Shevardnadze, who favors reform, succeeds hardline veteran Andrei Gromyko as foreign minister.

November   Gorbachev and Ronald Reagan meet in Geneva for the first U.S.-Soviet summit since 1979.

1986

February   Gorbachev denounces "years of stagnation" of former president Leonid Brezhnev and calls for a major overhaul of the country's centralized economy.

December   Andrei Sakharov, father of the dissident movement and winner of the Nobel Peace Prize, released after seven years of internal exile in Gorky.

1987

December   Gorbachev and Reagan meet in Washington to sign the intermediate-range nuclear forces (INF) treaty cutting Soviet and U.S. intermediate-range missiles.

1988

May   Reagan visits Moscow, praises Gorbachev's *glasnost* (openness) and *perestroika* (restucturing) initiatives.

October   Gorbachev is appointed president and promises to free all political prisoners.

December   Gorbachev announces unilateral cuts in Soviet conventional forces and withdrawal of 250,000 troops from Eastern Europe.

1989

February   Withdrawal of Soviet troops from Afghanistan completed.

April   Sakharov and other reformers elected to new Soviet parliament. Gorbachev ousts several hardliners from Politburo.

May   Gorbachev elected president of new Soviet parliament.

November   Popular revolutions sweep away communist regimes in East Germany and later in other countries in Eastern Europe. Berlin Wall that divided East and West since 1961 dismantled.

December   At summit in Malta, Gorbachev and President Bush hail the end of the Cold War.

1990

February   Communist party surrenders its constitutionally guaranteed monopoly on power. Parliament agrees to give Gorbachev an executive presidency.

March   Lithuania declares independence. Moscow imposes economic blockade. Estonia takes steps toward independence.

TABLE 4.3 (*continued*)

May	Latvian parliament declares independence.
December	Conservatives demand action to stop country's disintegration. Shevardnadze resigns as foreign minister in protest against "looming dictatorship."
1991	
February	Gorbachev says he is a dedicated communist and accuses hardline radicals of trying to seize power through force.
April	Warsaw Pact disbanded.
July	Gorbachev attends summit of leading industrial nations in London. In Moscow, Gorbachev and Bush sign treaty to reduce intercontinental nuclear weapons.
August	Alexander Yakovlev, one of the chief architects of Gorbachev's reforms, resigns as a top aide and quits the Communist party, warning that it plans a coup.
August	Hardline communist officials declare a state of emergency and announce they are replacing Gorbachev as president to prevent "a national catastrophe."
August	Coup collapses; Gorbachev issues edict barring communist cells from all military and government organizations.
August	Boris Yeltsin elected president by the Russian people.
September	Communist party rule ends and reforms to institutionalize democracy and capitalism announced.
October	Yeltsin and Gorbachev, hoping to prevent the union from dissolving as other republics declare their independence, agree to establish a transitional confederation in place of the old Soviet Union.
December	Ukraine holds referendum, votes for independence, and begins to print its own money and form its own army.
December	Except for Russia and Kazakhstan, all thirteen of the former Soviet republics proclaim their independence.
December	Desperate Mikhail Gorbachev warns that "disintegration is fraught with interrepublican clashes, even wars."
December	Russia, Ukraine, and Byelorussia declare the USSR "dead" as a subject of international law, and sign treaty establishing a new Commonwealth of Independent States (CIS) with the capital in Minsk.
December	Russian parliament approves Boris Yeltsin's plan to terminate the USSR and replace it with the Commonwealth of Independent States, which would include most of the former republics; Gorbachev, without a country to head, offers to resign, pledges to recognize the CIS.
December	Conflict erupts between Russia and nationalities of the former Soviet Union. The Independent States build up their armies as concern mounts about the command and control of nuclear weapons.

To seal the fate of the Cold War, Gorbachev followed the 1989 withdrawal of Soviet forces from Afghanistan with the announcement in 1991 that the Soviet Union would terminate its aid to and presence in Cuba. He also announced Soviet acceptance of a new strategic arms agreement (the START [Strategic Arms Reduction Talks agreement]), designed to reduce strategic arsenals, and a second treaty (the Conventional Forces in Europe [CFE] treaty), designed to reduce conventional forces in Europe and the threat of a surprise attack.

The failed conservative coup against Gorbachev in August 1991 put the nail in the coffin of Communist party control in Moscow, the very heartland of the international communist movement. As communism was repudiated, a new age began. Communism was in retreat everywhere (even in China, Cuba, and North Korea) and the face of world politics was irrevocably transformed.

The reform policies of *glasnost* (openness) and *perestroika* (restructuring) unleashed forces *within* the Soviet Union that were not a part of Gorbachev's plan, leading in December 1991 to the disintegration of the Soviet Union itself. Gorbachev had sought gradually to introduce some measure of democracy and a free market spirit into a society where incentive and growth had been crushed by communist rule. He never intended to commit political suicide by starting a revolution that would leave him without a country to lead. Yet that is precisely what happened: the forces of nationalism and frustration culminated in the disintegration of the fifteen Soviet republics as a single unit.

The future of the Commonwealth of Independent States (CIS), the successor of the Soviet Union, is impossible to predict. It could easily fail, as the republics could turn against each other. As George Bush lamented in November 1991, "The collapse of communism has thrown open a Pandora's Box of ancient ethnic hatreds, resentment, even revenge." What is certain is that the new Commonwealth, or its successor, represents a complete break from the state socialism the Bolshevik revolution institutionalized in 1917. In its place, and in most of the same space, a strikingly different confederation of quasi-independent republics now exists.

Each of the newly sovereign republics of the former Soviet Union initially pledged to respect political pluralism, to create a market economy, and to hold nationalist resentments in check. They promised to work together to construct joint economic and military policies. In January 1992 they verbally accepted Russian command over the huge nuclear arsenal spread over the territory of the former Soviet republics, an issue of special concern to the countries of Europe and the United States, and later agreed to abide by the provision of the START agreement.

Russia will figure prominently in any new configuration of the former Soviet state. As principal heir to the vast Soviet strategic arsenal, it remains a military superpower on the world stage. Moreover, it remains the largest country in the world in terms of landmass (see Map 4.4), and it is endowed with vast natural resources.

Some argued in the wake of the Soviet collapse that Russia was no longer vulnerable to "adventurous leaders who might try to resolve the economic crisis by resuming the imperialistic strategies of the past" (Barnet, 1992). In fact, the crisis produced by its long-neglected domestic problems appeared likely to compel a further retreat from

MAP 4.4 THE NEW EURASIAN LANDSCAPE, 1992

international affairs.[9] Russian President Boris Yeltsin signaled the changed times when, in 1992, he announced that Russia would stop targeting U.S. cities and military sites with nuclear weapons. The change in strategic policy reflected Yeltsin's position that Russia would "no longer consider the United States our potential adversary." It was reaffirmed in the 1992 Camp David Declaration on New Relations, in which Yeltsin and Bush stated that "from now on the relationship [between Russia and the United States] will be characterized by friendship and partnership, founded on mutual trust." Despite this promising development, however, some analysts worry about the possibility that, once the crisis produced by Russia's long-neglected domestic problems that now demand withdrawal from world affairs is resolved, Russia may again emerge as a superpower on the world stage. It stands at the heartland of Eurasia, a bridge between Europe and the Pacific Rim, with China and India to the south. And Russia stands tall—a power still to be reckoned with in world affairs (see Map 4.4).

In accepting the devolution of its external empire in Eastern Europe and elsewhere, Soviet leaders engineered the most dramatic peaceful retreat from power in history.

---

[9] On January 24, 1992, the Russian parliament approved an austere budget that Deputy Prime Minister Yegor Gaidar said would slash arms purchases to less than one-seventh the previous year's level. "We believe," he announced, "the state will no longer have money for armaments." The decline of the Russian military threat was underscored by Boris Yeltsin's prediction that the former Soviet army of 3.9 million would be halved within two years.

With the collapse of the Soviet Union in 1991 and its withdrawal from active intrusion in areas beyond its borders alongside the rejection of Marxism-Leninism, the Cold War had truly ended. No longer does the world face a powerful advocate of international communism with the ability to force its view on others. Russia could someday emerge to challenge those at the pinnacle of world power. But with the Soviet Union gone, the United States sat alone at the apex of the international hierarchy. The global distribution of power returned to a unipolar configuration, ephemeral though it may be.

Causes of the "Long Peace"

Unlike World Wars I and II, the Cold War ended with a clear victor but without mass destruction. Opinions differ on why the third great-power conflict of the twentieth century ended without bloodshed. What made the "long peace" (Gaddis 1986, 1991a) between the superpowers possible—the longest period of great-power peace in history without a global war—also stimulated much debate.

To some observers, the arguments elaborated by George Kennan in his famous "X" article now appeared prophetic. "The United States has it in its power," he wrote in 1947, "to increase enormously the strains under which Soviet policy must operate, to force upon the Kremlin a far greater degree of moderation and circumspection than it has had to observe in recent years, and in this way to promote tendencies which must eventually find their outlet in either the breakup of or the gradual mellowing of Soviet power." To many, that was precisely what *did* happen, albeit more than forty years later!

Others, however, focused attention on different influences, especially when trying to explain the absence of great-power war. They cited other characteristics of the Cold War era that may have exercised a stabilizing influence on the superpowers' behavior, including nuclear weapons, the distribution of military power, rigid bipolarity, crisis management capabilities, arms control agreements, legal and organizational restraints, and peace movements in Europe and elsewhere. Still, experts could not agree on the way these factors individually or in combination may have preserved peace or put an end to communism.[10]

A fundamental question sits at the center of this postmortem speculation, however. Did *militant* containment force the Soviet Union into submission? Or, instead, as Kennan urged, did Soviet leaders succumb to the inherent *political* weaknesses of communism, which caused an internal economic malaise that left them unable to conduct an imperial policy abroad or retain communist control at home? In other words, was the end of Communist party rule accepted because of intimidating U.S. military strength and political pressure? Or was the outcome produced by conditions such as the impact of "grassroots movements for global change" (Ekins, 1991) within the Soviet Union? The ideas recorded in Box 4.1 provide insights on these important, alternative viewpoints.

---

[10] For disscussions and comparisons of rival explanations, see Deudney and Ikenberry (1991–1992), Cox (1990), Gaddis (1992), and Kegley (1991).

Box 4.1
RIVAL IMAGES OF THE CAUSES OF COMMUNISM'S COLLAPSE AND THE COLD WAR'S END

• • •

THE PERSPECTIVE OF U.S. POLICYMAKERS

"There are few lessons so clear in history than this: only the combination of conventional and nuclear forces have ensured this long peace in Europe."

—President George Bush, 1990

"Those who argued for nuclear deterrence and serious conventional military capabilities contributed mightily to the position of strength that eventually led the Soviet leadership to choose a less bellicose, less menacing approach to international politics. . . . We're witnessing the rewards of the Reagan policy of firmness."

—Presidental adviser Richard Perle, 1990

THE PERSPECTIVE OF RUSSIAN POLICYMAKERS

"The version about President Reagan's 'tough' policy and intensified arms race being the most important source of perestroika—that it persuaded communists to 'give up'—is sheer nonsense. Quite to the contrary, this policy made the life for reformers, for all who yearned for democratic changes in their life, much more difficult. . . . In such tense international situations the conservatives and reactionaries were given predominant influence. That is why . . . Reagan made it practically impossible to start reforms after Brezhnev's death (Andropov had such plans) and made things more difficult for Gorbachev to cut military expenditures."

—Georgy Arbatov, Director,
Institute for the USA and Canada Studies, 1991

"The Reagan military buildup was only indirectly a factor in my country's rejection of communism and acceptance of its satellites' independence, and largely irrelevant."

—Cold War historian Vladislav Zubok, 1991

"The Cold War ended because it was no longer feasible. The U.S. and USSR had exhausted their capacity to carry on their global confrontation that engendered repeated and disastrous military interventions and extraordinarily expensive new weapons systems. These commitments had overburdened the socioeconomic and political bases for the East/West conflict."

—Peter Gladkov, Policy Analyst,
Institute for the USA and Canada Studies, 1991

Box 4.1 (*continued*)
THE PERSPECTIVES OF POLICY ANALYSTS

"Many of the demonstrators . . . who sought to reject communist rule looked to the American system for inspiration. But the source of that inspiration was America's reputation as a haven for the values of limited government, not Washington's $300-billion-a-year military budget and its network of global military bases."

—Ted Galen Carpenter, 1991

"There are ironies for Americans in the victory of democracy over Soviet communism. During the years of the Cold War . . . Washington consistently undervalued the attention of people elsewhere for the American system of constitutional government and individual rights."

—Anthony Lewis, 1991

"Some conservatives argue that the Reagan defense buildup forced Gorbachev to change his policies. And, clearly, the Soviets were concerned about having to compete with U.S. technological superiority. But it seems likely that internal pressures played as much, if not more, of a role in convincing the Soviet leader to agree to measures that cut his country's firepower more than they cut U.S. strength."

—Carl P. Leubsdorf, 1991

"The metamorphosis in the U.S.-Soviet relationship was the result of two interconnected factors: a formal recognition by the Soviet Union that to tackle its extraordinary economic difficulties it had to seek a permanent settlement with the capitalist world, and a growing recognition in Washington that to keep the world stable while it addressed its own economic problems (some the result of Reagan's policies) a deal with the Soviet Union would be highly desirable."

—Michael Cox, 1990

Still, the answers remain unclear.[11] Sorting out the contribution of different causes that ended the Cold War will doubtless intrigue historians for decades to come, just as determining the causes for its onset has done. The lessons derived are important nonetheless, as they will long shape thinking about the principles that should guide policy making in the post–Cold War world.

[11] Still other factors played a role:

Many Europeans claim that the Helsinki process, détente, and transnational ties within Europe caused change in the East. Members of the American peace movement also argue that their efforts to moderate Western extremism and to signal the Soviets that accommodation had a strong constituency in the West significantly contributed to the moderation of Soviet foreign policy. (Deudney and Ikenberry, 1991–1992: 79)

GREAT-POWER RIVALRY IN THE POST–COLD WAR WORLD . . . .

With the end of the Cold War both superpowers found themselves liberated from a rivalry that had exacted enormous resources, strained their economies, and impaired their power relative to the other great powers. Caught breathless, each found itself in an unfamiliar position without a clear vision in a now uncertain world. No longer was there "a clear and present danger to delineate the purpose of power, and this basic shift . . . invalidated the framework for much of the thought and action about international affairs in East and West since World War II" (Oberdorfer, 1991).

The end of the Cold War does not ensure a peaceful future. Nor does it promise that the current configuration of power and influence will remain. On the contrary, the insights of long-cycle theory promise that the last great-power conflict of the twentieth century, which finds the United States again in the advantageous position as the world's unambiguous hegemonic power in politics as well as economics, will witness the emergence of a new challenger—and the threat of a new war.

Many analysts have speculated about the range of new problems and potential threats caused by the end of the Cold War (see Box 4.2 on page 112). Thus the sea-changes caused by the end of the Cold War again raise the questions: What is new? and What is constant? As political scientist Robert Jervis explains,

> Cyclical thinking suggests that, freed from the constraints of the Cold War, world politics will return to earlier patterns. Many of the basic generalizations of international politics remain unaltered: it is still anarchic in the sense that there is no international sovereign that can make and enforce laws and agreements. The security dilemma remains as well, with the problems it creates for states who would like to cooperate but whose security requirements do not mesh. Many specific causes of conflict also remain, including desires for greater prestige, economic rivalries, hostile nationalisms, divergent perspectives on and incompatible standards of legitimacy, religious animosities, and territorial ambitions. To put it more generally, both aggression and spirals of insecurity and tension can still disturb the peace. (Jervis, 1991–1992: 46)

"Are the conditions that call these forces into being as prevalent as they were in the past?" Jervis continues. "Are the forces that restrain violence now as strong, or stronger, than they were?"

Answers to these questions depend in part on what analytical perspectives are brought to bear on the issues. To political realists, who see the drive for survival and power dictated by the anarchical international system, the future will doubtless resemble the past, as the state remains the preeminent actor in world politics and anarchy remains its defining characteristic.

Still, we must acknowledge the changing configuration of power. As it changes, uncertainty necessarily arises. The structures of world politics may persist, but the future of individual states and groups of states within the historical cycles that underlie the rise and fall of the great powers is by no means certain.

The distribution of power in the Cold War system was bipolar. The post–Cold War world promises to be very different. The United States found itself at the end of the Persian Gulf War in early 1991 basking in a "unipolar moment," arguably the

Box 4.2
GREAT-POWER RELATIONS AFTER THE COLD WAR:
MORE PERIL THAN PROMISE? POLICY ANALYSTS' PREDICTIONS

• • •

"We are witnessing today in Europe a return to history: a return to ethnicity, to nationalism, to self-determination, to the struggle for influence and power."

—Ronald Steel

"Far from ushering in a period of 'kinder, gentler,' and more purely cooperative relations among the industrial democracies, the end of the Cold War is likely to mark the dawning of the era of tougher bargaining and greater self-assertion."

—Aaron L. Friedberg

"The prospects of major crises, even wars, in Europe is likely to increase dramatically now that the Cold War is receding into history."

—John J. Mearsheimer

"By the year 2000 . . . there will be two dozen developing nations with ballistic missiles. In a shrunken world the divide between regional superpowers and great powers is radically narrowed . . . : relatively small, peripheral and backward states will be able to emerge rapidly as threats not only to regional but to world security."

—Charles Krauthammer

"Divergent perceptions of national interests in a world with fewer constraints on action by national governments will encourage individualism and opportunism that will threaten historic friendships and alliances."

— W. Y. Smith

All quotations are from Charles W. Kegley, Jr., and Eugene R. Wittkopf (eds.), *The Future of American Foreign Policy* (New York: St. Martin's Press, 1992), except Krauthammer, taken from Charles Krauthammer, "The Lonely Superpower," *The New Republic*, July 29, 1991.

"one first-rate power" with "no prospect in the immediate future of any power to rival it. . . . It is the only country with the military, diplomatic, political and economic assets to be a decisive player in any conflict in whatever part of the world it chooses to involve itself" (Krauthammer, 1991b).

A multipolar world is certain to emerge, however, and its future may not be distant. Japan and the European Community, and especially Germany, its most important member, are the obvious ascendant challengers of the United States. It is also important not to dismiss the potency of the independent states emerging from the former Soviet Union. The Ukraine, with 50 million people and a land mass larger than Germany, has the potential to play an assertive role in world affairs.

Russia is even more important. It is still the only actor in world politics able to challenge the United States militarily. Noteworthy in this respect is that Russian imperialism long predated the heavy hand of the former communist regime. As Mikhail Gorbachev warned on December 26, 1991, the day he resigned as leader of the now defunct Soviet Union, "Watch out for Russia."

Russia's democratic experiment is no guarantee that its imperial ambitions are dead. Germany is a possible parallel. "One recalls that after the First World War, Germany became a democratic nation free of its imperial burden. During its first four years, to be sure, the new Weimar Republic had a troubled time. . . . During the following five years, however, Germany enjoyed stable democratic government, vigorous economic growth, minimal unemployment, friendly relations with all its neighbors, and a burst of extraordinary cultural creativity. Europe and the world seemed at peace. Suddenly, the Great Depression and its wave of massive unemployment tilted the political forces in Germany (and in Japan as well) in favor of an ideology of violence and expansion" (Iklé, 1991–1992). If history is a guide, then, Russia could repeat this pattern. Thus the political configuration of the Eurasia emergent in 1992 may presage the reassertion of Russian expansionism.

There is an alternative path that Russia could follow, which also has historical precedent. It is a more benign and hence more peaceful path. At the Congress of Vienna in 1815, convened at the conclusion of the Napoleonic Wars, the European great powers created a Concert of Europe to manage the postwar peace. Russia was an active participant in this international effort to maintain the new world order. Today, Russia could play a similar role in the post–Cold War world, as it puts aside its ideological antagonism to democratic capitalism, participates with the other great powers in managing international conflict, and moves toward integration into the world political economy.

As noted, during the bipolarity of the Cold War the superpowers could maintain discipline among their allies and protégés. The fault lines were unambiguous, the behavior of the adversaries predictable, and incentives to drive enemies into submission weak. Arguably, the Cold War induced caution, because the risk of a nuclear exchange exceeded any benefits either superpower could derive from upsetting the status quo (Mearsheimer, 1990). Out of this, "rules of prudence" developed between the superpowers to assure that "the frictions between them did not become unmanageable" (Jervis, 1991).

The multipolarity of the post–Cold War era promises to be very different. In part this is because the emergent configuration of power itself introduces greater uncertainty, as the period leading up to World War I suggests. The issues will also be different, encompassing not only the high politics of peace and security that is the focus of political realism but also the low politics of material well-being to which neoliberal international relations theory speaks. "Security" will still be at issue, but the definition of security will change. "Now international security issues will exhibit themselves in all their variety once again—issues of markets, resources, technology, ethnic animosities, political philosophy, and different conceptions of world order, as well as armies and nuclear weapons" (Carter, 1990–1991).

In the chapters that follow, we will examine the interconnectedness of the "old" and "new" issues that comprise security in a post–Cold War world. We begin in Chapter 5 with a consideration of the history and characteristics of those at the bottom of the international system's hierarchy, the Third World, and of the foreign policy interests and goals that motivate their behavior in world politics.

SUGGESTED READINGS

Cox, Michael. "From the Truman Doctrine to the Second Superpower Détente: The Rise and Fall of the Cold War," *Journal of Peace Research* 27 (No. 1, 1990): 25–41.

Deudney, Daniel, and G. John Ikenberry. "The International Sources of Soviet Change," *International Security* 16 (Winter 1991–1992): 74–118.

Doran, Charles F. *Systems in Crisis: New Imperatives of High Politics at Century's End.* Cambridge: Cambridge University Press, 1992.

Jervis, Robert, and Seweryn Bialer, eds. *Soviet-American Relations After the Cold War.* Durham, N.C.: Duke University Press, 1991.

Kaldor, Mary. *The Imaginary War: Understanding East-West Conflict.* Oxford: Basil Blackwell, 1991.

Kegley, Charles W., Jr., ed. *The Long Postwar Peace.* New York: HarperCollins, 1991.

Kegley, Charles W., Jr., and Eugene R. Wittkopf, eds. *The Future of American Foreign Policy.* New York: St. Martin's Press, 1992.

Kennedy, Paul. *The Rise and Fall of the Great Powers.* New York: Random House, 1987.

LaFeber, Walter. *America, Russia, and the Cold War, 1945–1990,* 6th ed. New York: McGraw-Hill, 1991.

Oberdorfer, Don. *The Turn: From the Cold War to a New Era.* New York: Poseidon Press, 1991.

Rapkin, David P., ed. *World Leadership and Hegemony.* Boulder, Colo.: Lynne Rienner, 1990.

Rasler, Karen A., and William R. Thompson. *War and State Making: The Shaping of the Great Powers.* Boston: Unwin Hyman, 1989.

CHAPTER 5

. . .

THE NORTH-SOUTH CONFLICT: ROOTS AND CONSEQUENCES OF GLOBAL INEQUALITIES

. . .

The world is still hopelessly split into areas of wealth and poverty, with little prospect of narrowing the gap. The politics of international economic affairs in our lifetimes must therefore be a politics of inequality, inherently a politics of mutual suspicion and struggle.

Robert Heilbroner, Norman Thomas
Professor of Economics, 1991

Fundamentally, . . . the Third World is a state of mind. . . . In the circumstances, we should not be too surprised if the term "Third World" is widely used even in a post–Cold War world.

James O. C. Jonah, Under-Secretary
General of the United Nations, 1991

The end of the acceptability of colonialism as a form of political organization is one of the most remarkable developments in twentieth century world politics. As George Shultz observed in 1983 while serving as U.S. secretary of state, "Since the Second World War, the world has undergone a vast transformation as more than one hundred new nations have come into being. An international system that had been centered on Europe for centuries, and that regarded all non-European areas as peripheral or as objects of rivalry, has become in an amazingly short span of time a truly global arena of sovereign states."

Despite their legal status as sovereign entities, the new nations born since World War II found themselves thrust into an international system they had no voice in shaping but whose organization and operation they view as detrimental to the realization of their own goals. They are also typically beset by overwhelming political, economic, and social problems at home. Rising above their underdog status therefore seems remote. Herein lies the source of the North-South conflict, a struggle by those at the bottom of the international hierarchy to improve their position in the global pecking order. The rhetoric of debate in the conflict between the North and the South has stressed economic and related welfare issues, but the issues themselves are

. . .

115

intensely political. Hence economist Robert L. Heilbroner's (1991) pessimistic conclusion that "The politics of international economic affairs in our lifetimes must . . . be a politics of inequality, inherently a politics of mutual suspicion and struggle."

The nations of the South make up the *Third World*, a term commonly used to refer to the world's poorer, economically less developed countries, most of whom also share a colonial heritage. There are so many Third World nations that it takes less space to describe those nations that are developed than those that are not. The Third World includes all of Asia, the Middle East, and Oceania, except Australia, Israel, Japan, New Zealand, and Turkey; all of Africa except South Africa; and all of the Western Hemisphere except Canada and the United States. Thus it contains more than three-fourths of the world's population but accounts for less than a fifth of the goods and services produced in the world (as measured by gross national product [GNP]).

The industrialized nations of the North, otherwise known as the *First World*, account for most global production. The First World consists of Australia, Canada, Israel, Japan, Malta, New Zealand, South Africa, the United States, and the countries of Western Europe. These nations share a commitment to varying forms of democratic political institutions and free market economic principles, high standards of living, and (except Japan) a common cultural heritage. Reflecting their common economic characteristics, they are known in the idiom of international diplomacy as *developed market economies*.

During the Cold War it was commonplace to treat the First World as synonymous with the "free world." The purpose was to distinguish the "West" from the "East," also known as the *Second World*, which consisted of the Soviet Union and its politico-military allies in Eastern Europe. Second World nations were characterized as *centrally planned economies* because of their preference for state-owned and state-managed economic institutions. They not only organized their economies according to socialist principles but also shared an ideological commitment to the eventual victory of socialism over capitalism.

Although the nations in eastern Europe and the republics of the Commonwealth of Independent States that formerly made up the Soviet Union are still not properly regarded as market economies, the label once used to distinguish nonmarket economies from the First World is no longer appropriate. Today only a few centrally planned economies remain. As before, they are less developed nations (China, Cuba, Mongolia, North Korea, and Vietnam). (Even during the Cold War era the Second World largely disassociated itself from the North-South conflict, making it a North/West-South dispute.)

Our purpose in this chapter is to explore the divisions between North and South and the consequences they portend for world politics. We will find that the term Third World often masks important differences among the world's less developed (or developing) countries. Indeed, some analysts have seized on their growing diversity in combination with the end of the Cold War to pronounce the end of "third worldism." We will examine the reasons for that viewpoint in the concluding section of the chapter. First, however, we will examine the reasons underlying the "Third World" idea and inquire into its analytical utility.[1] We begin with an examination of colonialism and imperialism, historical experiences shared by most developing nations and ones that have shaped their contemporary world views in distinctive ways.

THE RISE AND FALL OF EUROPEAN EMPIRES

As noted, the emergence of the less developed world is primarily a post–World War II phenomenon. Although most Latin American nations were independent before that time, having gained their freedom from Spain and Portugal early in the nineteenth century, it was not until 1946 that the floodgates of decolonization were first opened. In the next four decades a profusion of new states joined the international community as sovereign entities, comprising by the 1980s a combined population exceeding 3.5 billion people. Nearly all of the new nations were carved from the former British, French, Belgian, Spanish, and Portuguese empires (see Figure 5.1 on pages 118 and 119). Often the areas granted independence had been colonized only since the late 1800s, when a wave of new imperialism swept the world. In other cases, the dependent relationships had existed for hundreds of years. Today, few colonies remain. A dozen or so remaining dependent territories may yet someday become independent members of the world community, but most of them have populations of less than 100,000. In short, decolonization is a distinctly contemporary phenomenon but as a political process is now complete.

But the vestiges of colonialism remain, with important consequences for the shape of contemporary world politics, as the needs, circumstances, interests, and objectives of Third World countries are often quite dissimilar from those of the older and more established states. For a variety of reasons these dissimilarities stem from the "gap"—the immense disparity in income and wealth between the world's rich and poor nations, between those that have advanced economically and those that have remained underdeveloped or only now may have begun to develop economically.

Differing perceptions of the causes of the gap and correspondingly different prescriptions for its cure lie at the heart of contemporary world politics. Indeed, as viewed through the nationalistic eyes of Third World leaders, the disparity between the rich North and the poor South is the consequence of "neocolonialism" or "neoimperialism," that is, of unequal exchanges that permit the advantaged to exploit others through the institutionalized processes of the contemporary international economic system. Thus the colonial heritage of the Third World is central to many explanations of the South's malaise.

The Emergence of the Modern State System

As a network of relationships among independent entities (and hence the term *international* relations), the *state system* was born with the Peace of Westphalia in 1648, which

---

[1] See Wolf-Phillips (1987) for a discussion of the derivation of the term *Third World* and how it came to be accepted in the development literature.

FIGURE 5.1 THE CHRONOLOGY OF DECOLONIZATION

Panel 1 — colonial powers: Belgium, Britain, France, Spain, Italy, Netherlands, USA

Year	Country
1946	Jordan
	Syria
	Philippines
1947	Bhutan
	India
	Pakistan
1948	Brunei
	Burma
	Ceylon (Sri Lanka)
	Palestine (Israel)
1949	Indonesia
	Laos
1951	Libya
1954	Cambodia
	Laos
	North Vietnam
	South Vietnam
1956	Morocco
	Sudan
	Tunisia
1957	Ghana
	Malaysia
1958	Guinea
1960	Benin
	Bukina
	Cameroon
	Chad

Panel 2 — colonial powers: South Africa, Britain, France, Spain, Portugal, Netherlands, USA

Year	Country
1963	Kenya
	Malaysia
	Singapore
	Zanzibar
	(part of Tanzania)
1964	Malawi
	Malta
	Zambia
1965	Gambia
	Maldives
	Singapore
1966	Barbados
	Botswana
	Guyana
	Lesotho
1967	Southern Yemen
1968	Equatorial Guinea
	Mauritius
	Nauru
	Swaziland
1969	Sidi Fini
1970	Fiji
	Tonga
1971	Bahrain
	Qatar
	Sierra Leone
	United Arab Emirates

Year	Country	1	2	3	4
	Central African Republic			•	
	Congo			•	
	Dahomey (Benin)			•	
	Gabon			•	
	Ivory Coast			•	
	Malagasy Republic (Madagascar)			•	
	Mali			•	
	Mauritania			•	
	Niger			•	
	Nigeria				•
	Senegal		•		
	Somalia	•			
	Togo			•	
	Upper Volta (Burkina)			•	
1961	Zaire (Congo)				•
	Cyprus			•	
	Kuwait			•	
	Sierra Leone			•	
1962	Tanganyika (Tanzania)			•	
	Algeria			•	
	Burundi				•
	Jamaica			•	
	Rwanda				•
	Trinidad and Tobago			•	
	Uganda			•	
	Western Samoa			•	

Year	Country	1	2	3	4
1973	Bahamas				•
1974	Grenada				•
	Guinea-Bissau		•		
1975	Angola		•		
	Cape Verde		•		
	Comoros			•	
	Mozambique		•		
	Papua New Guinea		•		
	Saõ Tomé and Príncipe		•		
	Surinam	•			
	Western Sahara			•	
1976	Seychelles				•
1977	Dijibouti				•
1978	Dominica				•
	Solomon Islands				•
	Tuvalu				•
1979	Kiribati				•
	St. Lucia				•
	St. Vincent				•
1980	Vanuatu			•	•
	Zimbabwe				•
1981	Antigua and Barbuda				•
	Belize				•
1983	St. Kitts-Nevis				•
1984	Brunei				•
1986	Marshall Islands	•			
1990	Namibia				•

Note: More than 100 dependent states acquired sovereign status between 1946 and 1989. One other new state was created during this period when Bangladesh (formerly the province of East Pakistan) seceded from Pakistan in 1971. A number of British dependencies in the Pacific had been administered by Australia or New Zealand.

Source: Peter J. Taylor (ed.), *World Government* (New York: Oxford University Press, 1990), pp. 16–17.

ended the Thirty Years' War in Europe. Thereafter, European potentates refused to recognize the temporal authority of the papacy (the Roman Catholic Church). A system of geographically and politically distinct entities that recognized no authority above them replaced the previous quasi-world government. Relations between the new entities were to be conducted according to the new rules of law, which entitled them to negotiate treaties and settle disputes without interference by, or recourse to, any institution transcending them. Moreover, all shared the same legal rights and responsibilities: the territorial inviolability of the state, its freedom from interference, its right to conduct foreign relations with other states as it saw fit, and its authority to rule its own population. The concept *sovereignty* captures these legal rights and responsibilities.

Although the new European states were assumed to be equal in law, they were not equal in military and economic capabilities. In fact, the international law that emerged in the post-Westphalia state system to regulate behavior legalized the drive for power and created rules by which states could compete with one another for rank in the international hierarchy. Some became great powers, such as Austria, England, France, Prussia, and Russia. Others remained minor powers, such as the various principalities in Germany and the Italian peninsula. And still others, such as the Netherlands, Portugal, and Spain, who once enjoyed great-power status but whose capabilities and influence had diminished noticeably by the time the state system emerged in 1648, enjoyed a secondary rank. Collectively, the major and secondary powers carried their competition for territorial control beyond the European arena, thereby transforming the European state system into a global one. Europeans controlled a third of the globe by 1800, two-thirds by 1878, and over four-fifths by 1914 (Fieldhouse, 1973: 3).

The First Wave of European Imperialism

The first wave of European empire building began during the fifteenth century, as the English, Dutch, French, Portuguese, and Spanish used their military power to achieve commercial advantage overseas. Innovations in a variety of sciences made the adventures of European explorers possible. Merchants followed in their wake, "quickly seizing upon opportunities to increase their business and profits. In turn, Europe's governments perceived the possibilities for increasing their own power and wealth. Commercial companies were chartered and financed, with military and naval expeditions frequently sent out after them to ensure political control of overseas territories" (Cohen, 1973).

The economic strategy underlying the relationship between colonies and colonizers during this era of classical imperialism was known as *mercantilism:* "the philosophy and practice of governmental regulation of economic life to increase state power and security" (Cohen, 1973). European rulers believed that state power flowed from the possession of national wealth measured in terms of gold and silver. Maintaining a favorable balance of trade (exporting more than is imported) was one way to accumulate the desired bullion. "Colonies were desirable in this respect because they afforded an opportunity to shut out commercial competition; they guaranteed exclusive access to untapped markets and sources of cheap materials (as well as, in some instances, direct sources of the precious metals themselves). Each state was determined to monopolize as many of these overseas mercantile opportunities as possible" (Cohen, 1973).

By the end of the eighteenth century, the European powers had spread themselves, although thinly, throughout virtually the entire world. But the colonial empires they had built had by that time already begun to erode. Britain's thirteen North American colonies declared their independence in 1776, and most of Spain's possessions in South America received theirs early in the nineteenth century. Between 1775 and 1825, ninety-five colonial relationships were terminated (Bergesen and Schoenberg, 1980: 236).

Concurrent with the breakup of colonial empires was the waning of the mercantilist philosophy that had sustained classical imperialism. As argued by Adam Smith in his treatise *The Wealth of Nations*, national wealth grew not through the accumulation of gold and silver but, rather, from the capital and goods they could buy. A system of free international trade consistent with the precepts of laissez-faire economics (minimal governmental interference) became the accepted philosophy governing international economic relations. European powers continued to hold numerous colonies, but the prevailing sentiment was now more anti- than pro-imperial.

The Second Wave of European Imperialism

Beginning in the 1870s and extending until the outbreak of World War I, a new wave of imperialism washed over the world as Europe (joined later by the United States and Japan) colonized new territories at a rate nearly four times faster than during the first wave of colonial expansion (Bergesen and Schoenberg, 1980). By 1914, nearly all of Africa was under the control of only seven European powers (Belgium, Britain, France, Germany, Italy, Portugal, and Spain). In all of the Far East and the Pacific only China, Japan, and Siam (Thailand) remained outside the direct control of Europe or the United States. Even China, however, was divided into spheres of influence by foreign powers, and Japan itself practiced imperialism with the acquisition of Formosa (Taiwan) and Korea. Elsewhere, the United States expanded across its continent, acquired Puerto Rico from Spain, extended its colonial reach westward to Hawaii and the Philippines, leased the Panama Canal Zone "in perpetuity" from the new state of Panama (an American creation), and exercised considerable political leverage over several Caribbean lands, notably Cuba. The British Empire, built by the preeminent imperial power of the era, symbolized the imperial wave that in a single generation engulfed the entire world. By 1900 it covered a fifth of the earth's land area and comprised perhaps a quarter of its population (Cohen, 1973: 30). As British imperialists were proud to proclaim, it was an empire on which the sun never set (see Map 5.1 on page 122).

In contrast with classical imperialism, extraordinary competition among the imperial powers marked the new imperialism of the late nineteenth century, as colonies

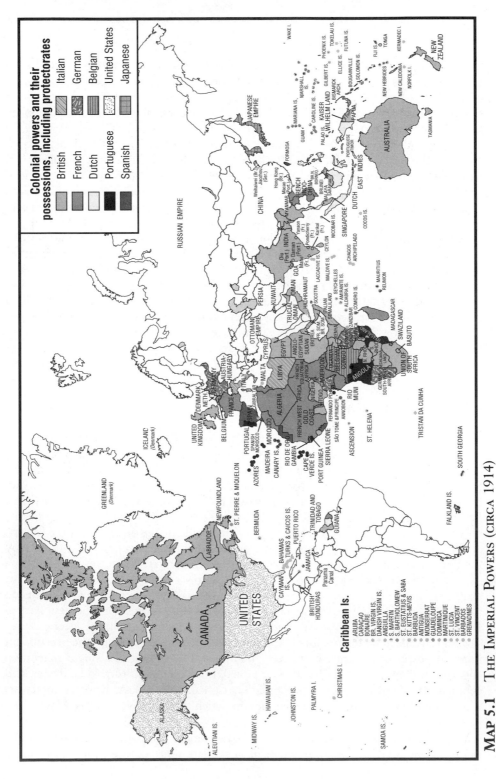

MAP 5.1 THE IMPERIAL POWERS (CIRCA 1914)
Source: Michael Dockrill, *Atlas of Twentieth Century World History* (New York: Harper-Perennial, 1991), pp. 12–13.

became an important symbol of national power and prestige. In the process, local inhabitants of the conquered lands were often ruthlessly suppressed. As Benjamin Cohen explains in his book *The Question of Imperialism:*

> The imperial powers typically pursued their various interests overseas in a blatantly aggressive fashion. Bloody, one-sided wars with local inhabitants of contested territories were commonplace; "sporting wars," Bismarck once called them. The powers themselves rarely came into direct military conflict, but competition among them was keen, and they were perpetually involved in various diplomatic crises. In contrast to the preceding years of comparative political calm, the period after 1870 was one of unaccustomed hostility and tension. (Cohen, 1973: 30)

Economic Explanations of the New Imperialism

Several explanations of the causes of the new imperialism exist. Marxists see the cause of imperialism as capitalism's need for profitable overseas outlets for surplus capital ("finance capital"). Thus V. I. Lenin viewed imperialism in his famous monograph *Imperialism, The Highest Stage of Capitalism* as the "monopoly stage of capitalism." From the Marxist perspective, the only way to end imperialism was to abolish capitalism. Classical or liberal economists, on the other hand, regarded the new imperialism "not [as] a product of capitalism as such, but rather [as] a response to certain maladjustments within the contemporary capitalist system which, given the proper will, could be corrected" (Cohen, 1973). What the two shared was the belief that economics explained the new imperialism. "The fundamental problem was in the presumed material needs of advanced capitalist societies—the need for cheap raw materials to feed their growing industrial complexes, for additional markets to consume their rising levels of production, and for investment outlets to absorb their rapidly accumulating capital. The rush for colonies was supposed to be the response of these capitalist societies to one or another of these material needs" (Cohen, 1973).

World-system analysts (see Chapter 2) also embrace an economic explanation of the new imperialism. They begin by noting that a single capitalist world-economy emerged during the "long sixteenth century" (roughly 1450–1640). During this time a world division of labor developed that demarcated "core" (industrial) political entities from those in the world's (nonindustrial) "periphery." Northwest Europe first emerged as the core. As the industrial revolution proceeded, the core states exchanged manufactured goods for agricultural and mineral products produced in the colonial territories at the periphery. From this perspective, colonization became a mechanism of imperial control that "was the principal political form of incorporating external areas into the capitalist world-economy" (Boswell, 1989). Imperialism expanded during periods of economic contraction in the core areas and contracted during periods of economic prosperity.

Despite the common world-system emphasis on economics, even its advocates recognize that the new imperialism of the late eighteenth century differed from the previous colonial period in important ways. "The earliest colonies were usually coastal trading posts for merchants involved in long-distance preciosity exchange with the contact periphery, such as the spice trade. Following rivers upstream, these were later superseded by settler colonies involved in the production of necessities, primarily mining and cash-crop agriculture using coerced labor. After 1870, 'occupation' colonies became common where a small number of European sojourners coerced an indigenous population into production for the world-economy" (Boswell, 1989).

Political Explanations of the New Imperialism

Political factors also explain the new imperialism. Especially important is the jockeying for power and prestige characteristic of the balance-of-power international political system that governed relations among the European powers for more than two centuries following the Peace of Westphalia.

By the 1800s Britain emerged as Europe's hegemonic (preponderant) core state. As the new leader in politics and economics, it became the chief promoter of free international trade (which, incidentally, promoted disproportionate economic growth in the core relative to the periphery) (McGowan, 1981). By 1870, however, Britain's superiority was on the wane. Germany emerged on the European continent as a powerful industrial nation, as did the United States in the Western Hemisphere. Accordingly, Britain's need to maintain its privileged position in the international division of labor in the face of growing competition from Germany and the United States, the newly emerging core states, helps to explain the second wave of imperial expansion, especially in Africa.

As Africa's partition illustrates, the European powers competed for power and prestige not in Europe itself but in the peripheral areas of the capitalist world-system. Competition for political preeminence led to economic domination and exploitation.[2]

> As in the days of mercantilism, colonies were integrated into an international economic system designed to serve the economic interest of the metropole [colonial power]. The political victors controlled investment and trade, regulated currency and production, and manipulated labor, thus establishing structures of economic dependency in their colonies which would endure far longer than their actual political authority. (Spero, 1990: 6–7)

Until the outbreak of World War I, the British-sponsored laissez-faire system of free international trade promoted rapid economic growth in many colonial territories. Even so, Western Europe, North America, Australia, and New Zealand were able to complete their industrial revolutions during this period and to advance as industrial societies. Thus the gap between the world's rich and poor nations began to take shape. After World War I the economies of North and South alike stagnated as worldwide

---

[2] Within Europe itself, the disintegration of political units into smaller ones was more prevalent than their integration into larger ones. (The unification of Germany and Italy are the principal exceptions.) Europe consisted of about fifteen sovereign states in 1871, twenty-five by the outbreak of World War I, and over thirty by the 1930s. The increase was due partly to the independence movements created by rising nationalistic aspirations and was fueled by the goal of national self-determination emulated worldwide after World War II.

The number of independent European states remained relatively constant from the late 1940s onwards. In the post–Cold War environment, however, the breakup of Yugoslavia and perhaps the successor to the Soviet Union, the Commonwealth of Independent States, would again accelerate the trend toward larger numbers of European states.

depression engulfed both, but there was an important difference between them. In most of the countries of the North, income levels remained comparatively high, for already by the time of the Great Depression in the 1930s it was evident that Western Europe, North America, and the southern Pacific were rich and that the rest of the world was poor (Higgins and Higgins, 1979).

Colonialism and Self-Determination in the Interwar Period

There was little movement toward the breakup of the colonial empires amassed in previous centuries between World War I and World War II. The Versailles peace settlement, which ended the First World War, incorporated the principle of national self-determination, which U.S. President Woodrow Wilson had espoused in justifying American participation in the war. Self-determination meant that nationalities would have the right to determine which authority would represent and rule them. Freedom of choice would lead to the creation of nations and governments content with their territorial boundaries and therefore less inclined to make war. In practice, however, the principle was applied almost exclusively to war-torn Europe, where six new states were created (Austria, Czechoslovakia, Hungary, Poland, Romania, and Yugoslavia) from the territory of the former Austro-Hungarian Empire. Most territorial adjustments elsewhere in Europe, many guided by the outcome of popular plebiscites, were also made, but the proposition that self-determination ought to be extended to Europe's overseas empires enjoyed little serious support.

However, the colonial territories of the powers defeated in World War I were not simply parceled out among the victorious allies. Instead, following the insistence of President Wilson, the territories controlled by Germany and the Ottoman Empire were transferred under League of Nations auspices to countries that would govern them as mandates pending their eventual self-rule. In the Middle East, France assumed the mandate for Syria and Britain assumed it for Iraq, Palestine, and Transjordan. In Africa, most of the German colony of Tanganyika went to Britain; the West African colonies of Cameroons and Togoland were divided between Britain and France; and the Union of South Africa gained responsibility for the mandate governing German South-West Africa. In the Pacific area, Australia, Japan, and New Zealand acquired jurisdiction over the former German colonies.

Many of these territorial decisions were destined to shape political conflicts for the next half-century or more. The decisions relating to the Middle East and Africa were especially crucial, as the League of Nations called for the eventual creation of a Jewish national homeland in Palestine and arranged for the transfer of control over South-West Africa (now called Namibia) to what would become the white minority regime of South Africa.

The principle implicit in the mandate system gave birth to the idea that "colonies were a trust rather than simply a property to be exploited and treated as if its peoples had no right of their own" (Easton, 1964). None of Germany's former colonies or provinces was annexed outright following World War I. This set an important precedent for the negotiations after World War II, when territories placed under the trusteeship system of the United Nations were not absorbed by others but were promised eventual self-rule.

The End of Empire

Imperialism threatened the world again in the 1930s and early 1940s, as Germany, Japan, and Italy sought to expand their political control in Europe, Asia, and Africa. With the defeat of the fascist powers, the threat of regional empire building receded, and the trend toward self-determination gained momentum. As noted earlier, in the space of a few short decades, more than a hundred new nations, representing perhaps three-quarters of humanity, gained their freedom in a display of political emancipation unprecedented in recorded history.

The post-colonial era began in earnest in 1947, when the British relinquished political control of the Indian subcontinent and India and Pakistan joined the international community as sovereign members. War eventually erupted between the new states as each sought to gain control over disputed territory in Kashmir, and it ignited twice more, in 1965 and again in 1971, when East Pakistan broke away from West Pakistan to form the new state of Bangladesh. Violence also broke out in Indochina and Algeria in the 1950s and early 1960s, as the French sought to reaffirm political control over colonial territories they had held before World War II. Similarly, bloodshed followed closely on the heels of independence in the Congo (later Zaire) when the Belgians granted their African colony independence in 1960, and it dogged the efforts of Portugal to battle—unsuccessfully—the winds of decolonization that swept over Africa as the 1960s wore on.

For the most part, however, decolonization was not only extraordinarily rapid but also remarkably peaceful. Arguably, this is explained by the fact that World War II sapped the economic and military vitality of many of the colonial powers. A growing appreciation of the costs of empire may also have eroded its support.[3] Regardless of the underlying cause, colonialism became less acceptable in a world increasingly dominated by rivalry between East and West. The Cold War competition for political allies and the fear of large-scale warfare militated against efforts to suppress revolution in the empire. Decolonization "triumphed," political scientist Inis Claude (1967) has written, "largely because the West [gave] priority to the containment of Communism over the perpetuation of colonialism."

The United Nations also played a role in the "collective delegitimization" of colonialism (Claude, 1967). With colonialism already in retreat, Third World nations took advantage of their growing numbers in the UN General Assembly to secure passage in 1960 of the historic Declaration on the Granting of Independence to Colonial Countries and Peoples.

---

[3] See Strang (1990, 1991) for an explanation of decolonization from a world-system perspective.

The General Assembly proclaimed that the subjection of any people to alien domination was a denial of fundamental human rights, contrary to the UN Charter, and an impediment to world peace and that all subject peoples had a right to immediate and complete independence. No country cast a vote against this anticolonial manifesto. . . . It was an ideological triumph. The old order had not merely been challenged and defeated in the field—its adherents were no longer willing to be counted in its defense. (Riggs and Plano, 1988: 228)

As the old order crumbled—and as Third World leaders found that political freedom did not translate automatically into political autonomy, economic independence, and domestic well-being—the North-South conflict between the rich nations of the First World and the newly emancipated nations of the Third World took shape.

PROFILES AND PROJECTIONS: GLOBAL DISPARITIES IN INCOME AND WEALTH . . . .

The unequal distribution of the world's wealth and people both reflects and explains the poverty of the South. As noted earlier, the more than three-quarters of humanity who live in the South account for only about one-fifth of the world's total economic product, whereas those in the North, making up less than a quarter of the population, account for nearly 80 percent of it. On a per-capita basis, this means (using 1988 data) that the average annual income for the Third World as a whole is less than $2,000 compared with nearly $14,000 for the First World—a ratio of nearly seven to one between the world's rich and poor. Figure 5.2 on page 128 lucidly illustrates how lopsided the world is, with its largest mass of people in the South and its greatest concentration of wealth in the North.

The discrepancies in wealth are even more stark when particular countries are compared. Consider, for example, the following comparison between the United States and Bolivia:

A child born in the United States will consume thirty to fifty times as many goods in his or her lifetime as one born in the highlands of Bolivia. . . . Rich is what we are when we are consuming thirty times as much as someone else—and that someone is managing to stay alive. Add a grain of salt to the statistics—add enough salt to take care of any quibbles about differing life expectancies or faulty measuring techniques—and say that our wealth exceeds that of the average Bolivian peasant by a ratio of twenty to one. (*New Yorker*, May 16, 1983: 32)

Third World Diversity

Table 5.1 on page 129 records differences in population and wealth for various countries and groups of countries. We have already commented on the overall differ-

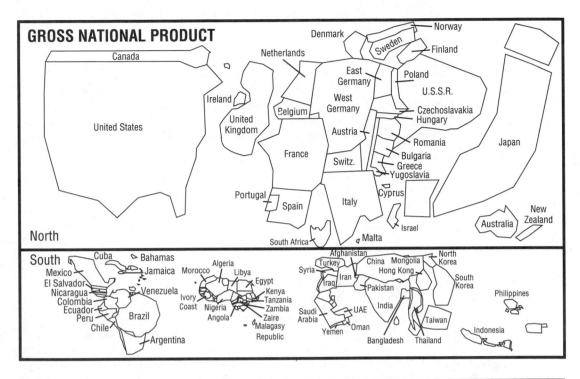

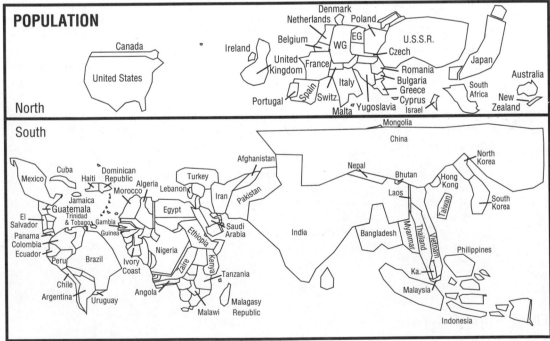

FIGURE 5.2 NORTH VERSUS SOUTH: GLOBAL DISPARITIES IN GROSS NATIONAL PRODUCT AND POPULATION, 1988

Table 5.1 The Distribution of World Population and Gross National Product Per Capita, by Selected Countries and Country Groups

Country or Group	Per-capita GNP 1988 ($)	Population, 1990 (millions)
Country data		
Switzerland	27,500	6.7
Japan	21,020	123.6
United States	19,840	251.4
France	16,090	56.4
United Arab Emirates	15,770	1.6
Soviet Union	4,550	291.0
Yugoslavia	2,520	23.8
Brazil	2,160	150.4
Thailand	1,000	55.7
Zimbabwe	650	9.7
China	330	1,120.0
Burundi	240	5.6
Mozambique	100	15.7
Group averages[a]		
First World	13,749	32.6
Third World	1,871	31.7
Least developed countries (LLDCs)	343	11.4
Oil-exporting countries	4,976	24.5
Organization of Petroleum Exporting Countries (OPEC)	5,075	35.6
Newly industrialized countries	5,014	47.8
Asian newly industrialized countries	7,165	17.9

Source: Based on data drawn from *Human Development Report 1991* (New York: Oxford University Press, 1991), pp. 122–123, 174. Data for Taiwan drawn from *Handbook of Economic Statistics, 1991* (Washington, D.C.: Central Intelligence Agency, 1991), p. 35, and *1988 World Population Data Sheet* (Washington, D.C.: Population Reference Bureau, 1988).

[a] Group averages are based on available data for Taiwan and the 161 independent and dependent territories commonly used by United Nations agencies for statistical purposes. Kiribati and Tuvalu, dependent territories among the forty-one entities classified as LLDCs, are omitted from the calculations; data for Andorra, Faroes Islands, Liechtenstein, Monaco, and San Marino, European entities that are part of the First World, are also excluded. Data for most remaining dependent territories, all of which belong to the Third World, are not available.

ences between the First and Third Worlds. Below we consider some groups within the Third World itself.

Least Developed Countries

Included among the more than 160 independent countries and dependent territories that make up the Third World is a group of forty-one regarded by the United Nations Conference on Trade and Development (UNCTAD) as the "least developed" of the less-developed countries (LLDCs). Nearly two-thirds are in Africa; most of the rest are in Asia. As shown in Table 5.1, for all of 1988 the average per-capita income of the LLDCs as a group was a minute $343.[4] Other characteristics accompanying this stark reality set the least developed countries apart from most others: agriculture (rather than manufacturing or services) is the dominant form of productive activity; two-fifths of the adult population is illiterate; life expectancy at birth is only fifty years; and infant mortality rates are among the highest in the world (United Nations Conference on Trade and Development, 1991: 3). Given their desperate present and bleak future, the least developed countries are properly candidates for designation as the *Fourth World*.

Oil-exporting Countries

The poverty of the LLDCs contrasts starkly with many of the world's oil-exporting nations, whose oil price increases during the 1970s compounded the problems of other developing economies. In 1988 the average per-capita income of the twenty major oil-exporting nations was roughly $5,000; the average income of the thirteen OPEC nations (Organization of Petroleum Exporting Countries) was similar, at $5,075.[5]

There are wide disparities in income even among the oil exporters, however. Indonesia and Nigeria, both members of OPEC, are at one end of the spectrum, with 1988 per-capita incomes of $440 and $290, respectively, and the United Arab Emirates and Kuwait are at the other end, with 1988 per-capita incomes of $15,770 and $13,400,

---

[4] We must exercise caution when interpreting per-capita income figures. They can understate the value of goods and services actually produced and consumed in poorer societies. It is absurd, for example, to think that a Burundian could actually live on an income of only $240 a year. Part of the problem is that the GNP measures only those goods and services that enter a society's monetary sector. Yet in many developing societies much economic activity exists outside the exchange economy, particularly in the agricultural sector. The problem is compounded by the fact that gross national products valued in domestic currencies are typically converted for international comparative purposes to a single currency unit, such as the U.S. dollar, using fixed rates of exchange (the rate at which one currency can be exchanged for another). Because exchange rates do not account for differences in a currency's purchasing power in different countries, cross-national comparisons of income probably overstate the magnitude of the difference between the world's rich and poor. Despite all of these difficulties, per-capita GNP remains the best single indicator available for making intercountry income comparisons.

[5] OPEC consists of Algeria, Ecuador, Gabon, Indonesia, Iran, Iraq, Kuwait, Libya, Nigeria, Qatar, Saudi Arabia, the United Arab Emirates, and Venezuela. The seven remaining major oil exporters are Angola, Bahrain, Brunei, the Congo, Oman, Syria, and Trinidad and Tobago.

respectively. These incomes approximate the incomes of many of the world's most advanced societies.

In part the differences within OPEC reflect not only the high concentration of rich oil deposits in the Middle East but also the much larger populations of Indonesia and Nigeria compared with Middle Eastern oil producers. For all the oil exporters, however, perhaps what is most notable is not how high their incomes are compared with other Third World countries but how far they have plunged since worldwide oil prices nose-dived in the mid-1980s. OPEC's average per-capita GNP dropped some 23 percent between 1981 and 1985. For particular members, such as Kuwait, the plunge in oil-based wealth was even more dramatic. And the downward spiral continued largely uninterrupted until the Persian Gulf War in early 1991, when oil prices shot upward dramatically (but only briefly).

Newly Industrialized Countries

Countries that have realized very rapid growth in their manufacturing sectors and have become important exporters of manufactures comprise a third important group among the developing nations, known as the *Newly Industrialized Countries* (NICs). The composition of the group varies somewhat depending on the criteria used to define it. Following UNCTAD's conventions, the calculations in Table 5.1 treat Brazil, Mexico, Singapore, South Korea, Taiwan, Yugoslavia, and the British crown colony of Hong Kong as the major Third World exporters of manufactured products, which describes the NICs. The Newly Industrialized Countries are essentially upper-middle-income countries, with annual per-capita incomes in 1988 ranging from $1,760 (Mexico) to $9,700 (Singapore). Moreover, some—particularly the four Asian NICs known as the "Asian Tigers" (Hong Kong, Singapore, South Korea, and Taiwan)—experienced rates of economic growth during the 1980s far greater than those of the more advanced industrial societies of the First World. As a result, they have become not only important exporters of manufactured goods (such as consumer electronics and automobiles) but also important markets for the major industrial countries that export capital goods. Those facts increasingly have made the Asian Tigers major players in the world political economy (see also Chapter 7).

The comparatively higher growth rates of the Asian NICs relative to the industrial societies of the First World reflect in part the fact that they began from a smaller base. It also means that their economies grew more rapidly than their populations, which is crucial if developing nations are to advance economically and to provide a better standard of living for their people.

The impact of population growth on the economic prospects of developing societies is central to understanding the gap between the world's rich and poor. Although developed and developing nations alike have experienced unprecedented economic growth since World War II, the developing nations as a whole have experienced higher growth rates, again in part as a result of the lower bases from which they began. Despite this, the gap between them and the world's rich has continued to widen, largely because of the much higher population growth of the developing nations (see also Chapter 9).

The widening absolute gap between rich and poor has become most apparent since World War II. One estimate (Brown, 1972: 42) puts the ratio between incomes in the industrializing societies of Western Europe and the rest of the world in 1850 at roughly two to one. By 1950 the gap had opened to ten to one, and by 1960 to nearly fifteen to one. Since 1950 the developed nations have nearly tripled their incomes, but the incomes of those at the periphery of the world political economy have remained largely unchanged (Durning, 1990: 136; also, *Human Development Report 1992*, 1992).

Narrowing the economic gap between the rich and poor countries requires that the poor continue to grow more rapidly than the rich. Yet only twenty-two developing nations fit this requirement on the basis of their performance from 1960 to 1975. Even if their relative growth rates remained constant, only a small proportion of this handful of nations could expect to close the gap within a reasonable time (Morawetz, 1977). For most, the process would take literally hundreds or even thousands of years, obviously not a realistic economic or political goal.

Measuring Economic Development and Standards of Living

Gross national product, per-capita GNP, and growth rates are the measures traditionally used to assess the progress of economic development. It is clear, however, that they offer too narrow a description of development. For example, even though developing nations as a whole have realized substantial gains in income since World War II, traditional measures fail to show that not everyone has enjoyed the fruits of progress because they cannot tell how evenly or unevenly income is spread.[6] Other factors must therefore be considered in weighing progress toward the reduction of poverty, such as improving the distribution of income within societies, increasing employment for everyone, and fulfilling basic human needs, including access to food, water, housing, health and health care, and education (see Box 5.1 for a personal perspective on the human dimensions of poverty).

The desirability of alternative measures to assess Third World living standards became especially apparent in the 1970s, when development economists and foreign aid donors shifted their attention from promoting economic growth toward meeting basic human needs. The Washington-based Overseas Development Council (ODC), a private research organization, developed at that time a Physical Quality of Life Index (PQLI), which uses life expectancy, infant mortality, and literacy rates to assess

---

[6] Widespread poverty within countries tends to be associated with extremely high concentrations of wealth in the hands of a few. Amin (1987: 1132) estimates that only 10 percent of the population in developing countries disposes of 25 percent of total income, compared with 50 percent of the population in developed nations, and that only a third of the population in developing nations disposes of half of total income, compared with 75 percent of the population in developed nations.

See the *World Development Report 1991* (1991: 262–263) and the *Human Development Report 1991* (1991: 152–153, 186) for supporting data on the income distribution in selected countries.

Box 5.1
An American Student Discovers the Meaning of the Third World

• • •

"I spent the first 24 years of my life in South Carolina. When I left . . . for Colombia [South America], I fully expected Bogota to be like any large U.S. city, only with citizens who spoke Spanish. When I arrived there I found my expectations were wrong. I was not in the U.S., I was on Mars! I was a victim of culture shock. As a personal experience this shock was occasionally funny and sometimes sad. But after all the laughing and the crying were over, it forced me to reevaluate both my life and the society in which I live.

"Colombia is a poor country by American standards. It has a per capita GNP of $550 and a very unequal distribution of income. These were the facts that I knew before I left.

"But to 'know' these things intellectually is much different from experiencing first-hand how they affect people's lives. It is one thing to lecture in air conditioned classrooms about the problems of world poverty. It is quite another to see four-year-old children begging or sleeping in the streets.

"It tore me apart emotionally to see the reality of what I had studied for so long: 'low per capita GNP and maldistribution of income.' What this means in human terms is children with dirty faces who beg for bread money or turn into pickpockets because the principle of private property gets blurred by empty stomachs.

"It means other children whose minds and bodies will never develop fully because they were malnourished as infants. It means cripples who can't even turn to thievery and must beg to stay alive. It means street vendors who sell candy and cigarettes 14 hours a day in order to feed their families.

"It also means well-dressed businessmen and petty bureaucrats who indifferently pass this poverty every day as they seek asylum in their fortified houses to the north of the city.

"It means rich people who prefer not to see the poor, except for their maids and security guards.

"It means foreigners like me who have come to Colombia and spend more in one month than the average Colombian earns in a year.

"It means politicians across the ideological spectrum who are so full of abstract solutions or personal greed that they forget that it is real people they are dealing with.

"Somewhere within the polemics of the politicians and the 'objectivity' of the social scientists, the human being has been lost."

Source: Brian Wallace, extracted from "True Grit South of the Border," OSCEOLA, January 13, 1978, pp. 15–16.

progress in meeting basic human needs.[7] The higher the score, the more favorable a country's social performance is thought to be.[8]

Table 5.2 lists the PQLI scores and their related data for several different countries falling into different income groups. The PQLI scores indicate that widely varying levels of social performance are possible, regardless of the income group into which a particular country falls. Sri Lanka is a particularly striking case. In income, it is among the poorest countries in the world, but its standard of living as measured by the PQLI is higher than that of most upper-middle-income countries. Similarly, Cuba's PQLI compares favorably with the world's richest nations, but its GNP per capita places it in the lower-middle-income group. On the other hand, Gabon (a member of OPEC) has a PQLI below that of most low-income countries, despite its upper-middle-income status.

The United Nations Development Program (UNDP) has also sought to measure *human development* using a combination of economic and noneconomic measures. As explained in its 1991 annual report:

> Human development is moving to centre stage in the 1990s. For too long, the question has been: how much is a nation producing? Now the question must be: how are its people faring?
>
> The real objective of development is to increase people's development choices. Income is one aspect of these choices—and an extremely important one—but it is not the sum-total of human existence. Health, education, a good physical environment and freedom—to name a few other components of well-being—may be just as important. (*Human Development Report 1991*, 1991: 13)

Recognizing that some distance separates the *concept* of human development from its *measurement*, the UNDP devised a *human development index* (HDI) that, like the PQLI, uses life expectancy and literacy to measure well-being. It adds the average number of years of schooling attained within societies, which helps to differentiate among countries at the top stratum on the human development scale. And it specifically incorporates income (using a strategy that measures its diminishing utility as countries become richer). Including income rests on the conviction that "a realistic view [of development] is that growth in income and an expansion of economic opportunities are necessary preconditions of human development. . . . Although growth is not the end of development, the absence of growth often is."

Table 5.3 on page 136 records the HDI for the sixteen countries shown in Table

---

[7] See Black (1991) and Sklair (1991) for critical evaluations of the PQLI and other indices of development.
[8] The PQLI is a composite index based on three indicators: infant mortality, life expectancy at age one, and literacy. Each of the components is indexed on a scale of 0 (the most unfavorable performance in 1950) to 100 (the best performance expected by the end of the century as estimated in 1979). The three are then averaged to create the PQLI for each country.

Using the PQLI in combination with income measures, the Overseas Development Council classifies a country as *developed* if it had per-capita income in 1988 of at least $4,530 and a high standard of living as indicated by a PQLI of 90 or more. It regards a country as *developing* if either its 1988 per-capita income is below $4,530 or if it achieves a PQLI score of less than 90. Hence, the oil-rich nations of OPEC and most of the Newly Industrialized Countries remain developing societies, for despite their often substantial per-capita incomes most fail to achieve a PQLI score of at least 90.

TABLE 5.2 PQLI AND RELATED ECONOMIC AND SOCIAL INDICATORS OF SELECTED COUNTRIES

Income Category[a]	Per-capita GNP 1988 ($)	Physical Quality of Life Index (PQLI) 1990	Life Expectancy at Birth (years)	Infant Mortality (per 1,000 births)	Literacy (%)
Low-income	319	68	63	66	60
Guinea-Bissau	190	36	44	140	37
China	330	84	71	27	73
India	340	60	60	88	48
Sri Lanka	420	90	72	24	88
Lower-middle-income	941	76	64	53	75
Philippines	630	83	65	40	90
Yemen, Arab Rep.	640	48	53	107	39
Zimbabwe	650	70	61	55	67
Cuba	1,170	96	76	13	94
Upper-middle-income	2,299	83	69	39	81
Poland	1,860	94	72	17	98
Brazil	2,160	79	66	57	81
Gabon	2,970	58	54	94	61
Korea, Rep.	3,600	92	71	21	96
High-income	14,421	97	75	12	97
Kuwait	13,400	87	74	15	73
United States	19,840	98	76	8	99
Japan	21,020	101	79	5	99
Switzerland	27,500	100	78	7	99

Source: Adapted from *U.S. Foreign Policy and Developing Countries: Discourse and Data 1991* (Washington, D.C.: Overseas Development Council, 1991), pp. 37–41.
[a] Income categories are based on the following criteria: *low-income*, a per-capita income of less than $515; *lower-middle-income*, $515–$1,304; *upper-middle-income*, $1,305–$14,529; *high-income*, $14,530 or above.

5.2. It also includes the HDI rank of each of the countries among some 160 independent polities, its PQLI in 1990, and its income group based on 1988 per-capita GNP data.

As with the PQLI, a comparison of the countries' human development performance with their income levels reveals some anomalies. China and Cuba, for example, perform better than expected on the basis of income alone, and Gabon does more poorly. Moreover, there is no one-to-one correspondence between income and non-income measures of development. Overall, however, a strong association exists between wealth and alternative measures of well-being. Map 5.2 on page 137, a PQLI map of the world, illustrates this general pattern. Note in particular the tendency for

TABLE 5.3 LEVEL OF HUMAN DEVELOPMENT, SELECTED COUNTRIES

	Level of Human Development			
HDI Category	HDI Rank[a]	HDI Value	PQLI	Income group[b]
Low Human Development (HDI value less than .50)				
Guinea-Bissau	151	.088	36	Low
Yemen	130	.242	48[c]	Low
India	123	.308	60	Low
Zimbabwe	111	.413	70	Low-Mid
Medium Human Development (HDI value .50 to .799)				
Gabon	97	.510	58	Up-Mid
Philippines	84	.613	83	Low-Mid
China	82	.614	84	Low
Sri Lanka	75	.665	90	Low
Cuba	62	.754	96	Low-Mid
Brazil	60	.759	79	Up-Mid
High Human Development (HDI .80 or above)				
Kuwait	48	.827	87	High
Korea, Rep.	35	.884	92	Up-Mid
Poland	41	.863	94	Up-Mid
United States	7	.976	98	High
Switzerland	5	.981	100	High
Japan	1	.993	101	High

Source: Adapted from *Human Development Report 1991* (New York: Oxford University Press, 1991), pp. 119–121. Physical Quality of Life Index (PQLI) and income categories are from Table 5.2.
[a] Rank among 160 independent nations.
[b] The income categories are based on the following criteria: *low-income* (Low), a per-capita income of less than $515; *lower-middle-income* (Low-Mid), $515–$1,304; *upper-middle-income* (Up-Mid), $1,305–$14,529; *high-income* (High), $14,530 or above.
[c] Arab Republic of Yemen only.

the highest living standards as measured by PQLI to occur in the North, where per-capita incomes are also generally high. Conversely, generally lower standards of living occur in the South, where per-capita incomes are measurably lower. Many, in fact, appear at the poverty end of the spectrum (those illustrated in dark gray and black). This is especially true in Sub-Saharan Africa and in South and Southeast Asia, where many nations described earlier as candidates for designation of the Fourth World are located.

Do political variables affect nations' economic and welfare performance? Western political leaders have long argued that market economies thrive in a political atmosphere that minimizes governmental interference in the economic laws of supply and demand. A corollary is that individual initiative in the marketplace is more likely to occur in an atmosphere of political freedom. The collapse of the socialist economies in Eastern Europe and the Soviet Union, in which the government sought to replace

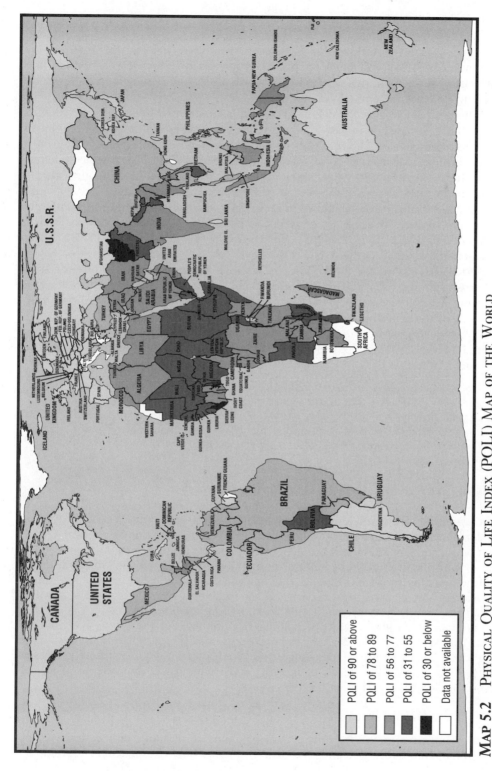

MAP 5.2 PHYSICAL QUALITY OF LIFE INDEX (PQLI) MAP OF THE WORLD

Source: Adapted from John W. Sewell and Stuart K. Tucker, and contributors, *Growth, Jobs, and Exports in a Changing World Economy: Agenda 1988* (New Brunswick, N.J.: Transaction Books). Copyright © 1988 by the Overseas Development Council, pp. 258–259. Reprinted with permission.

Legend:
- PQLI of 90 or above
- PQLI of 78 to 89
- PQLI of 56 to 77
- PQLI of 31 to 55
- PQLI of 30 or below
- Data not available

the market as the determinant of supply and demand and otherwise ruled with an iron hand, is consistent with this view, which holds that laissez-faire economics and political freedom go hand in hand.

The United Nations Development Program sought to address this matter in its 1991 report. It based its inquiry on the premise that "the goal of human development is to increase people's choices. But for people to exercise their choices, they must enjoy freedom—cultural, social, economic and political." Measuring freedom throughout the world is exceedingly difficult, but the UNDP concluded after a preliminary examination of the relationship between its human development index and the performance of (a limited number of) countries on some forty different indicators of freedom that "there seems to be a high correlation between human development and human freedom" (*Human Development Report 1991*, 1991; see also Pourgerami, 1991).

Others have asked whether differences in the character of political regimes account for cross-national variations in individual welfare. There are three basic ways that political processes are believed to affect differences in individual welfare: through the strength of the state apparatus, through democratic political processes, and through the ideological orientation of ruling elites (Moon and Dixon, 1985). Each is in fact related to variations in the welfare of individuals in different national settings as measured by the PQLI.

> Democratic processes are related to positive welfare outcomes irrespective of state strength and ideological norms. For regimes with a roughly centrist ideology, state strength appears to make little noticeable difference one way or another; for those on the [political] left, state strength promotes welfare performance; for those on the [political] right, state strength [inhibits] the provision of basic needs. (Moon and Dixon, 1985)

Impediments to Growth in a Typical Developing Country

The preceding discussion hints at the complexity of the development process. Raising a people's economic and social well-being involves the interaction of political, social, economic, and cultural factors, ranging from the level of resource endowment and the extent of industrialization to cultural norms about family size and the ability and willingness of governments to make difficult and often politically costly development decisions. The relations between rich and poor nations within the international political and economic systems also have a bearing on development.

We can better understand the political dispute between the North and South if we isolate some factors underlying the persistent underdevelopment that is today the plight of so many nations. Hans Singer and Javed Ansari (1988) identify high rates of population growth, low levels of income, and technological dependence as salient factors linked to several other considerations.

High Population Growth

High population growth is perhaps the single most important factor underlying the widening gap between rich and poor nations. Higher birthrates mean that developing nations have a far larger proportion of young people in their societies than do developed nations. Thus they "have to devote much more of their resources to the task of raising a new generation of producers, besides providing services of a given standard to an enlarged and rapidly urbanizing population" (Singer and Ansari, 1988).

Low Levels of Income

Low income levels distinguish the Third World from the First. They go hand in hand with impoverished economic and social conditions. More importantly, they also prevent poorer countries from generating enough economic surplus to make sizable investments in their future economic growth.

> New sectors of modern economic growth thus remain very small, especially in terms of employment, and are often foreign-controlled. The national economy at large remains deprived of new capital infusion. In the poor countries, agricultural production accounts for about 40–50 percent of GNP, while in the rich countries the ratio is about 5 percent. Moreover, about three-quarters of the total population of a poor country is engaged in the agricultural sector. (Singer and Ansari, 1988: 42–43)

It is widely assumed that when so many people work in the agricultural sector, many are in fact underemployed, and some perhaps are better classified as unemployed. This means, to use the economist's terms, that labor (which along with land and capital is one of the factors of production) is underutilized. Underutilization is not confined to agriculture, however. Many people in the Third World are deprived of meaningful employment opportunities or, more commonly, are engaged in unproductive labor. Singer and Ansari suggest that the underutilization of labor is "both the cause and effect of a distortion of the consumption and investment patterns and of high and rising inequalities of income distribution." The underutilization of all factors of production "is a central feature of the economy of a poor country" (Singer and Ansari, 1988). The result is inadequate investment in education, health, transportation facilities, credit facilities, and other socioeconomic infrastructure. Without this investment the poor remain poor, and the gap between them and the rich widens.

Technological Dependence

Developing countries have not been able to evolve an indigenous technology appropriate to their own resource endowments. Instead, they depend critically on powerful multinational corporations (MNCs) spawned in the North to transfer technical know-how from the world's rich to its poor. Not surprisingly, therefore, they are sensitive to the role that MNCs play in their economic and political lives.

The imbalance of technological development may be described thus:

> Almost all world expenditures on science and technology take place inside the richer countries, and research and development are therefore quite naturally directed towards solving *their* problems by methods suited to *their* circumstances and resource endowments. The problems of the poorer countries, however, are not the same; for instance, they need research to design simple products, to develop production for smaller markets, to improve the quality of and to develop new uses for tropical products, and above all to develop

production processes which utilize their abundant labour. Instead, emphasis is placed on sophisticated weaponry, space research, atomic research, sophisticated products, production for large high-income markets, and specifically a constant search for processes that save labour by substituting capital or high-order skills. (Singer and Ansari, 1988: 44)[9]

The causes and the consequences of technological dependence are among the principal concerns of Singer and Ansari's study, *Rich and Poor Countries.* "If the technological gap is not overcome," they conclude, "no form of assistance, trade concessions, aid, grants, technical assistance or fortuitous price rises will prove to be of lasting value. International cooperation policies must be devised which serve to remove this fundamental obstacle in the path of development."

Dualism in Developing Societies

Overall, *dualism* characterizes the social and economic structures of developing societies. It occurs when a society evolves into two separate sectors. Dual societies have a rural, impoverished, and neglected sector operating alongside an urban, developing, or modernizing sector. Typically, however, there is little interaction between the two:

> Most [developing countries] have a large, stagnant, agricultural sector which is linked to the small, modern, large-scale, industrial sector mainly through the supply of resources, both labour and capital, from the former to the latter. The growth of the industrial sector neither initiates a corresponding growth process in the rural sector nor generates sufficient employment to prevent a growing population in the stagnant sectors. (Singer and Ansari, 1988: 45–46)

The reasons for dualism in the developing countries' economic structures are lodged in their colonial past, when the metropolitan powers regarded themselves as the best producers of manufactured goods and their colonies as the best suppliers of basic foodstuffs and raw materials. This resulted in few "spread effects" in the colonial economies' secondary and tertiary sectors. Eventually, rapid population growth overwhelmed the ability of the colonies' rising incomes to produce continued economic growth (Higgins and Higgins, 1979). Yet the hope for a better life in the urban areas led to a flood of migrants from farm to city, resulting in decrepit urban slums and massive numbers of unemployed seeking work in the small industrial sector. Because the advanced technology of the industrial societies is almost always more capital

---

[9] In the late 1970s the Worldwatch Institute (Norman, 1979) provided data on global scientific priorities consistent with the crux of Singer and Ansari's arguments. It noted that worldwide, $150 billion was spent annually on research and development (R & D). About a quarter of this was spent on military R & D, which is about three times the amount that was spent on developing alternative energy technologies and more than was spent on energy, health, food production, and environmental protection combined. Moreover, only about $30 million was spent annually on research on tropical diseases. These maladies afflict perhaps a billion people in the Third World, but in the United States alone, nine times this amount was spent on cancer research. This disparity in medical R & D reflects the concentration of such efforts in the developed world. The United States at that time by itself accounted for a third of the world's R & D expenditures, Western Europe and Japan for another third, and the Soviet Union and Eastern Europe for about 30 percent (Norman, 1979: 14).

intensive than labor (that is, employment) intensive, it tends to exacerbate rather than alleviate the plight of the jobless.

Historically, population trends in the industrial world suggest that urbanization and industrialization are associated with declining, not rising, rates of population growth. One reason that developing societies do not mirror this pattern is that their death rates have fallen more precipitously than those in the industrial world. The difference is caused more by externally introduced measures to reduce death rates than by the changes in attitudes toward family size associated with urbanization and industrialization in the North. In addition, the industrialization experienced by colonial economies occurred mainly in the areas of basic foodstuffs and raw materials and therefore may not have altered the societal patterns of traditional colonialism. "Hence the checks on family size enforced by the urban industrialization of Europe and the New World operated less effectively in the underdeveloped countries" (Higgins and Higgins, 1979).

The persistence of dualism in the economic structures of the developing societies suggests that even in countries with incipient industrial sectors, the local population will not share widely in the benefits. In fact, "the industrial sector of the poor countries is really a periphery of the metropolitan industrial economies, critically dependent on them for the technology it uses" (Singer and Ansari, 1988). Benefits will be confined to those groups in developing societies that are able to link themselves to the rich countries:

> These will become oases of growth surrounded by a desert of stagnation, thus reinforcing other elements of dualism already present in the poorer countries. The way leads to polarization within the poor country, clashing with the objectives of national planning and national integration. This polarization expresses itself in widening internal income disparities, larger numbers exposed to extreme poverty, and rising unemployment. (Singer and Ansari, 1988: 28)

The problems faced by developing nations are thus characterized as a series of vicious circles, none of which seems capable of being broken because it is so closely intertwined with so many other difficult problems.

Dominance and Dependence in International Economic Relations

The discussion up to this point indicates that a combination of factors indigenous to Third World nations and inherent in their relationships with the First World causes the widening gap between the North and the South. Many theorists would not agree with that simple statement, however. In their attempt to explain the persistent underdevelopment of developing economies, some direct attention primarily toward what happens within Third World nations, while others focus on the position of developing nations in the world political economy. We identify and briefly discuss three variants on these viewpoints: the conventional (sometimes called "liberal") theory of economic development, dependency theory, and world-system theory.

Conventional Theory

Conventional theories of economic development first emerged in the early post–World War II era. These Western-oriented theories emphasized the factors indigenous to Third World nations in their efforts to understand the impediments to Third World development and to devise ways of overcoming them. Based on the assumption that growth meant increasing increments of per-capita GNP (rather than, say, meeting basic human needs), the task was to identify and remove obstacles to growth and supply various "missing components," such as investment capital (through foreign aid or private sources) (Todaro, 1989).

Once capital was accumulated sufficiently to promote economic growth, conventional theorists held that its benefits would eventually "trickle down" to other segments of society. In this way, everyone, not simply a privileged few, would enjoy the benefits of rising affluence. Walt W. Rostow (1960), an influential economic historian who would later play a key foreign policy role in the administration of U.S. President Lyndon Johnson, wrote an influential book entitled *The Stages of Economic Growth*, in which he maintained that traditional societies that entered the development path would inevitably pass through various stages. Eventually, they would become similar to the mass-consumption societies of the West. That prognosis proved wrong, of course, as did other conventional ideas about the route to economic development. Dependency and world-system theorists purport to explain why they failed.

Dependency Theory

Dependency theory builds on Lenin's theory of imperialism, described at the beginning of this chapter, but it goes beyond Lenin "by specifying the nature of imperialism more completely and by accounting for changes that have occurred since Lenin wrote [his treatise] at the beginning of the century" (Shannon, 1989).

A central proposition in dependency theory is that the relationship between the advanced capitalist societies and those at the periphery of the world political economy is exploitative.[10] From this viewpoint, underdevelopment "is not a stalled stage of linear development, a question of pre-capitalism, retarded or backward development, but rather a structural position in a hierarchical world division of labor." Hence, we need only to look "to contemporary relations with other societies to explain underdevelopment" (Bergesen, 1980). This viewpoint denies that development is merely a matter of passing through various stages, such as from the traditional society to the mass-consumption society, as Rostow had argued. As articulated by Andre Gunder Frank (1969), a leading dependency theorist, "The now developed countries were never underdeveloped, though they may have been undeveloped."

---

[10] For a sampling of some of the extensive dependency theory literature, see Amin (1974), Baran (1968), Emmanuel (1972), Frank (1969), and the special issue of *International Organization* on dependence and dependency in the global system edited by James A. Caporaso (1978). Todaro (1989) reviews the basic tenets of neo-Marxist views of dependency; Smith (1979, 1981) provides insightful critiques of dependency theory; and Caporaso (1980) discusses theoretical controversies surrounding the perspective.

In contrast with the "stages of growth" theory, Frank (and others) attributed "the development of underdevelopment" to the historical expansion of the capitalist system that "effectively and entirely penetrated even the apparently most isolated sectors of the underdeveloped world." *Dependentistas*, as they were frequently called, viewed the penetration process as fueled by capitalism's need for external sources of demand and profitable investment outlets. The overseas branches of the giant multinational corporations (MNCs), whose headquarters are in the North, were the agents of penetration. Foreign investment, whether made as private investments by MNCs or in the form of foreign economic and military aid by other governments, was also considered an instrument of penetration. Technological dependence and "cultural imperialism" perpetrated through ideas alien to the indigenous cultures of Third World societies were among the consequences. Ultimately, the MNCs' role was to transfer profits from the penetrated societies to the penetrators, as it is the profit motive that leads to the penetration of peripheral societies in the first place.

Once those that are underdeveloped have been penetrated by the advanced capitalist states, continues the dependency argument, the inherently exploitative linkages that bind them together are sustained by the local elites within the penetrated societies. Their own fortunes are tied to the dominant powers; therefore, they are co-opted by their desire to maintain their privileged positions in their own societies. One critic of dependency theory describes the role that the Third World's local elites play in the politics of dominance and dependence by noting that they structure their domestic position in ways that favor their international connections. "Thus, it is not the sheer economic might of the outside that dictates the dependent status of the South, but the sociological consequences of this power. . . . A symbiotic relationship has grown up over time in which the system [of dominance and dependence] has created its servants whose needs dictate that its survival be ensured, whatever the short-term conflicts of interests may be" (Smith, 1979). Implicit here is the notion that political repression, applied locally but often with foreign support, may be necessary to protect the privileges of the few.

Finally, dependency theorists also reject dualism as a description of the economic and social systems of the Third World countries. They attack that idea on two major counts:

1. The concept of dualism, with its division into "modern" and "traditional" sectors, suggests that there are two economic systems operating in (nonsocialist) [developing countries], whereas in fact there is only one; international capitalism, which makes the decision for the whole (nonsocialist) world and determines the outcome in social, economic and political terms.

2. Whereas standard or "Dualist" economists tend to suggest that the continuing poverty and growing gaps in developing countries reflect failure of developing policies adopted by governments of developing countries, . . . the truth is that the current situation in [developing countries] reflects the *success* of the policies imposed by international capitalism. The persistence of marginal

groups of poor workers and peasants in developing countries reflects a consciously planned system, designed to protect profits by keeping peasant incomes and wages down and reserving for capitalists of advanced countries production requiring advanced technology.[11] (Higgins and Higgins, 1979: 100)

World-System Theory

World-system theorists share some ideas with dependency theorists. Both, for example, view the world as divided into a core (the advanced capitalist states) and a periphery (the developing states). World-system theorists, however, take a longer-term perspective on the pattern of relationships between core and periphery, as suggested in our previous discussion of imperialism. They treat these relationships as a coherent, integrated whole in the context of a single capitalist world-system. Moreover, although world-system analysts concern themselves with the interaction of state power and economic forces in the global arena, they treat the actors in world politics in terms of classes, much as Karl Marx regarded class as the basic unit of social analysis. Immanuel Wallerstein, widely regarded as the intellectual father of world-system theory as it developed in North America (see Wallerstein, 1974a, 1974b, 1980, 1988),[12] rejects the charge that it is fundamentally a Marxist theory, but the label "neo-Marxist" is nonetheless often used to describe the perspective.

For world-system theorists, a critical issue is how states fit into the international division of labor.

> By claiming that there is a single division of labor, world-system theorists [reject] the more conventional approach, which [views] the world-economy as composed of isolated and independent national economies that just happen to trade with one another. . . . Economic activities in each part of a true world-economy depend on and make possible the activities of the other parts. . . . The result is an economic system that includes a number of cultural areas, states, or societies but constitutes a single economy based on a complex division of labor. Each part or area has acquired a specialized role producing goods that it trades to others to obtain what it needs. Thus, the world-economy is tied together by a complex network of global economic exchange. (Shannon, 1989: 21)

It is here that the core-periphery concept becomes important. "Within the world division of labor, core states specialize in the production of the most 'advanced' goods, which involves the use of the most sophisticated technologies and highly mechanized methods of production ('capital-intensive' production). At least until recently, this meant that core states specialized in the production of sophisticated manufactured goods" (Shannon, 1989). Core states, limited historically to Western Europe but joined

---

[11] Although Singer and Ansari (1988) subscribe to the dualism characterization, much of their analysis is consistent with dependency theory. Higgins and Higgins (1979), on the other hand, are critical of the dependency argument.

[12] In Europe the French historian Fernand Braudel (1981, 1982, 1984) developed many ideas germane to world-system theory.

in this century by the United States and, later, Japan, are also the most powerful militarily and the best organized administratively.

The periphery, of course, consists of those geographic areas that now make up the Third World. "Economic activities in the periphery are relatively less technologically sophisticated and more 'labor intensive' than those in the core. . . . For most of the modern era, production for export was concentrated on raw materials and agricultural commodities" (Shannon, 1989). Those on the periphery have historically been militarily inferior to core states and less well organized administratively, which limited their ability to compete with the capitalist states.

World-system theorists predict that in time a socialist world-system will replace the capitalist world-system, but they have difficulty explaining the industrialization now taking place in the periphery. To account for that, the *semi-periphery* has been introduced. This permits world-system theory to accommodate geographic areas or countries, such as the Newly Industrialized Countries, that do not fall neatly into either the core or the periphery in the current international division of labor.

Dependency theorists also have difficulty explaining the NIC phenomenon. For them, *dependent development* describes the industrialization of peripheral areas in a system of First World hegemony. As the term suggests, development (at least industrialization) is possible, but not outside the confines of the dominance-dependence relationship between North and South.

Each of the perspectives described above illuminates in important ways the nature of underdevelopment and development and prescribes methods of moving from the former to the latter. None, however, is entirely persuasive or able adequately to account for the current dire circumstances in which so many of the world's developing nations find themselves. Debates about theories and facts and about beliefs and perceptions therefore animate much of the North-South conflict. They also inform the motives underlying the foreign policy goals of Third World nations, to which we now turn.

BEYOND DEPENDENCE: THE FOREIGN POLICY GOALS OF THIRD WORLD NATIONS . . . .

The preceding discussion identifies many elements in the often contentious relations between the rich nations of the North and the poorer nations of the South, including such matters as trade, aid, and transnational pricing mechanisms. Together these have formed core issues in the North-South conflict that have spurred the Third World to adopt foreign policy strategies designed to move them beyond dependence.

A New International Economic Order

Developing nations believe that the present structure of international economic relations is responsible for their plight. They therefore want to change the regimes that shape the international movement of goods, services, capital, labor, and technology. The widely shared belief among Third World elites in the premises of dependency theory facilitates the pursuit of regime change. During the 1970s and early 1980s in particular, it galvanized the developing nations into a collective drive toward goals they were too weak to realize by traditional bilateral means (Krasner, 1981, 1985). Their collective demands culminated in a vociferous call for a New International Economic Order (NIEO).

The New International Economic Order sought by developing nations would be profoundly different from the Liberal International Economic Order (LIEO) created under the aegis of U.S. hegemony after World War II, which many Third World leaders viewed as an instrument of their continued oppression. Their goal was to be equal to the more advanced countries in fact, not just in law. Thus Third World nations saw the NIEO as an alternative to the prevailing exploitative system. Speaking for the Third World before the United Nations General Assembly in 1979, Cuba's Fidel Castro expressed this view in words commonly used to depict the Third World spirit. He demanded the creation of a "new world order based on justice, on equity, on peace" to replace "the unjust world system that exists today." Under the current system, he said, "wealth is still concentrated in the hands of a few powers" who profit from "exploitation" of the Third World.

The historical roots of the NIEO were grounded in the 1950s and 1960s, when the Third World, with support from the Second World, began forming a united front to deal with the industrial West on international economic issues. These efforts resulted in the first United Nations Conference on Trade and Development (UNCTAD), held in Geneva in 1964. The meeting became the forerunner of several later conferences that focused on various aspects of the relations between the world's rich and poor nations.

During the 1964 conference, the Group of 77 (known in diplomatic circles as simply G-77) was formed as a coalition of the world's poor countries to press for concessions from the world's rich. Now numbering over 120 developing countries, the G-77 continues to act in that capacity today. UNCTAD is also now a permanent organization in the United Nations' family of organizations. Building on the intellectual guidance and aggressive leadership of its first secretary general, Dr. Raúl Prebisch, it became an aggressive advocate for the world's less fortunate nations.

The issues addressed in the UNCTAD forum (and in other international bodies) have changed over time in response to changing international circumstances. Among the changes of the post–World War II period has been the ascendance of three independent centers of industrial power in the North: the United States, Western Europe, and Japan. Because each industrial center has different needs and interests, each has responded differently to the Third World's interests and demands. The United States is a continental power less heavily dependent on the rest of the world than most nations. Western Europe has strong historical ties and cultural bonds with many Third World countries. And Japan, an island nation, is critically dependent on raw-material imports. Conversely, among Third World nations different levels of development, differing degrees of economic and political affiliation with the North, differing colonial experiences,[13] and differing perceptions of national interests all affect both the stakes in and the positions of individual countries in the outcome of the North-South dialogue. Nevertheless, certain commonalities continue to pervade the foreign policy goals of developing nations.

Political Autonomy

Third World criticism of the existing international order does not focus on the exclusivity of the global system as much as on the manner in which the dispossessed are excluded from rank, status, and a fair share of global well-being. This ambivalence finds expression in developing nations' attitudes toward international law. Law cannot give them the status and rewards possessed by others, but it does help to ensure their survival in a threatening international environment, where the power of others could easily overwhelm them. Most are therefore vigorous supporters of the principles of self-determination and the inadmissibility of the acquisition of territory by force: one justifies their existence, and the other sustains it (Waldheim, 1984).[14]

Still, the Third World drive for equality of influence extends their interests beyond preservation of the status quo. As explained by a former U.S. ambassador to Sri Lanka, many Third World leaders "are hostile to the notion that the state system should be organized in its present sharply hierarchical fashion, in which a few with wealth, industrial and technological strength, and the capability to apply force regularly make decisions that so profoundly affect the conditions and well-being of even distant states" (Wriggins, 1978).

In addition to equality of influence, autonomy or independence is also sought. "Each state, it is held, should be able to manage its own political and economic affairs without interference from outside: each should be in a position to decide for itself how its resources should be utilized, what policies industrial and agricultural enterprises operating within its borders should follow, and such economic matters as interest rates for loans, rates of exchange, and export subsidies" (Wriggins, 1978). Transforming existing regimes is necessary, as the developing nations individually cannot change the environment that affects them adversely.

---

[13] Craig Murphy notes in his discussion of the history of Third World demands for a New International Economic Order that in the early 1970s the relative immediacy of the colonial experience helped split the South into "moderate" and "radical" camps, with the latter believing that the North owed the South restitution for past colonialism. "The radical camp included mostly Asian and African nations, nonaligned states, states that were recently independent, and other states that supported the restitution ethic. The moderate camp tended to be Latin American, aligned with the West, and included some states that had been independent longer, where people were relatively better off and whose governments rarely talked about the need for restitution for colonialism" (Murphy, 1983).

[14] Together these principles help explain the antipathy for Israel shared by many Third World nations, which is fueled by Israel's policies toward the Palestinian people and its occupation of Arab territory since the June 1967 war in the Middle East.

Nonalignment

In the same way that Third World nations have sought to erase the vestiges of dependent relationships implied by the terms *neocolonialism* and *neo-imperialism*, most were determined during the Cold War to avoid choosing between East and West because of fear that one form of domination might simply be replaced by another. Hence, they espoused a policy of *nonalignment*.

The nonaligned movement began in 1955, when twenty-nine Asian and African nations met in Bandung, Indonesia, to devise a strategy to combat colonialism. By 1961 it had grown into a permanent organization, and its membership later expanded to more than one hundred, with meetings scheduled every three years.

During its early years many leading world political figures were spokespersons for the nonaligned movement. Over time, however, it lost much of its unity and its corresponding political muscle as the diversity among Third World nations undermined its cohesiveness.

Diversity found expression in the various foreign policy roles that Third World nations adopted as they pursued their political goals,[15] even while they remained committed to the principle of nonalignment. Some, such as China, Algeria, and Cuba, adopted the role of *revolutionary liberator*. The task of the revolutionary liberator is "to liberate others or to act as the 'bastion' of revolutionary movements, that is, to provide an area which foreign revolutionary leaders can regard as a source of physical and moral support, as well as an ideological inspirer" (Holsti, 1970). Others, such as Burma (now Myanmar), pursued a policy of *isolation*. Instead of trying to reform the global structure, isolationism preaches withdrawal from world affairs.

Ally is a third orientation that some adopted. The incentives for association with a superpower patron during the Cold War were sometimes compelling. Ties to them produced not only an enhanced sense of national security but also sometimes the foreign aid needed for internal development and perhaps the arms to deal with enemies at home and abroad. Hence, some Third World leaders were willing to suffer a partial loss of freedom in return for the political and material compensations a close relationship gave them. Vietnam's one-time embrace of the Soviet Union as a shield from both China and the West is illustrative.

Few Third World nations chose to take on the role of ally in an open and formal way, however. This is understandable, as it runs directly counter to the avowed principles of the nonaligned movement. Nonetheless, many from time to time so openly supported one or the other of the superpowers that their nonaligned status became suspect. India and Cuba stand out on the Soviet side, while Pakistan, the Philippines, Thailand, the republics of China (Taiwan) and South Korea, and many Latin American states stand out on the U.S. side. Various Middle Eastern countries that were original members of the nonaligned movement, such as Egypt, Iran, Jordan, and Saudi Arabia, also aligned at one time or another with one of the superpowers. As noted, the superpowers provided economic and military aid to their clients and

---

[15] See Hermann (1987) for an application of role theory that links nations' foreign policies to the role orientations and personal characteristics of their leaders.

often granted them implicit or explicit security guarantees. In return they received the political support of their clients and sometimes more tangible benefits, such as military base rights.

The end of the Cold War signals the end of nonalignment. Even before that, nonalignment reflected more myth than reality, as the movement's claims of unity of purpose and principle became blurred in the face of growing Third World diversity. Differing interpretations of the foreign policy posture of nonalignment grew out of the sharply divergent foreign and domestic situations developing nations face. Varying degrees of industrialization and economic development are among them. Different cultures and traditions and varying threats of internal instability arising from religious and ethnic differences also influence their foreign policy postures. For some, the principal threat is internal—a lack of identity with the nation, separatism, or insurgency. For others, the primary threat is external—a powerful and obtrusive neighbor or one that might become so. No single interpretation of nonalignment could accommodate such diversity. Thus nonalignment often amounted to little more than a political slogan devoid of practical meaning.

Military Might

The Cold War is now history, but the Third World drive for autonomy and independence is not. That is nowhere more clear than in developing nations' determination to acquire the most sophisticated military weapons available anywhere. The passing of the Cold War may even encourage greater militarization among Third World nations, as many previously dependent on a superpower patron will have to fend for themselves in the face of diverse internal and external security threats (see Kemp, 1990).

Figure 5.3 on page 150 shows the value of arms imported into the Third World during the 1980s. Not surprisingly, the Middle East is the major importing region. In fact, Egypt, Iraq, Saudi Arabia, and Syria were among the world's twelve largest arms importers in the latter half of the 1980s. All Third World regions have joined the race to arm, however. Nearly half of the thirty largest arms importers are found in the Third World (Kidron and Smith, 1991: 68–69).

The Third World quest for national security is examined in greater detail in Chapter 11. Here it is sufficient to highlight that treatment with three points.

First, Third World nations increasingly produce arms themselves. Imports from more advanced industrial powers remain important. But now Argentina, Egypt, India, North Korea, South Korea, and especially Brazil and China have developed arms industries of their own that produce efficient weapons at accessible prices. And the weapons are for sale with few strings attached.

Second, the arms available to Third World nations in the global marketplace are the most sophisticated in the world—and their numbers are staggering.

Between 1981 and 1988, developing countries spent $345.6 billion (in 1988 dollars) to acquire over 37,000 surface-to-air missiles, 20,000 artillery pieces, 11,000 tanks and self-

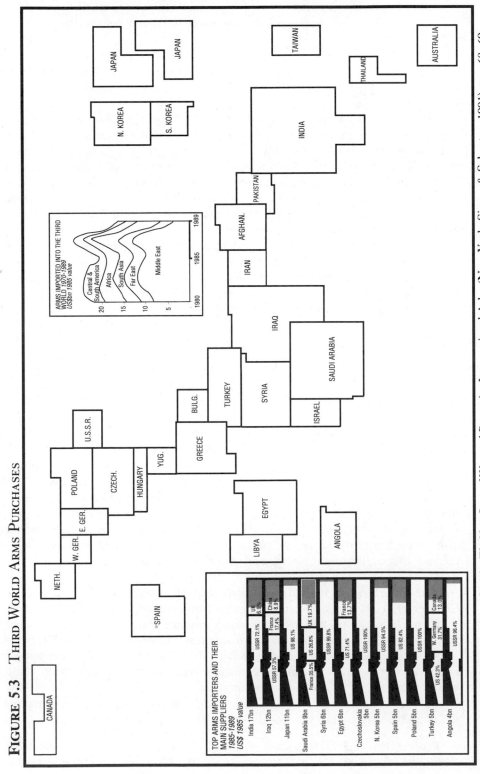

FIGURE 5.3 THIRD WORLD ARMS PURCHASES

Source: Michael Kidron and Dan Smith, *The New State of War and Peace: An International Atlas* (New York: Simon & Schuster, 1991), pp. 68–69.

propelled howitzers, 3,100 supersonic fighter planes, and 540 warships and submarines. . . .

To counter the growing incidence of ethnic conflict and guerrilla insurgency, Third World nations have also ordered vast quantities of small arms, infantry weapons, off-road vehicles, and police hardware. These "low-intensity" wars rarely produce major battles . . . , but they have nevertheless killed hundreds of thousands—perhaps millions—of people in Latin America, Southeast Asia, sub-Saharan Africa, Lebanon, Afghanistan, and the Philippines. Continuing economic problems will only worsen the social tensions that give rise to such conflicts in the [1990s]. (Klare, 1990b: 44–45)

The increased availability of ballistic missiles is a matter of particular concern. "Nations that possess ballistic missiles can fire large, destructive warheads deep into one another's territory with assurance that defenses have little likelihood of stopping an attack," the U.S. Arms Control and Disarmament Agency (1989) has noted.

By early 1990 more than twenty Third World countries either had surface-to-surface missiles or sought to buy or develop them. Ballistic missiles are especially prevalent in the Middle East, where at least ten countries have them and half that number have their own missile development programs (Carus, 1990: 12). Thus, as one analyst noted even before the 1991 Persian Gulf War, which further stimulated the desire for offensive missiles, "any country in the Middle East that aspires to be a military power possesses ballistic missiles" (Carus, 1990).

A related concern is the nature of the warheads being developed for the missiles. The proliferation of nuclear know-how has long been a matter of international concern. Now, alongside that danger, the dispersion of chemical and biological weapons capable of producing widespread damage at comparatively low cost poses a new danger.

Third, despite the relative poverty in which most developing nations find themselves, Third World countries spend tremendous sums of money on military acquisitions. The defense burden, the percentage of its GNP that a country spends on the military, is often highest among those least able to bear it (see Chapter 11). The opportunity cost (what is given up) of military spending impedes economic and social development. The actual resort to arms is even more costly, to say nothing of the lives lost.

> The 1969 Soccer War between Honduras and El Salvador lasted just 100 hours. About 2,000 people died. But 100,000 people became refugees. The fighting destroyed half of El Salvador's oil refining and storage facilities and paralyzed the Central American Common Market. Military expenditure and foregone output during the first five years [1980–1984] of the Iran-Iraq conflict cost more than $400 billion. The cost by the end of the war in 1988 was much higher. Economic disruption is similarly severe in civil wars. The conflict in northern Ethiopia's Eritrea territory has cut the labor force; bombs and mines have caused farmers to avoid some land, thus effectively taking it out of production—40 percent of the land was estimated to have been left idle in 1987, which partly explains the food shortfalls in the region. (*World Development Report 1991*, 1991: 141)

Despite the costs of war and preparations for it, both will continue as long as the reasons underlying the resort to arms persist. Among Third World nations these are legion.

THE END OF THIRD WORLDISM? . . . .

As we noted at the beginning of this chapter, some analysts have seized on the growing diversity of developing nations and the end of the Cold War to pronounce the death of "third worldism." "The Third World, as a political movement, has disintegrated," concludes Richard Bissell, an official at the U.S. Agency for International Development. "No vote was taken in an international body to disband the Third World. Rather," he continues, "the Third World lost its adherents [as] events disproved the value of its ideology. . . . In effect, the developing countries discovered what can be achieved through cooperation rather than confrontation with the rest of the world" (Bissell, 1990; see also Harris, 1987).

Several important developments during the 1980s in the Third World itself sustain that conclusion. Domestic economic policy reform, greater reliance on market mechanisms, and increased political freedom are among them. Internationally, the stridency of Third World demands so dominant in the 1970s gave way to greater pragmatism, and greater cooperation on North-South issues of mutual interest followed.

Unfortunately from the Third World viewpoint, the end of the Cold War threatens to suspend further North-South cooperation and progress on development and related issues, because it removes industrial nations' incentives to compete for favors among the developing nations. According to this argument, the end of the Cold War signaled "the end of the postcolonial era as well. For with no Cold War, there can be no 'Third World,' or rather, no 'Third Worldism.' And with no alignment—no sharp bipolarity within the international system—there can be no nonalignment either" (Falcoff, 1990).

Of course, there will be some sort of relationship between the former Third World and the erstwhile First and Second, but it will be very different from the past. First, because the fundamental centers of power will be more concerned with devising methods of cooperation than competing for dubious foreign clients, the capacity of peripheral societies to disrupt the system as a whole will be greatly diminished. . . . Second, these countries will find it increasingly difficult to extract concessions and resources from Western governments. Now that political influence in the former Third World is no longer a commodity worth bidding for, it will be possible to admit publicly something economists have known all along—that the majority of developing countries . . . are not developing at all and never have been. (Falcoff, 1990: 13)

The relationships between the world's more developed and less developed countries will doubtlessly change in the post–Cold War era. Exactly how remains uncertain, however. Some analysts in industrial societies see in the end of the Cold War an opportunity to practice a more isolationist foreign policy posture, one that would direct limited resources to domestic problems at the expense of those faced by Third World nations (see, for example, Buchanan, 1990). Should this happen, a posture of benign neglect of the Third World is probable. Others sense that "bipolarity's demise will allow the long-dormant seed of North-South cooperation to germinate as previously stymied North-South alliances emerge to forge solutions to common problems" (Feinberg and Boylan, 1991). From this perspective, the North will be required either to cultivate actively a closer relationship with the South or to risk "commercial, environmental, and security setbacks" (Feinberg and Boylan, 1992).

The differences between these viewpoints stem largely from differing perceptions of the importance of the South to the North. For some, security is paramount. For others, material well-being is more salient. The differences in viewpoints mirror the assumptions underlying the realist and neoliberal perspectives on world politics, as elaborated in Chapter 2.

As realists and neoliberals compete for prominence in decision-making circles, it is useful to remember the historical forces underlying the Third World as an analytical as well as political concept. Those who learned to regard themselves as members of the Third World shared important characteristics and experiences. Most were colonized by people of another race. They experienced varying degrees of poverty and hunger, and lost hope. They felt powerless in a world system dominated by the affluent nations that once—and perhaps still—controlled them.

It is also important to emphasize that, historically, the Soviet Union and the socialist states of Eastern Europe had little to do with the issues that separate North and South. In this sense, "third worldism" goes well beyond nonalignment, a specific foreign policy strategy pertinent to a specific historical era. Instead, it is a "state of mind" (Jonah, 1991) that will persist as a force in world politics as long as the divisions between North and South remain.

SUGGESTED READINGS

Black, Jan Knippers. *Development in Theory and Practice: Bridging the Gap.* Boulder, Colo.: Westview, 1991.

Caporaso, James A., ed. "Dependence and Dependency in the Global System." Special issue of *International Organization* 32 (Winter 1978): 1–300.

Cohen, Benjamin J. *The Question of Imperialism.* New York: Basic Books, 1973.

Elsenhans, Hartmut. *Development and Underdevelopment: The History, Economics, and Politics of North-South Relations.* New Delhi: Sage Publications, 1991.

Human Development Report 1991. New York: Oxford University Press, 1991.

Moon, Bruce E., and William J. Dixon. "Politics, the State, and Basic Human Needs: A Cross-National Study," *American Journal of Political Science* 29 (November 1965): 661–694.

Singer, Hans, W., and Javed A. Ansari. *Rich and Poor Countries: Consequences of International Economic Disorder,* 4th ed. London: Unwin Hyman, 1988.

Sklair, Leslie. *Sociology of the Global System.* Baltimore: Johns Hopkins University Press, 1991.

Todaro, Michael P. *Economic Development in the Third World,* 4th ed. New York: Longman, 1989.

Weiss, Thomas, G., and Meryl A. Kessler, eds. *Third World Security in the Post-Cold War Era.* Boulder, Colo.: Lynne Rienner, 1991.

CHAPTER 6

· · ·

Nonstate Actors in World Politics: The Role of International Organizations and Multinational Corporations

· · ·

The United Nations, if supported by . . . its membership, can help purge international relations of the lethal elements that lead to violent hostility between States or cause a pervasive sense of insecurity.

Javier Pérez de Cuéllar,
Secretary-General of the United Nations, 1991

Will nation-states fade away? I don't think so. Will state sovereignty fade? My answer is yes.

François Heisbourg, Director,
International Institute for Strategic Studies, 1990

Nation-states are the dominant form of political organization in the world. Their interests, capabilities, and goals significantly shape the contours of world politics. No mapping of the global political terrain would be complete, however, until it locates the role played by the increasing number of nonstate actors. International governmental and nongovernmental organizations, like the United Nations and the International Olympic Committee, have long been recognized as important nonstate actors. Today they are also joined by others that have assumed significant roles as part of the global topography. These include multinational corporations (like Exxon and IBM), transnational political movements and parties (like the Palestine Liberation Organization and the Social Democrats in the countries of Western Europe), and religious groups (such as the Roman Catholic Church).

Despite the obvious diversity among these groups, all share a common purpose: pursuing goals by operating across national boundaries, not just within them. This is obviously the case for the Palestine Liberation Organization, whose goal is the realization of a national homeland. It is also true of others, such as the Roman Catholic Church, whose transnational links together with its national hierarchies enable it to spread its religious and moral messages internationally as well as domestically. Even multinational corporations such as Ford Motor and British Petroleum, whose goals are profit maximization wherever possible, think of themselves as extraterritorial.

· · ·

This chapter examines the growth of nonstate actors, how states use them to realize perceived national interests, and whether they have become agents beyond the nation-state that propel the transformation of world politics.

THE GROWTH OF INTERNATIONAL ORGANIZATIONS . . . .

There are two principal types of international organizations, intergovernmental and nongovernmental. Governments are members of the first type, and private individuals and groups are members of the second. Neither type is peculiar to the twentieth century, but both are now more pervasive than ever.

The Rosicrucian Order, established in 1694, fits contemporary definitions of international nongovernmental organizations (INGOs), and the Central Commission for the Navigation of the Rhine, established by the Congress of Vienna in 1815, is the first modern international intergovernmental organization (IGO). The number of both types of organizations increased sharply during the latter part of the nineteenth century as international commerce and communications grew alongside industrialization. On the eve of World War I, nearly 50 IGOs and over 170 INGOs were in existence (Wallace and Singer, 1970: 272; *Yearbook of International Organizations, 1983*, 1983: 905). Thereafter, the pace of their growth quickened even more. By 1940 there were over 80 intergovernmental and close to 500 nongovernmental organizations. By the early 1990s these numbers had surged to roughly 300 and 4,600, respectively (Wallace and Singer, 1970: 272; *Yearbook of International Organizations, 1991/92*, vol. 2, 1991: 1667).[1]

---

[1] These figures imply that it is easier to identify international organizations than is in fact the case. In principle, IGOs are defined by a set of formal criteria:

> An international governmental organization is an institutional structure created by agreement among two or more sovereign states for the conduct of regular political interactions. IGOs are distinguished from the facilities of traditional diplomacy by their structure and permanence. International governmental organizations have meetings of representatives of the member states at relatively regular intervals, specified procedures for making decisions, and a permanent secretariat or headquarters staff. In some ways IGOs resemble governments, but they are not governments, for the capacity for action continues to rest predominantly with the constituent units, the member states. IGOs can be viewed as permanent networks linking states. (Jacobson, 1984: 8)

If, however, their permanence, regularly scheduled meetings, or some other criterion were eliminated, the number of IGOs in existence would far surpass the nearly three hundred "conventionally defined" organizations just cited, with some 1,500 additional international bodies qualifying for inclusion (see *Yearbook of International Organizations, 1991/92*, vol. 2, 1991: 1667). Furthermore, some international organizations have been created by others and thus do not fit the preceding definition, although clearly they are international organizations.

In principle, INGOs are easier to define than IGOs because the United Nations Economic and Social Council (ECOSOC) has followed the practice of granting these organizations consultative status before the council. Again, however, the Union of International Associations (*Yearbook of International Organizations, 1991/92*, vol. 2, 1991: 1668) has identified more than 11,400 other nongovernmental entities that share some characteristics with INGOs.

This growth has created a complex network of overlapping national memberships in transnational associations. In 1991, for example, the United States participated in more than 2,100 international organizations, over twice the number it participated in only two decades earlier. On a global scale, the national representations of some two hundred countries and territories in 4,917 international organizations numbered more than 118,000 (*Yearbook of International Organizations, 1991/92*, vol. 2, 1991: 1171–1669). These are "networks of interdependence" (Jacobson, 1984; Jacobson, Reisinger, and Mathers, 1986) whose activities span the entire panoply of activities associated with modern societies: trade, defense, agriculture, health, human rights, the arts, tourism, labor, education, the environment, telecommunications, science, and refugees, to name just a few.

International Intergovernmental Organizations

Even though more than 90 percent of the international organizations now in operation are nongovernmental, the remaining 10 percent are more important because their members are nation-states. The organizations nation-states create and join will remain preeminent as long as nation-states themselves persist as the principal centers of authority and legitimacy in world politics. Political scientist Harold K. Jacobson explains:

> Authoritative policies are more frequently made in and applied by governmental than by nongovernmental institutions; consequently in most political systems the former are more important than the latter. But the global system accords even greater importance to governmental institutions than is usually the case. States are the primary focal points of political activity in the modern world, and IGOs presently derive their importance from their character as associations of states. (Jacobson, 1984: 7)

The United Nations (UN) is doubtless the best known and most publicized international organization. It also has special characteristics that distinguish it from most others. First, its membership approximates universality. The end of the Cold War helped realize that goal, as Latvia, Lithuania, Estonia, North Korea, and South Korea, long denied a place in the UN, finally gained admission in 1991. Other former republics of the Soviet Union joined the organization in 1992, bringing the its membership to 175.[2]

Second, partly because nearly all states are members, the United Nations is a multiple-purpose organization. As stated in Article 1 of the United Nations Charter, the purposes of the organization are:

- to maintain international peace and security.
- to develop friendly relations among nations based on respect for the principle of equal rights and self-determination of peoples.

---

[2] With the complete breakup of the Soviet Union in late 1991, Russia became the legal successor to the USSR in the United Nations. Byelorussia (now Belarus) and Ukraine were already members of the United Nations due to a compromise reached between the United States and the Soviet Union in the 1940s, which effectively permitted the Soviet Union to occupy three seats in the UN.

- to achieve international cooperation in solving international problems of an economic, social, cultural, or humanitarian character, and in promoting and encouraging respect for human rights and for fundamental freedoms for all.
- to be a center for harmonizing the actions of nations in the attainment of these common ends.

These ideals have carried the United Nations into nearly every corner of the complex network of relations among nations. Its conference machinery has become permanent; the organization has provided a mechanism for the management of international conflict; and it has become involved in a broad range of global-welfare issues.

No international organization can claim the same extensiveness of purpose and membership as the United Nations. One study of several hundred IGOs extant in 1980, for example, found that only eighteen qualified as general-purpose organizations, and of these only the United Nations approximated universal membership. All of the rest, making up more than 97 percent of the total, were limited in their membership and purposes (Jacobson, 1984: 48).

Figure 6.1 provides examples of IGOs classified according to scope of membership and range of purpose. There is variation among the organizations falling into each quadrant, particularly the single-purpose, limited-membership one. The North Atlantic Treaty Organization (NATO), for example, is primarily a military alliance, while others, such as the Nordic Council, address both military security and economic cooperation issues. The latter therefore might be regarded as "political" IGOs.

Still, most IGOs engage in a comparatively narrow range of activities. The areas are usually economic and social in character, such as trade integration, common

Range of Stated Purpose

		Multiple purpose	Single purpose
Geographic Scope of Membership	Global	United Nations	World Health Organization International Labor Organization
	Interregional, regional, subregional	Organization of American States Organization of African Unity League of Arab States Association of Southeast Asian Nations	European Community Nordic Council North Atlantic Treaty Organization International Olive Oil Council International North Pacific Fisheries Commission

FIGURE 6.1 A Simple Classification of International Intergovernmental Organizations

services, and other types of functional cooperation. In this sense IGOs are agents as well as reflections of global social and economic interdependence.

International Nongovernmental Organizations

It is useful to think of INGOs as intersocietal organizations that help promote agreements among nation-states on issues of international public policy. One indicator of the relationship between INGOs and IGOs, operating as servants of the state, is that many INGOs interact formally with IGOs. For instance, many INGOs enjoy consultative status with various agencies of the extensive United Nations system, and they maintain offices scattered in more than a hundred cities throughout the world. The partnership between the two types of entities enables them to work (and lobby) together in pursuit of common policies and programs.

The United Nations also often relies heavily on nongovernmental organizations. As a result, the line between governmental and nongovernmental functions can become blurred. Examples include the United Nations Children's Fund (UNICEF), the United Nations Fund for Population Activities (UNFPA), and the United Nations University, which fulfill their missions in part through nongovernmental entities.

Although widespread geographically, INGOs' impact is greater in the advanced industrial states than in the developing world. "This is so because open political systems, ones in which there is societal pluralism, are more likely to allow their citizens to participate in nongovernmental organizations, and such systems are highly correlated with relatively high levels of economic development" (Jacobson, 1984). The composition of INGOs' membership therefore also tilts in the direction of the North rather than the South.

Because of their number and diversity, INGOs are even more difficult to classify than IGOs.[3] The Union of International Associations (itself an INGO) maintains comprehensive, up-to-date information about INGOs. It categorized 9 percent of some 4,600 INGOs as universal membership organizations, with most of the remaining 91 percent classified as intercontinental or regionally oriented membership organizations (*Yearbook of International Organizations, 1991/92*, vol. 2, 1991: 1667). Functionally, the organizations span virtually every facet of modern political, social, and economic life, ranging from earth sciences to health care, from language, history, culture, and theology to law, ethics, security, and defense.

International Organizations and the Politics of Peace and Security

The high politics of peace and security has figured prominently in the thinking of those responsible for shaping new international organizations during this century.

---

[3] For a discussion of the problems in classifying international organizations, see Bennett (1988) and the *Yearbook of International Organizations, 1991/92*, vol. 2 (1991: 1655–1660).

Following the onset of each of the world wars, world leaders mounted a concerted effort to create new institutions to cope with future threats to the peace. The first, the League of Nations, sought to prevent a recurrence of the catastrophe of 1914–1918 by replacing the balance-of-power system with one based on the principle of collective security (see Chapter 13). According to that principle, aggression by one state is an aggression against all others, who are then obliged to unite in collective action against the aggressor. When collective security failed to restrain Japan and Italy from waging war unilaterally during the 1930s, the League foundered. By the end of the decade global conflict broke out again. Nonetheless, with the restoration of peace in 1945, nations once more turned to an international organization—the new United Nations—as an instrument to maintain the peace.

A conviction at the core of political idealism—that war is not inevitable but can be eradicated by reforming the anarchical structures that encourage it—inspired both efforts to create a new world order. However, in the same way that the League of Nations proved incapable of stemming fascist aggression, the ability of the United Nations to maintain international peace and security quickly eroded. It soon became mired in the Cold War contest between the United States and the Soviet Union and, later, in the North-South dispute between the world's rich and poor nations. As before, then, the logic of *realpolitik* explained the diminishing prospects for international cooperation. And idealism again fell into disfavor as states relied, not on collective security, but on the timeworn balance of power to preserve order.

Because the United Nations, like the League before it, is a mirror of world politics, not an alternative to it, it reflects the forces outside the organization that have animated world politics since World War II. That is clear from a perusal of the issues that have dominated the UN's history over the past fifty years, to which we now turn.

THE UNITED NATIONS: BETWEEN EAST AND WEST, NORTH AND SOUTH

The United Nations was born as an organization of the victorious World War II allies. As early as 1941, and even before the United States had formally declared war on the Axis powers, U.S. President Franklin D. Roosevelt and British Prime Minister Winston Churchill referred in the Atlantic Charter, a document on war aims, to a postwar "general security" system. The name itself appears in the Declaration by United Nations, signed by twenty-six allied nations in January 1942, shortly after the Japanese attack on Pearl Harbor.

Given its wartime origins, it is not surprising that "maintenance of international peace and security" headed the list of the new organization's purposes. The Security Council was assigned primary responsibility for fulfilling this purpose.

The five major powers allied in war against Germany and Japan—the United States, the Soviet Union, Britain, France, and China—became permanent members of the Security Council with the right to veto its actions. This formula reflected the assumption that the major powers would act in concert to support the principle of collective security perceived necessary to maintain the postwar peace. Hence, unanimity among the permanent members was essential. Any disagreement signaled that the ingredient necessary to resolve a particular conflict was lacking.

The Security Council rapidly fell victim to the Cold War that erupted between the United States and the Soviet Union. Time and again the Soviet Union, unable to mobilize a majority on its side, exercised its veto power to prevent action on matters with which it disagreed. The Security Council was often paralyzed as a result, as the veto severely restricted the ability of the new organization to undertake collective action.

The Security Council is but one of six principal organs established by the United Nations Charter. The others are the General Assembly, the Economic and Social Council, the Trusteeship Council, the Secretariat, and the International Court of Justice. Among these, the General Assembly is the only body representing all the member states. Decision making there follows the principle of majority rule, with no state given a veto.

Unlike the Security Council, empowered by the UN Charter to initiate actions, including the use of force, the General Assembly can only make recommendations. Unforeseen by the founders of the United Nations, however, that limited mandate enabled the General Assembly to become a partner with the Security Council in managing security. It is also now the primary body for addressing social and economic problems.

As the latter issues grew in number and importance, the United Nations evolved into an extraordinarily complex set of political institutions. The United Nations today is not one organization but a conglomerate of countless committees, bureaus, boards, commissions, centers, institutes, offices, and agencies. The General Assembly, as the only principal UN organ representing all member states, now occupies the central role in the overall structure of the United Nations (see Figure 6.2).

The proliferation of United Nations bodies and activities parallels the growth of international organizations since World War II. It also parallels the expanding uses to which states have put the United Nations to accomplish their own aims. Third World nations, seizing advantage of their growing numbers under the one-state, one-vote rules of the General Assembly, now guide UN involvement in directions of particular concern to them.

They could not always do so, however. The United Nations began as a Western-dominated political organization. Only later did it evolve into one in which the Third World, often supported by the Second World (known in the UN as the socialist bloc), became the dominant voice. The forces underlying the shift are instructive.

Evolving Political Strategies in the Security Council and the General Assembly

In June 1950, North Korea launched a surprise attack against South Korea. The Security Council convened and promptly adopted a resolution supporting the use of force by the United Nations to repel the North Korean onslaught.

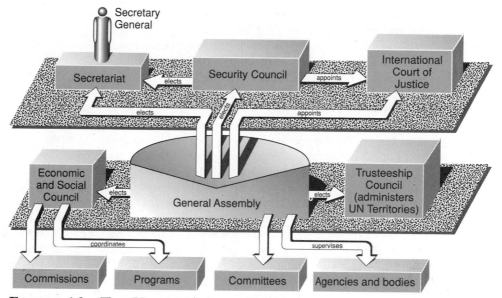

FIGURE 6.2   THE UNITED NATIONS SYSTEM
Source: Peter J. Taylor (ed.), *World Government* (New York: Oxford University Press, 1990), p. 40.

Because the Security Council authorized military force against the communist aggression, the defense of South Korea technically became a "police action" that bore some resemblance to the principle of collective security. However, the United States exercised command of the United Nations forces. It also supplied the bulk of the soldiers, money, and matériel, because combating the North Korean advance was consistent with the U.S. Cold War goal of containing communism. Although many UN members nominally supported U.S. policies, the net result of its actions was that the Korean police action was soon viewed as primarily a U.S. military operation aimed against the Soviet Union and the People's Republic of China, not an instance of effective collective security exercised by the world community.

The Security Council and the Unanimity Rule

Unique circumstances made the UN police action in Korea possible: the absence of the Soviet delegation from the Security Council meeting that authorized the use of force in protest of the world body's refusal to seat the Chinese Communist government (which had gained power on mainland China in 1949). Had it attended, it surely would have vetoed any UN role in Korea.

Before 1950 the Soviets' vetoes had repeatedly frustrated UN efforts to deal with emergent Cold War issues, such as the Berlin blockade and the 1948 coup that brought a communist government to power in Czechoslovakia. And it resumed its obstructionist behavior as soon as it returned to the Security Council. In fact, the Soviet Union quickly became the council's most prolific naysayer. It cast 77 vetoes between 1945 and 1955 and accounted for over 70 percent of the 144 vetoes cast in the first three decades of the United Nations' existence (Riggs and Plano, 1988: 77).

The Western powers began to use their veto more frequently when their ability to command a majority in the Security Council diminished. The United States did not cast a veto until 1970, on the issue of white minority control in Rhodesia (now Zimbabwe) and the extension of economic sanctions to South Africa. Since then it has vetoed proposals dealing with such issues as the Middle East, Rhodesia, South Africa, the Panama Canal, and the admission of Vietnam and Angola to the United Nations. In all, it exercised its veto power 98 times during the 1980s, twice as often as all other permanent council members combined (Alger, 1990: 19).

For years the United States prided itself on never having cast a veto in the Security Council. Now that it has done so frequently, it is clear that virtue had little to do with the U.S. position—nor was villainy the primary motivation of the Soviet Union's obstructionist behavior. Rather, the superpowers' respective voting behavior was a product of their differing parliamentary positions in the United Nations. Until 1960 the Soviet Union was clearly a minority power and the United States a majority power. In this environment, resort to rules the Big Three created in the 1940s to protect their power was virtually the only effective instrument available to the Soviet Union for protecting its national interests. In this sense the Soviet Union's frequent use of the veto in opposition to proposals put forward by the U.S.-dominated majority was a reflection, not a cause, of the United Nations' inability to organize a collective response to emergent threats to world order.

For its part, the United States assumed a more virtuous posture because it had other means of protecting its interests. During the UN's formative period, for example, the United States did not have to veto Security Council actions it opposed because it possessed a "hidden veto," an ability to persuade a sufficient majority of other council members to vote negatively so as to avoid the stigma of having to cast the single blocking vote (Stoessinger, 1977). This ability derived from the composition of the Security Council, among whose nine (later fifteen) members the United States could easily depend to provide a pro-Western majority.

The record shows that, long before the end of the Cold War, the United States no longer enjoyed a majority position in the Security Council and that the Soviet Union was no longer a defensive minority. Even so, the two powers found incentives in the wake of the Cold War to behave in a manner consistent with what the framers of the United Nations Charter contemplated when they adopted the unanimity principle, namely, that agreement among the major powers is essential to the maintenance of international peace. How far the United States and the Soviet Union had progressed became strikingly clear in 1990, when they joined forces in the United Nations to organize a collective UN effort to turn back Iraq's aggression in Kuwait. Other postures indicative of their changing attitudes included their mutual advocacy of "consensus" decision making in the Security Council (that is, without voting) and their push to revitalize the moribund Military Staff Committee.

The General Assembly and Majority Rule

As in the Security Council, the United States enjoyed a commanding position in the General Assembly during the early history of the United Nations, which caused the

Soviet Union frequently to deride the Americans' "mechanical majority." Figure 6.3 provides evidence of the dominant U.S. position. It shows the percentage of times the United States and the Soviet Union voted with the majority on roll-call votes in the General Assembly in each half-decade from 1946 to 1986.

These data do not portray the nuances of behavior underlying UN political processes. For example, they do not reveal the compromises that the United States often had to make to garner other nations' support or, indeed, the resolutions that never came to a vote because it could not find support (Holmes, 1977). Nor do they reflect the recent strategy of consensus decision making in the assembly, a development that highlights the apparent growing desire of states to compromise and cooperate. In 1986, nearly three-fifths of all assembly actions were decided by consensus, and the proportion increased in the following years, reaching 77 percent by 1990 (U.S. Department of State, 1990: 215; U.S. Department of State, 1991: 61). Still, some observers worry that, "in the search for common ground, nations will sign on to resolutions despite objections to particular provisions. Consensus resolutions frequently mask the diverging priorities of the developed North and the developing South" ("The Forgotten U.N.: An Inside Look at the 45th General Assembly," n.d.).

The data in Figure 6.3 also do not reveal different voting patterns on different types of issues. The United States, for example, frequently "found itself at odds with the majority in the General Assembly on issues involving decolonization and economic

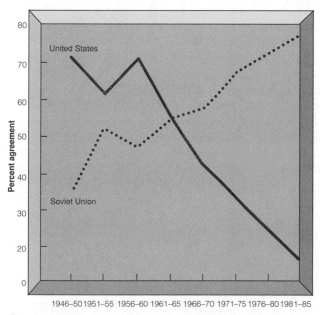

FIGURE 6.3 **Percentage Agreement of the United States and the Soviet Union with the Majority, United Nations General Assembly Roll-Call Votes, 1946–1985 (plenary sessions)**
Source: Robert E. Riggs and Jack C. Plano, *The United Nations: International Organization and World Politics* (Chicago: The Dorsey Press, 1988), p. 87.

development much more often than on issues concerning security" (Jacobson, 1984). The Soviet Union, on the other hand, found it easy to support the positions on decolonization advocated by the United Nations' anticolonial majority.

Related to issue voting is the salience states attach to different questions that come before the assembly. Recently, the U.S. Department of State has identified "important votes" on issues salient to the United States, many of which concern various Middle Eastern questions. On average, less than a quarter of the members of the assembly voted with the United States on these important votes in 1989, but the proportion jumped to nearly two-thirds in 1990. Similarly, when important consensus resolutions and important votes are combined, the proportions increased dramatically in both years, to 58 percent from 23 in 1989, and to 88 percent from 65 in 1990 (U.S. Department of State, 1990: 37, 224; U.S. Department of State, 1991: 40, 72).

The differences in the U.S. success rate between 1989 and 1990 reflect in part the issues that came before the General Assembly and how their sponsors framed particular votes on them. They also mirror the end of the Cold War and the unprecedented level of cooperation between the United States and the Soviet Union and Eastern European states made possible by it. From a long-term historical perspective, however, the overall impression remains unmistakable: Until the 1960s, the United States consistently enjoyed a majority position in the General Assembly, but since then it has aligned itself with prevailing sentiments in the General Assembly far less often.[4] Simultaneously, the Soviet Union increasingly found itself in step with majority sentiments.

The drop in U.S. success in relation to the majority following the Fifteenth General Assembly in 1960 is noteworthy, for it was then that seventeen new states joined the United Nations, nearly all of them African. Thereafter the Third World increasingly dominated the United Nations. By the 1980s, well over half of the organization's nearly 160 members came from Africa and Asia. In 1945 less than a quarter of them came from these two regions (see Figure 6.4).

Most Third World nations have used the UN forum to espouse aims and interests directly related to decolonization and economic development. They typically eschewed the U.S. view of the United Nations as a platform to pursue Cold War strategies vis-á-vis the Soviet Union. This did not mean they were pro-Soviet, for the Soviets, too, had used the United Nations to pursue their Cold War goals. In fact, the Soviet Union's increased voting success after 1960 was less a result of Soviet leadership than of its identification with the political priorities of the new Third World majority. It did mean that the Third World was less than enthusiastic about how the United States and the Soviet Union sought to use the United Nations. Thus the "mechanical majority" presumably enjoyed by the United States gradually eroded as it found itself increasingly on the defensive.

In 1971 the United States suffered a major defeat on a long-standing Cold War issue when the General Assembly voted to seat Communist China in the world body. Over the next decade it suffered other defeats. In 1983, for example, the

---

[4] Since 1985, the average voting coincidence of others with the U.S. position on UN resolutions ranged only between 15 percent (1988) and 24 percent (1986) (U.S. Department of State, 1991: 31).

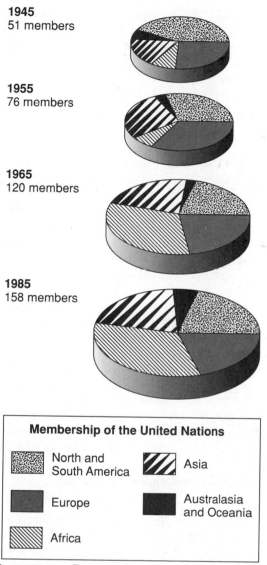

FIGURE 6.4 MEMBERSHIP PATTERNS IN THE UNITED NATIONS, 1945–1985
Source: Peter J. Taylor (ed.), *World Government* (New York: Oxford University Press, 1990), p. 17.

United States was the target of a resolution, approved overwhelmingly, that deplored its invasion of Grenada. In an earlier example, in 1974, it was in a distinct minority in opposing the extension by the General Assembly of permanent observer status to the Palestine Liberation Organization. And in 1975 it lost an important battle when the General Assembly went on record branding Zionism "a form of racism and racial discrimination." The vote outraged the U.S. ambassador to the United Nations, Daniel P. Moynihan, and led him to attack the United Nations bitterly. The phrase "tyranny of the UN's 'new majority' " captures his views.[5] Times had indeed changed![6]

Changing Superpower Fortunes: The Special Case of the United States

What was happening in the United Nations was little more than a microcosm of world politics. The reflection was not always perfect, of course, but by the 1970s and 1980s the United States could no longer control international issues and outcomes in the way it once did. Other states increasingly asserted themselves, and the diffusion of power in world politics gave greater voice to the aims and interests of others.

This reality posed special adjustment problems in U.S. attitudes toward the United Nations itself. After all, the organization was born in its image. The UN Charter, for example, reflects the same kinds of separation of power and sharing of responsibility embodied in the U.S. Constitution. Moreover, there is a strong case that the policies and programs of the United Nations and the political values and interests of the United States are compatible (Puchala, 1982–1983; see also the essays in Gati, 1983; and Ruggie, 1985). But how and why this is the case became increasingly opaque to the nation that provided the largest proportion of the money needed to run the United Nations while simultaneously finding itself on the defensive in the face of an antagonistic Third World and a Soviet-led socialist coalition.

The growing U.S. disaffection with what it regarded as the United Nations' anti-Western bias reflected itself in several ways. We will examine changes in U.S. attitudes as manifested in three issues: control of UN peacekeeping operations; financial support of UN operations; and membership in unaffiliated bodies.

Control of UN Peacekeeping Operations

The political tug-of-war between the Security Council and the General Assembly for political control of United Nations peacekeeping activities illustrates the impact of member states' foreign policies on the actions of the United Nations. It also illustrates how changing U.S. fortunes in the world organization stimulated changes in its attitudes toward multilateral peacekeeping activities.

---

[5] Moynihan's (1975) views of the Third World majority in the United Nations appeared in an article in the March 1975 issue of *Commentary*. Subsequently he wrote a book about his experiences at the United Nations. The title reflects Moynihan's view: *A Dangerous Place* (Moynihan with Weaver, 1978).

[6] President George Bush dramatized the sensitivity of the United States (and Israel) to the resolution branding Zionism as racism in a speech before the General Assembly during its 1991 opening session. He called for its repeal, saying it "mocks" the pledge of the UN Charter " 'to practice tolerance and live together in peace with one another as good neighbors' " and "the principles upon which the United Nations was founded." The General Assembly obliged the president later in the session, when, in a largely symbolic gesture designed to encourage the Middle East peace process then under way, it approved repeal of the resolution.

Following the return of the Soviet Union to the Security Council in 1950, responsibility for UN oversight of the Korean police action passed to the General Assembly. To ensure the permanence of this arrangement, the United States sponsored the Uniting for Peace Resolution, which, in the event a veto stymied the Security Council, empowered the General Assembly to meet in emergency session and to adopt collective measures to deal with "threats to the peace, breaches of the peace, and acts of aggression." The Soviet Union strenuously opposed the measure, because it implied that the United Nations might initiate enforcement measures against the wishes of a major power. The U.S. position prevailed overwhelmingly nonetheless.

The first use of Uniting for Peace procedures after the Korean War came in 1956. The General Assembly authorized the United Nations Emergency Force (UNEF) at that time in an attempt to restore peace in the Middle East following the eruption of war between Egypt, on one side, and Israel, Britain, and France, on the other. Interestingly, it was Britain and France, not the Soviet Union, that cast the negative votes that led to the emergency assembly session. Moreover, the General Assembly did not authorize the use of force in the same way it had in Korea. Instead, it created a "peacekeeping" force whose functions differed sharply from those implied in the principle of collective security. Collective security requires enforcement measures against an aggressor; peacekeeping implies no coercion but, instead, maintenance of the status quo (see also Chapter 14). In short, both the circumstances and the outcome of this first use of Uniting for Peace differed markedly from what the United States had envisioned only six years earlier.

Emergency special sessions of the General Assembly under the Uniting for Peace provisions have been called infrequently. A second session convened in 1956 to respond to the Soviet intervention in the Hungarian uprising, but no enforcement measures were adopted. In 1958 the assembly met to consider developments in Lebanon, where U.S. marines had intervened. In 1960, following a Soviet veto in the Security Council, the assembly took over direction of the United Nations Operation in the Congo (UNOC), which the Security Council had authorized earlier. In 1967 the General Assembly met in emergency session in yet another effort to contain the Middle East conflict. And in 1980 it convened in emergency session to consider the Soviet intervention in Afghanistan following a Soviet veto in the Security Council. As in Hungary in 1956, no enforcement procedures were authorized in a dispute directly involving one of the two most important members of the Security Council.

The use of the Uniting for Peace process in 1980, an initiative launched by Third World countries, was unexpected. The resolution's "transfer" provisions—those moving an issue from the Security Council to the General Assembly—appeared to have become a dead letter by that time for two reasons. First, there was a widespread view that the UN Congo operation (1960–1964) went too far in opposing the interests of one of the superpowers, namely, the Soviet Union. Second, given the erosion of the U.S. ability to command a majority for its policy positions in the expanding world forum, the United States by the mid-1960s was as apprehensive about the General Assembly as the Soviet Union had been in the 1950s. Noteworthy in both respects is that the Uniting for Peace resolution has never resulted in action by the General Assembly in quite the same way that the United States envisioned when it contemplated the lessons of Korea, namely, collective enforcement against aggressive actions initiated or backed by a major power (see Claude, 1971).

Control of UN Purse Strings

Growing U.S. apprehension about the General Assembly played itself out in two UN financial crises. The Soviet Union precipitated the first one, the United States the second.

THE FIRST UN FINANCIAL CRISIS The Soviet Union did not oppose creation of UNEF by the General Assembly in 1956, but it did refuse to pay for it, thus exercising a "financial veto." The Soviet Union also refused four years later to share the costs of the Congo operation. The United States built a convincing legal case that the Soviet Union and other recalcitrants were obligated to assume their share of the costs of these operations. The Soviet Union still refused, alleging that the issue was political, not legal. "Never had so many people argued so much about so little money," political scientist John Stoessinger (1977) remarked. "The financial crisis was in reality a political crisis over the proper role for the United Nations to play in the national policies of its member states, particularly the superpowers. Only secondarily was it a crisis over the costs of UN membership."

The crisis peaked in 1964. The United States threatened to deprive the Soviet Union of its vote in the General Assembly, which was possible according to Article 19 of the charter. But it refused to do so because it was no longer certain it could guarantee the General Assembly would not pursue actions detrimental to perceived U.S. interests.

In the two decades following the financial crisis of 1964–1965, the Soviet Union continued to withhold payments earmarked for certain United Nations activities, the most important of which were its share of the costs of UNEF and the United Nations Interim Force in Lebanon (UNIFIL). Its position on the peacekeeping issue remained the same for decades: that those responsible for creating the need for peacekeeping operations (Israel in the case of Lebanon) should bear the cost and that only the Security Council can apportion the cost of such operations, not the General Assembly (as in the case of UNEF).

Because of these positions, the financial arrears of the Soviet Union again placed it in potential violation of Article 19. Then, unexpectedly, the Soviet Union announced in 1987 that it would pay all of its outstanding debts as part of a foreign policy strategy designed to place greater emphasis on the United Nations.[7] This was the first sign among many that would follow that the superpowers' Cold War competition would no longer be an overriding factor in the world organization. The immediate effect was to alleviate the crisis atmosphere under which the United Nations had long operated.

THE SECOND UN FINANCIAL CRISIS Interestingly, the United States itself eventually emulated the Soviet strategy of withholding payments to programs with which it disagreed. During the 1980s in particular, the United States chose to withhold payment selectively from various UN programs as a way to register its resentment of the organization's activities and to change them.

---

[7] See Kozyrev (1990) for a discussion of the changed and changing attitudes of the Soviet Union toward the United Nations.

In December 1982, for example, the Reagan administration announced that it would not pay its $1 million annual assessment for implementing the deep-seabed mining provisions of the UN-sponsored treaty on the law of the sea. The treaty, concluded in 1982 after a decade of painstaking negotiations, envisions the creation of an international mining company called the Enterprise that would compete with private companies in mining the rich resources of the deep seabed and that would require a mandatory transfer of technology from private companies. In these and other ways, the International Seabed Authority created by the Law of the Sea Treaty, of which the Enterprise is one element, effectively tilts toward the developing nations at the expense of those in the industrial West (where the headquarters of multinational corporations with the technological capability to do the mining are located). Although the negotiations leading to the treaty were premised on the view that the oceans constitute a "common heritage of mankind," the Reagan administration chose instead to protect the interests of the private companies.

At a more basic level, the U.S. behavior on the Law of the Sea Treaty mirrored a general U.S. retreat from mutilateralism during the 1980s (Hughes, 1985–1986; Keohane and Nye, 1985). This withdrawal was also evident in the criticism the U.S. levied against the one-state, one-vote procedures used to apportion the UN's expenses among member states and the way those funds were spent. This forced a second UN financial crisis, which peaked in 1986.

As noted, the first UN financial crisis (1964–1965) arose out of the unwillingness of some states to pay for major UN peacekeeping activities. The second financial dispute was a regular-budget crisis.[8] It arose out of the natural tendency of governments (like individuals) to pay their bills as late as possible and, more importantly, out of the refusal of some to pay for activities that they vigorously opposed as a matter of principle (see Lister, 1986). Such opposition is natural in an organization that reflects a world marked by deep-seated antagonisms and often sharply divergent world views. But it immediately challenges the principle of the UN Charter embodied in Article 17, which states that "expenses of the Organization shall be borne by the members as apportioned by the General Assembly."[9]

---

[8] The United Nations' budget consists of three distinct elements: the regular budget (which includes the expenditures of the fifteen specialized agencies of the United Nations, each of which has its own budgetary procedures), the peacekeeping budget, and the budget for voluntary programs. States contribute to the voluntary programs and some of the peacekeeping activities as they see fit. The regular program and some of the peacekeeping activities are subject to assessments.

[9] The precise mechanism by which assessments are determined is complicated (see Lister, 1986), but generally assessments are designed to reflect states' capacity to pay. Thus the United States, which has the greatest capacity to pay, contributes 25 percent of the regular budget of the United Nations, whereas several dozen poor nations pay the minimum, which is 0.01 percent of the regular budget. The United States is also a prime contributor to the United Nations' peacekeeping and voluntary programs. In all, it paid $940 million of the costs of the United Nations in 1985, or 24 percent of the organization's $4 billion budget.

For comparative purposes, it is useful to note that the U.S. contribution to the United Nations in 1985 was roughly the same as the expenditures of the state of Rhode Island, whereas the budget of the entire United Nations system was roughly equal to the budget of the state of Louisiana. Outlays for U.S. national defense in 1985 were more than three hundred times greater than its expenditures on the United Nations.

When the General Assembly apportions expenses, it does so according to majority rule. The problem is that those with the most votes—the less developed nations—do not have the money, and those that do—the more developed nations—do not have the votes. Figure 6.5 illustrates these wide disparities. It shows that the main contributors to the United Nations command only fifteen votes, though they pay more than 85 percent of its costs.[10] At the other end of the spectrum, the poorer members of the United Nations, who collectively pay only about 2 percent of the organization's costs, command over one hundred votes. Thus the second financial crisis reflected "tension between the principle of sovereign equality of member states, permitting the more numerous developing countries to wield considerable influence over the kinds of issues on which the UN's attention and resources are focused, and the need to set priorities and manage more effectively the UN's limited monies and manpower, an increasing concern of the developed countries" ("Financing the United Nations," n.d.).[11]

At issue, of course, is not simply money—which remains, as in the crisis of the 1960s, a comparatively paltry sum[12]—but political influence. Most states that do not have the money vigorously embrace the principles embodied in the United Nations Charter, arguing that program needs should determine expenditure levels, rather than the other way around. The major contributors are sensitive to the amounts asked of them and the purposes for the funds (Lister, 1986). Often, Third World nations support the purposes but fail to generate broad political support for them among other important UN groups. Interestingly, however, many of the poor states have also fallen behind in their assessed payments. By 1992 80 percent of the UN members were in arrears (Schoettle, 1992: 15).

It is against the background of endemic cash-flow problems caused by often principled opposition to the sharply increased cost of the work of the organization that the United States precipitated a financial crisis in 1986. Due to several actions by the U.S. Congress, the Reagan administration withheld over half of the roughly $200 million U.S. regular-budget contribution. Principal among the congressional actions was the so-called Kassebaum amendment, which effectively cut the U.S. contribution from its assessed level of 25 percent to 20 percent pending the development of a system of weighted voting for financial decision making. Other congressional actions mandated across-the-board cuts in the United States' support of the United Nations, as well as cuts targeted at specific items.

The Kassebaum amendment challenged the principle on which the General Assembly makes its budgetary decisions. It effectively asked the United Nations either to adopt a system of weighted voting, in which those that pay more have more votes (as

---

[10] Brazil and Saudi Arabia are the only developing countries among the fifteen largest contributors.

[11] The choice of Boutros Boutros-Ghali of Egypt to succeed Javier Pérez de Cuéllar as Secretary-General of the United Nations in 1992 reflects in part sensitivity to these competing demands. Boutros-Ghali was one of several candidates put forward by African nations, who urged that Africa was the one remaining world region from which a Secretary-General had yet to be selected. The developed nations, on the other hand, found Boutros-Ghali, formerly deputy prime minister of Egypt, acceptable in part because they believed him to be more sensitive to management issues and the need to streamline UN operations than Pérez de Cuéllar had been.

[12] The entire regular budget of the United Nations for the 1991–1992 biennium was only $2.13 billion.

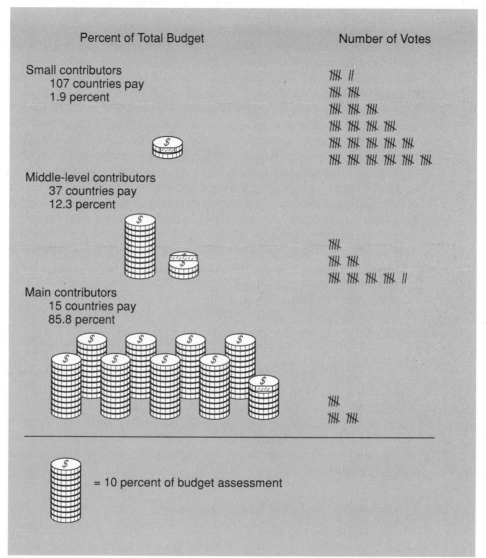

FIGURE 6.5 Relationship between UN Budget Assessments and Voting Strength in the General Assembly
Note: Based on UN scale of assessments for 1989–1991. The USSR, Byelorussian SSR, and Ukrainian SSR are considered one country for purposes of these analyses.

in other international organizations, like the International Monetary Fund and the World Bank), or to reduce the U.S. assessment. The former is virtually impossible, as it would require an amendment of the UN Charter, and the latter would require other comparatively impoverished states to pay more of the UN's costs, which they are unwilling to do.[13] The result, then, would be a reduction in the activities of the United Nations.

Progress was made during 1987 in devising a political solution to the UN's financial crunch that would avert insolvency, on the one hand, and placate the concerns of those that have to pay the most, on the other. Eventually the United States made a commitment to pay its debts to the United Nations over a five-year period. Coming as it did on the heels of the earlier Soviet promise to clear its accounts, the commitment eased the crisis atmosphere that had long plagued the UN's financial picture.

Budgetary stringency and a renewed sense of isolationism in the United States nonetheless continued to work against a final resolution of the world organization's own budgetary problems. By the end of 1991 the United States remained the largest UN debtor, with $2.7 million in unpaid regular-budget assessments and another $140.9 million in unpaid peacekeeping obligations (Lewis, 1992: A5).

Developments in world politics outside the organization, some of them augmented by the United Nations itself, helped to push U.S. policy—if not always practice—on financing the UN in new directions. The end of the Cold War and the positive contribution the United Nations made in repelling Iraq's aggression, in securing the release of American and European hostages held captive in Lebanon, in bringing the combatants in Cambodia together, and in ending the stalemate over Namibia all contributed to a reversal of the negativism long evident in U.S. attitudes toward the United Nations. For the organization as a whole, however, the distance between political and financial support remained troublesome. As UN Secretary-General Javier Pérez de Cuéllar lamented shortly before the end of his ten-year term in office, "It is a great irony that the United Nations is on the brink of insolvency at the very time the world community has entrusted the organization with new and unprecedented responsibilities."

Membership in Affiliated UN Agencies

Another way the United States registered its dissatisfaction with what it saw as the anti-Western drift of many UN bodies was to end its membership in them. In the 1970s, for example, the Carter administration withdrew for a time from the International Labor Organization in an attempt to influence the direction of its policies. The

---

[13] Granting some members of the United Nations special status in its deliberative bodies is commonly used to secure the political support of more powerful states and is one way in which the organization mirrors the structural inequalities found elsewhere in world politics. The special status (permanent membership) enjoyed by only five members of the Security Council is the clearest expression of these inequalities, but they apply to other limited-membership organs of the United Nations as well (see Jacobsen, 1969, 1978; Volgy and Quistgard, 1974). A weighted voting scheme would formalize these inequalities, although the precise ways in which they would reflect the "real world" would vary, depending on the weighting scheme chosen.

United States also at that time withheld payment of its UNESCO (United Nations Educational, Scientific and Cultural Organization) dues to protest an Arab-led effort to oust Israel from the organization. Later, during the Reagan administration, the United States withdrew from UNESCO in response to what it regarded as the politicization of UNESCO and its hostility toward Western values, including in particular freedom of communication, thereby depriving UNESCO of a quarter of its budget.[14]

In 1987 UNESCO came under new leadership, which sought to remove the obstacles toward reentry of the United States into the organization. It made efforts to undertake structural reforms in the organization and to streamline its management practices, both of concern to the United States. It also took steps to address the issue of freedom of communication, including encouragement of freedom of the press, freedom of journalists to report and have access to information, and promotion of private and independent news media. Despite these changes, the United States affirmed early in 1990 that it would not rejoin UNESCO, having concluded that too little progress had been made in the area of communications and that the organization continued to be mismanaged and to show bias against Israel.

The freedom of communications issue, which includes UNESCO but extends beyond it to other international organizations as well, warrants additional scrutiny, as it illustrates well the kinds of conflicts between the developed North and the developing South that are often played out in the United Nations.

The issue springs from Third World efforts to create a New World Information and Communication Order (NWICO). Their drive for a new order began, with the backing of the Soviet Union and other communist states, in the 1970s about the same time that the Group of 77 launched its drive for a New International Economic Order. The reform effort expressed the Third World's (and, to a lesser extent, the Soviet Union's) dissatisfaction with the media coverage provided by Western news agencies and its resentment of Western domination of other forms of communication, ranging from radio, television, and films to book publishing and satellite transmissions. Organizations in the advanced capitalist nations of the First World control virtually all of the world's means of communication today. That situation leads many Third World leaders to conclude that "the one-way inward flow of information will encourage consumerism and perpetuate economic dependency" (Mowlana, 1983).

The situation that Third World nations now face is, ironically, not unlike what the United States itself faced before it was a part of the international news monopoly.

At that time, a European news cartel—composed of the English Reuters, French Havas, and German Wolff agencies—controlled all foreign news sent into the U.S. and all American news to the world. Kent Cooper, then executive manager of the Associated Press, led the crusade to break up the European cartel. "Reuters decided what news was to be sent from America," he wrote. "It told the world about Indians on the warpath in the West, lynchings

---

[14] Ironically, the U.S. withdrawal from UNESCO came after most observers felt UNESCO had conformed to U.S. demands (Coate, 1988). The fact that the United States did not alter its decision to withdraw can be attributed to the Reagan administration's urge during its early years to reduce U.S. involvement in multilateral organizations generally.

in the South, and bizarre crimes in the North. The charge for decades was that nothing creditable to America was ever sent. American businessmen criticized the Associated Press for permitting Reuters to belittle America abroad." Cooper pointed out that Havas and Reuters always glorified their own countries. Today, the ironic parallel, as it is perceived, has not been missed by the Third World. (Mowlana, 1983: 43)

Of particular concern to the United States is the meaning of a "balanced" flow of communication that many Third World leaders advocate. The United States acknowledges that an imbalance between the North and the South currently exists (as attested by its programs to help develop communications infrastructures in the Third World). However, it fears any move toward government controls and the censorship to which they may lead, arguing "that no communication system in which the government has a share can truly be free" (Mowlana, 1983). This view places the United States in a rather peculiar situation in the NWICO debate, as even other First World countries practice various forms of direct government involvement in their communications industries.

The United States is especially important in this debate, for it is a massive supplier of media products to the rest of the world but consumes almost nothing produced abroad. At stake, therefore, is not only the issue of freedom of the press but also millions of dollars.

Even as the United States continues to register disaffection with some elements and actions of the United Nations and its affiliated agencies, we must be careful not to assume that its behavior is simply the bullied reaction of a nation otherwise without influence in the United Nations. As a practical matter, "little of substance can happen in the UN system without American cooperation—and little happens without American resources—so that it is not very surprising that negotiators often defer to United States preferences" (Puchala, 1982–1983). Noteworthy in this respect is that the Group of 77 decided not to push its call for a New World Information and Communication Order at the opening of the annual General Assembly session in 1990, thus paving the way for more cooperation with the United States on other issues.

The Third World: From Background to Center Stage

The United States and the Third World have each used the United Nations to shape the foreign policy goals and preferences of the other. In some respects, however, the Third World historically has been comparatively more effective than either the United States or the Soviet Union in using the United Nations' institutional structures and procedures, especially in the General Assembly, to advance its interests. For example, the General Assembly's one-state, one-vote rule helped the Third World to focus global attention on the issue of colonialism and to "delegitimize" it as a form of political organization (see Chapter 5).

Economic development has been another principal Third World aim advanced in United Nations forums. In the 1950s the then numerically smaller group of Third World nations pressed for organizational responses to its needs and realized some modest (if less than hoped for) results. The United Nations Special Fund, for example, was a partial response to Third World pressure for large amounts of UN economic development aid.

As their numbers in the United Nations increased in the 1960s, Third World nations pressed even more vigorously on economic development and related issues. By the early 1960s the group surpassed the two-thirds mark as a proportion of the total membership. This means that the Group of 77, if it can act as a cohesive coalition, can pass any measure it chooses. In doing so it runs the risk of alienating the minority of industrial nations that pays most of the costs of UN operations. In this respect the growing preference for consensus decision making better conforms to the "reality" of power outside the world organization. The one-state, one-vote rule in the General Assembly nonetheless gives the developing nations an important measure of institutional clout.

Third World interests have found expression in a host of world conferences and special General Assembly sessions held since the early 1970s. However, because these conferences frequently become forums for vituperative exchanges between North and South, their contribution to solving—not just articulating—global problems has been limited.

The range of subjects addressed nonetheless draws attention to the agenda of issues especially important to the Third World. Included, among others, have been conferences on the human environment (1972), law of the sea (1973), population (1974 and 1984), food (1974), women (1975, 1980, and 1985), human settlements (1976), basic human needs (1976), water (1977), desertification (1977), disarmament (1978 and 1982), racism and racial discrimination (1978), technical cooperation among developing countries (1978), agrarian reform and rural development (1979), science and technology for development (1979), new and renewable sources of energy (1981), least developed countries (1981), aging (1982), the peaceful uses of outer space (1982), Palestine (1982), the peaceful uses of nuclear energy (1983), the prevention of crime and the treatment of offenders (1985), drug abuse and illicit trafficking in drugs (1987), the protection of children (1990), and the environment and development (1992). The subjects covered in the world conferences during the past two decades are in effect a list of "the most vital issues of present world conditions," whereas the conferences themselves "represent a beginning in a long and evolving process of keeping within manageable proportions the major problems of humanity" (Bennett, 1988). In this the United Nations, spurred on by the Third World, can take some credit.

At another level, however, the conference technique represents an approach to global decision making marked with pitfalls. Developing nations prefer broadly based institutional settings, such as the global ad hoc conference forum, in which the one-state, one-vote principle gives them an advantage. In this way institutional procedures promote Third World interests. In contrast, the First World prefers small, functionally specific forums, usually outside the General Assembly, which, they believe, "are more likely to involve those states that have a real stake in the outcome of the deliberations." According to this viewpoint, "large, general-purpose bodies only encourage ill-informed participation by states uninvolved in the issue at hand and thus increase the likelihood of irresponsibly politicizing the agenda" (Gregg, 1977). Nonetheless, the conference strategy has become an accepted mechanism for pursuing a North-South dialogue on issues of particular interest to the Third World, whose effect has been "to change attitudes, to stimulate political will, and to raise the level of national and global interest in the subject. . . . The industrialized states, although reluctantly, in general continue the dialogue in their own enlightened self-interest" (Feld and Jordan, 1988).

The United Nations beyond the Cold War

The decision of the Security Council to authorize military enforcement measures against Iraq following its invasion of Kuwait in August 1990—the first time that it had done so since the Korean War—was widely heralded as infusing the United Nations with a new sense of purpose and power. The action was possible, of course, because the United States and the Soviet Union joined forces in their opposition to Saddam Hussein. As President George Bush proudly declared, "For the very first time on a matter of major importance, superpower competition was replaced with international cooperation." The steps on which the former Cold War antagonists agreed included condemnation of the invasion, the imposition and enforcement of a total trade embargo, the authorization of military action, and, finally, the terms of a final military settlement. Thus collective security arguably worked for the very first time since the San Francisco Charter gave birth to the United Nations in 1945.

The end of the Cold War holds out the promise that continued major-power cooperation will remove the single most important obstacle to an enhanced UN role in world affairs. The Security Council in particular "has shown that it has the capacity to initiate collective measures essential for the maintenance of peace in a new world order" (Russett and Sutterlin, 1991). The United States has also made clear by its commitments regarding the UN's precarious financial situation and in other ways that it now views the United Nations more favorably than it has for some time. As Thomas Pickering, the U.S. ambassador to the United Nations, observed in 1990, "Beyond its devotion to peace and security, there is increasing awareness and involvement of the United Nations in global and transnational issues which the U.S. considers important, such as the environment, drug trafficking, and human rights."

Against this background, we must recall that no United Nations forum is more congenial to the interests of the world's richest and most powerful states than the Security Council. As noted earlier, five of the council's fifteen members—China, France, the United Kingdom, the United States, and Russia (as legal successor to the Soviet Union)—enjoy the power of veto, and at least two of the remaining ten elected members are from the First World. Hence, "a more capable Security Council has aroused concern in the developing world about a marginalization of the General Assembly," and some fear that "the Security Council may emerge as an 'institutional bully'" ("The Forgotten U.N.: An Inside Look at the 45th General Assembly," n.d.).

THE EUROPEAN COMMUNITY AND OTHER REGIONAL ORGANIZATIONS . . . . .

The political tug-of-war between various states and groups of states within the United Nations over how the organization might best serve their national interests reveals an important fact—that the United Nations is a product of the interests of the nation-states that make it up. This severely circumscribes its ability to rise above global conflicts and to pursue an independent role. In the words of political scientist Inis Claude (1967), "The [UN] has no purposes—and can have none—of its own." Hence, the United Nations is better viewed as an instrument of states' foreign policies and an arena within which to debate issues than as an independent actor in world politics. Because the United Nations cannot act autonomously, it lacks the legitimacy and capability for independent, "competent global governance" (Alger, 1990).[15]

When states dominate international organizations, as they do the United Nations, they reduce the prospects for international cooperation because they typically resist any organizational actions that could conceivably curtail their autonomy or threaten their security. Thus, according to the theory of political realism, there are severe limits on the capacity of international organizations to engineer a more peaceful, just, and prosperous world order.

A rival hypothesis emerges from the neoliberal institutionalist world view. This perspective, described in Chapter 2, recognizes that states are dominant in international politics and that anarchy is its basic organizing principle, but neoliberals maintain that cooperation among states is still possible and that international organizations help produce it. That viewpoint is especially pertinent to the European Community.

The European Community

The European Community (EC) actually consists of three communities: the European Coal and Steel Community (ECSC, created in 1952), the European Atomic Energy Community (Euratom, 1958), and the European Economic Community (EEC, 1958). Since 1967, the three have shared common organizational structures (see Figure 6.6 on page 178). The members of the EC are Belgium, France, Germany, Italy, Luxembourg, and the Netherlands (who were the original "Six"), Denmark, Ireland, and the United Kingdom (who joined in 1973), Greece (1981), and Portugal and Spain (1986) (see Box 6.1 on page 180).

Organizational Components and Decision-making Procedures

A quadripartite institutional system consisting of an Executive Commission, a Council of Ministers, a European Parliament, and a Court of Justice governs the European Community.

The Council of Ministers is the system's central component. As the name implies, it consists of cabinet ministers drawn from the European Community's member states. The foreign ministers participate in the council when the most important Community decisions are made. In this respect the European Community is an association of

---

[15] Various secretaries-general have achieved some degree of autonomy and pursued quasi-independent roles in world politics, but such activities are more the exception than the rule. Individuals who participate in UN affairs have broadened their nationalistic perceptions (Alger, 1965; Riggs, 1977), but in the final analysis attachments to the nation-state reign supreme (see also Chapter 14 on the functional theory of peace).

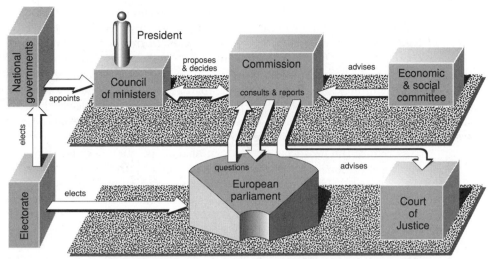

FIGURE 6.6 THE ORGANIZATION OF THE EUROPEAN COMMUNITY
Source: Peter J. Taylor (ed.), *World Government* (New York: Oxford University Press, 1990), p. 112.

nation-states that differs little from the United Nations. But the EC is more than an association of states. That is clear in part from an examination of its other elements and decision-making procedures.

Central among the other elements is the Commission, which consists of seventeen members (two each from Britain, France, Germany, Italy, and Spain, and one each from the remaining member states). A "Eurocracy"(professional staff) of more than ten thousand "Eurocrats" who, in principle, owe loyalty to the European Community, not to its national constituents, assists the Commission. The Commission proposes legislation, implements EC policies, and represents the Community in international trade negotiations. It also manages the EC budget, which, in contrast with most international organizations, derives part of its revenues from sources not under the control of member states.

The European Parliament is chosen by direct election of the citizenry of the EC's member states. Its 518 delegates debate issues in the same way that national legislative bodies do, but its legislative powers are less pervasive than in a typical domestic political system. Still, it, too, is distinctive in that most international organizations' legislative bodies represent states (as in the UN General Assembly), not individual citizens or transnational political parties.

The Court of Justice is also distinctive in this respect. Comprising thirteen judges, the court's functions include interpreting EC law for national courts and ruling on legal questions raised by the institutions of the EC communities, by member states, or, in an important deviation from traditional patterns, by individuals. Its decisions are binding, which also distinguishes the European Court of Justice from most other international tribunals.

Figure 6.7 on page 182 illustrates decision-making processes in the EC. As the figure shows, there are two procedures for the adoption of directives and regulations, a consultation procedure and a cooperation procedure. The procedure actually followed depends on the nature of the proposal, and a principal difference is that the European Parliament plays a greater role in the cooperative than in the consultative process. In both, however, the central role of the Commission in the EC's legislative process is evident; indeed, the Commission has been the driving force behind European integration (Ludlow, 1991).[16] It was under the imaginative leadership of Jacques Delors, president of the Commission, that the European Community in 1987 adopted the Single European Act, a major amendment to the 1957 Treaty of Rome that created the European Economic Community (popularly known for many years as the European Common Market). The Single European Act envisions the creation of a true European common market by the end of 1992, one free of internal borders similar to the way the United States is free of internal restraints.

Supranationalism or Pooled Sovereignty?

How, then, is the European Community, a nonstate actor, best characterized? That is, how are its structures and decision-making procedures best described, in comparison with the United Nations and the panoply of other international organizations that now dot the global terrain?

The EC has the power to make some decisions binding on its national members without being subject to their individual approval. In this sense it is a *supranational* entity. That is, it is not an organization of or between states—an international organization—but one that goes beyond them toward creation of a new political entity that supersedes the individual nations that make it up—a supranational organization. This characterization mirrors the visionary hopes of the founding fathers of the various European institutions that make up the EC. They saw on the horizon a "United States of Europe" that would ameliorate the bitter antagonisms, particularly between France and Germany, that had periodically plunged Europe into deadly warfare.

Although the EC incorporates some supranational elements, the term *pooled sovereignty* (Keohane and Hoffmann, 1991b) better captures its essence, because states remain paramount in its institutional structures and decision-making procedures.

Pooled sovereignty captures a central property of the European Community as now configured. No transfer of authority to a central body has occurred. Instead, critical decisions are still made in the Council of Ministers, where states dominate, and most decisions of the EC still depend on national governments for implementation. Sovereignty is nonetheless shared, in the sense that decision-making responsibility is now spread among governments and between them and community institutions.

Awareness of the fact that on some issues the EC members now decide by majority rule is critical to an understanding of pooled sovereignty. A major obstacle to effective

---

[16] It is also interesting to note that the Commission has been the center of a combined effort on the part of the principal Western economic powers (known as the Group of Seven, or simply G-7) to facilitate the process of economic liberalization in the socialist countries of Eastern and Central Europe.

Box 6.1
CHRONOLOGY OF EUROPEAN COMMUNITY EVENTS

• • •

1950

May 9 French Foreign Minister Robert Schuman proposes placing Europe's coal and steel under a common European authority.

1951

April 18 Treaty creating the European Coal and Steel Community (ECSC) is signed in Paris by the Benelux countries, France, Germany, and Italy.

1957

March 25 Treaties creating the European Economic Community (EEC) and the European Atomic Energy Community (Euratom) are signed in Rome.

1965

April 8 Signature of the treaty merging the institutions of the three European Communities.

1968

July 1 Customs union is completed 18 months early. Remaining industrial tariffs between the Six are abolished. Common external tariff enters into force.

1973

January 1 Denmark, Ireland, and the United Kingdom join the Community. Free trade agreements with European Free Trade Association (EFTA) countries begin to take effect.

1975

February 28 First Lomé Convention with African, Caribbean, and Pacific countries is signed.

1979

March 13 European Monetary System (EMS) becomes operative.

June 7–10 First direct elections to the European Parliament. Direct elections are held every five years.

1981

January 1 Greece joins the Community.

1985

June 29 E.C. Heads of State and Government endorse a "White Paper" outlining a strategy for creating a true common market by 1992.

1986

January 1 Spain and Portugal join the Community.

1987

July 1 The Single European Act, amending treaties, enters into force.

1989

May 21 President George Bush renews the U.S. commitment to a "strong united Europe" in a speech at Boston University.

June 26–27 The Heads of State and Government meeting in Madrid endorse a plan for Economic and Monetary Union.

July 14–16 Western Economic Summit in Paris asks the E.C. Commission to coordinate Western assistance to Poland and Hungary.

December 17 A new political partnership between the Community and the United States is outlined by Secretary of State James Baker in Berlin.

1990

October 3 The five Laender of the former German

Democratic Republic enter the Community as part of a united Germany.

November 20 The Community and the United States adopt a Transatlantic Declaration.

December 13–14 Opening of Intergovernmental Conferences of Economic and Monetary Union (EMU) and Political Union.

1991

October 21 The European Community and the European Free Trade Association (EFTA) agree to form the European Economic Area (EEA), a single market of 19 countries.

December 9–11 The European Council meeting in Maastricht agrees to treaties providing for economic and

monetary union, and closer political union.

December 16 Poland, Hungary, and Czechoslovakia sign far-reaching trade and cooperation agreements with the European Community.

1992

February 7 Treaty of Union and Final Act signed in Maastricht.

Source: The European Community in the Ninties (Washington, D.C.: Delegation to the United States, 1992), n.p.

decision making in the past has been that most substantive proposals required unanimous approval. That rule (also used in other international institutions, such as the UN Security Council) enabled member states to protect their national interests as they alone defined them. France took advantage of this provision to thwart Community action in the late 1960s by simply refusing to send a minister to its meetings. The resulting impasse, called the "empty chair" crisis, spurred the development of new decision-making procedures.

Today, in a radical departure from past practices, the Community requires only a qualified majority on most internal market decisions. Thus "unlike [typical] international organizations, the European Community as a whole has gained some share of states' sovereignty: The member states no longer have supremacy over all other authorities within their traditional territory, nor are they independent of outside authorities. Its institutions have some of the authority normally associated with institutions of sovereign governments: On certain issues individual states can no longer veto proposals before the Council [of Ministers]; members of the Commission are independent figures rather than instructed agents" (Keohane and Hoffmann, 1991b).

The EC's essence is also described by its functions. On the one hand, it is so distinctly different from traditional international organizations as to be virtually in a class by itself. On the other, however, it is clearly not (yet) a rival of the nation-state as the dominant form of political organization, even in Europe. The principle of sovereignty as a defining legal attribute holds that the state alone has dominion over its internal and external affairs. In the EC's case, its authority in external affairs is greatest in matters of international trade and related welfare issues, is seriously circumscribed in political affairs, and has yet to materialize in military affairs. That was nowhere more clear than during the 1991 Persian Gulf War, which demonstrated that the EC was both unwilling and ill-equipped to act quickly and decisively to protect the Community's economic and security interests that were at stake. Its

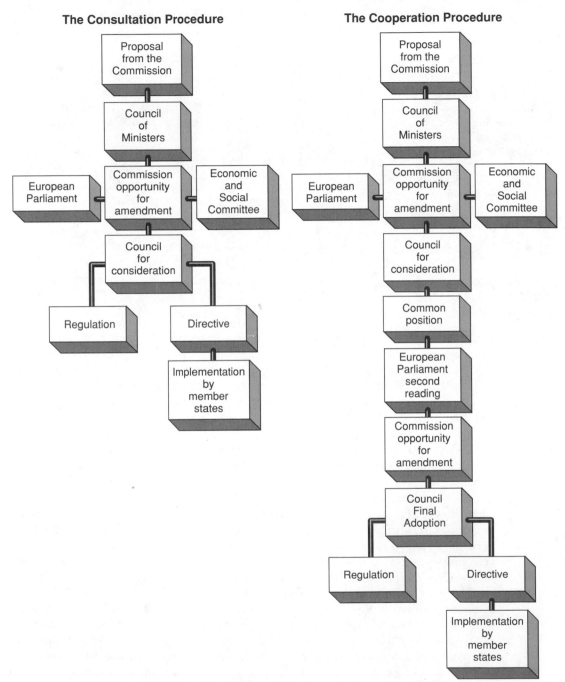

FIGURE 6.7 THE EUROPEAN COMMUNITY LEGISLATIVE PROCESS: CONSULTATION AND COOPERATION PROCEDURES

Source: Janet S. Zagorin, *Europe 1992: Navigating New Waters* (New York: Baker and McKenzie, 1990), p. 11.

unresponsiveness during the Gulf crisis led Belgium's Foreign Minister Mark Eyskens to conclude that Europe "is an economic giant, a political dwarf, and a military worm."

Europe: An Economic Giant

The historical development of the European Community is replete with evidence that the high politics of peace and security was uppermost in the minds of those who sought to forge a new Europe out of the ashes of World War II. Still, it is on the economic front—in the low politics of material well-being—that the EC has scored its most dramatic successes. Today, with a combined gross national product of more than $5 trillion and a combined population of 328 million, the European Community is the largest trading bloc in the world and rivals the United States as the largest market.

An even larger EC is in the offing (see Map 6.1 on page 184). The seven members of the European Free Trade Association (EFTA, created in 1960 as a counterpoint to the European Economic Community), have concluded a treaty with the EC, whose purpose is to create the world's largest trading area. The agreement foresees a single European "common market" embracing nineteen countries and more than 380 million people beginning in 1993. It does not call for the EC and the members of EFTA to maintain a common tariff wall against third parties, and thus does not extend the EC as a customs union. It does, however, ease the way for individual EFTA members to join the EC as full partners, as several doubtless will.

Already Austria, Finland, and Sweden, all members of EFTA, have formally applied for membership, and others are expected to follow suit. Switzerland, too, has sought to join the community in what would be a dramatic departure from its traditional policy of neutrality.

Elsewhere, Turkey, already an associate member, has applied for full membership, and the former socialist states of Eastern Europe have made ties with the EC a long-range goal. Negotiations on association agreements with Poland, Czechoslovakia, and Hungary are already under way. To the East, the Ukraine has voiced an interest in joining the EC. Thus a dramatically larger European Community may be in place by the turn of the century.[17]

The prospect of an enlarged European Community would not have been expected even a few short years ago. One reason for the change, of course, is the end of the Cold War, which has opened the prospect for the eventual integration of the socialist economies into the capitalist world political economy (see also Chapter 7). Even within

---

[17] The EC is also linked to sixty-nine African, Caribbean, and Pacific (ACP) countries through the Lomé Convention, first signed in 1975 and renewed at periodic intervals since, most recently in 1989 for a ten-year period. The Lomé Convention provides the ACP countries' exports with duty-free access to the EC without the necessity of reciprocal concessions for EC exports to their economies (see also Chapter 8). It also sets up a commodity price stabilization scheme and provides a framework for the allocation of EC foreign aid to these countries.

In addition to the ACP countries, the EC has agreements with several other countries throughout the Third World and has signed a cooperative agreement with ASEAN, the Association of South East Asian Nations, covering trade, economic, and development issues.

MAP 6.1 EUROPE AND THE EUROPEAN COMMUNITY
Source: The New York Times, December 9, 1991, p. A5.

the EC itself, however, expectations about the future of the Community are now much more optimistic than a decade ago. Then the commonly used term "Eurosclerosis" described Europe's stagnant political and economic environment. The Single European Act changed all that, breathing new dynamism into Europe with the prospect of achieving a true common market by the end of 1992 and, with that, promoting economic growth and an enhanced capacity to ameliorate differences between its more industrialized northern members and those in southern Europe. Thus "Europe 1992" replaced "Eurosclerosis" as the fashionable shorthand to describe the most innovative period of community reform since the 1960s.[18]

Europe 1992 promised to move the EC from a customs union, in which customs duties are eliminated, and from the free movement of workers, which the EC also enjoyed, to a genuine common market, in which the frontiers between member states are completely abolished. A genuine common market requires the removal of countless inhibitions long apparent in Europe, including exchange controls and restraints on the free movement of goods (many of which are nontariff barriers to trade, discussed in Chapter 7). It would also require the harmonization of product standards (for example, uniform socket sizes for electrical appliances), variations in rules governing taxation and capital movements, regulations on transport standards (such as rules governing truckers' driving hours, rest periods, and the makeup of teams of drivers), and the like. Such inhibitions safeguard national interests and autonomy. By inference, their elimination would abjure ancient nationalistic rivalries and promote the further pooling of sovereignty between the EC's national members and Community institutions. It is in this context that the commitment to majority rule in the Council of Ministers rather than the previous, common practice of consensus decision making takes on added meaning. Majority rule, reaffirmed in the Single European Act, restricts the ability of individual member nations to veto key decisions with which they disagree.

More than a few skeptics predicted that the EC's ambitious plans would fail. In fact, however, dramatic strides toward the economic objectives of Europe 1992 were realized, as national governments successfully implemented scores of directives issued by the Commission. As a result, attention turned increasingly to Europe beyond 1992.

The Single European Act had anticipated a number of significant developments beyond the completion of the single internal market, including initiatives in social, environmental, economic, and monetary policy—all with a view toward the eventual political union of Europe. Accordingly, the EC in 1990 embarked on a plan designed to create an Economic and Monetary Union, which would include a European central bank and a single European currency by the end of the century. European leaders reaffirmed those goals in a new agreement reached during a 1991 summit in the Dutch city of Maastricht. To preserve a façade of unity, however, they had to agree on a provision that would permit Britain to opt out of the monetary union at a later date.

The Single European Act also formalized procedures for cooperation in foreign policy that had been operational for some time but never institutionalized, in the hope of creating a common political identity for the Twelve. At issue is whether that more ambitious goal is attainable.

Europe: A Political Dwarf and Military Worm?

Members of the European Community have sought since 1970 to coordinate their efforts in hopes of devising a common EC position on foreign policy issues (see

---

[18] See the essays in Keohane and Hoffmann (1991a) for an examination of the forces giving rise to the Single European Act and those in Hufbauer (1990) for an assessment of Europe 1992 as seen from a U.S. perspective.

Knudsen, 1984). The practice, known as European Political Cooperation (EPC), emerged on the sidelines of the regularized procedures of the EC and in full recognition that the institutions of the EC would not enjoy the same powers in the domain of peace and security as in the low politics arena.

The amorphous character of EPC is acknowledged in the following description:

> In practical terms, the EPC essentially comes down to systematic and regular consultation and coordination among the people responsible for the definition, formulation, and implementation of national foreign policy, from the heads of governments to those responsible for regional departments in ministries of foreign affairs. This consultation process allows for defining common positions and organizing joint action as well as establishing a dialogue with other countries. The strength of the exercise derives from its synergistic development with the European. . . . Community, since, if a country wants to stay in the Community, it must accept the consultation process of EPC and, on the other hand, no country in Europe can be part of EPC it if is not first a member of the . . . Community. (De Ruyt, 1989: 11)

The European Community has enjoyed some success in framing community-wide positions on emergent foreign policy problems. Its efforts will doubtless intensify in the future, as the disappearance of the Soviet security threat, the need to rebuild Eastern Europe, and the blurring of the distinction between high and low politics increasingly push the Community to the forefront of European political and security affairs. The task will not be easy, however, as the foreign policy interests of the EC's member states seldom converge (see Dzordiak, 1991). Noteworthy in this respect is that Germany is now the undisputed European giant,[19] a new geopolitical fact certain to produce occasions in which Germany's aims and interests diverge from those of the other members of the European Community. Moreover, Britain, which has long enjoyed a "special relationship" with the United States, continues to harbor doubts about the wisdom of binding its own future to that of the continental European states.

The timidity of the European Community's response to Iraq's invasion of Kuwait and the subsequent Persian Gulf War illustrates the obstacles to forging a common European foreign policy posture.

> The Gulf War illuminated, like a conflagration, every crack and fissure between the Community's members on foreign policy matters. On one side of a fault line that runs along the Rhine are countries who see themselves as playing a world, or a least an Atlantic, role, however diminished by their relative economic decline that role may be. On the other side are those who have eschewed military action other than for their own defense and who feel uneasy about heroic political postures. The different response of a France, a Britain, an Italy, and a Germany to the Gulf War suggest that political cooperation on foreign policy will be very hard to realize and that the convergence of interests between the member states has a long way to go before it will be feasible. (Williams, 1991: 174–175)

EC Commission President Jacques Delors lamented in March 1991 that the Gulf War revealed "the limitations of the European Community." Another example of those limitations occurred with its response to the civil war that erupted in Yugoslavia

---

[19] The unification of Germany effectively expanded the size of the EC by sixteen million people without any formal action on the part of the Community.

in 1991, an area of primary interest to the Community and the very tinderbox in which the First World War ignited. More than in any previous conflict, the Community played a central role in monitoring ceasefires and mediating between the central Yugoslav government and the Croats and Slovenes. Nonetheless, divisiveness not only between contending forces in Yugoslavia but also among Community members themselves postponed a concerted, effectual European response to the conflict.

Complex issues also surround a future European security structure. For more than forty years the NATO alliance, under the leadership of the United States, provided Western Europe with protection from a possible Soviet invasion. At the same time, the members of the Atlantic alliance have always been reluctant to involve NATO in "out of area" disputes, as in the Persian Gulf. Without a Soviet security threat and the Cold War to consolidate the diverse members of the Community, the very existence of NATO is now at issue.

Members of NATO reaffirmed their commitment to the alliance on several occasions following the end of the Cold War. Simultaneously they moved, if only tentatively, to develop a European defense posture that, at some time in the future, could remove the need for NATO and distance European security from the protective U.S. security umbrella. Community leaders took a step in that direction during the 1991 Maastricht summit, when they agreed to build up the nine-nation European military pact known as the Western European Union (WEU). The WEU could eventually emerge as the military arm of the European Community.

While NATO exists there is little urgency to develop closer military cooperation among the EC members, but how long NATO can survive is problematic. As a collective defense (not a collective security) arrangement, NATO depends critically for the maintenance of alliance cohesion on the identification of a common external security threat. With that threat no longer visible, the future of NATO as the primary mechanism of European military cooperation is very much in doubt (see also Chapter 13).

Closer cooperation on foreign and national security policy is a prerequisite to the United States of Europe that the European Community's visionary founders once sought. National differences continue to make that an elusive goal. Even the form of a potential European government (for example, federal) is a divisive issue. Still, a single Europe remains a compelling idea for many Europeans. Thus the new agreement hammered out at the Maastricht summit, while avoiding any mention of a particular form of government, pictured the accord as "a new stage in the process creating an ever closer union among the peoples of Europe, where decisions will be taken as closely as possible to citizens."

Other Regional Organizations

In the decades following Europe's initiatives toward economic and political integration, a dozen or so regional economic schemes were created in various other parts of the world, notably among Third World nations. Most sought to stimulate regional economic growth. Exemplary of the major Third World regional organizations are the following:

- Latin American Integration Association (ALADI). Established in 1981 to promote freer regional trade, its members are Argentina, Bolivia, Brazil, Chile, Colombia, Ecuador, Mexico, Paraguay, Peru, Uruguay, and Venezuela.
- Association of South East Asian Nations (ASEAN). Established in 1967 to promote regional economic, social, and cultural cooperation, its members are Brunei, Indonesia, Malaysia, the Philippines, Singapore, and Thailand.
- Caribbean Community (CARICOM). Established in 1973 to promote economic development and integration, its members are Antigua and Barbuda, the Bahamas, Barbados, Belize, Dominica, Grenada, Guyana, Jamaica, Montserrat, St. Kitts-Nevis, St. Lucia, St. Vincent and the Grenadines, and Trinidad and Tobago.
- Council of Arab Economic Unity. Established in 1964 to promote economic integration of Arab nations, its members are Iraq, Jordan, Kuwait, Libya, Mauritania, the Palestine Liberation Organization, Somalia, Sudan, Syria, the United Arab Emirates, and Yemen.
- Economic Community of West African States (ECOWAS). Established in 1975 to promote regional economic cooperation, its members include Benin, Burkina Faso, Cape Verde, Gambia, Ghana, Guinea, Guinea-Bissau, Ivory Coast, Liberia, Mali, Mauritania, Niger, Nigeria, Senegal, Sierra Leone, and Togo.
- Southern African Development Coordination Conference (SADCC). Established in 1980 to promote regional economic development and reduce dependence on South Africa, its members are Angola, Botswana, Lesotho, Malawi, Mozambique, Swaziland, Tanzania, Zambia, and Zimbabwe.
- South Asian Association for Regional Cooperation (SAARC). Established in 1985 to promote economic, social, and cultural cooperation, its members are Bangladesh, Bhutan, India, Maldives, Nepal, Pakistan, and Sri Lanka.

It is hazardous to generalize about organizations as widely divergent in membership and sometimes in purpose as this brief list suggests (for a comparison, see Taylor, 1984). None has achieved anything approaching the same level of economic integration and supranational institution building as accomplished in Western Europe. The particular reasons underlying the modest success of the attempts vary, of course (see Chapter 14), but they share a common denominator: the reluctance of national political leaders to make the kinds of choices that would undermine their governments' sovereignty. Still, these attempts at regional cooperation demonstrate nations' belief that they are unable to resolve individually the problems that confront them collectively.

In this sense, the nation-state seems ill suited for both managing transnational policy problems and serving as an agent of organized efforts to do so. The effect of the collective problem-solving institutions on world politics is therefore problematic.

That viewpoint is reinforced by another transnational manifestation of the transformation of world politics, the multinational corporation, to which we now turn.

THE ROLE OF MULTINATIONAL CORPORATIONS . . . .

Since World War II the multinational corporation (MNC) has grown dramatically in size and influence alongside the expansion of the world political economy. As a result, multinational corporations have been the object of considerable discussion and often much animosity: Richard J. Barnet and Ronald E. Müller (1974) refer warily to the "global reach" of MNCs; George W. Ball (1971) coined the term *cosmocorp* to dramatize their increasing power; Robert Gilpin (1975) has attributed U.S. power to them; Robert S. Walters and David H. Blake (1992) ask the often-posed question whether they are a source of growth or underdevelopment for host countries; and Robert Reich (1990) asserts that they have lost their national identities.

The proliferation and tremendous size of MNCs add to the controversy surrounding their role and impact. It has been estimated that in the early 1980s about eighteen thousand MNCs worldwide controlled assets in two or more countries and that these corporations were responsible for marketing roughly four-fifths of the world's trade (excluding that of centrally planned economies). By the mid-1980s it was possible to identify the host-country location of some 104,000 MNC affiliates (Centre on Transnational Corporations, data tapes, July 29, 1987). (*Host country* refers to the country where a corporation headquartered in another country conducts its business activities.) As the tentacles of the MNCs spread, their combined share of the world's gross domestic product increased dramatically compared with previous decades (Clairmonte and Cavanagh, 1982).

The MNCs' expansion could not have occurred on such a massive scale without the financial contribution of the world's international banks. Indeed, the transnational bank (TNB) has itself become a major force in the world political economy. In 1986 the combined assets of the world's twenty-five largest banks stood at $3.7 trillion (Centre on Transnational Corporations, 1988: 546–548)—a figure more than triple the combined sales of the twenty-five largest industrial firms. Reflecting developments elsewhere in the world political economy, more than two-thirds of the world's largest banks in 1986 were headquartered in Japan (Centre on Transnational Corporations, 1988: 546–548).

As the MNC has grown in scope and power, it understandably has stimulated concern about whether it undermines the ability of ostensibly sovereign nation-states to control their own economies and therefore their own fates. Is it possible that MNCs are undermining the very foundations of the present international system? Or is this question perhaps based on exaggerated expectations of the MNCs' influence and therefore unwarranted?

The benefits and costs ascribed to MNCs as they emerged to a position of prominence since World War II, summarized in Box 6.2 on page 190, have been many and complex. Here we focus on four major issues: their global reach, their impact on host and home countries, their involvement in politics, and the question of their long-run impact on world politics.

Box 6.2
THE MULTINATIONAL CORPORATION IN WORLD POLITICS: A BALANCE SHEET OF CLAIMS AND CRITICISMS

• • •

POSITIVE	NEGATIVE
• Increase the volume of world trade.	• Give rise to oligopolistic conglomerations that reduce competition and free enterprise.
• Assist the aggregation of investment capital that can fund development.	• Raise capital in host countries (thereby depriving local industries of investment capital) but export profits to home countries.
• Finance loans and service international debt.	• Breed debtors and make the poor dependent on those providing loans.
• Lobby for free trade and the removal of barriers to trade, such as tariffs.	• Limit the availability of commodities by monopolizing their production and controlling their distribution in the world marketplace.
• Underwrite research and development that allows technological innovation.	• Export technology ill suited to underdeveloped economies.
• Introduce and dispense advanced technology to less-developed countries.	• Inhibit the growth of infant industries and local technological expertise in less-developed countries while making Third World countries dependent on First World technology.
• Reduce the costs of goods by encouraging their production according to the principle of comparative advantage.	• Collude to create cartels that contribute to inflation.
• Generate employment.	• Curtail employment by driving labor competition from the market.
• Encourage the training of workers.	• Limit wages offered to workers.

Positive	Negative
• Produce new goods and expand opportunities for their purchase through the internationalization of production.	• Limit the supply of raw materials available on international markets.
• Disseminate marketing expertise and mass-advertising methods worldwide.	• Erode traditional cultures and national differences, leaving in their place a homogenized world culture dominated by consumer-oriented values.
• Promote national revenue and economic growth; facilitate modernization of the less-developed countries.	• Widen the gap between the rich and poor nations.
• Generate income and wealth.	• Increase the wealth of local elites at the expense of the poor.
• Advocate peaceful relations between and among states in order to preserve an orderly environment conducive to trade and profits.	• Support and rationalize repressive regimes in the name of stability and order.
• Break down national barriers and accelerate the globalization of the international economy and culture and the rules that govern international commerce.	• Challenge national sovereignty and jeopardize the autonomy of the nation-state.

The Global Reach and Economic Power of Multinational Corporations

What is a multinational corporation? It is, typically, organized hierarchically and centrally directed. Beyond this, definitions differ. Nonetheless, they all agree that it is a business enterprise organized in one society with activities in another growing out of direct investment abroad (as opposed to portfolio investment through shareholding). "A distinctive characteristic of the [multinational corporation] is its broader-than-national perspective with respect to the pursuit of highly specialized objectives through a central optimizing strategy across national boundaries" (Huntington, 1973). The overseas network of affiliates of the Japanese electronics firm NEC Corporation (Nippon Electric Company) illustrates the transnational character of a multinational manufacturing and marketing firm (see Figure 6.8 on page 192).

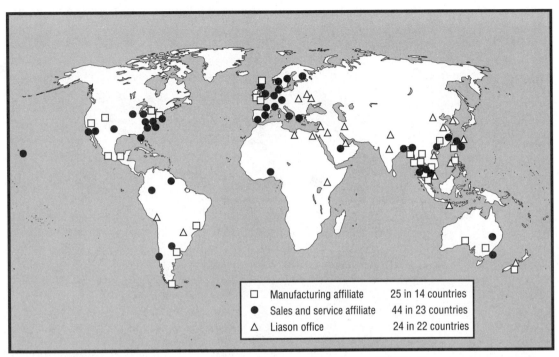

	Manufacturing affiliate	25 in 14 countries
●	Sales and service affiliate	44 in 23 countries
△	Liason office	24 in 22 countries

FIGURE 6.8 OVERSEAS NETWORK OF AFFILIATES OF THE NEC CORPORATION, 1989
Source: Centre on Transnational Corporations, *World Investment Report 1991: The Triad in Foreign Direct Investment* (New York: United Nations, 1991), p. 43.

The creation of the European Economic Community (EEC) in 1958 gave impetus to this form of business organization. Because the original six EEC members hoped to create a common external tariff wall around their common market, it made economic sense for U.S. firms to build production facilities in Europe. In this way they could remain competitive by selling their wares as domestic rather than foreign products, with their additional tariff costs.[20] Ultimately, of course, "the primary drive behind the overseas expansion of today's giant corporations is maximization of corporate

---

[20] The reasons for direct investments overseas are more complex than this simplified explanation suggests. The product-cycle theory is one example. According to this view, overseas expansion is essentially a defensive maneuver designed to forestall foreign competitors and hence to maintain the global competitiveness of domestically based industries. The theory views MNCs as having an edge in the initial stages of developing and producing a new product and then having to go abroad to protect export markets from foreign competitors that naturally arise as the relevant technology becomes diffused or imitated. In the final phase of the product cycle, "production has become sufficiently routinized so that the comparative advantage shifts to relatively low-skilled, low-wage, and labor-intensive economies. This is now the case, for example, in textiles, electronic components, and footwear" (Gilpin, 1975). See this source and especially Vernon (1971) for an elaboration of the product-cycle theory.

growth and the suppression of foreign as well as domestic competition" (Gilpin, 1975).[21]

Since the impetus given them by the EEC, the world's giant producing, trading, and servicing corporations have become the agents of the internationalization of production. Their economic and perhaps political importance in world politics is illustrated in Table 6.1 on page 194, which ranks billion-dollar-or-more firms and nations by the size of their gross economic product. The profile shows that over forty of the world's top one hundred economic entities are multinational corporations. Among the top fifty entries, multinationals account for only twelve, but in the next fifty, they account for thirty-three.

Patterns of Foreign Direct Investment

Although the growth of multinational firms is a global phenomenon, the developed areas making up the First World are the location for most transnational business enterprises. Historically, the United States has been the home country for the largest proportion of parent companies, followed by Britain and West Germany. Hence, the pattern of foreign direct investment was "bipolar" in nature, with the United States as one pole, and a handful of European nations (acting independently) as the other.

By the end of the 1980s Japan had emerged as a significant participant in the global investment picture. By then, Japan, the United States, and an increasingly integrated European Community accounted for 80 percent of world investment (compared with only 50 percent of world trade) (Centre on Transnational Corporations, 1991: 32). The developing countries' share of foreign direct investment grew in the 1970s but plummeted during the debt crisis of the 1980s (see Chapter 8), thus leaving the First World as the overwhelmingly dominant force in the pattern of global investments. (Foreign direct investment is measured in terms of stocks—investments already in place—and flows—investments that move across national boundaries.)

A TRIPOLAR INVESTMENT WORLD   The emergence of a "tripolar" investment world is one of the most significant investment developments of the 1980s (see Box

[21] As the world political economy has become more competitive, multinational corporations have had to adapt old investment strategies and develop new ones. As described by the UN Centre on Transnational Corporations (1991), two sets of forces are operative. One includes those factors that are converging across national borders, the other those diffusing through the world political economy. The convergent forces—the regionalization of developed market economies, the convergence of discrete technologies, and the convergence of consumer tastes—mean "that transnational corporations now face larger, more homogeneous markets and that the economic distance between countries, particularly developed countries, is narrowing. That implies new opportunities for the integration of international activities, along with greater returns stemming from those activities" (Centre on Transnational Corporations, 1991). On the other hand, the divergent forces—the diffusion of innovative activity and standardized technologies, the proliferation of production locations, and the diffusion of competition from domestic to international levels—mean "that the internationalization of activities is increasingly becoming a strategic imperative in a growing number of industries, rather than a profitable option open only to a handful of large firms" (Centre on Transnational Corporations, 1991).

Table 6.1 Countries and Corporations Ranked According to Size of Annual Product, 1989 (Countries) and 1990 (MNCs)

Rank	Economic Entity	Dollars (millions)
1	United States	5,445,825
2	Japan	3,140,948
3	Soviet Union	2,600,000
4	Germany (Federal Republic)	1,411,346
5	France	1,099,750
6	Italy	970,619
7	United Kingdom	923,959
8	Canada	542,774
9	Spain	429,404
10	China	415,884
11	Brazil	402,788
12	India	294,816
13	Australia	290,522
14	Netherlands	258,804
15	Korea, Republic of	231,132
16	Switzerland	219,337
17	Mexico	214,500
18	Sweden	202,498
19	Belgium	154,688
20	Austria	147,016
21	Finland	129,823
22	**GENERAL MOTORS** (U.S.)	125,126
23	Denmark	113,515
24	**ROYAL DUTCH/SHELL GROUP** (Britain, Netherlands)	107,204
25	**EXXON** (U.S.)	105,885
26	Indonesia	101,151
27	**FORD MOTOR** (U.S.)	98,275
28	Norway	98,079
29	Turkey	91,742
30	South Africa	90,410
31	Saudi Arabia[a]	86,898
32	Thailand	79,044
33	Argentina	76,491
34	Yugoslavia	72,860
35	**INTERNATIONAL BUSINESS MACHINES** (U.S.)	69,018
36	Hong Kong	66,666
37	**TOYOTA MOTOR** (Japan)	64,516
38	Poland	64,480
39	**IRI** (Italy)	61,433
40	Greece	60,245
41	**BRITISH PETROLEUM** (Britain)	59,541

TABLE 6.1 COUNTRIES AND CORPORATIONS RANKED ACCORDING TO SIZE OF ANNUAL PRODUCT, 1989 (COUNTRIES) AND 1990 (MNCs)

Rank	Economic Entity	Dollars (millions)
42	**MOBIL** (U.S.)	58,770
43	**GENERAL ELECTRIC** (U.S.)	58,414
44	**DAIMLER-BENZ** (Germany)	54,259
45	Algeria	51,585
46	Israel	50,866
47	Portugal	50,692
48	**HITACHI** (Japan)	50,686
49	Venezuela	50,574
50	Czechoslovakia	49,225
51	**FIAT** (Italy)	47,752
52	**SAMSUNG** (South Korea)	45,042
53	**PHILIP MORRIS** (U.S.)	44,323
54	Philippines	43,954
55	**VOLKSWAGEN** (Germany)	43,710
56	**MATSUSHITA ELECTRIC INDUSTRIAL** (Japan)	43,516
57	New Zealand	43,185
58	Pakistan	42,649
59	**ENI** (Italy)	41,762
60	Malaysia	41,524
61	**TEXACO** (U.S.)	41,235
62	Colombia	40,805
63	**NISSAN MOTOR** (Japan)	40,217
64	**UNILEVER** (Britain, Netherlands)	39,972
65	**E.I. DU PONT DE NEMOURS** (U.S.)	39,839
66	**CHEVRON** (U.S.)	39,262
67	**SIEMENS** (Germany)	39,228
68	Romania	38,025
69	Singapore	33,512
70	Ireland	33,467
71	**NESTLÉ** (Switzerland)	33,359
72	Kuwait[a]	33,089
73	**ELF AQUITAINE** (France)	32,939
74	United Arab Emirates	31,613
75	Egypt, Arab Republic	31,381
76	Nigeria	31,285
77	**CHRYSLER** (U.S.)	30,868
78	**PHILIPS' GLOEILAMPENFABRIEKEN** (Netherlands)	30,866
79	**TOSHIBA** (Japan)	30,182
80	**RENAULT** (France)	30,050
81	Hungary	30,047
82	**PEUGEOT** (France)	29,380

TABLE 6.1 COUNTRIES AND CORPORATIONS RANKED ACCORDING TO SIZE OF ANNUAL PRODUCT, 1989 (COUNTRIES) AND 1990 (MNCs) *(continued)*

Rank	Economic Entity	Dollars (millions)
83	**BASF** (Germany)	29,184
84	**AMOCO** (U.S.)	28,277
85	**HOECHST** (Germany)	27,750
86	**ASEA BROWN BOVERI** (Switzerland)	27,705
87	**BOEING** (U.S.)	27,595
88	**HONDA MOTOR** (Japan)	27,070
89	**ALCATEL ALSTHOM** (France)	26,456
90	**BAYER** (Germany)	26,059
91	Chile	25,504
92	Peru	25,149
93	**NEC** (Japan)	24,391
94	**PROCTER AND GAMBLE** (U.S.)	24,376
95	Morocco	23,788
96	**TOTAL** (France)	23,590
97	**PETRÓLEOS DE VENEZUELA** (Venezuela)	23,469
98	**IMPERIAL CHEMICAL INDUSTRIES** (Britain)	23,348
99	Bangladesh	22,579
100	**DAEWOO** (South Korea)	22,260

a Data are for 1989.

Source: Gross national product data are from *World Bank Atlas 1991* (Washington, D.C., 1991), pp. 6–9. Gross national product data for Czechoslovakia, Romania, and the Soviet Union are from *Handbook of Economic Statistics, 1991* (Washington, D.C.: Central Intelligence Agency, 1991), p. 34. Sales of industrial firms are from *Fortune*, July 29, 1991, p. 245.

6.3 on page 197). Wholly unexpected at the beginning of the decade, it grew out of the convergence of three important, interrelated trends: the rapid integration of Europe, which made it possible to treat the EC as a single investment entity; the growing importance of Japan as a source of foreign direct investment; and the declining role of the United States as a source of investments and its corresponding rise as a host country.[22] By the end of the decade Europe was on a par with the United States in terms of the stock of foreign direct investment, while Japan had surpassed the United States as a major source of foreign investment in terms of flows, with much of its outward investment directed to the United States itself (Centre on Transnational Corporations, 1991).

---

[22] Much of the foreign direct investment in the United States has taken the form of acquisitions by European and Canadian firms that already had some presence in the U.S. market, and the building of new production facilities by Japan (a trade-replacing form of foreign direct investment) in an effort to establish itself in a market in which it had little presence before 1970. Japanese investments in banking and real estate, such as hotels and office buildings, have also been substantial. The rapid growth of foreign investments has been controversial, as many U.S. policymakers worry that the "selling of America" will make the United States unduly vulnerable to foreign influence. For an alternative viewpoint, see Kapstein (1991–1992).

Box 6.3
TRANSNATIONAL INVESTMENT HIGHLIGHTS OF THE 1980s

• • •

- World foreign investment triples. Total global investment in stocks is now about $1.5 trillion. It was $550 billion in 1980.
- The United States emerges as the most important host country.
- The European Community emerges as the most important home region.
- Japan expands overseas investment sixfold during the decade.
- Developing countries' share in global flows declines. In spite of a near doubling of average annual flows to developing countries, their share fell from 25 percent to 17 percent.
- Latin America accounts for 80 percent of the declining share of developing countries' inflows. Some 40 percent of the inflows of large debtors was through debt-equity swaps.
- The Asian newly industrialized countries emerge as increasingly important foreign investors.
- The least developed countries, including much of Africa, are marginal to global trends, now as before, in spite of sizable policy reforms.

Source: Transnationals 3 (March 1991): 2.

Not only does the U.S.-Japan-EC triad dominate world investment patterns but, as the Japanese preference for the United States as an investment market suggests, the rate of growth of foreign direct investments within the triad itself has outpaced the growth of investments elsewhere. The patterns emerge from a corporate strategy in which each partner to the investment triad has sought to consolidate its own market hold and to gain a foothold in the other two regions.

Figure 6.9 on page 198 illustrates the investment amounts and preference patterns within the triad. It shows that the United States and the EC each prefer the other over Japan, and that Japan prefers to invest in the United States compared with Europe. It also highlights a serious imbalance between Japan and its other First World partners, with the outward flow of stocks much greater than the inward flow.[23] This imbalance parallels Japan's trade imbalance with other nations, notably the United States (see Chapter 7).

---

[23] As a relative newcomer to foreign direct investment, the value of Japan's outward stock of investments is less than that of Europe and United States but can be expected to rise dramatically during the 1990s as Japanese investments now dominate the foreign direct investment picture.

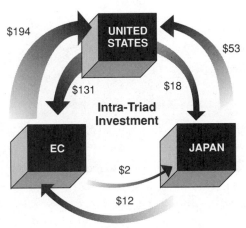

FIGURE 6.9 THE MAGNITUDE AND PATTERN OF INVESTMENTS AMONG JAPAN, THE EUROPEAN COMMUNITY, AND THE UNITED STATES (1988 STOCKS IN BILLIONS)
Source: Transnationals 3 (March 1991): 3.

A REGIONALIZED INVESTMENT WORLD   As major corporations in the United States, Europe, and Japan adopted market strategies designed to consolidate existing markets and to gain a foothold in other regions, they also adopted strategies that sought "to build up regionally-integrated core networks of affiliates, clustered around their home country" (Centre on Transnational Corporations, 1991). Figure 6.10, which depicts the automobile operations of Toyota Motor Company in four ASEAN countries, illustrates a regional clustering pattern in one industry.

As a result of this clustering strategy, global patterns of foreign direct investment are now increasingly regional in nature. Each of the principal host countries in Eastern Europe and the Third World receives the bulk of its funds from a single member of the investment triad, typically the one most proximate to it geographically. Countries in Central and South America tend to cluster around the United States; those in Eastern Europe tend to cluster around the EC; and those in East and Southeast Asia around Japan (see Figure 6.11 on page 200). The effect is to reinforce—perhaps cause—the growing regionalization of the world political economy across a range of dimensions considered not only in this chapter but also elsewhere in this book (notably Chapter 7).

Impact on Home and Host Nations

In addition to its global reach, the domestic impact of the MNC on both home and host countries is a matter of widespread concern.

The MNCs allegedly exercise their power at great cost to their home or parent countries. Charges against them include shifting productive facilities abroad to avoid labor unions' demands for higher wages. According to this view, because capital is

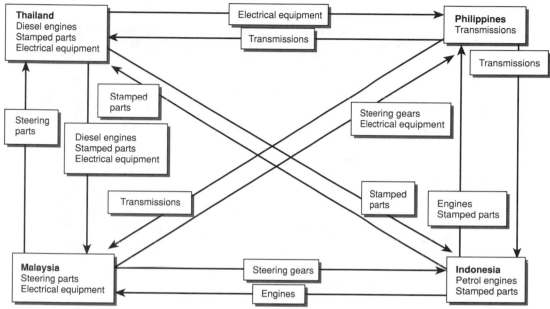

FIGURE 6.10   AUTOMOBILE OPERATIONS OF TOYOTA IN FOUR ASEAN COUNTRIES

Source: Centre on Transnational Corporations, *World Investment Report 1991: The Triad in Foreign Direct Investment* (New York: United Nations, 1991), p. 62.

more mobile than labor, the practice of exporting production from industrially advanced countries to industrially backward countries, where labor is cheap and unions weak or nonexistent, is the cause of structural unemployment in the advanced countries. In the case of the United States in particular, however, others contend that MNCs help reduce the nation's balance-of-payments deficit, create new employment opportunities, and promote competition in both domestic and foreign markets.

If home countries have incurred both costs and benefits, have host countries shared similar experiences? "As privileged organizations," David E. Apter and Louis W. Goodman (1976) note, MNCs "hold a unique position among growth-inducing institutions able to affect the direction of development." This implies that MNCs may benefit development as much as they impede it. It is nonetheless true that Third World nations have historically viewed multinationals with considerable and often emotionally charged suspicion. Although this viewpoint has changed noticeably in recent years—Third World nations now compete with one another to attract foreign direct investment—MNCs are comparatively more important to the developing nations' overall GNP and to their most advanced economic sectors than they are to the developed states' economies. We will therefore return in Chapter 8 to consider further the role of MNCs as seen from the perspective of developing nations. Here it is sufficient simply to note that the question of what weight to assign to the costs and

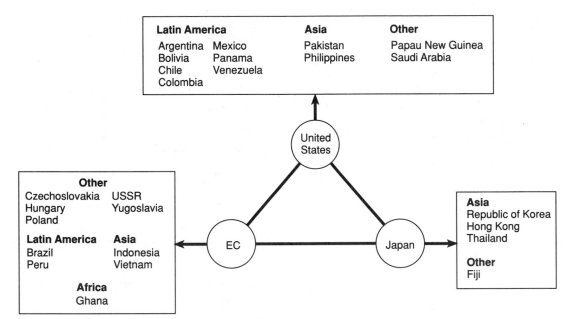

FIGURE 6.11 FOREIGN INVESTMENT CLUSTERS OF JAPAN, THE EUROPEAN COMMUNITY, AND THE UNITED STATES
Source: Centre on Transnational Corporations, *World Investment Report 1991: The Triad in Foreign Direct Investment* (New York: United Nations, 1991), p. 56.

benefits of MNCs has yielded different answers in different times and places, but none that is conclusive.

Politics and Multinational Corporations

Another aspect of the concern about the role of MNCs as nonstate actors concerns their involvement in political activities. The chief area of concern from the perspective of Third World nations is the obtrusive involvement of MNCs in local (host country) politics. MNCs have also involved themselves in the domestic politics of their home countries, lobbying home governments for policies that will enhance the profitability of their business activities abroad. And both host and home governments in turn have sometimes used them as foreign policy instruments.

Perhaps the most notorious instance of an MNC's intervention in the politics of a host state occurred in Chile in the early 1970s. There, International Telephone and Telegraph (ITT) tried to protect its interests in the profitable Chiltelco telephone company by seeking to prevent the election of Marxist-oriented Salvador Allende as president and by seeking his later overthrow. ITT's efforts to undermine Allende included giving monetary support to his political opponents and, once elected, attempting to induce the U.S. government to launch a program designed to disrupt the Chilean economy.

There are other instances in which MNCs have engaged in practices embarrassing to home countries—as when the West German government found that a German firm had sold mustard-gas manufacturing equipment to Libya—or that seemed to defy them—as when the French subsidiary of Dresser Industries of Dallas, Texas, exported energy technology to the Soviet Union in defiance of an effort by the U.S. government to thwart it.

MNCs also often lobby their home governments for policies that back the MNCs in disputes with host governments, though they are not always successful in these endeavors (see Spiegel, 1985). The U.S. stipulation made in the early 1970s that foreign aid would be cut off from any country that nationalized U.S. overseas investments without just compensation is exemplary of the tendency for home-state governments to support their own MNCs' overseas activities.

More broadly, MNCs have assisted in the maintenance of the Liberal International Economic Order (LIEO) that has been a prominent post–World War II goal of the United States, and have helped to shape the specific U.S. policies regarding trade and taxation that contributed to its effectiveness. In this sense, MNCs may influence the process by which national governments reach agreement on rules governing operation of the world political economy.

MNCs have also been used to enhance U.S. intelligence-gathering capabilities in other countries. In these cases it is almost as though the MNC is the captive of governments, not an autonomous political actor on the world stage. However, there are other instances where MNCs headquartered in one country actually work at cross-purposes with the parent government in serving the wishes of the host government. During the oil crisis of 1973–1974, for example, the governments of the Organization of Petroleum Exporting Countries (OPEC) effectively used the multinational oil companies to achieve OPEC's goal of using oil as a political weapon against the West.

Because the political role of the MNC in home and host countries is ambiguous, perhaps the conclusion that best characterizes its impact is one that pictures the MNC as "a stimulant to the further extension of state power in the economic realm" (Gilpin, 1985) rather than as a potential successor to the sovereign nation-state.

> Only the state can defend corporate interests in international negotiations over trade, investment, and market access. Agreements over such things as airline routes, the opening of banking establishments, and the right to sell insurance are not decided by corporate actors who gather around a table; they are determined by diplomats and bureaucrats. Corporations must turn to governments when they have interests to protect or advance. (Kapstein, 1991–1992: 56; see also Huntington, 1973; Waltz, 1970)

Still, the blurring of the boundaries between internal and external affairs adds potency to the political role that MNCs unavoidably play as actors at the intersection of foreign and domestic policy.

Controlling Multinational Corporations

Multinationals have become important actors in world politics in the sense that they make critical decisions over which national political leaders may not have complete control. Thus, the long-run impact of MNCs on a world in which nation-states alone claim sovereignty is a fourth significant question about the role of multinational corporations as nonstate actors.

The question of control is especially pertinent to Third World countries, but it is not confined to them. As one senior foreign policy official in the United States declared at the time of the Dresser Industries controversy, "Basically we're in an impossible situation. You don't want to get rid of the advantages of this international economic system, but if you try to exercise control for foreign policy reasons, you cut across sovereign frontiers." Furthermore, the MNCs' complex patterns of ownership and licensing arrangements mean that it is often difficult to equate the MNCs' interests with particular national jurisdictions (see Reich, 1990). General Electric, for example, one of the most "American" of all U.S. MNCs, has granted licenses for the production of energy-related equipment to Nuovo Pignone of Italy, Mitsubishi Heavy Industries and Hitachi of Japan, Mannessmann and AEG Telefunken of West Germany, John Brown Engineering of Great Britain, and Thomassen Holland of the Netherlands (U.S. Office of Technology Assessment, 1981). Controlling such a complex pattern of interrelationships, joint ventures, and shared ownership for any particular national purpose is nearly impossible. "The internationalization of the economy—which the U.S. spearheaded—has rendered obsolete old ideas of economic warfare," Richard J. Barnet, coauthor of *Global Reach*, observed in 1982. "You can't find targets any more, and if you aim at a target you often find it's yourself."

The potential long-run importance of MNCs for transforming world order is depicted in *Global Reach*:

> The global corporation is the most powerful human organization yet devised for colonizing the future. By scanning the entire planet for opportunities, by shifting its resources from industry to industry and country to country, and by keeping its overriding goal simple—worldwide profit maximization—it has become an institution of unique power. The World Managers are the first to have developed a plausible model for the future that is global. . . . In making business decisions today they are creating a politics for the next generation. (Barnet and Müller, 1974: 363)

Whether the corporate visionaries who manage the MNCs will help create a more prosperous, peaceful, and just world—as some hope, and others, whose interests are threatened by a new world political economy, fear—is questionable. "For some, the global corporation holds the promise of lifting mankind out of poverty and bringing the good life to everyone. For others, these corporations have become a law unto themselves; they are miniempires which exploit all for the benefit of a few" (Gilpin, 1975).

Those concerns remain as we contemplate the impact of multinational corporations on the transformation of world politics, but they are less prevalent in the thinking of political elites than during the 1960s and 1970s. The existence of multinational corporations "has become a fact of life. They are now permanent—and influential—players in the international arena" (Spero, 1990). Still, the challenge they pose to the existing international order should not be taken lightly. The United Nations Commission on Transnational Corporations forcefully poses the issue:

Over the past decade [the 1980s], a growing number of international norms has produced a body of international soft law on transnational corporations; it is, however, limited in scope and does not adequately match the globalization of business activity. In an era of globalization, it is increasingly difficult to distinguish between national and international issues of governance. The capacity of Governments to manage their economies and achieve national objectives in areas ranging from fiscal policy to environmental control is being strained by the growing importance of transnational corporations in the international economy. Many issues related to corporate responsibility cannot be resolved satisfactorily in the context of a single national legal regime. . . . The effective and stable governance of international economic relations requires not only the unleashing of market forces and private enterprise, but also effective international instruments to deal with the broad range of issues related to the globalization of business activity—problems that are beyond the capacity of national regimes of governance. (Commission on Transnational Corporations, 1991: 33)

NONSTATE ACTORS, INTERNATIONAL REGIMES, AND THE TRANSFORMATION OF WORLD POLITICS . . . .

Because multinational corporations challenge the nation-state, they also challenge the very foundations of the contemporary global system. States will not disappear quickly, however. Conflict between them and multinational corporations is, therefore, understandable. "What we seem to be witnessing," muses economist Robert Heilbroner (1977), "is a conflict between two modes of organizing human affairs—a 'vertical' mode that finds its ultimate expression in the pan-national flows of production of the giant international corporation, and a 'horizontal' mode expressed in the jealously guarded boundaries of the nation-state."

In the meantime, the rise of multinational corporations and the prodigious growth of other types of nonstate actors challenge the traditional state-centric theory of international politics, which holds that nation-states are the primary actors on the world stage. Because the state has "purposes and power," according to this view, it "is the basic unit of action; its main agents are the diplomat and soldier. The interplay of governmental politics yields the pattern of behavior that students of international politics attempt to understand and that practitioners attempt to adjust or to control" (Nye and Keohane, 1971).

Clearly such a view no longer adequately depicts the complexity of world politics. As described in Chapter 2, the behaviors of state and nonstate actors sometimes converge to form *international regimes.* Sovereign states are important members of international regimes. Oran R. Young (1980) argues, in fact, that "the members of international regimes are always sovereign states." Significantly, however, he quickly adds that "the parties carrying out the actions governed by international regimes are often private entities." In this sense the nonstate actors discussed in this chapter—IGOs, INGOs, and MNCs—are often the key participants in the regularized conduct of contemporary international relations encompassed by international regimes in such diverse areas as the law of the sea, nuclear nonproliferation, the global monetary and trade systems, and the global food system.

Moving from the level of cooperative international interactions to the level of foreign policy making within nation-states, an adequate conceptualization of contemporary world politics also must acknowledge the influence of nonstate actors on a government's ability to formulate public policy and on the ties among them. Nonstate actors help build and broaden the foreign policy agendas of national decision makers by serving as transmission belts through which one nation's policies become sensitive to another's (Keohane and Nye, 1975, 1989). At the same time, some nonstate actors are capable of pursuing their interests largely outside the direct control of nation-states while simultaneously involving governments in particular problems as a result of their activities (Nye and Keohane, 1971; Keohane and Nye, 1989).

These reflections invite this conclusion:

> There has developed on the global level an interconnected and intensified . . . complex of relationships . . . in which demands are articulated and processed through formal as well as informal channels, governmental as well as non-governmental organizations, national as well as international and supranational institutions. These processes of interaction are interdependent . . . and they perform a variety of functions, most prominently those of welfare and security. They are the structures through which governments perform a variety of functions; they are the way in which state and society seek to arrange their domestic and foreign environment. (Hanrieder, 1978: 1278)

The transformation of world politics manifests itself in these complex, interdependent relationships among diverse national and transnational actors. This by no means indicates that the nation-state is dead, however. Governments still retain the capacity to influence, indeed to shape, transnational interactions. It is not accidental that supranationalism (as in Europe) has been confined largely to economic interactions and that matters of national security are confined largely to government-to-government interactions.

Thus it is important not to exaggerate the impact of nonstate actors on world politics. Nation-states retain a (near) monopoly on the use of coercive force in the international system, and they retain enormous capacity to shape global and national welfare. The nation-state cannot be lightly dismissed, therefore; it still molds the activities of nonstate actors more than its behavior is molded by them. Moreover, it "may be anachronistic, but we have yet to develop an alternative form of societal organization that is able to provide its members with both wealth and power" (Kapstein, 1991–1992). Hence it would be premature to abandon the focus on the nation-state in international politics, just as it would be inadequate to regard the state as the only relevant actor or the sole determinant of its fate.

SUGGESTED READINGS

Barnet, Richard J., and Ronald E. Müller. *Global Reach: The Power of the Multinational Corporations.* New York: Simon & Schuster, 1974.

Centre on Transnational Corporations. *World Investment Report: The Triad in Foreign Direct Investment.* New York: United Nations, 1991.

Feld, Werner J., and Robert S. Jordan, with Leon Hurwitz. *International Organizations: A Comparative Approach,* 2nd ed. New York: Praeger, 1988.

Finkelstein, Lawrence S., ed. *Politics in the United Nations System.* Durham, N.C.: Duke University Press, 1988.

Fromuth, Peter, ed. *A Successor Vision: The United Nations of Tomorrow.* New York: United Nations Association of the United States of America, 1988.

Hanson, Eric O. *The Catholic Church in World Politics.* Princeton, N.J.: Princeton University Press, 1987.

Keohane, Robert O., and Stanley Hoffmann, eds. *The New European Community: Decisionmaking and Institutional Change.* Boulder, Colo.: Westview, 1991.

Nugent, Neill. *The Government and Politics of the European Community,* 2nd ed. Durham, N.C.: Duke University Press, 1991.

Riggs, Robert E., and Jack C. Plano. *The United Nations: International Organization and World Politics.* Chicago: Dorsey Press, 1988.

Russett, Bruce, and James S. Sutterlin. "The U.N. in a New World Order," *Foreign Affairs* 70 (Spring 1991): 69–83.

Taylor, Phillip. *Nonstate Actors in International Politics: From Transregional to Substate Organizations.* Boulder, Colo.: Westview Press, 1984.

Part III

Low Politics: Transnational Policy Issues

. . .

7.
The Transformation of the World Political Economy:
Perspectives from the First World

8.
The Transformation of the World
Political Economy:
Perspectives from the Third World

9.
The Global Commons:
Demography and the Environment
in World Politics

10.
Oil, Energy, and Resource Power

CHAPTER 7

$\bullet \quad \bullet \quad \bullet$

The Transformation of the World Political Economy: Perspectives from the First World

$\bullet \quad \bullet \quad \bullet$

The nation-state is just about through as an economic unit. . . . The world is too small. It . . . [does] not permit the sovereign independence of the nation-state in economic affairs.

Charles P. Kindleberger,
International Economist, 1969

I believe the 1990s will still be known as the decade of economics, and to that extent, the European Community will be a major geopolitical factor.

Robert Hunter, Vice-President of the
Center for Strategic and International Studies, 1991

Many analysts believe that economic contention will replace power politics as the dominant issue in post–Cold War international politics. "Except in those unfortunate parts of the world where armed confrontations or civil strife persist for purely regional or internal reasons," observes strategic analyst Edward N. Luttwak (1990), "the waning of the Cold War is steadily reducing the importance of military power in world affairs. . . . Everyone, it appears, now agrees that the methods of commerce are displacing military methods—with disposable capital in lieu of firepower, civilian innovation in lieu of military-technical advancement, and market penetration in lieu of garrisons and bases."

Although popular, Luttwak continues, that viewpoint ignores how inextricably linked politics and economics are. "The international scene is still primarily occupied by states and blocs of states that extract revenues, regulate economic as well as other activities for various purposes, pay out benefits, offer services, provide infrastructures, and—of increasing importance—finance or otherwise sponsor the development of new technologies and new products" (Luttwak, 1990). Thus politics—the exercise of power—determines economics—the distribution of material values.

The term *political economy* highlights the intersection of politics and economics, whose influence on world politics enjoys a long heritage. A combination of political and economic considerations gave rise to the nation-state more than three centuries ago and has helped to shape the patterns of dominance and dependence that have characterized relations between rich and poor states ever since. The relevance of the term today is captured in the extensive interdependent relationships between states that knit national and global welfare into a single tapestry.

Interdependence has doubtless produced benefits, but it has not been without costs. Increased trade can reduce as well as increase the number of available jobs, for example. Thus policymakers find that their domestic success is increasingly dependent on their ability to create a favorable political and economic environment abroad; and that in turn is often a product of what happens at home economically as well as politically (Mastanduno, Lake, and Ikenberry, 1989). More than ever, then, policymakers must play "two-level games" simultaneously, one at the domestic level, the other at the international (Putnam, 1988).

Two-level games are dictated by the fact that *interdependence* implies *mutual sensitivity* and *mutual vulnerability* (Keohane and Nye, 1988), conditions policymakers are as likely to deplore as to applaud. Even the United States, the principal architect of the post–World War II liberal economic order, now faces powerful domestic forces that challenge classical economic precepts, such as free trade, that have been the centerpiece of its foreign economic policy since the 1940s. Similar challenges to the norms and rules that have governed the conduct of international commerce since that time have been mounted elsewhere. Their breadth and intensity explain why international economic policy issues, such as trade protectionism, now figure so prominently on the global political agenda.

Our purpose in this chapter and the next is to explore the nature and implications of the challenges that now confront the world political economy. We begin with a brief discussion of the ideas and principles that link individual nations and their domestic welfare to the world political economy, including a consideration of the way the anarchical character of international politics affects international economic relations. Next, we examine the evolution of the international monetary and trade regimes that embrace the developed states of the North and the political economy issues that increasingly animate their policies at home and abroad. We conclude Chapter 7 with a consideration of the prospects for the entry of the Commonwealth of Independent States and the former socialist states in eastern Europe into the capitalist world political economy as seen through the eyes of the First World. Then, in Chapter 8, we examine the economic relationships between the more developed nations of the North and the less developed nations of the South, and political economy issues that arise from them.

NATIONAL ECONOMIES IN THE WORLD POLITICAL ECONOMY . . . .

World exports now exceed $3 trillion annually and account for roughly 15 percent of world economic output. The dramatic increases in world trade since World War II that these numbers reflect have fueled the unprecedented growth in global welfare the world has experienced since then; indeed, one could not have occurred without the other.

Both increases are the product of the victorious World War II Allies' success in avoiding a repetition of the economic disaster that followed World War I. The lessons the Allies drew from the interwar years, particularly the Great Depression of the 1930s, influenced their wartime deliberations about the shape of the post-war international economic structure, even as they continued their struggle against the Axis powers. The main lesson was that the United States could not safely isolate itself from world affairs as it had after World War I. Thus the United States now actively led in the creation of the various rules and institutions that were to govern post–World War II international relations. The result in the economic sphere was the Liberal International Economic Order (LIEO) in which barriers to the free flow of trade and capital were progressively reduced, thus promoting today's interdependent world political economy.

The postwar Liberal International Economic Order rested on three political bases: "the concentration of power in a small number of states, the existence of a cluster of important interests shared by those states, and the presence of a dominant power willing and able to assume a leadership role" (Spero, 1990).

Power was concentrated in the developed countries of Western Europe and North America. Neither Japan nor the Third World then posed an effective challenge to Western dominance, and the inclusion of the then-communist states of Eastern Europe and the Soviet Union in the international economy was limited. The concentration of power thus restricted the number of states whose agreement was necessary to make the system operate effectively.

The shared interests of these states facilitated the operation of the system. They included a preference for an open economic system combined with a commitment to limited government intervention, if this proved necessary. The onset of the Cold War was a powerful force cementing Western cohesion on economic issues. Faced with a common external enemy, the Western industrial nations perceived economic cooperation as necessary not only for prosperity but also for security. The perception contributed to a willingness to share economic burdens. It was also an important catalyst for the assumption of leadership by only one state—the United States—and for the acceptance of that leadership role by others.

The open (liberal) economic order created after World II promises benefits to everyone, but states still seek through unilateral action to enhance their individual welfare, arguably at the expense of others, rather than cooperating with one another so all can benefit. Such behavior flows naturally from the fact that governments want to increase the beneficial domestic effects of international economic transactions and to lessen their adverse consequences. The tactics they use in pursuit of these goals will be shaped by domestic factors, notably how they organize their national economies, and by external factors, particularly their position relative to other states.

Open versus Closed Economies

States' responses to the economic challenges they face depend in part on how they organize their domestic economies. Some have *open* economic systems. These allow the "invisible hand" of the marketplace to determine the flow of economic transactions within and across the state's borders. Such countries are commonly known as *market economies*.

Closed systems are at the opposite end of this spectrum. Because they rely on government intervention to regulate and manage the economy, closed systems are also called *centrally planned* or *command* economies. Policymakers in closed systems use taxes, wage and price controls, monetary regulations, tariffs, and other policy instruments to prevent competitive market forces from determining economic transactions.

For many states, trade is their most important international economic transaction. A deficit in their *balance of trade* results from an imbalance between exports and imports, that is, when they buy more abroad than they sell. The *balance of payments* is a more inclusive summary statement of a state's financial transactions with the rest of the world. In addition to imports and exports, the balance of payments includes such items as foreign aid transfers and the income of citizens employed abroad who send their paychecks home. If more money flows out of the country than comes in, then it will suffer a balance-of-payments deficit. When this happens, some kind of corrective action is required. Policies that modify either the level of imports or the value of one's currency (relative to others') are possible options, but neither is without costs.

Where a nation falls along the open-closed continuum helps to shape the options policymakers perceive as viable as they seek to adjust imbalances in their nation's economic transactions with the rest of the world.[1] For countries with closed economies, adjusting international income to international expenses is comparatively easy. The government can simply mandate an increase or decrease in the importation of certain commodities, for example.

Countries with comparatively open economic systems can use similar devices to restrict imports or capital flows to balance their international payments, but such measures would make their economies less open and policymakers therefore usually avoid them. More often, nations committed to maintaining an open economy cope with balance-of-payments problems by trying to reduce the level of their economic activity at home or to adjust their currency's exchange rates.

States can finance balance-of-payments deficits if they have access to financial assets in the form of foreign currency reserves or loans from multilateral agencies or other countries. The International Monetary Fund (IMF), a specialized agency of the United Nations, is an important source of funds for states experiencing temporary balance-of-payments shortfalls. Often, however, the IMF will provide assistance only if the borrowing state promises to undertake domestic reforms to correct the economic problems that may have caused the deficits. Such reforms are usually difficult to institute politically because they typically require domestic sacrifices that affect employment opportunities and the standard of living. Indeed, whether a state's economic

---

[1] "Open" and "closed" are useful conventions for classifying differences between economic systems, but they are relative terms. No economy is completely open or closed, as every system has, to a greater or lesser extent, ingredients of both types. Which political model for the management of national economies is most conducive to growth and welfare is the subject of much controversy (see Lindblom, 1977; Olson, 1982; Reich, 1983).

system is open or closed, adjustments in international economic transactions produce important domestic consequences. For this reason, all states are sensitive to the organization and conduct of their commercial relations with others.

Realism, Relative Gains, and International Cooperation

Rules governing international commerce—like those governing international politics—often evolve according to the wishes of the stronger players. Historically, these have been the advanced capitalist societies of the Western industrialized world, particularly Britain in the nineteenth century and the United States in the twentieth century. Both used their military superiority and economic advantage to create international economic regimes in which market forces played a powerful role and enjoyed more legitimacy than state intervention and control. The economic order created following World War II is described as an "open" or "liberal" international regime because it minimized government interference in its operation.

How states respond to economic challenges is dependent not only on how they organize their domestic structures but also on their position in the international pecking order governed by rules often made by others. Concern for their position in the pecking order helps to explain why states sometimes pursue goals that may be rational in the short run but that can easily undermine the prospects for international cooperation, and hence the long-term benefits that cooperation with others might bring. In other words, it helps us to understand why international cooperation designed to achieve mutual gain is so difficult.

According to the theory of political realism, described in Chapter 2, the anarchical character of the international system explains why states shun cooperation. Anarchy creates fear. Because states fear one another, they are wary of any movement on the part of others that might threaten the realization of their goals. Moreover, because the international system is a self-help system, states alone are responsible for their survival and well-being. Thus, fear and uncertainty explain why each "spends a portion of its effort, not forwarding its own good, but in providing the means of protecting itself against others" (Waltz, 1979).

The fear that breeds competition and militates against cooperation is especially evident in the high politics of peace and security, but it also applies to the low politics of material well-being and explains why even here cooperation may fall victim to calculations of short-term benefit. "Even if nation-states do not fear for their physical survival, they worry that a decrease in their power capabilities relative to those of other nation-states will compromise their political autonomy, expose them to the influence attempts of others, or lessen their ability to prevail in political disputes with allies and adversaries" (Mastanduno, 1991). Thus states are concerned not only with *absolute gains* in their material well-being but also with how they fare in comparison with others, their *relative gains*.

Concern for relative gains explains why states seek not only to increase their own power but also to prevent the relative power advancement of others (Grieco, 1988a,

1988b, 1990). Thus they often behave in a *defensively positional* manner on issues of international economic policy. Hence the distinction between absolute and relative gains provides insight into the way that politics shapes economics, even in an interdependent world, and why states in an anarchical society often recoil from cooperation as they seek to promote and protect their parochial interests.

Hegemony and Hegemonic Stability

Without the regulatory authority of a government, nation-states must rely on self-help measures to protect their interests. Still, they routinely engage in various forms of cooperation, notably economic transactions, and they can do so because, paradoxically, order and predictability characterize the anarchical international system.

The theory of political realism explains the anarchy-order paradox by drawing attention to the role that power balances play in thwarting the aspirations of dominance-seeking powers. *Hegemonic stability theory*, on the other hand, focuses not on a balance of power among contending states but on the preponderance of one, a hegemon, which serves as the stabilizer of the system. In particular, the theory captures the special roles and responsibilities of the major economic powers in a commercial order based on market forces.

Hegemons' Roles, Responsibilities, and Benefits

Hegemony refers to a preponderance of power and influence. As applied to the world political economy, it describes a "preponderance of material resources," of which four sets are especially important. "Hegemonic powers must have control over raw materials, control over sources of capital, control over markets, and competitive advantages in the production of highly valued goods" (Keohane, 1984).

From their vantage points as preponderant powers, hegemons are able to promote rules for the system as a whole that protect their own interests. Capitalist hegemons, like Britain and the United States, prefer open systems because their comparatively greater control of technology, capital, and raw materials gives them more opportunities to profit from a system free of nonmarket restraints. More broadly, the "ideology [of capitalism] is cosmopolitan. Capitalism in just one state would undoubtedly be an impossibility" (Gilpin, 1987).

Capitalist states also have special responsibilities. They must ensure nations facing balance-of-payments deficits that they will find the credits necessary to finance their deficits. If the most powerful states cannot do this, they are likely to move toward more closed domestic economies, which may undermine the open international system otherwise advantageous to them (Block, 1977). Generally, hegemonic powers must "be willing and able to furnish an outlet for distress goods, maintain the flow of capital to would-be borrowers, serve as a lender of last resort in financial crises, maintain a structure of exchange rates, and coordinate macroeconomic politics" (Isaak, 1991). In short, those most able to influence the system also have the greatest responsibility for its effective operation.

As hegemons exercise their responsibilities they confer benefits known as public or collective goods.[2] National security is a public or *collective good* that governments provide to all of their citizens, regardless of the resources that individuals contribute through taxation. In world politics, "international security, monetary stability and an open international economy, with relatively free and predictable ability to move goods, services and capital are all seen as desirable public goods. . . . More generally, international economic order is to be preferred to disorder" (Gill and Law, 1988).

Those who enjoy the benefits of collective goods but pay little or nothing for them are *free riders*. Hegemons typically tolerate free riders, partly because the benefits hegemons provide encourage other states to accept their dictates.

Analysts regard the international economist Charles Kindleberger (1973) as the father of hegemonic stability theory because he was the first to theorize about the order and stability that preponderant powers provide as he sought to explain the Great Depression of the 1930s. Kindleberger concluded that "the international economic and monetary system needs leadership, a country which is prepared, consciously or unconsciously, . . . to set standards of conduct for other countries, and to seek to get others to follow them, to take on an undue share of the burdens of the system." Britain played this role from the Congress of Vienna in 1815 until the outbreak of World War I in 1914, and the United States assumed the British mantle in the decades immediately following World War II. In the interwar years, however, Britain was unable to play its previous role as leader, and the United States, although capable of leadership, was unwilling to exercise it. The lacuna, Kindleberger concluded, was a principal cause of the national and international economic traumas of the 1930s. Thus he attributed the "width and depth" of the Great Depression "to the absence of a leading power willing and able to bear a disproportionate share of the costs to discharge the responsibilities of a stabilizer" (Isaak, 1991).

As argued by Kindleberger, the leadership Britain and the United States provided was positive and their hegemony "benign." Other theorists take a different view. Indeed, the term "hegemony" itself often has negative connotations, suggesting an oppressive, exploitative, and sometimes coercive relationship between a leader and those it leads.

Those who subscribe to the "malign" view of hegemony (for example, Gilpin, 1981) argue that, even though hegemons provide order (a public good) that benefits subordinate states, they do so through coercive rather than benevolent leadership. That is, a hegemon enforces rules with positive and negative sanctions. The United States, for example, allegedly acted as "a quasi-government by providing public goods *and* taxing other states to pay for them" (Snidal, 1985). Subordinate states may have been reluctant to be taxed, but the preponderant power of the United States forced them into submission. "The focus of the theory [of hegemonic stability from this viewpoint] thus shifts from the ability to provide a public good to the ability to coerce other states" (Snidal, 1985). In this sense there is a close correspondence between the

---

[2] It is sometimes useful to distinguish between public and collective goods. Here we treat them synonymously. Both may be defined as goods that are jointly supplied and from which it is not possible to exclude beneficiaries on a selective basis.

stability and order that hegemons provide and that ensured by power balances among dominance-seeking states or coalitions.[3]

International Stability and Hegemonic Decline

What happens when hegemonic powers decline? If the theory of hegemonic stability is correct, instability and disorder will result. In the extreme, global war may follow, much as the hegemonic decline of Britain and absence of U.S. leadership may have precipitated the two world wars of the twentieth century.

The United States assumed the leadership mantle following World War II, of course, and it was clearly preponderant from then until the mid-1970s (see Kennedy, 1987). Hegemonic stability theory predicts that this, then, should have been an orderly period, and for the most part it was. Since the 1970s, however, instability and disorder have racked the world political economy. Simultaneously the relative power position of the United States has declined measurably.

An array of evidence points to the changing role of the United States in the world political economy. In 1947 it accounted for 50 percent of the combined gross world product. It was also the world's preeminent manufacturing center and leading exporter, and its monopoly of the atomic bomb gave it military superiority. By 1960, however, the U.S. share of gross world product had slipped to 28 percent, by 1970 to 25 percent, and by 1980 to 23 percent. During the 1980s the proportion hovered around the 24–26 percent mark, but the U.S. share of both "old manufactures," such as steel and automobiles, and "new manufactures," such as microelectronics and computers, continued to decline. Moreover, labor productivity was often greater in other industrial nations, which also exhibited personal saving rates that far surpassed those in the United States. At the same time the U.S. share of world financial reserves declined precipitously and its dependence on foreign energy sources, first evident in the early 1970s, continued unabated into the 1990s.[4] Thus in all the areas essential to hegemony—control over raw materials, capital, and markets, and competitive advantages in the production of valued goods—U.S. preponderance has waned.

Despite this and other evidence of U.S. decline relative to other advanced industrial states (notably Germany and Japan, which are regarded as the principal economic competitors of the United States), controversy rages over the meaning of the evidence

---

[3] Hegemonic stability theory is a form of realist theory, known as structural realism, not an alternative to it. Although many structural realists are more concerned with cooperative international behavior than with conflict and emphasize the role of international regimes in the maintenance of order (see, for example, Keohane, 1984), their primary emphasis is on the role that the distribution of economic capabilities plays in promoting cooperation and in the creation and maintenance of international regimes. The impact of domestic politics on international outcomes, a central concern of the transnational and complex interdependence perspective outlined in Chapter 2, is generally ignored. For an effort to incorporate domestic politics into realist theory, see Mastanduno, Lake, and Ikenberry (1989).

[4] Data on U.S. energy dependence are examined in Chapter 10. The U.S. share of world financial reserves is from Goldstein (1988: 354). The other data cited here are from Block (1981: 13–14) and U.S. Central Intelligence Agency (1988: 30, 16, 18, 58).

and the probable impact of the seeming decline of the United States on its national security and foreign economic policies.[5]

Not in dispute, however, is that the United States no longer controls international outcomes in the way that it once did. This is especially so in the world political economy, where economic policy coordination and a sharing of leadership among multiple centers of power have become the norm. Still, cooperation in the maintenance of the LIEO has often been strained, as the interests of individual states and groups of states have led them to pursue policies that run counter to the (classical) liberal conviction that free markets and free trade will produce global economic prosperity.

The role of the United States in the world political economy relates intimately to the relative gains problem and to the calculus that leads states to cooperate or not to cooperate in pursuit of material welfare under conditions of anarchy. Hegemonic powers typically are less concerned about their relative power position than others. Thus they are unlikely to behave in a defensively positional manner on international economic policy issues, especially compared with aspiring hegemons or others that may feel that their relative power position is deteriorating. As a hegemon's preponderance erodes, however, its behavior on trade and related welfare issues can be expected to change.

> As [the hegemon's] relative economic power declines, it will feel that it is less able to afford, and thus less likely to tolerate, "free riding" by its allies that works to its relative economic disadvantage. Furthermore, as commonly perceived military threats diminish [as has happened with the end of the Cold War], the hegemonic state will be less inclined, in economic disputes with its allies, to subordinate its national economic interests to the pursuit of political harmony or solidarity within the alliance. In short, the transformation of international economic and security structures should inspire a dominant state to act more as an "ordinary country," and strive for relative economic advantage in relations with its allies. (Mastanduno, 1991: 81–82)

In this new context the order and stability that the United States once provided alone is now often attributed to the influence of *international regimes* (see Chapter 6). Most of the international regimes that today govern the world political economy were created during the era of U.S. preponderance, but they have continued to flourish as the world has grown more interdependent. This may explain why the magnitude and extent of disruptions predicted by the relative decline of U.S. power have not (yet?) materialized.[6] Nonetheless, many developments in the world political economy are

---

[5] For contrasting viewpoints, see Dietrich (1992), Kennedy (1987), Nau (1990), and Nye (1990). Although especially relevant to American foreign policy, these studies are part of a large corpus of theory and evidence that speaks to the causes and consequences of the rise and decline of hegemonic powers. In addition to Robert Gilpin's (1981) work cited above, Goldstein (1988), Modelski (1987), and Thompson (1988) are illustrative.

[6] The role that international institutions play in promoting order and stability under conditions of anarchy is a hotly debated issue among neorealists. Axelrod and Keohane (1985) make a theoretical case for cooperation under conditions of anarchy. Other studies relevant to the debate cited here and elsewhere in this chapter include Grieco (1988a, 1988b, 1990), Keohane (1984), Mastanduno (1991), Mastanduno, Lake, and Ikenberry (1989), Snidal (1991a, 1991b), and Waltz (1979).

potentially disruptive. It is to these, and to the historical context in which they emerged, that we now turn, beginning with changes in the international monetary regime.

The Transformation of the International Monetary Regime . . . . . .

The international and domestic economies are different because nations do not use the same currencies. In the absence of an international government, there is no common currency all states can use to carry on their financial transactions and settle their international accounts. If nations are to trade or engage in other financial transactions with one another, they must devise a mechanism to determine the relative value of their currencies. Thus the monetary system establishes a common framework for commercial interactions in the presence of a multitude of individual, national currencies.

Currency rates of exchange express the value of one currency (say, the German mark) in relation to another (such as the U.S. dollar). A combination of governmental and market forces typically determines a currency's rate of exchange.

Because currency rates are somewhat under the control of governments (more so in closed economies than in open ones), changes in them become potential adjustment mechanisms to deal with other economic problems. Changes will affect the relative attractiveness of a country's exports to foreign buyers and of its imports to domestic consumers. A currency *devaluation*, for example, will make exports cheaper and imports more expensive. As with a reducton in imports of goods or capital, a currency devaluation will not change the market, but it can change the quality of social life. If a country has a balance-of-payments deficit, for instance, lowering either the level of economic activity (deflation) or the exchange rate (devaluation) will reduce its international expenditures while increasing its revenues. Both adjustment techniques work by lowering the level of employment and the level of income in the deficit country.

Devising mechanisms to determine the value of nations' currencies in relation to one another was among the tasks the World War II Allies faced as they began planning for the postwar world. In the international economic sphere the rules, institutions, and decision-making procedures they devised became known as the Bretton Woods system. The name comes from the New Hampshire conference site where, in 1944, agreements were negotiated that sought to create a postwar international monetary regime characterized by stability, predictability, and orderly growth. The agreements assigned governments primary responsibility for enforcing the rules and otherwise making the system work effectively. They also anticipated that the International Monetary Fund, created at Bretton Woods, would serve as a formal mechanism to help states deal with such matters as maintaining equilibrium in their balance of payments and stability in their exchange rates with one another. The International Bank for Reconstruction and Development (IBRD), now commonly known as the World Bank, was also created to facilitate recovery from the war. The IMF continues to perform the functions expected at the time of Bretton Woods, but the primary purpose of the World Bank has since shifted to promoting Third World economic development (see Box 7.1 on page 220).

The U.S. Role in the Bretton Woods Regime

Although the International Monetary Fund and the World Bank have become important instruments for the effective operation of the international economic system, they enjoyed too little authority and had too few financial resources in the immediate post–World War II period to cope with the enormous devastation the war had caused. For these reasons they proved incapable of managing postwar economic recovery. The United States stepped into the breach.[7]

Unchallenged Hegemony

The U.S. dollar became the key to the role that the United States assumed as manager of the international monetary system. Backed by a vigorous and healthy economy, a fixed relationship between gold and the dollar (that is, $35 per ounce of gold), and a commitment by the government to exchange gold for dollars at any time (known as *dollar convertibility)*, the dollar became "as good as gold." In fact, it was preferable to gold for use by other countries to manage their balance-of-payments and savings accounts. Dollars earned interest, which gold did not; they did not incur storage and insurance costs; and they were needed to buy imports necessary for survival and postwar reconstruction. Thus the postwar economic system was not simply a modified gold standard system; it was a dollar-based system. Dollars became a major component of the international reserves used by national monetary authorities in other countries and of the "working balances" used by private banks, corporations, and individuals for international trade and capital transactions.

In addition to these functions, the dollar became a *parallel currency:* It was universally accepted as the "currency against which every other country sold or redeemed its own national currency in the exchange markets" (Triffin, 1978–1979). To maintain the value of their currencies, central banks in other countries either bought or sold their own currencies, using the dollar to raise or depress their value. Such intervention was often necessary, because under the Bretton Woods agreement states had committed themselves to keeping fluctuations in their exchange rates within very narrow limits. In other words, the Bretton Woods monetary regime was based on *fixed exchange rates*, which ultimately required a measure of government intervention for its preservation.

A central problem of the immediate postwar years was how to get U.S. dollars into the hands of those who needed them most. One vehicle was the Marshall Plan, which provided Western European nations with $17 billion in assistance with which to buy the U.S. goods necessary to rebuild their war-torn economies. The United

---

[7] Our discussion of the international monetary system draws on Spero (1990). See also Walters and Blake (1992).

Box 7.1
The Bretton Woods Conference and Its Twin Institutions

• • •

The International Monetary and Financial Conference of the United and Associated Nations was convened in Bretton Woods, New Hampshire, on July 1, 1944. By the time the conference ended on July 22, 1944, based on substantial preparatory work, it had defined the outlines of the postwar international economic system. The conference also resulted in the creation of the International Monetary Fund (IMF) and the International Bank for Reconstruction and Development (IBRD, or the World Bank)—the Bretton Woods twins.

The World Bank was to assist in reconstruction and development by facilitating the flow and investment of capital for productive purposes. The International Monetary Fund was to facilitate the expansion and balanced growth of international trade and to contribute thereby to the promotion and maintenance of high levels of employment and real income. Also discussed at Bretton Woods were plans for an International Trade Organization (ITO). This institution did not materialize, but some of its proposed functions are performed by the General Agreement on Tariffs and Trade (GATT), which was established in 1947.

The discussion at Bretton Woods took place with the experience of the interwar period as background. In the 1930s every major country sought ways to defend itself against deflationary pressures from abroad—some by exchange depreciation, some by introducing flexible exchange rates or multiple rates, some by direct controls over imports and other international transactions. The disastrous consequences of such policies—economic depression with very high unemployment—are well known. The participants in the Bretton Woods conference were determined to design an international economic system where "beggar-thy-neighbor" policies, which characterized the international economic community when World War II began, did not recur. There was also a widespread fear that the end of World War II would be followed by a slump, as had the end of World War I.

Thus the central elements of the system outlined at Bretton Woods were the establishment of convertibility of currencies and of fixed but adjustable exchange rates, and the encouragement of international flows of capital for productive purposes. The IMF and the World Bank were to assist in the attainment of these objectives. The economic accomplishments of the postwar period are in part the result of the effectiveness of these institutions.

Source: World Development Report, 1985. *Copyright 1985 by The International Bank for Reconstruction and Development/The World Bank. Reprinted by permission of Oxford University Press, Inc., p. 15.*

States also encouraged deficits in its own balance of payments as a way of providing international liquidity in the form of dollars.

In addition to providing liquidity, the United States assumed a disproportionate share of the burden of rejuvenating Western Europe and Japan. It supported European and Japanese trade competitiveness, permitted certain forms of protectionism (such as Japan's restrictions against products imported from the United States), and condoned discrimination against the dollar (as in the European Payments Union, a multilateral European group that promoted intra-European trade at the expense of trade with the United States). The United States willingly incurred these short-run costs because the growth that they were expected to stimulate in Europe and Japan was expected eventually to provide widening markets for U.S. exports. The perceived political benefits of strengthening the Western world against the threat of communism helped to rationalize acceptance of these economic costs.

"The system worked well. Europe and Japan recovered and then expanded. The U.S. economy prospered partly because of the dollar outflow, which led to the purchase of U.S. goods and services" (Spero, 1990). Furthermore, the top currency role of the dollar facilitated the U.S. ability to pursue a globalist foreign policy. Indeed, U.S. foreign economic and military aid programs were made possible by acceptance of the dollar as the means of paying for them. Business interests could readily expand abroad because U.S. foreign investments were often considered desirable, and American tourists could spend their dollars with few restrictions. In effect, the United States operated as the world's banker. Other countries had to balance their financial inflows and outflows. In contrast, the United States enjoyed the advantages of operating internationally without the constraints of limited finances. The dominant position of the United States also meant that its internal economic circumstances affected other nations in significant ways. Through the ubiquitous dollar, the United States thus came to exert considerable influence on the political and economic affairs of most other nations.

Yet there were costs. The enormous number of dollars held by others made the U.S. domestic economy vulnerable to financial shocks abroad. U.S. policymakers of course sought to insulate the U.S. economy from these shocks, but their task was made more difficult because some tools available to others were proscribed by the status of the dollar as a reserve currency.

For most countries an imbalance in their balance of payments is readily corrected by raising or lowering their currency exchange rate. But this simple mechanism, which lies at the heart of international financial adjustments, was more difficult for the United States because of the dollar's pivotal role. Devaluation of the dollar, for example, would adversely affect political friends and military allies who had chosen to hold large amounts of dollars as reserve currency—and who were especially important in the context of U.S. competition with Soviet communism. Furthermore, a devaluation could easily be offset by others adversely affected by the U.S. action simply by devaluing their own currencies. Understandably, therefore, the United States was reluctant to devalue the dollar.

By the late 1950s concern began to mount about the long-term viability of an international monetary system based on the dollar (see Triffin, 1978–1979). Analysts worried that such a system would be unable to provide the world with the monetary reserves necessary to ensure growing economic activity. They also feared that the number of foreign-held dollars would eventually overwhelm the ability of the United States to convert them into gold. This undermined the confidence others had in the soundness of the dollar and the U.S. economy and led eventually to a severing of the link between the dollar and gold.

Hegemony under Stress

As early as 1960 it was clear that the dollar's top currency status was on the wane. Subsequently, the dollar-based international monetary system unilaterally managed by the United States became increasingly a multilaterally managed system under U.S. leadership. There are several reasons for the dollar's declining position.

If too few dollars was the problem in the immediate postwar years, by the 1960s the problem became one of too many dollars. The costs of extensive U.S. military activities, foreign economic and military aid, and massive private investments produced increasing balance-of-payments deficits. Although encouraged earlier, the deficits were by this time out of control. Furthermore, U.S. gold holdings in relation to the growing number of foreign-held dollars fell precipitously. Given these circumstances, the possibility that the United States might devalue the dollar led to a loss of confidence by others and to their unwillingness to continue to hold dollars as reserve currency. Under the leadership of Charles de Gaulle, France went so far as to insist on exchanging dollars for gold, although admittedly in part for reasons related more to French nationalism than to the viability of the U.S. economy.

Along with the glut of dollars, the increasing monetary interdependence of the First World's industrial economies led to massive transnational movements of capital. The internationalization of banking, the internationalization of production via multinational corporations, and the development of a Eurocurrency market outside direct state control all accelerated this interdependence.[8] An increasingly complex relationship between the economic policies engineered in one country and their effects on another was the result. This in turn spawned a variety of comparatively formal groupings of the central bankers and finance ministers from the leading economic powers who devised various *ad hoc* solutions to their common problems. The decision was also made to create a form of "paper gold" known as Special Drawing Rights (SDRs) in the IMF to facilitate the growth of international liquidity by means other than increasing the outflow of dollars.[9]

Although the United States was the chief proponent and supporter of the various management techniques devised during the 1960s, none proved sufficient to counter the "dollar crises" that surfaced in the late 1960s and early 1970s. An important reason

---

[8] Eurocurrencies are dollars and other currencies held in Europe as bank deposits and lent and borrowed outside the country of origin.

[9] SDRs are reserve assets that nations' central banks agree to accept to settle their official financial transactions. Because their value is set in relation to a "basket" of major currencies, SDRs tend to be more stable than either gold or a single currency.

underlying these crises is that the Bretton Woods regime never operated in quite the way it was intended.

The Bretton Woods system obligated each country to maintain the value of its currency in relation to the U.S. dollar (and through it to all others) within the confines of the agreed-upon exchange rate. The purpose was to stabilize and render predictable the value of the currencies needed to carry on international financial transactions. The rules permitted states to devalue their currencies if maintenance of the agreed-upon rates became difficult due to persistent structural weaknesses in a nation's economy. Despite this provision, devaluations "proved to be traumatic politically and economically. . . . [They] were taken as indications of weakness and economic failure by states and, thus, were resisted" (Walters and Blake, 1992).

Other changes in the international political economy also contributed to states' unwillingness to continue to hold U.S. dollars. By the 1960s the European and Japanese recovery from World War II was complete, which meant that U.S. monetary dominance and the dollar's privileged position were no longer politically acceptable. The United States nonetheless continued to exercise a disproportionate influence over these others states, even while it was unreceptive to their criticisms.

The Europeans and Japanese especially came to resent the prerogatives that the United States derived from its position as the world's banker and from its ability to determine the level of international liquidity through its balance-of-payments deficits. Not only did these prerogatives affect their economies; they also enabled the United States to spend money for foreign policy purposes with which they disagreed. U. S. involvement in Vietnam was a primary example. Détente between the United States and the Soviet Union, the superpowers' official policy beginning in 1969, also eroded the willingness of others to follow U.S. leadership. In this case the reason is that it lessened the military threat that had induced the industrial powers to subordinate their economic disagreements to enhance Western security.

The United States, of course, had enjoyed its preponderant status for years. It therefore came to see its own economic health and that of the world political economy as one and the same. In the case of the monetary regime in particular, U.S. leaders treasured the dollar's status as the top currency and interpreted attacks on it as attacks on international economic stability (see Walters and Blake, 1992). That view in turn reflected the interests and prerogatives of a hegemon. Fred L. Block elaborates:

> The exercise of American political and military power on a global basis [had] been designed to gain foreign acceptance of an international monetary order that institutionalizes an open world economy, giving maximum opportunities to American businessmen. It would be absurd for the United States to abandon its global ambitions simply to live within the rules of an international monetary order that was shaped for the purpose of achieving these amibitions. So it [was] hardly surprising that the United States continued to pursue its global ambitions despite the increasing strains on the international monetary order. The fundamental contradiction was that the United States had created an international monetary order that worked only when American political and economic dominance in the capitalist world was absolute. That absolute dominance disappeared as a result of the reconstruction of Western Europe and Japan, on the one hand, and the accumulated domestic costs of the global extension of U.S. power, on the other. With the fading of the absolute dominance,

the international monetary order began to crumble. The U.S. [balance-of-payments] deficit was simply the most dramatic symptom of the terminal disease that plagued the postwar international monetary order. (Block, 1977: 163)

Hegemony in Decline

The United States sought to stave off challenges to its leadership role, but its own deteriorating economic situation made that increasingly difficult. Mounting infla-tion—caused in part by the unwillingness of the Johnson administration to raise taxes to pay either for the Vietnam War or the Great Society at home—was particularly troublesome, as it reduced the competitiveness of U.S. goods overseas.

Historically, the United States had enjoyed favorable balances of trade. This was important, because the trade surpluses were used to offset its balance-of-payments deficits, which by the end of the 1960s had become chronic. In 1971, for the first time in the twentieth century, the United States actually suffered a modest trade deficit (of $2 billion). This deficit worsened thereafter. As a result, demands by industrial, labor, and agricultural interests for protectionist trade measures designed to insulate them from foreign economic competition began to grow.

Policymakers laid partial blame for the trade deficit at the doorstep of major U.S. trading partners. Japan and West Germany in particular were criticized for maintaining undervalued currencies (that is, currencies that did not accurately reflect the cost of goods in those countries). This made their goods attractive internationally (and to the American consumer), which in turn enabled these countries to generate balance-of-payments surpluses by selling more overseas than they bought. At the same time, the relative position of the United States in international trade was deteriorating, as the U.S. share of international trade declined and Europe's and Japan's increased.

Faced with these circumstances, the United States took several steps to shore up the sagging U.S. position in the world political economy. In August 1971 President Richard M. Nixon abruptly announced that the United States would no longer exchange dollars for gold. He also imposed a surcharge on imports into the United States as part of a strategy designed to force a realignment of others' currency exchange rates. These startling and unexpected decisions, which came as a shock to the other Western industrial nations, marked the end of the Bretton Woods regime.

A system of free-floating exchange rates replaced the Bretton Woods fixed exchange-rate system. In this kind of system, market forces rather than government intervention determine currency values. The theory underlying the Bretton Woods replacement is that a country experiencing adverse economic conditions will see the value of its currency in the marketplace decline in response to the choices of traders, bankers, and business people. This will make its exports cheaper and its imports more expensive, which this in turn will pull the value of its currency back toward equilib-rium—all without the need for central bankers to support their currencies (see Box 7.2 on page 226).

Based on the theory underlying a free-floating exchange-rate system, policymakers hoped that the politically humiliating devaluations of the past could be avoided. What they did not foresee was that the new system would introduce an unparalleled degree of uncertainty and unpredictability into international monetary affairs.

The strident actions taken by the U.S. in 1971 were in part a reaction to its growing dependence on the rest of the world and its realization that it could no longer unilaterally regulate international monetary affairs. In this sense its actions were a predictable response to the U.S. decline in the world political economy. For the political economy as a whole, it was now clear that the political basis on which the Bretton Woods system had been built lay in ruins. U.S. leadership was no longer accepted willingly by others or exercised willingly by the United States. Power had come to be more widely dispersed among states, and the shared interests that once bound them together had dissipated.

From Hegemony Toward Multilateral Management

The world political economy would face serious challenges in the wake of Bretton Woods' demise. Where hegemony once reigned, various groups of industrial nations now evolved a series of quasi-official negotiating forums to cope with monetary and other economic stresses.

The OPEC Decade

Formal negotiations on reform of the international monetary system began in 1972. Before new agreements were devised, however, policymakers faced new crises in the form of two oil shocks administered by the Organization of Petroleum Exporting Countries (OPEC). The first came in 1973–1974, shortly after the 1973 Yom Kippur War in the Middle East, when the price of oil increased fourfold. The second occurred in 1979–1980 in the wake of the revolution in Iran and resulted in an even more dramatic jump in the world price of oil.

Since the U.S. is the world's largest energy consumer, the impact of the two oil shocks on the United States was especially pronounced, all the more so as each coincided with a decline in domestic energy production and a rise in consumption. A dramatic increase in U.S. dependence on foreign sources of energy to fuel its advanced industrial economy and a sharp rise in the overall cost of U.S. imports resulted.

As dollars flowed abroad to purchase energy resources (a record $40 billion in 1977 and $74 billion in 1980), others began to worry about the dollar's value—which augmented its marked decline on foreign exchange markets in the late 1970s and early 1980s. Demand for oil in the United States and elsewhere softened in the early 1980s as a consequence of conservation measures, economic recession, and a shift to alternative sources of energy. Oil prices also began to ease as a result and then plummeted in 1986, due largely to the worldwide oil glut that followed the decision of key members of OPEC to increase their output in an effort to regain market shares lost earlier to others. The decline in oil prices helped to contain inflation and stimulated economic growth in the United States and elsewhere. Simultaneously, the dollar experienced a rapid surge in value (see Figure 7.1 on page 228). Thus the world political economy weathered the immediate effects of the two OPEC oil shocks. However, their long-term effects would persist for years.

Box 7.2
WHY DO EXCHANGE RATES FLUCTUATE?

• • •

Money works in several ways and serves different purposes: It must be acceptable, so that people earning it can use it to buy goods and services from others. It must serve as a store of value, so that people will be willing to keep some of their wealth in the form of money. And it must be a standard of deferred payment, so that people will be willing to lend money knowing that when the money owed them is repaid in the future, it will still have purchasing power.

Inflation occurs when the government creates too much money in relation to the goods and services produced in an economy. As money becomes more plentiful and hence less acceptable, it cannot serve well as a store of value or a medium of exchange to satisfy debts. Governments work to make certain that their currencies do the jobs intended for them, which means, among other things, that they try to maintain an inflation-free environment.

In the international monetary system, movements in a nation's exchange rate occur in part when changes occur in assessments made of the underlying economic strength of a country or the ability of its government to maintain the value of its money change. A deficit in a country's balance of payments, for example, would likely cause a decline in the value of its currency relative to others, because the supply of the currency would be greater than the demand for it. Similarly, when those engaged in international economic transactions change their expectations about the future value of a currency, they might reschedule their lending and borrowing; fluctuations in the exchange rate could follow.

Speculators—those who buy and sell money in an effort to make it—may also affect the stability of a nation's currency internationally. Professional speculators make money be making guesses about the future. If, for example, they believe that the Japanese yen will be worth more in, say, three months than it is now, they can buy yen today and sell them for a profit three months hence. Conversely, if they believe that the dollar will be worth less in ninety days, they can sell some number of yen today for a certain number of dollars and then buy back the same yen in ninety days for fewer dollars, thus making a profit.

On what basis do speculators make these kinds of decisions? One is their reading of the health of the currency in which they are speculating. If they believe the U.S. dollar is weak because the U.S. economy itself is weak, they may conclude that the U.S. government will permit a devaluation of the dollar. Another, closely related consideration is whether a government is perceived as having the political will to devise effective policies to ensure the value of its money, particularly against inflation. If speculators think that it does not, they would again be wise to sell dollars today and buy them back tomorrow at the (anticipated) lower price. In the process, of course, speculators may create self-fulfilling prophecies: They may "prove" that the dollar needs to be devalued simply because of the volume of seemingly unwanted dollars offered for sale.

In the same way that governments seek to protect the value of their currencies at home, they try to protect them internationally by intervening in the marketplace. Their willingness to do so is especially important to importers and exporters, who depend on orderliness and predictability in the value of the currencies they deal in to carry on their transnational exchanges. Governments intervene when nations' central banks buy or sell currencies to change the value of their own currencies in relation to others. Unlike speculators, however, they are pledged not to manipulate exchange rates so as to gain unfair advantage.

The Aftermath of the OPEC Decade

Global economic recession followed each oil shock. The close relationship between the changing fortunes of the dollar and the price of oil was due in part to the way in which the leading industrial powers chose to cope with the recessions. In response to the first, they relied on fiscal and monetary adjustments to stimulate economic recovery and to avoid unemployment levels deemed politically unacceptable. In response to the second, which proved to be the longest and most severe economic downturn since the Great Depression of the 1930s, they shifted their efforts to controlling inflation through strict monetarist policies (that is, policies designed to reduce the money supply in the economy). Large fiscal deficits and sharply higher interest rates resulted. Both were particularly apparent in the United States. The other industrial nations also experienced higher levels of unemployment than they had been willing to tolerate before.

In an era of complex interdependence, none could escape the impact of these developments, including Third World nations. In response to the two oil shocks, many developing countries borrowed extensively from abroad to pay for the increased cost of energy as a way to prevent reductions in domestic economic activity. Borrowing was possible because of the billions of "petrodollars" that flowed to the oil-producing states and that private banks and various multilateral institutions helped to recycle. In the process, however, the debt burden of many nations assumed ominous proportions, particularly as interest rates climbed following the second oil shock. The threat of massive defaults by countries unable to service their debts pushed the international monetary regime to the brink of crisis in the early 1980s and again at mid-decade. The crisis atmosphere receded later, but the debt problem persisted (see Chapter 8).

High interest rates in the United States compared with others not only contributed to the debt burden of Third World states; they also contributed measurably to the changing fortunes of the U.S. dollar as increased demand for dollars drove up the exchange rate. Renewed economic growth in the United States, a sharp reduction in inflation, and the perception that the United States was a safe haven for financial investments in a world otherwise marked by political instability and violence also helped to restore faith in the dollar. Foreign investors therefore rushed to acquire the dollars necessary to take advantage of profitable investment opportunities in the United States. This situation

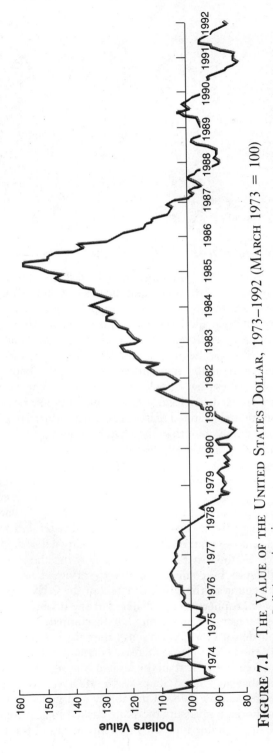

FIGURE 7.1 THE VALUE OF THE UNITED STATES DOLLAR, 1973–1992 (MARCH 1973 = 100)

Source: Federal Reserve Bulletin, various issues.

Note: The index is the weighted average value of the U.S. dollar against the currencies of the other nine major industrialized nations plus Switzerland.

contrasted sharply with the 1970s, when the huge foreign indebtedness of the United States, often called the "dollar overhang," was a principal fear.

For the United States, the appreciation of the dollar was a mixed blessing. On the one hand, it reduced the cost of imported oil. On the other hand, it increased the cost of U.S. exports to foreign buyers, thus reducing the competitiveness of U.S. products in overseas markets. This meant the loss of tens of thousands of jobs in U.S. industries that produced for export. It also resulted in a series of record trade deficits—$122 billion in 1985, $145 billion in 1986, and $160 billion in 1987—as imports from abroad became relatively cheaper and hence more attractive to American consumers.

The budget deficit of the U.S. government also reached record portions at this time, topping $200 billion annually. Simultaneously, the United States became for the first time in more than half a century a debtor nation as it moved in the short span of only five years from being the world's biggest creditor to being its largest debtor. The debt legacy would eventually constrain the policy choices the government could draw upon to deal with later economic downturns (Aho and Levinson, 1988–1989; Aho and Stokes, 1991), as happened with the prolonged recession that began in 1990.

For a time during the 1980s the high levels of U.S. government spending alongside its staggering budget deficits sustained high interest rates, which in turn triggered a rise in the value of the dollar. Eventually, however, the chronic trade and budget deficits became overwhelming, precipitating a long decline in the value of the dollar from the lofty heights it had achieved by mid-decade (see Figure 7.1). A renewed sense of global economic uncertainty plagued decision makers in the advanced industrial societies, whose economic fates had become increasingly intertwined. Their interdependence was dramatized in October 1987, when stock prices in markets throughout the world plummeted overnight, resulting in billions of dollars in lost equity throughout the world. The shocking events demonstrated the existence of an interdependent global market, as well as the extent to which its health critically depended on the value of the U.S. dollar and the underlying health of its economy.

Macroeconomic Policy Coordination

Historically, the United States had been loath to intervene in the international marketplace to affect the value of the dollar. By 1985, however, the erosion of U.S. trade competitiveness in overseas markets due to the overvalued dollar had become unpalatable domestically (Destler and Henning, 1989). In response, the Group of Five (the United States, Britain, France, Japan, and West Germany) met secretly in the Plaza Hotel in New York and decided on a coordinated effort to bring down the overvalued dollar. The landmark agreement proved important not only because it signaled an end to the benign neglect toward the consequences of interdependence that the United States had previously exhibited. It also committed the major economic powers to a coordinated effort to manage exchange rates internationally and interest rates domestically, and it signaled the emergence of Japan as a full partner in international monetary management (Spero, 1990).

The Plaza agreement failed to realize all the goals that had been intended, however. The Group of Five financial ministers therefore reconvened in Paris at the Louvre in early 1987 to again discuss international monetary management. Japan moved in the aftermath of Louvre away from its export-led economic strategy toward one designed to stimulate domestic demand (see Balassa and Noland, 1988). On the whole, however, the Louvre meeting was a disappointment, as the important goal of macroeconomic policy coordination among the industrial nations remained unfulfilled (see Mead, 1988–1989, 1989).

The inability of the United States to devise a politically acceptable budget-deficit reduction strategy was a critical factor in the disintegration of macroeconomic policy coordination. It was in this environment of domestic and international policy failure that the 1987 stock market crash occurred (Spero, 1990). That event stimulated a renewed effort among the Group of Seven (the Group of Five plus Canada and Italy) to coordinate their domestic and international efforts to stabilize the dollar. A degree of success was finally achieved, aided in part by some reductions in the twin U.S. deficits.

Despite this temporary victory, "the long-term success of international monetary cooperation of the Group of Seven continued to depend on the ability of the key monetary actor, the United States, to pursue policies that would reduce its twin deficits" (Spero, 1990). That prospect remained dim as federal budget projections early in the 1990s showed that the U.S. budget deficit would actually *widen* before beginning a gradual descent sometime during mid-decade. At the same time, U.S. dependence on foreign energy sources again grew to ominous proportions, contributing not only to the U.S. trade deficit but also to its vulnerability to oil supply or price disruptions caused by some kind of crisis—which struck in August 1990 when Iraq invaded Kuwait.

The Persian Gulf War temporarily pushed concern about U.S. budgetary problems aside. With victory and the Bush administration's promise of a "new world order," however, attention returned to U.S. domestic economic and political problems widely perceived as having been neglected too long—to the detriment of the United States and the world alike (see Kuttner, 1991b).

Two facts are noteworthy in this respect. First, a marked downward trend in the value of the dollar was evident even before the Persian Gulf War, but unlike the situation following the 1987 stock market crash, this time there was little disposition among the other industrial nations to cooperate with the United States to rescue the dollar. Second, the value of the U.S. dollar in the international marketplace declined precipitously in the weeks following the onset of the Persian Gulf crisis. The normal pattern is that a country viewed as a "safe haven" for investments during times of crisis will see the value of its currency appreciate. Typically this had been the United States. In the Persian Gulf case, however, investors concluded Europe and Japan were better bets.

Toward a Regionalized Monetary Arrangement

The dollar remains preeminent in the world political economy, as does the U.S. economy, but the continuing challenges to U.S. preeminence reflect long-term processes that are impossible to ignore. Reinforcing those are movements that portend the possible emergence of a monetary order in which the dollar will play a less pervasive role. Potentially the most important change involves Europe, where the European Community has launched a European Monetary System (EMS) designed to stabilize the currency values of the European Community's member nations against one another and against the dollar. Although the promise and performance of the EMS have sometimes diverged, the goal of securing a "zone of monetary stability in Europe" has been reached (Spero, 1990).

Moving beyond currency stability toward monetary union is now the goal. A three-stage process has been put in motion by the European Community, whose ultimate goals are the creation of a European System of Central Banks (ESCB) and a single European currency unit (ECU) (see also Chapter 6). In the eyes of many, monetary union may also foster the eventual political union of the EC.

Whether these lofty goals are achievable is by no means certain (see Ferguson, 1991). The history of the EC is replete with postponed and unrealized plans. In part this is because emergent problems have often deflected the European Community from pursuit of its most visionary unification goals. The strains caused by the merger of the two Germanies are the most recent example. Still, the EMS may contain the seeds of a regional international monetary arrangement based on a single European currency in which the European Community will emerge dominant in Europe and in those areas of Africa and the Caribbean linked by treaty to the EC. That development in turn could stimulate similar arrangements in Asia and the Western Hemisphere, where Japan and the United States dominate.

As the preponderant economic power in the 1990s and as in previous decades, the United States is likely to resist regionalization, at least rhetorically, but it can no longer realize its preferences unilaterally. The United States is necessary for effective management of the monetary regime, but it is not sufficiently dominant to fulfill its earlier hegemonic role. Negotiations with others, most notably Europe and Japan, are necessary to manage successfully the competing and sometimes contradictory demands that economic interdependence and the desire for sovereign autonomy impose. In short, "the U.S. economy and American economic decision-making must now be adapted to an emerging global economy that no longer revolves around the United States" (Aho and Stokes, 1991).

TRADE STRATEGIES IN AN INTERDEPENDENT WORLD

The exponential expansion of the volume and value of international trade has been one of the primary engines driving economic growth and raising living standards throughout the world to levels never before achieved. Continuation of these trends is problematic, however. Increased trade protectionism and the corresponding prospect of regionalization, already apparent in capital markets, the monetary system, and even the trade regime itself, now threaten to dampen further trade growth.

Trade protectionism threatens closure of the open (liberal) multilateral trade regime created after World War II. *Nondiscrimination* is the central norm of the regime, and the General Agreement on Tariffs and Trade (GATT) is the principal international organization that seeks to promote and protect it. Nondiscrimination is embodied in the *most-favored-nation* (MFN) principle. According to that principle, the tariff preferences granted to one nation must be granted to all others exporting the same product. That is, everyone is to be treated the same as the most favored one (provided, of course, that the trading partners have previously agreed to grant one another MFN status). Thus the principle stands for nondiscrimination in the way that nations treat one another; its purpose is to eliminate preferential treatment in trade concessions.

Despite widespread enthusiasm for free, nondiscriminatory trade, the political case for trade protectionism is often compelling. When, for example, during the recession of the early 1980s an estimated 30 million people in the industrial world were unemployed, it was easy to conclude that imports were responsible for the loss of domestic jobs.[10] However, cutting off imports denies the benefits that free trade promises. It has been estimated, for instance, that by the early 1990s "trade barriers were costing American consumers $80 billion a year—[a sum] equal to more than $1,200 per family" (Bovard, 1991: 13).

Free Trade and Protectionism

As noted, there is a clear correlation between the growth of world trade and global welfare. Moreover, because the costs of protectionism are high and the benefits of free trade clear, the rise of protectionist sentiment in the world political economy is puzzling.

Classical (liberal) economic theory shows conclusively that when all states specialize in the production of those goods in which they enjoy a *comparative advantage* and trade them for goods in which others enjoy an advantage, a net gain in welfare will result. Still, states sometimes practice *neomercantilism* in an effort to enhance domestic welfare, even if it undermines their relations with their trade partners. Furthermore, classical theory does not comprehend the possibility that states may create comparative advantages. That is the purpose of the *strategic trade* policies now widely practiced by Japan and others. These reflect states' sensitivities to their *relative gains* from trade, not just their absolute gains.

Comparative Advantage

In principle, economic relations between states are voluntary exchanges that nations, either through private entities or public enterprises, enter into freely for mutual benefit. Indeed, the *raison d'être* of foreign trade is that it offers advantages to both parties in the exchange.

According to the principle of *comparative advantage*, any two nations will benefit if each specializes in those goods it produces comparatively cheaply and acquires,

---

[10] Consider, for example, the U.S. position in the steel and automobile industries. In 1955 the United States produced 39 percent of the world's steel, but by 1981 that proportion had slipped to 15 percent. In the same year, employment declined 25 percent compared with its level twenty years earlier. In the case of autos, the American proportion of world production declined from 68 percent in 1955 to only 21 percent in 1981. Between 1978 and 1981 alone, 275,000 jobs were lost in the American auto industry (Walters, 1983: 27).

through trade, goods that it can only produce at a higher cost. Trade is encouraged because those countries most efficiently producing cars, textiles, wines, or other products will, because of their lower cost, make them attractive to foreign consumers. Those that produce for export will also have incentives to import other goods that may be acquired at lower cost from foreign sources. Specialization and trade therefore permit each to enjoy a higher standard of living than would be possible without them. Thus, when trade is unfettered by nonmarket forces or politically imposed barriers, all nations stand to share in the gains in welfare that trade produces, as illustrated in Box 7.3 on page 234. This simple conclusion—that the net gain in welfare to most countries is greater as a consequence of their exchange of goods with one another—is the basis of classical (liberal) international trade theory.

The actual operation of the international economic system is, of course, far more complicated than this simple illustration suggests. Under a free trade regime, states should specialize in the production of goods in which they enjoy cooperative advantages, but in practice they routinely interfere with free trade for a variety of political reasons. Moreover, because they are not equal economically (some are endowed with greater resources and productive capacities than others), political motives among unequals shape the international economy. Indeed, the search for self-advantage at the expense of others—captured in the phrases "beggar-thy-neighbor policies" and "neomercantilism"—is commonplace, not the exception.

Neomercantilism

Beggar-thy-neighbor policies are designed to enhance domestic welfare by promoting trade surpluses that can be realized only at other countries' expense. They reflect the efforts by one country to reduce its unemployment through currency devaluations, tariffs, quotas, export subsidies, and other strategies that adversely affect its neighbors.

Beggar-thy-neighbor policies enjoy a long history. During the 1890s, for example, the United States imposed the McKinley tariff in response to high European agricultural tariffs. France retaliated with the Meline tariff that levied still higher duties.

National economic strategies such as these were especially prevalent during the 1930s. Currency devaluations, foreign exchange controls, and restrictive tariffs, such as the U.S. Smoot-Hawley Act of 1930, were implemented at that time to improve states' domestic economic conditions at the expense of other nations. In the end, their efforts to generate trade surpluses by cutting imports led to a breakdown of the entire international trade system.[11]

Neomercantilism describes today's beggar-thy-neighbor strategies. The term itself derives from the mercantilist policies that imperial states pursued early in the history of the modern state system, when they sought supremacy over others by the accumulation of precious metals and by exporting as much and importing as little as possible.[12] In the contemporary context, it refers to "a trade policy whereby a state seeks to

---

[11] For a contrasting view, see Strange (1985), where the author argues it was not protectionism but financial uncertainty and the shrinking of credit that slowed trade and growth in the 1930s (and again in the recession of the 1980s).

[12] See Chapter 5 for a discussion of classical mercantilism.

Box 7.3
COMPARATIVE ADVANTAGE AND THE GAINS FROM TRADE
• • •

Start with two countries, for example, the United States and the United Kingdom. Each produces steel and cloth. The hypothetical figures below show output per hour for workers in each country. It's clear that the U.S. has an absolute advantage; American workers are more productive in turning out both products than the British workers.

WORKER
PRODUCTIVITY

	U.S.	U.K.
Steel, units of output/hour	9	4
Cloth, units of output/hour	3	2

Does this mean that there is no possibility for trade between the two countries? If the U.K. wants to trade with [the U.S.], should it try to produce something else in which it has an advantage? And if trade occurs, should the U.S. continue to allocate its scarce resources in the same way it has done? The answer to all these questions is no.

Each country should specialize in those items in which it has the best comparative cost advantage or least comparative cost disadvantage, and trade with others. Here's why.

Since the U.S. is three times more productive in steel than cloth, it should direct more of its resources into steel. One cost of producing more steel is lost cloth output. But the U.S. can turn out three additional units of steel for every unit of cloth production given up, while the U.K. can obtain only two units of cloth.

In the U.K. workers are also more productive in steel than in cloth making. But greater emphasis should be placed on cloth production because Britain is at a smaller disadvantage, compared with America, in this area. If the U.K. specializes in cloth and the U.S. in steel, and they trade, each will benefit.

The chart shows that by moving resources in the U.S. to steel production and in the U.K. to cloth production, the same total inputs will cause steel and cloth output to rise 10 units each. This gain indicates a more efficient allocation of resources. Benefits to both countries can be realized when the U.S. trades its extra steel for British cloth. Indeed, the U.S. ends up with more steel than before specialization and trade and with the same quantity of cloth. The U.K. finds itself with more cloth and the same amount of steel. More output in both countries means higher living standards.

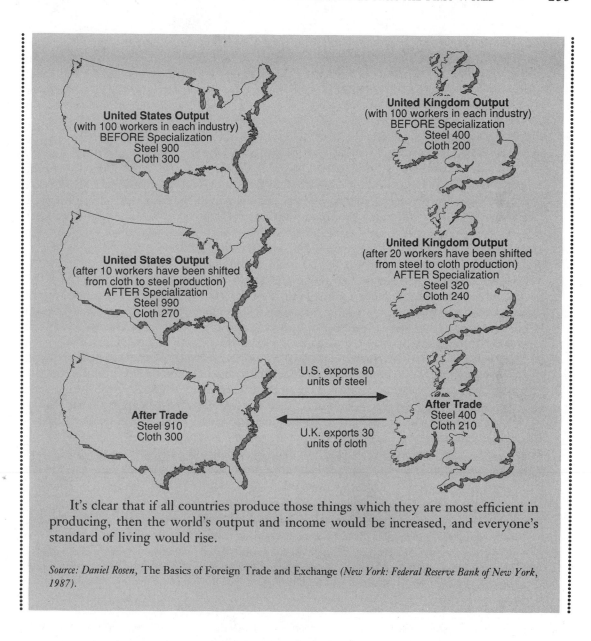

It's clear that if all countries produce those things which they are most efficient in producing, then the world's output and income would be increased, and everyone's standard of living would rise.

Source: Daniel Rosen, The Basics of Foreign Trade and Exchange *(New York: Federal Reserve Bank of New York, 1987).*

maintain a balance-of-trade surplus and to promote domestic production and employment by reducing imports, stimulating home production, and promoting exports" (Walters and Blake, 1992). More broadly, neomercantilism is state intervention in economic affairs to enhance the state's economic fortunes. Japan is frequently described as a neomercantilist power, having achieved tremendous export growth in the postwar years as a consequence of an intimate government-business alliance.

IMPORT QUOTAS Among industrial states, neomercantilism—and the case against free trade—is commonly rationalized by the perceived need for protection from cheap foreign labor, or perhaps from more technologically sophisticated producers. Already established industries may, for example, seek safeguards in the form of government assistance or trade restrictions targeted at specific foreign producers as a way to protect domestic producers.

Import quotas usually specify the quantity of a particular product that can be imported from abroad.[13] Governments impose quotas to protect domestic producers, regardless of their efficiency relative to foreign producers. In the late 1950s, for example, the United States established import quotas on oil, arguing that they were necessary to protect U.S. national security. Hence the government, rather than the marketplace, determined the amount of imports, and from whom. Sugar is another commodity that the United States has subjected to quotas in pursuit of its foreign policy objectives, particularly in the Caribbean (see Krasner, 1978).

EXPORT QUOTAS *Export quotas* also impose barriers to free trade. In this sense they are similar to import quotas, but the two differ in important respects. Import quotas are unilateral instruments of policy while export quotas are imposed as a result of negotiated agreements between producers and consumers. The United States and the European Community, in particular, routinely press other countries to accept *Orderly Market Arrangements* (OMAs) and *Voluntary Export Restrictions* (VERs) in an effort to protect domestic industries threatened by foreign imports.[14] Of the roughly one hundred major known VERs in operation in the mid-1980s, fifty-five restricted exports to the European Community, and thirty-two restricted exports to the United States (Boonekamp, 1987: 3). Sectors subject to OMAs and VERs include automobiles, footwear, steel, ships, electronic products, and machine tools.

In some cases there are even networks of agreed-upon export restrictions. The classic example is in textiles and clothes, which has a long history.

> In the 1950s, when domestic interests began putting pressure on the U.S. Government for protection against cheap cotton-textile imports from the Far East, Washington negotiated several informal VERs with Japan and, later, Hong Kong. Ostensibly "temporary," they soon were imitated by major European importers; and in 1961 all were formally consolidated into the first of a series of multilateral cotton-textile agreements later expanded to include woolens and synthetic fibers as well. Now called the Multifiber Arrangement, and involving some forty countries in all, the scheme has evolved into an elaborate international market-sharing agreement that allows virtually no room at all for significant structural adjustment.

---

[13] Import quotas differ from voluntary export restraints (VERs), discussed later, in that the former are normally applied on a global, nondiscriminatory basis, whereas the latter are negotiated bilaterally.

[14] Voluntary export restriction (or restraint) is a generic term for all bilaterally agreed restraints on trade. It usually arises from pressure on an exporting country by an importing country and can be thought of as "voluntary" in the sense that the exporting country may prefer it to other trade barriers that the importing country might impose. An OMA is a voluntary export restriction that involves a government-to-government agreement and often specific rules of management and consultation rights and calls for monitoring trade flows (Boonekamp, 1987). Boonekamp (1987) discusses the nature of VERs, why they were introduced, and their economic effects.

Importing countries troubled by excess domestic capacity and deteriorating demand are determined not to allow lower-cost Third World exporters to threaten employment at home. Consequently, a disproportionate fraction of their workers remain tied to a stagnant industry. (Cohen, 1983: 10)[15]

Estimates suggest that some 10 percent of total world trade is subject to the distorting effects of OMAs and VERs (Boonekamp, 1987: 3). Moreover, their prevalence grew substantially in the 1980s, particularly as applied to the exports of Japan and the Newly Industrialized Countries (NICs) of East Asia. Although these restrictions on exports are arguably not illegal under GATT's rules (compare Isaak, 1991), which are concerned primarily with governmental actions affecting imports, they doubtless contravene its broad goal of trade liberalization.

NONTARIFF BARRIERS Import and export quotas are two examples of a class of trade restrictions known as *nontariff barriers* (NTBs). NTBs are now a more important form of protection than tariffs, which, in the area of industrial products, at least, are now comparatively inconsequential.

NTBs have become particularly ubiquitous with the rise of the welfare state. Their effects, sometimes inadvertent and sometimes intentional, often restrain trade. As complex societies strive to protect the welfare of their citizens through numerous and often complex government regulations regarding health and safety, foreign-produced goods frequently cannot compete. Examples are the emission-control and safety standards imposed on the auto industry by the United States government in order to reduce air pollution and the risk of serious injury. When initiated, these standards, although meeting domestic needs, put burdens on certain foreign auto producers.

Health and safety standards are now regarded as necessary and legitimate forms of government regulation. They have no necessary bearing on international trade, but if their purpose is to limit external competition—and only secondarily, if at all, to safeguard domestic welfare—then they become legitimate objects of attack by free-trade advocates. The problem lies in the difficulty of distinguishing legitimate NTBs from regulations designed primarily to limit foreign competition. The French and British, for example, suspect that U.S. noise regulations imposed some years ago to restrict the supersonic Concorde passenger plane were really an attempt to limit competition in the aircraft industry after the decision of the United States not to produce the Boeing supersonic transport.

NTBs range widely in their extensiveness and variety. Over 40 percent of First World imports are subject to the nontariff measures, and the proportion has grown sharply since the mid-1960s (*World Development Report 1991*, 1991: 104–105). Just as health and safety regulations may be legitimately designed to protect a nation's citizens, measures taken to limit foreign imports in contravention of what liberal trade theory would otherwise see as mutually beneficial to all—a liberal multilateral trade regime—

---

[15] The Multifiber Arrangement was renegotiated in 1986 and was scheduled for renewal again in 1991. Negotiators had hoped to bring textile trade into the GATT framework during the Uruguay Round of multilateral negotiations, but their efforts were put on hold when the Uruguay Round stalled in late 1991.

are often deemed justified (see Box 7.4 on page 240 for an amusing illustration). Even though the goods produced by one nation may be superior in quality and cheaper in price than those produced in another, the latter may still use import quotas, export quotas, and other nontariff barriers to keep out the superior, less expensive, foreign-produced goods. It will do so if it perceives that the foreign goods' superior performance results not from purely market forces but from government subsidies granted to the export industries in the producing country.

INFANT INDUSTRIES   The neomercantilist practices described above are widespread among industrialized nations. Among developing nations, for whom the absence of protection from the more efficient Western firms prohibits the realization of their domestic industrialization goals, the *infant industry* argument is more often used to justify policies restricting free trade. According to this argument, tariffs or other forms of protection are necessary to nurture young industries until they can mature and until their eventually lower-cost production enables them to compete effectively in the world marketplace. Protectionism is the product.

THE COSTS OF PROTECTIONISM   One of the costs of trade protectionism is that it may postpone needed structural changes in national economies, as technological changes alter the relative efficiencies of different industries. A well-known international economist makes the case against protectionism this way:

> Import protection is like the toadstool—superficially attractive but potentially deadly. What protectionists prefer to ignore is that while individual industries might well profit from protectionism, at least for a time, the economy as a whole will suffer as increasingly more resources are locked into inefficient, low-growth activities. A healthy economy must be capable of adapting continuously to changes in the competitive environment. Capital and labor must be able to shift readily into growing, high-productivity sectors. Otherwise overall economic growth—the ultimate guarantor of jobs—gradually will be stifled. History is replete with tragic examples of economies that have choked on a diet of protectionism. (Cohen, 1983: 10)

Although they are commonplace, beggar-thy-neighbor trade strategies cannot work for everyone; not everyone can run a balance-of-trade surplus. As in the case of balances of payments, when one country is in a surplus position, another must have a deficit. Moreover, a contrary view to that described above maintains that the consequences of protectionism may be less devastating than the advocates of free trade sometimes allege (see Box 7.5 on page 242). In either event, the practice of neomercantilism with varied tactics is widespread. Often this means consumers either pay higher prices or must settle for commodities inferior to those otherwise available from abroad.

Strategic Trade

In contrast with policies designed to protect inefficient industries, advocates of strategic trade policy see it as a means of ensuring that a nation's industries will remain competitive in the rapidly changing, high-tech environment of the future.

Classical international trade theory shows how international trade contributes to the welfare of trading partners. By implication, it also demonstrates why states may choose to cooperate with one another to reduce trade barriers. What classical theory does not deal with is the fact that comparative advantages may change.

Classical theory attributes the basis for trade to underlying differences among states: Some are better suited to the production of agricultural products, such as coffee, because they have vast tracts of fertile land, for example, while others are better suited to the production of labor-intensive goods, such as consumer electronics, because they have an abundance of cheap labor. Increasingly, however, economists now recognize that comparative advantages take on a life of their own.

> Much international trade . . . reflects national advantages that are created by historical circumstance, and that then persist or grow because of other advantages to large scale either in development or production. For example, the development effort required to launch a new passenger jet aircraft is so large that the world market will support only one or two profitable firms. Once the United States had a head start in producing aircraft, its position as the world's leading exporter became self-reinforcing. So if you want to explain why the U.S. exports aircraft, you should not look for underlying aspects of the U.S. economy; you should study the historical circumstances that gave the United States a head start in the industry. (Krugman, 1990: 109)

If the contemporary pattern of international trade reflects historical circumstances, then states may conclude it is in their interests to try to create advantages that will redound to the long-run benefit of their economies. Curiously, then, the logic of comparative advantage can itself be used to justify government intervention in the economy. This rationale underlies *strategic trade*—a form of industrial policy that seeks to create comparative advantages by targeting government subsidies toward particular industries (for example, computers, semiconductors, high-definition television) so as to gain a competitive edge vis-à-vis foreign producers. Although studies indicate that the returns on strategic trade policies are often marginal (Krugman, 1990), the fact that some states (such as Japan) engage in such practices encourages others to do likewise.

Free Trade and Hegemonic Decline

Economic considerations encourage states to pursue strategic trade policies, but important political considerations also motivate them. As noted above, the absence of an international government encourages states to be more concerned with how they fare in relation to others—their relative gains—than with how they fare individually—their absolute gains. Strategic trade, because of "its emphasis on how economies of scale in industries present states with incentives to interfere in trade to gain market shares" (Snidal, 1991b), illustrates how the pursuit of relative gains may interfere with the logic of comparative advantage and free trade. Thus it shows why states are prone in the economic as well as military sphere to "forgo some of the benefits of cooperation or economic exchange in the short run, in order to assure security, broadly defined, over the long run" (Mastanduno, 1991; see also Chapter 2).

Box 7.4
The "Poitiers Effect"

• • •

The "new protectionism" usually refers to the use of nontariff barriers such as VERs and orderly marketing arrangements. But it only takes a little ingenuity to introduce an administrative regulation which can be an effective barrier to trade.

In October 1982, citing a "Japanese invasion" in consumer electronics, the French government decreed that all imports of videocassette recorders (VCRs) would have to pass through Poitiers. Although not the most obvious point of entry, Poitiers could hardly be better suited to the purpose. It is a town hundreds of miles inland from France's northern ports where the VCRs are landed. It has a tiny customs crew that is obviously inadequate to the task of clearing hundreds of thousands of VCR imports. As the town where the French repelled an earlier invader, the Moors, Poitiers seemed an apt choice.

Moreover, a particularly long and tedious set of customs regulations were strictly enforced at Poitiers. All the accompanying documents were thoroughly examined and each container opened. A large number of VCRs were taken out of their boxes by the customs inspectors, who carefully checked their serial numbers and made sure that the instructions were written in French. Finally, a number of VCRs were dismantled to make sure that they were actually built in their reported country of origin. The regional customs director responsible for Poitiers said of the new regulations: "Before the new policy, it took a morning to clear a lorry-load of video recorders. Now it takes two to three months. We are still clearing consignments that arrived here [three months ago] when the policy went into effect. . . . "

As planned, the "Poitiers effect" severely limited VCR imports into France. Before the use of Poitiers, more than 64,000 VCRs, mostly from Japan, entered France each month for the first ten months of 1981. Afterward, less than 10,000 VCRs cleared the customs point at Poitiers each month, while the rest of the supply waited in bonded warehouses throughout the town. Exporters did not passively concede to the French barriers. Denmark, the Federal Republic of Germany, and the Netherlands, which also export VCRs to France, filed a complaint with the EC Executive Committee in Brussels, which in turn brought charges against France at the European Court of Justice for breach of EC free trade rules. Japan brought its complaint to the GATT and then suspended or curbed VCR shipments to France.

It is not clear what the French hoped to gain from the use of the Poitiers weapon. The French electronics firm Thomas-Brandt did not make its own VCRs, but sold Japanese VCRs under its own label. It experienced a shortage of these when the government required all the imports to go through Poitiers. Shortly after the establishment of Poitiers, the EC Commission negotiated a VER limiting Japan's exports to the entire European Community. This was followed by an agreement between Thomas-Brandt and Japan's JVC to manufacture component parts in France and later the lifting of the Poitiers restrictions. It is likely that several complex issues concerning intragovernment and government-industry relations played a role in the Poitiers scheme. Yet, although the motives remain somewhat obscure, the protective effect of it is clear.

Source: World Development Report 1987. *Copyright 1987 by The International Bank for Reconstruction and Development/The World Bank. Reprinted by permission of Oxford University Press, Inc., p. 141.*

Relative gains and states' concern for position in their relations with others also sheds light on the reasons why the United States, the principle advocate of free trade in the post–World War II era, has increasingly engaged in trade practices that make it look less like a hegemon and more like an "ordinary country." Thus an understanding of the changing role of the United States in the international trade regime, as in the international monetary regime, is essential to understanding the transformation of the international trade system.

THE TRANSFORMATION OF THE INTERNATIONAL TRADE REGIME . . . .

Many of the same forces that nudged the crisis-prone international monetary system away from the precepts of the postwar Liberal International Economic Order also induced states to adopt more narrowly construed foreign economic policies. Increasingly, they pursued policies designed to meet their domestic economic goals but detrimental to the maintenance of the LIEO. In this sense the very success of the open, multilateral trade regime undermined its continuation, as growing interdependence increased policymakers' incentives to protect their national interests. The demise of U.S. hegemony contributed to closure of the system simultaneously, as the United States arguably is no longer willing or able to bear the costs of leadership, as it had previously.

The forces that now challenge the liberal trade regime can be better understood by examining its postwar history and the role played by the United States in shaping it.

Creating the Liberal Trade Regime: America's Leadership Role

The importance of the United States to the international trade system derives from the size of its economy and the value of its production sold abroad. In 1988, for example, U.S. exports equaled 7 percent of its gross national product. This contrasts sharply with the exports of many other countries that are comparatively more "involved" in the world economy. Japan's exports-to-GNP ratio in the same year, for

Box 7.5
The Costs of Trade Conflict
• • •

A hypothetical scenario may be useful for understanding what the costs of protection are, and why they are more modest than many people seem to think.

Let's imagine that most of the world's market economies were to group themselves into three trading blocs—one centered on the United States, one centered on the European Economic Community, and one centered on Japan. And let's suppose that each of these trading blocs becomes highly protectionist, imposing a tariff against goods from outside the bloc of 100 percent, which we suppose leads to a fall in imports of 50 percent.

So we are imagining a trade war that cuts the volume of world trade in half. What would be the costs of this trade war?

One immediate response would be that each bloc would lose jobs in the industries that formerly exported to the others. This is true; but each bloc would correspondingly gain a roughly equal number of jobs producing goods it formerly imported. There is no reason to expect that even such a major fragmentation of the world market would cause extra unemployment.

The cost would come instead from reduced efficiency. Each bloc would produce goods for itself that it could have imported more cheaply. With a 100 percent tariff, some goods would be produced domestically even though they could have been imported at half the price. For these goods there is thus a waste of resources equal to the value of the original imports.

But this would be true only of goods that would have been imported in the absence of tariffs, and even then 100 percent represents a maximum estimate. Our three hypothetical trading blocs would, however, import only about 10 percent of the goods and services they use from abroad even under free trade.

A trade war that cut international trade in half, and which caused an *average* cost of wasted resources for the displaced production of, say, 50 percent, would therefore cost the world economy only 2.5 percent of its income (50 percent × 5 percent = 2.5 percent).

This is not a trivial sum—but it is a long way from a Depression. (It is roughly the cost of a 1 percent increase in the unemployment rate.) And it is the result of an extreme scenario, in which protectionism has a devastating effect on world trade.

If the trade conflict were milder, the costs would be much less. Suppose that the tariff rates were only 50 percent, leading to a 30 percent fall in world trade. Then 3 percent of the goods originally used would be replaced with domestic substitutes, costing at most 50 percent more. If the typical domestic substitute costs 25 percent more, then the cost of the trade conflict is 0.75 percent of world income (25 percent × 3 percent = .075 percent).

Source: Paul Krugman, The Age of Diminished Expectations: U.S. Economic Policy in the 1990s *(Cambridge, Mass.: MIT Press, 1990), p. 105.*

example, was 9 percent, Britain's 18 percent, West Germany's 27 percent, the Netherlands' 46 percent, and Taiwan's 51 percent. Despite these higher ratios, however, only West Germany's exports rivaled in value the more than $321 billion of U.S. production sold abroad. In fact, the ranking among these seven countries according to their exports-to-GNP ratio is nearly the opposite of their ranking according to the size of their economies.

In 1988 the gross national product of the United States was four times West Germany's and more than forty times greater than Taiwan's. In general, therefore, and despite the relative decline in American economic dominance, the U.S. economy and its foreign economic policies are much more important to other nations than their economies and policies are to the United States. As the U.S. trade representative, Reuben Askew, put it in 1980, "True, we are no longer the single, pre-eminent economic power in the world. But we are still the strongest."

The U.S. Role in the Bretton Woods Period

The importance of the United States to the world political economy was especially pronounced in the immediate post–World War II period. Today the United States accounts for roughly a quarter of the world's aggregate GNP. In 1947 it accounted for half of all world production. Not surprisingly, therefore, it became the dominant voice in trade as well as monetary affairs.

As with the monetary system, the liberal trading system the United States promoted drew on the lessons policymakers perceived in the 1930s. The zero-sum, beggar-thy-neighbor policies associated with the intensely competitive economic nationalism of the interwar period were widely regarded by those concerned with postwar reconstruction to have been a major cause of the economic catastrophe of the 1930s that ended in global warfare. To avert its repetition, priority was assigned to removing barriers to trade, particularly tariffs.

The United States envisioned that an International Trade Organization (ITO) would be created to seek lower restrictions on trade and set rules of commerce. Thus the new organization would perform the role in trade policy that the IMF and World Bank were designed to perform in international monetary management. But the ITO was stillborn. It failed to win approval when the liberal trading system envisioned in its proposed charter, popularly known as the Havana Charter, generated congressional opposition: "Protectionists opposed the arrangement for being too liberal, and liberals were against it for being too protectionist. . . . Without U.S. support the ITO was dead" (Isaak, 1991). In its place, the United States sponsored a new multilateral treaty that created the General Agreement on Tariffs and Trade (GATT). GATT became the cornerstone of the liberalized trade regime originally embodied in the ITO.

Under GATT and the most-favored-nation principle, states initiated a series of multilateral trade negotiations aimed at tariff reductions with broad national participation. The eighth of these sessions, the Uruguay Round, began in 1986 in Punta del Este, Uruguay. It was to have been completed in 1990, but the negotiating partners failed to reach agreement on all of the important issues. The negotiations were therefore extended indefinitely.

The high point of postwar momentum toward a liberalized trading system, notably on industrial products, was the Kennedy Round of negotiations, which actually took place during the Johnson administration (1964–1967). In this, as well as in all previous multilateral trading conferences, the United States was the principal mover.

As hegemony demands, the United States was willing to accept fewer immediate benefits than were its trading partners in anticipation of the longer-term benefits of freer international trade. In effect, the United States was the locomotive of expanding world production and trade. By stimulating its own growth, the United States became an attractive market for the exports of others, and the outflow of U.S. dollars stimulated the economic growth of other nations in the "American train." Evidence that supports the wisdom of this strategy, particularly the association between tariff reductions and export growth, is the fact that as the average duty levied on imports to the United States declined by more than half between the late 1940s and the early 1960s, world exports nearly tripled.

The Kennedy Round did not deal successfully with tariff barriers on agricultural products, however. Lack of progress on this issue, and later disagreements over it, began to raise doubts among U.S. policymakers about the wisdom of the United States' expansionary policies. The immediate challenge was posed in 1966 in the Common Agricultural Policy (CAP) instituted by the European Economic Community (EEC). To outsiders, the CAP was seen as a protectionist tariff wall designed to maintain politically acceptable but artificially high prices for farm products produced within the EEC. It effectively curtailed U.S. agricultural exports to the EEC (which by the 1960s had become a principal trading partner of the United States).

The Trade Expansion Act of 1962, passed by the U.S. Congress in an effort to improve the U.S. competitive trade position in relation to that of the European Economic Community, provided the U.S. domestic base for the Kennedy Round. The president's authority to negotiate trade matters under the earlier Trade Expansion Act expired with the end of the Kennedy Round. Thereafter, Presidents Johnson and Nixon fought a rearguard action against the rising protectionist forces that bombarded Congress with trade-restriction demands.

The challenge of an economically revitalized and politically uniting Europe was among the factors that led to the waning of U.S. support for a multilateral free-trade regime. Other contributing factors included the EC's extension of preferential trade treatment to nations in Africa, the Mediterranean, and the Caribbean; the expansion of the Common Market from six members to nine in 1973; the extension of associate status to others; and the growing perception that Japan's highly protectionist trade policies violated the liberalized trading scheme in which others remained in voluntary compliance (Spero, 1990).

At a broader level, the postwar trade regime was undermined by many of the same forces that were eroding the international monetary system. Its collapse also contributed to the lack of progress on trade matters, as did the shifting constellation of political forces within the Western world and between it and the communist world. The loss of U.S. leadership was finally the consequence.

The Regime under Stress

In much the same way that the monetary disorder of the 1970s reflected the inability of the Bretton Woods system to master the international economic forces then unleashed, the erosion of the liberal trade regime of the 1950s and 1960s reflected the inability of GATT to keep pace with the new developments. As described by a former counsel to the U.S. special trade representative:

> GATT was formed to promote free-market competition among a maximum number of countries under a relatively few simple rules: nondiscrimination (the United States must treat Japanese and European products equally, for example); no barriers to imports other than declining tariffs; and no protection of faltering industries from import competition except through temporary measures taken publicly in emergency cases. These were rules for a simpler era, when trade was a fraction of its present volume, tariffs were the main trade barrier, a few Western countries dominated international trade and postwar optimism for international free enterprise was high—at least in the United States, which was the preeminent economic superpower. Although by the 1970s all of these circumstances had changed drastically, the GATT rules remained substantially the same and, as a result, were widely ignored. Without viable international rules, trade relations quickly revert to the law of the jungle. (Graham, 1979: 52)

Challenges to American Leadership and the Liberal Trade Regime

The European Community's agricultural policies maintain product prices above market values, but they also reveal an important underpinning of protectionist logic: It appeals to influential domestic political interests that perceive the costs of free trade as greater than its benefits.

The Tokyo Round of Multilateral Trade Negotiations

In part to cope with growing protectionist sentiments in the United States, the Nixon administration sought a new grant of authority from Congress to negotiate lower tariff barriers with other nations. The result was the Tokyo Round of multilateral trade negotiations, which was concluded in 1979 after nearly five years of bargaining.

The Tokyo Round began in a radically different environment from that of the previous GATT sessions. The world political economy had experienced an exponential growth in trade value, the level of economic interdependence among the world's leading industrial nations stood at unprecedented levels, tariffs no longer posed the principal barriers to trade, and the United States no longer enjoyed the prerogatives of an economic giant without rivals. In this new environment, addressing nontariff barriers to trade and reducing barriers to the free flow of agricultural products took on greater urgency.

The Tokyo Round produced new international rules to deal with such issues as subsidies and countervailing duties, dumping, government purchasing, product standards, custom valuation and licensing, and trade with developing nations. Still, it did not clearly reaffirm the precepts underlying GATT and the liberal trade regime (see Graham, 1979; Krasner, 1979). Nor did it deal effectively with agricultural trade issues and with the growing incidence of neomercantilist and strategic trade practices that were of special concern to the United States.

It was clear by the time the Tokyo Round concluded that the promise and practice of free trade diverged widely. Part of the reason is that states differ in their assessment of the role that government should play in regulating economic behavior. Where they fall along the continuum between an open and a closed economic system, in other words, and what they therefore view as appropriate government intervention in market-oriented economies, predicts their position on international trade issues.

The United States became increasingly reluctant to assume the costs of leadership in an environment in which others were perceived to be playing by a different set of rules. Lee Iacocca, the president of the Chrysler Corporation, reflected popular sentiment by charging in 1983 that "because the U.S. government still clings to free trade rules, America lacks a trade policy responsive to new realities of international competition. For American businessmen and workers—sent out into the global marketplace to compete without government help—the playing field is not level; it's tilted against them." The playing field analogy stresses not the issue of free trade but *fair trade*.

The Uruguay Round of Multilateral Trade Negotiations

It was against the background of a trade system increasingly rife with restrictive barriers, subsidies, the intentional use of product standards that others cannot meet, and other unfair trade practices that go beyond the principles of GATT that the United States urged a new round of trade negotiations to "level the playing field."

FREE TRADE VERSUS FAIR TRADE   The trade policies of the continental European states, Japan, and less-developed countries were of special concern to the United States. Governments there routinely intervene actively in economic life and play entrepreneurial and developmental roles. Such action violates what the United States, in principle, regards as government's proper role in economic policy making.

By the time the Uruguay Round was in full swing, on the other hand, others began to view the United States as part of the problem. By then it had become the world's largest debtor; its trade deficit ranged well beyond $100 billion annually; and its trade imbalance with particular countries, notably Japan, had burgeoned to seemingly intractable levels.[16] Furthermore, the U.S. role as a principal exporter of foodstuffs had eroded, as world food production, fed by high levels of government

---

[16] In 1990, for example, U.S. imports from Japan were just under $90 billion, but its exports to that island nation were less than $49 billion. However, the bilateral trade deficit peaked in 1987 and has since declined measurably. U.S. exports to Japan grew by more than $20 billion from 1987 to 1990, thus outpacing the overall growth of U.S. exports during this period.

subsidies, markedly stimulated competition for foreign markets. In such an environment, other nations were not quick to accept the U.S. analogy of an uneven playing field skewed in their favor (see Walters, 1983; Kuttner, 1991a). As one observer put it caustically, "the more inefficient and backward an American industry is, the more likely the U.S. government will blame foreign countries for its problems" (Bovard, 1991).

Despite their understandable concern and pique, others were sensitive nonetheless to the need to keep protectionist sentiments in the United States at bay. Because U.S. imports stimulated the economic growth of its trade partners, which enabled the United States to act as the engine of Western economic growth, America's trade partners conceded that new trade talks were necessary to cope with issues of special concern to the United States. The Reagan administration simultaneously used the proposed trade talks to thwart growing protectionist sentiments at home, where, at one time during 1985 (when Congress began to debate what eventually became the Omnibus Trade and Competitiveness Act of 1988), some 300 trade protection bills were pending before Congress. These bills offered protection to almost every industrial sector, ranging from steel, copper, lumber, and automobiles to shoes, textiles, neckties, and waterbeds.

NEW ISSUES, OLD PROBLEMS Coping with traditional tariff issues and bringing VERs (voluntary export restrictions) and other forms of the new protectionism under multilateral management were of special concern to the United States in the Uruguay Round. In addition, it pushed hard to reduce barriers to trade in services (for example, insurance), intellectual property rights (for example, computer software), and investments. These areas have traditionally been outside the GATT framework, but they are of special concern to the United States and other advanced industrial societies who enjoy comparative advantages in them.

As the comparative advantage in the production of manufactured goods, such as consumer electronics and automobiles, moves toward advanced developing nations like the Newly Industrialized Countries (NICs), the importance of trade in services and intellectual property will grow. The task as seen by the United States and others is to develop rules that protect their present or potential advantages and that enable them to yield the production of manufactures to developing countries. From the viewpoint of the developing countries, on the other hand, severe impediments to the enhancement of their advantages in manufactured products already exist in the form of nontariff and other barriers to access to markets in the First World. That perception doubtless hardened their bargaining position on issues salient to the industrial societies of the First World.[17]

Agriculture is another issue of special importance to the United States. World trade in agriculture evolved outside the main GATT framework and thus has not experienced the same liberalizing influences as industrial products (Spero, 1990). It is

---

[17] See Spero (1990) for a discussion of the issues faced in the Uruguay Round, the positions taken by various nations and groups of nations on them, and the factors that enhance or impede agreement on them. Preeg (1989) usefully summarizes the broader range of issues that challenge the GATT trading system itself.

especially controversial because it is deeply enmeshed in the domestic politics of producing states.

At the core of differences on agricultural trade are the enormous subsidies that governments of the leading producers in the First World pay farmers to keep them competitive in world markets, where prices are often much lower than in Europe or North America. In 1986, for example, the European Community spent over $20 billion, or more than two-thirds of its budget, on agricultural subsidies. The United States, for its part, spent about $30 billion in farm support programs, an amount that exceeded the net income of U.S. farms (Wallis, 1986: 2).

The perceived need for such subsidies reflects fundamental structural changes in the global system of food production. As with textiles, these subsidies are difficult to manage because of the potentially adverse domestic political consequences in those countries for which the global market is an outlet for surplus production, such as the United States and members of the European Community. The difficulty is exacerbated by the emergence of new competitors among Third World producers and by the shrinkage of traditional First World markets as a consequence of technological innovations. The latter have enabled expanded agricultural production in countries that previously experienced food deficits (see also Chapter 9).

During the Uruguay Round the United States aggressively proposed to phase out all agricultural subsidies and farm trade protection programs within a decade. It gained the support of some other producing states but was opposed by the European Community, which viewed the proposal as unrealistic and sought instead to maintain its own Common Agricultural Policy. The dispute over agriculture led eventually to an impasse in the Uruguay Round negotiations.

U.S. Bilateral and Unilateral Initiatives   At the same time that the United States pursued resolution of outstanding trade issues via the multilateral GATT mechanism, it also undertook important bilateral and unilateral measures perceived by many to be at variance with the spirit if not the letter of GATT. Among them was conclusion of free-trade agreements with Israel and Canada. Although these initiatives were rationalized as consistent with GATT, analysts worried that they violated the rule of nondiscrimination (otherwise known as general reciprocity) underlying the liberal trade system.[18]

The United States also pursued unilateral remedies in response to what it regarded as the unfair trade practices of other governments. The 1988 omnibus trade act required that the president identify countries believed to engage in unfair trade practices and to seek negotiated remedies or face U.S. retaliation. Although the Super 301 provisions of the law were "almost unamimously viewed abroad as a clear violation of the GATT" (Walters and Blake, 1992), they reflected particular U.S. resentment of the trade policies of Japan and the four Asian NICs (Hong Kong, Singapore, South Korea, and Taiwan). The intent of Super 301 was to level the playing field with those

---

[18] Vernon (1982) points out that the United States continues to preach free trade even though it has knowingly violated the rule of nondiscrimination because "it has had trouble envisaging a coherent world trading system without such a rule."

perceived most in violation of the rules of free trade, so as to right the overall U.S. imbalance of trade.

The persistent U.S. trade deficit underlies the determination of the United States to take unilateral action against those deemed to play unfairly. The causes of the deficit, however, include factors besides trade.

As noted earlier, the dollar exchange rate also is important to an understanding of the trade deficit. As the dollar soared in the first half of the 1980s, the ability of U.S. exporters to compete in the global marketplace plummeted, resulting in thousands of lost jobs among those who depend on exports. Even as the dollar declined in the latter half of the decade, however, the deficit, while reduced, persisted. U.S. imports from abroad continued their upward trend in response to the aggressive strategies of major exporters to the U.S. market, who sought to protect their coveted market shares. Moreover, capital flows now play a more dominant role than trade in the global political economy, with the result that exchange rate fluctuations no longer vary in tandem with changes in the direction of international trade (Bhagwati, 1991).

In addition, the deficit is influenced by the long-term decline in U.S. productivity resulting from a loss to Japan and others of the technological edge that the United States enjoyed in the 1950s and 1960s. Insufficient domestic savings and insufficient investment in civilian research and development as well as in basic education contributed to the erosion of the nation's trade competitiveness (see Hufbauer, 1989–1990; Thurow, 1985).

As noted earlier, analysts and policymakers alike often attribute Japan's spectacular export growth since the 1960s to an intimate government-business alliance, which leads many to conclude that Japan is the world's preeminent neomercantilist power. The enormous trade imbalance between Japan and the United States in recent years reinforces the belief that Japan's trade policies are inherently detrimental to U.S. business.

The United States and Japan have engaged in protracted negotiations designed to right their trade imbalance (the Structural Impediments Initiative [SII] is among the most recent), but the goal has proved elusive. A number of factors explain this, including the preference of millions of Americans for products made in Japan, Japanese tariff and nontariff barriers that limit the ability of U.S. producers to penetrate the Japanese market, and a cultural tradition in Japan that views foreign products as ill-suited to the Japanese consumer. Furthermore, the domestic savings rate in Japan is considerably higher than the average savings rate among the other Western industrialized nations. Its domestic consumption is also low. This means Japanese industry must look overseas for growth. In other words, its surplus of savings over investment, and of production over consumption, gravitates abroad (Feldstein, 1985).

Since the mid-1980s Japan's policymakers have emphasized an economic strategy focused on domestic demand rather than export promotion, as previously noted. Still, their policies have not rectified Japan's chronic trade imbalance with the United States and others. Until policies are designed to offset the impact of Japan's high savings rate, Japan will continue to have an important impact on the world political economy generally—and on the U.S. economy in particular, for the United States has become Japan's most important overseas market (see Rosecrance, 1990).

Japan will play an important role in the world political economy even beyond its relations with the United States. "Because of its size and its role in world trade, reestablishing a reasonable balance between Japan and its trading partners, as well as integrating Japan into the management of the international trading system, will be a central challenge for the remainder of the century" (Spero, 1990).

From Multilateralism to Regionalism

For some time the possibility that the multilateral trading system will splinter into several regional trading blocs has concerned analysts. They worry that regionalism will push the open trading regime central to the Liberal International Economic Order toward closure.

The European Community in particular is often perceived as the greatest threat to the open, liberal regime. Its determination under the slogan "Europe 1992" to create a market completely free of internal barriers reinforced that fear. As George Bush put it early in his presidency, "We must all work hard to ensure that the Europe of 1992 will adopt the lower barriers of the modern international economy, not the high walls and the moats of medieval commerce."

At the same time that the United States expressed concern about trends in Europe, the 1988 U.S.-Canada Free Trade Agreement raised fear that the United States was moving toward the same kind of regionalized monetary and trade system that it opposed in Europe. That concern was further heightened in 1991, when the leaders of Canada, Mexico, and the United States announced that they had begun negotiations to conclude the North American Free Trade Agreement (NAFTA).[19] Each of the partners to a potentially integrated North American free trade area with completely free internal barriers was motivated by a combination of political and economic motives (see Baer, 1991). Regardless, the effect would be to create the largest free trade area in the world, a trade bloc that would encompass 360 million people with an annual output exceeding $6 trillion (see Table 7.1).

At present there is no official movement toward creation of a formal Asian trading system centered on Japan, but developments in North America and the continuing integration of Europe may nudge that eventuality forward. More than a third of total world trade already takes place within these three (nascent) trading blocs, as illustrated in Figure 7.2 on page 252. The intraregional trade in the total exports of the European Community is especially striking. Thus, as a 1991 report of the United Nations (1991a) concluded, "Today the question is not whether these blocs will be formed, but rather how encompassing they will be and how to ensure that they will not harm the [global] trading system."

Regional trade schemes like those in Europe and the proposed North American free trade area do not necessarily contravene GATT's rules regarding nondiscrimination in

---

[19] The Bush administration anticipated an eventual free trade area encompassing all of the Western hemisphere. Realization of that goal may be facilitated by the Mercosur talks among Argentina, Brazil, Paraguay, and Uruguay, whose purpose is the integration of their economies by 1995.

TABLE 7.1 GROSS NATIONAL PRODUCT, POPULATION, AND PER-CAPITA GROSS NATIONAL PRODUCT WITHIN POTENTIAL TRADING AREAS, 1990

	GNP, 1990 (billions)	Population, 1990 (millions)	Per-Capita GNP, 1990
Asia-Pacific	$3,592.8	248.3	$14,467
European Community	$5,517.4	342.5	$16,107
North America	$6,203.1	363.6	$17,060

Source: Adapted from The World Bank Atlas 1991 (Washington, D.C.: The World Bank, 1991), pp. 6–9.
Note: North America: Canada, Mexico, United States; European Community: Belgium, Denmark, France, Greece, Ireland, Italy, Luxembourg, the Netherlands, Portugal, Spain, United Kingdom, West Germany; Asia-Pacific: Hong Kong, Japan, Malaysia, Republic of Korea, Singapore, Thailand.

trade. Nor are analysts agreed on the question of whether regionalization is good or bad from the point of view of the effective functioning of the world political economy. But some do worry about the adverse effects that rival trading blocs may have on individual countries, including in particular the United States.

According to this viewpoint, the regionalization of the world trade (and monetary) regimes into three primary blocs—in Europe, Asia and the Western Hemisphere—would find the United States the leader of the weakest bloc of the three (Mead, 1990). The conclusion is that "the United States and Canada are too much like twins to grow rich trading largely with each other"; that prolonged economic weakness characterizes many of the other economies in the Western Hemisphere, whose cultures in any event direct them more toward Europe rather than the United States; that the U.S. dollar, while remaining "the key international currency" is "but a ghost of its former self"; and that the United States is, and will remain, dependent on oil imports from the volatile Middle East (Mead, 1990).

What effect will the end of the Cold War have on the regionalization of the multilateral trade system and, more generally, on the world political economy? Many analysts see the eventual integration of the nations of Eastern Europe into the European Community or perhaps some other, even larger, European economic entity as both possible and probable. Less certain is the fate of the now fragmented Soviet Union. What is clear is that many elites in Moscow and elsewhere in the republics that once made up the Soviet Union now see their integration into the world capitalist system as essential to their prosperity.

FROM SOCIALISM TO CAPITALISM

For more than seventy years the Soviet Union sought to build a domestic economy based on centralized state planning. The Soviet system, which after the formation of

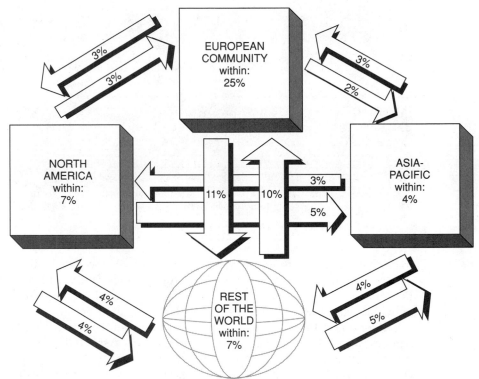

FIGURE 7.2 SHARE OF WORLD EXPORTS WITHIN AND BETWEEN TRADING
AREAS, 1990
Source: United Nations, *World Economic Survey 1991* (New York: United Nations, 1991), p. 6.
Note: North America: Canada, Mexico, United States; European Community: Belgium,
Denmark, France, Germany, Ireland, Italy, Luxembourg, the Netherlands, Portugal, Spain,
United Kingdom; Asia-Pacific: Hong Kong, Japan, Malaysia, Republic of Korea, Singapore,
Thailand.

the Council for Mutual Economic Assistance (CMEA) in 1949 incorporated the countries in Eastern Europe as well as the Soviet Union itself, was "based on the proposition
that social gain is maximized by the state's commands." The economic systems in
most Western countries, on the other hand, were "fashioned on the proposition that
as individuals pursue their private gain, the benefits for the country will exceed its
costs, yielding a social gain" (Vernon, 1979). Thus, in contrast with the market
economies of the Western industrial world, the governments of the socialist states
made all production and distribution decisions, and they did not allow prices to play
a role in encouraging production and regulating the distribution of goods and services.
These characteristics underscore the marked contrast in concept and performance
between closed (command or planned) and open (market) economies.

The End of Empire

State planning was always inefficient in the Soviet Union, but the economic trends apparent when Mikhail Gorbachev came to power in 1985 were especially ominous. Declines in worker productivity were widespread, the social and economic infrastructure was deteriorating badly, growing consumer demands outpaced the ability of state planning mechanisms to meet them, and the technological gap between the East and West, already wide, was growing (Bunce, 1991). Decades of centralized state planning, in short, had been economically disastrous, as the Soviet Union in many ways resembled a Third World developing country.[20]

The burden that the maintenance of Soviet hegemony in Eastern Europe placed on the Soviet economy was also significant (see McGwire, 1991; also Naylor, 1991). The Warsaw Pact and the Council for Mutual Economic Assistance together had been constructed to ensure Soviet security and contribute to Soviet economic well-being, but by the 1980s there was no denying that "the Soviet empire in Eastern Europe was . . . an acquisition generating fewer and fewer returns."

> The extensive trade subsidies offered to Eastern Europe, the considerable burden of regional defense . . . , the degree to which East European economic weaknesses merely duplicated those in the Soviet Union, the economic crises in Poland, Hungary, and Romania, and, finally, East European resistance to Soviet pressures to reform the bloc in ways more beneficial to Soviet economic interests—all these circumstances had the effect of increasing an already weighty burden on the Soviet economy. (Bunce, 1991: 225)

The burden of competing with the United States militarily compounded the economic difficulties the Soviet system experienced. The role that the U.S. military buildup in the 1980s and the U.S. containment policy pursued since the 1940s played in the decision of Soviet leaders to repudiate communism and to end the Cold War may never be known with certainty (see Chapter 4). What is clear is that the Soviet Union's extraordinary military spending distorted priorities and placed a heavy burden on its economy. Military spending in turn retarded growth in many sectors, as the drastic decline during the 1980s in Soviet citizens' standard of living dramatized. Technological prowess at home, which military spending might have been expected to stimulate, lagged far behind the West. To cite but one example, in the late 1980s the Soviets were manufacturing a computer called the Agat similar to the old Apple II personal computer produced in the West, but which was 30 percent slower and cost $17,000 (cited in Snow, 1991: 72).

To prevent assignment of the Soviet Union to the rank of a "permanently developing country" (Winiecki, 1989), and to halt the erosion of living standards apparent

---

[20] For assessments of the state of the Soviet economy prior to its collapse, see Schroeder (1991); *The Economy of the USSR*, prepared by the International Monetary Fund, the World Bank, Organisation for Economic Co-operation and Development, and European Bank for Reconstruction and Development (1990); and "Beyond Perestroyka: The Soviet Economy in Crisis" (1991), prepared by the U.S. Central Intelligence Agency.

for some years, leaders in the (now former) Soviet Union and elsewhere in Eastern Europe embarked on a bold path to transform their moribund economies into market systems and to end the isolation of the command economies from the Western world by seeking integration into the capitalist world economy. The transition promises to be difficult, and success is by no means assured (see Box 7.6; also Collins and Rodrik, 1991). The sobering fact is that the twentieth century provides leaders with no prior experience on which they can draw to transform their socialist economies into market ones.

What are the consequences for other nations of the revolutionary changes now taking place in the former socialist economies? On the economic front, several broad generalizations have been advanced:

> Demand for capital in the newly liberalizing countries will put upward pressure on world interest rates; developing countries' access to international capital markets will become more restricted; [the collapse of] the Council for Mutual Economic Assistance (CMEA) [will reorient the region's] trade toward the West; trade tensions will increase in many "sensitive" sectors such as agriculture, steel, textiles, and clothing as producers in the developing and the industrialized countries come under competitive attack by new exporters in Eastern Europe. (Collins and Rodrik, 1991: 2)

In addition to these consequences, aid to developing countries from Russia and the other successor republics of the Soviet Union may vanish altogether. In 1991 Soviet President Mikhail Gorbachev pledged to terminate Soviet aid to Cuba, one of the few remaining communist bastions. The disintegration of the Soviet state virtually precludes any substantial foreign aid to others.

The industrial nations of the First World, and the world political economy generally, cannot insulate themselves from the revolutionary political and economic changes that have swept the Soviet Union and Eastern Europe. The question, then, is how to accommodate those changes. This is especially troublesome for the United States, the long-time leader of the "free world."

For more than a generation, the pattern of commercial relations between the United States and the Soviet Union and its allies was shaped almost exclusively by political and national security concerns. Indeed, economic collaboration and political-military confrontation were incompatible, and the latter dictated the pace of the former. Now, however, it seems that economics is increasingly the driving force in relations between the West and the former Soviet republics joined in the Commonwealth of Independent States.

To accommodate this dramatic shift in priorities, the United States has had to ask how far it is willing to go to assist the former socialist states. There are historical precedents for assisting nations defeated in war, as the United States did with the reconstruction of Germany and Japan after World War II. Doing so again will, however, require a painful reexamination that also necessitates reassessing the wisdom of prior policies designed to promote political and security objectives that may no longer be pertinent. Trade in strategic goods and the manipulation of trade policy to promote changes in internal policies in the former Soviet republics stand out. A brief historical sketch of the commercial relations between East and West during the Cold War era will place these issues in proper perspective.

Box 7.6
FROM A CENTRALLY PLANNED ECONOMY TO A MARKET ECONOMY
• • •

Transforming a centrally planned economy into a market economy requires complex and unprecedented reforms. There is no experience to guide transitions of the current magnitude. And most countries in transition are simultaneously creating a new political order. There is relatively little disagreement that the transitions have to be made, but there is much controversy about the theory, timing, scope, speed, and sequencing of reforms.

Three sets of issues arise. One concerns the economic implications of a policy sequence: will one kind of reform achieve its objectives while other economic distortions remain? Another question is political: will mounting opposition derail reforms scheduled near the end of the sequence? Finally, there is technical feasibility. New legal, accounting, and financial systems will require greater technical expertise and longer gestation periods than reforms that include only price deregulation.

One school of reform proposals puts change in ownership at the head of the sequence before or alongside changes that address macroeconomic stability and markets. The rationale is partly political. With early privatization, there is less risk that the economy will remain state-controlled and greater pressure for complementary market-oriented reforms. But another school of thought begins with macroeconomic and market-building reforms: it leaves privatization—at least for large state enterprises—to a second stage. . . . The rationale is that private ownership requires financial institutions, experience, and expertise that do not yet exist in the transitional economies. Without this infrastructure, rapid privatization could lead to widespread corruption and economic and political chaos. Within each school there are further differences on the proper order for addressing particular distortions.

No single reform sequence will fit all the transitional economies. Reform histories vary; unlike others, Hungary has had more than two decades of experience with decentralized economic decisions. Macroeconomic conditions range from great instability (the Soviet Union) to relative stability (Czechoslovakia). Private sector activity has been relatively higher in predominantly agricultural countries such as China and Viet Nam but negligible in more industrialized nations. . . .

Reforms will surely involve painful adjustments. Inflation and unemployment will worsen as price controls are removed and the real economic losses of some activities are revealed. Political opposition may mount with these developments and with the rise in income inequality that comes after radical change in the incentive structure. But progress in exports and the availability of consumer goods could soon follow. And, given the relatively strong human resource endowments in Eastern Europe, prospects for growth could be excellent.

Source: World Development Report 1991 *(New York: Oxford University Press, 1991), pp. 145–146.*

East-West Commercial Ties in Historical Perspective

During World War II, Western planners expected that the Soviet Union would participate in the postwar international economic system, just as they initially counted on Soviet cooperation in maintaining the postwar political order. The Soviet Union had taken part in the Bretton Woods negotiations. Moreover, trade between Eastern and Western Europe had been extensive before the war, and after the war the Soviet Union and the Eastern European states under its domination were invited to participate in the U.S.-sponsored European Recovery Program, popularly known as the Marshall Plan. However, because the Marshall Plan was largely framed as part of the emerging U.S. design to thwart the spread of communism in Europe, the Soviet Union and its "satellites" understandably refused. Instead, they embarked on the creation of a regional economic system isolated from the West, one designed to augment the Soviet Union's capability to compete politically and militarily with the West.

The Isolation of East from West

Under U.S. leadership, the West actively discouraged economic ties between the socialist and capitalist worlds. The United States sought to curtail trade in so-called strategic goods that might bolster Soviet military capabilities and thus threaten Western security. It sponsored the Coordinating Committee (Cocom) as a multilateral mechanism designed to induce its NATO allies to join in a unified embargo effort. Although the allies were never enthusiastic about using economic instruments to fight the Cold War, Cocom became—and remained even in the early 1990s—a primary vehicle for restricting the export of high-technology goods from West to East.

In 1951, during the Korean War, the United States also moved to strip the Soviet Union and other communist countries of any trade preferences. Thus it denied the East markets for its own products as well as access to Western goods and finances (see Spero, 1990). Economics joined hands with politics in creating and perpetuating the Cold War.

During the 1960s there were signs in the economic sphere that some thawing of the Cold War was in the offing. On the economic front, a desire for access to Western technology, rising demand in the socialist countries for consumer goods, and the continued inability of the Soviet agricultural system to meet its production goals stimulated increased interest among Soviet leaders for commercial ties with the West. These same concerns dominated the East-West commercial agenda in the 1970s, when détente became the official policy of both the United States and the Soviet Union.

From Détente to Renewed Hostility

Each of the partners to détente had different priorities. Commercial ties were comparatively unimportant to the United States (for whom political issues were more salient), somewhat more important for other Western nations, and a paramount concern to the Soviets. For some time the Soviet Union had sought (unsuccessfully) to move away from reliance on heavy industry and toward reliance on improved technology as a means of stimulating higher productivity and greater economic growth. To rejuvenate the sluggish Soviet economy, access to Western technology and the credits necessary to buy it were required. Similarly, to supplement the persistent shortfalls in Soviet agricultural production, grain imports were necessary.

During the 1972 summit in Moscow, at which the superpowers initialed their first strategic arms control agreements, U.S. and Soviet leaders paved the way for the United States to grant the Soviet Union most-favored-nation (MFN) trade status and to extend the Soviet regime U.S. government-backed credits. Both, however, fell prey to U.S. domestic politics and, more broadly, to the overriding political interests that the United States attached to its commercial ties with the Soviet Union. The U.S. Congress limited the extension of credits to the Soviet Union, and the granting of most-favored-nation status was made contingent on the liberalization of communist policies regarding Jewish emigration. Although the Soviet Union did tacitly signal its willingness to permit freer emigration of Soviet Jews, early in 1975 it reversed its position on the understandings, labeling them a violation of agreements made earlier and an unwarranted interference in Soviet domestic affairs.

In the years that followed, the granting of MFN status was held hostage to improved political ties between the superpowers. It was not until 1990 that the United States and the Soviet Union reached a new accord that would offer the Soviet Union significantly lower tariffs on goods sold in the United States. Even then, it was more than a year later before the Bush administration submitted the agreement to Congress. Only with its approval could earlier restrictions on U.S.-Soviet trade be eased and the Soviet Union, through the granting of MFN status, be placed on an equal footing with other U.S. trade partners.[21] This finally occurred in 1992, when the United States granted Russia MFN status, apparently in return for a major Russian concession on strategic arms agreed to in June of that year.

The desire for improved commercial relations between the superpowers and their allies persisted through much of the 1970s, but the Soviet invasion of Afghanistan in 1979 dashed any hope for normalizing East-West commercial relations. Even before then, the United States saw the Soviets' desire for high-technology goods as leverage it might use to realize U.S. foreign policy goals in the human rights area.

As Soviet-American relations deteriorated, the Carter administration used economic instruments to counter the Soviet Union's continued high levels of military spending, its overseas military buildup and arms transfers to the Third World, and its backing of Cuban intervention in Angola, Ethiopia, and elsewhere in Africa. As new sanctions were imposed on the Soviet Union following Afghanistan, the commercial ties that a decade earlier had been built to cement détente became the victim as well as the instrument of renewed Soviet-American rivalry.

---

[21] The freedom-of-emigration conditions that must be met before MFN status can be granted to the Soviet Union and the other nonmarket economies are contained in the Jackson-Vanik amendment to the Trade Act of 1974. The president is empowered to grant a temporary waiver of those provisions, or he may determine that compliance with the amendment has been met by virtue of a country's emigration laws and practices. At this stage, a bilateral trade agreement between the United States and the other party is necessary before MFN status is granted. With the exception of Romania, nearly all of the Eastern European countries enjoyed MFN status by 1991.

Underlying the strategy of détente was the expectation that a web of economic and political relationships between East and West would cause both to moderate their political hostility. During the 1980s U.S. policymakers came to the conclusion that the logic underlying détente was flawed, arguing that détente "was no barrier at all when Soviet decisionmakers saw opportunities to advance their strategic position through overseas adventurism or outright military aggression" (Wallis, 1983). Thereafter, the Reagan administration's confrontational policies included restrictions on the export of energy technology to the Soviet Union as the United States sought, first, to punish the Soviets for their presumed complicity in the imposition of martial law in Poland in the early 1980s and, second, to win cancellation of the planned Soviet-Western European pipeline that would eventually bring natural gas from Soviet Siberia to markets in Western Europe. At the same time, however, Reagan lifted a ban that the Carter administration had placed on grain sales to the Soviet Union, and in 1983 Washington and Moscow concluded a new long-term grain sales agreement. The accord contained language that effectively pledged the United States not to interrupt future grain shipments in pursuit of its self-defined national security policy goals. Eventually efforts to block completion of the trans-Siberian pipeline were also dropped, but not before they had produced a serious split in the Atlantic alliance.

The differences between the United States and its NATO allies on the pipeline issue cast in sharp relief the differences on the issue of East-West trade that often separated—and still separates—the United States from its allies in the industrial world. The legacy of established trade with Eastern Europe and the Soviet Union, geographical proximity, differences in import needs, and perceived marketing possibilities led Europe and Japan to actively cultivate East-West commercial ties. For a more self-sufficient and security-conscious United States, for whom trade with the Soviet Union and Eastern Europe had always been comparatively insignificant as a proportion of overall U.S. trade, commercial concerns were less important (Spero, 1990).

A major conclusion about East-West commerce suggested by recent decades is that trade expands when political tensions ease and contracts during periods of animosity. The record also indicates a prudent Western readiness, even on the part of the United States, to jettison trade as an instrument of political influence and to reduce restrictions if and when economic conditions made them excessively costly. The latter lesson may prove important in contemplating the prospects for integrating the former socialist economies into the world political economy.

Integrating the Socialist Economies into the World Political Economy

Earlier in this chapter we introduced the notion of "two-level games" to describe the fact that policymakers must often contend simultaneously with challenges and constraints posed by both domestic and international politics. The concept is especially apt in understanding the forces that led to the end of the Cold War, to the reform of Soviet politics and economics that the Gorbachev regime initiated, and to the role that the former socialist states are likely to pursue in the world political economy.

On the Soviet side, the Gorbachev regime made an about-face on the issue of linking the Soviet economy to the world capitalist system that was every bit as dramatic as was its about-face on key security issues (such as the unification of Germany). Shortly after coming to power, Gorbachev warned that "increased trade with the West would leave the Soviet Union 'vulnerable to pressure and blackmail on the part of imperialism' " (Kramer, 1991a). Nonetheless, as early as 1986 the Soviet Union sought observer status in GATT. Gorbachev also made a radical departure from the past in calling for "full participation by the USSR in the global economy." Toward this end, he sought Soviet membership in the International Monetary Fund and the World Bank, initiatives that "once seemed inconceivable because of the organizations' requirements regarding free-market reforms, data disclosure, and currency convertibility" (Kramer, 1991a).

To facilitate Soviet entry into the world political economy, Gorbachev pledged to make the ruble a fully convertible currency. He also repeatedly sought Western financial assistance to resuscitate the moribund Soviet command economy and ease its conversion to a market economy.

The industrial nations of the First World responded positively but with varying degrees of enthusiasm to these initiatives. They granted the Soviet Union observer status in GATT in 1991, but they denied it full membership, presumably until further domestic reforms could be put into place. They also permitted the Soviet Union to join the IMF and World Bank as an associate member, which enabled it to receive technical assistance, but they denied it the full membership that would qualify the Soviet Union for financial aid. Finally, the industrial powers targeted the Soviet Union with various forms of financial assistance, but both the mix of assistance and its level remained tentative as policymakers debated the stake that the industrial nations had in the Soviet future and, correspondingly, where and how to help it (see Allison and Blackwill, 1991; Layne, 1990–1991).

As in the case of commercial relations during the Cold War era, Germany and some of the other Western European nations moved more rapidly than the United States in responding to Moscow's pleas. In addition to the billions the government in Bonn dedicated to the task of integrating the former East German communist state into the German federal republic, by 1991 it accounted for nearly a third of the more than $18 billion dollars in Western government credits that had been offered to the Soviet government. The United States, on the other hand, proceeded more cautiously. As noted above, it took steps to remove the prohibitions on trade with the Soviets that Congress had mandated in the 1970s. It also undertook time-consuming reassessments of existing policies designed to restrict trade in strategic goods with the Soviet Union and the other states in Eastern Europe. But it remained reluctant to grant the outright aid to the Soviet government that the Gorbachev regime sought.

The U.S. policy position was underscored at an early 1992 meeting of the major powers providing aid to the former Soviet republics, when the United States agreed only to a modest increase in its humanitarian assistance. As before, political considerations dominated economic policy. And the imperative of two-level games in Washington seemed to dictate a much slower pace of policy change in the United States than the new Commonwealth of Independent States preferred. Eventually, however, the

United States did agree to participate with the other Western industrial nations in a $24 billion aid package for Russia. It also supported full membership in the International Monetary Fund and the World Bank for Russia and most of the other former Soviet republics, thus bringing them into the capitalist fold they had shunned for seventy years. Membership in the multilateral institutions made them eligible for additional financial backing.

THE TURBULENT 1990s: TRIUMPH AND TROUBLE . . . .

Late in 1991 Israel and its Arab foes sat down together at a historic peace conference many hoped would end the bloodshed that for so long had marked politics in the Middle East. Gorbachev, having only recently survived a coup attempt, seized that occasion to remind the world of the central role that the Soviet Union played in the transformation of world politics then under way. "The world community is becoming increasingly aware," he declared, "that what is happening in the Soviet Union has a larger bearing than any regional conflict on the vital interest of the greater part of today's world." There was an element of hyperbole in so bold a statement, but policymakers throughout the Western world remained keenly aware of the potential and actualized power of the Soviet state and many of its constituent republics. In this sense, accommodating the former Soviet republics' desire to become full partners in the capitalist world economy is only one dimension of the larger need to facilitate the peaceful transformation of the communist world to a new form of political, economic, and social organization. The process will extend well into the future.

The world also will need to come to grips with the changing role of the United States in world politics. Some voices in the United States see in the demise of Soviet communism an opportunity for U.S. disengagement from world politics so as to rebuild U.S. power and leadership capabilities without the burdens of past commitments (Buchanan, 1990; also Tonelson, 1991). Others see this as a unique period in world history, a "unipolar moment" that finds the United States unchallenged in the world and "the only country with the military, diplomatic, political and economic assets to be a decisive player in any conflict in whatever part of the world it chooses to involve itself" (Krauthammer, 1991b).

Still others worry that the very exercise of U.S. power throughout the world is a misapplication of its resources that could spell its ultimate demise. "Although the United States is at present still in a class of its own economically and perhaps even militarily," historian Paul Kennedy (1987) writes, "it cannot avoid confronting the two great tests which challenge the *longevity* of every major power that occupies the 'number one' position in world affairs: whether, in the military/strategical realm, it can preserve a reasonable balance between the nation's perceived defense requirements and the means it possesses to maintain those commitments; and whether . . . it can preserve the technological and economic bases of its power from relative erosion in the face of ever-shifting patterns of global production" (see also Kennedy, 1992).

The many issues and problems discussed in this chapter touch directly on the shifting patterns of economic power that shape the contours of contemporary world politics. "Low politics is becoming high politics" (Moran, 1991). Moreover, if "welfare, not warfare, will [increasingly] shape the rules . . . and dictate the agenda" (Joffe, 1990), as many analysts believe, political leaders will have incentives to substitute "an ethics of 'shared sovereignty' and mutual assistance for the conventional realpolitik ethics of self-help and national competition" (Kegley, 1992).

The prospect of further competition is more likely, however. In an interdependent world the decisions of policymakers on issues affecting the material well-being of their own citizenry and their states' relative power position abroad will surely affect other national actors and their citizens. In this sense, interdependence is, paradoxically, a force promoting economic nationalism.

Economic nationalism threatens to undermine the overall prospects for the world economy's growth. It also encourages states to focus on short-term issues rather than to confront long-term problems (see Stewart, 1984). Thus the principles on which the liberal international economic order have rested are under attack precisely when, as in the period following World War II, they may be most needed, and by the very First World nations whose interests they have most clearly served. "The industrial countries," former U.S. Secretary of State Henry A. Kissinger (1982) has noted, "are still groping to reconcile the imperatives of their domestic policies with the realities of interdependence." How they finally manage that will have profound effects throughout the world.

SUGGESTED READINGS

Baer, M. Delal. "North American Free Trade," *Foreign Affairs* 70 (Fall 1991): 132–149.

Bergsten, C. Fred. "The World Economy after the Cold War," *Foreign Affairs* 69 (Summer 1990): 96–112.

Bhagwati, Jagdish. *The World Trading System at Risk*. Princeton: Princeton University Press, 1991.

Block, Fred L. *The Origins of International Economic Disorder*. Berkeley: University of California Press, 1977.

Bovard, James. *The Fair Trade Fraud*. New York: St. Martin's Press, 1991.

Collins, Susan M., and Dani Rodrik. *Eastern Europe and the Soviet Union in the World Economy*. Washington, D.C.: Institute for International Economics, 1991.

Gilpin, Robert. *The Political Economy of International Relations*. Princeton, N.J.: Princeton University Press, 1987.

Hormats, Robert D. *Reforming the International Monetary System: From Roosevelt to Reagan*. New York: Foreign Policy Association, 1987.

Isaak, Robert A. *International Political Economy: Managing World Economic Change*. Englewood Cliffs, N.J.: Prentice Hall, 1991.

Spero, Joan Edelman. *The Politics of International Economic Relations*, 4th ed. New York: St. Martin's Press, 1990.

Thurow, Lester C. *Head to Head: Coming Economic Battles Among Japan, Europe, and America*. New York: Morrow, 1992.

Walters, Robert S., and David H. Blake. *The Politics of Global Economic Relations*, 4th ed. Englewood Cliffs, N.J.: Prentice Hall, 1992.

CHAPTER 8

• • •

THE TRANSFORMATION OF THE WORLD POLITICAL ECONOMY: PERSPECTIVES FROM THE THIRD WORLD

• • •

The challenge of development . . . is to improve the quality of life. Especially in the world's poor countries, [it] calls for higher incomes—but it involves much more. It encompasses . . . better education, higher standards of health and nutrition, less poverty, a cleaner environment, more equality of opportunity, greater individual freedom, and a richer cultural life.

World Development Report 1991, 1991

Bilateral military and economic assistance will remain an essential tool in advancing U.S. interests through the 1990s . . . . Our interests in political pluralism, market-driven economic development, peace-making, and strengthening alliances—can all be advanced by prudent use of bilateral assistance resources.

James A. Baker, U.S. Secretary of State, 1991

The international monetary and multilateral trading regimes that evolved during the postwar decades served the interests of the First World industrial nations that built them. The Soviet Union and the socialist states in Eastern Europe had minimal ties with the Western nations. Developing nations on the periphery of the First World were also outside the privileged circle. Yet the remaining vestiges of colonial economic linkages entangled the Third World in industrial nations' systems, over which, however, they had little control. From their perspective, the end of colonialism merely ushered in a period of more subtle and devious exploitation that existing international economic structures helped to perpetuate.

The most strident effort by developing nations to alter their position in the world political economy occurred in the 1970s, when they called for a New International Economic Order (NIEO). The debate that followed engaged primarily the First and the Third Worlds. The communist countries formed political alliances with one side or the other from time to time, as their political advantage dictated. However, because of their own lack of economic ties with the South and their belief that the so-called socialist nations bore no responsibility for colonialism, Second World countries were not active participants in the most intense debates between the North and the South about the structure and operation of the world political economy.

Today the New International Economic Order rhetoric is little more than a footnote to the North-South debate as played out primarily from 1973-1981. Now the central issue is what impact the end of the Cold War will exert on the developing world. Will it lead to a period of benign neglect, as the industrial nations turn their attention to their own domestic problems and to those of the fledgling democracies in Eurasia? Or will the policy and financial resources once devoted to the high politics of peace and security be redirected toward the urgent needs of the South and toward resolution of long-standing problems that bind North and South in a common fate?

In this chapter we will examine trade, aid, development, and debt issues as they relate to the politcal economy of North-South relations as seen through the eyes of the Third World. The inquiry includes an examination of the historical roots of the issues raised in the context of the NIEO debate, how they have evolved since then, and how they now animate the goals and interests of Third World nations. In Chapters 9 and 10 we will examine demographic, environmental, and resource issues, all of which also involve North and South but extend beyond the world political economy.

THE NEW CLIMATE FOR ECONOMIC DEVELOPMENT . . . .

The 1980s was a period of economic expansion. Still, by the time it ended, the Third World remained far from being a full partner in the world political economy. With nearly 80 percent of the world's population, it accounted for less than 20 percent of its economic output, and its share of world trade was only 17 percent (*World Development Report 1991*, 1991: 17). As a group, therefore, the developing nations "still have a long way to go before they are fully integrated with the global economy" (*World Development Report 1991*, 1991).

The 1990s promise to be pivotal for the Third World. As noted, a critical question is whether in the post–Cold War world the industrial nations will pay attention to the developing world. "The South itself is seized by the profound anxiety that the termination of the East-West struggle will cause the industrial democracies to forget about it. Accustomed to an age where conflict proved a magnet for . . . foreign policy attention, the developing world now fears falling off the North's agenda" (Feinberg and Boylan, 1991; see also Chapter 5).

Many arguments can be advanced to support the thesis that the South will continue to be important to the North, even in an environment where strategic considerations no longer dominate (see Sewell, 1991, 1992). Nonetheless, because policymakers' world views are colored by subjective as well as objective reality, the perception that the North will lose interest in the South for all except perhaps humanitarian reasons is a cause for concern among Third World leaders.

Beyond security interests, developments in world trade, finance, capital flows, energy, the environment, and the like will affect the prospects for Third World development in the post–Cold War world. Even here, however, no clear direction is apparent. As summarized in Box 8.1, the anticipated climate for development in the 1990s is amenable to both pessimistic and optimistic interpretations. As in the past, the eventual nature of the development environment will depend in part on forces beyond the control of individual Third World nations and even the South as a whole.

We can begin to understand the forces that affect Third World development prospects and the obstacles developing nations face as they seek to become full partners in the world political economy with a retrospective look at the issues and events surrounding their drive for a New International Economic Order.

THE NORTH-SOUTH DIALOGUE: A HISTORICAL OVERVIEW . . . .

The end of colonialism freed Third World nations from their political bondage but it did not end their economic dependence on the former imperial powers. Nor did it guarantee self-sustained economic development. Thus, as noted in Chapter 5, Third World leaders came to believe that the structure of the international economic system was responsible for their plight. Increasingly they sought structural reforms of the world political economy to make it more responsive to their interests and needs.

Many Third World nations believed that existing international economic institutions, such as the International Monetary Fund (IMF) and General Agreement on Tariffs and Trade (GATT), and the political processes they govern, were "deeply biased against developing countries in their global distribution of income and influence" (Hansen, 1980). The perception was buttressed by the legacy of colonial exploitation and the continued existence in many parts of the Third World of levels of poverty and deprivation unknown in the North. Thus, not only a redistribution of income and wealth from rich nations to poor but also a similar transfer of political influence propelled the North-South conflict. Simply put, the goal sought by many Third World leaders was *regime change*—a revision of the rules, norms, and procedures of the Liberal International Economic Order to serve the interests of the Third World rather than the industrial North (Krasner, 1985). From this perspective, a New International Economic Order (NIEO) governing the transnational flow of goods, capital, and technology would replace the inherently exploitative Liberal International Economic Order (LIEO).[1]

The New International Economic Order

The historical roots of the developing nations' demands for a new order can be traced to the 1964 United Nations Conference on Trade and Development (UNCTAD),

---

[1] The developing nations did not challenge the state system itself, only how it functions. Thus, the choice of the word *international* rather than *global* or *world* is significant. "The growing assertiveness of the developing countries cannot be found to herald the beginning of a new world," declared Robert W. Tucker (1980). "It is not the state system per se that is condemned, but the manner in which the system operated in the past and presumably continues to operate even today. It is primarily through the state that the historically oppressed and disadvantaged nations seek to mount a successful challenge to what governing elites of developing countries view as persisting unjust inequalities."

Box 8.1
The Climate for Development in the 1990s

• • •

Pessimistic	Optimistic
World trade	
GATT negotiations collapse; unilateral policies by large industrial countries lead to trade wars; trade declines overall, though by less within regional blocs.	GATT makes real progress; regional GATT-compatible agreements produce dramatically greater integration in Europe, Asia, and the Western Hemisphere; world trade expands rapidly.
Capital flows	
International capital markets are overcautious, and transfers to developing countries fail to pick up.	Capital flows to the developing countries resume; greater confidence spurs direct foreign investment.
World finance	
Major institutions fail in Japan and the United States, leading to high risk premiums, low investment, a prolonged economic slowdown, and possibly higher inflation; the debt crisis continues to impede growth in the developing regions.	Major institutions muddle through; financial reforms and regulatory changes reduce systemic risks; economic recovery is rapid; Brady Initiative and its successors gradually reduce developing-country debt burdens.
Industrial–country policy	
Large industrial countries fail to cooperate; they follow poor macroeconomic policies, and financial instability and low growth result.	Macroeconomic policies of the large industrial countries stabilize financial markets and lead to sustained growth.
Security	
The decline of the superpowers leads to regional crises and ethnic strife within and among countries; arms races divert economic resources; terrorism, drugs, and poverty undermine internal security.	End of Cold War reduces tensions among superpowers; new international security arrangements are developed through a strengthened United Nations.
Technology	
Technologies required for competitive products become more and more sophisticated and labor-saving; technology flows are restricted by protectionist policies and firm strategies; developing-country advantages resulting from cheap labor and raw materials diminish.	New technologies improve health and productivity (especially in agriculture); multinationals develop wider global production networks; computers reduce advantages of large markets; better communications make it easier for countries with adequate human capital to catch up in productivity.

Energy ————————————————————————————————

Oil prices remain volatile because of ongoing political and social instability in the Middle East, which continues to be the main supplier of oil.

New political arrangements in the Middle East, combined with constructive dialogue between producers and consumers of petroleum, lead to a period of unusual stability in real oil prices.

Environment ————————————————————————————————

Damage to the environment mounts, with economic repercussions; global resources dwindle; the frequency of local environmental disasters increases.

Environmental ill effects prove less costly and less immediate than predicted; new national and international policies take adequate steps to protect scarce resources.

Source: World Development Report 1991 *(New York: Oxford University Press, 1991), p. 22.*

when the developing nations banded together to form the Group of 77 as a coalition of the world's poor to press for concessions from the rich. Known in diplomatic circles as the G-77, the coalition effectively joined the nonaligned movement during the 1973 Algiers summit of nonaligned nations, when issues relating to economic as well as political "liberation" came to the fore. Algeria, then the spokesperson for the nonaligned countries, led the call for what became in 1974 the Sixth Special Session of the United Nations General Assembly. Using their superior numbers, the G-77 succeeded in passing the Declaration on the Establishment of a New International Economic Order.

Significantly, both the special United Nations session and the declaration on the NIEO occurred during the food and energy crises of the 1970s. Until then, the advanced industrial nations of the North did not give serious attention to the demands of the developing nations of the South, but they could not ignore OPEC's (Organization of Petroleum Exporting Countries) success in cartelizing the world market for oil.

For the nations of the South, OPEC's success augmented the stridency of their demands for a new order. Inspired by the belief that "commodity power" endowed the Third World with the political strength necessary to challenge the North, the developing nations felt that their superior numbers would enable them to wield influence in the United Nations, UNCTAD, the IMF, the World Bank, the Third United Nations Law of the Sea Conference, and various other global and regional forums. They sought a North-South dialogue on general issues, such as more rapid economic development, increased transfers of resources from industrial to developing nations, and a more favorable distribution of global economic benefits. And they provoked debate on a host of more specific issues dealing with aid, trade, foreign investment, foreign ownership of property, multinational corporations, debt relief, commodity price stabilization, compensatory financing mechanisms, price indexation, and the like.

Although the South forced the industrial nations to pay some heed to Southern demands, the North rejected—and still does reject—the view that the Third World's economic woes are a product of structural deficiencies in the existing economic order. Instead, it locates the causes (and potential cures) of those problems in the domestic systems of Third World countries themselves. Accordingly, proposals to radically alter existing international economic structures as well as the more modest elements of the Third World program met with resentment and resistance. Intransigence was especially apparent during the 1980s in the United States, as the Reagan administration approached the Third World primarily from the vantage point of its role in the East-West conflict. It showed little concern for those aspects of Southern aims and interests as they related to the transformation of the Liberal International Economic Order. Thus the North-South dialogue gradually degenerated into a dialogue of the deaf.

The Demise of the NIEO

Because UNCTAD has long served as a spokesperson of the world's poor, it has been a central forum for the North-South dialogue. Ever since the G-77 was first formed, the periodic meetings of UNCTAD focused attention on Third World problems and priorities. Box 8.2 on page 268 summarizes the principal issues addressed during the eight UNCTAD meetings held between 1964 and 1992.

This brief summary illustrates the extent to which the demands and concerns of the Third World nations have changed over time. For instance, UNCTAD VI (1983) and VII (1987) exhibited greater concern with immediate issues than with the long-term goals of structural reform and regime change that had dominated the agenda in earlier meetings. The new mood was summarized by Farouk Sobhan of Bangladesh, chairman of the Group of 77, in 1983: "We cannot change institutions overnight. We have to do this gradually with a sense of purpose and pragmatism." It is an attitude that extended into the eighth UNCTAD conference, held in Cartagena de Indias, Colombia, in early 1992, where structural reform of UNCTAD itself was a primary issue. The debate took place against the background of a broad consensus on the importance of market-oriented economic policies and political pluralisms as the basis for development (Taplin, 1992).

What accounts for the Third World's apparent retreat from its earlier, militant posture toward regime change?

First, the economic climate faced by most Third World nations changed sharply. North and South alike experienced a general and prolonged economic slump in the early 1980s, but for many Third World nations the effects were especially damaging. Economic growth rates deteriorated in many of them, and in some developing regions, particularly Africa, they actually reflected "negative growth." The prices of the commodities exported by Third World nations fell sharply compared with the prices they had to pay for their imports. Faced with reduced export earnings and higher interest rates, the debt burdens of many Third World nations assumed ominous proportions. Thus acute economic problems at home caused many Third World leaders to focus pragmatically on immediate policy problems rather than ideologically on the longer-term drive for structural reform launched a decade or more earlier.

Box 8.2
THE EVOLVING STAGES OF UNCTAD

• • •

UNCTAD I, GENEVA 1964

- The creation of a forum to attract attention to issues supporting the developing countries, not covered by existing institutions.
- The formulization of the Group of 77 and beginning of discussion on a few issues such as terms of trade, resource gap, and Generalized System of Preferences (GSP).

UNCTAD II, NEW DELHI 1968

- Between 1964 and 1968 the UNCTAD secretariat focused more seriously but still sporadically on GSP, the needs of the developing countries for assistance, terms of trade, technology transfer, and selected development policies.
- The Conference led the OECD to initiate work on a scheme of preferences.
- Dr. Raúl Prebisch retired in 1969 as the Secretary-General of the UNCTAD.

UNCTAD III, SANTIAGO 1972

- Unlike the Geneva and New Delhi meetings, where these issues were considered separately, UNCTAD III saw discussion on interrelationships between trade, money, finance, and development at a technical level.
- Initiation of an effort by Mr. Robert McNamara, President of the World Bank, to mobilize global support for the poor, suggesting ways to integrate the bottom 40 percent of the population in the development process.

UNCTAD IV, NAIROBI 1976

- Stocktaking of progress in various forums (CIEC, GATT) on decisions taken at the Sixth and Seventh Special Sessions of the UN General Assembly in 1974 and 1975, respectively, particularly in the light of the oil price increase, monetary instability, recession, inflation, increased balance of payments gap of the non-oil developing countries, decline in commodity prices, and the uncertainty that the minimum development needs in many developing countries would be met.
- Main emphasis on commodities (Integrated Programme for Commodities–Common Fund) and to a lesser degree on external debt.
- Resolution on a Common Fund symbolized G-77 unity.

UNCTAD V, MANILA 1979

- Emphasis on trade and financial flows aspects of the relationships between developed and developing countries.

- Emphasis on growing interdependence between different parts of the world economy.
- Efforts to bring socialist countries into the dialogue on economic issues.
- Emphasis on trade liberalization and concern about expanding protectionism.

UNCTAD VI, BELGRADE 1983

- Movement by G-77 toward immediate issues relating to the global economy and Third World development and away from demands for structural reform.
- Emphasis on a common analysis of the world economic situation and an agreed strategy for economic recovery and development.
- Continued concern for the issue of trade protectionism.
- Recognition of the important role of the World Bank and International Monetary Fund as multilateral development institutions.

UNCTAD VII, GENEVA 1987

- Broad agreement on the need for macroeconomic policy coordination among major industrial countries.
- Acceptance of the need for growth-oriented adjustment among developing countries, including the need for adequate external support.
- Focus on four substantive issues: resources for development, including the Third World debt problem; commodity prices; the role of trade in economic development; and the problem of the Least Developed of the Less Developed Countries (LLDCs).

UNCTAD VIII, CARTAGENA DE INDIAS, 1992

- Emergence of a broad consensus on importance of market-oriented economic policies and political pluralism as basis for development.
- Reform and revitalization of UNCTAD to ensure its continuing relevance on trade and development issues.
- Agreement to place future emphasis on consensus building and appropriate domestic policies rather than negotiations aimed at binding international agreements.

Sources: Summary description of UNCTAD I through UNCTAD V from Mahmud A. Burney, "A Recognition of Interdependence: UNCTAD V," Finance and Development 16 (September 1979): 18; summary description of UNCTAD VI and UNCTAD VII adapted from Shahid Javed Burki, "UNCTAD VI: For Better or Worse?" Finance and Development 20 (December 1983): 18–19; and Carlston B. Boucher and Wolfgang E. Siebeck "UNCTAD VII: New Spirit in North-South Relations?" Finance and Development 24 (December 1987): 14–16. Grant B. Taplin, "Revitalizing UNCTAD," Finance and Development 29 (June 1992): 37–38.

Second, the erosion of the Third World's bargaining leverage added to the softening of its militancy. The denouement of the OPEC decade in the face of a worldwide oil glut in the 1980s removed any reason the North might have had to make major concessions to Southern demands. Thus the NIEO fell victim to "the lack of will on the part [of the] powerful, and the lack of power on the part of the willing" (Laszlo et al., 1980).

Third, as the unifying force of commodity power receded and the changing economic climate of the 1980s affected different countries in different ways, latent fissures and growing diversity within the Group of 77 became more evident (see also Chapter 5). As a result, the South no longer spoke as a unified group. The differences between the more advanced of the developing nations, on the one hand, of which the Newly Industrialized Countries (NICs) stand out, and the less well-off, especially the least developed of the less developed countries (LLDCs), on the other, became especially pronounced. Others among the more advanced developing nations, particularly in Latin America, were hardest hit by the debt crisis (discussed below). This, too, had the effect of dividing the Third World into competing groups rather than uniting them behind a common cause.

Finally, an increased preference for market mechanisms and a corresponding decline in "statism" as a development strategy undermined the NIEO ideology, including in particular the belief that the structure of the world political economy was the source of all Third World ills.

Against the background of these changes, the Third World drive for a New International Economic Order might properly be conceived not as the "beginning of the end" of the Liberal International Economic Order but "as the 'end of the beginning,' a period of transition to a more complex order with a different international division of labor and different economic and political prospects for different Third World states" (Rothstein, 1988).

The Political Economy of North-South Relations . . . .

Historically, many Third World leaders found four elements in their economic relationships with the North particularly irksome. W. Arthur Lewis, the Nobel Prize–winning economist, summarizes them as follows:

> First, the division of the world into exporters of primary products and exporters of manufactures.
> Second, the adverse factoral terms of trade for the products of the developing countries.
> Third, the dependence of the developing countries on the developed for finance.
> Fourth, the dependence of the developing countries on the developed for their engine of growth. (Lewis, 1978: 3).

Third World nations no longer actively seek to address these items through structural reforms of the world political economy, but all remain central to an understanding of the evolving international division of labor and the economic and political prospects of different Third World countries within it. Thus we will examine each in greater detail.

Exporters of Primary Products and Manufactured Goods

Trade-related issues are at the core of many of the Third World's complaints about the structure of the world political economy. The trade relationships between many developed and developing nations formed during the age of imperialism, when colonies existed for the presumed benefit of their colonizers. Frequently this meant that the colonies were sources of primary products, such as agricultural products and mineral resources, and markets for the finished manufactured goods produced in the metropole. This pattern continued long after the death of imperialism as a form of political organization.

As shown in Table 8.1 on page 272, the developing countries rely on primary products for their export earnings (the money necessary to buy goods from abroad) to a much greater extent than do developed countries. In 1980, for example, nearly 80 percent of Third World exports were primary products, and only about 20 percent were manufactured goods. The developed countries in the First World, in contrast, relied on primary products for less than a quarter of their earnings, with manufactured products accounting for nearly 75 percent.

A New International Division of Labor?

Although many developing nations continue to depend heavily on primary product exports, during the past two decades the export composition of the Third World as a whole has shifted sharply toward manufactured goods. In 1989, for example, manufactured products accounted for two-thirds of the exports of non-OPEC developing countries (United Nations, *Monthly Bulletin of Statistics* 45 [May 1991]: Special Table C). Thus, it is no longer accurate to picture developing countries as simply exporters of primary products and importers of manufactures.

The shift in the composition of Third World exports challenges empirically the rhetoric many Third World leaders used during the height of the NIEO debate. As a World Bank official observed, "The developing countries . . . persistently argued their case for changing the structure of a global economic order on the grounds that . . . they are unequal partners with the industrial nations. While this concept may be politically attractive, it is increasingly inaccurate as a framework for analysis of the dynamics of current world economic development" (Burki, 1983).

Thus a "new international division of labor" may be replacing the one characterized by the terms *core* (the industrial world) and *periphery* (the developing world) central to both world-system theory and dependency theory (see Chapter 5). In this new international division of labor, the developing nations, traditionally the suppliers of primary and semiprocessed goods, provide First World nations with many manufactured and processed goods, and the latter provide the developing nations with raw materials and agricultural products (see Sanderson, 1984).

TABLE 8.1 First and Third World Trade Composition, 1970–1989 (Percentages)

	Third World					First World				
	1970	1975	1980	1985	1989	1970	1975	1980	1985	1989
Exports										
Primary Products	74.2	82.6	77.6	62.1	41.9	22.5	23.3	24.0	22.2	17.4
Mineral fuels and related materials	32.4	59.4	59.7	43.2	23.2	3.4	5.1	7.0	7.9	3.7
Other primary products[a]	41.8	23.2	17.9	18.9	18.7	19.1	18.2	17.0	14.3	13.7
Manufactured Products	23.7	17.0	21.5	36.9	55.6	75.4	75.2	73.8	75.4	79.4
Other	2.1	0.3	0.9	1.1	2.4	2.1	1.5	2.2	2.3	3.2
Imports										
Primary products	26.6	31.0	34.7	33.5	24.2	34.8	42.5	43.5	34.1	23.5
Mineral fuels and related materials	7.5	14.6	18.0	17.8	9.2	9.8	22.2	27.1	19.2	9.1
Other primary products[a]	19.1	16.4	16.7	15.7	15.0	25.0	20.3	16.4	14.9	14.4
Manufactured Products	68.8	65.8	62.8	62.9	71.0	63.5	56.3	54.4	64.1	73.7
Other	4.6	3.2	2.5	3.6	4.7	1.6	1.2	2.1	1.9	2.8

[a] Food, beverages, tobacco, crude materials (excluding fuels), oil and fats.
Source: Adapted from United Nations, *Monthly Bulletin of Statistics*, various issues.

Growth Strategies

Third World nations have purused two strategies in an effort to build their own industrial bases: *import-substitution industrialization (ISI)* and *export-led industrialization (ELI)*.

Import-substitution industrialization was once the preferred strategy for realizing industrial growth and reducing dependence on imports. Particularly popular in Latin America, the strategy involved encouraging domestic entrepreneurs to manufacture products otherwise imported from abroad. ISI eventually fell into disfavor, however, in part because Third World manufacturers often found that they still relied on technology and even component parts imported from the North to produce goods for their domestic markets (Sklair, 1991; also Black, 1991).

More recently, the preference has been for the development of export industries capable of competing in overseas markets. "The idea behind this was the mirror image of ISI. What had enriched the rich was not their insulation from imports (rich countries do, in fact, import massively all sorts of goods) but their success in manufactured exports, where higher prices could be commanded than for Third World raw materials" (Sklair, 1991).

The remarkable strides achieved since the late 1960s by the Newly Industrialized Countries, notably the four Asian Tigers (Hong Kong, Singapore, South Korea, and Taiwan), is testimony to the success of export-led industrialization. Others have therefore tried to emulate the NICs' experience, but how many will succeed is questionable. The conditions in the world political economy are no longer as favorable as when the NICs embarked on their development strategies (Broad and Cavanagh, 1988). Massive debt now burdens many would-be NICs, for example. In addition, competition for limited external markets is intense in an environment where the growth of world trade has slowed and protectionist sentiments are on the rise. Thus, as one observer put it, "few of the countries undertaking structural adjustment have turned into tigers. Most have turned into turkeys" (Massing, 1990–1991).

Some analysts also question how "new" the new international division of labor really is. As noted in Chapter 5, world-system and dependency theorists use *semiperiphery* and *dependent development* to describe the emergence of industrial powers within the Third World. The terms imply the perpetuation of long-standing patterns in the relations between rich and poor countries. "Even when manufactures are exported to the core," one analyst notes, "they remain of the sort that has always defined the semi-periphery's role in the world division of labor. The new industries of the semi-periphery are the old, declining industries of the core. By relying on the now easily transferred technology of traditional mass production using semiskilled labor, the semi-periphery can use the advantage of low wages to capture a segment of the market. . . . Hence, world-system theorists view recent developments in the semi-periphery not as some sort of unprecedented economic breakthrough, but as extensions of the normal role of that zone in the world-economy" (Shannon, 1989).

Preferential Trade

Because of the importance of trade to the realization of Third World aspirations, gaining access to markets in the industrial world is an important goal. Indeed, "trade, not aid" is a persistent Third World plea, as many developing nations believe the industrial nations have systematically denied them access to First World markets through both tariff and nontariff barriers.

Beginning as early as 1964, during the first UNCTAD conference, Third World nations sought preferential (as opposed to most-favored-nation) trade treatment as a means to overcome the obstacles to their access to First World markets. Preferential treatment, they believe, will enable them to build diversified export industries capable of competing on equal terms with those of the North.

In partial response to that view, the industrial nations agreed in the 1970s to establish within GATT a system of trade preferences for developing nations. Known as the Generalized System of Preferences (GSP), the scheme permits First World nations to grant preferences to developing nations without violating GATT's nondiscrimination principle, long a centerpiece of the LIEO.

Despite this apparent Northern concession, its effects are in dispute. For example, some of the countries that have benefited most from the trade preferences, such as Hong Kong and South Korea, have needed them least (Spero, 1990; also *World Development Report 1990*, 1990). In addition, following the insistence of the United States, the GSP provisions approved during the Tokyo Round of GATT negotiations included a "graduation clause." It stipulated that, as developing countries reached higher levels of development, they would receive less special treatment and have to compete on a more equal footing with Northern states. No precise guidelines were formulated to determine when graduation would occur, a matter of concern to the South, but it was on the basis of this provision (written into U.S. law in 1984) that the United States in 1989 revoked the preferential treatment earlier granted the Asian NICs.

The Tokyo Round of GATT trade negotiations that legitimized the GSP also failed to grapple with the protectionist sentiments in the North often directed at products in which some developing nations already enjoyed comparative advantages, such as clothing, footwear, textiles, and steel. In 1986, for example, 21 percent of the imports of industrial countries from the Third World were subject to "hard-core" nontariff barriers,[2] compared with only 16 percent of the imports from industrial countries from the North (*World Development Report 1991*, 1991: 105). If other restraints are added, such as health and safety standards, the proportion would be even larger—and the trends point toward more restraints, not fewer.

Because of their belief that the Tokyo negotiations did not address protectionist sentiments in the North, the developing nations, many of which do not belong to GATT, generally shunned the accords. However, the greater attention to nontariff barriers in the Uruguay Round of negotiations sparked considerable interest among the developing nations and drew some of the most important of them into fuller participation in the deliberations. Still, it remains problematic whether the outcome of those deliberations will ultimately prove beneficial to the aims and interests of Third World nations.

---

[2] "Hard-core" NTBs comprise that subset of all NTBs most likely to have significant restrictive effects, including "important prohibitions, quantitative restrictions, voluntary export restraints, variable levies, MFA restrictions, and nonautomatic licensing" (*World Development Report 1987*, 1987).

Other developments have also stimulated a change in Third World attitudes toward GATT. As noted above, historically developing nations have viewed GATT with suspicion. Now, ironically, the possibility of a regionalized trade regime (see Chapter 7) has stimulated a very different view of the organization and its principles. "For the developing countries, the prospect of a world divided into separate regional centers is disconcerting. It leaves too many countries out of the system altogether, and even those it encompasses are left relatively weaker as their bargaining power is divided. So, even though developing countries in the past have regarded the GATT as a 'rich man's club,' today they see it as a guardian for the clear and fair rules they need if they are to enter the international arena successfully" (Philips and Tucker, 1991).

Commodity Exports and the Terms of Trade

As noted, a large proportion of manufactured product exports now originate in the Third World. For many countries, however, primary products continue to dominate their exports. The poorest of poor countries, particularly in Africa, are typically among them (see Figure 8.1). And often it is a single export commodity that dominates.

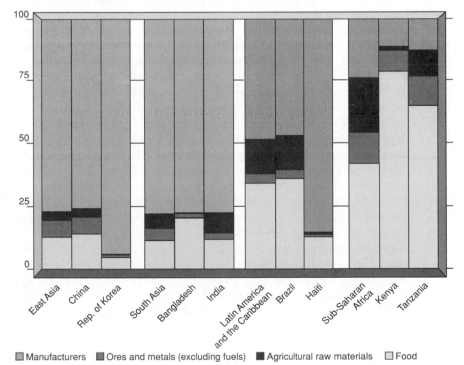

■ Manufacturers   ■ Ores and metals (excluding fuels)   ■ Agricultural raw materials   ☐ Food

FIGURE 8.1   COMMODITY COMPOSITION OF DEVELOPING NATIONS' EXPORTS, 1988 (PERCENTAGE OF TOTAL VALUE IN DOLLARS)
Source: World Development Report 1990 (New York: Oxford University Press, 1990), p. 125.
Note: The data for Sub-Saharan Africa do not include Botswana and Lesotho.

Coffee, for example, accounts for three quarters of Burundi's exports and more than 96 percent of Uganda's. It is iron ore in Liberia (57 percent), alumina and bauxite in Jamaica (58 percent), fish and iron ore in Mauritania (59 and 41 percent, respectively), and copper in Zambia (86 percent).[3] Thus each of the exporting countries is particularly susceptible to external forces that affect both short- and long-term commodity prices.

The Terms of Trade

The dependence of many developing nations on a narrow range of primary-product exports gives urgency to the forces that affect the *terms of trade* between North and South. The phrase refers to the ratio of export prices to import prices. The developing nations believe that the prices they receive for their exports vary erratically in the short run and fall in the long run, while the prices of the manufactured goods that they import increase steadily.

According to world-system and dependency theory, structural characteristics of the international economic order are among the alleged causes of the deteriorating terms of trade. The South remains critically dependent on the North not only for manufactured goods but also for technology (see Head, 1989; also Chapter 5). The greater technological sophistication of the North causes natural resources to flow into markets where they are transformed efficiently into finished goods. Powerful labor unions and giant corporations institutionalize (through wage and fringe benefit programs) the comparatively high cost of the technologically sophisticated products produced in the North. Meanwhile, worldwide advertising campaigns sustain demand for these products.

Developing nations are unable to compete on similar terms with the North, the argument continues. They cannot bid up the prices for the materials produced in developing nations. In a system where those with the most money determine prices, Third World nations find themselves unable to determine the terms of trade for their products.

There is no question that the developing nations' primary product exports are subject to sharp price fluctuations. Non-oil commodity prices dropped sharply in the early 1980s during the recession induced by the second oil shock, for example, when they fell to a lower level in real terms (after adjusting for the rise in prices of manufactured goods imported by developing nations) than at any time since World War II (*World Development Report 1983*, 1983). Prices rebounded somewhat between 1984 and 1986, as shown in Figure 8.2, only to continue their fall later. The near free-fall of oil prices beginning in 1985 is also shown in Figure 8.2, which charts the downward trend of the terms of trade for the developing nations during the 1980s.

Other evidence is consistent with the terms-of-trade argument. Between 1900 and 1986, for example, non-fuel commodity terms of trade declined an average of 0.6 percent a year (*World Development Report 1991*, 1991: 106). There are reasons to be cautious with such data, however. For one thing, the choice of the base year for

---

[3] Data are from the *International Financial Statistics Yearbook* (1991) and refer to either 1989 or 1990 data.

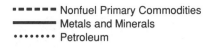

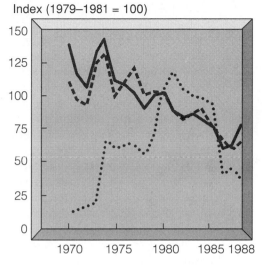

Index (1979–1981 = 100)

FIGURE 8.2 COMMODITY PRICES, 1970–1988

Source: World Development Report 1989 (New York: Oxford University Press, 1989), p. 11.
Note: Real prices are annual average prices in dollars, deflated by the annual change in the manufacturing unit value (MUV) index, a measure of the price of industiral country exports to developing countries. Prices for nonfuel primary commodities are based on a basket of thirty-three commodities.

comparison matters. If one chooses 1920 rather than 1900, for example, the terms of trade declined only 0.3 percent per year, rather than 0.6 percent (*World Development Report 1991*, 1991: 106).

Also unclear is whether trends over shorter periods are due to a structural deterioration in the terms of trade or to short-term perturbations related to changes in the business cycle. Moreover, the quality of manufactured products has increased over time, and the increase in the volume of trade offsets some of the decline in the terms of trade (*World Development Report 1991*, 1991). Regardless, to the extent that beliefs and perceptions influence Third World leaders, these, rather than reality, dictate policy. As political scientist Robert L. Rothstein notes (1979), "Many economists doubt that there has been a secular decline in the terms of trade for commodities, but what is believed or assumed—taken on faith—is more important here than analytical argument."

Price Stabilization

Reversing the unfavorable terms-of-trade pattern is a long-term goal of the Third World nations. A more immediate goal is reducing the fluctuations in the prices they receive for their commodities.

Creation of a new commodities regime was a principal objective of the Group of 77 and UNCTAD during much of the 1970s. It was the central issue during the

UNCTAD IV meeting in Nairobi, Kenya, in 1976, when the G-77 won adoption of a proposed Integrated Programme for Commodities. As originally formulated, the Integrated Programme called for a revolutionary approach to international decision making and management of trade in commodities (see Rothstein, 1979).

Eventually, attention focused on proposals for a Common Fund designed to stabilize prices of several commodities. The Common Fund would finance creation of buffer stocks that could be bought and sold as supply and demand dictated.[4] The G-77 pushed for a $6 billion fund and a significant voice in its management.[5] The industrial nations opposed both the amount, most of which they would have to finance, and the management proposals, which favored the South.

What finally emerged was far different from the ambitious goals that the Group of 77 and the UNCTAD secretariat had originally set out to achieve. A 1979 agreement created a $750 million arrangement consisting of a kind of bank to help inidividual commodity organizations purchase buffer stocks of raw materials, which would be used to keep commodity prices within predetermined ranges. The agreement also anticipated creation of an international aid organization to help poorer developing nations expand, diversify, and market their commodity exports.

It would be another decade before the Common Fund secured the number of signatories and ratifications necessary to make it operational. Even then, some key actors, notably the United States, were not among them. Furthermore, the fund's ability to deal successfully with commodity prices so critical to Third World nations remained doubtful. Successful operation is hampered because only individual international commodity agreements involving producers and consumers may be parties to the arrangement, but agreements do not exist in all of the commodities envisaged by the fund. Moreover, concluding new ones has proved difficult, and even those that do exist have been comparatively ineffective.

Other avenues are available for dealing with the developing nations' commodity problems. Associations of producing countries, for example, avoid the difficulties inherent in international commodity agreements, which require balancing consumer and producer interests. Compensatory financing arrangements, which seek to stabilize export earnings through financial aid rather than buffer-stock manipulation of prices, are another alternative. The International Monetary Fund, for example, maintains a Compensatory and Contingency Financing Facility designed to assist Third World nations with balance-of-payments difficulties caused by shortfalls in their export earnings or unforseen price increases (as in the case of oil following Iraq's invasion of Kuwait in 1990).

The European Community operates a compensatory financing scheme known as STABEX, the intellectual forerunner of UNCTAD's original proposal for an integrated commodity program (Hart, 1978). It is part of the Lomé Convention, concluded

---

[4] As originally envisaged, eighteen products were to be covered by the Common Fund: bananas, bauxite, cocoa, coffee, copper, cotton, hard fibers, iron ore, jute, manganese, meat, phosphates, rubber, sugar, tea, tropical timber, tin, and vegetable oils.

[5] See Rothstein (1979) and Schechter (1979) for examinations of objectives and the evolution of strategies regarding the Integrated Programme and the Common Fund in particular.

in 1975 (and since extended to 1999) between the European Community and sixty-six African, Caribbean, and Pacific nations (the so-called ACP nations), mostly former European colonies. Through the convention the EC granted the ACP nations preferential trade access to the European market without the requirement of reciprocity for the EC nations. It also increased the amount of foreign aid available to the ACP countries while giving them a voice in the management of aid projects. But the centerpiece of Lomé is STABEX, a compensatory financing arrangement designed to stabilize ACP export earnings in forty-eight agricultural products (mineral exports are covered in a separate agreement[6]). "Ground-breaking" and "politically genuinely significant" were terms describing STABEX at its inception (Gruhn, 1976).[7]

Despite this initial optimism, the contribution of STABEX to the goal of commodity price stabilization is unclear. As the World Bank (*World Development Report 1986*, 1986) put it in commenting on both STABEX and the IMF compensatory financing facility: "To be successful, compensatory schemes must have clear objectives, permit quick identification of shortfalls, and provide prompt payments without complicated conditions. Neither the [IMF scheme] nor STABEX has been ideal in these respects." Furthermore, it became apparent at the time Lomé was first renegotiated that the very economic problems that make compensatory financing mechanisms attractive to producing countries can breed conflict between producing and consuming countries over the coverage and operation of the system (Islam, 1982).

Thus, just as the Common Fund seems unlikely to have the measurable impact on commodity trade once sought by advocates of the New International Economic Order, the STABEX experience suggests that alternative approaches to commodity price stabilization are also unlikely to produce easy solutions to Third World commodity problems. The reason is simple: "Supporting and stabilizing the prices of commodities and providing compensatory financing for Third World exporters both require that resources be transferred from consuming to producing countries, which invariably means from developed to developing countries. Here the major obstacle has been, and remains, Northern unwillingness to make the required transfers" (Puchala, 1983).

Finally, it should be noted that changes in the world political economy raise the possibility that stabilizing commodities' prices may not offer realistic solutions to the problems of Third World commodity exporters. Commodities have increasingly become "uncoupled" from industrial economies as the material intensity of manufacturing has steadily diminished (Drucker, 1986). Hence, commodities are simply less important than previously.

Development Finance

The developing nations may prefer trade to aid, but aid has a long heritage in the relations between rich and poor nations. Moreover, in many ways it remains a pre-

---

[6] The minerals scheme is known as MINEX. It was negotiated in 1979 and designed to give mineral producers the same benefits that STABEX earlier granted to producers of agricultural commodities, principally tropical products (see Shonfield, 1980).

[7] See also Bywater (1975) and Ravenhill (1984) for further discussions of the Lomé Convention and STABEX.

ferred weapon in the developed nations' arsenal for coping with the South, in part, perhaps, because it is more easily tailored to the pursuit of specific foreign policy objectives.

The developing nations, for their part, often view aid as a moral obligation of the rich to the poor necessary to redress the injustices of the imperial past. Not surprisingly, therefore, they are sensitive to the "strings" sometimes attached to the aid they receive. They have also been critical of what they regard as the comparatively meager resources channeled from the rich countries to the poor.

The Form and Purposes of Foreign Aid

"Foreign aid" comes in a variety of forms and is used for a variety of purposes. Some aid consists of outright grants of money, some consists of loans at concessional rates, and some consists of shared technical expertise. Most foreign aid is bilateral, meaning it flows directly from one country to another, but some is channeled through international institutions like the World Bank, and hence is known as multilateral aid.

The purposes of aid are as varied as its forms. Security objectives are typically pursued through military assistance of one kind or another, but economic aid is also used for these purposes. The United States, for example, "paid" for military base rights in many Third World countries during the Cold War with varying amounts of economic as well as military aid. It also continues to target Israel and Egypt as major recipients of U.S. economic assistance because of their critical role in furthering U.S. political and security goals in the Middle East.[8]

Disaster relief and other humanitarian purposes are also served with grants and loans, but the economic development of the Third World has been a primary aim of most foreign aid donors since World War II. The assumption is that development will enhance prospects for the realization of other goals, such as commercial advantage and the growth of free markets and democratic political systems (see Table 8.2).

The Volume and Value of Foreign Aid

Developing nations charged during the height of their drive for a New International Economic Order that the volume and value of foreign aid flowing from North to South was "unjustifiably low" (Hansen, 1979). How do those charges stack up against the evidence?

Certainly by some standards the largess funneled to developing nations has been considerable. The United States alone has provided more than $212 billion in economic assistance since World War II. On an annual basis its allocation of "official development assistance"—a term used to capture the concessional element in donors' aid allocations—has averaged about $9 billion annually since the early 1980s.

Today the United States is only one of many major foreign aid donors. Various multilateral institutions are among the others, including the World Bank, the United

---

[8] In 1990 Egypt and Israel received 47.1 percent of U.S. overseas loans and grants, down from a high of 67.5 percent in 1979, when the Camp David accords leading to peace between the regional antagonists went into effect (Philips and Tucker, 1991: 35; see also Sewell and Contee, 1987).

TABLE 8.2 THE FOREIGN POLICY AND ECONOMIC GOALS OF FOREIGN AID DONORS

Time Frame	Primary Objectives	Expected Byproducts	Types of Donors
Long-range	1. Economic development; reduce poverty 2. Eventual self-sufficiency of recipient	1. Political Stability 2. Democratization 3. Speed up historical trend toward socialism 4. Arab/Muslim solidarity	1. Western 2. Western 3. Soviet Union 4. Arab (OPEC)
Medium-range	1. Maintain diplomatic presence in recipient 2. Symbolize friendships and commitments to, and support for, recipients 3. Maintain access to, and influence over, recipients' domestic and foreign policies	1. Commercial, trade opportunities 2. Enrich bilateral relations 3. Great powers	1. All donors 2. All donors 3. Great powers
Immediate	1. Change recipient's current domestic or foreign policies 2. Sustain a recipient's regime in power 3. Humanitarian emergency relief	1. Obtain support for donor's foreign policies 2. Protect donor's core objectives 3. Possible future goodwill	1. Great powers 2. Great powers 3. All donors

Source: K. J. Holsti, *International Politics: A Framework for Analysis* (Englewood Cliffs, N.J.: Prentice Hall, 1992), p. 199.

Nations Development Program, the Inter-American, Asian, and African Development banks, the European Community, and various OPEC and Arab institutions.

Also included are the major industrial powers, who are also the major donors of foreign aid. Collectively, they make up the Development Assistance Committee (DAC) of the Organization for Economic Cooperation and Development (OECD).[9] As shown in Figure 8.3, the official development assistance of DAC members grew from less than $30 billion annually in 1970 to nearly $50 billion two decades later. Interestingly, Japan replaced the United States in the early 1990s as the world's foremost aid donor.

Although the members of DAC are the principal aid donors, others have also played a role in the aid effort. The communist countries, for example, made grants of between $2 billion and $3 billion annually from the early 1970s until well into the 1980s, when their own domestic ills caused them to turn increasingly inward. That in turn led to a rapid decline in their aid effort, with sometimes dramatic effects on recipient countries, notably Cuba. The OPEC countries have also been significant

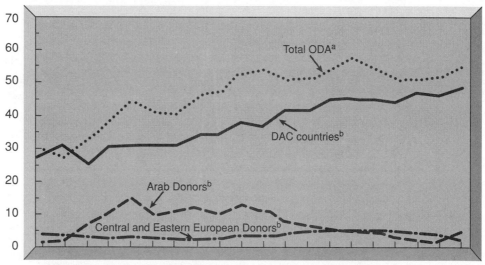

FIGURE 8.3 OFFICIAL DEVELOPMENT ASSISTANCE BY MAJOR DONOR GROUPS, 1971–1990 (BILLIONS $ AT 1989 PRICES AND EXCHANGE RATES)
Source: Development Cooperation: 1991 Report (Paris: Organization for Economic Co-operation and Development, 1991), p. 127.
a Bilateral ODA from all sources and concessional loans from multilateral agencies.
b Bilateral ODA and ODA contributions to multilateral agencies.

---

[9] DAC members are Australia, Austria, Belgium, Canada, Denmark, Finland, France, Germany, Ireland, Italy, Japan, the Netherlands, New Zealand, Norway, Sweden, Switzerland, the United Kingdom, the United States, and the Commission of the European Community. Members of the OECD include the above countries plus Greece, Iceland, Luxembourg, Portugal, Spain, and Turkey.

players in the aid game, particularly when global oil prices were high. OPEC's role diminished following the decline of oil prices in the mid-1980s, however. In fact, many OPEC countries found themselves seeking external sources of funds to cope with the balance-of-payments deficits they suddenly faced.

Against this background, what is the basis for the charge that the volume and value of foreign aid received by developing nations has been unjustifiably low? In one sense, of course, the charge is simply wrong: The flow of aid has been substantial and increasing. In other ways, however, the charge has merit.

Consider, for example, the "aid burden." The generally agreed-upon standard for measuring the burden of aid is the ratio between aid and a donor's income as measured by gross national product. The principle widely accepted in diplomatic circles is that rich nations should transfer to poor nations resources equivalent to 0.7 percent of their GNP. The OPEC nations generally exceeded this target until the mid-1980s, but the DAC donors and particularly the communist countries have fallen far short of it. Furthermore, the trend has been flat rather than upward, largely a consequence of the downward turn in the relative aid effort of the United States, long the largest aid donor. Between 1965 and the mid-1980s, U.S. development assistance as a proportion of its GNP declined by more than half—plummeting from 0.58 percent in 1965 to 0.15 percent in 1989 (*World Development Report 1991*, 1991: 240). The United States now ranks at the bottom of the list of DAC donors in the proportion of its income devoted to foreign aid.

The rapid decline in the *relative* volume of U.S. foreign economic aid reflects a failure to increase aid commensurately with real increases in GNP or with rising prices. A combination of three factors explains the failure: "donor fatigue" with the seeming intractability of the development process, a conviction that domestic needs should take priority over foreign ones, and, from time to time, disenchantment with the performance of the multilateral lending agencies. Most recently, the end of the Cold War has stimulated questions about the continued pertinence of aid as an instrument of foreign policy (see Bissell, 1991; Eberstadt, 1990; Graves, 1991; Sewell, 1991).

Furthermore, the United States, like most aid donors, "ties" its aid to purchases in the United States, even though it may not be the lowest-cost producer of the goods that the developing nations need.[10] At the same time, developing nations have experienced dramatic population increases in recent decades, which tends to erode the per-capita impact of aid. Adding these two facts to the picture, it becomes clear that the volume of foreign aid received by Third World countries is comparatively small and that its value is shrinking.

Finally, a consideration of other expenditures magnifies the comparative insignificance of foreign aid. Global military spending, for example, outpaced official government-to-government economic aid flows during much of the 1980s by a margin

---

[10] Tying means that the aid recipients are required to spend their aid dollars to purchase goods produced in the donor country. C. Fred Bergsten (1973: 104) noted some years ago that "tying alone reduces the real value of aid by 10 to 30 percent below its nominal value." For recent data on the proportion of aid tied by individual DAC donors, see *Development Cooperation: 1991 Report* (1991: 206).

of roughly twenty to one. The disparity is more conspicuous in particular cases, as in the United States. Furthermore, even after U.S. military spending began a downward trend in 1990, Americans still spent more than three times as much on tobacco products and nearly five times as much on alcoholic beverages as their government spent on official development assistance (Philips and Tucker, 1991: 34).

Conditionality

Beyond criticism of the meager volume and value of aid, complaints about its political strings are legion. The complaints grow out of a long (and understandable) history of donors' efforts to use foreign aid to serve the multiple foreign policy goals summarized in Table 8.2.

We noted above, for example, that the United States has used aid to foster its foreign policy goals in the Middle East. It pursued similar strategies in the Caribbean and Central America during the 1980s, where security considerations were overriding concerns. The United States has also gone on record declaring that it will consider states' voting records in the United Nations in assessing their qualifications for U.S. foreign assistance (see Kegley and Hook, 1991).

The behavior of the United States is not unusual. OPEC allocates the largest percentage of its aid to Arab countries, with much of the rest spread among Asian and African nations with sizable Muslim populations (see *Development Cooperation: 1991 Report*, 1991). Similarly, Britain and France give much of their aid to their former colonies. Noting the failure of many recipients of foreign aid to improve their economies, some observers (Hayter, 1971, for example) have even suggested that foreign aid is often a tool used by the North to perpetuate neocolonial and neo-imperial ties, thus further subordinating the weak and poor while promoting the welfare of those already strong and rich.

Although developing nations are sensitive to the strings attached to foreign aid flows, conditionality is widespread and often involves not only changes in recipients' economic systems but also political reforms. Japan, for example, has guidelines for development assistance that "include reductions in recipient countries' military expenditures (including arms production and trade), introduction of market-oriented economies, promotion of democracy, and respect for human rights" (Philips and Tucker, 1991).

The trend toward Third World democratization, which the Japanese guidelines seek to encourage, is an appropriately heralded positive development. As shown in Figure 8.4, the number of elected Third World heads of state has increased dramatically since the mid-1980s. But will the democracies survive?

Ensuring a successful transition to democracy "has triggered an intense debate about what role [the industrial democracies] and the international financial institutions [IMF and the World Bank] should play in supporting this process." In this context, the view now increasingly shared in the North is that "political democracy is not only compatible with, but even a precondition for, economic development" (Philips and Tucker, 1991). There are reasons to question this emerging conventional wisdom.

Neither empirical evidence nor historical experience substantiate the view that democracy

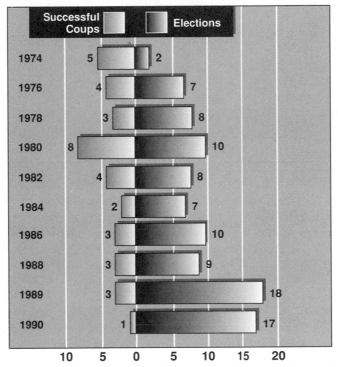

FIGURE 8.4 THE TREND TOWARD DEMOCRACY IN THE THIRD WORLD, 1974–1990

Source: Rosemarie Philips and Stuart K. Tucker, *U.S. Foreign Policy and Developing Countries: Discourse and Data 1991* (Washington, D.C.: Overseas Development Council, 1991), p. 16.

is a necessary precondition for development. Where powerful special interests or a small self-serving elite control the electoral process; where patronage is a significant force in the political parties; where ethnic or regional tensions could provoke conflict or disintegration; or where terrorists, guerrillas, or drug barons control much of public life, rapid political liberalization could result in disproportionate influence on the part of some, rather than increased influence on the part of all. Moreover, political pluralism may conflict with other important policy goals such as economic reform, poverty-oriented development measures, environmental protection, control of the drug trade, or control of terrorism. (Philips and Tucker, 1991: 17)

From this perspective, democracy should be defined not in terms of political institutions, such as legislatures and political parties, but in terms of people-involvement in political decision making.

The connection between democracy and development may be unclear, and the role that foreign aid might play in encouraging democracy may prove as elusive as its role in promoting economic development. Nonetheless, it is clear that donor countries will use whatever leverage they have to encourage Third World reforms designed to promote democratic capitalism.

Engines of Growth

The preceding discussion demonstrates how profoundly developed nations of the North affect developing economies of the South. Whether those effects are purposeful or not, beneficial or adverse, remain controversial questions. Dependency theory, to which many Third World leaders once subscribed, purports to have the answer. Recall from Chapter 5 the core arguments of dependency theory:

- the relationship between the advanced capitalist societies and those at the periphery of the world political economy is exploitative;
- underdevelopment is a structural position in a hierarchical world division of labor explained by the relationship between core and peripheral states in the world political economy;
- capitalism's need for external sources of demand and profitable investment outlets leads to the penetration of peripheral societies;
- penetration leads to technological dependence and "cultural imperialism";
- multinational corporations, driven by the profit motive, are a primary agent of the penetration process;
- multinational corporations transfer profits from the penetrated societies to their home states, thus retarding growth in peripheral societies;
- local elites within the penetrated societies, whose own fortunes become tied to the dominant powers, sustain the inherently exploitative linkages that bind core and periphery together.

Multinational corporations (MNCs) figure prominently in dependency theorists' arguments, as the preceding summary shows. Thus it is appropriate to return to the question of the costs and benefits of multinational corporations that we raised in Chapter 6, but this time from the perspective of Third World economies.

The Benefits of Multinational Corporations

Multinational corporations doubtless play a dominant role in developing nations, but are they necessarily detrimental to economic growth? Some analysts think not.

> For all the talk (and the reality) of imperialist domination, most of the underdeveloped nations want domestic foreign investment, European and/or American, for a variety of reasons. The multinationals pay higher wages, keep more honest books, pay more taxes, and provide more managerial know-how and training than do local industries. Moreover, they usually provide better social services for their workers, and certainly provide fancy career opportunities for a favored few of the elite. They are, in addition, a main channel through which technology, developed in the West, can filter into the backward nations. To be sure, the corporations typically send home more profits than the capital that they originally introduce into the "host" country; but meanwhile that capital grows, providing jobs, improving productivity, and often contributing to export earnings. (Heilbroner, 1977: 345–346)

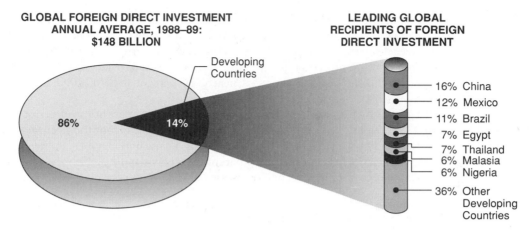

GLOBAL FOREIGN DIRECT INVESTMENT ANNUAL AVERAGE, 1988–89: $148 BILLION

86%   14%   Developing Countries

LEADING GLOBAL RECIPIENTS OF FOREIGN DIRECT INVESTMENT

16% China
12% Mexico
11% Brazil
7% Egypt
7% Thailand
6% Malasia
6% Nigeria
36% Other Developing Countries

FIGURE 8.5   FOREIGN DIRECT INVESTMENT IN DEVELOPING NATIONS
Source: Rosemarie Philips and Stuart K. Tucker, *U.S. Foreign Policy and Developing Countries: Discourse and Data 1991* (Washington, D.C.: Overseas Development Council, 1991), p. 33.

These reasons may explain the widespread quest for multinational investment. Increasingly, as we have noted, multinationals invest not in Third World economies but in First World economies (see Figure 8.5). Developing nations nonetheless actively seek to attract them, especially states committed to export-led industrialization. One observer explains the attractiveness of and "nearly universal demand for substantial MNC activity":

In many fields the most attractive technology and expertise does not come in "unbundled" form; the advantages in foreign market access that are inherent in most manufacturing MNCs often cannot be duplicated except at a very high price. A rapid and premature jettisoning of the MNC—even in natural resource industries—has led some countries to economic disaster. (Kudrle, 1987: 241)

The Costs of Multinational Corporations

From another Third World perspective, however, the costs associated with MNCs have been excessive. "The capital, jobs and other benefits they bring to developing economies are recognized, but the terms on which these benefits come are seen as unfair and exploitive and as robbing the new nations of their resources" (Cutler, 1978).

One of the alleged costs is technological dependence. According to one argument, technology imported from the North impedes local development. Technology transferred to the Third World is often inappropriate to the local setting, and the diffusion effects of industrial activity within the developing nations in particular are limited (see also Chapter 5).

Another argument points to the repatriation of profits by multinationals. Because MNCs seek to maximize profits for their shareholders, who more often than not live in the parent state rather than in the host state, there is little reinvestment in the country of production. Instead, capital finds its way into someone else's hands. Moreover, the returns are sometimes excessive. Between 1975 and 1978, for example, the profit on U.S. direct foreign investment in the First World averaged 12.1 percent, but in the Third World it averaged nearly 26 percent (Spero, 1990: 241; compare Drucker, 1974).

Critics also charge that profits represent only a small part of the effective return to parent companies. "A large part of the real return comes from the licensing fees and royalties paid by the subsidiary to the parent for the use of technology controlled by the parent" (Spero, 1990). Admittedly, parent companies must absorb the research and development costs of new technologies used abroad. Nonetheless, critics argue that

> subsidiaries in less-developed countries pay an unjustifiably high price for technology and bear an unjustifiably high share of the research and development costs. The monopoly control of technology by the multinational corporation enables the parent to exact a monopoly rent from its subsidiaries. And the parent chooses to use that power and to charge inordinately high fees and royalties to disguise high profits and avoid local taxes on those profits, according to the critics. (Spero, 1990: 242)

Critics also point to the *transfer-pricing mechanism* as another device used by MNCs to increase their profits and minimize their tax burdens. The raw, semiprocessed, or finished materials produced by a parent's subsidiaries located in different countries are in effect traded among the subsidiaries. Because the same company sits on both sides of the transaction, it can manipulate the sales or "transfer" prices of these import-export transactions so as to benefit the parent firm. "Some firms do this as objectively as they can, without regard to tax considerations. But there are also some who exercise this discretion so as to minimize their global taxes and maximize their after-tax earnings. Since tax rates vary around the world, they accomplish this by recording profits in jurisdictions where taxes are relatively low" (Cutler, 1978; see also Centre on Transnational Corporations, 1985a). Increased capital flow from South to North is the net effect. Poverty in the host country is allegedly the primary product (Müller, 1973–1974).

Much of the critical literature considers "the remission of 'excessive' profits the key mechanism by which the host country's balance of payments is adversely affected by multinational corporations." Political economist Raymond Vernon argues instead "that the annual income remissions are insignificant compared to the local value added annually by such corporations" (cited in Bierstecker, 1978). He also challenges the capital-outflow and technology dependence arguments, alleging that the former "is fallacious because of its failure to measure the implications of changes in domestic output" (cited in Bierstecker, 1978), while the latter is subject to "an overwhelming propensity on the part of well-trained and well-informed critics to oversimplify the issue and to disregard the nonconforming evidence" (Vernon, 1975). In a similar vein, international economist Charles Kindleberger (1969) contends that, despite MNCs' monopolistic and exploitative tendencies, multinationals as a whole have, paradoxically, expanded competition and enhanced world economic efficiency.

In sum, then, the economic consequences of MNCs' activities are not always discernible or easily agreed upon, which is perhaps why evaluations do not point to consensus. As political economist Joan Spero (1990) observes, "It is impossible to reach any general or definitive conclusion about the overall effect of multinationals on development. The influence of foreign investment varies from country to country, from firm to firm, and from project to project. Some case studies demonstrate the beneficial impact of direct foreign investment; others, the detrimental effects." She continues by noting that "the principal effect of the criticism of multinationals that began in the 1970s has been to alter the political reality of foreign investment in the developing countries. No longer do governments assume that foreign investment will automatically promote development. Instead, . . . developing country governments have tried to regulate that investment to maximize the rewards and minimize the costs to the host economy" (see also Leyton-Brown, 1990; Sklair, 1991; Walters and Blake, 1992).

THIRD WORLD DEBT AND THE MANAGEMENT OF INTERDEPENDENCE . . . . . .

As noted above, OPEC's success in cartelizing the global oil regime during the 1970s galvanized the non-oil-producing developing nations into the belief that commodity power would enable them to "force" the North into replacing the Liberal International Economic Order with one more amenable to their goals and interests. Ironically, however, the two oil shocks of the 1970s created an environment in which many Third World nations thought it was prudent to borrow heavily from abroad, while they simultaneously eroded the economic bases on which repayment of those loans depended. The result was a "debt crisis" that "dominated—some would say 'consumed'—international economic discussions in the 1980s" in what effectively became the "debt decade" (Nowzad, 1990). Its causes and consequences weave together many of the strands of the tapestry of North-South relations in the world political economy.

As it first emerged in the early 1980s, the debt crisis spread to a broad group of countries, ranging from Poland in Eastern Europe to Brazil in Latin America, from the Philippines in the Far East to Nigeria in West Africa. It grew out of a combination of heavy private and public borrowing from private and public sources during the 1970s that led to an accumulated debt estimated to have been over $600 billion by 1980 and more than twice that amount a decade later. Many debtor nations found that they needed to borrow more money not to finance new projects but to meet their debt service obligations (interest and principal payments) on previous loans.

The specific event that triggered the debt crisis was the threat in August 1982 that Mexico would default on its loans. In addition to Mexico, others with the largest debts, including Poland, Argentina, and Brazil, required special treatment to keep them from going into default when they announced they did not have the cash necessary to pay their creditors. Eventually Third World debtor nations, especially those in Latin America, received the most attention.

Averting Disaster

The foreign debt accumulation of the 1970s was part of a process that saw private loans and investments and official nonconcessional loans become more important than public foreign aid for all but the poorest of the poor countries (Burki, 1983).[11] The first oil shock gave impetus to the "privatization" of Third World capital flows. As dollars flowed from oil consumers in the West to oil producers in the Middle East and elsewhere, the latter, unable to invest all of their new-found wealth at home, "recycled" their "petrodollars" by making investments in the First World. In the process the funds available to private banks for lending to others increased substantially.

Many of the non-oil-exporting developing nations became the willing consumers of the private banks' investment funds. The fourfold rise in oil prices induced by the OPEC cartel hit these nations particularly hard. To pay for the sharply increased cost of imported oil along with their other imports, they could either tighten their belts at home to curb their economic growth or borrow from abroad to sustain that growth and pay for needed imports. Many chose the latter, and they often preferred private banks to other governments or multilateral agencies because the banks usually placed fewer restrictions on the use of the borrowed money than did the public sources. Private banks for their part were willing lenders, as they believed "sovereign risk"—the risk that governments might default—was virtually nonexistent.

Just as many of the now industrial states were net borrowers from the world when they were building their own economies in the past, countries that seek to industrialize today must often rely on external capital. As long as the exports needed to earn the money to pay back the loans grows at the same rate, the accumulation of more debt is no problem. Moreover, there can be long-run payoffs in that investments made today in development projects, such as roads, hydroelectric dams, and steel plants, may eventually more than make up the cost of the original loans by generating new income, employment, and exports.

Whether developing nations always spent their borrowed money wisely is questionable. Argentina, for example, spent billions of dollars on sophisticated military equipment later used against Britain during the Falkland Islands (Malvinas) War. And Brazil, the largest debtor, used foreign loans to finance several extraordinarily expensive "white elephants," including three nuclear power plants, the world's largest hydroelectric dam, and a railroad that were all either unworkable or never completed (Henry, 1987).

Massive capital flight from debtor nations was another problem. Unscrupulous

---

[11] During the 1970s private financial institutions surpassed not only official bilateral aid but also multilateral institutions as the principal source of financial capital available to Third World countries. The result in many cases was a condition of "indebted industrialization" (Frieden, 1981) as governmental agencies in state-capitalist regimes became actively involved in promoting industrial growth. A decade later many observers (for example, Kuczynski, 1987) as well as some state-capitalist regimes (such as Mexico) came to the conclusion that disengagement of the state from direct involvement in industrialization activities, often through a process of "privatization," was a necessary component of the internal reforms needed to cope effectively with the debt crisis. That process has now spread widely in the Third World as well as in Eastern Europe and the former Soviet Union.

political leaders or well-heeled elites funneled much of the money into private accounts in the very banks extending the loans to the governments in the first place. The outflow of money reduced what was available for the investments that create new jobs and new wealth.

At the same time that developing nations' debt mounted during the 1970s, however, so did the resources needed to service it. As a result, the burden of the growing debt was essentially the same in 1980 as it was in 1970. But that situation changed sharply after 1980 as the drop in commodity prices associated with the worldwide recession caused the ratio of Third World debts to exports to rise markedly between 1980 and 1982. Economic growth slowed as the prices of the commodities needed to pay for the debt dropped and the money needed to pay off the loans simply failed to materialize.

The appreciation of the dollar in foreign exchange markets added to the debt burden, as many developing nations' loans are denominated in dollars. Similarly, the strict monetarist policies adopted by the Western industrial nations as a way of coping with their persistent inflation caused interest rates to rise, with the result that developing nations' debt obligations, tied to those rates, also inched upwards. For developing nations as a whole, the ratio of debt service obligations to export earnings rose sharply. The magnitude of the debt also grew to staggering proportions, increasing from $634 billion, or 82 percent of exports in 1980, to $850 billion, or 120 percent of exports, two years later (International Monetary Fund, 1987: 181, 186).

The International Monetary Fund assumed a leadership role in securing debt relief for many Third World countries, but it did so at the cost of imposing strict conditions for domestic reform on individual debtors. Included were programs designed to curb inflation, limit imports, restrict public spending, expose protected industries, and the like. It also typically urged those it helped to increase their exports. Thus the label "export-led adjustment" described the IMF's approach to the debt problem.

Because the conditions attached to the IMF's help added so clearly to the strains on the political and social fabric of debtor nations, some commentators asked whether its policies might not have been self-defeating. The IMF austerity program pushed vigorously until 1985 could claim considerable success from a strictly financial viewpoint (see Amuzegar, 1987), but its domestic burdens and the political costs they imposed simply proved too overwhelming (Sachs, 1989). Analysts blamed austerity for the overthrow of the Sudanese government of President Jaafar Nimeri in 1985, for example. Debt and related financial issues also inflamed domestic political conflict in many others among the most heavily indebted nations, including Argentina, Brazil, Chile, Mexico, and Nigeria. Meanwhile, proposals surfaced for creating a "debtors' cartel" that would confront the creditor nations with a unified approach for easing their problems, as political leaders in the debtor nations began adopting a more defiant posture toward the predicament they faced.

The Search for Long-term Solutions

In this emotionally charged atmosphere the United States abandoned its earlier arm's-length policy and proposed a new plan, known as the Baker initiative, to deal with the debt crisis. The plan sought new loans from private banks and coupled these with renewed efforts to stimulate Third World economic growth via domestic economic reforms in debtor nations. Thus it emphasized a "market approach" to the debt problem rather than the austerity imposed through IMF conditionality. It failed, however, when it proved incapable of delivering the promised new resources. In fact, new loans of all sorts became increasingly scarce from 1982 onward, with the result that developing countries were paying more to their creditors than they were receiving in new loans (see Figure 8.6). Moreover, because most foreign direct investment occurs in the industrial countries, not the Third World (see Figure 8.5 and Chapter 6), most developing nations had to rely on their own resources for investment capital and debt servicing.

Two events in 1987 added renewed urgency to the imperative of finding long-term solutions to the debt problem. In February Brazilian President José Sarney announced that his country would suspend interest payments on the bulk of its $108 billion debt, declaring, "We cannot pay the debt with our people's hunger"; and in May Citicorp Chairman John Reed astonished the financial world when he announced that the giant U.S. bank would take a billion-dollar loss to cover its shaky international loans. Other major U.S. banks quickly followed suit. Meanwhile, the debt burden of the most

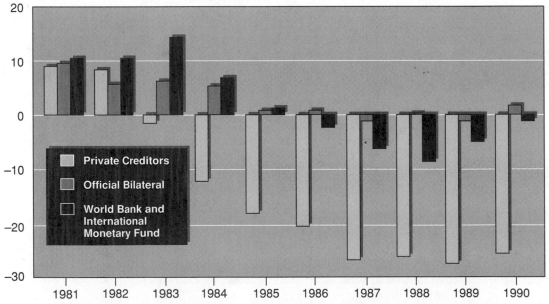

FIGURE 8.6 The Collapse of Net Lending to Developing Countries, 1981–1990

Source: Rosemarie Philips and Stuart K. Tucker, *U.S. Foreign Policy and Developing Countries: Discourse and Data 1991* (Washington, D.C.: Overseas Development Council, 1991) p. 31.
Note: Data refer to net debt transfers which are principal received minus payments of principal and interest. 1990 data are projected.

hard-pressed debtors continued to mount, as did bitterness among the debtor nations toward their creditors, who resented being told that the poor should not borrow more than they could repay. Peruvian President Alan Garcia reflected the sentiments when he asserted in 1987 that "Each of us has the right . . . to not pay more than what its economy can pay. . . . That is the moral law of the debtors."

Events in 1989 again underscored the explosive domestic situation exacerbated by foreign indebtness, as widespread rioting broke out in Venezuela in protest of the government's austerity measures. "In the course of a few days an estimated 300 people died. This was particularly shocking since Venezuela had long been regarded as one of the most stable Latin American democracies" (Sachs, 1989). Yet the occurrence could easily have been repeated elsewhere.

Again the United States stepped forward to offer a new plan. The Brady initiative, announced in early 1989, pursued debt reduction as a strategy to cope with the debt crisis. Specifically, it sought to reduce the debt of all debtors by as much as 20 percent over three years. In focusing on debt relief rather than debt restructuring, the plan signaled that "the foreign policy concerns over the deteriorating situation in the debtor countries finally came to the fore" (Sachs, 1989). Previously, concern for the banks had taken precedence. Still, the initiative did not fully break with the Baker plan in that it depended on voluntary actions by creditors to bring about the debt reductions, which, for a number of reasons (see Cohen, 1989; Sachs, 1989), are difficult to achieve. In this respect the Brady initiative was an extension of the strategy of containing the debt crisis, not an alternative to it (Cohen, 1989).

The adverse impact of the debt crisis on the commercial interests of the industrial nations is underscored by the fact that their exports to Third World nations fell from 30 percent of all exports in 1981 to only 20 percent in 1987 (Spero, 1990: 198). Thus developed nations share an interest in reducing the debt burden of the Third World as a way to stimulate developing nations' economic growth and the markets they provide for many First World exports (such as U.S. agricultural exports).

The Debt Decade in Retrospect

Among debt-burdened developing nations, the debt decade exacted a devastating toll. Figure 8.7 on page 294 provides some sense of its cost by charting trends in the per capita gross domestic product of the industrial countries and two groups of developing countries, those burdened by debt service difficulties, and those free of them. The differences are striking: The per-capita income of those without debt-servicing difficulties soared by more than 60 percent between 1978 and 1991, while the incomes of those burdened by debt were actually less than they had been in 1978. The reality is especially acute in Latin America, where the 1980s are known as "the lost decade."

The trauma and hostility caused by the debt crisis that first exploded in August 1982 is difficult to exaggerate. "It called into question the soundness of the international financial and banking system. It was accused of stunting economic growth in the developing countries. It was blamed for social and political instability, specifically for

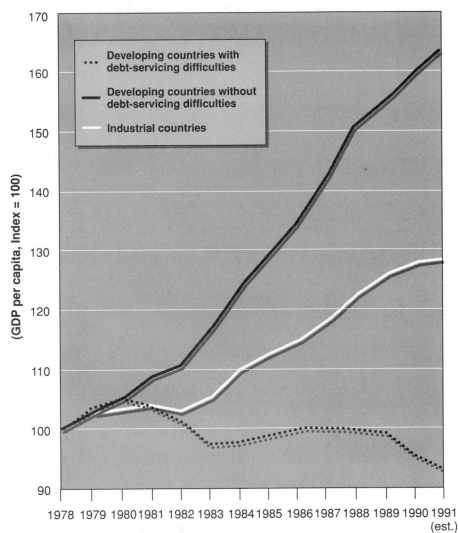

FIGURE 8.7 PER CAPITA ECONOMIC PERFORMANCE BY COUNTRY GROUPS, 1978–1991

Source: Rosemarie Philips and Stuart K. Tucker, *U.S. Foreign Policy and Developing Countries: Discourse and Data 1991* (Washington, D.C.: Overseas Development Council, 1991), p. 32.

endangering nascent democratic tendencies in certain countries. It mobilized religious, environmental, and other interest groups that usually remain outside the financial fray. It led to calls for repudiation, solidarity, the formation of debt cartels, and the exploitation of financial obligations to obtain concessions in unrelated areas" (Nowzad, 1990).

The debt crisis has not been fully resolved, but its prominence has receded as various strategies to contain and redirect it are in place. Included alongside the Brady plan framework are various debt forgiveness and debt rescheduling initiatives by governments and multilateral institutions, such as the World Bank, many directed toward the severely strained countries in Africa.

The debt decade reveals several lessons that may apply to the future (see Fischer and Husain, 1990; Nowzad, 1990). Among them is that developing nations have a responsibility to pursue sound policies. A second is that, regardless of how sound their policies may be, developments in the industrial world will affect them. In this sense the debt crisis echoes issues raised in the debates over the proposed New International Economic Order. Developing nations blamed the structure of the world political economy for their ills, and the First World responded with the charge that forces indigenous to the Third World were at fault. The lessons of the debt crisis suggest that both may be right.

NORTH-SOUTH RELATIONS IN THE 1990S

How might Third World aspirations for development in all of its manifestations be satisfied and properly managed? Despite the contentious rhetoric surrounding the North-South debate in the past and the persistent global inequalities on which it was based, it is clear that the South cannot force the North to submit to its demands, nor will the North do so voluntarily. A more reasonable scenario depicts piecemeal adjustments in North-South relations born of the realization that the well-being of each is dependent on the health of the other.

The end of the Cold War creates new opportunities for a realistic assessment of where the interests of North and South intersect. The diversity inherent among Third World nations ensures less uniformity of outlook than in the past. Similarly, the emergence of three major economic clusters in the First World, centered on Europe, Japan, and the United States, portends diverging interests as they assess the challenges and opportunities posed by the developing nations. The competition for allies and influence in the Third World characteristic of the Cold War rivalry between the United States and the Soviet Union is history, but divergent interests and perspectives in North and South alike ensure that conflict of one form or another will continue.

As in the past, political economy issues will likely spark conflict between North and South. Other issues relating to population growth, resource consumption, environmental stress, and sustainable development will also define the future parameters of North-South conflict and cooperation. It is to these issues that we now turn.

SUGGESTED READINGS

Bhagwati, Jagdish N., and John Gerard Ruggie, eds. *Power, Passions, and Purpose: Prospects for North-South Negotiations.* Cambridge, Mass.: MIT Press, 1984.

The Challenge to the South. The Report of the South Commission. Oxford: Oxford University Press, 1990.

Eberstadt, Nicholas. "U.S. Foreign Aid Policy—A Critique," *Foreign Policy Association Headline Series* 293 (Summer 1990):1–64.

Feinberg, Richard E., and Delia M. Boylan. *Modular Multilateralism: North-South Economic Relations in the 1990s*. Washington, D.C.: Overseas Development Council, 1991.

Head, Ivan L. *On a Hinge of History: The Mutual Vulnerability of South and North*. Toronto: University of Toronto Press, 1991.

Helleiner, G. K. *The New Global Economy and the Developing Countries*. Brookfield, Vt.: Edward Elgar, 1990.

Krasner, Stephen D. *Structural Conflict: The Third World Against Global Liberalism*. Berkeley, Calif.: University of California Press, 1985.

Nossiter, Bernard D. *The Global Struggle for More: Third World Conflicts with Rich Nations*. New York: Harper & Row, 1987.

Sewell, John W. "The Metamorphosis of the Third World: U.S. Interests in the 1990s," pp. 222–238 in Charles W. Kegley, Jr. and Eugene R. Wittkopf, eds., *The Future of American Foreign Policy*. New York: St. Martin's Press, 1992.

Sklair, Leslie. *Sociology of the Global System*. Baltimore: The Johns Hopkins University Press, 1991.

Weisband, Edward, ed. *Poverty Amidst Plenty*. Boulder, Colo.: Westview Press, 1989.

CHAPTER 9

• • •

THE GLOBAL COMMONS: DEMOGRAPHY AND THE ENVIRONMENT IN WORLD POLITICS

• • •

The final binding thought is to shape a more satisfying future for the coming generations, a global society in which individuals can develop their full potential, free of capricious inequalities and threats of environmental degradation.

Rafael M. Salas, Executive Director,
United Nations Fund for Population Activities, 1984

Overconsumption by the wealthiest fifth of humanity is an environmental problem unmatched in severity by anything but perhaps population growth. The surging exploitation of resources threatens to exhaust or unalterably disfigure forests, soils, water, air, and climate.

Alan Durning, Senior Researcher,
Worldwatch Institute, 1991

Interdependence is a key to understanding the transformation of the Liberal International Economic Order. Because the concept challenges the efficacy of national solutions to global problems, it also enables us to comprehend the relationship between humankind and the biological and geophysical environments within which human interactions occur.

The *ecological perspective* on world politics views the global environment as a system of delicately and tightly integrated components. Its central concern is the interrelatedness of biological, economic, political, social, technological, and geographic subsystems. This obvious but often ignored linkage underscores the limits nature imposes, namely, that the planet's *carrying capacity*—its ability to support human and other life forms—is not infinite.

How many people can the earth support? What is its ultimate carrying capacity? These questions have been asked for millennia, but the answers remain elusive, in part because rapidly advancing technology has continuously stretched the boundaries. Thus the earth will doubtless accommodate the growth projected for today's more than five billion inhabitants into the next century, but at what cost—to human

• • •

freedom, human welfare, and ultimately to the environment necessary to sustain humankind?

The *tragedy of the commons* is a metaphor widely used to explain the impact of human behavior on ecological systems. It was first articulated in 1833 by the English political economist William Foster Lloyd and later popularized and extended to contemporary world problems by the human ecologist Garrett Hardin (1968). If we assume that the search for self-advantage and personal benefit drives humankind, the metaphor provokes inquiry about the probable human approach to resources held in common in the absence of regulation. If advancing their personal welfare is the primary interest that motivates individuals, what consequences should be anticipated for the finite resources held in common, and hence for all?

Consider, as Hardin did, what occurred in nineteenth-century English villages. The village green was typically common property on which all herders were permitted to graze their cattle. Sharing the common grazing area worked well as long as the number of cattle did not exceed the land's carrying capacity, for if that occurred, the pasture would be ruined, and the number of cattle it could support would decline drastically. Still, individual herders had powerful incentives to increase the size of their herds as much as possible, because this was the only way they could maximize their individual gain. If pushed, individual herders might concede that reductions in the size of their herds would serve the collective interest of all, which was to preserve the commons. Without guarantees that other herders would follow suit, however, self-restraint was costly. There were few incentives to voluntarily reduce the number of one's own cattle to relieve the pressure on the common village green. Indeed, no one could guarantee that others would follow suit.

On the other hand, the addition of one more animal to the village green would produce a personal gain whose costs would be borne by everyone. Hence, rational economic behavior encouraged all herders to increase indiscriminately the size of their herds, and it discouraged self-sacrifice for the common welfare. In the end, the collective impact of the effort by each herder to maximize individual gain was to place more cattle on the village green than it could sustain. Destruction of the common village green was the inevitable result. "Ruin is the destination toward which all men rush," Hardin concluded, "each pursuing his own best interest in a society that believes in the freedom of the commons."

The tragedy of the commons is widely used to understand environmental politics because it illuminates so well the sources of many human predicaments. Its relevance to global ecopolitical problems is obvious when we draw an analogy between the village commons in England before the enactment of closure laws and contemporary planetary "common property," such as the oceans, fisheries, and the atmosphere, from which individual profit is maximized on the basis of a first-come, first-serve principle but which largely remain beyond regulation. Overuse, even abuse, of common property is apparent when some nations take more fish from ocean fisheries than their yields are able to sustain or when the oceans and atmosphere become sinks for environmental pollution perpetrated by a few but whose costs are borne by many. The task in both instances becomes one of devising regulations for an ecopolitical environment that thrives on freedom of choice (see Soroos, 1992).[1]

A major unregulated freedom of choice on which Hardin focused in his well-known article is the human freedom to propagate. "The most important aspect of necessity that we must now recognize," he wrote, "is the necessity of abandoning the commons in breeding. Freedom to breed will bring ruin to all. . . . The only way we can preserve and nurture other and more precious freedoms is by relinquishing the freedom to breed, and that very soon. . . . Only so, can we put an end to this aspect of the tragedy of the commons."

Not everyone will agree with the moral and ethical implications of Hardin's arguments. Few decisions, in fact, are more intensely personal or more intimately tied to the social and cultural fabric of a society than those of individual couples about marriage and the family. Furthermore, just as the ultimate carrying capacity of the global ecosystem has proved elastic, the impact of unregulated population growth on environmental quality remains unclear (see Repetto, 1987). Nonetheless, the balance of both theory and evidence points to a world in which unrestrained population growth will result in lost economic opportunities, environmental degradation, domestic strife, and incentives—perhaps imperatives—for governmental restraints on individual choice (see Choucri, 1972; Choucri and North, 1975; Diaz-Briquets, 1986; McNamara, 1984).

A world interdependent ecopolitically as well as economically is certain to share the consequences (see Homer-Dixon, 1991). Even those countries not experiencing excessive population growth contribute to the problems by placing a disproportionate strain on global resources and the ability of the ecosystem to withstand environmental abuse. That is nowhere more clear than with global warming, a quintessential transnational problem whose causes and potential solutions are presently lodged not in the world's most populous nations but in its most prosperous.

Our purpose in this chapter and the next is to explore how developments in demography, the environment, and resources interact with political considerations to propel the transformation of world politics. Here we focus on demographic variables and their correlates. We direct particular attention to how present and projected global trends in births, deaths, and migration will shape the character of our world for the duration of this century and into the next. This sets the stage for Chapter 10, where we examine the political role of resources in the world political economy, the implications that trends in global patterns of oil production and consumption portend for world politics, and the uses made of economic sanctions to realize national and global political objectives.

GLOBAL DEMOGRAPHIC PATTERNS AND TRENDS . . . .

The dramatic growth in world population in the decades following World War II is without historical precedent. As Figure 9.1 on page 300 illustrates, it took from the

---

[1] Thomas Schelling (1978) observes that the commons image is widely used as a kind of shorthand "for situations in which people so impinge on each other in pursuing their own interests that collectively they might be better off if they could be restrained, but no one gains individually by self-restraint." He goes on to point out that "the commons are a special but widespread case out of a broader class of situations in which some of the costs or damages of what people do occur beyond their purview, and they either don't know or don't care about them."

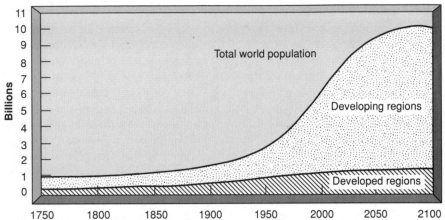

FIGURE 9.1 World Population Growth, Global and Regional Trends, 1750–2100

Source: Thomas W. Merrick, "World Population in Transition," *Population Bulletin*, vol. 41, no. 2 (Washington, D.C.: Population Reference Bureau, Inc., January 1988 reprint), pp. 4, 19.

beginning of time until the early 1800s for world population to reach one billion people. Because of substantial declines in death rates, world population reached two billion about 130 years later, around 1930. Since then, additional billions have been added even more rapidly: Three billion was reached by 1960, four billion in 1975, and five billion in 1987. As present trends unfold, the world will reach the six-billion figure before the turn of the twentieth century and finally stabilize at more than eleven billion sometime in the twenty-second century. That projection depends, however, on the assumption that the norm worldwide will have become an average family size of no more than two children, as is presently the case in most of the more developed nations but rarely elsewhere.

The rapid growth of world population since World War II is described by a simple mathematical principle articulated in 1798 by the Reverend Thomas Malthus, namely, that population when unchecked increases in a geometric or exponential ratio (1 to 2, 2 to 4, 4 to 8, and so forth), whereas subsistence increases in only an arithmetic ratio (1 to 2, 2 to 3, 3 to 4). When population increases in such an accelerating fashion, the compound effect can be staggering.

Consider, for example, the results that flow from the simple decision of whether to have two children or three. If parents decide to have three children and if each of their children and their children's children also decide to have three, by the third generation thirty-nine people will have been born—three in the first, nine in the second, and twenty-seven in the third. If, however, the initial decision is to have two children instead of three, and if each child makes the same choice, in three generations only sixteen people will have been born (two in the first, four in the second, and eight in the third). Extrapolating these patterns to whole societies, the cumulative results can be enormous. For example, the population of the United States in 1968 was 200 million. Assuming two-child families (and no immigration), U.S. population will grow to 300 million by the year 2015. However, if we assume three-child families, 300 million will be reached before the turn of the century, and the population will have doubled to over 400 million by 2015. Extending these projections over a century, the population of the United States in 2068 will exceed 800 million if three-child families are the rule but will remain well under 400 million with two-child families.

Another way to contemplate how sensitive world population is to even small, incremental changes in its rate of growth (the difference between births and deaths) is to consider how long it will take the population to double given a particular growth rate. Just as money deposited in a savings account will grow more rapidly if it earns interest not only on the original investment but also on the interest payments, population growth is a function of increases in the original number of people plus those accruing from past population growth. Thus a population growing at a 1 percent rate will double in sixty-nine years, while a population growing at a 2 percent rate will double in only thirty-five years[2] (see Box 9.1 on page 302).

Worldwide, the rate of population growth peaked at slightly over 2 percent in the late 1960s and then declined to 1.7 percent by the 1980s. The dip, though modest, is an important step toward stabilizing the world's ultimate population size. It means, for example, that by the year 2000 the world's population will be 20 percent less than the 7.5 billion people that the birth and death rates of the 1950s would have produced had they continued uninterrupted. Still, the pressures associated with population growth continue. In the early 1990s world population was growing by nearly 95 million people annually, an amount equivalent to adding the entire population of Austria every month or populating the Bahamas again each day. Even more will be added each year in the future. In fact, as Figure 9.2 on page 303 illustrates, more people will be added to the world's population in the last fifth of the twentieth century than at any other time in history.

Not all nations will share equally in the phenomenon, however. In fact, rapid population growth in the Third World is the most striking demographic development in the post–World War II era, and it will persist into the future at the same time that the more developed nations of the world move toward zero population growth (see Figure 9.2). Ours has become a demographically divided world, with the low-growth nations in the North and the high-growth nations in the South. As with other fissures between North and South, the demographic divisions of the world promise to widen even further in the decades ahead. We can better understand the inevitability of this result—and how demographic trends will affect world politics—if we go beyond the simple arithmetic of population growth and explore its dynamics.

Factors Affecting National and Regional Variations in Population Growth

The population growth rate in the United States in 1991 was 0.8 percent. This is an annual rate similar to that of other industrial nations of the North, where births and

---

[2] This is merely another way of saying that the population grows exponentially rather than arithmetically. The impact of different growth rates on doubling times can be calculated by dividing sixty-nine by the percentage of growth. Thus a population growing at 1 percent will double in sixty-nine years, but a population growing at 3 percent will double in twenty-three years.

Box 9.1
The Secret of the Persian Chessboard
• • •

The way I first heard the story, it happened in ancient Persia. But it may have been India, or even China. Anyway, it happened a long time ago. The Grand Vizier, the principal adviser to the King, had invented a new game. It was played with moving pieces on a board of 64 squares. The most important piece was the King. The next most important piece was the Grand Vizier—just what we might expect of a game invented by a Grand Vizier. The object of the game was to capture the enemy King, and so the game was called, in Persian, *shahmat*—*shah* for king, *mat* for dead. Death to the King. In Russia it is still called *shakhmaty*, which perhaps conveys a lingering revolutionary ardor. Even in English there is an echo of the name—the final move is called "checkmate." The game, of course, is chess.

As time passed, the pieces, their moves and the rules evolved. There is, for example, no longer a piece called the Grand Vizier—it has become transmogrified into a Queen, with much more formidable powers.

Why a king should delight in the creation of a game called "Death to the King" is a mystery. But, the story goes, he was so pleased that he asked the Grand Vizier to name his own reward for such a splendid invention. The Grand Vizier had his answer ready: He was a humble man, he told the King. He wished only for a humble reward. Gesturing to the eight columns and eight rows of squares on the board he had devised, he asked that he be given a single grain of wheat on the first square, twice that on the second square, twice *that* on the third, and so on, until each square had its complement of wheat.

No, the King remonstrated. This is too modest a prize for so important an invention. He offered jewels, dancing girls, palaces. But the Grand Vizier, his eyes becomingly lowered, refused them all. It was little piles of wheat he wanted. So, secretly marveling at the unselfishness of his counselor, the King graciously consented.

When the Master of the Royal Granary began to count out the grains, however, the King was in for a rude surprise. The number of grains starts small enough: 1, 2, 4, 8, 16, 32, 64, 128, 256, 512, 1024. . . . But by the time the 64th square is approached, the number becomes colossal, staggering. In fact the number is nearly 18.5 quintillion grains of wheat. Maybe the Grand Vizier was on a high-fiber diet.

How much does 18.5 quintillion grains of wheat weigh? If each grain were 2 millimeters in size, then all the grains together would weigh around 75 billion metric tons, which far exceeds what could have been stored in the King's granaries. In fact, this is the equivalent of about 150 years of the world's present wheat production. . . .

A sequence of numbers like this—where each is a fixed multiple of the previous one—is called an exponential increase. Exponentials show up in all sorts of places. Compound interest, for example: If an ancestor of yours put $10 in the bank for you 200 years ago, and it accrued a steady 5% annual interest, then by now it would be worth $10 \times (1.05)^{200}$, or $172,925.81$—where $(1.05)^{200}$ simply means 1.05 times itself 200 times. If that ancestor could have gotten a 6% rate, you'd now have over $1 million; for 7%, over $7.5 million; and for an extortionate 10%, a tidy $1.9 billion.

Source: Carl Sagan, "The Secret of the Persian Chessboard," Parade, February 14, 1989, p. 14.

deaths have nearly stabilized. Hence, the difference between a typical industrial nation and the world growth rate of 1.7 percent is largely attributable to a population surge in the less developed nations of the South, where sharply lower death rates since World War II have resulted from advances in medical science, agricultural productivity, and public sanitation. The paradox posed by reduced death rates is that this favorable development has contributed to an accelerating rate of population growth in precisely those nations least able to support a burgeoning number of people.

Variations in national and regional population growth virtually ensure that today's demographic division of the world will grow wider in the future. As illustrated in Figure 9.1, the 3.7 billion people who inhabited the Third World in 1985 will have grown to 4.8 billion by the year 2000, while the comparable increase among the developed nations will be only from 1.2 billion to 1.3 billion (Merrick, 1986: 13). High fertility rates in much of the Third World today combined with increases in the sheer number of children that will be born underlie these projections.

Fertility Rates

In 1991 the average woman in the world gave birth to 3.4 children. In the developed world the total fertility rate (the average number of children a woman would have in

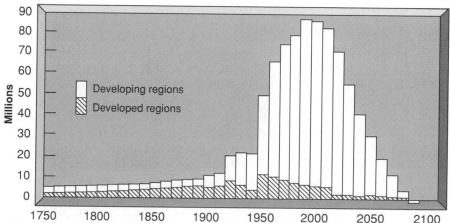

FIGURE 9.2   AVERAGE ANNUAL INCREASE IN WORLD POPULATION IN NUMBERS PER DECADE, GLOBAL AND REGIONAL TRENDS, 1750–2100
Source: Thomas W. Merrick, "World Population in Transition," *Population Bulletin*, vol. 41, no. 2 (Washington, D.C.: Population Reference Bureau, Inc., January 1988 reprint), pp. 4, 19.

a lifetime) stood at 1.9, which is actually below "replacement fertility" (one couple replacing themselves with two children), but in the developing world it stood at 3.9 (Population Reference Bureau, *1991 World Population Data Sheet*). In many Third World countries, notably in Africa, the preferred family size is actually much larger than this.[3] But world population will not stabilize until replacement fertility is reached everywhere, for only then will the number of births equal the number of deaths.

The developing countries' high fertility rates derive from a variety of sources. Besides the pleasures that children provide, religious norms often sanction and encourage parenting, prescribing the bearing of children (particularly male offspring in some cultures) as both a duty and a path to a rewarding afterlife. In addition, cultural traditions sometimes ascribe prestige and social status to women according to the number of children they bear. And most important perhaps, high fertility rates are explained by economic factors. Large families add more hands to a family's labor force today and may be a future source of social security for parents who live in societies that have no public programs to provide for the elderly. Under such conditions, parents usually try to have as many children as possible so their family income can be enhanced today and they can be cared for in their old age. When the infant mortality rate is high, the incentives for many progeny are even greater—the larger the number of children born, the greater the chance that some will survive.

Even in the face of increasing life expectancy throughout the world, over fourteen million children die each year before they reach the age of five (World Resources Institute, 1990: 253). Child death rates remain particularly high in much of Asia and Africa. In Afghanistan, for example, more than 30 percent of the children will die before the age of five, and in many places in Africa more than 20 percent will die by that age. Thus the logic underlying high fertility rates is often most compelling where poverty in all its manifestations is most widespread; the tragedy is that such high rates often reinforce the persistence of poverty.

Population Momentum

Even more important to understanding the implications of today's population surge in the Third World (which is a result of high, but declining, birthrates and rapidly falling death rates) for tomorrow's world is the "momentum" factor. It halps explain why in the last quintile of the twentieth century more people will be added to the world's population than at any other time in history. Like the momentum of a descending airliner when it first touches down on the runway, population growth simply cannot be halted even with an immediate, full application of the brakes. Instead, many years of high fertility mean that more women will be entering their reproductive years than in the past. Even if all of them gave birth to only two offspring, the absolute number of children born would continue to grow well into the future.

---

[3] Excluding China from this figure, the total fertility rate among developing nations stood at 4.4. China's rate was 2.3, the product of a vigorous national population policy designed to slow the growth of China's huge population, estimated in 1991 to be 1.15 billion. It should also be noted, however, that the desired family size has declined measurably during the past two decades in every world region, even in high-fertility, low-contraceptive areas in Asia and Africa (United Nations Fund for Population Activities, 1991).

The process will continue until the size of the generation giving birth to children is no larger than the generation among which deaths are occurring.

Consider, for example, the three age and sex population profiles shown in Figure 9.3. Kenya's profile shows a "rapid growth" population, because each new age group or cohort contains more people than did the one before it. In contrast, the United States has a "slow growth" profile, because recent cohorts have been smaller than preceding ones and the society as a whole has been aging. Finally, Austria's profile is that of a "declining" population, because it has both low birthrates and a large number of people who survive middle age. Thus Austria's "mature" or "old" age structure reflects an extended period of low birthrates and low death rates.

Although most nations of the developed world have moved toward zero population growth (and many toward Austria's negative growth profile), developing nations as a whole mirror the Kenyan pattern. Because each cohort is typically larger than the one before it, the number of young men and women entering their reproductive years will

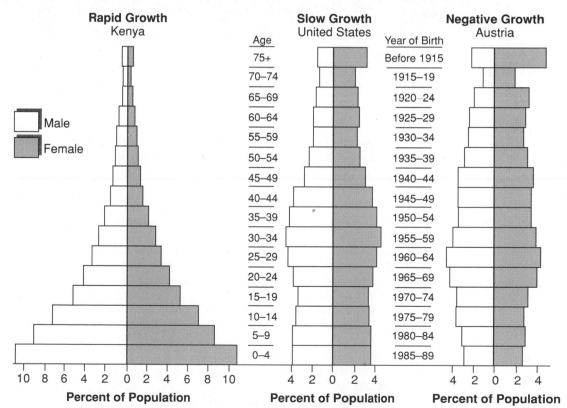

FIGURE 9.3 Three Patterns of Population Change

Source: Population Reference Bureau, *World Population: Fundamentals of Growth* (Washington, D.C.: Population Reference Bureau, 1990), p. 9.

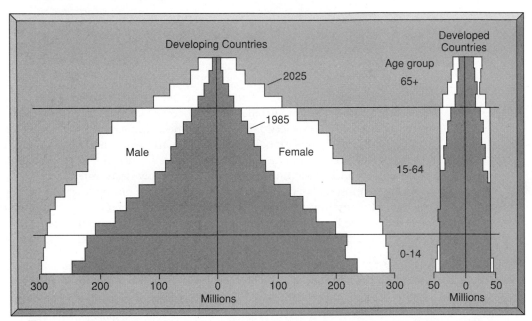

FIGURE 9.4 POPULATION AGE PYRAMIDS FOR DEVELOPED AND DEVELOPING COUNTRIES, 1985 AND 2025
Source: Thomas W. Merrick, "World Population in Transition," *Population Bulletin*, vol. 41, no. 2 (Washington, D.C.: Population Reference Bureau, Inc., January 1988 reprint), pp. 4, 19.

also grow. Thus the developing nations' age profiles explain the sheer momentum of population growth in the Third World. Figure 9.4 demonstrates the importance of this momentum by projecting into the future the larger proportion of fertile age groups in the developing world. It also underscores why the demographic patterns already in place will produce quite different population experiences in the developed and the developing worlds.

In general, population growth will continue after replacement-level fertility is achieved for as many as fifty to seventy years. If the goal of replacement-level fertility is reached worldwide around the year 2020, some seventy years later this would lead to a steady-state population of around eleven billion people (see Figure 9.5). If replacement-level fertility is not reached by this time, of course, the world's ultimate population size will be much greater. Conversely, if replacement-level fertility could be achieved earlier, the impact would be equally substantial. As Robert S. McNamara (1984), former president of the World Bank, has pointed out, "if the date at which replacement-level fertility is reached could be advanced from 2020 to 2000 . . . the ultimate population would be approximately 3 billion less, a number equivalent to 75 percent of today's world total. This reveals in startling terms the hidden penalties of failing to act, and act immediately, to reduce fertility."

The obvious question, then, is how to achieve replacement-level fertility. The demographic transition theory, which is the most widely accepted explanation of population changes over time, contains important insights.

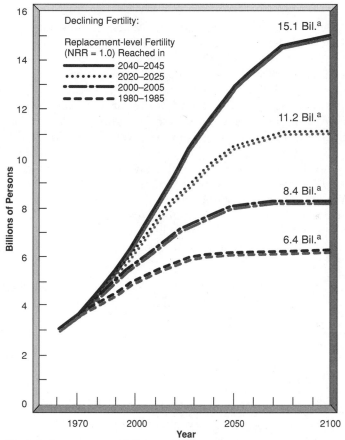

FIGURE 9.5 MOMENTUM OF WORLD POPULATION GROWTH
*Source:*U.S. Department of State, "World Population: The Silent Explosion—Part I,"
Department of State Bulletin 78 (October 1978): 50.
[a] Stabilization level.

The Demographic Transition Theory

The demographic transition theory explains the change that Europe and later North America experienced between 1750 and 1930, when a condition of high birthrates combined with high deathrates was replaced by a condition of low birthrates and low deathrates. The transition started when deathrates began to fall, presumably because of economic and social development, especially rising standards of living and improved control of disease. In such circumstances, the potential for substantial population growth was, of course, great. But then birthrates also began to decline, and during this phase population growth slowed.

According to the theory, these declines in birthrates occurred because economic growth alters people's attitudes toward family size. In preindustrial societies, children are economic bonuses. As industrialization proceeds, they become economic burdens, as they inhibit social mobility and capital accumulation.[4] The move from large to small families, with the associated decline in fertility, is therefore usually assumed to arise in industrial and urban settings.

The fourth stage in the demographic transition was achieved in Europe and North America when both the birth and death rates reached very low levels. With fertility rates near the replacement level, the result was a very low rate of population growth, if any at all. The panel on the left in Figure 9.6 depicts the demographic transition experienced by most nations in the developed world.

By contrast, the panel on the right in Figure 9.6 makes clear that the developing nations have not yet experienced rapidly falling birthrates, despite the extraordinarily rapid increase in life expectancy that has occurred in the Third World since World War II. In fact, the precipitous decline in death rates was largely the result of more effective "death-control" measures introduced by the outside world.[5] The decline in the developing nations' death rates thus differs sharply from the long-term, slow declines that Europe and North America experienced. They have been the result of

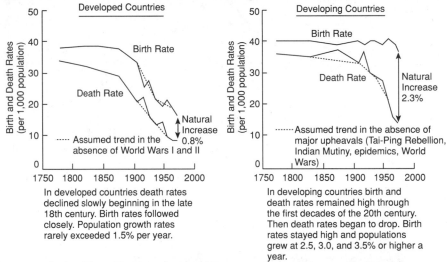

FIGURE 9.6 THE DEMOGRAPHIC TRANSITION IN DEVELOPED AND DEVELOPING COUNTRIES

Source: U.S. Department of State, "World Population: The Silent Explosion—Part I," *Department of State Bulletin* 78 (October 1978): 52. Based on United Nations data.

---

[4] In the United States, for example, the estimated cost of raising a child in an urban setting in the late 1980s ranged from $100,000 to $112,000, depending on the region of the country (*Family Economics Review*, 4 [1988]: 24).

[5] Sri Lanka illustrates the effect of public-health measures on the developing nations' death rates. Malaria and malaria-related diseases were a major cause of the historically high death rates in Sri Lanka, which in 1945 stood at twenty-two per one thousand. In 1946 the insecticide DDT was introduced to eradicate the mosquitoes that carry malaria. In a single year the death rate dropped 34 percent, and by 1955 it had declined to about half the 1945 level (Ehrlich et al., 1977: 197).

externally introduced and rapid environmental changes rather than the fundamental and evolutionary changes that affect a nation's policies, institutions, or ways of life. In particular, the developing nations have not experienced the more or less automatic decline in fertility rates that follows the decline in the rate of mortality assumed to be associated with economic development. A population "explosion" is the inevitable result.

Population Projections

Although developing countries have yet to move toward replacement-level fertility, demographers expect this will happen. Consider the projections in Figures 9.1 and 9.2 (pages 300 and 303). They predict that the transition to low fertility and mortality will occur by the year 2025 and that fertility will decline to replacement level by 2040. Based on those assumptions, it is possible to foresee a stable population of slightly more than ten billion people early in the twenty-second century. In fact, however, recent United Nations projections show that world population will grow well into the twenty-second century before it stabilizes at more than 11.6 billion (United Nations Fund for Population Activities, 1991: 3).

Uncertain Deathrates

Projections far into the future are inevitably subject to error. Uncertainty about death rates is one reason. A "limited" nuclear war, for example, could occur, inducing a climatic catastrophe through "nuclear winter" (see Sagan and Turco, 1991) that would dramatically reduce long-term population projections. The destructiveness of modern weapons guarantees that even a conventional war would result in substantial deaths. During the Persian Gulf War in early 1991, for example, between 100,000 and 120,000 Iraqi soldiers were killed in only forty-three days, and an estimated 49,000 to 76,000 Iraqi civilians lost their lives (Barnaby, 1991: 167).

A more populous world is also a more vulnerable one. Consider, for example, the difference in population density in Bangladesh and the state of Louisiana in the United States, two delta lands of similar size. Four and a half million people lived in Louisiana in 1990; 115 million lived in Bangladesh, giving it a population density of over two thousand people per square mile. A natural disaster in Bangladesh—where typhoons are commonplace—carries a proportionately greater threat to life and property. In fact, a 1988 typhoon in Bangladesh killed over a thousand people and made twenty-five million homeless.

Death due to malnutrition and starvation and from inadequate health care also may affect the long-term growth of the world's population. Twice in recent years, in the 1970s and again in the 1980s, broad stretches of the Sahel area in Africa experienced life-threatening drought and famine. Africa is also more threatened than other regions by AIDS (acquired immune deficiency syndrome). "More than 1 percent of the people of Sub-Saharan Africa, aged 15 to 49, are infected with the human immunodeficiency virus (HIV), which gives them a high risk of contracting AIDS" (*Human Development*

Report 1991, 1991: 36). The World Health organization predicts that life expectancy in Africa, which had been expected to climb to nearly 60 by 2010, will actually drop to less than 50, while increases in child mortality due to AIDS will cancel out the positive effects of health programs introduced over the past two decades (*Washington Post National Weekly Edition*, December 23–29, 1991, p. 18). Projections that AIDS could nearly double the current death rate in Africa are not unrealistic (United Nations Fund for Population Activities, 1991: 35).[6]

Eight to ten million people throughout the world are now thought to be infected by the HIV virus. Half are expected to develop AIDS by the end of the century. Fifteen million new HIV infections will also occur in the 1990s, more than half of them in the developing world (*Human Development Report 1991*, 1991: 27–28). In addition to Africa, the potentially fatal virus is spreading steadily in Asia, Latin America, and the Caribbean. The United States has the largest number of reported AIDS cases at the present time.

Whether AIDS will become the plague of the twenty-first century comparable to the Black Death of the Middle Ages, as some predict, remains problematic, but the claim AIDS will make on the world's health resources and its contribution to rising mortality in many areas of the world will doubtless grow. Lack of information will make developing nations particularly vulnerable to the spread of the AIDS virus (see Lewis et al., 1991).

Uncertain Birthrates

World population projections will also be affected by birthrates. Here incompleteness in the demographic transition theory, which is based primarily on the European experience prior to World War II, may affect their accuracy.

The demographic transition theory envisages four phases: (1) high birthrate, high deathrate; (2) high birthrate, falling deathrate; (3) declining birthrate, relatively low deathrate; (4) low birthrate, low deathrate. The experience in Europe since the 1970s suggests a possible fifth phase: low deathrate, declining birthrate. Some have called this Europe's "second" demographic transition (van de Kaa, 1987).

The fertility rate in Europe during the past two decades did not stabilize at the replacement level, as the demographic transition theory predicts. Instead, for Europe as a whole it stands at 1.7, with the highest rate in Romania (2.3) and the lowest in Italy and Spain (1.3) (in most of Africa, by comparison, it is over 6) (Population Reference Bureau, *1991 World Population Data Sheet*). As a result, a secular decline of Europe's population is now in motion: It will take over a thousand years for Italy's population to double, and a German population less than three-fourths its current size—80 million and the largest in Europe—is now foreseeable (Heilig, Büttner and Lutz, 1990: 34).

A second puzzle that the theory of demographic transition does not solve applies

---

[6] AIDS is a particular threat to Africa because "it appears to have spread among its limited pool of professional and technical elite. . . . AIDS could, in a sense, decapitate some African countries. The growing epidemic . . . aggravates an already severe shortage of skilled people and raises the prospect of economic, political and social disorder" (Harden, 1987).

to developing nations; some are seemingly stuck somewhere between the second and third stages of the transition. In such widely separated places as Costa Rica, Korea, Sri Lanka, and Tunisia, for example, death rates have fallen to very low levels, but fertility rates seem to have stabilized well above the replacement level (Merrick, 1986). Perhaps the reason lies in the absence of change in social attitudes toward family size of the sort Europe and North America experienced.

Developing cultural attitudes that favor smaller families is important in environments where social and economic improvements are taking place. The status of women in society, and especially their education, have an important influence on preferences toward family size.

> Women who have completed primary school have fewer children than those with no education. Having an education usually means that women delay marriage, seek wage-paying jobs, learn about and have more favorable attitudes toward family planning, and have better communication with their husbands when they marry. Educated women have fewer infant deaths; high infant mortality is associated with high fertility. Similarly, when women have wage-paying jobs, they tend to have fewer children (and conversely, women with fewer children find it easier to work). (Population Reference Bureau, 1981: 5)

Despite the positive impact of education, women throughout the world continue to be disadvantaged relative to men across a broad spectrum of educational statistics, such as literacy rates, school and college enrollments, and targeted educational resources. Women also enjoy less access to advanced study and training in professional fields, such as science, engineering, law, and business; within occupational groups they are almost always in less prestigious jobs; and "everywhere women are paid less than men" (United Nations, 1991b). A major United Nations (1991b) study on *The World's Women 1970–1990* concludes that in many parts of the world these and other differences between men and women have narrowed in recent decades, but in most countries the complex social, cultural, economic, and political forces that underlie them remain firmly rooted. Enhancing the educational opportunities of women and changing their status in society as a route toward lower fertility rates will not be easily achieved.

Global Patterns of Emigration and Immigration

Fertility, mortality, and migration are the three basic demographic variables that determine all population changes. Migration often receives less attention than the other variables, but its political importance was nowhere more dramatically evident than in the massive migration of Germans from East to West in 1989 in what became a precursor to the fall of the Berlin Wall, a symbol for nearly three decades of the Cold War division of Europe. Whether migration from one side of the "Iron Curtain" to the other precipitated its final collapse may never be known for sure, but the dissatisfaction with their political and economic fate that so many thousands demonstrated could not be ignored by the political leaders in the former socialist states. Nor should we overlook the consequence of the political unification of the German people.

Because of unification, the Federal Republic of Germany today ranks with the United States, Japan, and the Commonwealth of Independent States (notably Russia) as one of the most powerful nations in the world according to such traditional measures of capabilities as population size, territorial breadth, and economic vitality.

Germany is a dramatic case, but transnational migration has also affected many other nations in Europe and elsewhere. Israel has absorbed a flood of migrants during recent years, particularly from the Soviet Union, who promise to shape the nature of Israeli politics and society for years to come. The Middle Eastern oil producers have also received large numbers of migrants in recent years, and of course the United States has traditionally provided refuge and opportunity for millions from throughout the world (see Map 9.1).

Causes of Migration

Migrants are of two types: political refugees who move because of threats to their convictions or fear for their lives, and those who move for economic reasons. The United Nations High Commission for Refugees keeps tabs on more than eleven million refugees throughout the world, a number that has grown dramatically in recent years. More than half are in the Middle East, and about a third are in Africa. Refugees are often byproducts of war. Many of the Asian immigrants to the United States in the early 1980s were victims of the Vietnam War, for example. Political turmoil and civil strife in El Salvador, Guatemala, Nicaragua, and elsewhere in Central America and the Caribbean caused an influx of migrants from these areas as well. And with the end of communist party control in the Soviet Union and Eastern Europe in 1991 and the liberalization of the new governments' immigration policies, a wave of humanity left their homelands in search of a better way of life.

Other than refugees, migrants, both domestically and internationally, typically are in search of a better standard of living and way of life. Increasingly, many are also "environmental refugees"—people forced to abandon lands no longer fit for human habitation due to environmental degradation. Their number is estimated to be at least ten million, which rivals the number traditionally classified as political refugees by various national and international agencies (Jacobson, 1989: 60). Some become environmental refugees due to catastrophic events, such as the explosion of the nuclear power plant at Chernobyl in the Ukraine in 1986; others suffer the consequences of long-term environmental stress, such as excessive land use that results in desertification (discussed below).

Consequences of Migration

Migrants are often willing to take jobs in faraway lands shunned by local inhabitants. Typically this means they earn less than do the native people but more than they would earn in their homelands, even performing the same tasks. Host (receiving) countries often welcome migrants, not only because they accept low wages for jobs that natives do not want, but also because the host pays little if anything for migrants'

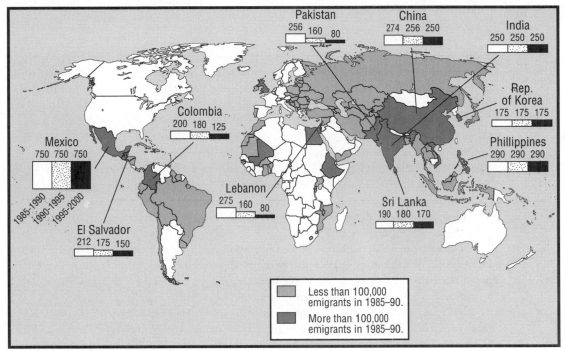

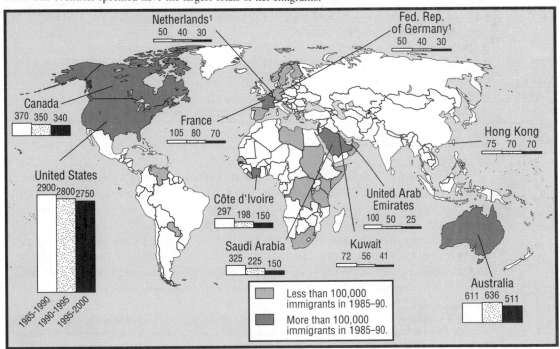

[1] Tied for tenth place.

Note: The countries and territories specified receive the largest totals of net immigrants.

MAP 9.1 **PATTERNS OF EMIGRATION AND IMMIGRATION, 1985–2000**
Source: Fred Arnold, "International Migration: Who Goes Where?" *Finance & Development* 27 (June, 1990): 46–47.

health, education, and welfare needs.[7] On the other hand, the home (sending) countries sometimes encourage people to emigrate as a way of reducing unemployment and because migrants usually repatriate considerable portions of their income to their families at home.

Although receiving countries often benefit from migration, its extent and consequences have been matters of growing concern in Europe, the Middle East, and the United States, as the demographic composition of their societies undergoes change. Among the industrial societies in particular, where fertility levels are already below the replacement level, major cultural changes can be expected, as a larger proportion of their future populations will be made up of recent immigrants from nations culturally different from their descendants. In fact, for Northern countries, migration, not growth, is *the* population problem.

Consider the United States. With fertility in the United States below the replacement level, immigration is now the primary demographic variable stimulating U.S. population growth. During the 1980s immigrants accounted for a third of its growth, a proportion higher than at any time since early in the twentieth century.

Even more important is the dramatic shift in the origins of the immigrants over recent decades. Most U.S. citizens came from Europe during its first 150 years. This was true even into the mid-twentieth century. Between 1931 and 1960, for example, nearly three-fifths of all immigrants to the United States were of European origin. During the 1980s, by contrast, Europeans counted for little more than 10 percent of new Americans, with immigrants from Asia (40 percent) and Latin America (38 percent) accounting for the bulk of them (De Vita, 1989: 9). Most were legal immigrants, but the United States has also absorbed large numbers of illegal aliens—estimates vary from as few as 200,000 to as many as two million annually—most of whom enter through Mexico.

In Europe, immigrants were especially important after World War II when they provided much of the unskilled labor needed to aid in reconstruction. Others migrated from former colonies, notably the British Commonwealth, to settle in the "mother" country.

The mid-1970s was the peak of the "guest worker" era, when one of every seven manual workers in Germany and Britain was a migrant, as were a quarter of those in France, Belgium, and Switzerland (Barnet, 1979: 56). However, as unemployment became the primary economic problem in Europe, migrants were no longer as welcome. In Germany, for example, where the West German government once offered incentives to entice people of other nationalities to emigrate to the Federal Republic, and which in the early 1980s was the home of some four million guest workers, new incentives to encourage emigration were devised. Many, however, in Germany and

---

[7] Foreign workers are also likely to be the first victims of bad economic conditions. In early 1983, for example, Nigeria expelled upwards of two million foreign workers. The official reason was the alleged involvement of alien workers in bloody religious riots that earlier had rocked sections of the country. Others viewed the expulsion as a response to the growing unemployment problem in Nigeria, as its economic development projects were curtailed following the loss of oil revenues caused by the worldwide oil glut of the early 1980s (see *Washington Post*, January 31, February 2, and February 4, 1983).

elsewhere, prefer to stay despite the difficulties they experienced assimilating into the local society and culture.[8] Clashes between Germans and Turks, between Britons and Indians and Pakistanis, and between French people and migrants from North Africa are recurrent (*Population in Perspective*, 1986).

The Middle East is also the scene of migrant-related tensions. Here oil money attracted immigrants, where in many of the host countries they comprised two-thirds of the labor force during the 1980s (*Population in Perspective*, 1986: 27). Many came from other Arab countries, but large numbers also came from outside the region, mainly from India, Pakistan, Thailand, and South Korea. Concern for the impact of non-natives on Arab culture and religion is evident, but here the large majority of aliens who are not citizens can never hope to be citizens. Whether the immigrants will be able to stay in the oil-rich countries as the fortunes of the oil producers change is likely to prove controversial among the peoples and nations concerned.

The United States is a nation born of immigrants. Despite this, public attitudes in recent years indicate a strong preference for limiting the number of legal immigrants and preventing the influx of illegal aliens into the country. As elsewhere, such attitudes reflect a growing concern about the impact of immigrants on traditional values. Others worry that U.S. immigration laws, which use kinship as the primary basis for determining who will be permitted to enter the United States and who will be denied access, are insensitive to the skills workers will need if the United States is to remain competitive in the world political economy. Current regulations, they argue, do not give enough weight to the potential contributions immigrants offer to the U.S. economy (see Chiswick, 1990).

The situation faced by the United States offers but a glimpse of the larger demographic forces that will shape national politics and economics for decades to come (see Masson, 1990). Population growth in the developing nations of the South will create pressures toward outward movement, and the aging of the industrial societies of the North will encourage them to search for new sources of labor. These forces promise to place migration at the center of national political agendas.

OPTIMISTS, PESSIMISTS, AND PUBLIC POLICY . . . .

The demographic transition theory and the forces that prompt transnational migration both underscore the critical linkages between population changes and changes in the larger socioeconomic environment within which they occur. Government policies often seek to change the former through the latter.

In 1974, the United Nations sponsored a World Population Conference to address

---

[8] East Germany also encouraged immigrant workers, who were hired to work in now defunct state-owned economic enterprises. By the end of the 1980s there were about 100,000 foreign workers in eastern Germany, most from Asia and Africa. With unemployment in the region on the rise following unification, most of the foreign workers sought to return to their homelands, but some, estimated at 10 to 12 percent, sought to remain in Germany by seeking refugee status or political asylum (Heilig, Büttner, and Lutz, 1990: 28–29).

the population "problem," which essentially meant population growth in Third World countries. The lessons of the demographic transition theory informed the view of many of the delegates from the Third World. If declining fertility follows more or less automatically from improvements in the standard of living, the appropriate approach to the population problem is first to attack the problems of economic and social development that inhibit improvements in the quality of life. The population problem will then take care of itself. The slogan "development is the best contraceptive" reflects this view. It summarizes the early European experience, when industrialization and the wealth it promoted coincided with rapid declines in fertility rates.

Other views were apparent among Third World countries, including, for example, various Marxist propositions that ascribed the lack of economic progress not to population growth but to the absence of equitable income distributions globally as well as nationally.

Many First World nations, on the other hand, sought a more direct attack on the population problem than the protracted solution implied by the "development is the best contraceptive" approach. Led by the United States, they conceded that economic development could encourage declining fertility rates, but they also argued that the control of birthrates could by itself substantially address the immediate problem and thus contribute to subsequent economic development. This policy position echoed the emphasis placed on family planning programs until that time by the United States, other governments, international organizations, and various nongovernmental organizations through their foreign aid and development assistance programs.

A decade later, in 1984, a second World Population Conference was held in Mexico City. By that time a new consensus had converged around the proposition that family planning could make an important contribution to the realization of other goals. Curiously, the United States, previously a major advocate of this viewpoint, now found itself out of step with global sentiments. Reflecting the conservative political sentiments prevalent in Washington at the time, the U.S. delegation asserted that free-market principles ought to take precedence over government intervention in economic and population matters. It also vigorously opposed abortion as an approach to family planning, a policy position that persisted into the 1990s. As a result, the United States withheld support for multilateral as well as bilateral efforts to assist family planning programs in developing nations.

Although the views of the United States in 1984 were clearly in the minority, they reflected a growing sense of dissatisfaction with the conclusions and policy prescriptions of earlier analyses of the global ecopolitical implications of population growth, especially *The Limits to Growth*, published in 1974 by a private group known as the Club of Rome (Meadows et al., 1974), and *The Global 2000 Report to the President*, published by the United States government in 1980 (see also Ehrlich and Ehrlich, 1990). Both came to be characterized as products of "Neo-Malthusians" or "growth pessimists" (many of whom are human ecologists), whose arguments were informed by the metaphor of the tragedy of the commons described earlier. The position reflected by the U.S. delegation to Mexico City, on the other hand, was that of the "growth optimists" (see, for example, Simon, 1981; Simon and Khan, 1984; also Wattenberg, 1989), who criticized the earlier limits-to-growth analyses. Sometimes called "cornucopians," optimists (many of whom are economists) argue that markets effectively maintain a balance among population, resources, and the environment. They point out that human ingenuity has developed resource-saving (or -substituting) innovations in response to shortages created by population growth, so that population growth is a stimulus, not a deterrent, to economic advancement.

The debate between optimists and pessimists carries with it important policy implications. When dealing with complex social scientific questions, however, determining who is right is difficult. We can appreciate this by considering some correlates of demographic changes.

CORRELATES OF DEMOGRAPHIC CHANGES . . . .

As trends in births, deaths, and migration unfold worldwide during the remainder of this century and beyond, demographic developments will promote changes in world politics. At issue is how trends in our demographically divided world will affect traditional national security considerations, economic development opportunities, the prospects for achieving global food security, and world resources and the global commons.

The Impact of Demographic Trends on National Security

As noted earlier, rapid population growth in the Third World is the most striking demographic development of the post–World War II era. Because nearly all future population growth will also occur in the developing world, the twenty-first century will witness the rapid emergence of a world in which only a tiny fraction of its population will live in the developed world. National security planners in Washington and other national capitals in the industrial world may rightly be concerned about the foreign and national security policy implications of the widening demographic division between the world's have and have-not nations. As one observer noted,

> Current UN projections for the year 2025 depict an American population slightly smaller than Nigeria's, an Iranian population almost as large as Japan's and an Ethiopian population nearly twice that of France. Today's industrial democracies would almost all be "little countries." Canada, one of the Big Seven industrial democracies today (alongside the United States, Germany, Japan, Britain, France and Italy), would have a smaller population than such countries as Madagascar, Nepal and Syria. (Eberstadt, 1991: 128)

Political realists argue that a country's size is an important source of political power. Given this, diminution of the world's most populous states to a lesser rank may itself be a concern. Moreover, the low fertility rates in developed states combined with their aging populations will make it more difficult to recruit and maintain standing armies. Before the breakup of Soviet power in Eastern Europe and the unification of Germany, for example, military planners in the NATO alliance worried about West Germany's ability to perform its critical role on the central front in the face of a diminishing pool of military personnel.[9] In contrast, the abundant youth in developing societies provide ample human resources for waging war and rebellion.

Some suggest that even more menacing than the changing relative size of states may be the consequences for the values and interests of the industrial democracies of the erstwhile Western world: "Even without the rise of new blocs or alignments, one can envision a fractious, contentious and inhumane international order: liberal precepts could have steadily less impact on international action and belief in human rights could prove a progressively weaker constraint on the exercise of force. . . . Even without an aggressive or hostile Soviet bloc, or the invention of new weapons, this world could be a very dangerous and confused place" (Eberstadt, 1991; see also Wattenberg, 1989).

Specific challenges to the established political order within as well as between states also emerge from differential fertility rates among various ethnic populations. In Israel, for example, the Jewish population may one day become the minority, as fertility rates among Arabs and Palestinians within Israel's borders outstrip those of Israel's Jews. Analogous trends are already evident in South Africa, where the white population has become a progressively smaller minority and is expected by the year 2020 to comprise only one-ninth to one-eleventh of the total population compared with the one-fifth it accounted for in the early 1950s (Eberstadt, 1991: 121). The proportion of ethnic Russians in the Commonwealth of Independent States may likewise decline, as fertility rates among non-Russians, particularly Muslims, are measurably higher. Demographic trends will thus reinforce other challenges to the ruling authority of ethnic Russians in the fragile successor to the Soviet state. Already Russians are less than a majority of the military-age population and will make up less than a majority of the working-age population by the turn of the century (Eberstadt, 1991:122).

It is difficult to determine but equally difficult to ignore the stimulus to domestic political strife and external political conflict that changes in the ethnic composition of societies provoke. In virtually every world region and within every major power, demographic developments either ignite or fan the flames of political and social unrest, with corresponding implications for the national security interests of states throughout the world (Foster, 1989).

The Impact of Demographic Trends on Economic Development

Lost economic opportunities caused by excessive population growth are among the sources of political and social instability many nations face. Growth pessimists in particular place considerable emphasis on the adverse effects of population growth on economic development. What they often ignore, however, is that the world has enjoyed unprecedented levels of economic growth and unparalleled population increases simultaneously. Even those nations with the highest rates of population increase are arguably better off economically today than they were at the dawn of the

[9] See Heilig, Büttner, and Lutz (1990) for a demographic prospective on the united Germany.

twentieth century. That is certainly the case in the area of public health, where the very forces that drive population growth—declining infant mortality and rising life expectancy—demonstrate the improvement of living standards throughout the world.

The views of growth pessimists are not easily dismissed, however. Population growth contributes to the widening income gap between the world's rich and poor nations. It also contributes to lower standards of living at the individual level, as poor people tend to have more children to support than do those who are relatively better off. Furthermore, by depressing wage rates relative to rents and returns to capital, "rapid population growth devalues what poor households have to sell—their labor. Property owners gain relative to wage earners when the labor force grows quickly" (Repetto, 1987).

It is also true, however, that "politics and economic policies influence the distribution of income within countries far more than population growth rates do" (Repetto, 1987). This fact lies close to what is emerging as the conventional view among demographers and development economists about the effects of population growth on economic development. Contrary to the view of growth pessimists, the emerging consensus casts population "not as the sole cause of underdevelopment, but an accomplice aggravating other existing problems" (*The New Population Debate*, 1985; see also *World Development Report 1984*, 1984, especially Chapter 5). The larger proportion of young people in developing countries places strains on certain social institutions, for example, whereas the larger proportion of older people in the developed countries creates other problems.

The Third World

In developing countries, dependent children (those younger than fifteen years old) typically make up about 40 percent of the total population (compared with 22 percent in the developed world) (Merrick, 1989: 9). This means there is only about one working-age adult for each child under fifteen in the Third World, compared with nearly three working-age adults in the developed countries. Such a large proportion of dependent children places a heavy burden on public services, particularly the educational system. It also encourages the immediate consumption of economic resources rather than their reinvestment in social infrastructure to promote future economic growth.

As the children mature, the demands for new jobs, housing, and other human needs multiply, but the resources to meet them are typically scarce and inadequate. In Mexico, for example, a million new jobs are required every year to absorb the wave of young people entering the labor market. On a global scale, the International Labor Organization estimates that the total labor force in developing countries will be 600 million to 700 million larger in the year 2000 than it was in 1980. "To employ all those additional workers, the developing countries would have to create more jobs than now exist in Western Europe, Japan, the United States, the [Commonwealth of Independent States], and the other industrialized nations combined" (Fallows, 1983).

The search for jobs augments the growth of urban areas, which has proceeded at an unprecedented rate in recent decades. In 1950 less than a third of the world's population lived in cities; by 1990 the proportion had grown to over 40 percent; and by the year 2020 as many as 60 percent will live in urban areas. Urbanization is a global phenomenon, but increasingly the world's largest cities will be in the Third World. London, New York, and Shanghai were the only cities with populations of ten million or more in 1950. By the turn of the century some two dozen cities will be this large—all but six of them in the less developed nations of Africa, Asia, and Latin America, where a combination of natural population growth and a desire to escape poverty in the countryside will fuel the expansion of the megalopolises.

Wherever urbanization occurs it taxes severely the capacity for effective governance. It places added pressures on the demand for expanded social services associated with rapid population growth, as urban development requires more investment in infrastructure than does rural development. It also increases the pressures on local agricultural systems, because there are fewer hands in the countryside to feed the growing number of mouths in the city. Urbanization thus adds to the need to import food from abroad, further straining already limited resources. And within the urban areas themselves, the often deplorable living conditions contain the seeds of social unrest and political turmoil. Already thousands upon thousands of urban dwellers live in cramped, shantytown hovels without adequate water, sanitation, health, education, and other social services. Being outside the urban elite and middle class, they are "acutely aware of the great disparity in wealth and poverty about them," which "contributes to alienation and frustration on a massive scale" (U.S. Department of State, 1978b).

Alienated and frustrated urban masses can be dangerous, which arouses fear in political leaders.

> The larger the city population, the more governments have to be concerned. . . . and the more they must make concessions in setting prices and creating employment. And so they strain to provide low-priced food and adequate schools for the newcomers, not to mention streets, houses, clean water, and jobs. They know the political pressure, in the form of strikes and riots, that the concentrated millions can exert. At the same time they cannot improve conditions for the existing population without attracting further immigrants, and these increase further the pressure on governments. (Keyfitz, 1991: 66)

Figure 9.7 illustrates the political dynamic underlying urban growth. The figure highlights the important fact that foreign aid and trade with other nations may enable political leaders to meet the demands of growing urban crowds. In some cases, however, as in undermining incentives to local food production, ties to the world political economy may prove dysfunctional in the long run.

A number of developing countries, particularly in Asia and Latin America, are now poised for a reduction in their dependency ratios (the number of people under fifteen and over sixty-five). If the experience of Europe, North America, and especially Japan is a guide, this should facilitate the realization of economic gains (Woods, 1989). Ironically, however, the demographic life cycle also portends that the countries that now have the greatest burden of a burgeoning population of young people also will be those with a growing number of older dependents as today's youth grow to maturity and old age fifty years hence. Although the Third World today contains more than

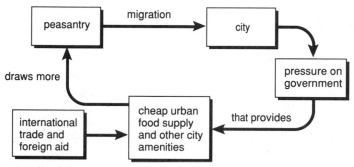

FIGURE 9.7 THE POLITICAL DYNAMIC OF THIRD WORLD URBANIZATION
Source: Nathan Keyfitz, "Population Growth Can Prevent the Development That Would Slow Population Growth," Jessica Tuchman Mathews (ed.), *Preserving the Global Environment* (New York: Norton, 1991), p. 67.

three-quarters of the world's people, it contains only half of those over sixty. By 2025, the population pyramid for developing regions shown in Figure 9.4 will begin to turn upside down because of declining birthrates and increased longevity, and the Third World will increase its share of the "gray generation" to three-quarters ("The Age of Aging," 1982: 82). As the experience of the more developed economies demonstrates, demands for social services, particularly expensive health care, will again multiply.

The First World

As noted earlier, the United States has recently moved toward zero-population growth, but in many other parts of the industrial world below-replacement fertility is now the norm. Population *decline* is the inevitable result (see Austria's population profile in Figure 9.3). As longevity increases, an aging population is also inevitable.

The aging of the First World is especially striking in Japan, where the demographic transition began later than elsewhere but was completed more rapidly. Today Japan is the most rapidly aging society in the world. The number of elderly (over 65) Japanese is expected to increase from 12.5 million in 1985 to 31.5 million in 2025, by which time they will comprise nearly a quarter of the population (Martin, 1989: 7). Already the median age of Japanese workers is over forty (Merrick, 1989: 11). As it continues to rise, Japan will have to confront worrisome questions about its ability to continue the vigorous economic productivity and high domestic saving rates that have been key factors in the projection of its economic power abroad.[10]

Beyond the particular case of Japan's export-oriented economy, some gerontologists (those who study aging and its consequences) argue that the move toward zero or negative population growth in advanced industrial societies will have untoward effects on growth in their aggregate demand, on which their economies depend. Others speculate that a gradually aging society will be a more conservative one

---

[10] These and related demographic issues surfaced in a 1985 Japanese government white paper on economic planning. The issues are discussed in Martin (1989).

politically. Evidence refutes both of these views (see Weller and Bouvier, 1981). Still, what is beyond dispute is that older people will increasingly pose a social and potential political force worldwide that will escalate the demand for age-related social services.

Providing for the increasing number of dependent elderly people relative to the number of productive workers is already a political concern throughout the First World. "Child shock" is the Japanese term used to draw attention to the growing crisis forecast by the decline in workers and growth in pensioners. The Japanese government and private-sector groups have joined forces to promote pronatalist attitudes among the Japanese people, whose purpose is to raise fertility rates. However, unlike similar efforts undertaken during the 1930s (when war between Japan and the United States loomed on the horizon), other socioeconomic forces in Japan have dampened efforts to stimulate birthrates.

In Western Europe the wisdom of pursuing pronatalist policies has been a matter of intense political debate. Much of the dialogue turns on questions of individual versus collective welfare (van de Kaa, 1987; see also Wattenberg, 1989). Proponents of pronatalist measures are concerned with the "continued vitality of national popula-tions that do not replace themselves: no children, no future, is the key phrase" (van de Kaa, 1987). National pride, concern for the nation's place among the world powers, and sensitivity to the vitality of European culture in a world where non-European countries grow much faster are also at issue. It was in this context that NATO planners worried in the 1980s about West Germany's ability to continue to perform its defense mission.

Opponents of pronatalist measures, on the other hand, "dismiss as exaggerated the specter of Europe as a decrepit society of ruminating octogenarians." They "attach no special value to their own cultures" and oppose stimulating population growth in a world where this is already a serious problem. They believe that "economic resources rather than military resources or population size determine a country's international standing" and that "economic integration is a much more effective way to maintain Europe's international position than stimulating the birth rate." Finally, they question whether it makes sense to stimulate births when Europe already suffers from high levels of unemployment. "With modern technology eliminating jobs, workers are encouraged to work shorter hours, part-time, or retire early and immigration is halted," the argument continues, "so why should we have more people?" (van de Kaa, 1987).

Pronatalist policies have not been at issue in the United States—although right-to-life issues have long dominated the national political scene. The aging of society is nonetheless pertinent to both domestic and international politics as the United States struggles to remain competitive in the world political economy. Educational skills must be enhanced as the economy shifts from manufacturing toward high technology and service industries, but the government will be pressured simultaneously to distrib-ute a greater share of limited resources, drawn from a declining pool of productive workers, to care for the elderly. Immigrants from throughout the world will seek to enter the United States in search of political freedom and economic opportunity, as they have for more than two hundred years, but jobs will continue to be "exported" to youthful, labor-rich countries "off-shore," where the costs of production are markedly lower. Thus the aging of the United States, like that of the rest of the industrial world, will prove to be profoundly important not only domestically but also internationally.

The Impact of Demographic Trends on Global Food Security

The gloomiest of Thomas Malthus's predictions made nearly two centuries ago was that the world's population would eventually outstrip its capacity to produce enough food to sustain its growing numbers. As noted above, Malthus based his prognosis on what he regarded as the simple mathematical fact that population grows exponentially, while agricultural output grows only arithmetically. What he did not foresee is that agricultural output would also grow at an increasing rate due to technological innovations.

Trends in Agricultural Production

Increases in the world's food output have been particularly impressive since World War II. In the thirty-five years from 1950 to 1985, world grain harvests increased from less than 750 million tons to 1.7 billion tons. Even though the world experienced unprecedented population growth during this period, the growth in food production was so spectacular that it permitted a 25 percent increase in per-capita food supplies and a corresponding increase in meeting minimum nutritional standards (O'Brien, 1988: 395).

The greatest increases in food production occurred as a result of the increased productivity of farmers in the developed world, but impressive gains were also recorded in many countries of the Third World as a result of expanding acreage devoted to agriculture and, later, the Green Revolution (the introduction of new high-yield strains of wheat and rice) in such countries as Bangladesh, India, Indonesia, Mexico, Pakistan, and the Philippines. By the 1980s Indonesia, once a massive importer of food, had largely been removed from the import market, and India, once regarded as a permanent candidate for the international dole, had actually become a modest grain exporter.

Whether world food production will continue to grow as it has in the past is uncertain, yet that will have to happen if output is to keep pace with an expanding world population and improvements in living standards. "In the next two to four generations, world agriculture will be called on to produce as much food as has been produced in the entire 12,000-year history of agriculture" (Freeman, 1990: 16). Growth optimists confidently predict the challenge will be met, believing that technology, particularly genetic engineering, will provide the basis for sharply improved agricultural productivity. Growth pessimists, on the other hand, worry that the impressive gains of the past few decades cannot be repeated as returns from the further application of existing technology diminish and the environmental costs of modern agricultural techniques begin to take their toll.

As pessimists emphasize, few further gains have occurred in agricultural productivity since the mid-1980s. Noting that "many countries have reached the point where using additional fertilizer does little to boost food output," they conclude that "the diminishing crop response to the additional use of fertilizer, the negative effect of environmental degradation on harvests, and the lack of any new technology to replace fertilizer as the engine of agricultural growth are each contributing to a potentially hungry future for much of humanity" (Brown, 1991).

The pessimists' views are reinforced by what has happened to the world stock of surplus grains (large amounts of which are produced in the North America) since the mid-1980s. As global food production flattened out, these carryover stocks, which in effect provide the world with a food-security buffer during lean years, dwindled. Climate trends produced a lean year in 1988, as excessive heat and drought in the United States and elsewhere sharply reduced global food production. By 1989 world stocks of grain had fallen below 1983 levels (World Resources Institute, 1990: 86), when drought and famine were visited on broad stretches of the Sahel in Africa. Noteworthy, however, is that little rebuilding occurred during 1990, despite record harvests that year. The experience of the 1970s suggests that falling carryover stocks will result in instability in the price of agricultural products worldwide. In this sense "agriculture is likely to be the sector that first illustrates how profoundly environmental degradation will eventually shape global economic trends" (Brown, 1991).

Food Security

Ensuring against wide swings in the availability and price of food underlies the goal of realizing global food security now widely embraced by the world's food producers and consumers. *Food security* is usefully defined as the "access by all people at all times to enough food for an active, healthy life."

> Its essential elements are the availability of food and the ability to acquire it. Conversely, food insecurity is the lack of access to sufficient food and can be either chronic or transitory. Chronic food insecurity is a continuously inadequate diet resulting from the lack of resources to produce or acquire food. Transitory food insecurity, on the other hand, is a temporary decline in a household's access to enough food. It results from instability in food production and prices, or in household incomes. The worst form of transitory food insecurity is famine. (Reutlinger, 1985: 7)

Achieving food security became an item on the North-South agenda during the 1970s when, at about the same time as the first OPEC-induced oil crisis, the ability of the multitude of nationally based agricultural systems to produce sufficient food for the world's growing billions was severely challenged. However, despite a widespread commitment nationally and globally to the goal of food security since then, its realization remains elusive. More food is produced now than ever before, but its distribution remains uneven and its accessibility beyond the reach of many.

UNEVEN DISTRIBUTION   As noted above, global food production has increased since World War II, but increases in the per-capita availability of food are unevenly spread. Among the developed countries of the North, increases in per-capita food production since the 1950s have generally moved upward in tandem with increases in total food production. But among the developing nations of the South per-capita food production has generally lagged behind. Moreover, even in countries where the Green Revolution has produced spectacular production gains, the distribution of its rewards has often been quite uneven (R. Hopkins et al., 1982; Shiva, 1991; Wolf, 1986).

As a generalization, population growth accounts for the difference between total

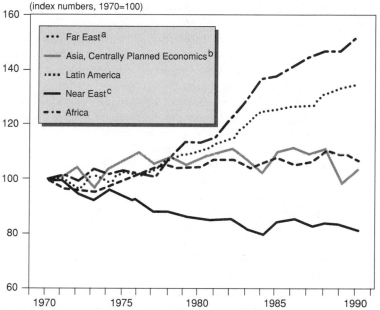

FIGURE 9.8 INDEX OF PER-CAPITA FOOD PRODUCTION IN DEVELOPING REGIONS, 1970–1990

Source: Food and Agriculture Organization of the United Nations (FAO), unpublished data, March 1991.

Notes: [a] Far East = Bangladesh, Bhutan, Brunei Darussalam, East Timor, Hong Kong, India, Indonesia, Republic of Korea, Lao People's Democratic Republic, Macao, Malaysia, Maldives, Myanmar, Nepal, Pakistan, Philippines, Singapore, Sri Lanka, Thailand; [b] Asia, Centrally Planned Economies = Cambodia, China, Democratic People's Republic of Korea, Mongolia, Vietnam; [c] Near East = *Africa:* Egypt, Libyan Arab Jamahiriya, Sudan. *Asia:* Afghanistan, Bahrain, Cyprus, Gaza Strip (Palestine), Islamic Republic of Iran, Iraq, Jordan, Kuwait, Lebanon, Oman, Qatar, Kingdom of Saudi Arabia, Syrian Arab Republic, Turkey, United Arab Emirates, Yemen Arab Republic, Democratic Yemen.

and per-capita production of food in developed and developing countries. Yet, as Figure 9.8 illustrates, there exist widely differing experiences among developing nations themselves. Using 1970 as the baseline for comparison, the figure demonstrates that China and other Asian centrally planned economies (notably Vietnam) have experienced dramatic increases in per-capita food availability; that the other nations in Asia have been able to keep slightly ahead of the population curve; that Near Eastern and Latin American nations have seen their total food production move roughly in tandem with their population growth; and that Africa has experienced a serious and prolonged deterioration in its food-population equation.

Most analysts believe that the introduction of market incentives was critical in stimulating increased food production in China and, somewhat later, in Vietnam. In 1978 the Chinese government shifted from a commune-organized to a market-based agricultural system that offered more financial incentives to farmers to produce. The reform seems to have been the missing piece in China's agricultural puzzle, as increases in agricultural productivity and farm income became widespread (Spivack and Florini, 1986). A decade later Vietnam experienced similar famine-to-feast increases in rice production in response to changes in government policies regarding land tenancy and related economic reforms (Richburg, 1990).

Africa stands in stark contrast. Nowhere does Malthus's grim prediction that population growth would outstrip food production appear more apt than here. During the 1970s, Africa's food production increased by only 1.8 percent annually, but its population grew at a rate of 2.8 percent. Starvation and death became daily occurrences in broad stretches of the Sahel, ranging from Ethiopia in the east to Mauritania in the west. The situation was repeated a decade later, when in Ethiopia in particular world consciousness was awakened by the tragic specter of tens of thousands suffering from malnutrition and dying of famine at a time of unprecedented food surpluses worldwide. As population growth has moved hand in hand with desecration of the environment, sub-Saharan Africa has experienced the tragedy of the commons in all of its most remorseless manifestations.

Two other causes of the African crisis warrant attention. Civil strife and war are one. At various times during the past two decades civil unrest and major armed conflict affecting tens of millions of people have ravaged a third or more of the nations in sub-Saharan Africa. In some cases, as in Ethiopia and the Sudan, food was actively used as a weapon. In the words of Shun Chetty of the United Nations High Commission for Refugees, "He who controls roads controls food. He who controls food controls the people."

Government policies toward agriculture are a second cause of Africa's crisis that warrants comment. Many African governments have promoted policies that reduce incentives for domestic production and increase incentives to import food from abroad (see World Resources Institute, 1990). Often their purpose is to promote domestic tranquility and prevent political turmoil, but the effect is not only to reduce farmers' incentives to produce food but also to encourage migration from farms to cities (see Figure 9.7). This increases the strain on local agricultural systems. Western countries have compounded the problem by providing food imports at subsidized prices: "By controlling the food policies of their respective governments, a powerful minority in the North (rural producers) has joined in a curious alliance with a powerful minority in the South (urban consumers), the result being a 'North-to-South' flow of food that misrepresents production efficiencies and drags against the urgent task of agricultural development in poor countries" (Paarlberg, 1982).

UNEQUAL ACCESS Poverty is an important cause of the perpetuation of millions of chronically hungry people in a world of (relative) plenty. According to the microeconomic principle known as Engel's law, poorer families typically spend a much greater percentage of their budget on food than do higher-income groups. Thus, as Richard Barnet (1980) has observed, "Most people who stop eating do so not because there is insufficient food grown in the world but because they no longer grow it themselves and do not have the money to buy it." This is what *effective demand* means: The ability to acquire more food depends on having the income necessary to buy more food. Many people in the developing countries are simply incapable of registering an effective demand for food because they do not have the purchasing power necessary to secure an adequate diet.

The people who live in *absolute poverty* are least able to register effective demand for food in the global marketplace. Robert McNamara used that term when he was president of the World Bank to describe "a condition of life so limited by malnutrition, illiteracy, disease, squalid surroundings, high infant mortality, and low life expectancy as to be beneath any reasonable definition of human decency." In the early 1980s the number estimated to be living in absolute poverty varied from 700 million to 1 billion; by the end of the decade estimates stood at 1.2 billion, or nearly a quarter of humanity (Durning, 1990: 136, 139; see also *World Development Report 1990*, 1990).

At the other end of the spectrum are the world's affluent. Many of the agricultural products produced in developing nations, such as sugar, tea, coffee, and cocoa, are routinely exported to industrial societies, where they are dietary supplements (with little nutritional value) for the world's rich.

Wealth also affects dietary habits. As personal income rises, individuals tend to shift from the direct toward the indirect consumption of grain, with substantial increases in beef and poultry consumption the most visible result. Thus, as global patterns of grain consumption indicate, one of the characteristics of social and economic development is that people climb the *food ladder* as well:

> In the poorer countries the average person can get only about 180 kilograms of grain per year—about a pound per day. With so little to go around, nearly all grain must be consumed directly if minimal energy needs are to be met. But as incomes rise, so do grain comsumption levels. In the wealthier industrial societies such as the United States . . . the average person consumes four-fifths of a ton of grain per year. Of this, only 90 to 140 kilograms is eaten directly as bread, pastries, and breakfast cereals; most is consumed indirectly as meat, milk, and eggs.
>
> In effect, wealth enables individuals to move up the biological food chain. Thus, the average . . . American uses roughly four times the land, water, and fertilizer used by an Indian, a Colombian, or a Nigerian. (Brown, 1978: 134)

The changing consumption patterns described by the food ladder concept have had an important impact on the overall food picture since World War II. "While fewer than 200 million people had made the transition to diets with a quarter or more of their calories from livestock products by the mid-1950s, more than 600 million people had made the transition by the early 1980s. An added 650 million consumers in the middle-income countries had also begun the transition" (O'Brien, 1988: 398). Whether the world will be able to sustain a similar transition up the food ladder for billions more in the future is, however, problematic. Regardless, the food ladder concept underscores the fact that affluence and rising consumption place greater strains on the ability of food producers to ensure global food security than does population growth. This proposition applies to other resources as well.

The Impact of Demographic Trends on the Global Commons

The environmental toll of population growth and rising affluence seemingly binds humanity in a common fate, but, as the tragedy of the commons suggests, nations do not share the costs and benefits associated with the exploitation equally. Herein lies important insight into what many have described as the "planetary predicament."

The Third World

Soil erosion, desertification, and deforestation are worldwide phenomena, but they are often most acute where population growth and poverty are most evident (see Durning, 1989). The search for fuelwood is a major source of deforestation and a primary occupation in many parts of the developing world. Deforestation and soil erosion also occur when growing populations without access to farmland push cultivation into hillsides and tropical forests ill-suited to farming. In the Sahel area of Africa, growing populations of livestock as well as humans hastened the destruction of productive land, producing a desert that led to famine—a graphic illustration of the tragedy of the commons.

Where population growth rates remain high a kind of "ecological transition" occurs that is "almost the reverse of the demographic transition in that its end result is disastrous."

> In the first stage, expanding human demands are well within the sustainable yield of the biological support system. In the second, they are in excess of the sustainable yield but still expanding as the biological resource itself is being consumed. And in the final stage, human consumption is forcibly reduced as the biological system collapses. (Brown et al., 1987: 26–27)[11]

Tragically, an ecological transition applies to much of the developing world, particularly sub-Saharan Africa, where more than a quarter of the land area is "moderately to very severely desertified" and vast areas have "permanently" lost their agricultural potential (World Resources Institute, 1990: 91).

---

[11] The process of desertification demonstrates how overshoot of the carrying capacity of biological systems multiplies.

Once the demand for fuelwood exceeds the sustainable yield of local forests, it not only reduces tree cover but also leads to soil erosion and land degradation. When grasslands deteriorate to where they can no longer support cattle, livestock herders often take to lopping foliage from trees, thus putting even more pressure on remaining tree cover. Both contribute to a loss of protective vegetation, without which both wind and water erosion of soil accelerate, leading to desertification—a sustained decline in the biological productivity of land.

A decline in the diversity of plant and animal communities marks the onset of desertification. This in turn leads to a reduction of soil organic matter, a decline in soil structure, and a loss of water retention capacity. It also lowers soil fertility, reduced further by increasing wind and water erosion. Typically the end result is a desert: a skeletal shell of soil consisting almost entirely of sand and lacking in the fine particles and organic matter that make soil productive. (Brown et al., 1987: 26)

The First World

Excessive population growth doubtless strains the environment and contributes to destruction of the global commons, but excessive consumption is even more damaging. In this respect it is not the disadvantaged four-fifths of humanity in the burgeoning South who place the greatest strains on the global habitat but the affluent one-fifth in the consumption-oriented North. Consider some evidence:

- A typical resident of the industrialized . . . world uses 15 times as much paper, 10 times as much steel, and 12 times as much fuel as a Third World resident. The extreme case is . . . the United States, where the average person consumes most of his or her own weight in basic materials each day—18 kilograms of petroleum and coal, 13 kilograms of other minerals, 12 kilograms of agricultural products, and 9 kilograms of forest products. (Durning, 1991: 161)

- The average Japanese consumes nine times as much steel as the average Chinese, and Americans use more than four times as much steel and 23 times as much aluminum as their neighbors in Mexico. U.S. paper consumption per person is over a dozen times the average for Latin America, and Americans use about 25 times as much nickel apiece as someone who lives in India. (Young, 1991:40)

A consuming society is also a throwaway society. "The Japanese use 30 million 'disposable' single-roll cameras each year, and the British dump 2.5 billion diapers. Americans toss away 180 million razors annually, enough paper and plastic plates and cups to feed the world a picnic six times a year, and enough aluminum cans to make 6,000 DC-10 airplanes" (Durning, 1991: 161). Each American threw away an average of 1,460 pounds of garbage in 1988, and the amount is expected to grow to nearly 1,800 pounds per person by 2010 (Young, 1991: 28). As the mountains of garbage grow, disposing of it has become increasingly difficult.

The growing volume of solid waste in the North mirrors the dramatic increase in consumption that has occurred in industrial societies since World War II. Again consider some evidence:

- In the United States . . . people today own twice as many cars, drive two-and-a-half times as far, use 21 times as much plastic, and travel 25 times as far by air as did their parents in 1950. Air conditioning spread from 15 percent of households in 1960 to 64 percent in 1987, and color televisions from 1 to 93 percent. (Durning, 1991: 154)

- The Japanese of today consume more than four times as much aluminum, almost five times as much energy, and 25 times as much steel as people in Japan did in 1950. They also own four times as many cars and eat nearly twice as much meat. (Durning, 1991: 155)

- Taken together, France, West Germany, and the United Kingdom almost doubled their per capita use of steel, more than doubled their intake of cement and aluminum, and tripled their paper consumption since mid-century. (Durning, 1991: 155)

Military Preparedness and War

Disposing of industrial societies' solid wastes is now more difficult not only because of their magnitude but also because the proportion of plastics and toxic substances has increased markedly (Young, 1991). Peacetime military preparations magnify the problem even further. One analyst concludes that "the military is quite likely the largest operator of hazardous wastes in the United States and, rivaled by only the [former] Soviet armed forces, the world. In recent years, the Pentagon generated between 400,000 and 500,000 tons of toxics annually, more than the top five U.S. chemical companies. Its contractors produced tens if not hundreds of thousands of tons more. And these figures do not even include the large amounts of toxics spewing from the Department of Energy's nuclear weapons complex" (Renner, 1991: 143).[12]

War itself often precipitates environmental desecration. Rome sowed salt on a defeated Carthage to prevent its resurgence; the Dutch breached their own dikes to allow ocean saltwater to flood fertile farmlands in an attempt to stop the advancing Germans during World War II; and the United States used defoliants on the dense jungles in Vietnam in an effort to expose enemy guerrillas. More recently, Iraq engaged in what the United States called an act of "environmental terrorism" without military purpose when it released millions of gallons of oil into the Persian Gulf during the 1991 Gulf War. Retreating Iraqis also set nearly 600 oil wells on fire and blew up hundreds of other wells, storage tanks, refineries, and other facilities. Extinguishing the fires took months. Meanwhile, tons of smoke with toxic pollutants belched thousands of meters skyward, from where environmental experts expected they would affect near-term the regional climate, food production, and water quality. Experts also expected the disruption of the delicate desert ecosystem caused by military activities in the Persian Gulf region before and during the war to last for decades (Barnaby, 1991).

It would be impertinent to suggest that the United States, the (former) Soviet Union, and the other members of NATO and the now-defunct Warsaw pact are alone responsible for the adverse environmental consequences of military preparedness, but it is a viewpoint not easily dismissed. These are precisely the nations that have spent the most on military preparedness since World War II and even today remain among the largest suppliers of arms to other nations (see Chapter 11).

Global Warming

What are the long-term consequences of the disproportionate impact of the world's rich nations on global resource consumption, particularly fossil fuels (examined in

---

[12] The extensiveness of toxic contamination by the U.S. military has hampered efforts by the Department of Defense to sell or lease obsolete military bases. Military officials estimate it will cost more than $1 billion and take at least a decade to clean up just eighty-six military bases that were slated in 1988 for closing (*New York Times*, June 30, 1991, p. 1).

Chapter 10)? During the 1970s, growth pessimists warned that the exhaustion of global resources was inevitable. Today the concern lies "less in running out of resources . . . than in the continuing damage that their extraction and processing impose on the environment" (Young, 1991). The consequence of continued heavy dependence on oil in transportation and industry is illustrative: "Rising levels of carbon dioxide in the atmosphere make it unlikely the world will run out of oil before the environmental cost of its use—in the form of global warming—becomes prohibitive" (Young, 1991).

"Global warming" is shorthand for the prospective climate changes that the insulating effect of the earth's atmosphere may cause. The atmosphere permits radiation from the sun to penetrate to the earth, but gas molecules form the equivalent of a greenhouse roof by trapping heat remitted from earth that would otherwise escape into outer space. Carbon dioxide (CO_2) accounts for about half of the greenhouse gases. Methane (natural gas), nitrous oxide, ozone, and chlorofluorocarbons (CFCs) make up the rest. (CFCs are artificial chemicals widely used in refrigerators and air conditioners as refrigerants, in Styrofoam cups, in cleansers for computer components, and as aerosol propellants for such things as deodorants.)

In all cases consumption patterns are the chief cause of the volume of greenhouse gases released into the atmosphere.[13] Thus the developed countries of the North are the chief perpetrators of the growing amount of greenhouse gases in the atmosphere. As Figure 9.9 on page 332 shows, the developed nations, who make up about a quarter of the world's population, are responsible for 54 percent of the heating effect caused by greenhouse gas emissions. In contrast, developing nations, who make up nearly 80 percent of the world's population, account for less than half. Among the developed nations the United States again stands out, accounting for nearly 18 percent of the heating effect of the greenhouse gases emitted but less than 5 percent of world population. Brazil is the main culprit among developing nations because of the adverse consequences of deforestation of the Amazon basin.[14]

There is widespread agreement on the theory underlying global warming and on

---

[13] Carbon dioxide, CFCs, and methane are the three most important greenhouse gases. The carbon dioxide in the atmosphere is now growing at a rate of 0.05 percent per year, CFCs by 5 percent, and methane by 1 percent (Mathews, 1992: 367). As noted below, fossil fuel combustion and deforestation account for the bulk of the increased concentration of CO_2, and the source of CFCs (which can remain active in the atmosphere for more than a century) is well known, as they are man-made chemicals. The causes of the buildup of methane concentration are unclear, however. "It may be that there are so many links between methane and human activity—from cattle ranching to rice paddies to leaky gas pipelines—that methane emissions are simply tracking population growth" (Mathews, 1992). At present rates of increase, the concentration of greenhouse gases would double by 2030 (Topping, 1990: 5).

[14] The data on greenhouse gas emissions graphed in Figure 9.9 are an index designed to ascertain the contribution individual countries and regions make to global warming. The index is designed to measure two elements: "first, the proportion of the annual release of each greenhouse gas which remains in the atmosphere at the end of a given year and, second, a factor which measures the instantaneous effect of this amount of gas on the earth's energy balance" (McCully, 1991). The prestigious World Resources Institute, which designed the index, argues that it provides an important policy-making base by permitting inter-country comparisons that demonstrate the global proportions of the problem of global warming in both cause and effect, but critics argue that the index assigns disproportionate responsibility for global warming to developing nations and thus directs the attention of policymakers away from the primary source of the problem, which is the industrial world (see McCully, 1991).

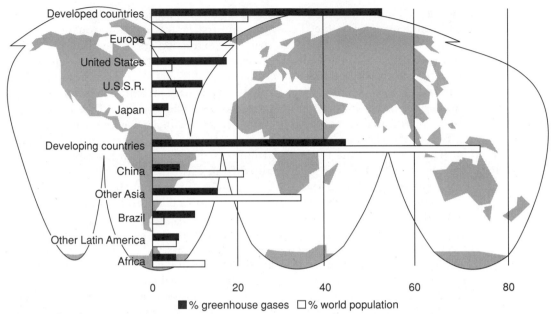

FIGURE 9.9 NET ADDITIONS TO THE GREENHOUSE HEATING EFFECT AND WORLD POPULATION (PERCENTAGES)

Source: Based on data drawn from World Resources Institute, *World Resources 1990–1991* (New York: Oxford University Press, 1990), pp. 348–349; and Population Reference Bureau, *1991 World Population Data Sheet*. *Note:* Population data are for 1991; greenhouse gas data are circa 1985–1987. Greenhouse gas heating effects are based on an index of carbon dioxide and methane emissions and chlorofluorocarbon use; the index includes an estimate of carbon dioxide emissions caused by changes in land use, principally deforestation.

the fact that the gases that cause heat to be trapped in the atmosphere are increasing at unprecedented rates. What remains in dispute is whether continued high rates of greenhouse gas emissions will lead to global warming (and, we might add, with what consequence), in part because too many determinants of climate change are inadequately understood.[15] Not surprisingly, therefore, global warming is a contentious issue on the global agenda.

CAUSES OF GLOBAL WARMING Deforestation is one of the human activities that accelerate global warming. Green plants routinely remove carbon dioxide from the atmosphere during photosynthesis. The natural processes that remove greenhouse gases are destroyed when forests are cut down, and, as the forests decay or are burned, the amount of CO_2 discharged into the atmosphere increases. This makes deforestation doubly destructive. Yet many governments have permitted the destruction of forests, which are being depleted at an alarming rate. For many years it was believed that an

---

[15] *World Resources 1990–91*, published by the World Resources Institute (1990), is a useful treatment of the theory and evidence about global warming.

area the size of Austria was deforested every year, but recent evidence indicates that the magnitude of the destruction of the world's forests may be even greater (World Resources Institute, 1990: 101–104). Tropical deforestation is notably acute in places like Indonesia, Myanmar (formerly Burma), Cameroon, Costa Rica, and especially Brazil (see Figure 9.9), where vast tracts of rain forests have been cleared and burned to make room for farms and ranches (whose cattle, incidentally, add to the staggering volume of methane released into the atmosphere).

Although deforestation contributes heavily to the greenhouse process, the burning of fossil fuels is an even greater culprit. It accounts for three-quarters of the excess carbon released into the atmosphere, or roughly a ton of atmospheric CO_2 for every man, woman, and child on earth. (Deforestation, in contrast, accounts for 25 percent of the excess carbon [Mathews, 1992: 367]).

Along with manufacturing, the utilities industry is often believed especially responsible for atmospheric pollution. In part this is because it is known to produce atmospheric sulfur and nitrogen oxides. These pollutants return to earth, typically after traveling long distances, in the form of "acid rain," which adds to the acidification of lakes, the corrosion of materials and structures, and the impairment of ecosystems. (Acid rain has fallen in measurable amounts in the Scandinavian countries and in the United States and Canada, where it has been a source of transnational controversy.) And the burning of coal, widespread among utilities, releases more CO_2 than does the burning of other fossil fuels. Automobiles also emit large quantities of greenhouse gases. The average American car driven an average ten thousand miles a year releases its own weight in carbon into the atmosphere every year (McKibben, 1989: 48).

Energy is the engine of economic growth and improved living standards throughout the world. Today the industrial nations of the North consume over seventy percent of the world's energy. Moreover, their access to the world's energy supplies has materially benefited their societies. Interestingly, however, the greatest increases in the *rate* of energy consumption now occur in the developing nations of the South. This also means that the greatest increases in atmospheric pollution due to fossil-fuel combustion will result from Third World policies and achievements. If, for example, China were to increase its per capita gross national product to just fifteen percent of the U.S. per capita GNP, it would have to burn so much fossil fuel that "the increase in CO_2 emissions would equal the total CO_2 released from all the coal currently consumed by the United States" (Owen, 1989: 40).

Even without economic growth, the expected doubling of the world's present population of more than five billion people will require an enormous increase in fossil fuel consumption simply to maintain living standards at their current levels. Thus the unfolding of demographic patterns now in place may seriously disrupt the world's climate and delicate ecosystems in the decades ahead even in the unlikely event that the process of global warming has not already begun.

CONSEQUENCES OF GLOBAL WARMING   Is the temperature of the world's atmosphere rising inexorably? The 1980s witnessed the six warmest years on record, and the decade as a whole was the hottest ever. These facts are consistent with a trend evident over the past century, when the average temperature rose by as much as .7

degrees Celsius (World Resources Institute, 1990: 20). During the same period the amount of CO_2 in the atmosphere increased by twenty-five percent and the amount of methane doubled (Schneider, 1989: 72). Still, scientists do not agree on whether the heat wave of the 1980s was itself a consequence of the greenhouse effect taking hold. Nonetheless, it may provide a glimpse of the future.

As the greenhouse gases in the atmosphere mount, global temperatures will rise. Some researchers predict that by 2050 global temperatures will reach an average level four degrees (Celsius) higher than now. The consequences are not easily predicted (see Woodwell, 1990; Wyman, 1991), but some that are widely discussed include a melting of the polar ice caps, which will raise ocean levels significantly and lead to the destruction of coastal areas and wetlands; an increase in the frequency and severity of droughts, dust storms, forest fires, and hurricanes; and a marked alteration of rainfall and other traditional weather patterns critical to economic processes.

While not all projected changes will be detrimental, collectively they will lead to dramatic changes in global patterns of production, trade, capital flows, and migration. The global power pyramid may be transformed in the process. The desertification of the rich agricultural lands in the heartland of the United States and the emergence of Siberia as a major food-producing region are common prognoses; if they occur, important economic and political changes will follow. Similarly, a warmer Canada could induce large numbers of Americans to migrate there, with the result that Canada may emerge as the global hegemon of the twenty-first century. Thus changes in the world's climate promise to alter world politics profoundly.

Toward a Managed Commons Arrangement

Other examples of environmental stress associated with affluence include soil erosion caused by the expansion of energy-intensive, mechanized agriculture to marginal lands; water shortages caused by the massive requirements of modern agriculture, industry, and residential living; and depletion of ocean fisheries caused by technology-intensive overfishing and pollution of spawning beds. In Eastern Europe and the former Soviet Union, decades of central planning and authoritarian rule that placed intense emphasis on rapid industrialization also led to widespread abuse and destruction, which now requires extensive environmental reconstruction (French, 1990). Still, global warming may be the ultimate tragedy of the commons. It was intended by none yet is seemingly beyond the control of all who will bear its costs.

The Prospects for International Cooperation

The unequal distribution of power in the international system and the sovereign equality of its members both ensure that national interests will dominate considerations of the common (global) interest. Nonetheless, as the world has become increasingly interdependent ecologically as well as economically, there is a greater awareness that what is in the best interest of all may also be in the best interest of each (see Renner,

1989). The changes taking place are reflected in the "greening" of politics in many nations, particularly in the industrial world, as sensitivity to environmental issues multiplies, as well as in the growing commitment worldwide to the principle of *sustainable development* (Helman, 1990).

Sustainable development is the central concept in *Our Common Future*, the 1987 report of the World Commission on Environment and Development (1987), popularly known as the Brundtland Commission after the Norwegian prime minister who was its chair. The commission concluded that the world cannot sustain the growth required to meet the needs and aspirations of the world's projected population unless it adopts radically different approaches to basic issues of economic expansion, equity, resource management, energy efficiency, and the like. The commission did not embrace the "limits of growth" maxim popular among growth pessimists during the 1970s; instead, it emphasized "the growth of limits." Thus sustainability means learning to live off the earth's interest, without encroaching on its capital (see MacNeill, 1989–1990, 1992; World Resources Institute, 1992).

The Brundtland Commission report is an important landmark in the rapid emergence of environmental concerns as a central issue on the global political agenda. The process began in 1972, when the UN General Assembly convened the first United Nations Conference on the Human Environment in Stockholm. In the ensuing years other conferences were held on a wide range of topics related to the environment, including, for example, population, desertification, food, and the oceans. New international agencies were created to monitor developments in their respective areas and to promote international cooperation in dealing with both national and transnational problems within their jurisdictions. In the process new principles were articulated that direct the world's nations toward the goal of preserving the global habitat for future generations.

Many of these helped set the stage for the Second United Nations Conference on Environment and Development, held in Rio de Janeiro, Brazil, in 1992, the twentieth anniversary of the first conference. Preparing for the conference, popularly known as the Earth Summit, proved difficult, as many of the differences between the world's rich and poor nations shaped perceptions of their national interests in environmental issues. Still, the conference marked another milestone in the development of basic principles of national conduct designed to promote a sustainable future for all of humankind.

Although the machinery for international cooperation on environmental issues is extensive, its past effectiveness in dealing with environmental problems, and especially its ability to cope with emerging problems, notably those related to climate change, are questionable (Sand, 1991; Soroos, 1992). If there is cause for optimism, it is perhaps best exemplified by the concerted action that depletion of the stratospheric ozone layer has stimulated.[16]

Coping with Ozone Depletion

Ozone is a pollutant in the lower atmosphere, but in the upper atmosphere it provides the earth with a critical layer of protection against the sun's harmful ultraviolet

---

[16] The discussion of the ozone-depletion issue that follows is based on Benedick (1991).

radiation. Scientists have discovered a marked depletion of the ozone layer—most notably an "ozone hole" over Antarctica that grows at times to be larger than the continental United States—and they have conclusively linked the thinning of the layer to chlorofluorocarbons and a related family of compounds known as halons. Depletion of the ozone layer exposes humans to increased health hazards of various sorts, particularly skin cancer, and threatens other forms of marine and terrestrial life. The release of CFC gases in turn adds measurably to the accumulation of greenhouse gases that threaten dramatic climate change through global warming.

Scientists began to link CFCs to ozone depletion in the early 1970s. Even before their hypotheses were conclusively confirmed, the United Nations Environment Programme (a UN agency created in the aftermath of the 1972 Stockholm conference) began to seek some form of regulatory action. The scientific uncertainty surrounding the issue eased the sense of urgency some felt, and differences between the interests of the chemical industry in the United States (where bans were placed on some CFCs, such as aerosol propellants) and Europe (where they were not) slowed efforts to devise controls. Nevertheless, in 1985 an agreement (the Vienna Convention on Protection of the Ozone Layer) was concluded whose purpose was to control ozone-modifying substances. This landmark decision "represented the first international effort to deal formally with an environmental danger before it erupted" (Benedick, 1991).

Two years later a second and even more significant agreement was reached, the Montreal Protocol on Substances That Deplete the Ozone Layer, signed by twenty-three nations and the Commission of the European Community. The signatories agreed at that time to reduce their CFC emissions to half of their 1986 levels by the turn of the century. The agreement was widely heralded, as those who participated in the negotiations accounted for more than 80 percent of global CFC emissions. Even further cuts were proposed later, and in 1990 an agreement was reached that pointed toward the rapid phaseout of CFCs altogether. The unexpected discovery in early 1992 of an ozone hole over the Northern Hemisphere will probably move even this timetable up, as the United States decided unilaterally to phase out production of all CFCs by 1995.

The rapid move between 1985 and 1987 to restrict the use of CFCs and related compounds reflected growing scientific certainty about the connection between CFCs and ozone depletion. Still—and unlike what the tragedy of the commons metaphor would lead us to expect—the success depended on the ability of national negotiators to put aside short-term interests, which included large investments in important segments of the chemical industry and thousands of related jobs.

> Perhaps the most extraordinary aspect of the Montreal Protocol was that it imposed substantial short-term economic costs in order to protect human health and the environment against speculative future dangers—dangers that rested on scientific theories rather than proven facts. Unlike environmental agreements of the past, this was not a response to harmful developments or events, but rather *preventive* action on a global scale. (Benedick, 1991: 129)

Can the success achieved in reducing ozone-depleting gases be repeated to reduce the emissions that threaten to change the world's climate through global warming? That experience contains important lessons, to be sure, but there are also reasons to be cautious, even skeptical (Grubb, 1990; Sebenius, 1991). They have to do with the magnitude of the problem and the distribution of costs and benefits associated with alternative solutions. The scientific uncertainty surrounding the evidence on global warming even further muddles efforts to deal with it.

Coping with Global Warming

The magnitude of the problems related to global warming are truly enormous, not simply because of the global character of climate change and its anticipated consequences but also because of who will be affected by policy choices designed to slow it. These facts distinguish global warming from the process that dealt with ozone depletion.

> Negotiating and sustaining serious substantive actions to mitigate greenhouse gas emissions will be far more difficult. . . . The number of significant CFC-producing countries was small. The economic costs, required institutional changes, and affected industries were relatively limited. Those firms that expected to be able to produce CFC substitutes could benefit compared with their competitors and thus could even gain from the treaty. Few of these conditions apply to limits on carbon and other greenhouse emissions. (Sebenius, 1991: 118)

The expected consequences of reducing carbon emissions could be especially severe in the United States, the world's largest consumer of fossil fuel energy. The Bush administration—characterized as "wed to the gloomiest economic predictions"—estimated that the U.S. GNP would decline by 3 percent (roughly $150 billion) as a result of efforts to halt global warming through increased energy efficiency (Weisskopf, 1991: 33). This perhaps explains why the United States—at least until the surprising discovery of significant ozone depletion over North America—talked more of the uncertain extent and consequences of global warming than of positive steps to halt it. Accordingly, the United States "took a hang-tough, U.S.-against-the-world approach toward the Earth Summit," demanding and winning "a weekend version of a treaty on climate change on the grounds that accepting tough new rules to limit carbon dioxide emissions would hurt economic growth" (Greenhouse, 1992). Specifically, the United States refused to join other industrial nations in a commitment to reduce carbon dioxide emissions to 1990 levels by the year 2000.

At the same time that the United States waxed uncertain about the future, nations in western Europe and even Japan (which previously had followed the U.S. lead on greenhouse policy) began to formulate national policies designed to reduce radically carbon dioxide emissions, which are the largest source of greenhouse heating. Thus, "without intending to, or even fully realizing that it has done so, Europe has assumed the mantle of international leadership on this central environmental issue, leaving the United States increasingly isolated" (Mathews, 1990; see also French, 1991). Furthermore, "if Japan and the West Europeans are correct and the greenhouse phenomenon proves to be a trend that must soon be reversed, their recent decisions to take remedial action could hold bad news for U.S. economic competitiveness. The means by which carbon dioxide emissions will be cut depend on advances in energy supply technologies, in transportation, agriculture, industry, appliances, building construction—in short in every corner of the economy where energy use is important" (Mathews, 1990).[17]

The industrial nations of the North (including members of the Commonwealth of Independent States and the nations in eastern Europe) today account for the bulk of greenhouse gas emissions, but, as noted earlier, the most rapid rate of increase in carbon emissions is among the developing nations of the South. Even if the industrial nations are able to reduce their carbon dioxide emissions by 20 percent over the next three decades, the volume would still nearly double as a result of Third World carbon output (Stetson, 1991: 24).

Developing nations are understandably wary about efforts by the rich nations to solve environmental problems they (the developing nations) did not cause, all the more so if they are denied access to the very technologies that stimulated the economic growth of the now developed world. "Leaders struggling with the hand-to-mouth survival of millions find that 'sacrifice today to save tomorrow' is bitter medicine, especially when those administering it have already reaped the benefits of unlimited greenhouse effusions" (Stetson, 1991). They also regard efforts to blame developing countries for what some see as an emerging ecological crisis as a form of "environmental colonialism."

> The bulk of Third World contributions to climate change . . . comes from agriculture and forests, in the form of methane from cows and rice paddies and carbon released from burning trees. These "survival emissions," as Third World countries call them, are the by-products of life-sustaining activities that generate food and income. They are different from the "luxury emissions" of the North, which come from cars and electricity for appliances in every home. (Stetson, 1991: 23)

During 1991, as preparations continued for the 1992 UN Conference on Environment and Development, substantial efforts were made to hammer out a global climate treaty that would balance the interests of the developed and developing worlds. With the notable exceptions of the United States and the Soviet Union, a consensus among the industrial nations favoring a rapid reduction of carbon emissions seemed to emerge.

Third World participation in such efforts is critical if the rate of global temperature increases projected for the next century is to be slowed. Importantly, many Third World nations expressed a willingness to consider voluntary reductions in their carbon dioxide emissions, provided, however, that the industrial nations also reduced their emissions. Developing nations also looked for assistance from the North in acquiring the technology to reduce their own pollutants (Stetson, 1991; also Sebenius, 1991). The strategy was similar to that devised in 1990 for dealing with ozone depletion, when an agreement was reached on the creation of a special fund (to be administered through the World Bank) that would finance the introduction in developing countries of products and technologies that would substitute for those known to cause depletion

---

[17] Mathews (1992) argues elsewhere that even in the face of uncertainty, "much of what we need to do to limit further commitment to global warming will benefit us as a nation and as a species even if our greenhouse predictions should turn out to be wrong."

of the ozone. Thus halting steps were taken toward a managed commons arrangement even in the absence of a regulatory (supranational) agency.

THE FREEDOM OF THE COMMONS ....

Garrett Hardin (1968) warned in his well-known popularization of the tragedy of the commons metaphor that "ruin is the destination toward which all . . . rush . . . in a society that believes in the freedom of the commons." Will the world's nations give up that measure of individual freedom necessary to avert global disaster? The tentative steps toward a managed commons arrangement to cope with climate change are reassuring, but optimism must be tempered by a recognition that the issue of global warming involves "the interaction of two vast and complex systems, the planet's ecosystem and the human socioeconomic system" (Skolnikoff, 1990). Substantial inertia that works against policy change in the best of circumstances characterizes both.

Global warming is an inherently transnational policy problem. Its solution, however, continues to rest in the hands of nations, as the generally tentative steps taken at the 1992 Earth Summit amply demonstrated. Maurice Strong, organizer of the twelve-day conference, worried that the summit's outcome reflected "agreement without sufficient commitment." "I believe," he lamented, "we are on the road to tragedy." Thus, the logic of state sovereignty (read individual freedom) continues to militate against global action in a society where the benefits of inaction are shared nationally but the costs are borne transnationally.

SUGGESTED READINGS

Benedick, Richard Elliot. *Ozone Diplomacy: New Directions in Safeguarding the Planet*. Cambridge, Mass.: Harvard University Press, 1991.

Brown, Lester R., et al. *State of the World 1992*. New York: Norton, 1992.

Caldwell, Lynton Keith. *International Environmental Policy: Emergence and Dimensions*, 2nd ed. Durham, N.C.: Duke University Press, 1990.

Ehrlich, Paul R., and Anne H. Ehrlich. *The Population Explosion*. New York: Simon & Schuster, 1990.

Fletcher, Lehman B., ed. *World Food in the 1990s: Production, Trade, and Aid*. Boulder, Colo: Westview, 1992.

Homer-Dixon, Thomas F. "On the Threshold: Environmental Changes as Causes of Acute Conflict," *International Security* 16 (Fall 1991): 76–116.

Leggett, Jeremy, ed. *Global Warming: The Greenpeace Report*. New York: Oxford University Press, 1990.

Mathews, Jessica Tuchman, ed. *Preserving the Global Environment*. New York: Norton, 1991.

Meissner, Doris. "Managing Migrations," *Foreign Policy* 86 (Spring 1992): 66–83.

Porter, Gareth, and Janet Welsh Brown. *Global Environmental Politics*. Boulder, Colo: Westview, 1991.

Wattenberg, Ben J. *The Birth Dearth*. New York: Pharos Books, 1989.

World Commission on Environment and Development. *Our Common Future*. New York: Oxford University Press, 1987.

World Resources Institute. *World Resources 1992–93*. New York: Oxford University Press, 1992.

CHAPTER 10

• • •

OIL, ENERGY, AND RESOURCE POWER

• • •

Whoever controls world resources controls the world in a way that mere occupation of territory cannot match.

Richard J. Barnet,
political scientist, 1980

Vital economic interests are at risk. . . . An Iraq permitted to swallow Kuwait would have the economic and military power, as well as the arrogance, to intimidate and coerce its neighbors—neighbors who control the lion's share of the world's remaining oil reserves. We cannot permit a resource so vital to be dominated by one so ruthless.

George Bush,
U.S. President, 1990

In April 1990, the average price for a barrel of internationally traded crude oil was less than $15. Five months later, in September, it was more than $40. Thus, for the third time in less than two decades, the world suffered an "oil shock" as the price paid for the most widely used commercial energy source skyrocketed.

The first oil shock occurred in 1973–1974, when, shortly after the 1973 Yom Kippur War, the price of oil increased fourfold as a result of the collective action of the major Middle Eastern oil producers. The second, again stimulated by oil-exporting countries, occurred in 1979–1980 in the wake of the revolution in Iran and resulted in an even more dramatic jump in the world price of oil. Iraq's invasion of Kuwait on August 2, 1990, caused the third shock.

Iraq's aggression catapulted the foremost military power in the Arab world into control of a fifth of the oil produced by the Organization of Petroleum Exporting Countries (OPEC) and more than a quarter of its proven reserves of crude oil. In part for this reason, the world community, under the leadership of the United States, launched a dual response. The United Nations first authorized economic sanctions against Iraq in an effort to force its withdrawal from Kuwait. Failing this, on November 29, 1990, the UN Security Council took an unprecedented step when it authorized the use of "all necessary means" to force Iraq from Kuwait. Seven weeks later, on January 16, 1991, the Persian Gulf War began when a coalition of UN forces launched

• • •

the most intensive aerial bombardment ever. Then, in February, coalition forces easily routed Iraqi troops in a 100-hour ground campaign. With Iraq's surrender, the United Nations again used economic sanctions to prod Iraq's compliance with the terms of the truce. Meanwhile, the price of oil reverted to its prewar levels.

The recurring rise and fall of world oil prices is a major source of the financial and political disruptions experienced by the world political economy in recent years. Moreover, states regard secure access to oil at reasonable prices as a major national security concern, as the Persian Gulf War proved. OPEC is no longer able to utilize oil to exercise "commodity power" as it once did, but the repeated use of economic sanctions as an instrument of states' foreign policies underscores the centrality of economic rewards and punishments in contemporary world politics.

The purpose of this chapter is to explore the causes and consequences of the three oil shocks the world has experienced since the early 1970s and the role that economic sanctions play as instruments of foreign policy. The inquiry will embrace several related topics, including policies toward alternative energy sources and the relationship between resource dependence and national security threats. We begin with an examination of the forces giving rise to the OPEC decade.

THE POLITICAL ECONOMY OF OIL: THE MAKING OF THE OPEC DECADE . . . .

The phrase *OPEC decade* captures the centrality of OPEC in the world political economy in recent years. The OPEC decade began in October 1973, when members of the organization, in response to the outbreak of war in the Middle East, imposed an embargo on the supply of oil and cut overall production levels. It then chose to raise the price of its oil—a decision that precipitated the first of three oil shocks.

The OPEC decade ended in March 1983, when, in response to a worldwide oil glut, OPEC for the first time in its history agreed to cut its official price of oil and set a ceiling on its aggregate production levels. For the remainder of the 1980s and into the 1990s the production, price, and supply of energy exhibited much variation, adding uncertainty to a world political economy already buffeted by other problems, thus reducing policymakers' ability to make decisions based on reliable forecasts. This "post-OPEC decade" ended with the Persian Gulf War, but, as we will see, uncertainty continues to characterize the global energy environment.

Global Patterns of Energy Consumption

The behavior of individuals in different national settings influences the dynamics that govern energy supply and demand, price and production. Just as people in the world's rich nations place a disproportionate burden on the global commons, they also consume a disproportionate share of its energy resources. Figure 10.1 illustrates the enormous gap between the developed and the developing worlds in the energy consumed per person. Western Europe uses more than three times as much energy per capita as the developing world, the former centrally planned economies in Eastern Europe and the Soviet Union more than four times as much, and Canada and the United States nearly eight times as much. The differences parallel the gap between the world's rich and poor nations apparent in so many other dimensions of contemporary world politics.

Energy consumption is critical to the production of goods and services. Thus it tends to move in tandem with changes in the gross national product (GNP). During the roughly fifty years from the 1930s to the 1980s, the world's demand for energy increased at almost the same rate as did the aggregate world gross domestic product (GDP) (International Energy Agency, 1982: 69), reflecting in important ways the substitution of energy for labor in the industrial societies of the North. In industrial production, in transportation, and in the distribution of goods and services, intensive uses of energy have become the hallmark of the modern industrial society. Not surprisingly, therefore, the developing nations of the South, which have not yet become as mechanized as the industrial societies, see higher rates of energy use as the

Tons oil equivalent

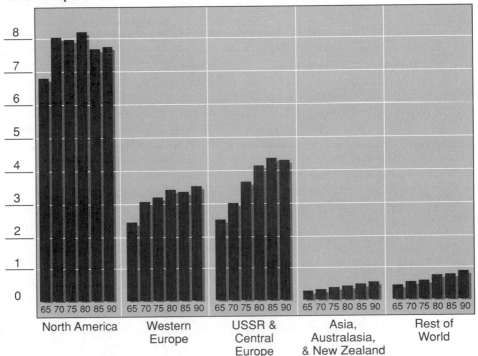

FIGURE 10.1 ENERGY CONSUMPTION PER CAPITA, 1965–1990
Source: BP Statistical Review of World Energy (London: British Petroleum Company, 1991), p. 36.

key to more rapid economic development and higher standards of living. Moreover, the greatest increases in energy consumption today are occurring in the developing nations.[1]

Although the correlation between income and energy use is high, wide differences within given levels of economic output are apparent. Pakistan and Sri Lanka, for example, had similar per-capita incomes in 1989, but Pakistan used over 20 percent more energy per capita than Sri Lanka. Similarly, Argentina used more than twice as much energy per capita as Uruguay but enjoyed a per-capita GNP only four-fifths as great (*World Development Report 1991*, 1991: 204–205, 212–213).

Even more striking are the differences among developed nations. In 1989, for example, the United States used more than twice as much energy per capita as Switzerland, but its per capita income was $9,000 less (*World Development Report 1991*, 1991: 205, 213). Japan also enjoys a higher living standard than the United States even though it uses considerably fewer energy resources. Instead, as Figure 10.2 illustrates, it has proven itself to be dramatically more energy efficient than the United States despite (or perhaps because of) its heavy dependence on imported oil.

The Development of Fossil Fuel Dependence

Rapid increases in the rate of energy usage in general and petroleum in particular are primarily post–World War II phenomena. In 1950, when world population stood at roughly 2.5 billion people, world energy consumption was 2.5 billion tons of coal-equivalent energy. Population increased rapidly during the next quarter-century, but energy use increased even more dramatically. By 1979 the world's 4.4 billion people were consuming 8.7 billion tons of coal-equivalent energy (Sivard, 1981: 6). This increase was closely tied to the unprecedented level of economic growth that the world experienced in the postwar era. From 1950 to 1973, the world economy expanded at a rate of 4 percent annually, spurred by the 7 percent growth in world oil output during this period (Brown, 1979: 17). On a per-capita basis, this meant that the amount of oil available increased from an average of 1.5 barrels per person in 1950 to over 5.3 barrels in 1973 (Brown, 1979: 18). (One barrel of oil equals forty-two U.S. gallons.) The dramatic rise in production has made oil the principal source of commercial energy in the world today.

The Development and Impact of Inexpensive Oil

Little more than a century ago, fuelwood was the principal energy source. As the mechanical revolution altered the nature of transportation, work, and leisure, coal began to replace fuelwood. Early in the twentieth century, coal became the dominant

[1] The burden of growing energy use in the Third World on total energy supplies deserves attention. As Timothy E. Wirth (1991–1992), a Senator in the U.S. Congress, observed, "To provide today's population of 5.3 billion people with the amount of energy used by industrialized societies would require a tripling of global energy use, which is impossible as long as we use the current energy mix."

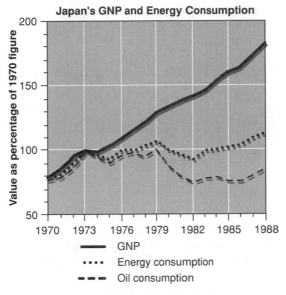

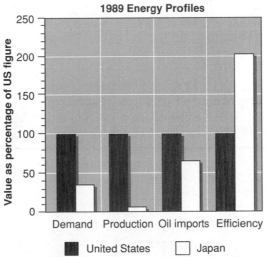

FIGURE 10.2 JAPANESE ENERGY CONSUMPTION AND EFFICIENCY
Source: Ronald A. Morse, "Japan: Crafting an Energy Strategy of Competitiveness in the World Market," *Harvard International Review* 14 (Winter 1991–1992): 15.

source of energy throughout the world. By 1913 it accounted for 75 percent of global energy consumption (Sivard, 1979a: 7).

New technological developments, particularly the internal combustion engine, spurred the shift from coal to oil and, somewhat less so, natural gas. The United States, well endowed with petroleum resources, led the development of oil-based technologies, above all in the automotive and petrochemical industries. Although oil accounted for less than a third of world energy production in 1950, by 1965 it equaled coal production. In the next decade it rapidly outpaced coal as the main energy source. Everywhere the reasons were the same. Energy derived from oil (and gas) was cleaner and less expensive than coal. (The cost of once inexpensive coal also rose in response to labor demands for higher wages, rules to protect the environment, and more costly safety standards.) From the end of the Korean War until the early 1970s, world oil prices actually declined compared with the prices of other commodities. Natural gas prices showed a similar decline in the United States, where it was used more extensively than elsewhere.

The long-term stability of world oil prices is striking. As shown in Figure 10.3, World Wars I and II each produced small, step-level increments in the price of oil, but essentially it remained stable. As the price of other commodities as well as manufactured goods rose, oil became relatively cheaper. It therefore made good economic sense to use it in large quantities. As a result, by 1979—the peak year of world oil consumption since the first well was drilled in the middle of the nineteenth century—over 31,000 gallons of petroleum were used every second. The United States alone consumed more than a fourth of this amount. Not until the onset of the

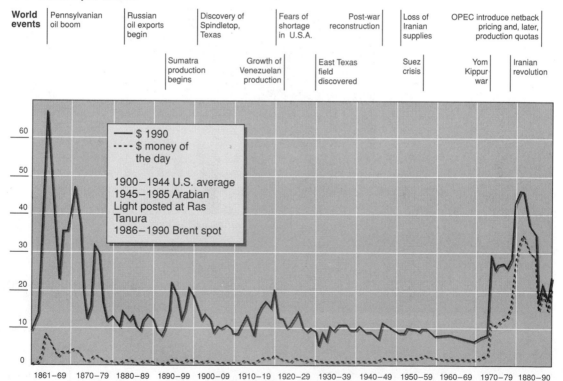

FIGURE 10.3 CRUDE OIL PRICES SINCE 1861
Source: BP Statistical Review of World Energy (London: British Petroleum Company, 1991), p. 12.

OPEC decade was the continuation of this upward consumption trend seriously challenged.

The Role of the Majors

The chief actors propelling the worldwide shift from coal to oil were eight multinational corporations known as the "majors"—Exxon, Gulf, Mobil, Standard Oil of California, Texaco (all U.S. based), British Petroleum, Royal Dutch Shell, and Compagnie Française des Petroles. In the mid-1970s these eight firms (the first seven of which are often referred to as the *seven sisters*) controlled nearly two-thirds of the world's oil production (Abrahamsson, 1975: 80). Their operations encompassed every aspect of the business from exploration to the retailing of products at their gas stations.

The majors were largely unhindered in their search for, production of, and marketing of low-cost oil. Concessions from nations in such oil-rich areas as the Middle East were easy to get. The communist states were virtually the only ones that barred the majors.

A buyer's market existed, which meant that the majors had to control production to avoid glut and chronic oversupply. They did this by keeping other competitors, known as *independents*, out of the international oil regime, by engaging in joint ventures and otherwise cooperating among themselves to restrict supply, and by avoiding price competition (Spero, 1990). The oil companies were thus able to manage the price of oil at a level profitable for themselves even though it declined relative to other commodities.

An abundant supply of oil at low prices facilitated the recovery of Western Europe and Japan from World War II and encouraged consumers to adopt energy-intensive technologies, such as the private automobile. The overall result was an enormous growth in the worldwide demand for and consumption of energy.

To sustain the high growth rates, there was a continual need to find and exploit new oil deposits. The incentives for developing petroleum reserves outside the Middle East waned, however, as the real cost of oil failed to keep pace with increases in the cost of other commodities, goods, and services. And incentives for developing technologies for alternative energy sources, such as coal, were virtually nonexistent. Thus, when OPEC increased the price of oil fourfold in the winter of 1973–1974, consumers had no recourse but to absorb the costs because of the absence of energy alternatives.

The Rise of OPEC

Several factors explain the emergence of OPEC as a successful commodity cartel. One, already noted, was the absence of energy alternatives in the face of growing worldwide demand for oil. A second factor was the growing dependence of much of the world on Middle Eastern oil. By 1979, the Middle East accounted for a third of the world's oil supply (production) but less than 3 percent of its demand (consumption).

Before the 1979 Iranian revolution, Iran and Saudi Arabia alone accounted for nearly a quarter of the entire world's production of oil.

In contrast, Japan and Western Europe accounted for over 30 percent of the world demand for oil but produced less than 4 percent domestically. U.S. dependence on foreign energy sources was less, but as domestic supplies of oil were depleted during the OPEC decade, the United States increasingly turned to foreign suppliers. The resulting shortfalls in the noncommunist nations of the industrial world were met by increased OPEC production.

A third factor that contributed to OPEC's success was its ability to wrest control of production and pricing policies from the multinational oil companies. This occurred gradually, as the bargaining advantages enjoyed by the multinationals vis-à-vis the host governments of the producing countries deteriorated. OPEC's formation in 1960 was part of the process whereby the oil-producing nations sought to increase their own economic returns as well as their leverage with the majors. Their efforts were bolstered by an increase in the number of independents in the oil field between the 1950s and the 1970s, whose presence made for a more competitive market.

Libya provided the catalyst for the first oil shock. Following a coup in September 1969 that brought to power a radical government headed by Colonel Muammar Qaddafi, Libya targeted Occidental Petroleum, an independent, as it moved to assert control over its resources by cutting oil production and increasing prices. Other oil-producing states quickly learned from Libya's action. They discovered both "the vulnerability of the independent oil companies . . . and the unwillingness of the Western consumers or the majors to take forceful action in their support" (Spero, 1990). The foundation was also being laid for using production controls, not just pricing policies, to generate oil revenues for the governments of the producing countries.

The possibility of using oil as a political weapon to affect the outcome of the unsettled Arab-Israeli dispute intrigued the Arab members of OPEC. Their common desire to defeat Israel was a principal element uniting them. Thus, when the Yom Kippur War broke out between Israel and the Arabs on October 6, 1973, the stage for using the oil weapon was set.

Less than two weeks after the outbreak of war, the OPEC oil ministers seized the right to determine prices unilaterally, and the Arab producing countries decided to reduce their production levels. Thus, control over production and prices—which quadrupled between October 1973 and January 1974—was transferred from the oil companies to the host governments. Furthermore, the political goals sought by the Arab members of OPEC were pursued by their production cuts and the imposition of an embargo on exports to consuming countries considered too pro-Israeli, principally the Netherlands and the United States.

The events of 1973–1974 suggested several lessons. One was that the oil weapon, apparently brandished successfully, could be used again.[2] The inability of the major

---

[2] There are isolated instances in later years when individual members of OPEC sought to use the oil weapon, defined as an instrument for the realization of political objectives. Generally, however, OPEC is less a politically cohesive organization than a collection of states motivated simply by economic gain.

multinational oil companies to control the international oil regime, as they had done for decades, was a second.[3] Finally, the events showed that even the world's foremost economic and military power, the United States, had become vulnerable to foreign economic pressures as it moved away from relative self-sufficiency in oil production and consumption.

The U.S. Role in Shaping the OPEC Decade

Given the enormity of overall U.S. consumption, its policies and practices exert a powerful influence on the entire global energy picture, including OPEC's role within it. Growing U.S. vulnerability to OPEC's production and pricing actions during the OPEC decade and the shift from a buyer's to a seller's market facilitated OPEC's rise to prominence as a world political actor.

The United States has long been a major producer as well as consumer of oil. In 1938 it accounted for nearly two-thirds of the world's crude-oil production and over 70 percent of production in the noncommunist world (Darmstadter and Landsberg, 1976: 33). By 1973, however, these proportions had slipped to 16 and 19 percent, respectively (*BP Statistical Review of World Energy*, 1984: 5).

U.S. oil production began to decline precipitously in the early 1970s at the same time that domestic demand increased. Imported oil made up the balance, accounting for over a third of consumption by 1973 (compared with about 20 percent in the mid-1960s) (Darmstadter and Landsberg, 1976: 31). Growing U.S. oil import dependence thus helped make possible the OPEC price hikes and production controls of 1973–1974.[4]

Historically, energy has been abundant and cheap in the United States, a circumstance that removed incentives to develop efficient energy practices and conservation programs. Americans' personal preferences for automobiles and trucks as their principal modes of transportation also fueled increases in consumption rates in the post–World War II era.

Despite the adverse economic consequences of the first oil shock, U.S. oil consumption continued to grow between 1973 and 1978, while domestic production declined

---

[3] During the crisis, in fact, the oil companies responded "with the conditioned reflexes of entrepreneurs minimizing their risks at the margin." As Raymond Vernon (1976), an expert on multinational corporations, explained: "The patterns of oil distribution in the crisis . . . were curiously non-national. Anyone looking for confirmation of the view that it paid a country to have an oil company based within its own jurisdiction would have found scant support for such a hypothesis in this brief episode in the oil industry's history."

[4] Several factors contributed to this increased dependence, including an "accelerated demand for energy in the aggregate; a dramatic falling off of reserve additions of oil and natural gas; severe constraints, largely for environmental reasons, on the use of coal; lags in the scheduled completion of nuclear power plants; and protracted delays in oil and gas leasing" (Darmstadter and Landsberg, 1976).

The growing demand for oil, particularly gasoline, was the core of the problem. The demand for oil in turn was related to price, which, as noted earlier, actually declined relative to other commodities from the 1950s to the 1970s. Hence, there was little incentive for, or public interest in, conservation measures. On the supply side, however, U.S. domestic oil production did not keep pace with trends in consumption, and U.S. reserves relative to total world reserves declined steadily (Darmstadter and Landsberg, 1976).

further. This increased U.S. dependence on foreign sources of oil and made it especially vulnerable to exporters' pricing decisions. It also set the stage for the second oil
shock, which came in 1979–1980 in the wake of the Iranian revolution that ousted
the government of Shah Muhammad Reza Pahlavi and led to the creation of the
revolutionary Islamic republic headed by the Ayatollah Khomeini. The global
economic recession that followed the oil price increases laid the basis for the
Third World debt crisis and other dislocations in the world political economy (see
Chapters 7 and 8).

THE POLITICAL ECONOMY OF OIL: THE UNMAKING OF THE OPEC DECADE . . . .

Reducing dependence on foreign supplies of oil became a major policy preoccupation
among the Western industrial nations during the OPEC decade. By the early 1980s,
conservation measures, economic recession, and a shift to alternative sources of energy
combined to push down the demand for oil. As Figure 10.4 shows, the consumption
of oil by industrial nations declined to 58 percent of total world consumption by 1983,
compared with 70 percent of total consumption in 1973.

Oil prices also began to soften following their 1981 peak and went into a near free-
fall in 1986 (see Figure 10.3 and Figure 8.2 in Chapter 8). Many pressures accelerated
the drop (see Morse, 1986), but the most important was a worldwide oil glut resulting
from the decision of key members of OPEC, notably Saudi Arabia, to increase their
output in an effort to regain the market share lost to others during the OPEC decade.[5]

By the early 1990s, however, a sense of *déjà vu* punctuated many discussions of
the global energy environment. Demand increased steadily from the trough of the
early 1980s, surpassing the 1979 peak in 1989 (see Figure 10.4). Prices generally
moved upward with increased demand. Although subject to short-term gyrations, they
increased from a low of about $8 per barrel in 1986 to around $20 during most of
1990. Moreover, nearly all of the increase in world demand for oil was met by OPEC
producers (Amuzegar, 1990). Earlier predictions of "a coming crisis" (for example,
Pirages, 1986) suddenly seemed prophetic.

The crisis occurred when Iraq invaded Kuwait. The scenario was surprising, but
suddenly and unexpectedly, the world experienced a shortage of 4 million barrels of
oil per day, or approximately 6 percent of the world oil supply (Sterner, 1990–1991:
43). The shortfall caused the price of oil to skyrocket to more than $40 per barrel.

Thus the Persian Gulf crisis again riveted policymakers' attention on the costs and
consequences of dependence on fossil fuel energy, notably oil, in an environment

[5] Ironically, OPEC nations themselves were among the principal victims of the decline in oil prices, as the
revenues on which they had staked important domestic development objectives disappeared. Saudi Arabia,
for example, saw its oil income plummet from $113 billion in 1981 to only $28 billion in 1985 (Morse, 1986:
796). Non-OPEC oil exporters suffered similarly. Mexico, an emergent oil exporter, for example, lost
considerable revenue on which it depended to pay its enormous foreign debt (but it benefited from interest
rate reductions made possible in part by the reduced cost of oil internationally).

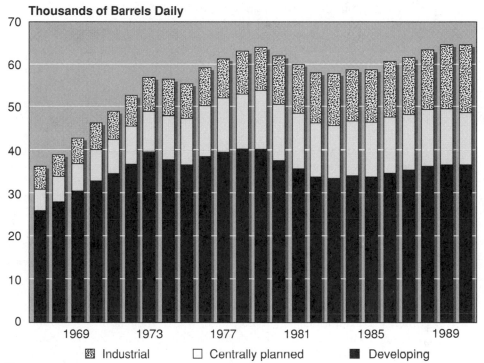

FIGURE 10.4 OIL CONSUMPTION BY INDUSTRIAL, CENTRALLY PLANNED, AND DEVELOPING ECONOMIES, 1967–1990

Source: 1967–1979 adapted from *BP Statistical Review of World Energy* (London: British Petroleum Company, 1987), p. 9; 1980–1990 adapted from *BP Statistical Review of World Energy* (London: British Petroleum Company, 1991), p. 8.

Note: Data before 1980 may not be entirely comparable to data beginning with that year.

characterized by highly uneven distributions of supply and demand. The domestic turmoil in and subsequent collapse of the Soviet Union, the world's largest oil producer and its second largest exporter, added to the sense of urgency.

Consumption: The Changing Demand Picture

Conservation measures contributed importantly to the softening demand for oil in the 1980s. They took two forms in response to changing prices, *irreversible* and *reversible* (Mossavar-Rahmani, 1983). Irreversible measures translate into improved energy efficiency resulting from the turnover of capital stock or from retrofitting, such as driving automobiles with improved mileage standards, building more energy-efficient commercial buildings and industrial plants, and improving the insulation in existing residential buildings. Reversible effects derive from behavioral changes, such as turning the thermostat lower in the home or office during the winter or driving in a commuter car pool.

Conservation clearly reduced the energy intensiveness of the industrial nations' economies during the OPEC decade. As noted above, the linkage between increases in demand for energy and increases in economic output was particularly evident before the first oil shock, where among First World nations a nearly one-to-one correspondence existed. From 1960 to 1973 every 1 percent increase in energy consumption was associated with the same percentage increase in GNP (International Energy Agency, 1982: 69). Since 1973, however, this correspondence has declined measurably. Figure 10.5 illustrates the change. It also shows that energy intensity (the ratio of energy consumption to GNP) among the industrial nations is expected to continue its downward trajectory until the end of the century. Among the developing nations, on the other hand, a moderate increase in energy intensity will likely accompany their modernization efforts.

Reversible conservation measures, by definition, may not be permanent. Instead, their continuation is affected by the price of energy. As prices decline, incentives to conserve diminish. Similarly, economic fortunes affect energy use. The demand for oil fell dramatically during the early 1980s, for example, in part as a result of recession-induced reductions in national income. Once economic growth was restored, however, energy consumption again moved upward. In a healthy economic environment, income-induced conservation measures disappear, and the behavioral changes stimulated by high energy prices may be reversed. The trend in U.S. oil consumption following the 1981–1983 recession illustrates the pattern: Consumption rose an average

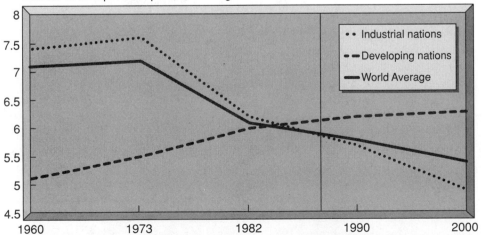

FIGURE 10.5 Energy Intensity and Economic Development, 1960–2000
Source: U.S. Congress, Office of Technology Assessment, *Energy in Developing Countries* (Washington, D.C.: Government Printing Office, 1991), p. 33.

of 1,850 barrels per day between 1983 and 1990 (*BP Statistical Review of World Energy*, 1991: 8). The result, of course, is that U.S. vulnerability to another oil shock increased markedly.[6]

Reduced U.S. production since the early 1980s magnified its vulnerability. The combination of rising consumption and declining production meant that U.S. imports increased "from about one-third of total U.S. consumption in 1983 to over 40 percent in 1990. Moreover, the fraction of total oil imports coming from the Persian Gulf nations . . . increased from about 4 percent of total U.S. oil consumption (10 percent of total U.S. oil imports) to over 11 percent (25 percent of gross U.S. oil imports in 1990)" (U.S. Office of Technology Assessment, 1991b: 4).

Production: The Changing Supply Picture

OPEC accounted for 53 percent of the world's oil output in 1973, but by 1986 this proportion dropped to less than a third (*BP Statistical Review of World Energy*, 1987: 6). In effect OPEC moved from being a principal supplier of oil to being a residual supplier, as consumers first sought energy resources elsewhere.

Several factors account for the shift away from OPEC. One, of course, was the reduced demand for oil. A second was the discovery during the 1970s of new sources of oil outside the OPEC framework. The development of the North Sea oil fields by Britain and Norway, the completion of the Alaskan pipeline by the United States, and Mexico's increased oil output were elements in the changing global oil environment. The result is that the share of world oil produced outside OPEC and other traditional suppliers, such as the United States and the Soviet Union, declined dramatically. By 1990, however, OPEC's share of world oil production had inched upward once more, to 38 percent (*BP Statistical Review of World Energy*, 1991: 5).

A shift to alternative energy sources contributed to the reduced reliance on OPEC oil. Coal, for example, again became a major source of energy in the United States. Similarly, Japan increased its import of coal to meet a growing proportion of its electrical generation and industrial needs, and China relied heavily on coal as its primary source of fossil fuel. Elsewhere, nuclear power was the alternative. The French, for example, increased their electrical generation through nuclear power more than seventeenfold between 1973 and 1986 (U.S. Department of Energy, 1987a: 118) as part of an ambitious nuclear energy program designed to help reduce dependence on imported oil. Brazil invested heavily in the generation of fuel ("gasohol") extracted from agricultural products. And the West German government encouraged a shift from oil to natural gas.

---

[6] Morse (1990–1991) notes that demographic developments in the North contributed to the decline in demand for oil during the 1980s ("Older drivers do not use cars as much as those 18 to 35 years old, and the number of people in the younger age groups in industrial countries declined during recent years") but that "another era of demographic growth in the United States is set for the 1990s and this, too, will profoundly affect the supply-demand balance."

In addition to the reduced demand for oil and a lessening of dependence on OPEC, a third outgrowth of the OPEC decade was a shift in the character of the international oil market (see Morse, 1986, 1990–1991). During the first phase of the post-OPEC decade, the major multinational oil companies lost control of pricing and production decisions, as these shifted to the oil-producing countries themselves, thus completing a process that had been in motion for some time. During the second phase, however, producing countries once more turned to the multinationals as a source of venture capital and modern technology to discover and exploit new oil fields (Amuzegar, 1990; Morse, 1990–1991). Thus a new partnership between the major multinational oil companies and the oil-producing countries is in the offing.

THE POLITICAL ECONOMY OF OIL: THE SHAPE OF THE FUTURE . . . .

A major lesson of the OPEC decade and its aftermath is that the future cannot be predicted with confidence. Still, the dramatic changes in the global energy environment during the past two decades portend further adjustments in the 1990s that will doubtless have global ramifications.

The World Bank (*World Development Report 1983*, 1983: 29–30) estimated in the early 1980s that by 1995 petroleum will account for only 35 percent of global energy consumption, compared with 46 percent in 1980, even though total energy consumption will grow from 135 million to 191 million barrels of oil-equivalent energy during this same period. Assuming an absence of environmental constraints—which, however, are growing—coal is expected to supply the largest portion of the projected increase in global energy demand, followed by nuclear and hydroelectric power.

Despite petroleum's declining share of world energy consumption, it will still play a key role in the global energy picture for the remainder of this century and perhaps beyond. This in turn raises questions about OPEC's role as a price setter and production leader.

OPEC's Changing Fortunes

OPEC's members differ widely in their financial needs, oil reserves, political regimes, foreign policy goals, and political aspirations. They are also geographically distant, with widely disparate sociocultural systems, population sizes, levels of income, internal problems, and external challenges. These factors have always made OPEC a fragile organization. A new partnership between oil-producing countries and the oil multinationals may help perpetuate OPEC, but the organization has little prospect of exercising the kind of "commodity power" toward political issues that some of its members once cherished.

Even OPEC's ability to control prices has waned. The "spot market" and oil "futures" are now more important than official posted prices in determining the value of oil traded internationally (see Lippman and Potts, 1991).

Leading OPEC producers are quite potent in driving oil prices down to low levels almost anytime because they have the capacity to flood the market. But they find it much more difficult, if not impossible, to force prices up by much for an extended period, because their critical dependence on oil revenues keeps them from cutting output to very low levels. Sharp price rises are now often triggered by political events. (Amuzegar, 1990: 44)

Because of these and other changes, "OPEC, long regarded as a major hub of the international oil markets, . . . appears to be in institutional decay, its role increasingly outmoded by the economic and political logic of the petroleum sector's evolution. Yet whether OPEC will be replaced by new institutional arrangements, and what they might look like, remain open issues" (Morse, 1990–1991).

Oil Supply and Demand

Apart from its institutional forms, OPEC oil will remain, indeed, will grow in importance. As noted above, the rise in demand for oil since the mid-1980s has been met largely by OPEC oil. In 1990 it accounted for 38 percent of world production, up from a low of 30 percent in 1985.

Oil Reserves

Increasingly, the six Persian Gulf members of the thirteen-member organization will matter most. Two-thirds of the world's proved reserves of oil are in the Middle East (see Figure 10.6 on page 356), virtually all in the territories of OPEC's Persian Gulf members. They also control nearly two-thirds of OPEC's production (in 1990) (*BP Statistical Review of World Energy*, 1991: 2, 5).

Third World Demand

Growing demand for fossil fuel energy in the developing world will contribute to the enhanced position of the Persian Gulf states. Hastened by rapidly rising population, high economic growth rates, and structural changes resulting from the development process, Third World energy consumption in 2020 could be as much three times higher than in 1985 (U.S. Office of Technology Assessment, 1991a: 34; also Munasinghe, 1991–1992) (see Figure 10.7 on page 357). As these and related changes take place in the oil-producing countries themselves, some of them—such as Algeria, Ecuador, Gabon, Indonesia, and Nigeria—will need to direct their production to domestic needs rather than the export market (Ebinger, 1985).

Although the long-term trend is toward greater energy use in the Third World, fluctuations in the supply and price of oil will exact a toll. As noted in Chapter 8, seeds of the Third World debt crisis were sown by the first two oil shocks. Many Third World nations borrowed heavily from abroad to cover higher energy costs, only to find that the resources necessary to repay the loans failed to materialize in the recessionary environment of the early 1980s. On the other hand, when oil prices in

FIGURE 10.6 PROVED RESERVES OF OIL, 1990
Source: BP Statistical Review of World Energy (London: British Petroleum Company, 1991), p. 3.

turn fell, import-dependent countries, such as Brazil and Chile, benefited from re-duced energy costs. Furthermore, as inflation caused by the rising costs of oil eased, interest rates also eventually declined, reducing the burden of many debt-ridden Third World countries whose obligations were tied directly to the cost of borrowing. To many of these same countries, the threat posed by Iraq's attack on Kuwait was that the process would revert to its earlier form.

As it turned out, the Persian Gulf crisis was relatively short-lived. Even so, its costs (apart from the war itself) both globally and locally were high. World oil prices averaged $30 per barrel between August 1990 and January 1991. The Overseas Development Council (1991: 1) estimates that reduced world economic activity during this period caused a 1 percent cut in developing nations' exports, amounting to a $6 billion cut in earnings. It also estimates that the effects of "higher oil import costs, loss of migrant remittances, and loss of export markets" for a group of thirty-five low- and middle-income countries exceeded $12 billion, or 1 percent of their GNP—" a UN criterion used in assessing the need for disaster relief" (Overseas Development Council, 1991: 2; see also Murphy, 1990). Future threats to energy security and price

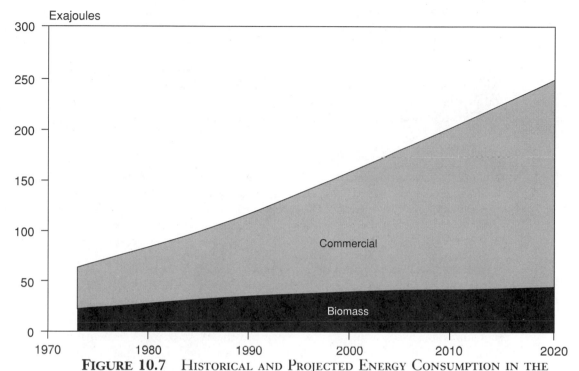

FIGURE 10.7 HISTORICAL AND PROJECTED ENERGY CONSUMPTION IN THE DEVELOPING COUNTRIES

Source: U.S. Congress, Office of Technology Assessment, *Energy in Developing Countries* (Washington, D.C.: Government Printing Office, 1991), p. 34.

stability are difficult to predict, but the experience of Third World nations with the three prior oil shocks proves they will be costly indeed.[7]

Non-OPEC Production

A second development that will enhance the importance of OPEC's Persian Gulf producers is the expected decline of production among the non-OPEC states. As the North Sea and Alaskan oil finds of the 1970s reach their maximum production levels and then begin to drop in the years ahead, the enormous concentration of oil in the Middle East will loom larger in importance.

> Certainly, there are signs of new production coming on stream in places like Yemen, Brazil, India, Norway, Angola, Malaysia and Papua New Guinea. These sources may provide a total of 1.5 million to 2 million barrels a day of incremental supply by 1995. But there is nothing on the horizon to match the giant oil fields discovered in the 1960s and 1970s in

---

[7] The oil shocks produced winners as well as losers. During the crisis over Kuwait, for example, Saudi Arabia's average daily revenues from oil exports increased by $178 million over pre-crisis levels. Other Persian Gulf exporters doubled their incomes compared with 1989 (Murphy, 1990: 18).

non-OPEC countries. These discoveries enabled Alaska's North Slope production to go from scratch to nearly 2 million barrels daily, Mexican production to rise by 2 million barrels daily, and North Sea output to add nearly 4 million. (Morse, 1990–1991: 44)

In a related development, the output of "mature" non-OPEC producers, including Mexico and the United States and the former Soviet Union, two of the world's largest oil producers, will drop rapidly during the 1990s (Morse, 1990–1991). This in turn will create upward pressure on prices and production elsewhere.

Soviet Energy Production

Energy developments in the former Soviet Union have long been of concern to policymakers in the industrial West, largely due to their national security implications.

The largest oil producer in the world throughout the OPEC decade and until its collapse in 1990 was the Soviet Union. Its domestic consumption was high, but the Soviet Union was also a net exporter of oil. Many of its resources were funneled to its Eastern European allies, where they comprised a significant element in the economic linkages among the Comecon nations. Thus the Warsaw Pact countries were jointly self-sufficient in energy.

As in other areas of international economic affairs, the Soviet Union was generally a bystander in matters that influenced developments in the global oil regime. It was not unresponsive, however, as oil exports to the West were its principal source of "hard" (convertible) currency earnings, accounting for roughly half of them in the mid-1980s (U.S. Department of Energy, 1987b: 227). Oil was also the principal link between the Soviets' command economy and the world political economy.

Eventually natural gas was also to become an important export commodity and source of foreign exchange. This was to have been accomplished by the trans-Siberian pipeline, which, when made fully operational in the 1990s, would provide much of Western Europe access to Soviet gas supplies.

Whether the Soviet Union would be able to sustain its enviable position as a net oil exporter became questionable during the OPEC decade. In 1977 a U.S. Central Intelligence Agency (1977) report predicted that the Soviets' productive capacity would peak in the early 1980s and then fall sharply. It also predicted that by 1985 the Soviet Union and Eastern Europe would be required to import several million barrels of oil daily, speculating that this might cause the Soviet Union not only to reduce its exports but also to compete for OPEC oil for its own use. Later analyses indicated that Soviet oil production did, indeed, begin to slow in the early 1980s and that it actually declined between 1984 and 1985 (which was the first time that had happened since World War II).

As the Soviet domestic crisis deepened in the late 1980s, evidence mounted that it had difficulty meeting its energy production targets, whether because of mismanagement, outmoded technology, or a decline in the productivity of the most easily accessible oil fields. As Soviet output dropped, exports to its one-time Warsaw Pact allies at subsidized prices were slashed, creating hardship in the former socialist states. Further declines in production, widely predicted, will force the successors of the former Soviet leaders to choose between cuts in domestic production to maintain hard-currency exports or perhaps cuts in both domestic consumption and exports. Some predict that by 1995 the Commonwealth of Independent States will become a net oil importer (see Lippman and Potts, 1991).

To stem current production declines and increase future output, Western companies have been invited to enter into joint ventures and otherwise provide capital and technology to exploit the vast resources of the former Soviet Union. The risks to Western firms are great (see Potts, 1991), but the change in attitude is extraordinary. "The Soviet Union . . . nationalized its oil industry nearly three-quarters of a century ago," observed the publisher of the authoritative *Petroleum Intelligence Weekly* shortly before the breakup of the Soviet Union. "Reopening the Soviet oil sector portends a phenomenal reversal of the sometimes rampant resource nationalism of the past twenty years" (Morse, 1990–1991).

U.S. Oil Import Vulnerability and Dependence

There is nearly universal agreement among experts that oil prices will rise during the 1990s, even without the kinds of crisis conditions that provoked the three oil shocks of the recent past. Due to the uneven distribution of oil resources, some will benefit from the rise in prices, and some will pay its costs. *Oil import dependence* and *import vulnerability* are among the costs. The former may contribute to the latter, but the terms are not synonymous. "A growing level of imports contributes to import vulnerability, but import dependence alone does not translate into a serious threat to energy security" (U.S. Office of Technology Assessment, 1991b).

As the world's largest energy consumer, the United States is sensitive to the impact that its growing import dependence exerts on its import vulnerability. Growing dependence on oil imports from the politically volatile Middle East is cause for special concern for several reasons.

1. Greater reliance on oil from foreign sources magnifies the potential impacts of import curtailments on U.S. oil supplies and the economy.

2. Oil imports contribute to U.S. balance of payments deficits, and as oil imports (and/or prices) rise, more U.S. export earnings must be allocated to paying for oil rather than devoted to domestic consumption. In 1990 the bill for oil imports amounted to $65 billion, more than half of [the U.S.] $101 billion balance of payments deficit.

3. The threat of potential economic and social dislocations that could accompany major oil supply or price disruptions could constrain U.S. policymakers in foreign affairs, national security and military matters where oil supplies might be affected.

4. The ready availability of cheap imported oil in the United States is a powerful financial disincentive for oil-saving investments in efficiency and alternative energy sources or the development of higher cost domestic oil. Unlike Japan

and most Western European countries that are highly dependent on oil imports and where oil is heavily taxed, U.S. oil prices are comparatively low and do not fully reflect many of the external costs of oil use. Among the most notable of these externalities are, for example, the environmental damage from production, oil spills, and emissions from refining and combustion, and the costs of maintaining and deploying military forces to protect supplies. The defense costs in particular have applied disproportionately to the United States relative to European countries and Japan. (U.S. Office of Technology Assessment, 1991b: 12–13)

In light of these considerations, it is not surprising that the United States has seen a strong link between oil and national security.

OIL AND NATIONAL SECURITY . . . .

U.S. President George Bush never openly admitted that oil was a principal factor propelling the decision of the United States to oppose Iraq's Saddam Hussein. However, in early September 1990 he did acknowledge that short-sighted policies had made the United States unduly dependent on Middle Eastern oil to fuel its industrial economy. "We had moved in the wrong direction," he said. "Now we must act to correct that trend."[8]

Oil and the Persian Gulf War

Oil did figure prominently in Iraq's decision to invade Kuwait. Its eight-year war with Iran, which ended in 1988, caused severe economic dislocations, including an $80 billion foreign debt. Lower oil prices, caused in part by increased production by other OPEC members, made it more difficult for Iraq to meet its obligations. "In theory, Iraq might have managed the economic pressures by trimming its costly military program, by tightening its belt, and by intimidating its brethren in the Organization of Petroleum Exporting Countries to curtail their production in order to push prices higher. . . . Saddam [Hussein], however, saw a quicker fix for the economic ills of his country—sharply higher oil prices and the vast wealth of Kuwait, including its $100 billion in foreign assets" (Quandt, 1991).

> By the spring of 1990 he was making his demands known. He wanted Saudi Arabia and Kuwait to write off the billions of dollars of loans extended during the Iran-Iraq War; he wanted Kuwait to come up with an additional $10 billion in aid; he wanted OPEC to push oil prices to $25 per barrel; and he wanted Kuwait to yield two islands that controlled access

---

[8] See Renner (1987) for a critical appraisal of the energy policies (or lack thereof) of the Reagan administration and of the need to devise a strategy whose "short-term task is to avoid the recurrence of another oil crisis in the 1990s" and whose "long-term task is to manage the transition from the present heavily oil-reliant energy system to a future system based on renewable energy sources."

to Iraq's port at Umm Qasr, as well as to pay some $2.4 billion for oil taken from the Rumailah oil field. At a meeting of the Arab League in May, and later in a letter from his foreign minister, Saddam made these points explicit. According to Arab sources, Saddam acknowledged at the Arab League meeting that his demands might sound like blackmail, but he did not care. Iraq was determined to get its way. (Quandt, 1991: 52)

There were political as well as economic reasons motivating Saddam Hussein, including an insatiable drive to achieve hegemony over the Arab world. Thus control over Kuwaiti oil was a means to an end as well as an end in itself. Nonetheless, the Middle East was once more plunged into open warfare, causing alarm throughout the world. In the end, nearly forty countries contributed to the UN-authorized military response to Iraq's aggression.

The Gulf crisis touched the entire world through skyrocketing oil prices, but this was only a symptom of the causes of the world's collective response.

Three factors distinguished the Iraqi invasion of Kuwait as a situation that demanded an international response. First, Kuwait's importance to the international economy is far beyond its size. It sits atop the fourth largest oil reserve in the world. If Saddam Hussein could have added Kuwait's oil reserves to Iraq's and used his superior military might to bully Saudi Arabia and the smaller Gulf oil states into supporting Iraq's positions in [OPEC], he could have dominated oil production and pricing policies. Oil prices still would have been tied to supply and demand, but Hussein would have been in a position to push prices up, thereby straining the world economy. Second, Iraq's efforts to acquire nuclear weapons and its existing conventional, chemical, and biological weapons capabilities made that country a long-term military threat to the entire Middle East and perhaps beyond. Third, Iraq's government had demonstrated an appetite for military conquest and a capacity for brutality. Since 1980, Iraq had invaded Iran, resorted to the use of chemical weapons against Iranian soldiers and ballistic missiles against Iranian citizens, and used poison gas against its own Kurdish population during a campaign to snuff out the Kurdish resistance movement. (*The Middle East*, 1991: 315–316)

The Persian Gulf War culminated two decades of Middle Eastern turmoil which saw the United States become increasingly involved militarily in the ongoing conflict between the Arabs and Israel and among the Arabs themselves. The war itself was also important in a larger theoretical sense, as it bridged the gap between high politics and low.

The Western liberal economy was predicated on the separation of high politics (i.e., the use of force and other security concerns) from low politics (the economic rules whereby participating nations skirmished with one another principally over the rules of distribution, but in which everyone basically agreed that all parties could benefit from an ever-increasing economic pie). The use of force was permissible outside this "lower" realm, but it was deemed illegitimate and too costly to use within it. Iraq's takeover of Kuwait and its threatened domination of other key oil-producing countries in the Persian Gulf [breached] this wall between high and low politics over issues of international distribution. (Morse, 1990–1991: 37)

These developments had their origins just prior to and during the OPEC decade.

The Emerging Security Threat

As noted earlier, the first oil shock occurred in the wake of the 1973 Yom Kippur War. During the war itself the United States substantially increased its shipment of weapons to Israel, enabling it to counter Soviet-supplied Egyptian and Syrian forces. U.S. military aid continued at much higher levels than previously in the years that followed. The 1978 Camp David agreements solidified the U.S. commitment to Israel as part of a package that also included U.S. military support for Egypt, in return for a peace treaty between the two historic antagonists. Thus the United States became a key actor in efforts to maintain regional stability.

During the OPEC decade many analysts concluded that the most likely threat to Middle Eastern oil supplies was that posed by internal instability in a key oil-producing country. The events in Iran leading to the second oil-price shock in 1979 reinforced this belief. As noted earlier, domestic political turmoil there led to oil production cutbacks and a sharp upturn in the price of oil (fed by consumers' anticipation of severe supply shortages). The new round of OPEC-mandated price increases underscored the Western countries' new levels of vulnerability to disruptions in prices and supplies from abroad.

The Iranian situation was particularly troublesome for the United States. For years before the Iranian revolution the United States had pumped billions of dollars' worth of sophisticated military equipment into Iran—transfers premised on the belief that the shah's government would use Iranian military might to protect the oil-rich Persian Gulf area from outside—namely, Soviet—interference, thus ensuring a continual flow of Persian Gulf oil to the West. Similar motivations were behind the massive U.S. arms shipments sent to Saudi Arabia both before the Iranian revolution and since. The revolutionary government that came to power in Iran in 1979 was, however, resolutely anti-American. With Iran removed from the ranks of pro-Western nations in the region, Saudi Arabia's position as a Western-oriented oil supplier gained added significance. At issue was not only Saudi Arabia's ability to protect its vast oil fields from terrorist or other attacks (see Map 10.1) but also averting a repetition of the internal political disruptions that Iran experienced.

The threat of internal upheaval now preoccupied Western policymakers. The related threat of regional conflict intensified the concern, as the two phenomena are often indistinguishable. Following the Israeli invasion of southern Lebanon in 1982, for example, a multinational peacekeeping force of British, French, Italian, and U.S. soldiers was dispatched to Lebanon. As it became embroiled in Lebanon's continuing political and religious strife, the peacekeeping force eventually found itself the target of not only political opposition by some Arab governments but also a terrorist attack by pro-Iranian Shi'ite militants. Simultaneously, the protracted Iran-Iraq war threatened to engulf other Persian Gulf oil-producing states in a wider war.

Concern for ensuring Western oil supplies heightened in 1979, when the Soviet Union intervened militarily in Afghanistan, poising it perilously close to the Middle Eastern oil lifeline to the West. In response, U.S. President Jimmy Carter enunciated the doctrine bearing his name, pledging that "an attempt by an outside force to gain

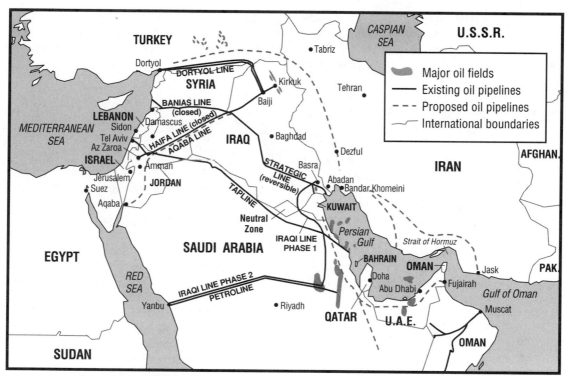

MAP 10.1 MAJOR MIDDLE EAST OIL FIELDS AND PIPELINES, CIRCA 1987
Source: The Middle East (Congressional Quarterly, Inc., 1991), p. 95.

control of the Persian Gulf region will be regarded as an assault on the vital interests of America and such an assault will be repelled by any means necessary, including military force." The Bush administration effectively made good on that pledge when it dispatched 200,000 troops to Saudi Arabia in August 1990—although the threat was now from Iraq, not the Soviet Union.

Some Western policymakers interpreted the Soviet invasion of Afghanistan as a prelude to a major invasion of the Persian Gulf area. That view eventually gave way to one that saw Moscow's aims "not as getting Middle East oil for itself, but as making Western access more tenuous and dependent on Soviet forbearance" (Gelb, 1983) so that the Soviets could be assured of a greater voice in the Middle East.[9] The assessment

---

[9] The superpowers' competition for influence and allies through arms exports and various other means extended beyond the Middle East to Africa and Asia, with much of it taking place in areas near the major oil sea-lanes of transportation from the Middle East to Europe, North America, and Japan. There is no apparent reason to believe that the Soviet Union consciously sought to extend its influence so as to interdict the supply of Middle East oil to Western markets (for assessments of Soviet Third World objectives in the aftermath of its invasion of Afghanistan, see Halliday, 1987; Papp, 1986; Shulman, 1986; and Whelan and Dixon, 1986). Nonetheless, by the mid-1980s the Soviet Union enjoyed power-projection capabilities far greater than ten or twenty years earlier, putting it in a position to strike at Western interests in ways and in places not previously possible.

was grounded in part on projections that the Soviet Union's domestic supplies of oil would be sufficient to meet demand for the foreseeable future. That remained accurate throughout the OPEC decade, but, as we saw earlier, the oil picture in the former Soviet Union is far from optimistic.

Ensuring Energy Security

The United States responded to its own growing oil import dependence by developing a strategic petroleum reserve from which it could draw stockpiled oil in the event of a supply interruption.[10] It also sponsored creation of the International Energy Agency, designed to oversee the sharing of oil among the Western industrial nations in an emergency. In a related move, it embarked on a diplomatic offensive to enhance its ability to ensure the security of supply routes out of the volatile and geopolitically sensitive Middle East to oil-short markets in Japan, Western Europe, and elsewhere (see Map 10.2).

Ensuring global energy security and an adequate supply of oil requires not only access at the wellhead but also secure routes to refiners and consumers.[11] The two most important routes are from the Persian Gulf area to the Cape of Good Hope at the tip of Africa and from there to Europe and North America, and eastward from the Persian Gulf through the Strait of Malacca to Japan. The importance of the African route grew just before and during the OPEC decade. In 1965 most of the crude oil going to Europe traveled through the Suez Canal, but after its closure during the 1967 Arab-Israeli War (it was reopened in 1975), the canal receded in importance and, a decade later, became less critical as a sea-lane with the creation of supertankers too large to pass through it. Thus the African route became far more important and remains so today (see Map 10.3 on page 366).

In 1987, in response to the fear that the continuing war between Iran and Iraq might widen and thereby threaten the continued flow of oil from the Middle East, the United States substantially increased its naval presence in the Persian Gulf region and made the controversial decision to escort Kuwaiti oil tankers through the Persian Gulf and the perilous Strait of Hormuz, where oil tankers had become routine targets in the war. Nothing could have underscored more dramatically the importance that the United States attaches to the Middle Eastern oil lifeline to the West and the security of its sea-lanes of communication.

Other means to ensure energy security were tried, including, as noted earlier, a shift to alternative energy sources to reduce reliance on OPEC oil. As part of that strategy, Western European nations agreed to help the Soviet Union build a pipeline designed to transport natural gas from Siberia to markets in Germany and elsewhere.

---

[10] Small amounts of oil were withdrawn from the reserve during the 1990 Persian Gulf crisis.

[11] It is interesting to note that in 1990 Canada, the United States, and Western Europe accounted for 39 percent of the world's crude oil–refining capacity. The Middle East, in contrast, accounted for only 7 percent (*BP Statistical Review of World Energy*, 1991: 14). The discrepancies were even more striking during the OPEC decade, when (in 1976) the Western nations accounted for 53 percent of the world's refining capacity and the Middle East only 4 percent (*BP Statistical Review of World Energy*, 1987: 16).

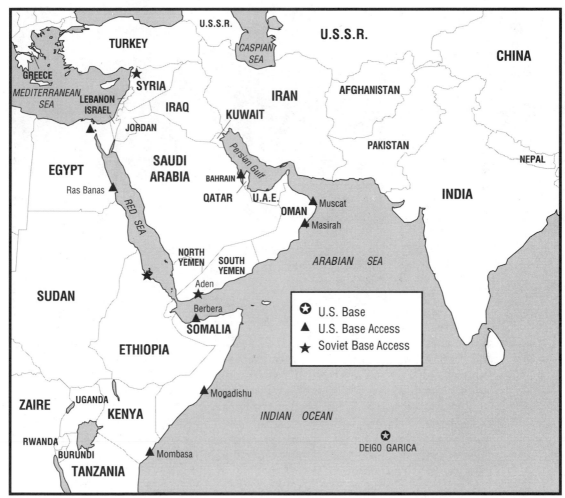

MAP 10.2 SOVIET AND AMERICAN MILITARY PRESENCE IN THE MIDDLE EAST, CIRCA 1989
Source: The Middle East (Congressional Quarterly, Inc., 1991), p. 71.

The United States in the early 1980s imposed stiff controls on the export of oil and gas technology to the Soviet Union in an effort to dissuade Western Europe from completing the pipeline and to punish the Soviet Union for its role in imposing martial law in Poland. To the United States, Western European dependence on Soviet energy supplies would compromise Western security by making Europe subject to Moscow's dictates and providing it with much-needed hard currency. European leaders did not agree and argued that in the end Soviet gas would account for a relatively small proportion of Europe's total energy use. Furthermore, the alternative—greater dependency on politically insecure sources of gas and oil in Africa or the Middle East—was

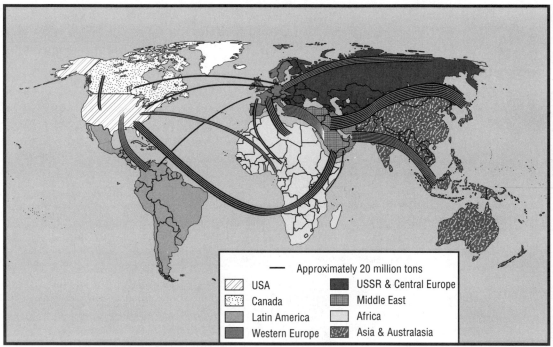

MAP 10.3 Main Oil Trade Movements, 1990
Political borders may not reflect actual country sources or destinations of oil trade movements.
Source: BP Statistical Review of World Energy (London: British Petroleum Company, 1991), p. 17.

less palatable (Ebinger, 1982).[12] Eventually the United States backed away from its efforts to stop the Siberian pipeline project, but the fracas with its NATO allies underscored how much Cold War considerations alongside Middle Eastern developments shaped U.S. efforts to ensure the flow of oil to the West.

Oil and the Middle East in the New World Order

The end of the Cold War may change the strategic calculations over oil, but it will not end them. The Middle East is a highly volatile region where the threats of internal conflict and war are ever present, and from which a political or military event might erupt to trigger a future energy crisis. Various national and subnational groups in the region also harbor deep-seated hostility toward the United States. Moreover, the

---

[12] Noteworthy is that the most important political and military allies of the United States are far more dependent on oil imports than is the United States. This fact figured prominently in the debate over who should pay the cost of the defense of Kuwait, as many in the United States believed Japan, Germany, and others in Europe should have borne a greater share of the cost of collective action due to their stakes in the outcome.

Middle East remains an area of immediate security concern to the Commonwealth of Independent States, as it shares an extended border with Iran and otherwise finds the region in its own backyard. As in the past, then, the fact that the United States defines the Middle East as critical to its national security poses a potential threat to the former Soviet republics as they define their own security interests and needs in the post–Cold War world.

Even as the war against Iraq raged, George Bush spoke of a new world order, "a new era, freer from the threat of terror, stronger in the pursuit of justice, and more secure in the quest for peace. An era in which the nations of the world, east and west, north and south, can prosper and live in harmony." Underscoring the unprecedented cooperation between the Soviet Union and the United States during the crisis over Kuwait, he declared, "We are united in the belief that Iraq's aggression must not be tolerated," adding, "no longer can a dictator count on East-West confrontation to stymie concerted UN action against aggression."

The new world order envisaged by Bush would require U.S. leadership, including a continuing role in the Middle East: "Our interest, our involvement in the Gulf, is not transitory. It predated Saddam Hussein's aggression and will survive it. Long after our troops come home . . . there will be a lasting role for the United States in assisting the nations of the Persian Gulf. Our role, with others, is to deter future aggression. Our role is to help our friends in their own self-defense."

As before, Saudi Arabia figured prominently among the friends Bush had in mind. Saudi Arabia had itself made a historic about-face with the unprecedented decision to let Western nations station troops on its soil. Thus it moved even closer to the United States in the sometimes fluid, always fractious process of Middle East coalition building, while the United States embraced the Saudis even more warmly as the guarantor of the oil lifeline to the First World.

ALTERNATIVE ENERGY SOURCES

During the OPEC decade considerable discussion revolved around the need for comprehensive energy policies that would ease dependence on oil and, more broadly, encourage the development of alternatives to fossil fuel energy. Two decades later, following the third oil shock, the issues and prescriptions remained much the same as after the first shock. "Excluding some sort of accommodation with major oil exporters, major oil importing countries . . . still . . . have to adopt a comprehensive domestic energy policy to reduce consumption and increase fuel efficiency, and they must embark on serious efforts to develop alternative, renewable energy sources" (Amuzegar, 1990). The new wrinkle in the 1990s is the dramatically greater concern over the environmental hazards of burning fossil fuels.[13]

On the basis of current ratios of production to known reserves, oil will last only

[13] The series of articles in the *Harvard International Review* (1991–1992) by Flavin, Laskshmanan and Andersson, Morse, Munasinghe, Watkins, and Wirth provides a useful overview of energy policies in various parts of the world.

until about the year 2035 (see Figure 10.8). Declining oil supplies will not lead to declining energy supplies if economically and politically viable energy alternatives are found and utilized. In addition to increased reliance on coal and natural gas, greater use of nuclear and hydropower could ease the transition to a non-oil-based energy system. Oil derived from unconventional sources such as tar sands and shale, and renewable forms of energy, such as solar, tidal, and wind power, geothermal energy, and bioconversion, might also become viable technologically and economically.[14]

Most economists agree that higher oil costs will encourage the development of alternative sources of energy such as these. How high prices must rise is uncertain, but clearly the decline of oil prices (both absolutely and relative to other goods) in the post-OPEC decade stifled efforts to devise energy alternatives. Indeed, those who staked resources on the development of unconventional energy technologies were among the principal losers in the denouement of the OPEC decade. Coal, natural gas, hydropower, and nuclear power are therefore the major alternatives to oil. Each, however, is beset with economic, environmental, and political uncertainties.

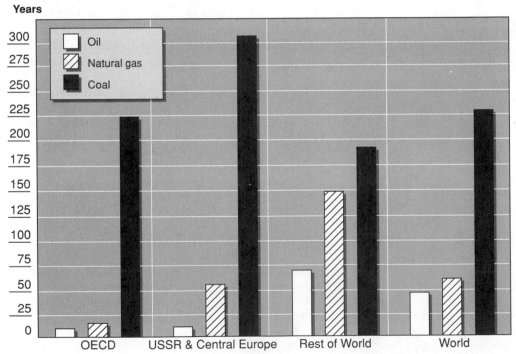

FIGURE 10.8 RATIO OF FOSSIL FUEL RESERVES TO PRODUCTION, 1990
Source: BP Statistical Review of World Energy (London: British Petroleum Company, 1991), p. 36.

---

[14] Stobaugh and Yergin (1979) provide a useful discussion of the economic and political factors associated with alternative energy strategies. A somewhat more technical discussion can be found in Ehrlich, Ehrlich, and Holdren (1977).

Coal

Estimates of the world's reserves of fossil fuels are imprecise, but all agree that coal is vastly more abundant than either oil or natural gas. Based on the current ratio of reserves to production, coal will last for more than two centuries.

China, the United States, and the former Soviet Union account for more than 60 percent of world reserves of coal. Trade in coal increased by 40 percent during the 1980s and, unless constrained by growing environmental concerns, is expected to increase another 40 percent by the year 2000 (World Resources Institute, 1990: 143). Still, most coal is consumed where it is produced, making it less susceptible to supply disruptions than oil. China, in fact, "is trying to do something that is nearly unique today—fueling its rapid economic expansion almost entirely with coal. Indeed, coal now accounts for a remarkable 76 percent of the country's total commercial energy supply" (Flavin, 1992: 30).

As noted earlier, coal use increased sharply as an alternative to oil in the aftermath of the first two oil shocks, growing 30 percent since the mid-1970s (Flavin, 1991–1992: 4). Coal is now the leading alternative to oil, accounting for 27 percent of the world's primary energy use in 1990, compared with 39 percent for oil and 22 percent for natural gas (*BP Statistical Review of World Energy*, 1991: 34). The social costs or "externalities" associated with its widespread use are substantial, however, which has caused a slowdown in the coal boom as environmental concerns and tighter regulations make it less attractive.

As noted in Chapter 9, coal contributes heavily to the acidification of precipitation and to the release of carbon that contributes to global warming. "Because coal has a higher carbon content than other fossil fuels, rising levels of coal combustion accounted for more than half the increase in carbon emissions between 1975 and 1990. By then coal was responsible for 42 percent of the world's carbon emissions from fossil fuels, virtually the same share as oil" (Flavin, 1991–1992: 4).

Because of coal's environmental hazards, its heavy use by China is a growing international concern. "Carbon emissions [in China] have increased 60 percent in the past decade and account for 37 percent of the Third World total. China is already the world's third largest carbon emitter, and is likely to surpass the [Commonwealth of Independent States] within the decade. Redirecting China's energy economy is fast becoming as important to the global atmosphere as changing those of Europe and the United States" (Flavin, 1992: 30–31).

Natural Gas

Natural gas is cleaner and more convenient to use than either oil or coal (see Flavin, 1992). Natural gas supplies, based on the current reserve/production ratio, will last for nearly sixty years (Figure 10.8). Unlike coal, however, natural gas is distributed very unevenly on a regional basis, which means that its continued development will depend on export trade.

The two largest natural gas markets are the United States and the former Soviet Union, which consumed, respectively, 28 percent and 33 percent of total world production in 1990 (*BP Statistical Review of World Energy*, 1991: 22). The former Soviet Union is also a major producer of gas and possesses the largest reserves, with 38 percent of the world's proved reserves in 1990. The United States, on the other hand, has only 4 percent of the world's gas reserves (*BP Statistical Review of World Energy*, 1991: 18). Historically the United States has met virtually all of its need for gas from domestic sources, but it seems likely that it will increasingly have to look to imports to sustain its high demand. As with oil, the Middle East is a likely source, as it holds nearly a third of the world's proved reserves but consumes less than 6 percent of world production.

Getting gas from the wellhead to consumers is a primary problem. Pipelines are the preferred method of transport, but they are expensive and massive engineering projects that also pose environmental dangers and thus encounter resistance. Liquefied natural gas is an alternative, perhaps the only one for transshipment from the Middle East to North America or to the growing European and Japanese markets, but experts disagree about its safety. That concern combined with cost considerations and sensitivity to dependence on OPEC sources has limited the development of new liquefied natural gas projects, at least in the United States (Stobaugh and Yergin, 1979). Still, because natural gas produces considerably less carbon emissions than either coal or oil, its attractiveness will grow, thus providing incentives to increase its useability throughout the world.

Hydropower

Hydropower accounts for about 7 percent of world energy use. North America is the primary consumer of electricity generated by hydropower, followed by Latin America, Europe, and Asia (*BP Statistical Review of World Energy*, 1991: 34). Severe drought in the 1980s curtailed water supplies, particularly in the United States, thus reducing the amount of energy available from hydropower. Hydropower has distinct advantages over fossil fuels in that it does not pollute the atmosphere, but water availability, land management issues, and financial considerations, especially in the developing world, will constrain its further development.

Nuclear Energy

In 1990 nuclear power accounted for 5.7 percent of global energy use. By the end of 1988 some 420 commercial reactors were in operation in 25 countries. In roughly half of these countries, electricity derived from nuclear power accounted for at least a quarter of their electrical use (World Resources Institute, 1990: 144). The United States is the single largest consumer of nuclear energy (followed by France, Japan, and the former Soviet Union), but France uses it most intensively, deriving 30 percent of its total energy use (in 1990) from nuclear power (*BP Statistical Review of World Energy*, 1991: 34).

Among known technologies, nuclear energy was once seen as the leading alternative to dependence on fossil fuels, but that is no longer the case. Technical and financial problems have forced some countries to reduce or abandon their programs, and in others the political climate has turned markedly against nuclear power, with safety a principal point of contention. Two well-publicized nuclear accidents, one in the United States at the Three Mile Island nuclear power plant in Pennsylvania in 1979, and a second at Chernobyl in the Ukraine in 1986, dramatized the risks and seemed to vindicate the skeptics who had warned about the dangers posed by nuclear energy.

Catastrophe was averted at Three Mile Island, but even without the threatened meltdown of the reactor core, the accident released the largest-ever level of radioactive contamination by the U.S. commercial nuclear industry. At Chernobyl, however, catastrophe did strike—and only now is the full magnitude of the world's worst nuclear disaster being revealed. "The fallout from Chernobyl—the equivalent of 10 Hiroshima bombs—has left a swath of agricultural land the size of Holland permanently poisoned. About 200,000 people have already been evacuated from their homes. Nearly 4 million people live in contaminated areas. . . . The official death toll remains 31, which was the number of Chernobyl workers and firefighters killed in the immediate aftermath of the explosion. But unofficial estimates run between 5,000 and 10,000" (Dobbs, 1991: 10).

The effects of the Chernobyl explosion ranged well beyond the Ukraine. Within days "much of Europe was experiencing the highest levels of radioactive fallout ever recorded there, and within two weeks, minor radioactivity was detected throughout the northern hemisphere. . . . The health of Europe could be affected for decades. Estimates of resulting cancer deaths by researchers in the field range from less than 1,000 to almost 500,000. . . . Rarely have so many countries been so affected by a single event" (Flavin, 1987: 5).

No new reactors were commissioned in the Soviet Union following Chernobyl, construction on thirty-nine others was halted, and the Ukrainian parliament voted to shut down the three remaining reactors at Chernobyl by 1995 and switch to alternative sources of energy (Dobbs, 1991: 11)—all of which increase pressures on existing oil resources. Moreover, the secretive, clumsy, inept, and inhumane response of Soviet leaders and the Soviet command system to the disaster may have hastened the collapse of the Soviet Union. "The disaster, and the subsequent cover-up, radicalized public opinion [in the Ukraine and Byelorussia] and helped create a sense of aggrieved nationalism. 'Chernobyl woke us up,' says Yavorivskii, the Ukrainian legislator and writer. 'It made us understand that we were not masters of our own land. The union and republic leadership treated the Ukraine like a colony that could be exploited as mercilessly as possible. What happened here was an indictment of the imperialist system of government'" (Dobbs, 1991).

Chernobyl dramatized the risks of nuclear power, but other issues beyond the safety of nuclear energy, narrowly defined, work against its further development as technology is now configured. How and where to dispose of highly radioactive nuclear wastes, for example, is a contentious political issue. It has been prominent in Europe and Japan as well as the United States. Spent fuel from nuclear-generating facilities must be removed periodically. It is then "cooled" in water to remove some of the most intense radioactivity before being reprocessed, a procedure that separates still-useful uranium and plutonium from other waste materials. No safe procedure for handling nuclear waste—some of which remains dangerous for hundreds of thousands of years—has yet been devised. In the meantime, large quantities have accumulated, posing a substantial threat to environmental safety.

A related fear is that nuclear know-how might be acquired by countries that do not already possess it, thereby giving them the means to develop nuclear weapons. Proliferation is essentially a national security issue, but it has a bearing on the use of nuclear power for peaceful purposes. Nuclear-generating facilities produce weapons-grade material, specifically highly enriched uranium and plutonium. Neither of these materials, which can be used to create a nuclear explosive device, is used commercially as fuel in the current generation of nuclear power reactors.[15] Yet at current and projected rates of production, the amount of such material created will eventually make available enough weapons-grade material to place within reach the construction of tens of thousands of nuclear bombs every year. Preventing the spread of nuclear weapons is therefore tied to the development of safeguards in the commercial nuclear industry, which, however, are lax because other foreign and economic policy objectives often take priority over nonproliferation (see also Chapter 11).

Even before Chernobyl and Three Mile Island, these and related issues caused the role of the nuclear industry in the world's energy future to be scaled down from previous plans. Virtually all of the industrial world determined in the wake of the first oil shock that a rapid buildup of nuclear power was necessary, but only in France did the nuclear industry develop as planned (Stobaugh, 1982). In the United States, in contrast, many of the earlier orders for nuclear power plants were either canceled or deferred, and since 1978 no new plants have been ordered by the utilities industry. Faced with soaring costs, regulatory log jams, and political opposition, the industry also halted construction of numerous plants already under way. Elsewhere, the growth of West Germany's nuclear industry came to a virtual standstill, and earlier ambitious plans to develop nuclear power in Australia, Austria, Denmark, New Zealand, and Norway were postponed indefinitely. Even where nuclear power continued to expand, as in Japan, the Soviet Union, and the United Kingdom, the pace was much slower than once anticipated. The number of nuclear power plants that developing countries had planned to build was also cut to less than half the number expected in the mid-1970s (Stobaugh, 1982). Three Mile Island and Chernobyl merely reinforced already stiff resistance to the further development of nuclear energy.

This brief exploration of alternatives to energy derived from oil demonstrates that

---

[15] Commercial generating facilities generally use natural uranium, in which the fissile isotope U-235 occurs in low concentrations (less than 1 percent), or slightly enriched uranium (3 to 4 percent). Nuclear weapons, by contrast, require highly enriched uranium, which at present can be produced by only a few states.

Plutonium is an artificial element produced as a by-product of uranium-burning reactors. If separated from spent fuel by chemical reprocessing, it can be used to produce additional electrical generating capacity. However, only about ten kilograms of plutonium are needed to make a nuclear weapon (U.S. Arms Control and Disarmament Agency, 1979: 23).

the "energy problematique" is a complex mixture of technical, economic, environmental, political, and security issues. Preparing for a postpetroleum world therefore requires a frontal attack on a multitude of well-entrenched challenges, not the least of which is preservation of the standard of living to which much of the developed world has grown accustomed and to which others aspire. Mustering the political will to address the challenges constructively may prove the most formidable task.

ON THE (DIS)UTILITY OF RESOURCE POWER . . . .

The impact of oil price and production policies on the world political economy derives from the uneven distribution of the demand for and supply of oil, an essential resource. Should there be another oil crisis, it, like the previous ones, will spring from this imbalance. Are there other commodities with similar characteristics? Are other OPECs therefore possible? Might they, too, become vehicles for the use of commodity power to enhance the economic welfare of their members or to realize political purposes?

Table 10.1 on page 374 shows the volume and share of world commodity exports of Third World countries in the early 1980s. The data appear to support the proposition that developing nations hold substantial commodity power. Note, for example, that they account for 97 percent of the world's exports of rubber, 90 percent of its cocoa, 89 percent of its coffee, 82 percent of its tea and bananas, and 78 percent of its palm oil and tin. Such an apparently high degree of global dependence on a few exporters of commodities, some regarded as "critical" or "strategic" resources, has been a serious concern among policymakers in many importing countries, especially after their experiences with the OPEC cartel. In the early years of the Reagan administration U.S. policymakers frequently talked about an impending "resource war" as resource-dependent industrial nations clamored to ensure secure access to resources vital to their advanced economies. Yet no resource war has broken out. And even though producers' associations have at one time or another existed in many of these commodity markets,[16] none has come under monopoly control in the same way that oil once did. Why not? And what do these apparently failed prognoses regarding impending war and dashed hopes about commodity power portend for the future?

Resource Dependence and Commodity Power

The ability of Third World producers to wield commodity power—and the incentives that the First World importing countries might have to use force of arms to ensure their access to essential resources—depends on a peculiar combination of circumstances.

---

[16] Several studies consider the possibility of other resource markets becoming cartelized, and most agree that oil is unique. Among them are Arad and Arad (1979), Krasner (1974), Pirages (1978), Smart (1976), Spero (1990), Stern and Tims (1976), and Varon and Takeuchi (1974).

TABLE 10.1 MAJOR PRIMARY COMMODITY EXPORTS OF DEVELOPING COUNTRIES, 1985–1987 ($ BILLIONS AND PERCENTAGES)

Developing-Country Exports

World Exports of Commodities

Commodity	$	%	Commodity	$	%
Rubber	3.1	97.4	Rice	1.9	58.2
Cocoa	2.7	90.2	Oilseed cake and meal	2.8	53.1
Coffee	11.0	89.0	Cotton	2.9	48.8
Bananas	1.4	82.4	Tobacco	1.9	48.7
Tea	1.8	81.6	Iron ore	3.0	44.0
Palm oil	1.6	77.9	Aluminum and bauxite	3.1	24.8
Tin	1.2	77.8	Soybeans	1.4	24.8
Sugar	6.9	72.9	Maize	1.7	23.1
Phosphate rock	.9	64.3	Timber	3.9	21.9
Copper	5.0	64.0			

Major Developing-Country Suppliers 1985–1987

Percentage of World Exports of Commodities

Country	%	Country	%	Country	%	Country	%
Malaysia	41.5	Ghana	14.3	Brazil	9.9	Sri Lanka	3.0
Côte d'Ivoire	30.7	Brazil	17.1	Mexico	5.3	Nigeria	7.2
Colombia	17.2	Ecuador	13.8	Costa Rica	12.5	Indonesia	5.2
Honduras	16.7	Sri Lanka	17.3	China	15.2	Colombia	10.9
India	23.2	Indonesia	8.9	Papua and	1.9	Kenya	10.7
Malaysia	64.0	Indonesia	12.0	New Guinea		Côte d'Ivoire	1.6
Malaysia	26.8	Brazil	3.8	Brazil	10.7	Thailand	8.7
Cuba	48.3	Jordan	12.3	Thailand	3.0	Mauritania	2.8
Morocco	28.8	Zambia	9.5	Togo	5.9	Senegal	3.4
Chile	24.2	Pakistan	8.8	Zaire	7.2	Peru	6.1
Thailand	25.3	Argentina	12.9	China	6.2	India	5.1
Brazil	25.0	Pakistan	7.0	Bangladesh	6.1	China	2.8
China	9.2	Turkey	7.7	Egypt	6.4	Sudan	2.6
Brazil	10.7	India	6.7	Greece	5.4	India	2.6
Brazil	23.8	Guinea	4.1	Liberia	3.6	Uruguay	3.4
Brazil	4.3	Argentina	7.9	Venezuela	3.4	Jamaica	2.5
Brazil	9.3	China	7.5	China	5.5	Paraguay	1.6
Argentina	7.7	Indonesia	2.6	Thailand	3.5	Greece	1.3
Malaysia	10.3	Thailand	19.7	Philippines	0.9	Brazil	0.8
Indonesia	25.2						

Source: Based on unpublished World Bank data.

Dependency is the critical factor, but it can take on various manifestations. As political scientist Bruce Russett observes:

> Fears of dependence in industrialized economies arise from several different economic and political possibilities. The first involves changes in market conditions that suppliers impose deliberately, for economic reasons: in effect, the possibility of significant price increases imposed by a single supplier or, more likely, by a cartel in order to reap monopoly (or oligopoly) profits. . . .
>
> A second possibility concerns changes in market conditions imposed deliberately, but for political purposes, by suppliers or hostile third parties. Here we refer chiefly to embargoes, boycotts, or trade sanctions, such as the American economic sanctions against the Soviet Union for its action in Poland and Afghanistan [described later in this chapter]. . . . (Russett, 1984: 483)

As we noted earlier, OPEC's behavior during the OPEC decade was motivated by political and economic aspirations, both of which created fears of resource dependence in the North. The oil embargo against the United States and the Netherlands in the immediate aftermath of the Yom Kippur War sought to alter their support of Israel. Thereafter, most of OPEC's efforts were motivated by a desire to maximize economic returns to its members. To understand why these actions succeeded, if only to a limited extent, and to predict whether they might be repeated in other commodity markets, several factors critical to the exercise of a commodity power need to be evaluated.

Economic Factors

The two market conditions necessary for effective monopoly power are (1) a lack of responsiveness to prices by consumers, and (2) a lack of responsiveness in the supply of the commodity growing out of increases in its price. These conditions are known technically as the *price inelasticity of demand and supply*.

The demand for a commodity is price inelastic if the amount consumed changes little in response to price increases. The price inelasticity of demand is essential to a producers' cartel whose goal is to maximize the amount of foreign exchange it earns from its product. If the demand is price elastic, the total money earned will be less at the new, higher price than at the old, lower price, because of reduced consumption. If, however, the demand is price inelastic, the total revenues will be greater at the higher prices.

The price inelasticity of supply operates in much the same way. If the supply of a commodity is price inelastic, new producers will not (or cannot) enter the market to take advantage of the higher rates of return. If new producers do enter the market, meaning the supply is price elastic, the increased supply will likely drive prices back down, making the foreign exchange earned no greater (and perhaps less) than before. Even if prices do not return to previous levels, producers' monetary receipts will diminish because of the reduced market share each will control. Clearly, then, the price inelasticity of supply is also essential.

OPEC's experience illustrates how important these economic factors are. The crucial role that oil had come to occupy in the world energy picture by the onset of the OPEC decade was apparent by the near absence of any change in global demand following the fourfold increase in the price of oil during the winter of 1973–1974 (Smart, 1976). On the supply side, the long lead time required to develop new petroleum sources (demonstrated by the time required to bring the Alaskan and North Sea finds into production) combined with the absence of energy alternatives to prevent rapid movement away from dependence on OPEC oil. Eventually both the demand for and supply of oil proved to be more price elastic than most analysts had predicted, as consumers responded to higher prices by reducing consumption and new energy producers entered the marketplace more rapidly than expected. Both forces contributed substantially to the denouement of the OPEC decade. But in the immediate aftermath of the first oil shock, supply, like demand, generally proved price inelastic.

How do other commodities compare with oil? In the near term it would appear that many commodity producers could enjoy the benefits of monopoly control, as both demand and supply are sufficiently price inelastic that the producers could enjoy the benefits of increased export earnings if they could cooperate to control prices and output (Krasner, 1974). In the long term, however, the price elasticity of demand for many of the major commodities traded internationally, particularly minerals, is clearly not conducive to effective cartelization (see Varon and Takeuchi, 1974). Three factors capable of altering market conditions are important in explaining this: stockpiles, recycling, and substitutes.

Many commodities are easily stockpiled. The United States, for example, has maintained since 1939 large "strategic stockpiles" of certain minerals. As noted earlier, it now maintains a strategic petroleum reserve as well. These inventories give the United States a cushion against the actions of foreign producers.

Recycling is another means of affecting commodity supplies. Recovering metal from scrap material is one example; recycling aluminum soft-drink cans is another. Developing recycling capacity may take time, and the resulting product may be comparatively expensive, but the important point is that many minerals are not completely used when they are consumed.

Substitution is a third way to undermine producers' cartels. If aluminum becomes too expensive for making cans, tin can be substituted. If tin becomes too expensive, glass or plastic might be used. Even oil has its substitutes in coal, natural gas, hydropower, and nuclear energy. In the long run, then, there exist few Third World commodities whose potentials for market control are not undermined by simple economic forces.

Political Factors

What about political factors? Is there some combination of these that might enhance the poor nations' bargaining power by increasing the rich nations' fear of them?

Several "political" factors are necessary for translating control over the supply of a commodity (especially nonrenewable resources compared with renewable resources, such as agricultural products) into effective political power (defined as the use of resource power for realizing political returns, not simply economic or commercial benefits). Three are especially important: (1) *scarcity*—"the global, physical availability of the raw material in question, relative to other natural resources as well as possible substitutes"; (2) *distribution*—"the political and economic character of the market for the specific raw material, its existence in reserve form among the consuming nations, and its pattern of consumption"; and (3) *essentiality*—"the intrinsic importance of the raw material . . . either in security or in economic terms" (Arad and Arad, 1979).

One survey of the applicability of these prerequisites to a range of nonrenewable natural resources concluded that oil was the only resource that met all three criteria (Arad and Arad, 1979; see also Russett, 1984). (Even oil, however, as the experience of the 1980s showed, proved not to meet these three basic requirements.) Several circumstances explain why.

First, many First World countries depend on imports of mineral and other products to sustain their sophisticated economies, but this does not mean they are dependent on Third World exports. Canada is a principal source of many critical U.S. mineral imports, for example. Similarly, other developed nations are suppliers of commodities that enter world trade. Australia is an important producer of bauxite and alumina; South Africa is an important source of manganese, chromium, platinum, and gold; and the republics of the former Soviet Union are important producers of these same four minerals. In fact, the major exporters of most minerals in the world today generally include developed as well as developing countries. This situation is unlikely to change. (The producers of many internationally traded agricultural commodities that enhance the dietary intake of people in the world's rich nations are concentrated in the Third World, but their products fail to meet the criterion of product essentiality.)

Second, because the exporters of many essential products are diverse economically, the prospects of their building effective producers' cartels are diminished. Add to this the fact that many of the principal producers of the minerals traded internationally consist of such traditionally politically antagonistic states as South Africa and the former Soviet Union, and it becomes obvious that the possibility of creating effective producers' cartels is remote indeed.

Finally, just as many First World nations depend on foreign imports to sustain their economies, many Third World commodity producers depend on exports to sustain theirs (see Chapter 8). Few, therefore, can afford the financial and potential political risks that efforts to cartelize export markets may entail. Indeed, one of the striking lessons from the OPEC experience is that its success depended in large part on the ability of the cartel's key members to bear the brunt of production reductions so as to maintain higher oil prices. This meant that the "swing producers," mainly Saudi Arabia and, less so, Kuwait, had to have enough money (foreign exchange) "in the bank" so as to absorb the costs of production cutbacks.

But the second lesson is more important: OPEC's success as a political force depended on shared political values (at least among its most important members, the Arab ones) that enabled it to be transformed at least for a short time from simply another commodity producers' association into an effective political force. Antipathy toward Israel was the shared value. It was buttressed by the desire of OPEC's most important members to use the oil weapon to affect the outcome of the long-standing and bitter Middle East conflict. Perhaps more than anything else, this political factor distinguished OPEC from other producers' cartels.

Economic Sanctions as Instruments of Foreign Policy . . . .

When the Arab members of OPEC placed an embargo on the shipment of oil to the United States and the Netherlands in 1973, their purpose, as noted, was to change these countries' policies toward the Arab-Israeli conflict. When the United Nations Security Council decided in August 1990 that members of the world organization should cease trade with Iraq, its purpose was to accomplish the immediate and unconditional withdrawal of Iraqi forces from Kuwait. Both are examples of the use of *economic sanctions*, that is, "deliberate government actions to inflict economic deprivation on a target state or society, through the limitation or cessation of customary economic relations" (Leyton-Brown, 1987).[17]

Economic sanctions are part of the broad array of instruments of economic state-craft available to governments (see Baldwin, 1985). Their general purpose is to demonstrate resolve and to exercise influence in a manner short of the actual use of military force. Since the beginning of World War I sanctions have been deployed for foreign policy purposes 120 times (Hufbauer, Schott, and Elliott, 1990), an expression of their widespread popularity with policymakers.

Despite their frequent use, most efforts to apply economic sanctions have failed. This fact has led many policy analysts to conclude that economic sanctions are not very useful instruments of policy (see, for example, Knorr, 1975, 1977). Why is this the case? And why, then, do policymakers continue to rely on economic sanctions as instruments of influence? Let us address each of these questions by looking at some prominent sanctions cases.

Cold War Competition

Three conspicuous cases of the application of economic sanctions in the context of the U.S.-Soviet rivalry illustrate their shortcomings: those applied against Castro's Cuba beginning in 1960; against the Soviet Union following its intervention into Afghanistan in 1979; and against Poland and the Soviet Union between 1981 and 1982 following the imposition of martial law in Poland in December 1981.

Cuba

The United States placed sanctions on the Castro regime shortly after it assumed power in 1960. They began with a cut in the amount of sugar permitted to enter the United States under its quota system. Later the United States extended the sanctions to a full ban on all U.S. trade with Cuba, and it pressured other nations to follow suit. The U.S. goals were twofold. Initially, it sought the overthrow of the Castro government. Failing that, from about 1964 onward the aim was containing the Castro revolution and Cuban interventionism in Central and South America and Africa (Roca, 1987).

---

[17] Economic sanctions are a subgroup of "negative nonviolent sanctions," which also include diplomatic, political, and cultural measures and organizational penalties (Doxey, 1990).

Clearly the United States was unsuccessful in securing Castro's overthrow, and it was only marginally successful in containing Cuba's ability to pursue its own revolutionary brand of foreign policy abroad. "The major accomplishment of the U.S. economic embargo . . . consisted of increasing the cost to Cuba of surviving and developing as a socialist country and of pursuing an international commitment" (Roca, 1987). That Cuba was able to do so was largely due to the willingness of the Soviet Union to support Cuba economically, to the inability of the United States to persuade other Western nations to curtail trade and financial relations with Cuba, and to Castro's charismatic leadership and the Cuban government's domestic political control at home (Roca, 1987; see also Schreiber, 1973).

The Soviet Union and Afghanistan

Following the Soviet Union's intervention in Afghanistan in 1979, the United States imposed several economic sanctions on the Soviet Union and undertook other measures, including a boycott of the 1980 Summer Olympics scheduled for Moscow. The most celebrated of U.S. efforts was a partial embargo on the sale of grain to the Soviet Union. Among other aims, the actions sought "to punish the Soviet Union while at the same time limiting the damage to the economic interests of important domestic groups" (Falkenheim, 1987; see also Paarlberg, 1980).

The grain embargo failed to stop the flow of grain to the Soviet Union, largely because other nations (principally Argentina) increased their exports to make up the shortfall in U.S. exports. What the (partial) embargo and the other sanctions hoped to accomplish remains a matter of dispute, however, partly because the reasons for the Soviet intervention in Afghanistan were themselves open to conflicting interpretations. If the goal was "to punish the Soviet Union for its invasion of Afghanistan in order to moderate future Soviet foreign policy behaviour" (Falkenheim, 1987), sanctions may have been an appropriate response, assuming that the Kremlin's intention was to push into the remote Southwestern Asian land as a prelude to a further advance toward the rich Persian Gulf oil fields. If, on the other hand, Moscow's behavior was merely the defensive reaction of a major power seeking to maintain a client regime in a bordering state, thus preventing it from being neutralized or falling into the "enemy camp," sanctions arguably were quite irrelevant.

In any event, the evidence suggests that the U.S. sanctions extracted a cost on Soviet society but did not have a meaningful impact on its foreign policy. There are two reasons for this. First, the Soviet economy was largely self-sufficient, which lessened the impact of external events on its economic system. Second, Soviet leaders were determined to resist external pressures on their foreign policy behavior. Economic sanctions thus served to increase their resolve to do as they pleased rather than to diminish it (Falkenheim, 1987).

The Soviet Union and Poland

Similar lessons apply to Poland. Following the imposition of martial law by the Polish government in 1981 to forestall continued labor and related unrest, the Reagan administration imposed a series of sanctions against both Poland and the Soviet Union, including, among others, restrictions on U.S. government credits for the purchase of food and other commodities by Poland, restrictions on high-technology exports to Poland, and suspension of its most-favored-nation status with the United States (Marantz, 1987). Regarding the Soviet Union, one goal was to restrict the flow of Western goods and technology necessary to proceed with the trans-Siberian gas pipeline designed to bring Soviet energy resources into Western European markets.

As in the other cases, several purposes motivated the Polish sanctions. Hope that the severity of Polish martial law might be lessened was among them. Moreover, "doing nothing" was morally reprehensible. Instead, the United States had to stand up to the Soviet Union. Thus economic pressure would increase the economic strains under which the Soviet system would have to operate (Marantz, 1987). As in the case of Afghanistan, by "doing something," the sanctions enabled the Reagan administration to satisfy domestic constituencies with measures short of more forceful actions preferred by conservative critics of U.S. policies toward the Soviet Union and Eastern Europe (see Marantz, 1987).

In the end, the Reagan administration was forced to seek a face-saving compromise with its European allies on the pipeline issue, which permitted its continued construction. The compromise preserved a degree of unity in the Atlantic alliance in the face of the inability of the sanctions imposed by the United States (and others in varying degrees) to alter the behavior of the Soviet Union. The absence of consensus among the NATO allies was itself a factor contributing to the sanctions' failure. Other factors were also at work, however, including the Soviet Union's ability and willingness to support its client, namely Poland, and the relative invulnerability of the Soviet economic and political systems to external pressures (Marantz, 1987). Thus sanctions in the end may have had some liberalizing influence on Poland, but the Soviet Union was unmoved.[18]

South Africa and *Apartheid*

Even without the special circumstances involved in Western efforts to impose economic sanctions on the Soviet Union and its allies, the utility of economic sanctions as instruments of foreign policy enjoys a checkered history at best. Notable in this regard is the long history of efforts by various nations and groups of nations to impose international economic sanctions on South Africa as a way to influence the Pretoria regime to liberalize its policies regarding racial separation, known as *apartheid*, with a

---

[18] "Don't bite off more than you can chew" is one of the conclusions by Hufbauer, Schott, and Elliott (1990) in their study of more than a hundred attempts to use economic sanctions in pursuit of foreign policy goals: "Sanctions are seldom effective in impairing the military potential of an important power, or in bringing about major changes in the policies of the target country. . . . Excluding the two world wars and the two civil wars [involving India and Nigeria], we have found only three cases in which economic coercion was effective in changing a major policy of the target country." Interestingly, the sanctions against Poland (as distinct from those imposed on the Soviet Union because of Poland) was among the three. In this instance "sanctions exacerbated a deteriorating economic situation and encouraged the gradual softening of the Communist government's crackdown on the Solidarity union movement."

view toward its eventual elimination (see Shepherd, 1991). For example, at the behest of Third World nations, the United Nations imposed a voluntary arms embargo against South Africa in 1963, which became "mandatory" in 1977. More recently South Africa became the object of an oil embargo.

The attitude of the United States toward South Africa has been of special concern to the opponents of *apartheid*, because the United States has major investments in South Africa and is a primary importer of the many critical minerals of which South Africa enjoys vast reserves. A frequent argument in the United States during the long years of debate about the appropriate response of the United States to *apartheid* focused on who would be the targets of internationally applied sanctions: South African blacks, already the victims of a policy of systematic racial discrimination, or the white minority regime who perpetuated *apartheid*? On assuming office in 1981, the Reagan administration adopted a policy of "constructive engagement" toward South Africa, whose broad purpose was a diplomatic approach to the Pretoria regime on the *apartheid* issue. In 1985, however, in an unusual domestic political development, the Congress of the United States legislated, over a presidential veto, mandatory sanctions against South Africa, hoping to change the policies that Congress found objectionable.

Four years later, in 1989, F. W. de Klerk assumed power in South Africa. He promised to release Nelson Mandela, leader of the African National Congress (ANC) and a political prisoner for twenty-seven years. He also lifted the ban on the ANC and other anti-*apartheid* groups, which opened the way for negotiations on political reforms between the South African government and the ANC. Thus the process of dismantling *apartheid* appeared to have begun, which led the European Community and several countries to ease the economic sanctions they had earlier imposed on the Pretoria regime.

Were sanctions responsible for setting South Africa on a path toward reform and perhaps eventual majority rule? Most analysts conclude they were not. "By 1987 a wide variety of sanctions against South Africa had been approved by many governments and organizations; but they remained uncoordinated, and the level of implementation was often unsatisfactory. There were some unwelcome effects for South Africa, chiefly in terms of international isolation (pariah status) and as a result of disinvestment and other financial sanctions, but there was no indication . . . that the sanctions were exerting any significant coercive effect on South African government policy" (Doxey, 1990; also Hufbauer, Schott, and Elliott, 1990; but cf. Claiborne, 1990, and Minter, 1986–1987).

Iraq and the Crisis over Kuwait

The first response of the international community to the crisis over Kuwait was the imposition of sanctions. All exports to and imports from Iraq were prohibited except humanitarian shipments of medicine and some food.[19]

---

[19] Sanctions often impose costs on the initiators as well as the targets. Poland, for example, reportedly stood to lose $1 billion in arms sales and construction contracts with Iraq, its main economic partner in the Middle East, as a result of the Iraqi sanctions (Burgess and Auerbach, 1990: 21). Earlier, in the case of the U.S. grain embargo against the Soviet Union, American farmers who depend on exports were especially hard hit by Washington's policies.

The embargo was designed to cause economic hardship in Iraq that would compel the Iraqi government to withdraw from Kuwait. It also was intended to weaken Iraq militarily by creating shortages of spare parts, munitions, and fuel and by stalling further progress on its chemical weapons and ballistic missile industries and its pursuit of nuclear weapons. Finally, the United States and its allies hoped that the embargo might foment enough discontent within Iraq to cause the ouster of the Hussein regime. (*The Middle East*, 1991: 321)

In the months that followed, a vigorous debate took place at the United Nations and in various national capitals over the utility of the sanctions. Would they force Saddam Hussein from Kuwait? How long should they be applied before resorting to military power?

Iraq was especially vulnerable to a total embargo because it imported nearly three-quarters of its food and depended almost completely on oil exports for its foreign exchange (*The Middle East*, 1991: 321). Its oil could pass through only two routes, by ship through the Persian Gulf, which was easily blockaded, or overland through pipelines across other countries (see Map 10.1). In December 1990, the director of the U.S. Central Intelligence Agency reported that "more than 90 percent of imports and 97 percent of exports have been shut off." He also reported, however, that "we see no indication that Saddam is concerned at this point that domestic discontent is growing to levels that may threaten his regime or that problems resulting from the sanctions are causing him to rethink his policy on Kuwait. . . . There is no assurance or guarantee that economic hardships will compel Saddam to change his policies or lead to internal unrest that would threaten his regime." Little more than a month later, military power replaced economic sanctions to force Iraq from Kuwait.

During the debate over force and sanctions, two former chairmen of the U.S. Joint Chiefs of Staff urged that sanctions be given a year or more to work. "If in fact the sanctions will work in twelve to eighteen months instead of six months, the trade-off of avoiding war with its attendant sacrifices and uncertainties would, in my view, be worth it," Admiral William J. Crowe testified before the Senate Armed Services Committee of the U.S. Congress. Historically, however, sanctions applied over long periods enjoy less success than others.

> Sanctions imposed slowly or incrementally may simply strengthen the target government at home as it marshals the forces of nationalism. Moreover, such measures are likely to be undercut over time either by the sender's own firms or by foreign competitors. Sanctions are generally regarded as a short-term policy, with the anticipation that normal relations will be reestablished after the resolution of the crisis. Thus, even though popular opinion in the sender country may welcome the introduction of sanctions, the longer an episode drags on, the public support for sanctions dissipates. (Hufbauer, Schott, and Elliott, 1990: 100–101)

Concern for how long the coalition against Iraq would hold together did shape the decision to resort to force more quickly than some would have preferred.

Why Sanction?

The long and generally unsuccessful history of international economic sanctions led many observers to conclude that the sanctions against South Africa mandated by the

U.S. Congress or those against Iraq authorized by the United Nations would have little material impact on their intended targets in Pretoria or Baghdad. One reason is that a typical response to economic coercion in the sanctioned society is a heightened sense of nationalism, a *laager* mentality (circle the ox wagons to face oncoming enemies), which stimulates resistance in the target state. Another, perhaps more important reason, at least in the South African case, is that governments act in many ways to support the sanctioned state covertly even as they profess their support of sanctions publicly.

The Soviet, South African, and Iraqi experiences also raise questions about the suitability of sanctions as foreign policy instruments.

> Policymakers often have inflated expectations of what sanctions can and cannot accomplish. . . . At most there is a weak correlation between economic deprivation and political willingness to change. The *economic* impact of sanctions may be pronounced, both on the sender and the target country, but other factors in the situational context almost always overshadow the impact of sanctions in determining the *political* outcome. (Hufbauer, Schott, and Elliott, 1990: 94)

If sanctions are generally ineffective, why do governments seemingly persist in using them?

In a provocative study that focuses not on the broad array of economic sanctions employed by states during the twentieth century but on a narrower number that focus on the use of trade sanctions as instruments of policy, political scientist James M. Lindsay (1986) argues that the goals of the sanctioning countries fall into five basic categories:

- *compliance* ("to force the target to alter its behavior to conform with the initiator's preferences"), as in the case of the 1982 U.S. embargo of Libya designed to force it to end its support of terrorism;

- *subversion* ("to remove the target's leaders . . . or overthrow the regime"), as in the case of the early U.S. trade embargo on Cuba;

- *deterrence* ("to dissuade the target from repeating the disputed action in the future"), as in the case of the Soviet grain embargo by the United States;

- *international symbolism* ("to send messages to other members of the world community"), as in the case of the British sanctions against Rhodesia following its unilateral declaration of independence in 1965; and

- *domestic symbolism* ("to increase its domestic support or thwart international criticism of its foreign policies by acting decisively"), as in the case of U.S. sanctions against Iran following its seizure of U.S. diplomats in 1979.

The cases described earlier suggest that *symbolism* is a primary motivation behind the use of international economic sanctions. It will often be the most important motivation supporting sanctions over other policy options, particularly military force. "When military options are not feasible or desirable and the initiator wants to respond forcefully to the target's behavior, sanctions provide a means of 'doing something' " (Lindsay, 1986).

Whether the "symbolic utility" of economic sanctions in the face of their otherwise "apparent disutility" is a cause for applause or concern may be disputed. "Critics may deride the symbolic uses of trade sanctions as empty gestures, but symbols are important in politics. This is especially so when inaction can signal weakness and silence can mark complicity" (Lindsay, 1986). Thus economic sanctions often fail to achieve the most visible aims for which they are implemented, but they serve important functions nonetheless. Providing a policy alternative to the use of force to publicize and condemn another's unacceptable behavior is principal among them.

TOWARD THE FUTURE

Although economic sanctions often fall short of the objectives their proponents seek, they will continue to be used as instruments of foreign policy when states seek to register protest and force compliance by means short of military force. In this sense resource power is an instrument nations use to influence one another in international politics. A world interdependent economically multiplies the opportunities to use economic instruments, but because interdependence implies mutual sensitivity and vulnerability, resorting to resource power will also result in domestic disruptions.

Among Third World countries, the euphoria that once greeted OPEC's efforts to convert resource power into political leverage has dissipated. Nations that once thought of reliance on commodity exports as a form of dependence viewed OPEC's experience as a demonstration that commodity cartels might enable them to use their very dependence as a form of strength. That idea has proved illusory. Still, commodity associations of one form or another may be pursued by developing nations as they seek to cope with their underdog status in the global pecking order, and they may cause disruptions in various national economies as well as the global marketplace (Spero, 1990). The oil supply and price disruptions that began with the OPEC decade suggest that if a future crisis in the oil regime occurs, the disruptions could be great.

The world's present, crisis-prone energy environment, characterized by dependence on fossil fuels, is being forced in new directions by three major considerations.

The first is the availability of fossil fuels, particularly the most economic and versatile one—petroleum. The constraint is not the global resource base but the geographical and political limits of having nearly two-thirds of the world's current oil reserves in the Persian Gulf region.

The second limit is environmental—the capacity of the world to cope with the overwhelming burden of pollution that is emitted by a $20-trillion world economy run on fossil fuels. The most intractable load is the nearly 6 billion tons of carbon added to the atmosphere each year. As no technical fix appears likely for this problem, slowing global warming will mean placing limits on fossil fuel combustion.

The third constraint is social and political. In recent years, citizens around the globe have rebelled against the energy "solutions" their governments pursued. . . . Political leaders around the world are beginning to realize that people's passionate concerns cannot be swept aside by a tide of technocratic policymaking. (Flavin and Lenssen, 1991: 21–22)

These constraints will become more severe as we move toward the dawn of the twenty-first century and a postpetroleum world. The shape of that future remains clouded nonetheless, as the disjointed energy policies and practices of the world's nations often work at cross-purposes with the reality of an increasingly ecologically interdependent world. The challenge political leaders face is shaping a postpetroleum world beneficial to all and harmful to none. The challenge is creating a sustainable energy future.

SUGGESTED READINGS

Adelman, M. A. "Oil Fallacies," *Foreign Policy* 82 (Spring 1991): 3–16.

Arad, Ruth W., et al. *Sharing Global Resources*. New York: McGraw-Hill, 1979.

Bromley, Simon. *American Hegemony and World Oil*. University Park, Penn.: Penn State University Press, 1991.

Ebinger, Charles K. *The Critical Link: Energy and National Security in the 1980s*. Cambridge, Mass.: Ballinger, 1982.

Flavin, Christopher. "Building a Bridge to Sustainable Energy," pp. 27–45 in Lester R. Brown, Christopher Flavin, Sandra Postel, Linda Starke, Alan Durning, Hilary F. French, Jodi Jacobson, Marcia D. Lowe, Michael Renner, Holly B. Brough, Nicholas Lenssen, John C. Ryan, and John E. Young. *State of the World 1992*. New York: Norton, 1992.

Hufbauer, Gary Clyde, Jeffrey J. Schott, and Kimberly Ann Elliott. *Economic Sanctions Reconsidered: History and Current Policy*, 2nd edition. Washington, D.C.: Institute for International Economics, 1990.

Leyton-Brown, David, ed. *The Utility of Economic Sanctions*. New York: St. Martin's Press, 1987.

Morse, Edward L. "The Coming Oil Revolution," *Foreign Affairs* 69 (Winter 1990–1991): 36–56.

Odell, Peter R. *Oil and World Power*. New York: Penguin, 1983.

Quandt, William B. "The Middle East in 1990," *Foreign Affairs* 70 (No. 1, 1990): 49–69.

Yergin, Daniel. *The Prize: The Epic Quest for Oil, Money, and Power*. New York: Simon & Schuster, 1991.

Youngquist, Walter. *Mineral Resources and the Destinies of Nations*. Portland, Ore.: National Book Company, 1990.

Part IV

High Politics: National Security, Arms, and War

. . .

11.
The Quest for National Security:
Trends in Military Capabilities

12.
Resort to Force: Armed Conflict
and Violence in World Politics

13.
Military Paths to Peace:
Alliances, the Balance of Power,
and Arms Control

14.
Political Paths to Peace:
International Law, Organization,
and Integration

CHAPTER 11

· · ·

THE QUEST FOR NATIONAL SECURITY: TRENDS IN MILITARY CAPABILITIES

· · ·

The adversaries of the world are not in conflict because they are armed. They are armed because they are in conflict and have not yet learned peaceful ways to resolve their conflicting national interests.

Richard M. Nixon,
U.S. President, 1969

Instead of the vanished Cold War issue of "first use," the United States, its allies, and Russia will together have to cope with a different and growing problem of first use stemming from the proliferation of weapons of mass destruction.

Fred Charles Iklé,
former U.S. Undersecretary of Defense, 1992

The pervasive sense of fear that characterizes world politics explains the pre-occupation of nation-states with threats to their security and why they engage in extensive preparations for war. The nature of the international system requires that nations rely on themselves for protection. *National security*—a nation's psychological freedom from fear of foreign attack—is a paramount value. Without the ability to ensure survival, all other values are vulnerable. Thus policymakers typically assign national security the most prominent place on their foreign policy agendas.

In this chapter we examine why states feel threatened by others and how they respond to those threats. We begin with the *security dilemma* states face and follow this with an examination of *power* and how it relates to military preparedness and other capabilities. We then consider states' practices designed to diminish threats to their national security. Specifically, we examine trends in military spending, the arms trade, and weapons technology as they relate to the quest for power and security. We also explore states' defense strategies and doctrines regarding offense (compellence) and defense (deterrence).

· · ·

THE SECURITY DILEMMA . . . .

What breeds the competition that propels the search for security through preparations for war? In the eighteenth century Jean-Jacques Rousseau argued that "the state . . . always feels itself weak if there is another that is stronger. Its security and preservation demand that it make itself more powerful than its neighbors. It can increase, nourish and exercise its power only at their expense. . . . Because the grandeur of the state is purely relative it is forced to compare itself to that of the others. . . . It becomes small or great, weak or strong, according to whether its neighbor expands or contracts, becomes stronger or declines."

Concern for relative power derives from the fact that nations want many of the same things—self-preservation, national identity, freedom from the dictates of others, status, and wealth. They seek these in an anarchical system that affords none protection from the hostile designs of others. Believing their own strength will make them secure, most therefore attempt to build as much military might as their resources allow.

Although states typically arm for ostensibly defensive purposes, others perceive their military might as threatening. Alarmed, this provokes them to arm as well. Thus, as Rousseau perceptibly observed, security is a relative phenomenon. Such fear and its reciprocated behaviors create a predicament known as the *security dilemma* (Herz, 1951).

Some scholars also describe this syndrome as the *spiral model* (Jervis, 1976). The imagery is apt, as it captures the tendency of defense-enhancing efforts to result in escalating arms races, which diminish the security of all. Sir Edward Grey described this process well:

> The increase in armaments, that is intended in each nation to produce consciousness of strength, and a sense of security, does not produce these effects. On the contrary, it produces a consciousness of the strength of other nations and a sense of fear. Fear begets suspicion and distrust and evil imaginings of all sorts, til each government feels it would be criminal and a betrayal of its own country not to take every precaution, while every government regards every precaution of every other government as evidence of hostile intent. (Grey, 1925: 92)

As noted, insecurity for all is the unintended result of an unrestrained arms race. The irony is that no one consciously seeks this unanticipated outcome. Indeed, even without the desire or intention to attack another, fear still prevails.

> None can be sure that others' intentions are peaceful, or will remain so; hence each must maintain power for defense. Since no state can know that the power accumulation of others is defensively motivated only, each must assume that it might be intended for attack. Consequently, each party's power increments are matched by the others, and all wind up with no more security than when the vicious cycle began, along with the costs incurred in having acquired and having to maintain their power. (Snyder, 1984: 461)

Despite the security dilemma that affects all states, leaders still refuse to accept vulnerability and therefore search for strength. They often proceed from the assumptions that (1) security is a function of power, (2) power is a function of military capability, and (3) military might is a measure of national greatness. Each of these assumptions is, of course, consistent with the logic of *realpolitik*.

Reformers in the neoliberal tradition (recall Chapter 2) question the logic that causes states to engage in the behavior that creates and sustains the security dilemma. To them, "the central theme of international relations is not evil but tragedy. States often share a common interest, but the structure of the situation prevents them from bringing about the mutually desired situation" (Jervis, 1976).

To escape the predicament, reformers call for changes in customary approaches to the problem of national security. Seeing weapons as "indefensible" (see Lifton and Falk, 1982; also Karp, 1991), they argue that unarmed or defenseless countries enjoy a flexibility in their foreign policies that their armed neighbors do not, as they are freed from the responsibilities that (military) power imposes and do not have to worry about controlling it. Although they might have to live in the constant shadow of others' missiles, they can take comfort in knowing that they are not the targets of the missiles. Appropriate in this context is U.S. President John F. Kennedy's sober warning that, in the event of another total war, regardless of how it might begin, those most heavily armed would automatically become the primary targets of destruction.

Not surprisingly, realists are less than sanguine about the idealists' views. Even if leaders and defense planners recognize the costs that arming for security imposes, they argue, international anarchy requires that they be borne. Because, by definition, there is no escaping a dilemma, the security dilemma explains why states sharing a common interest in security nonetheless engage in individual actions that prevent them from realizing it. Instead, *insecurity* is often the product of their actions.

POWER IN INTERNATIONAL POLITICS

What is this abstraction called *power*, the quest for which political realists depict as states' primary motive? Although definitions abound, power remains an ambiguous concept (see Baldwin, 1989; Claude, 1962; Wolfers, 1952).

Most foreign policy leaders assume that power will give them the ability to promote and protect their countries' national interests, to win in bargaining situations, and to shape the rules governing the international system. From this perspective, power is a political phenomenon. It manifests itself in the ability of one actor to persuade another to do what it otherwise would not do. Thus, power is the ability to exercise influence. Some also equate power with coercion, and others see influence as manipulation (which is perhaps why politics is often regarded as "dirty"). Indeed, to say that nations pursue power is to say that they seek to control others.

When we view power as the means to control, it is reasonable to ask, Who is stronger and who is weaker? and Who will get their way and who will give in?

These invite the more fundamental question: What enables states to achieve their goals?

The Elements of National Power

To ascertain the comparative power of states, analysts conventionally rank them according to the kinds of capabilities or resources presumed necessary to attain influence over others. For such purposes, multiple factors measure states' relative *power potential*. If we could weigh comparatively each state's total capabilities, according to this logic, we could then rank nations according to their ability to draw on these resources to exercise influence. Such a ranking would reveal the international system's hierarchy of power, differentiating the strong from the weak, the great from the nongreat.

Of all the components of national power, military capability is typically thought to be the most important. Political realists in particular regard it as the central element in states' power potential. "Throughout history, the decisive factor in the fates of nations has usually been the number, efficiency and dispositions of fighting forces," they argue. "National influence bears a direct relationship to gross national strength; without that, the most exquisite statesmanship is likely to be of limited use" (German, 1960).

Figure 11.1 illustrates two parallel rankings of the world's most powerful states (in 1988) as seen from the vantage point of military spending and the size of armed forces. On the eve of the Cold War's end, the United States and the Soviet Union rank at the top of the military spending list, as expected, with the other members of NATO (North Atlantic Treaty Alliance) and the Warsaw Pact and several Middle Eastern and Asian nations making up most of the rest. The size-of-force ranking, on the other hand, contains more developing nations, where military personnel are often in greater supply than financial resources, but even here the members of the Cold War alliances that then competed and the antagonists in the Middle East's ongoing conflicts dominate. Thus both rankings conform to what most people would likely regard as the world's most "powerful" states.

From the viewpoint of political realists, economic capabilities are secondary to military strength as a source of power. Realists assume that the ability to coerce is more important than the ability to reward. Accordingly, they believe that military capability is more important than economic capability in international politics.

In addition to military capability, power potential also derives from such factors as population and territorial size, geographic position, raw materials, degree of dependence on foreign sources of materials, technological capacity, national character, ideology, efficiency of governmental decision making, industrial productivity, volume of trade, savings and investment, educational level, and national morale.

There is, however, no consensus on how best to weigh these factors, what their relative importance should be in making comparisons across nations, or what conditions affect the contribution that each makes in the equation that converts capabilities

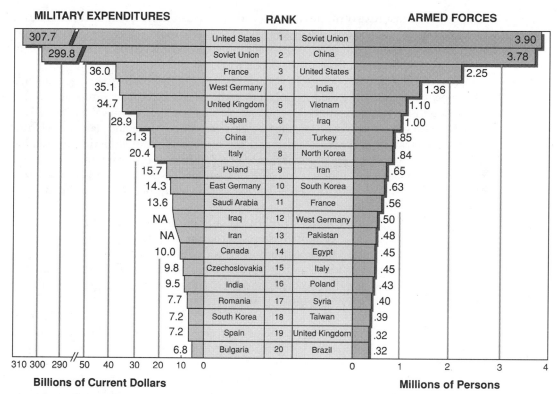

MILITARY EXPENDITURES	RANK	ARMED FORCES

FIGURE 11.1 LEADING MILITARY POWERS, 1988
Source: U.S. Arms Control and Disarmament Agency, *World Military Expenditures and Arms Transfers 1989* (Washington, D.C.: U.S. Government Printing Office, 1990), p. 3.

into influence. Most analysts agree that nations are not equal in their ability to influence others, but few agree on how to rank their power potential.

Inferring Power from Capabilities

Part of the difficulty of defining the elements of power is that their potential impact depends on the circumstances in a bargaining situation between actors, and especially on how leaders perceive those circumstances. Such judgments are subjective rather than concrete, as power ratios are not strictly products of measured capabilities. Perceptions matter more.

In addition, power is not a tangible commodity that states can acquire. It has meaning only in terms of others. Power is relational—a state can have power over some other actor only when it can prevail over that actor. Both actual and perceived strength determine who wins in a political contest. To make a difference, an adversary must know its enemy's capabilities and willingness to mobilize them for coercive purposes. It must regard the adversary's threat to use military capabilities as credible, for example. Intentions—and especially perceptions of them—are critically important in this respect. The mere possession of weapons does not increase a nation's power if its adversaries do not believe they will be used.

Noteworthy in this context is that, historically, those with the largest arsenals have not necessarily prevailed in political conflicts. Weaker states often successfully resist pressure from their military superiors. A Vietnam that was weak in the conventional military sense succeeded against a vastly stronger France and, later, the United States. An armada of U.S. missiles and bombers capable of inflicting horrendous destruction did not prevent the emergence of a communist government in Cuba only ninety miles from U.S. shores. And superior military power did not prevent seizure of the USS *Pueblo* by North Korea in 1968 or the taking of American diplomats as hostages by Iran a decade later.

Similarly, the Soviet Union's inability, prior to its disintegration, to control political events in Afghanistan, or in its Eastern European satellite empire, or even over its own constituent republics, despite its awesome weapons arsenal, shows that the impotence of military power is not peculiar to the United States. In these and other important instances, so-called second-rate military powers have exerted more influence over the great powers than the great powers have over them.

Despite these caveats, the quest for security through arms and the belief in the utility of military force continue unabated. In fact, "while it could be a mistake to assume that political influence is proportional to military strength, it would be an even bigger mistake to deny any connection between the two" (Majeed, 1991). The reason, many believe, is that military capability is a prerequisite to the successful exercise of "coercive diplomacy," that is, the employment of "threats or limited force to persuade an opponent to call off or undo an encroachment" (Craig and George, 1990). In fact, the link between military power and foreign policy "is now more pervasive and more comprehensive than in earlier periods of history when war was less dangerous" (Majeed, 1991).

The Changing Nature of World Power

Military power remains a central element in world politics. As noted in previous chapters, however, analysts now argue that "the sources of power are, in general, moving away from the emphasis on military force and conquest that marked earlier eras. In assessing international power today, factors such as technology, education, and economic growth are becoming more important, whereas geography, population, and raw materials are becoming less important" (Nye, 1990). In part this is because military force has often proven ineffectual against certain forces, notably politically mobilized populations.

Economics figure prominently in much of this new thinking. Traditionally, military power was viewed as the basis for the acquisition of wealth, rather than vice versa. That is, military capabilities enabled states to project power abroad and enhance their political leverage over others, thus permitting them to gain economic resources. Now, however, economic capability is increasingly viewed as the foremost power. On some issues, at least, the capacity to mobilize capital and resources and to compete successfully in garnering a share of world markets confers political power. Japan's rise to influence as the world's preeminent trading state stands out in this regard.

Political scientist Richard Rosecrance (1986) compares military-political and trade strategies as alternative methods for realizing national security. Increasingly, he argues, the latter has been more effective as a strategy toward political power and material advancement. "Since 1945 a few nations have borne the crushing weight of military expenditure," he observes, "while others have gained a relative advantage by becoming military free-riders who primarily rely on the security provided by others. While the United States spent nearly 50 percent of its research and development budget on arms, Japan devoted 99 percent to civilian production."

In addition to sacrificing other economic opportunities, Rosecrance continues, military spending has direct costs because expensive equipment quickly becomes outdated in the face of rapid technological innovations. Tanks routinely cost $2 million or more per copy. Fighter planes cost upward of $10 million each. Even these demands pale in comparison with the cost of missiles and ships. The estimated cost to produce the Trident II missile was "a cool $40 billion" (Sivard, 1991: 64). Thus the costs of defense may erode what policymakers hope to defend with military might. It is a troublesome idea to which we will return below.

In addition to economic capability, other, less tangible sources of national power now figure more prominently in world politics. "Political leaders and philosophers have long understood that power comes from setting the agenda and determining the framework of a debate. The ability to establish preferences tends to be associated with intangible power resources such as culture, ideology, and institutions." These intangible resources constitute "soft power," in contrast with the "hard power usually associated with tangible resources like military and economic strength" (Nye, 1990). As "soft power" grows in relative importance, military force ratios will no longer translate into power potential in the way that they once did.

THE QUEST FOR MILITARY CAPABILITIES . . . .

How people spend their money reveals their values. Similarly, how governments allocate their revenues reveals their priorities. Examination of national budgets discloses an unmistakable pattern. Although the sources of world political power may be changing, nearly all states seek security by spending substantial portions of their national treasures on arms.

Trends in Military Spending

Not only is the commitment to purchase military protection nearly universal, it is also growing, as many nations spend increasing amounts of national wealth for arms and armies. Globally, some $880 billion was spent on military preparedness in 1990. "Although down slightly, expenditures in 1990 still ranked among the largest military outlays on record, exceeding annual totals in constant dollars in all but five of the past 30 years" (Sivard, 1991: 11). The amount, even after adjusting for inflation, is twice that spent in the 1960s and "60 percent above the average annual outlays in the 1970s" (Sivard, 1991: 8).

Increases in military spending were especially evident during the 1980s, but on closer inspection it is apparent that they merely continued trends in place throughout the twentieth century. Military spending has increased fifteenfold since the mid-1930s, for example, a rate of growth exceeding the growth of world population, the global economy, and even prices since that time (Sivard, 1991).

Historically the rich nations spent the most money on arms acquisitions.[1] The pattern continues today. The developed nations spent $867 billion for defense in 1989, in contrast with the developing nations' $168 billion (U.S. Arms Control and Disarmament Agency [hereafter ACDA], 1992: 1) (see Figure 11.2). Thus the developed countries' share of the world total is more than 83 percent (ACDA, 1992: 2).

Although the leading military powers are among the largest and wealthiest countries (see also Figure 11.1), the drive to arm militarily is a universal phenomenon, as the developing nations now mimic the budgetary habits of the rich. Third World military expenditures accounted for less than 5 percent of the world's total in 1960, but the proportion grew to 16 percent by 1989 (Luckham, 1984: 355; ACDA, 1992: 2). Third World military spending has increased sixfold since 1960 (in constant dollars). This exceeds the growth in world military expenditures generally.

The dramatic increase in developing nations' military spending is apparent in the enlargement of Third World armies. Between 1960 and 1987, the armed forces of the developed world remained constant at a little more than 10 million, but the total in the developing world nearly doubled, growing from 8.4 to 16.4 million—or more than 60 percent of the world total (Sivard, 1991: 51; also ACDA, 1992: 5).

Trends in Military Capabilities

The growing militarization of the Third World manifests itself in other ways. Military capabilities are now more widely spread than ever. "The most striking geostrategic phenomenon of the past few decades," political scientist Michael Klare (1990a) posits, "is the extraordinary diffusion of war-making capabilities from the industrial North to the largely agrarian South. Nations which as recently as 1970 were equipped with a few obsolete tanks and subsonic aircraft, acquired as gifts from the major powers, [now have] large numbers of modern aircraft, tanks, and missiles." Parallel developments in the international arms trade and in the destructiveness of modern weapons underlie this diffusion.

[1] The United States, for example, spent nearly $3 trillion on defense in the 1980s, or $45,000 for each American household (Sivard, 1991: 3). In 1990, preparations for nuclear war still cost the United States more than $1 billion a week (*The Defense Monitor*, Vol. 19, no. 1, 1990, p. 1).

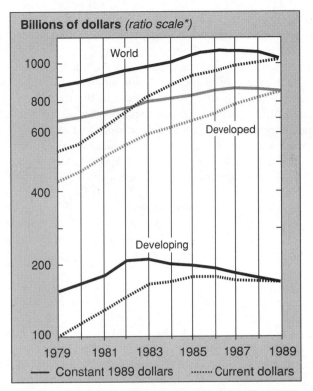

FIGURE 11.2 WORLD MILITARY EXPENDITURES, 1979–1989

Source: U.S. Arms Control and Disarmament Agency, *World Military Expenditures and Arms Transfers 1990* (Washington, D.C.: U.S. Government Printing Office, 1992), p. 1.
* The logarithmic or ratio scale used in this figure is designed to facilitate growth rate comparisons. A ratio scale is compressed as values increase so that, anywhere on the chart, equal vertical distances show equal ratios of value and equal slopes represent equal growth rates.

Trends in the Arms Trade

Kenneth N. Waltz (1975) observes that "states imitate the military innovations contrived by the country of greatest capability and ingenuity. And so the weapons of major contenders, and even their strategies, begin to look much the same all over the world." The international trade in arms, spurred by developing nations' energetic search for armaments commensurate with those of the industrial nations, has fueled the diffusion of military capability throughout the globe. In 1988, 116 countries were recipients of imported weapons, 84 of them in the developing world (*The Defense Monitor*, Vol. 20, no. 4, 1991, p. 6).

Growth in the value of arms sales attests to the present character of arms trafficking. In 1960 weapons exports were valued at $2.4 billion (Sivard, 1991: 50). By 1991, they had become a $45-billion-a-year business (Pearlstein, 1991: 8). The 1980s witnessed a slight dip in the upward trend in arms sales, but the surge in new spending following the Persian Gulf war dispelled any notion that a permanent reduction in arms trafficking was in the offing.

As noted, the developing nations have been the leading market for the traffic in arms, accounting since the late 1970s for three-fourths of all trade. They ordered an estimated $406.7 billion in armaments in the decade ending in 1989 (ACDA, 1992: 89), including a diverse range of sophisticated equipment. Today, in the face of fierce competition among an expanding number of suppliers, some of the world's most advanced weapons enter the marketplace. Sales during the 1980s included 11,000 tanks and self-propelled cannon, 20,000 artillery pieces, 3,100 supersonic combat aircraft, 37,000 surface-to-air missiles, and 540 warships and submarines (Klare, 1990b: 44).

The sale of advanced technologies is also now commonplace. This permits Third World states themselves to manufacture sophisticated weapons either for their own use or for export to others. The spread of ballistic missiles is one result (see Carus, 1990; Nolan and Wheelon, 1990).

Arms Importers Figure 11.3 portrays temporal changes in global arms imports and exports, contrasting the distribution of arms transfers by supplying countries and recipient regions between 1967 and 1989.

The increase in arms imports by Middle Eastern nations is particularly noteworthy. In 1967, they accounted for 11 percent of world arms imports. By 1989 the proportion had mushroomed to more than 26 percent (ACDA, 1992: 9). The dramatic increase reflects a combination of security concerns and economic developments.

Economically, the dramatic surge in world oil prices following OPEC's price shocks in the 1970s enabled the Middle Eastern oil exporters to buy virtually anything they wished. The drop in world oil prices in the 1980s undermined their ability to continue their arms splurge, but the Middle East remains the most important recipient region. In 1988 five of the world's top six arms-importing states were in the Middle East or Southwest Asia: Afghanistan, Iran, Iraq, Israel, and Saudi Arabia (ACDA, 1990: 10).

Strategically, the Middle East is the locus of intense strife and chronic national security problems. It includes many pairs of competitive states, including Egypt and Israel, Egypt and Libya, Iran and Iraq, Iran and Saudi Arabia, Iraq and Kuwait, Iraq and Syria, Iraq and Turkey, and Israel and Syria. The two superpowers played on this competitive environment during the Cold War to foster their own security interests. Thus they competed for allies and influence and, as the world's largest arms merchants, used arms grants and sales as policy instruments toward these ends. The Middle Eastern countries for their part were eager arms consumers.

Arms Exporters In 1963 the two superpowers supplied four-fifths of world arms transfers, but by the 1970s they began to face competition from other great powers, notably, Britain, France, Italy, and West Germany. Still, the superpowers continued to dominate the market. Between the late 1970s and late 1980s their share of global arms exports varied between one-half and three-quarters. Since the demise

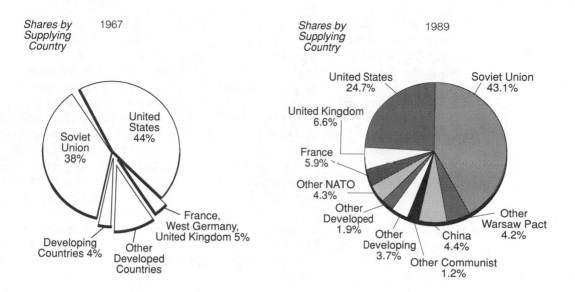

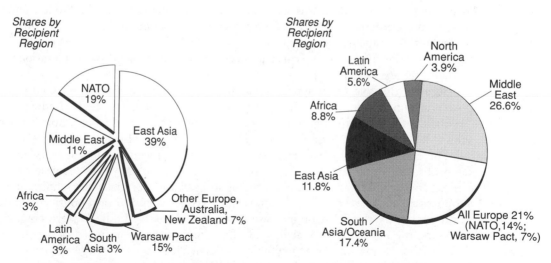

FIGURE 11.3 ARMS TRANSFERS BY SUPPLYING COUNTRIES AND RECIPIENT REGIONS, 1967 AND 1989

Sources: 1967 adapted from U.S. Arms Control and Disarmament Agency, *World Military Expenditures and Arms Transfers 1967–1976* (Washington, D.C.: U.S. Government Printing Office, 1978), pp. 115–156; 1989 from U.S. Arms Control and Disarmament Agency, *World Military Expenditures and Arms Transfers 1990* (Washington, D.C.: U.S. Government Printing Office, 1990), pp. 10, 15.

of the Soviet Union, however, the United States has recaptured its position as the "arms merchant of the world" (a phrase used by U.S. President Jimmy Carter to deplore what he sometimes regarded as an unsavory business).

Although the most powerful states in the world dominate the arms market, the number of new suppliers has grown steadily, as many developing countries now produce arms for export. The latter's share of world arms exports grew from 4 percent in 1979 to 10 percent in 1989 (ACDA, 1992: 15). By 1990 more than sixty states had entered the business of "peddling arms" (Sivard, 1991: 11). Still, most of these were small producers struggling for a share of the lucrative conventional armaments trade.[2]

A consequence of the increased competition for arms markets is that export controls designed to protect suppliers' (and others') security interests have been relaxed. The illicit export of Western nuclear, ballistic missile, and chemical weapons technology is illustrative (Timmerman, 1991). Diversification has also ended many supplier-consumer ties that earlier had cemented patron-client diplomatic relationships. Saudi Arabia, for example, turned toward Britain in the late 1980s as it sought to ease its dependence on the United States as an arms supplier (albeit also, in part, because of U.S. support for Israel).

Motives for Arms Trade Economic gain is an important rationale for foreign military sales. Israel sells arms abroad to subsidize its arms production at home (Frankel, 1987).[3] The United States uses arms exports to offset its chronic balance-of-payments deficits. And Russia, following the disintegration of the Soviet Union, sought to raise desperately needed hard currency by selling its one product mix still in demand—weapons, weapons technology, and weapons expertise. Cash is also the primary motive among other arms suppliers, for whom ideological considerations are virtually nonexistent.

Because the sale of weapons is big business, arms manufacturers comprise a powerful domestic lobby for the continuation of arms sales. In the United States a "gunbelt" military-industrial complex profits at home and abroad from continued arms sales (Markusen, Hall, Campbell, and Deitrick, 1991; see also Kapstein, 1992).

The end of the Cold War promises to increase the incentives to sell arms merely for profit, not in pursuit of foreign policy goals, as historically was the case for the United States and the Soviet Union. States still sell arms (or make outright grants) to support friendly governments, to honor allies' requests, and to earn political loyalty, as illustrated by the dramatic increase in arms deals with Middle Eastern countries following the Persian Gulf War in 1990. But the profit motive, fueled in part by the desire of defense contractors to maintain profits in a less hostile strategic environment, will increasingly dominate in the post–Cold War world.

---

[2] At the end of the 1980s the major arms suppliers were the Soviet Union, the United States, United Kingdom, France, and China, followed by West Germany, Czechoslovakia, Israel, Sweden, Canada, North Korea, Poland, Egypt, East Germany, and Bulgaria (ACDA, 1992: 16).

[3] Arms manufacturing is, by its very nature, an expensive proposition. One way to reduce the per-unit cost of a particular weapons system is to produce for foreign consumption as well as for the immediate security needs of the producing state. Selling weapons abroad is thus an attractive option.

Ironically, the treaty on Conventional Armed Forces in Europe (CFE), signed in 1990, will accelerate the arms trade. The treaty calls for the elimination from Europe of thousands of tanks, artillery pieces, armored personnel carriers, infantry fighting vehicles, and heavy armament combat vehicles. Many will be sold rather than destroyed. Czechoslovakia alone marked for export more than three-quarters of the equipment it was required to dispose of under the CFE treaty (*The Defense Monitor*, Vol. 20, no. 4, 1991, pp. 6–7). Other Eastern and Western European states can be expected to follow suit.

Whether the arming of other nations has accomplished all of its intended goals is open to dispute. During the Cold War, for example, the United States and the Soviet Union thought they could maintain peace by spreading arms to politically pivotal recipients. Between 1983 and 1987 the United States provided arms to fifty-nine Third World countries while the Soviet Union supplied forty-two (Klare, 1990a: 12). Yet many of the recipients engaged in war with their neighbors or were the targets of internal rebellion. Of the top twenty arms importers in 1988, more than half "had governments noted for the frequent use of violence" (Sivard, 1991: 17). The toll in lives from the wars among Third World arms importers since 1945 exceeds 25 million people (Sivard, 1991: 22–25). Nonetheless, over thirty conflicts using conventional weapons, many doubtless imported from abroad, were fought around the globe in 1990 (*The Defense Monitor*, Vol. 20, no. 4, 1991, p. 3).

The questionable ability of arms suppliers to control the uses to which their hardware is put is also troublesome. The United States armed both sides in several Third World conflicts since World War II, as did the Soviets on occasion. Moreover, loyalty is often a fragile commodity, and supplying weapons can backfire. In 1982 Great Britain found itself shipping military equipment to Argentina just eight days before Argentina's attack on the British-controlled Falkland Islands (Sivard, 1982). Similarly, the day before Iraq sent its troops pouring into Kuwait, the United States approved the sale to the Iraqi government of nearly $700,000 worth of advanced data transmission devices with military applications. "The sale was just one item in $1.5 billion in advanced U.S. products that the Reagan and Bush administrations allowed Iraq to buy from 1985 to 1990" (Auerbach, 1991: 11).

The problem these examples suggest is that the uses of arms by recipients are often beyond the control of the supplier. Betrayal can result when arms sold to an ally, or by an ally to a third party, are later used for purposes that challenge the national interests of the supplier. During the 1980–1988 Iran-Iraq war, for example, the United States supplied arms to both sides, to the detriment of its own security, as it turned out. Iran continued to regard the United States as a hostile world power, and U.S. forces sent to the Persian Gulf in 1990 to turn back Iraq's invasion of Kuwait found themselves facing an aggressive force armed with weapons from the West (Timmerman, 1991).

Arms buyers seek weapons for compelling reasons. Many Third World leaders prize military capabilities to symbolize their country's statehood, power, and prestige in the world's pecking order or to deal with internal opposition. Others willingly pay the price because they feel threatened or because they treasure the ability to exercise "forceful persuasion" (George, 1992). Noteworthy is the tendency of arms shipments to gravitate toward regions (notably the Middle East and Africa) where the potential for armed conflict is high and the desire to redress grievances strong. The absence of security in these trouble spots, and not merely suppliers' greed or the recipients' modernization plans, whets states' appetites for more efficient weapons systems. Through arms, threatened states hope to protect their national security and aggressive states hope to retaliate for perceived past injustices.

Trends in Weapons Technology

The quest for national security has led to a potentially explosive global political environment. The description is especially apt when we consider not only trends in defense expenditures and the arms trade but also trends in the destructiveness of modern weapons.

NUCLEAR WEAPONS   Technological research and development has radically expanded the destructiveness of national arsenals. The largest "blockbuster" bombs of World War II delivered a power of ten tons of TNT. The atomic bomb that leveled Hiroshima had the power of over 15,000 tons of TNT. Less than twenty years later the Soviet Union built a nuclear bomb with the explosive force of 57 megatons (million tons) of TNT. Today, the world's 52,000 nuclear warheads contain the equivalent of well over 1 million Hiroshima bombs. The combined nuclear stockpiles of the known nuclear powers contains "an explosive force *1,600 times* the firepower released in three major wars (World War II, Korea, Vietnam) that killed 44,000,000 people" (Sivard, 1991: 16). The use of such weapons could destroy not only entire cities and countries but, conceivably, the world's entire population.[4] Albert Einstein, the Nobel Prize–winning physicist whose ideas laid the basis for the development of nuclear weapons, was well aware of the threat they posed. He professed uncertainty about the weapons that would be used in a third world war, but in a fourth they would be "sticks and stones."

More bucks have led to more bombs with more bang, making ours an age of overkill. "A nuclear-headed cruise missile, launched from a submarine 1,500 miles at sea, carries thirteen times as much TNT-equivalent explosive as the nuclear bomb that levelled Hiroshima" (Sivard, 1991: 5). A single U.S. bomber can deliver a force level equal to nearly twice the tonnage delivered by all of the participants in World War II. "Far more powerful, of course, are the intercontinental ballistic missiles, which travel 8,000 miles at an incredible speed of 15,000 miles per hour, loaded with multi warheads and enough explosive force (up to 5,900,000 tons of TNT, over 300 times the power of the Hiroshima bomb) to destroy not just one but several major cities" (Sivard, 1991: 13).

The six (known) nuclear states—the United States, the Commonwealth of Independent States, Britain, France, China, and India—have continuously refined the

[4] Estimates of the number of people who would perish in the event of a nuclear clash vary widely. Former U.S. Secretary of Defense Harold Brown (1983) predicted that the "destruction of more than 100 million people in each of the United States, the Soviet Union, and the European nations could take place during the first half-hour of a nuclear war." For other estimates and scenarios, see Bunge (1988).

deadliness of these weapons through testing. Between July 1945 and 1991 they "detonated a combined total of at least 1,910 nuclear explosives at some 35 sites around the world, an average of one explosion every nine days" (*The Defense Monitor*, Vol. 20, no. 3, 1991, p. 1).

The nuclear arsenals of the United States and the former Soviet Union are particularly extensive and sophisticated. When World War II ended, the United States possessed the one atomic bomb still in existence. In 1988, when the level of U.S. strategic forces peaked, the United States had 13,000 warheads in its arsenal, and in 1989, when the Soviet Union was at its peak, it had 11,000 (*The Bulletin of Atomic Scientists* 48 [May 1992]:49).[5] In addition, during the Cold War the United States and the Soviet Union each deployed somewhere between 10,000 and 20,000 tactical nuclear weapons designed for the direct support of combat operations. The 1987 Intermediate-range Nuclear Force (INF) treaty began the elimination of short- and medium-range delivery vehicles from Europe. Still, "mini-nukes"—nuclear weapons so small they can be carried in a suitcase—may still pose a threat.

CONVENTIONAL WEAPONS AND DELIVERY SYSTEMS   Advances in weapons technology have been rapid and extraordinary. Already technological refinements enable states to deliver weapons as far away as nine thousand miles within a few hundred feet of their targets in less than thirty minutes. Other technological improvements have broadened the spectrum of available weapons. The United States and the former Soviet Union, for example, equip their ballistic missiles with MIRVs (multiple independently targetable reentry vehicles). These enable a single missile to launch multiple warheads toward different targets simultaneously and with great accuracy. One MIRVed U.S. MX (Peacekeeper) missile carries ten nuclear warheads—enough to wipe out Moscow and everything else within a fifty-mile radius. The Minuteman III missile carries three warheads; missiles on Trident submarines carry eight. As a result of MIRVing, the number of deliverable nuclear warheads in the nuclear powers' arsenals increased far more rapidly than the number of delivery vehicles.

Further technological improvements will lead to steady increases in weapons' speed, accuracy, range, and effectiveness. As Ruth Leger Sivard notes,

> Now, with the improved yield-to-weight ratio, nuclear warheads can be incorporated in artillery shells with a weight of 95 pounds and a range of 18 miles. These have a yield of 2,000 tons of TNT equivalent. More powerful is the nuclear-headed cruise missile which weighs 2,650 pounds. Launched from a submarine at sea, it can travel 1,500 miles under its own power, and release up to 200,000 tons of explosives on the target. (Sivard, 1991: 13)

Other technologies also alter the character of weapons. Laser weapons, "hunter-killer" satellites, and antisatellite (ASAT) weapons that can project force in and wage war from outer space have become a part of the military landscape.

Further advances will make obsolete both orthodox ways of classifying weapons

---

[5] In 1991, the French reportedly held 600 warheads, the British 300, and the Chinese about 350 (*U.S. News & World Report*, October 21, 1991, p. 54).

systems and prior equations for measuring power ratios. As an influential U.S. strategic report predicted:

> Dramatic developments in military technology appear feasible over the next twenty years. They will be driven primarily by the further exploitation of microelectronics, in particular for sensors and information processing, and the development of directed energy. The much greater precision, range, and destructiveness of weapons could extend war across a much wider geographic area, make war much more rapid and intense, and require entirely new modes of operation. Application of new technologies to both offensive and defensive systems will pose complicated problems for designing forces and assessing enemy capabilities. (Commission on Integrated Long-Term Strategy, 1988: 8)

The 1990 Persian Gulf War provided a glimpse of the future of high-tech weaponry with a dazzling display of military capabilities not previously tried in war. The war revealed elements of the two dimensions of the technological revolution that have transformed the character of so-called conventional weapons:

> One is range coupled with precision guidance. The emphasis is on computerized radars, remotely-piloted vehicles, laser- and television-guided bombs. Satellites and air-borne radar can see far into enemy territory. Targets can be destroyed from great distances. A plane flying at a height of 40,000 feet can hit a target on earth with remarkable precision. A soldier firing a wire-guided weapon can destroy a tank two miles away. A submarine submerged 120 miles at sea can pinpoint a land target with a missile which is guided by the terrain map in its nose. In the war against Iraq in early 1991, the smart bombs and precision-guided missiles quickly established the coalition's air superiority. . . .
>
> On the other hand, the capability for massive destruction has been markedly improved. In one sortie a bomber can drop 50 or more bombs of 500–1,000 pounds each. Explosive power has been greatly enhanced. A single cluster bomb detonates into several hundred bomblets. Fuel air explosives disperse fuel into the air and then detonate the fuel cloud. Both in lethality and in area covered, so-called conventional weapons today approach small nuclear weapons in destructive power. (Sivard, 1991: 13)

Changes in military capabilities, in short, have revolutionized the nature of warfare. Today's conventional weapons are increasingly destructive, and the precision and power of their means of delivery have improved exponentially. At the same time, the nuclear powers have emphasized quality over quantity, precision and miniaturization over blast and bigness.

For decades a "firebreak" has separated conventional from nuclear wars. The term comes from the firebreaks that fire fighters build to keep forest fires from racing out of control. In the context of modern weaponry, it is a psychological barrier whose purpose is to "prevent even the most intensive forms of conventional combat from escalating into nuclear war" (Klare, 1985). As both nuclear and conventional weapons technologies advance, there is danger that the firebreak is being crossed from both sides—by a new generation of "near-nuclear" conventional weapons capable of "levels of violence approximating those of a limited nuclear conflict," and by a new generation of "near-conventional" nuclear weapons able "to inflict damage not much greater than that of the most powerful conventional weapons" (Klare, 1985).

Unconventional Weapons Chemical and biological weapons pose a special and growing threat. Each is sometimes regarded as a "poor man's atomic bomb" because of its potential for widespread injury and death at comparatively small cost. Already twenty Third World states are regarded as "possible" or "likely" candidates for developing chemical weapons, and another four as "likely" candidates for developing biological weapons (Fetter, 1991).

Among the industrial states, the United States and the Commonwealth of Independent States maintain the largest stockpiles of chemical weapons, but in 1990 the United States and the Soviet Union agreed to stop their production and significantly reduce their numbers. "No nation is known to possess biological weapons today, but the United States, the United Kingdom, and Japan are known to have developed several types of biological weapons in the past (such stocks have since been destroyed), and Iraq and Syria are strongly suspected of stockpiling such weapons" (Fetter, 1991).

Chemical weapons (gas) were used during World War I, "producing about 100,000 fatalities and over 1,000,000 total casualties" (Fetter, 1991: 15). The only significant recent experience with such weapons occurred during the war between Iran and Iraq (1980–1988), when both sides apparently used them, although precisely when and where remains uncertain (McNaugher, 1990). A number of factors affect the military utility of chemical weapons, including weather conditions and the ability to defend against them. Thus the "poor man's atomic bomb" analogy, while appropriate for biological weapons, does not aptly describe chemical weapons, as their characteristics as weapons of "mass destruction" are limited (Fetter, 1991).

Chemical weapons are nonetheless capable of causing widespread death and suffering. And what makes them so fearful is the proliferation of ballistic missiles, particularly among regional antagonists as in the Middle East. Already some twenty Third World countries enjoy a ballistic missile capability, with others likely entrants into the field.

The psychological effects of ballistic missiles, particularly because of the absence of effective defenses against them, are greater than their military effects. During World War II, for example, Germany used V-2 rockets in its assault against Britain. Each rocket was loaded with a one-ton warhead (the same size as on the Soviet-built SCUD-B missile, a modified version of which Iraq used during the Persian Gulf War). "The average V-2 missile landing in London killed five people, injured 13, and damaged 40 buildings" (Fetter, 1991: 15). Missiles with payloads such as these "would only be useful in strategic attacks against cities, but a truly strategic threat (or a strategic deterrent) would require a capability to launch tens of thousands of such missiles. Conventionally armed missiles cannot be decisive militarily, and a nation certainly could not hope to deter nuclear attack by fielding a force of conventionally armed missiles" (Fetter, 1991).

Thus the military capability of conventional warheads on ballistic missiles is minimal. The nuclear powers have long recognized this, as demonstrated by MIRV and related technological enhancements designed to improve warhead performance. Third World nations also recognize this. Hence, a close correspondence exists between countries with ballistic missile capability and those with aspirations for chemical, biological, or nuclear weapons.

The Proliferation Problem

Do arms acquisitions promote violence and war? "Many amply supplied armed forces may incline governments to use force rather than to negotiate to resolve conflicts." Even so, "the possession of weapons does not guarantee their use" (Ball, 1991). In fact, as we will discuss in more detail below, the purpose of arming for deterrence is to prevent the use of force, not encourage it. Hence, as Michael Klare (1987) argues, "it would be foolish to argue that increased arms transfers automatically increase the risk of war—the decision to wage war is determined by numerous factors."

Still, he continues, "there is no doubt that the widespread availability of modern arms had made it *easier* for potential belligerents to choose the military rather than the diplomatic option when seeking to resolve local disputes." Huge arms purchases by Iraq, for example, may have set the stage for its invasion of Kuwait and the subsequent Persian Gulf War. Iraq purchased $75 billion in military equipment during the 1970s and 1980s, or nearly ten percent of all arms transfers. "The weapons. . .may have encouraged Saddam Hussein to believe that his invasion of Kuwait would not be challenged" (Ball, 1991: 20). Thus, even if the arms trade does not necessarily make the world more violent, it does make it less secure. Hence the proliferation of arms is a serious issue on the global agenda.

Ballistic Missiles and Unconventional Weapons

Despite its seriousness, there are comparatively few restraints on the spread of arms. Those that do exist deal primarily with nuclear weapons.

During the 1970s the United States initiated a series of talks aimed at stopping the spread of conventional arms, but the negotiations ended in failure. For example, the Carter administration initiated the U.S.-Soviet Conventional Arms Transfer Talks (CATT) but suspended them in 1979. And in 1987, eight Western nations (Britain, Canada, France, Italy, Japan, Spain, the United States, and West Germany) that manufactured ballistic missiles, their components, and their production facilities established the Missile Technology Control Regime (MTCR). But this consensual cartel includes only a fraction of the current suppliers of missile technology, and lacks an institution to monitor and enforce compliance with the voluntary agreement. In 1991, following the Persian Gulf War, the United States again sought to stem the flow of conventional arms to the Middle East, but the effort was short-lived, as even the United States pushed arms sales to Saudi Arabia and other states in the region to record heights. Thus not only the highly threatening ballistic missile continues outside meaningful international restraints but virtually every other conventional weapon as well. As a result, the threat of another Iraq, that is, another new "Weapon State"—whose characteristics, among others, include "deep grievances against the West and the world order that it has established and enforces" (Krauthammer, 1990–1991)—has grown.

International law prohibits the use of unconventional weapons (the 1925 Geneva Protocol prohibits chemical weapons, for example), but these legal restraints have not constrained their use, as Iran's and Iraq's recent use of gas in warfare demonstrates. (Iraq even used chemical weapons against its own Kurdish people.) Thus the firebreak, the taboo against the use of unconventional weapons, has already been breached.

The 1972 Biological Weapons Convention prohibits the development, production, and stockpiling of biological weapons, and biological weapons at present pose a less serious threat than chemical weapons. Accordingly, international efforts to control unconventional weapons have focused on the latter. Among them are efforts by the United Nations Conference on Disarmament to devise a chemical weapons convention and by the "Australian Group" of chemical suppliers to tighten export controls on chemical agents. Individual states, notably the United States, also have sought in various ways to stem the spread of unconventional weapons technology.

"The dual uses of chemical technologies for fertilizers, pesticides and herbicides as well as weapons is even closer than the overlap between commercial and military nuclear facilities" (Nye, 1989–1990; also Dunn, 1989). The dual use of chemical agents hampers verification efforts, a principal stumbling block in most arms control efforts. Moreover, the United States, while strongly supportive of a chemical weapons treaty proposed by the UN Disarmament Conference, insists that it "must retain a small stockpile of chemical weapons for deterrent purposes until all other states capable of manufacturing chemical weapons have joined the treaty. As might be expected, this provision has come under heavy criticism by those who claim that it smacks of the division between the 'haves' and the 'have nots' that has undermined adherence to the nuclear Non-Proliferation Treaty (NPT)" (Fetter, 1991). Nonetheless, in what may turn out to be a significant breakthrough, negotiators in Geneva reached an agreement in 1992 on a draft treaty designed to ban not only the use of chemical weapons—already prohibited under international law—but also their production and stockpiling.

Nuclear Weapons

The addition of new nuclear states is commonly referred to as the Nth country problem. The increase in the number of nuclear states is called *horizontal proliferation*, in contrast with increases in the capabilities of existing nuclear powers, known as *vertical proliferation*.

Most countries dread the chain reaction that might lead to widespread horizontal proliferation, for it increases the likelihood that one or more states will choose to use nuclear weapons or that an accident or miscalculation will lead to catastrophe. Estimates vary, but experts agree that perhaps as many as thirty other states now have the economic and technological potential to become nuclear powers. By the year 2000, the number could grow to forty (Klare, 1990a; also Clausen, 1991).

NUCLEAR POWERS, NUCLEAR ASPIRANTS   As Map 11.1 on page 408 indicates, presently there are only six "official" members of the nuclear club—the United States, the Commonwealth of Independent States, Britain, France, China, and India—but many others are de facto or emerging nuclear states.

It is widely believed, for example, that both Israel and South Africa have already acquired nuclear weapons clandestinely.[6] In addition, experts generally regard Algeria, Argentina, Brazil, Iran, Iraq, Libya, North Korea, Pakistan, South Korea, and

---

[6] Seymour Hersh (1991) argues that Israel's nuclear arsenal far exceeds that suspected by the U.S. Central Intelligence Agency, that the Soviet Union has been a principal target, and that the Israelis wheeled their nuclear missiles out of silos and put them on launchers on full alert on at least three separate occasions.

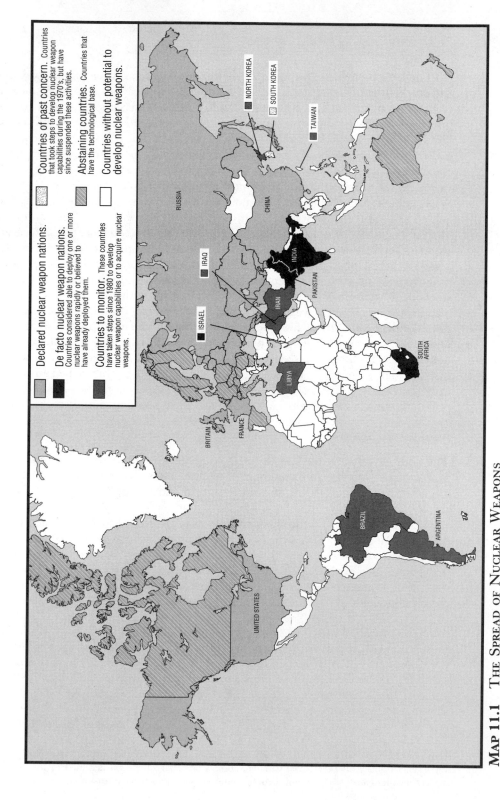

MAP 11.1 THE SPREAD OF NUCLEAR WEAPONS
Source: Adapted from Michael T. Klare, "An Arms Control Agenda for the Third World," *Arms Control Today* 20 (April 1990): 9.

Taiwan as emerging or "threshold" states. Recent political agreements between Argentina and Brazil, India and Pakistan, and North and South Korea, historic antagonists with deep-seated suspicions of one another, reduce somewhat the proliferation threat, but it remains a potent global security issue that is not easily controlled.

THE NONPROLIFERATION REGIME The Nuclear Nonproliferation Treaty (NPT), first signed in 1968, seeks to prevent further proliferation by prohibiting the transfer of nuclear weapons technology from the now nuclear states to the non-nuclear states. At the same time, however, the nuclear states are obligated to provide others with nuclear information and technology for peaceful purposes. All of the six "official" nuclear states are now members of the NPT regime, and none of the thirty remaining nonsignatories has chosen to violate its provisions openly.

Despite the apparent success of the NPT regime, the obstacles to further proliferation are fragile, and the incentives to join the nuclear club are strong. There are several reasons.

First, the materials needed to make a nuclear weapon are widely available. In part this is due to the widespread use of nuclear technology for generating electricity. Long-standing concerns about Pakistan's nuclear intentions, for example, intensified in early 1992, when China announced it would export a 300-megawatt nuclear power plant to Pakistan.

Today more than 850 nuclear generating plants are in operation in more than sixty countries (Sivard, 1991: 14). In addition to spreading nuclear know-how, states could choose to reprocess the uranium and plutonium that power plants produce as waste. As U.S. President Jimmy Carter warned, "We know that by the year 2000 nuclear power reactors could be producing enough plutonium to make tens of thousands of bombs every year."

Second, scientific expertise necessary to weapons development has spread with the internationalization of advanced scientific training. "In the near future it will be possible to duplicate almost all past technology in all but the most forlorn of Third World backwaters, and much of the present state-of-the-art will be both intellectually and practically accessible" (Clancy and Seitz, 1991–1992).

Third, export controls designed to stop technology transfer for military purposes are weak. "A large and growing number of states can now export material, equipment, technology, and services needed to develop nuclear weapons" (Potter, 1992), and the leaks in nuclear export controls makes "a mockery of the long-revered nuclear nonproliferation regime" (Leventhal, 1992). Conversion of peacetime nuclear energy programs to military purposes could occur either overtly or, as in the case of India, covertly. The safeguards built into the nonproliferation regime are simply inadequate. The ease with which Pakistan made a successful end run around the technology-export controls of the United States and Western European governments illustrates the problem of control. In 1979 Pakistan quietly bought all the basic parts—allegedly with funds supplied by the radical government of Libya—necessary for a uranium-enrichment plant. Similarly, UN inspectors discovered after the Persian Gulf War that Iraq was much closer to building an atomic weapon than previously suspected. Yet Iraq "remained a member [of the nonproliferation regime] in good standing for more than a decade. This was possible because the [NPT] treaty allows members legally to get much too close to weapons capability. . . . The Iraqi experience suggests that it is impossible to effectively safeguard weapons-grade materials" (Mathews, 1991).

Fourth, other states have strong incentives to develop nuclear weapons similar to those once cited by the members of the nuclear club. French President Charles de Gaulle averred that, without an independent nuclear capability, France could not "command its own destiny." Similarly, Britain's Labour party leader Aneurin Bevan asserted that without the bomb Britain would go "naked into the conference chamber."

Many non-nuclear states want the same command of their own fate and the same diplomatic influence. Why, they ask, should they adhere to a nonproliferation agreement that dooms them to others' domination and security guarantees? Consider Iran's sentiments. In January 1992 its spiritual leader, the Ayatollah Ali Khamenenei, declared that the United States had no business questioning his country's nuclear weapons program designed to make it the most powerful military force in the Persian Gulf. "Iran's revolutionary Muslim people recognize no false hegemony for America or any other power," he exclaimed.

Fifth, the breakup of the Soviet Union encourages the spread of nuclear weapons. Nuclear weapons were on the soil of four of the former Soviet Republics—Russia, Ukraine, Belarus, and Kazakhstan—when the Soviet Union dissolved and was reconstituted as the Commonwealth of Independent States. Each had incentives to assert continued control over the weapons, although all of them made genuflections in the direction of a joint command over them. Still, many analysts, drawing on the experience of other confederal arrangements, pointed toward the possibility that such an arrangement would not survive. Noteworthy is the position Ukrainian defense planners staked out in late 1991: "There is no way Ukraine will give nuclear weapons that are on its territory to the Russians. Nuclear weapons . . . are very good nuclear security."

Nuclear Disarmament?   Some see the end of the Cold War as an opportunity to move toward the elimination of nuclear weapons. Leaders in the former Soviet Union and in Russia, for example, embraced the goals of complete nuclear disarmament. Moreover, the United States and Russia have undertaken a number of important steps toward meaningful disarmament (see Chapter 13), something unheard of even a few short years ago. Perhaps this will set the stage for expanding the nonproliferation regime, when the parties to the NPT treaty gather in 1995 to consider its renewal.

The NPT treaty was reviewed in 1990 at Geneva. At that time the contracting parties were unable to reach a consensus on nuclear testing issues. That does not augur well for extending, or even maintaining, the nonproliferation regime, much less eliminating nuclear weapons. They, like gods of old, have become symbols of limitless power to which weak states attribute qualities of awe and omnipotence to compensate for their sense of powerlessness (Chernus, 1987). Thus few reasons exist to expect that the nuclear threat will cease with the diminution of great-power tensions. "There's not a snowball's chance in hell we'll eliminate all nuclear weapons from the face of the earth," explains Matthew Bunn, editor of *Arms Control Today*. "That genie is long since out of the bottle and there's no chance of ever getting him back in." Moreover, the security problem posed by a disarmed world is compelling. "The problem is, if you eliminate them all, then any country that built just a few nuclear weapons would have enormous blackmail potential" (Davidson, 1991).

THE SOCIAL AND ECONOMIC CONSEQUENCES OF MILITARY SPENDING . . . . .

Global patterns of military spending and arms acquisitions testify to the belief that power can be purchased. What are the effects of this conviction on national well-being?

The *relative burden* of military spending, defined as the ratio of defense spending to gross national product, is one way to measure the sacrifices military spending requires. In 1989 the relative defense burden for the world as a whole was 4.9 percent, with 5 percent the average among developed countries and 4.3 percent among developing countries (ACDA, 1992: 18).

For comparative purposes, Table 11.1 on page 412 groups the world's nations according to their share of GNP devoted to the military on the vertical axis and their GNP per capita on the horizontal axis. The data show wide variation among countries. Some comparatively wealthy states (for example, Israel, the United Arab Emirates, and the United States) bear a heavy burden for defense, but others (Austria, Finland, and Japan) do not. Likewise, some very poor countries (Cambodia, Ethiopia, and Laos) are heavily burdened, while others (Nepal and Sierra Leone) are not. Thus it is difficult to generalize about the precise relationship between a country's defense burden and its income level or stage of development. Still, the data do suggest two general patterns.

First, those most burdened by the costs of defense include a disproportionate share of poor countries experiencing civil or international war or threats to their security (ACDA, 1990: 19). Second, the burden of defense in relation to income is more than three times greater in developing than in developed countries. "At 1988 levels of GNP per capita, . . . the countries least able to afford it bore the major share—close to four-fifths—of the world's military burden" (Sivard, 1991: 11). It seems, then, that those least able to afford weapons have made the greatest sacrifices to get them. Hence the costs of arming for security pose "a formidable barrier" to economic development, concludes Ruth Leger Sivard (1991:11), because the developing nations "lost to the arms race in a single year the equivalent of 187 million human-years of income."

Military Spending and Social Priorities

The comparatively greater resources military preparedness commands in relation to other problems manifests itself in other ways, as indicated by the data in Box 11.1 on page 414.

The data in Box 11.1 show that most countries are more concerned with defending their citizens from foreign attack than they are with protecting them from social,

(Text continues on page 415.)

Table 11.1 Relative Burden of Military Expenditures, 1989

ME/GNP* (%)	GNP PER CAPITA (1989 dollars)					
	Under $200	$200–499	$500–999	$1,000–2,999	$3,000–9,999	$10,000 and over
10% and over	Ethiopia Cambodia+		Yemen (Aden)+ Angola+ Lebanon+	Iraq+ North Korea Jordan Syria	Oman Saudi Arabia Libya Bulgaria Soviet Union	Qatar+ Israel
5–9.99%	Laos+ Mozambique	Vietnam+ Nicaragua+ Afghanistan+ Pakistan	Yemen (Sanaa)+ Zimbabwe Cape Verde+ Morocco	Mongolia+ Algeria Egypt	Poland East Germany Czechoslovakia Bahrain Hungary Romania Greece Taiwan	Kuwait United States Un. Arab Emir. Singapore
2–4.99%	Tanzania Guinea-Bissau+ Burundi Malawi	Liberia Burma Togo Sri Lanka Chad+ India Equat. Guinea+	Bolivia Mauritania Congo+ China Honduras Philippines Sudan	Gabon South Africa Albania Turkey El Salvador Yugoslavia Argentina	South Korea Cuba Portugal Suriname Spain	United Kingdom France Norway Netherlands West Germany Sweden Belgium

ME/GNP						
		Guyana, Kenya, Zaire+, Lesotho+, Burkina Faso+, Mali	Senegal	Panama, Chile, Iran+, Malaysia, Tunisia, Botswana, Thailand, Fiji, Colombia, Uruguay+		Italy, Australia, Denmark, New Zealand, Switzerland, Canada
1–1.99%	Bangladesh, Somalia+, Nepal	Benin, Haiti, Rwanda+, Indonesia, Cen. Afr. Rep., Uganda+, Madagascar, Niger, Guinea+	Ecuador, Swaziland, Guatemala, Ivory Coast, Papua N. Guinea, Paraguay, Zambia+	Trinidad & Tobago, Peru+, Cameroon, Jamaica	Ireland, Brazil+, Malta	Finland, Austria, Japan
Under 1%	Sierra Leone+	The Gambia, Ghana, Nigeria, Sao Tome & Prin.+	Dominican Rep.	Venezuela, Mexico, Costa Rica, Mauritius	Cyprus, Barbados	Luxembourg, Iceland

* Countries are listed within blocks in descending order of ME/GNP.
+ Ranking is based on a rough approximation of one or more variables for which 1989 data or reliable estimates are not available.
Source: U.S. Arms Control and Disarmament Agency, *World Military Expenditures and Arms Transfers 1990* (Washington, D.C.: U.S. Government Printing Office, 1992), p. 20.

Box 11.1
Military and Other Social Priorities

• • •

- World military expenditures from 1960 to 1990 add up to $21 trillion ($21,000,000,000,000) in 1987 dollars, equivalent in size to the value of all goods and services produced by and for the 5.3 billion people on the earth [in 1990]. (p. 11)

- The price of one ballistic submarine ($1,453,000,000) would double the education budget of 18 poor countries with 129,110,000 children to educate. (p. 5)

- In recent decades military expenditures have taken $5 of every $100 of goods and services produced in the world, a share of gross product five times as large as that allocated to defense before World War II. . . . $15 to $20 of every $100 spent by central governments now goes to military purposes, triple their budgets for education, eight times their budgets for housing. (p. 26)

- For military objectives, governments now invest an average of $36,000 per year per member of the armed forces, thirty times more than they invest in the education of a child enrolled in school. The formidable gap between the two underscores the serious neglect of human capital, and with it, of economic development, in favor of unlimited military power. (p. 27)

- The world's armed forces are the single largest polluter on earth; in the US they produce more toxics annually than the top five chemical companies combined. (p. 5)

- Despite some retrenchment in military spending recently, [Third World] annual outlays still take the equivalent of 180 million man-years of income vs. 56 million man-years for the developed countries. (p. 11)

- Developing countries have eight times as many soldiers as physicians. (p. 5)

- [If present downward trends in military spending continue] it could be 125 years before annual education expenditures per school-age child match the current level of military expenditures per soldier. (p. 6)

Source: Ruth Leger Sivard, *World Military and Social Expenditures 1991* (Washington, D.C.: World Priorities, 1991).

educational, and health insecurities. They also suggest that military spending reduces social welfare. The connection is not direct, but military spending and global deprivation are linked.

Consider, for example, how the United States, first in military spending, ranks (in 1988) among all nations across various social indicators (Sivard, 1991: 46):

	U.S. RANK COMPARED WITH OTHER COUNTRIES
• Literacy rate	4
• Per-capita public expenditure for education	8
• Per-capita GNP	8
• Maternal mortality rate	13
• Per-capita public expenditure for health	14
• Life expectancy	15
• Infant mortality rate	18
• Population per physician	18
• Total fertility rate	20
• Percent population with access to sanitation	20
• Under 5 mortality rate	22
• Percent infants with low birth weight	36

These rankings alongside the data in Box 11.1 suggest that high military spending reduces the quality of citizens' lives. Security in the broadest sense means security in the expectation that one will live a full life. Yet arms do not contribute to increased life expectancy or freedom from want. Instead, when expenditures for arms go up, so do disease, illiteracy, and suffering. Thus, high rates of military spending reduce social welfare (see Nincic, 1982; Russett, 1982; Wolpin, 1983). As U.S. President Dwight D. Eisenhower observed, "the world in arms is not spending money alone. It is spending the sweat of its laborers, the genius of its scientists, the hopes of its children."

Military Spending and Economic Growth

How are military expenditures and social welfare linked? Many politicians and experts argue that a trade-off exists between "guns and butter," that is, between military spending and economic growth. Ruth Leger Sivard (1979b), for example, observes that evidence on the relationship between military spending and economic growth points to "retarding effects through inflation, diversion of investment, use of scarce materials, misuse of human capital." One econometric study found that every additional dollar spent on arms in the Third World reduced domestic investment by 25 cents and agricultural output by 20 cents (Klare, 1987: 1279–1280). For most developing countries, when military spending rises the rate of growth declines (Lipow, 1990; also Deger and Smith, 1983) and debt increases (Snider, 1991).

Despite this evidence, the guns-versus-growth issue remains controversial. "Previous research on the impact of military spending on the economy has produced disparate, inconsistent, and unstable results" (Chan, 1987). It has not established a strong correlation that holds for all countries. "The effects of military expenditure on the economy," conclude Ron P. Smith and George Georgiou (1983), "depend on the nature of the expenditure, the prevailing circumstances, and the concurrent government policies."

Even if a linkage cannot be shown to hold across all countries, there is reason to believe that the strain of military spending on economic growth may be especially severe in the most advanced industrial societies. Consider, for example, the data in Figure 11.4, which charts the level of military spending and manufacturing productivity among ten industrial powers. The data show unambiguously that the two are negatively correlated. That is, as military spending goes up, economic productivity declines. The contrast between Japan, on the one hand, and the Soviet Union, on the other, is especially striking. Indeed, excessive military spending was a primary cause of the Soviet Union's demise. "No other industrialized state in the world [had] for so long spent so much of its national wealth on armaments and military forces. Soviet militarism, in harness with communism, destroyed the Soviet economy and thus hastened the self-destruction of the Soviet Empire" (Iklé, 1991–1992: 28).

"The problem in defense spending," President Eisenhower observed in 1956, "is to figure how far you should go without destroying from within what you are trying to defend from without."[7] Paradoxically, the demise of the Soviet Union has added a new wrinkle to the question of the impact of defense spending on the economy. Now the concern is how "downsizing" military establishments geared toward Cold War competition will affect employment levels and research, development, and production opportunities in industries that provide for defense.[8] The goal is "bedeviled by two conflicting objectives: how to shift firms out of defense and into civilian pursuits, and how to preserve a mobilization base to meet conceivable future defense needs" (Adelman and Augustine, 1992). Even the absorption of large numbers of military personnel into the domestic economy has been a matter of concern on both sides of the one-time East-West divide. Just as there may be costs associated with excessive military spending, conversion to a much smaller, "peace-maintaining" military posture may also exact a domestic economic toll.

---

[7] The lingering costs of previous wars also exact a toll. For example, the ratio of U.S. funds spent fighting a war to the funds spent on that war's veterans' benefits are 1:3 (*Harper's*, May 1991, p. 17).

[8] See Renner (1990b) for an examination of some of the issues involved in the conversion of war-making capabilities to other priorities without causing social and economic dislocations. Paul Dunne and Ron Smith (1990) present evidence showing that "the fear that reductions in the share of military expenditures will be associated with higher average unemployment levels is misplaced." In addition, Murray Weidenbaum (1992), former Chairman of the President's Council of Economic Advisors, shows that in the United States military spending increases tend to be inflationary, but that following cuts in military spending we can expect a temporary rise in unemployment to be followed by a long-term growth in the economy.

**Military Expenditures and Productivity
1960-1988**

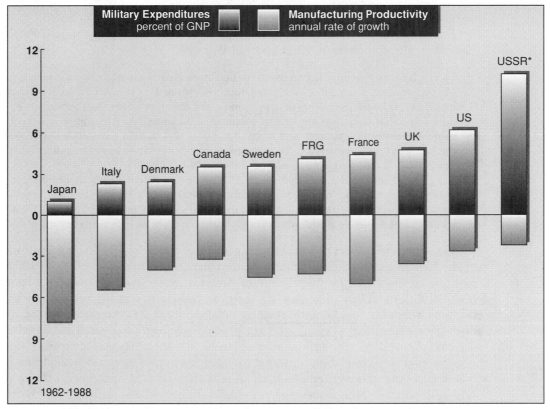

FIGURE 11.4 MILITARY EXPENDITURES AND PRODUCTIVITY IN THE ADVANCED INDUSTRIALIZED COUNTRIES, 1960–1988
Source: Adapted from Ruth Leger Sivard, *World Military and Source Expenditures 1991* (Washington, D.C.: World Priorities, 1991), p. 27

The end of the Cold War poses special problems for the United States, which now stands alone at the pinnacle of world power. What commitments and responsibilities should engage the United States now that the challenge of communist ideology and Soviet expansionism have dissipated? What resources, military and other, should the nation devote to those ends? Should the ends sought determine what resources are devoted to the task? Or should the level of available resources dictate the choice of commitments and responsibilities?

There are no easy answers to these questions, but even before the end of the Cold War many analysts worried that U.S. commitments exceeded the nation's ability to fulfill them. As noted in previous chapters, historian Paul Kennedy (1987) used the term "imperial overstretch" in his influential book *The Rise and Fall of the Great Powers* to symbolize concern about a growing imbalance between the ends and means of U.S.

foreign policy and the possibility that this imbalance parallels that which led to the fall of hegemonic powers in previous historical periods, notably the Spanish at the turn of the seventeenth century and the British at the turn of the twentieth.

Kennedy reiterated that concern in a response to his critics during the 1991 Persian Gulf War, the first crisis of the post–Cold War era:

> So much of the "decline" debate seems to be obsessed with where America is now. . . . My own concern is much more with the future, a decade or more down the road, if the trends in national indebtedness, low productivity increases, mediocre educational performance and decaying social fabric are allowed to continue at the same time that massive American commitments of men, money and material are made in different parts of the globe. Like the late Victorians, we seem to be discovering ever-newer "frontiers of insecurity" in the world that we, the number one power, feel impelled to guard.
>
> . . . It is no use claiming that America is completely different from those earlier great powers when we are imitating so many of their habits—possessing garrisons and bases and fleets in all parts of the globe and acting as the world's policeman on the one hand, running up debts and neglecting the country's internal needs on the other. (Kennedy, 1992: 345–346)

Even those who reject the thesis of "imperial overstretch" worry about the solvency of the United States. Political commentator Charles Krauthammer (1990–1991), for example, responds to the question "Can America long sustain its unipolar preeminence?" with the observation that "an American collapse to second-rank status will be not for foreign but for domestic reasons." Among them are "America's low savings rate, poor educational system, stagnant productivity, declining work habits, rising demand for welfare-state entitlements and new taste for ecological luxuries."

Others worry about the ability of the United States to compete in an environment where economic power is emerging as more potent than military power. Given the "rising importance of economic power in world affairs," Alan Tonelson (1991) writes, "indifferences to domestic decay" and "disregard for the home front [have] entailed enormous risks and costs" that arguably erode the ability of the United States to guarantee "its safety and well-being."

Maintaining a balance between military preparedness and economic revitalization is a challenge, however. Former U.S. Undersecretary for Defense Fred Charles Iklé (1991–1992) warns that thinking about future security problems and requirements (in the former Soviet Union as well as the United States) remains "heavily burdened by the Cold War legacy," which includes "old habits of the mind, reinforced by old bureaucratic practices."[9]

---

[9] *The New York Times* (February 17, 1992, pp. A1, A5) reported that "the Pentagon envisions seven scenarios for potential foreign conflicts that could draw United States forces into combat over the next 10 years." The seven scenarios are: (1) Iraq invades Kuwait and Saudi Arabia; (2) North Korea invades South Korea; (3) the Iraqi and North Korean invasions occur simultaneously; (4) Russia attacks Lithuania through Poland with help from Belarus; (5) a coup in the Philippines threatens U. S. citizens there; (6) a coup in Panama threatens access to the canal; and (7) a new expansionist superpower emerges. Many members of the U.S. Congress objected that some of the scenarios bordered on the preposterous, but there seemed to be widespread agreement that the Pentagon's exercise was part of its effort to maintain a large military establishment in the post–Cold War environment.

Among the "old habits of mind" influencing U.S. thinking about its foreign policy goals in the post–Cold War world are a continuation of "the policy of peace through nuclear strength" and maintenance of "the 'stability' of mutual deterrence" (Iklé, 1991–1992). The centrality of those ideas in U.S. and Soviet thinking about arms and influence during the Cold War deserves special attention.

STRATEGIC DOCTRINE DURING THE COLD WAR AND BEYOND . . . .

The dropping of the atomic bomb on Japan in August 1945 is the most important event distinguishing pre– from post–World War II international politics. In the blinding flash of a single weapon and the shadow of its mushroom cloud the international arena was transformed from a "balance-of-power" to a "balance-of-terror" system. In the decades that followed, policymakers in the nuclear states had to grapple with two central policy questions: Should they use nuclear weapons? and How can their use by others be prevented? The questions were especially pertinent to the United States and the Soviet Union, Cold War adversaries who were also the two most heavily armed nuclear powers.

Although the existence of weapons of mass destruction has been a constant since World War II, the United States and the Soviet Union adopted varying postures toward them. For analytical convenience, we can treat those postures in terms of two periods. The first began at the end of World War II and lasted until the Cuban missile crisis. U.S. nuclear superiority was the dominant characteristic of this period. The second began in 1962 and lasted until the breakup of the Soviet Union in 1991. Growing Soviet military capability was the dominant characteristic of this period, which meant that the United States no longer stood alone in its ability to annihilate another nation without fear of its own destruction.

A third phase in the posture of the nuclear powers toward nuclear weapons began in 1992, as the former Cold War antagonists began to restructure their forces and revise their doctrines to deter not each other's attack but other kinds of threats to their national security. We will examine the outlines of this new thinking later. First, however, we will examine the superpowers' strategic policies during the Cold War itself.

Coercive Diplomacy, 1945–1962

Nations that enjoy military superiority vis-à-vis their principal adversaries often think of weapons as instruments in diplomatic bargaining, that is, as tools for the political purpose of changing others' behavior. The United States, the world's first and, for many years, unchallenged nuclear power, is no exception. *Compellence* (Schelling, 1966) describes U.S. strategic doctrine when it enjoyed a clear-cut superiority in the nuclear balance of power. Compellence makes nuclear weapons instruments of influence, used not for fighting but to get others to do what they might not otherwise do. Thus it refers to the use of nuclear weapons as instruments of "coercive diplomacy" or "forceful persuasion" (George, 1992).

The United States sought during the Cold War to gain bargaining leverage by conveying the impression that it was actually willing to use nuclear weapons. The posture was especially evident during the Eisenhower administration in the 1950s. To win political victories for the United States, Secretary of State John Foster Dulles practiced *brinkmanship*, portraying a willingness, if necessary, to pursue U.S. objectives to the very brink of war by threatening U.S. adversaries with nuclear destruction.

Brinkmanship made sense only as long as the United States enjoyed a position of preponderant strength. It was part of the overall U.S. strategic posture known as *massive retaliation*, employed by the Eisenhower administration as the nuclear arm of the U.S. foreign policy goal of containing communism and Soviet expansionism. Massive retaliation was a *countervalue* posture because it targeted U.S. weapons on objects that the Soviets presumably valued most, their industrial and population centers. The alternative is a *counterforce* strategy, one that targets the enemy's military forces and weapons, thus sparing the general civilian population from immediate destruction.

Massive retaliation and brinkmanship heightened Soviet fears. The Soviet Union had earlier broken the U.S. atomic monopoly, but now, faced with U.S. belligerence, it pursued a twofold response. Following Nikita Khrushchev's assumption of power in the mid-1950s, the Soviets ceased speaking of the utility of military power. Instead, they promoted peaceful coexistence as an alternative means of doing battle with democratic capitalism. Yet, fearing that a nuclear exchange would destroy the Soviet Union but permit the survival of the United States, Soviet leaders also accelerated their efforts to augment their own nuclear capabilities. In 1957 the Soviet Union successfully launched the world's first space satellite *(Sputnik)*, demonstrating its potential ability to deliver nuclear weapons far beyond the Eurasian landmass. Thus the superpowers' strategic competition took a new turn, as the United States for the first time began to face a credible military threat to its own geophysical security.

Mutual Deterrence, 1962–1983

As U.S. strategic superiority eroded, policymakers in the United States began to question the assumption that they could actually use weapons of mass destruction as instruments of foreign policy. They recoiled in horror at the thought of the destruction that could result should compellence provoke a nuclear exchange. The nearly suicidal Cuban missile crisis of 1962 dealt coercive diplomacy a serious blow. Thereafter, the object of nuclear weapons shifted from their potential use toward reliance on strategic capabilities to prevent an attack. That is, strategic policy shifted from compellence to deterrence. In contrast to forceful persuasion, *deterrence* is a strategy designed to prevent an adversary from doing what it would otherwise do.

Both superpowers also pursued a posture of *extended deterrence*. The goal was to prevent an attack not only on oneself but also on one's allies. Thus, the superpowers sought to protect not only their homelands but also targets outside their adversary's own defense perimeter and alliance network.

Extended deterrence was especially critical to the United States, as its allies were far from its own shores and geographically proximate to the Soviet Union itself. Despite repeated U.S. assurances that it would defend its allies, however, the credibility of its guarantee to the NATO countries in particular was often questioned. Former U.S. Secretary of State Henry Kissinger punctuated the doubt when he noted (in 1979) that the promise to defend Europe, with nuclear weapons if necessary, involves "strategic assurances that we cannot possibly mean or if we do mean, we should not execute because if we should execute, we risk the destruction of civilization." The dubious credibility of the U.S. deterrent led some critics to advocate "decoupling" Europe from the U.S. strategic security umbrella and encouraging individual NATO countries to develop their own nuclear capability.

Ironically, the shift from compellence to deterrence stimulated, rather than inhibited, the U.S.-Soviet arms race. A deterrent strategy depends on the ability to deliver without question unacceptable damage on an opponent. It requires a *second-strike capability* that enables a country to withstand an initial strike by an adversary and still retain the ability to retaliate with a devastating second blow. Such a capability will assure a potential aggressor of destruction, thus deterring the contemplated preemptive attack. To ensure a second-strike capability and an adversary's awareness of it, deterrence rationalized an unrestrained search for sophisticated retaliatory capabilities. Any system that could be built was built, because, as President Kennedy explained in 1961, "only when arms are sufficient beyond doubt can we be certain without doubt that they will never be employed."

Mutual Assured Destruction

Policymakers coined the phrase *mutual assured destruction* (MAD) to characterize the strategic balance that emerged during the 1960s and early 1970s. The term accurately described the superpowers' essential military stalemate, for mutual deterrence, based on the principle of assured destruction, rested on the military potential for and psychological expectations of widespread death and destruction for both combatants in the event of a nuclear exchange. Peace—or at least stability—was the product of mutual vulnerability; if one attacked the other, it would do so at the price of its own destruction. Thus nuclear deterrence was "like a gun with two barrels, of which one points ahead and the other points back at the gun's holder. If a burglar should enter your house, it might make sense to threaten him with this gun, but it could never make sense to fire it" (Schell, 1984).

As the United States and the Soviet Union competed with each other, the differences in their strategic capabilities narrowed. By the early 1970s a kind of parity (equality) existed in the capabilities of the two superpowers, which solidified the strategic assumptions of MAD. Thereafter both armed, not to gain superiority but to preserve a rough equivalence in their strategic arsenals. Soviet Premier Leonid Brezhnev in 1978 declared the Soviets' belief that "approximate equilibrium and parity are enough for defense needs. We do not set ourselves the goal of gaining military superiority. We also know that this very concept loses its meaning with the present enormous stockpiles of nuclear weapons and systems for their delivery." Thus the superpowers tacitly "agreed to stop comparing their overall national power in terms of the size of their respective nuclear arsenals" (Hunter, 1988).

The balance in the superpowers' strategic arsenals laid the basis for negotiations on limiting strategic arms. Two SALT (Strategic Arms Limitations Talks) agreements were concluded during the détente phase of the U.S.-Soviet rivalry. Both attempted to guarantee each superpower's second-strike capacity, on which stable deterrence rested. Although the pursuit of this shared goal posed difficulties, a precarious peace resulted. Despite the superpowers' sometimes tacit, sometimes formal acceptance of the principles on which assured destruction rested, differences in their interpretation and practical application inevitably led to disagreements. Thus the strategic arms race continued into the 1980s. As it did, the concepts governing the competition began to revert from the principle of deterrence to the previous principle of compellence—which implied the actual utilization of nuclear weapons.

Nuclear Utilization Theory

Political relations between the superpowers deteriorated rapidly in the early 1980s, as confrontation replaced cooperation. A new debate about the role and purpose of nuclear weapons accompanied the change. Should nuclear weapons still be used exclusively for purposes of defense and deterrence? Or, assuming that a first-strike capability could be achieved, might they be used for offensive purposes?

Neither adversary had reason to trust the other. Each assumed that, unless deterred, its opponent would be tempted to use its arsenal for attack. Bad faith and "worst case" analyses governed the reformulation of doctrine.

From the Soviet perspective, U.S. statements about the practicability of preemptive strikes and the "winnability" of a nuclear exchange were alarming. U.S. leaders spoke boldly of *damage limitation*, predicated on the belief that one way to avoid the destructive effects of nuclear weapons was to be the first to use them to destroy a portion of the adversary's weapons so that they could not be used in a retaliatory strike.

As U.S.-Soviet relations worsened, debate in the United States about the best way to protect national security with strategic weapons divided into polar positions. MAD continued to dominate the thinking of some, but others advocated *nuclear utilization theory*, or a NUTs approach to the role of nuclear weapons. For the proponents of NUTs, nuclear weapons would not play simply a deterrent role; the United States could also use them in war. Such a posture was necessary, it was argued, because the Soviet Union was preparing to fight—and win—a nuclear war (Pipes, 1977; in contrast, see Holloway, 1983, and Kennan, 1984b). Furthermore, the advocates of NUTs argued that any use of nuclear weapons would not necessarily escalate to an unmanageable, all-out nuclear exchange. Instead, they reasoned that it was possible to fight a protracted nuclear war. By making nuclear weapons more usable, they argued, the United States could make nuclear threats more credible and hence lessen the chance that nuclear weapons would actually be used.

The proponents of MAD, on the other hand, held that deterrence remained the only sane purpose for nuclear weapons. Any use of nuclear weapons, they argued, however limited initially, would surely escalate to an unrestrained exchange. "It is inconceivable to me," former U.S. Secretary of Defense Robert McNamara reflected, "that limited nuclear wars would remain limited—any decision to use nuclear weapons would imply a high probability of the same cataclysmic consequences as a total nuclear exchange." According to this view, the technical requirements necessary to wage a protracted limited nuclear war would surely exceed the human capacity to control it.

Furthermore, the advocates of MAD felt that, because the threatened use of even tactical nuclear weapons would lower the nuclear threshold, a nuclear strategy premised on the usability of nuclear weapons in war in fact made war more likely, not less, and thereby diminished the weapons' deterrent capability. From this viewpoint, both superpowers were destined to live in a MAD world, even if, ironically, this meant they would remain bound in the "mutual hostage relationship" in which their earlier weapons decisions had imprisoned them (Keeny and Panofsky, 1981).

As the nuclear debate raged in the early 1980s, political leaders in the United States and the Soviet Union both professed their commitment to avoiding nuclear war because it was "unthinkable." This meant expanding the capabilities of both defensive and offensive systems. Accordingly, each superpower continued developing and deploying the kinds of weapons that NUTs required—so-called discriminating low-yield nuclear weapons made possible by new technologies in guidance and precision. These prepared the contestants for warfare short of a massive all-out nuclear attack and sought to provide them with effective deterrents against a conventional war.

Yet this search for new weapons and new ideas to govern their use did little to calm fears. Instead, a vigorous peace movement swept Europe and North America, as mass publics on both sides of the Atlantic expressed their desire for an alternative to the threat posed by nuclear weapons. Accordingly, the purposes that NUTs strategists assigned nuclear arsenals fell into disfavor. As the U.S. Commission on Integrated Long-Term Strategy (1988) concluded, keeping a limited war within bounds involved "a reckless gamble with fate."

From Offense to Defense, 1983–?

A new challenge to strategic thinking was launched in 1983, when U.S. President Reagan proposed building a space-based defensive shield against ballistic missiles.

The Strategic Defense Initiative (SDI), as it was known officially, called for the development of a "Star Wars" ballistic missile defense (BMD) system using advanced space-based technologies to destroy offensive weapons launched in fear, anger, or by accident. Reagan sought the development of technologies that would free the world from the threat of nuclear weapons by making them "impotent and obsolete." Thus the aim of the Strategic Defense Initiative was to shift U.S. nuclear strategy away from reliance on offensive missiles to deter attack—that is, away from dependence on mutual assured destruction, which President Reagan deemed "morally unacceptable."

Considerable uncertainty surrounded the ambitious goals of Star Wars from the start. Scientists doubted the feasibility of a technological fix to the security dilemma posed by strategic weapons. If nothing else, it would take decades to produce the required technologies but with no assurance that a reliable system was possible (see Slater and Goldfischer, 1988). Critics also warned that SDI was prohibitively expensive ($24 billion was spent by 1991, and at least another $100 billion in additional costs was projected [*The Defense Monitor*, Vol. 20, no. 5, 1991, p. 2]). They also thought it dangerous, for it could induce an unwarranted sense of safety when in fact it might not work. Worse still, they warned that SDI would stimulate development of a new generation of offensive weapons designed to overwhelm the defensive ones.

Despite this uncertainty, the United States continued to support SDI even after the end of the Cold War and the demise of the Soviet Union. In the view of the Bush administration, SDI still had a mission in the post–Cold War world. Rather than deter a massive Soviet missile attack on the United States, SDI was now needed to protect the United States against limited missile strikes by lesser powers. SDI, President Bush asserted, could defend against "attacks from the many countries that, regrettably, are acquiring ballistic missile capabilities. In the 1990s strategic defense makes much more sense than ever before."

This rationale reaffirmed the conviction that mutual assured destruction could not provide an adequate defense against missile attacks. SDI was better, Bush claimed, because it could provide "protection from limited ballistic missile assaults, whatever their source," rather than relying on "some abstract theory of deterrence" (Barnes, 1991). Yet questions remain. The Pentagon, for example, still "generally looks askance at SDI" because of the enormous costs, uncertain technological reliability, and the inability of a space-based system to protect against the many other ways that an enemy can deliver tactical weapons (Barnes, 1991) including "short-range missiles or intermediate-range ballistic missiles that fly slightly depressed trajectories" (Fetter, 1991).

The New Strategic Balance

Even as the United States pursued its own strategic defense posture, it continued policies designed to limit arms competition with the Soviet Union and its successor, the Commonwealth of Independent States, as MAD remained a central strategic concept.

Mikhail Gorbachev assumed power in the Soviet Union in 1985, not long after Reagan's Star Wars speech. In subsequent years the superpowers negotiated a series of dramatic new arms control agreements (see Chapter 13). Reduced fears of an attack in Europe stripped away the rationale for tactical weapons. The precedent-setting Intermediate-range Nuclear Forces (INF) treaty, followed by the Conventional Armed Forces in Europe (CFE), and then the Strategic Arms Reduction Treaty (START), hastened the reduced sense of fear.

The consequences of the START agreement for the strategic arsenals of the United

States and the former Soviet Union are depicted in Figure 11.5 on page 426. Later disarmament initiatives by the United States and Russia promised to cut their arsenals even further. Particularly noteworthy was the agreement reached in 1992 in which the two nuclear powers pledged to drastically reduce their offensive capabilities by the year 2003. If this and other "deep cuts" occur, the geostrategic landscape at the turn of the twenty-first century will look radically different. In turn, this would require rethinking old assumptions underlying strategic doctrines.

U.S.-Soviet Strategic Competition: Retrospect and Prospect

The history of the superpowers' military competition reveals several patterns. It suggests that mutual fears feed arms races; that states believe that arms strengthen national security; that each partner to the arms competition is extraordinarily sensitive to the other's advances in military capabilities; and that technological advances can undermine the fragile military balance by making one partner vulnerable to attack by the other.

Mutual assured destruction also showed how perceptions, not military hardware, technology, and destructive capabilities, often matter most. As the U.S. Commission on Long-Term Strategy (1988) observed, "Deterrence is not an abstract notion amenable to simple quantification. . . . Deterrence is a set of beliefs in the minds of . . . leaders, given their own values and attitudes, about capabilities and will."

The United States and the Soviet Union also demonstrated other proclivities. One was the tendency to pursue an arms race and arms control simultaneously. Another was the search for peace while preparing for war. And a third was the inclination to regard the price of national security as never too high.

The assumptions underlying the superpowers' quest for national security shaped their decisions about force postures and doctrines. In much the same way that reciprocity characterized their diplomatic and political interactions, their strategic systems grew increasingly alike as each superpower stimulated—and simulated—the other's nuclear weapons development (Holloway, 1983).

Box 11.2 on page 427 documents this convergence, tracing the dynamics of the competition during the Cold War. Note how the strategic choices of one superpower predicted the choices of the other. Every weapons procurement initiative by one side stimulated a compensatory response by the other. As a result, the superpowers' strategic capabilities converged. There is an element of irony here, for this action-and-reaction strategic competition created similar threats to both superpowers' survival. Each became a victim of the strategic security dilemma, as "nuclear weapons . . . brought the superpowers both great security and enormous insecurity" (Jervis, 1986).

The prospect of a U.S.-Russian alliance raised by the 1992 Camp David Declaration on New Relations transforms the defense requirements of both states. In "a new era," in which "Russia and the United States do not regard each other as potential adversaries," the purpose of the two great powers' remaining arsenals is no longer the

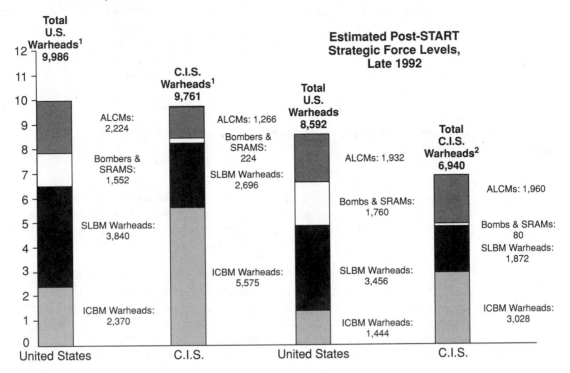

Figure 11.5 U.S. and C.I.S. Strategic Forces, March 1992, and Estimation for Late 1992 under START
Source: The Arms Control Association, *Fact Sheet*, December 1991, and March 1992 (Washington, D.C.: The Arms Control Association).

Note: ALCM = air-launched cruise missiles; SRAM = short-range attack missiles; START = Strategic Arms Reduction Talks.

[1] The current total warhead figures for the United States and the C.I.S. do not reflect the unilateral reductions announced by Presidents Bush and Gorbachev on September 27, 1991 and October 5, 1991, respectively.
[2] The estimated C.I.S. total warhead figure does not take into account President Gorbachev's announcement that the C.I.S. would unilaterally reduce its accountable warhead number under START to 5,000.

Box 11.2
CONVERGENCE IN THE SUPERPOWERS' WEAPONS SYSTEMS:
A CHRONOLOGY OF RECIPROCAL DEVELOPMENTS

• • •

ACTION ⇌ REACTION

IN THE SUPERPOWER COMPETITION

Conventional Weapons

USSR **1949**	main battle tank	**1952** U.S.
U.S. **1955**	nuclear-powered submarine	**1958** USSR
U.S. **1955**	large-deck aircraft carrier	**1975** USSR
USSR **1955**	wire-guided anti-tank missile	**1972** U.S.
U.S. **1959**	photo reconnaissance satellite	**1962** USSR
U.S. **1960**	supersonic bomber	**1975** USSR
U.S. **1960**	computer-guided missile	**1968** USSR
U.S. **1961**	nuclear-powered aircraft carrier	**1992** USSR
USSR **1961**	surface-to-air missile	**1963** U.S.
U.S. **1962**	long-range fighter bomber	**1973** USSR
U.S. **1964**	air-to-surface missile	**1968** USSR
USSR **1970**	high-speed attack submarine	**1976** U.S.
U.S. **1972**	television-guided missile	**1987** USSR
USSR **1972**	heavy attack helicopter	**1982** U.S.
U.S. **1975**	jet-propelled combat aircraft	**1983** USSR
U.S. **1976**	large amphibious assault ship	**1978** USSR
USSR **1978**	multiple-launch rocket system	**1983** U.S.
U.S. **1987**	binary (chemical) weapons	**199?** USSR

Nuclear Weapons

U.S. **1945**	atomic bomb	**1949** USSR
U.S. **1946**	electronic computer	**1951** USSR
U.S. **1948**	intercontinental bomber	**1955** USSR
U.S. **1952**	thermonuclear bomb	**1953** USSR
USSR **1957**	intercontinental ballistic missile (ICBM)	**1958** U.S.
USSR **1957**	man-made satellite	**1958** U.S.
USSR **1958**	early-warning radar	**1960** U.S.
U.S. **1960**	submarine-launched ballistic missile (SLBM)	**1968** USSR
U.S. **1966**	multiple warhead (MRV)	**1968** USSR
USSR **1968**	anti-ballistic missile (ABM)	**1972** U.S.
U.S. **1970**	multiple independently-targeted warhead (MIRV)	**1975** USSR
USSR **1971**	sea-launched cruise missile	**1982** U.S.

U.S. **1983**	neutron bomb	**199?** USSR
U.S. **1985**	new strategic bomber	**1987** USSR
USSR **1987**	single warhead, mobile ICBM	**1992** U.S.
U.S. **1990?**	stealth bomber	**199?** USSR

Source: Ruth Leger Sivard, *World Military and Social Expenditures 1987–88* (Washington, D.C.: World Priorities, 1987), p. 14.

same. As U.S. Secretary of Defense Richard Cheney wrote in 1991, "the threat of a short-warning, global war starting in Europe is now less likely than at any time in the last 45 years."

Without their threat to each other, deterrence no longer requires an ability to prevent massive destruction. Instead, deterrence shifts to combating other types of attack. In this context, it is apparent that agreements to cut strategic and tactical nuclear stockpiles serve the interests of both the United States and Russia.

DETERRENCE AFTER THE COLD WAR

The Cold War, the third global conflict of the twentieth century, concluded without bloodshed. To some, this remarkable achievement was attributable to the efficacy of the superpowers' deterrence strategies—the intimidating power of their weapons that made aggression suicidal, and the rationality of leaders inspired by their awareness that survival was preferable to victory. To others, the superpowers averted apocalypse despite their awesome arsenals and deterrence doctrines, not because of them (see Johansen, 1991; Vasquez, 1991). Thus, like the causes of the onset and end of the Cold War, the explanations of the long superpower peace will doubtless puzzle historians for decades.

Regardless of its causes, the end of the Cold War and the collapse of the Soviet Union have altered dramatically the strategic environment and perceptions of the threats to national security (see Box 11.3).

Few expect a war between the great powers in the foreseeable future. Most expect wars to continue in the Third World, however, and perhaps in the (re)developing countries in eastern Europe and the Commonwealth of Independent States. To deal with the threat to world order presented by this raging disorder, the great powers in 1992 sought to restructure their armed forces to deal with the kinds of threats and weapons with which adversaries will fight such wars. This calls for further reducing nuclear (strategic) arsenals, helping the former Soviet republics destroy their nuclear weapons, and keeping them out of the wrong hands.

It also calls for increasing the capacity to wage conventional wars in emergent trouble spots. Military preparations have not ceased. Instead, there is a redirection toward the conduct of short-term wars fought with increasingly sophisticated conventional weapons. The emerging strategies of the great powers reflect the shift in emphasis from superpower conflict toward containment of regional conflicts.

Box 11.3
Redefining the Post–Cold War Security Environment of the United States

• • •

Old World	New World
U.S. Perceptions	
Soviet military power	Spread of nuclear weapons
	Terrorism
	Regional thugs
	Drug traffickers
Deliberate Soviet attack	Instability in the former Soviet republics
Economic power assumed	Japanese economic power
High defense budgets	Declining defense budgets
Global security concerns paramount	Domestic security concerns paramount
Geopolitical Context	
Bipolar rigidity	Multipolar complexity
Predictable	Uncertain
Communism	Nationalism/religious extremists
U.S. dominant Western power	U.S. militarily no. 1, not economically
Fixed alliances	Ad hoc coalitions
"Good guys and bad guys"	"Gray guys"
UN paralyzed	UN viable
The Threat	
Single (Soviet)	Diverse
Survival at stake	Interests/Americans at stake
Known	Unknown
Deterrable	Nondeterrable
Strategic use of nukes	Terroristic use of nukes
Overt	Covert
Europe-centered	Regional, ill-defined
High risk of escalation	Little risk of escalation
Military Forces	
Attrition warfare	Decisive attacks on key nodes
War by proxy	Direct involvement
High tech dominant	High-medium-low tech mix
Forward-deployed	Power projection
Forward-based	U.S.-based
Host-nation support	Self-reliant

Source: Rep. Les Aspin, "National Security in the 1990s: Defining a New Basis for U.S. Military Forces," Address before the Atlantic Council of the United States, January 6, 1992, p. 21.

U.S. Strategy in the New World Order

The Persian Gulf War was a learning experience, a "defining event in the new post–Cold War world," in the words of U.S. Secretary of Defense Dick Cheney. It revealed the outlines of a reconstructed post–Cold War U.S. strategy. As Cheney put it, "The fact is that we . . . faced in the Persian Gulf . . . exactly the kind of situation that we had been focusing on as we developed a strategy and the adjustments to the new world situation that we are now facing."

Even as the United States debated strategies and force structures for the new world order, continuities with the past were apparent. The United States rededicated itself to the role of world policeman (see Tunander, 1991).[10] President Bush explained in March 1992 that in the new world order "the United States has a burden to bear. . . . We are the leaders and we must continue to lead" to keep the dangers of disorder at bay. This would require military might; as the president put it, "America must possess forces able to respond to threats in whatever corner of the globe they may occur. . . . U.S. interests can be protected only with a capability which is in existence and which is ready to act without delay."

The new U.S. strategy for the next century reveals several properties.

- It moves U.S. strategy from preparing for a war with the Soviet Union and the use of nuclear weapons to preparing for wars that do not threaten the use of these weapons.

- It accepts the vision of a nuclear-free Europe. The Bush administration's cancellation of its previous commitment to develop a new short-range nuclear-tipped missile to defend Europe helps realize the vision.

- It will rely on force. "There will be no gradualism, no restraint on firepower" (Klare, 1991). U.S. plans call for short, decisive wars. As President Bush put it, the United States would not fight any more Vietnams: "If one American soldier has to go into battle, that soldier will have enough force behind him to win, and then get out as soon as possible."

- It will mobilize a balanced force structure "to meet any challenge that might emerge." These range from short, small engagements to prolonged, large-scale deployments. It would "keep a large standing military establishment and rely less on rapid mobilization than during the interwar period, although more than it did during the Cold War. . . . The basic elements of American deployment would remain unchanged" (Cohen, 1991).

- It will use modern conventional (non-nuclear) weapons for strategic purposes "to achieve air superiority in a combat theater and then to exploit that superiority

[10] Critics of the Pentagon's proposed post–Cold War strategy revealed in early 1992 (see footnote 9) focused attention on proposal's advocacy of "the perpetuation of a one-superpower world in which the United States would work to prevent the rise of any 'competitors' to its primacy in Western Europe and East Asia." In the face of that criticism, a revision of that planning document sharpened "the American commitment to collective military action" (Tyler, 1992).

to . . . destroy the adversary's capability to sustain its war effort" (Nitze, 1991).

- It calls for a rearmament to conduct what Pentagon officials call "mid-intensity conflict" (MIC). To deal with the perceived emerging threat presented by the rise of Third World powers such as Iraq, the U.S. will fund the development of a plethora of new weapons. "The MIC posture," observes Michael Klare (1991), "carries profound dangers for the United States. This country will have to maintain a mammoth military establishment, keep military budgets at peak Cold War levels, and eliminate hope that a significant 'peace dividend' can be garnered from the Cold War's end."

These anticipated changes and continuities preserve deterrence as the cornerstone of a revised post–Cold War U.S. strategy. The enemy changes. New threats are identified, and powerful conventional weapons will meet and deter them. But the purpose remains the same: deterring the aggression not of another great power but of militarized Third World powers. This strategy would also preserve a global policeman role for the United States. As General Colin Powell summarized in 1991, "we no longer have the luxury of having a threat to plan for. What we plan for is that we are a superpower. We are the major player on the world stage with responsibilities around the world, with interests around the world."

Russian Strategy in the New World Order

For Russia, the purpose of weapons looks much different. The primary threat with which the newly independent Russia and the independent republics associated with it must deal is internal, not external. The greatest threat is not an external attack, it is the threat of civil violence. The possibility of escalation to violence *between* the independent republics of the commonwealth is also a present danger.

Russian strategic planning must confront several tasks. First, it must ensure control over the panoply of nuclear weapons. This requires managing the military establishment, preventing internal differences within the officer corps and between it and enlisted soldiers, institutionalizing civilian authority over the armed forces, and preserving command of the nuclear warheads based outside the Russian republic (pending their possible removal altogether). Second, Russia must assure that no foreign actor will attack it or intervene militarily to restore order. Third, Russia must cement the commonwealth into an integrated confederation that can deter attack by the neighbors on its borders. In this regard China, India, the Muslim countries to the south, and Germany present potential, if unknown, threats.

The direction that Russian strategy will take to confront these national security challenges is far from certain. Most likely is that Russian leaders will restructure their forces and strategies to prepare for the mid-level violence that is now most probable. They will not continue to invest what remains of their scarce resources in preparations to deter (or fight) a nuclear war.

What, then, are the probable revisions in Russian strategy and force structures?

First, like the United States, Russian leaders will seek to keep the Russian arsenal "formidable" (Raphael, 1991). As former Soviet Foreign Minister Alexander Bessmertnykh pledged in January 1992, "Russia will remain a great power. It may not be a superpower, but it will be a great military power and part of the global strategic balance." "Russia will be the continuation of the Soviet Union in the field of nuclear weapons" was the way Russian Foreign Minister Andrei Kozyrev phrased this goal.

Second, Russian force reconstruction will seek to produce "a more efficient military, but one that is less threatening to the world." Russia fears wars among its neighbors, along its borders, and even on the territory of the Commonwealth of Independent States. "Having emerged from the Cold War," lamented Russian strategist Sergei Karaganov in February 1992, "we now face the prospect of hot war and even several hot wars. All our efforts in diplomacy and defense should be concentrated on avoiding those wars. What were nasty little domestic disputes are now international with the independence of all the former Soviet republics." For this, an overpowering, intimidating strategic arsenal is not needed.

This Russian strategy is likely to focus on the proliferation of weapons of mass destruction, and to place special emphasis on preserving Russian command of existing nuclear weapons and preventing the loss of their control to the three other commonwealth republics while they remain deployed. Their use against Russia must be deterred. For this we can expect a shift from strategic to tactical weapons.

Fourth, Russian military planners

> have also paid close attention to the lessons of the Gulf War, particularly because of their persistent past shortcomings in both the strategic and tactical fields. They are applying these lessons even now to a basic revision of their strategic ideas and to their air doctrine. . . . They emphasize the use of advanced non-nuclear weapons throughout the depth of the opponent's military deployment and against all critical means of sustaining the war effort. In fact, they assert that such weapons are capable of accomplishing all of the missions previously reserved for strategic nuclear forces. (Nitze, 1991: A6)

This reconstruction meets the pressing Russian need to reduce spending on defense. It calls for a new security strategy that resembles the new thinking in U.S. strategy. Some dimensions of Russian strategy are radically different, however. The end of the Cold War ended Russia's perception of a threat from the West. Today, Russian leaders look to the West for support and friendship and no longer see the United States as an enemy. They no longer see arming against it as necessary. As Russian strategist Andrey Kokoshin (1992) put it, "The huge military potential of the two superpowers plays repeatedly against their long-term interests." To rectify this, Russia has begun to disarm its strategic arsenal, and has asked to join NATO. The military "has shown that they reciprocate" the eagerness of U.S. military leaders "to develop cordial and cooperative relations with their [Russian] counter-parts; to speak to them 'as a friend—no longer as an enemy,' as General Colin Powell . . . told a group of visiting Soviet officers" (Iklé, 1991–1992).

Times have indeed changed. It is now possible to envision formation of a "Russian-American Defense Community." "America's and Russia's armed forces have never fought a war against each other; they fought together as allies in two world wars." Thus "the day has come," asserts defense analyst Fred Charles Iklé (1991–1992), for Russia and the United States "to work together as comrades in arms for the sake of both their nations and the world at large."

ESCAPING THE SECURITY DILEMMA? . . . .

The search for national security through preparation for war continues. The quest is understandable in a world where states alone remain responsible for their own self-defense. As President Eisenhower once noted, "until war is eliminated from international relations, unpreparedness for it is well nigh as criminal as war itself." Hence the security dilemma persists.

The fears engendered by visions of national vulnerability also explain why defense planners base their plans on "worst-case" analyses of others' capabilities and intentions. The urge to arm is further stimulated by the ubiquitous influence of defense planners in the policy-making process of most countries and the tendency of political leaders to adopt the vocabulary and concepts of their military advisers.

Asking whether military preparedness risks rather than increases national security raises an uncomfortable question. It challenges the orthodox approach to national security prevalent throughout much of the world's history. Yet questioning is required. Many experts today recommend redefining national security (for example, Sorensen, 1990; Allison and Treverton, 1992) (see Box 11.4, page 434). To their way of thinking, reconceptualization is needed to answer the ultimate questions—Can the world escape the security dilemma and can it remove its vulnerability to annihilation? Less apocalyptically, how can new conceptions of national security gain acceptance? Some believe that in the twenty-first century we should define "security" broadly to include all threats to national survival, both military and nonmilitary. If this is so, the dangers posed by the erosion of states' economic and ecological well-being must receive greater attention.

If the pursuit of military might does, indeed, lead to a decrease in national and global security, how then can states escape this dilemma and free themselves from the prospect of destruction?

The security dilemma grants little room for maneuvering. The world has yet to accept "common security" and "nonoffensive defense," strategies that would eliminate offensive capabilities (Møller, 1992). States still build weapons of attack for deterrence, even though conventional deterrence has failed frequently in the past (Huth, 1988; Mearsheimer, 1983). Moreover, deterrence remains an uncertain theory based on a peculiar, almost illogical premise that requires the continuing vulnerability of all states. Despite this, most believe that the threat system must be preserved to counter the threat. Thus security may depend as much on the control of force as on its pursuit. As H. G. Wells long ago prophesied it would, human destiny may be becoming more and more a race between self-restraint and survival.

Box 11.4
Redefining "Security" in the "New World Order"

• • •

The concept of "security" must include protection against all major threats to human survival and well-being, not just military threats. Until now, "security"—usually addressed as "national security"—has meant the maintenance of strong military defenses against enemy invasion and attack. This approach may have served us well in the past, when such attack was seen as the only real threat to national survival; today, however, when airborne poisons released by nuclear and chemical accidents can produce widespread death and sickness (as occurred with the Bhopal and Chernobyl disasters), and when global epidemiological and environmental hazards such as AIDS and the "greenhouse effect" can jeopardize the well-being of the entire planet, this perspective appears increasingly obsolete. As individual economies become ever more enmeshed in the world economy, moreover, every society becomes more vulnerable to a global economic crisis. And, as modern telecommunications bring us all closer together, we are made acutely aware of the pain and suffering of those living under oppression, tyranny, and injustice.

Given the fact that our individual security and well-being will depend to an ever-increasing extent on the world's success in mastering complex political, economic, environmental, and epidemiological problems, we must redefine "security" to embrace all of those efforts taken to enhance the long-term health and welfare of the human family. Defense against military aggression will obviously remain a vital component of security, but it must be joined by defenses against severe environmental degradation, worldwide economic crisis, and massive human suffering. Only by approaching the security dilemma from this multifaceted perspective can we develop the strategies and instruments that will be needed to promote global health and stability.

Given the multiplicity of pressing world hazards, the concept of "national security" must be integrated with that of "world security." Until now, most people have tended to rely on the nation-state to provide protection against external threats, and have viewed their own nation's security as being conversely affected by the acquisition of power and wealth by other nations. Thus, in the interests of "national security," nation-states have often engaged in a competitive struggle to enhance their own economic and military strength at the expense of other nations' capabilities. This us-versus-them, zero-sum competition for security is naturally biased toward unilateral solutions to critical problems, frequently entailing military and/or economic coercion. In today's interdependent world, however, the quest for security is rapidly becoming a *positive-sum* process, whereby national well-being is achieved jointly by all countries—or not at all.

Source: Michael T. Klare and Daniel C. Thomas, *World Security: Trends and Challenges at Century's End* (New York: St. Martin's Press, 1991), p. 3.

SUGGESTED READINGS

Allison, Graham, and Gregory F. Treverton, eds. *Rethinking America's Security: Beyond Cold War to New World Order*. New York: W. W. Norton, 1992.

Baldwin, David A. *Paradoxes of Power*. New York: Basil Blackwell, 1989.

Booth, Ken., ed. *New Thinking About Strategy and International Security*. London: Unwin Hyman Academic, 1991.

Friedberg, Aaron L. "The Changing Relationship Between Economics and National Security," *Political Science Quarterly* 106 (Summer, 1991): 265–276.

Kapstein, Ethan Barnaby. *The Political Economy of National Security: A Global Perspective*. New York: McGraw-Hill, 1992.

Karp, Regina Cowen, ed. *Security with Nuclear Weapons? Different Perceptions of National Security*. New York: Oxford University Press, 1991.

Kegley, Charles W., Jr., and Eugene R. Wittkopf, eds. *The Nuclear Reader: Strategy, Weapons, War*, 2nd ed. New York: St. Martin's Press, 1989.

Klare, Michael T., and Daniel C. Thomas, eds. *World Security: Trends and Challenges at Century's End*. New York: St. Martin's Press, 1991.

Prestowitz, Clyde V., Jr., Ronald A. Morse, and Alan Tonelson, eds. *Powernomics: Economics and Strategy After the Cold War*. Lanham, Md.: Madison Books, 1991.

Sullivan, Michael P. *Power in Contemporary International Politics*. Columbia: University of South Carolina Press, 1990.

Tarr, David W. *Nuclear Deterrence and International Security: Alternative Nuclear Regimes*. New York: Longman, 1991.

Weidenbaum, Murray. *Small Wars, Big Defense: Paying for the Military After the Cold War*. New York: Oxford University Press, 1992.

CHAPTER 12

• • •

RESORT TO FORCE: ARMED CONFLICT AND VIOLENCE IN WORLD POLITICS

• • •

Only the dead have seen the end of conflict.

George Bush, U.S. President, 1992

Mankind must put an end to war or war will put an end to mankind.

John F. Kennedy, U.S. President, 1961

Every day, newspapers and television report that human activity revolves around the use of force to settle disputes. Since 1945 not a single day has gone by without war (Sivard, 1991). It is little wonder so many people equate world politics with violence.

In *On War*, the Russian strategist Karl von Clausewitz advanced his famous dictum that war is merely an extension of diplomacy by other means. This insight underscores the fact that war is an instrument states use to resolve their conflicts. It is also the deadliest instrument. War's onset means that persuasion and negotiations have been unsuccessful. War is, in this sense, as Clausewitz stated, "a form of communication between nations," albeit an extreme form.

This definition pictures war as the use of military force against an adversary to achieve political goals, as distinct from conflict.[1] With this distinction in mind, this chapter examines five ways that force is used in world politics: wars between states (and their causes), crises involving "coercive diplomacy," "low-intensity conflict," civil wars, and terrorism.

THE FREQUENCY OF WAR . . . .

To trace changes in the frequency and character of war between states, we will break the state system since 1815 into five historical periods, with 1848, 1881, 1914, and

---

[1] *War* and *conflict* are different. Conflict occurs when two parties perceive differences between them and seek to resolve those differences to their own satisfaction. Conflict is an intrinsic product of communication and contact. Because when people interact some conflict is inevitable, we should not regard conflict as abnormal. Paradoxically, close contact leads to both friendship and enmity: Cooperation may produce conflict, and conflict may promote cooperation (Coser, 1956). Nor should we regard conflict as altogether undesirable. Conflict promotes social solidarity, clarifies values, stimulates creative thinking, and encourages learning. If managed properly, these functions are constructive to human progress.

• • •

TABLE 12.1 FREQUENCY WITH WHICH
181 WARS HAVE BEGUN OVER FIVE
HISTORICAL PERIODS, 1816–1988

Period	No. of Wars	Average No. of States in the International System
1816–1848	33	28
1849–1881	43	39
1882–1914	38	40
1915–1944	24	59
1945–1988	43	117

Source: Data provided courtesy of the Correlates of War Project at the University of Michigan under the direction of J. David Singer and Melvin Small, as retrieved and aggregated by Ricardo Rodriguez.

1945 demarcating the significant "turning points" scholars conventionally regard as major transition points in contemporary history (with a sixth, that following the end of the Cold War in 1991, too recent for the purpose of monitoring the amount of war). Table 12.1 summarizes the data that speak to comparisons across these five successive periods.

This evidence measures only sustained wars *between* sovereign states resulting in at least one thousand battle deaths (see Small and Singer, 1982). Measured in this restricted way, the data show that 181 interstate wars erupted between 1816 and 1988, but that the frequency has been fairly stable over time.[2] Furthermore, if we take the expanding number of countries in the system into account, the frequency of the outbreak of wars since 1816 "actually declines from 4 per state per decade prior to World War II to 2 per state per decade since. And if we control not for the number of states but the number of *pairs*, the decline appears even more dramatic" (Singer, 1991: 57). Thus, when we adjust for the increasing number of nations, the post–World War II era has been comparatively more peaceful than were the periods that preceded it.

Or has it? A different picture emerges when attention focuses on the number of wars *under way*, rather than on the number of wars that start. Interstate war has been

---

[2] Estimates of the amount of war depend on the criteria used to define war. Quincy Wright (1942) identified 278 wars from 1480 to 1940; Lewis Fry Richardson (1960b) over 300 from 1820 to 1949; Pitirim Sorokin (1937) 862 from 1100 to 1925; William Eckhardt (1990, 1991) 589 from 1500 to 1990; and R. Paul Shaw and Yuwa Wong (1989: 3) 14,500 over the last 5,600 years, with peace comprising "only 8 percent of the entire recorded history of mankind."

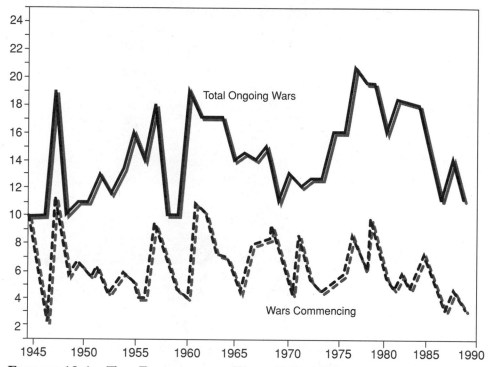

FIGURE 12.1 THE FREQUENCY OF WAR, 1945–1988
Source: Adapted from evidence summarized in Herbert K. Tillema, *International Armed Conflict since 1945* (Boulder, Colo.: Westview, 1991).

under way almost continuously over the past 175 years. Although there were eighty-two years between 1816 and 1988 in which no wars began, there were only twenty in which none was under way (Small and Singer, 1982: 149; Singer, 1991: 60–75). The so-called "outbreak of peace" in 1991 is no exception, for at the start of that year "40 or more countries [had] forces engaged in wars" (Sivard, 1991: 12).

Let us look at the period since 1945 more closely. Defined broadly to include all occasions in which one or more states undertook overt military actions beyond their borders, we observe 269 such incidents between September 1945 through the end of 1988 (Tillema, 1991). Thus, the number of wars commencing and under way world-wide has remained high. Figure 12.1 portrays the pattern for the nuclear era punctuated by Cold War confrontation.

THE NATURE OF WAR

War has been recurrent in history, but its character has changed markedly in the twentieth century. The reason is found in the nature of modern weapons.

The Destructiveness of War

One of the most disquieting long-term global trends is the exponential increase in the destructiveness of war, as measured by the loss of human life.

[Since 1500, the world] has lived through 589 wars and lost 141,901,000 lives to them. . . . Beginning with the 17th, every century has registered an increase in the number of wars and in the number of deaths associated with them. The rise in war deaths has far outstripped the rise in population. The 20th century in particular has been a stand-out in the history of warfare. Wars now are shockingly more destructive and deadly. So far, in the 90 years of this century, there have been over four times as many war deaths as in the 400 years preceding. (Sivard, 1991: 20)

Since 1945 all wars either have been between Third World countries or entailed military intervention of the great powers in them; none has occurred *between* the great powers. This is why scholars term the post-1945 period the "long postwar peace" (Gaddis, 1991a). Still, the fact that, without exception, all wars have erupted in the Third World does not mean that war has ceased to be destructive and bloody. "The pattern is tragically unambiguous." Since 1945 18.2 million fatalities can be attributed to wars, "virtually all . . . suffered outside the central system of major powers" (Singer, 1991: 59).

New, more destructive but nondiscriminating weapons and aerial bombardment have increasingly made noncombatants and civilians wars' main victims. "In this century many more unarmed civilians than professional soldiers have died in wars. In the decade of the 1980s, the proportion of civilian deaths jumped to 74 percent of the total and in 1990 it appears to have been close to 90 percent. The 16 wars that were going on in 1990 . . . killed 2,632,000 civilians" (Sivard, 1991: 20, 26).

Nuclear weapons create new dangers that threaten to worsen this trend beyond imagination. Described in Chapter 11, today's nuclear weapons are far more destructive than those used against Japan during World War II. The U.S. National Security Council estimated in the late 1970s that a superpower exchange at that time would have killed nine times as many Americans and Soviets, not counting the ravaging effects of radiation, as the number who died in all their previous wars (*The Defense Monitor*, February 1979, p. 8). The effects of a "limited" war with today's nuclear arms would not be limited. Studies of the immediate and delayed effects of nuclear war (see Sagan and Turco, 1990; also Bunge, 1988) picture a postnuclear environment repugnant to contemplate (see Box 12.1, on page 440). Life as we know it could cease.

The increasing destructiveness of modern weapons has transformed the character of contemporary warfare in other ways. The length of interstate wars steadily increased between 1816 and World War II, for example, but then began a drastic decline. Wars since 1945 have simply been shorter. Similarly, the average number of nations participating in major wars (which had been rising steadily since 1815) has fallen sharply since World War II (Singer, 1991).

Wars are also more confined geographically and usually involve small countries: Since 1945 about 75 percent of wars have been between minor states (Singer, 1991: 59; also Holsti, 1988: 399). Hence, major wars have ceased to occur, but the number

Box 12.1
Two Views of the Aftermath of a Nuclear Attack

• • •

A Physician's View

A 20-megaton nuclear bomb . . . would create a fireball 1½ miles in diameter, with temperatures of 20 million to 30 million degrees Fahrenheit. . . . All living things would be vaporized within a radius of "ground zero." Six miles from this point, all persons would be instantly killed by a huge silent heat flash traveling at the speed of light. . . . Within a 10-mile radius, the blast wave would slow to 180 mph. In that area, winds and fires would probably kill 50 percent of the population, and injure another 40 percent. . . . Within 20 miles of the center, 50 percent of the inhabitants would be killed or injured by the thermal radiation and blast pressures, and tens of thousands would suffer severe burn injuries. . . . Medical "disaster planning" for a nuclear war is meaningless.[a]

An Astronomer's View

A nuclear war, even a fairly modest one, now seems likely to trigger a period of hemispheric, and possibly global, subfreezing cold and dark that would have catastrophic consequences for our planetary civilization and perhaps for our species. The cause would be absorption of sunlight at altitude by dust from high yield ground bursts and, particularly, by soot from the burning of cities and forests. . . . This effect [has been called] Nuclear Winter. . . . A quite "small" nuclear war, involving 1,000 weapons, each of 100-kiloton yield, all exploded over cities, could produce virtually the full Nuclear Winter effects. . . . Vast numbers of survivors would soon starve to death.[b]

[a] *International Physicians for the Prevention of Nuclear War, "The Medical Consequences of Nuclear War," as reported by the Associated Press, March 8, 1980.*
[b] *Carl Sagan, from the* Wall Street Journal, *February 16, 1984, p. 35, and "Nuclear War and Climatic Catastrophe,"* Foreign Affairs 62 (Winter 1983–1984): 271.

of smaller ones has increased. This reverses the historic pattern that characterized the previous century, when war between the major powers was comparatively frequent and took a large toll in human lives.

Weapons and the Obsolescence of Great-Power War?

Paradoxically, perhaps, the world's most powerful nations have been the most constrained in their use of their military strength against one another. The destructiveness of modern weapons may have reduced their practical utility and restrained their use. Winston Churchill articulated this thesis in 1953 when he confessed that on occasion he had "the odd thought that the annihilating character of [nuclear weapons] may bring an utterly unforeseeable security to mankind. . . . It may be that when the advance of destructive weapons enables everyone to kill anybody else no one will want to kill anyone at all." As Churchill mused, "After a certain point has passed, it may be said, the worse things get the better. . . . Then it may be that we shall, by a process of sublime irony, have reached a stage in this story where safety will be the sturdy child of terror, and survival the twin brother of annihilation."

This predicament provides a plausible explanation for the virtual absence since 1945 of wars among the major powers.[3] It was perhaps the incredible costs and risks of fighting that led U.S. President Richard Nixon to say, in the context of the Vietnam War and implicitly in reference to wars between major powers, "I seriously doubt that we will ever have another war. This is probably the very last one." Others also voice this sentiment. Writing "On the Obsolescence of War," John Weltman (1974) asserted, for instance, that "violence as an instrument of foreign policy has increasingly become highly inefficient, if not counterproductive." Even more confidently, Werner Levi (1981) predicted in *The Coming End of War* that the day was nearing when "weapons [will] wipe out war."

Since the Cold War, the great powers appear to have engaged in a "retreat from doomsday" (Mueller, 1989). In early 1992, U.S. President George Bush observed at the United Nations that "today the threat of global nuclear war is more distant than ever before." This does not mean, however, that the threat has disappeared. Increasing numbers of countries stockpile weapons of mass destruction (see Chapter 11). Warfare is not necessarily the intended purpose, because military strategies today often emphasize not winning in war but deterring an adversary from starting it. Yet there is no guarantee that deterrence will succeed forever. Still, the self-defeating nature of nuclear might has reduced its utility as a tool of coercive diplomacy. As Melvin Laird, U.S. secretary of defense in the Nixon administration, observed, "Nuclear weapons . . . are useless for military purposes." Today nuclear states want not so much to win as to avoid loss.

A rival, more pessimistic explanation is also worth contemplating. The world may have escaped nuclear devastation by sheer luck—"less a consequence of intelligent policy than a fortunate concatenation of conditions" (Singer, 1991). By the laws of probability, so this reasoning goes, the longer nuclear arsenals exist, the more likely it is that a nuclear exchange will occur, as any event that can possibly happen eventually will. The question is not if, but when, for deterrence is inherently unstable and cannot persist forever. The odds for nuclear holocaust through a fatal error, whether of judgment, performance, miscalculation, or accident, are not low simply because the world has avoided that tragedy until now. Moreover, the limits to rationality under conditions of crisis heighten the potential dangers (Holsti, 1989a).

---

[3] And it fulfills a prediction made by Alfred Nobel (the Swedish armaments manufacturer whose endowments fund the Nobel Peace Prize and other awards), who speculated in 1892 that "perhaps my dynamite plants will put an end to war sooner than your congresses. On the day two army corps can annihilate each other in one second, all civilized nations will recoil from war in horror."

These apocalyptic thoughts suggest that the widespread belief that nuclear weapons have preserved peace—a *pax atomica*—may be a fanciful "myth" (see Vasquez, 1991). We may also question the corollary proposition that as "the fear of escalating nuclear power reaches further down, [it will inhibit] also the use of lesser force for lesser ends and goals" (Majeed, 1991).

These speculations lead to a related set of questions about the causes of war. Accordingly, it is useful to review contending ideas about the sources from which wars originate.

THE CAUSES OF WAR: CONTENDING PERSPECTIVES

The resort to force has prompted efforts throughout history to understand its causes. Inventories of the causes of war invariably conclude that they are incomplete (see Blainey, 1988; Howard, 1983; Waltz, 1954), in part because most agree that war is rooted in multiple sources at various "levels of analysis" (recall Chapter 2).

War and Human Nature

In one sense, of course, all wars originate from the decisions of national leaders. The choices they make ultimately determine whether war will occur. It is therefore common in discussions of the roots of war to consider the relationship of war to individuals and human choice. For this, questions about human nature are central.

The repeated outbreak of war has led some, such as the famous psychologist Sigmund Freud (1968), to conclude that aggression stems from humans' genetic programming and psychological makeup. Noting that Homo sapiens is the most deadly species, ethologists (those who study animal behavior in order to understand human behavior) such as Konrad Lorenz (1963) similarly argue that humankind is one of the few species practicing "intraspecific" aggression (routine killing of its own kind). Most other species practice "interspecific" aggression (they kill only other species, except in the most unusual circumstances—cannibalism in certain tropical fishes is one exception).

Many question these theories on both empirical and logical grounds. If aggression is an inevitable impulse deriving from human nature, they ask, then should not all humans exhibit this genetically determined behavior? Some people are consistently nonaggressive, however. Genetics also do not explain why individuals are belligerent and nonbelligerent at different times.

Many social scientists thus conclude that war is a learned trait, that it is a part of humankind's cultural heritage, not its biological nature.[4] For example, the 1986 *Seville Statement* endorsed by more than a dozen scientific and professional associations maintains that "it is scientifically incorrect" to say that "we have inherited a tendency to make war from our animal ancestors," "that war or any other violent behavior is

---

[4] The controversy over the nature-nurture question regarding the biological basis of aggression has not been resolved. For reviews of discourse about the issue, see Nelson (1974) and Somit (1990).

genetically programmed into our human nature," "that humans have a 'violent brain,'" or "that war is caused by 'instinct' or any single motivation" (see Somit, 1990). As Ted Robert Gurr (1970) puts it, "The capacity, but not the need, for violence appears to be biologically entrenched in men." Aggression is a propensity acquired early in life as a result of socialization and, therefore, is a learned rather than biologically determined behavior.

Scholars also question the belief that entire nations are predisposed to war—that "national character" predetermines national aggression. National character can express itself in different ways. And it can change; for example, Sweden since 1809 and Switzerland since 1815 have managed conflict without recourse to war, whereas formerly they were aggressive. This suggests that violence is not an inborn national trait that predestines periodic outbreaks of national aggression. Many countries have escaped the tragedy of war. In fact, since 1500 more than one in five states have never experienced war (Sivard, 1991: 20). This variation across different countries over 400 years suggests that war is not endemic and unavoidable. "A vision of a ubiquitous struggle for power or of a determining systemic structure explains recurrence without accounting for non-recurrence or the great deviations from an average pattern of recurrence" (Holsti, 1991).

Nobel Prize–winner Ralph Bunche argued in an address to the United Nations that "there are no warlike people—just warlike leaders." But explaining the role of leaders in making war is not quite that simple. Leaders usually make foreign policies within groups. Both the social-psychological and bureaucratic setting for decision making and the global environment may exert "an influence independent of the actions and beliefs of individual policymakers. . . . War seems less like something decision makers choose than something that somehow happens to them," even as it happens "through them," through the choices they make (Beer, 1981).

The decision for war is better explained, then, not by individual leaders' aggressiveness or by aggressive national characters, but by the many political pressures that influence the government leaders who "ultimately decide the great questions of war and peace" (Holsti, 1991). Therefore, it is relevant to ask, what domestic factors encourage policymakers to choose war?

Internal Characteristics and War Involvement

Conventional wisdom holds that variations in states' size, ideology, geographical location, population dynamics, ethnic homogeneity, wealth, economic performance, political institutions, military capabilities, and level of educational attainment influence whether they will engage in war.[5] Drawing on the possibility suggested by the

---

[5] Implicit in this approach is the assumption (embraced by "the comparative study of foreign policy" perspective identified in Chapters 2 and 3) that the differences in the types or classes of nations will determine whether they will engage in war. A (perhaps dubious) corollary is that the leaders' personalities and perceptual idiosyncrasies are relatively immaterial—that the prospects for war will be conditioned more by the effects of national attributes than by the impact of leaders on the countries they lead. The decision for war, in other words, will be affected more by the circumstances that leaders encounter than by their preferences.

Russian political theorist Peter Kropotkin in 1884 that "the word *state* is identical with the word *war*," let us next examine some theories addressing the internal characteristics of states that influence leaders' choices about the use of force.

Duration of Independence

New nations are more likely to initiate wars than are mature states (Wright, 1942). Newly independent nations usually go through a period of internal political upheaval. This has often served as a catalyst to external aggression. As the recent national rivalries within and conflicts between the newly independent republics of the former Soviet Union indicate, drives to settle long-standing internal grievances and territorial disputes by force often follow the acquisition of independence. Since 1945, all but one of the sixty civil wars were fought in emergent nations, and fourteen of them became internationalized as the internal bloodletting expanded across borders (Singer, 1991: 59, 79). It is thus not coincidental that wars since World War II have been prevalent among the newly independent states of the Third World.

National Poverty

A nation's level of economic development also affects the probability of its war involvement. Advanced industrial societies with comparatively high standards of living tend to be satisfied states less apt to start a war that might risk that valued status. (There are exceptions, of course, such as Germany in 1939.) On the other hand, historically the most warlike states have been poor, and this pattern persists, as the locale of warfare has shifted since 1945 to the developing nations at the periphery. As U.S. Secretary of Defense Robert S. McNamara explained in 1966, "there is no question but that there is evidence of a relationship between violence and economic backwardness." Aggression is a response to frustration and relative deprivation. When peoples' expectations of what they deserve rise more rapidly than their material rewards, the probability of conflict grows. That, of course, applies to most of the Third World today.

Before we conclude that poverty breeds war, however, we must note that the *most* impoverished nations have been the least prone to start wars. The poorest countries cannot vent their frustrations aggressively because they lack the military or economic resources to sustain its costs. Thus the poorest nations, like the wealthiest, cannot afford to wage war, but for quite different reasons. The former lack the means; the latter hold weapons too destructive to use.

This pattern does not mean that the poorest nations will always remain peaceful. Indeed, if the past is a guide to the future, then the impoverished nations that develop economically will be those most likely to acquire arms and engage in future wars (Chouchri and North, 1975).

Power Transitions

An extension of the preceding theory reasons that war is most likely when competitive states' power ratios—the differentials between their capabilities—narrow. Dubbed the *power transition* theory, this holds that an even distribution of political, economic, and military capabilities between contending groups of states is likely to increase the probability of war; peace is preserved best when there is an imbalance of national capabilities between disadvantaged and advantaged nations; the aggressor will come from a small group of dissatisfied strong countries; and it is the weaker, rather than the stronger, power that is most likely to be the aggressor. (Organski and Kugler, 1980: 19)

During the transition from developing to developed status, emergent challengers can achieve through force the power and recognition their new-formed muscles permit them. Conversely, established powers often are willing to employ force to arrest their relative decline. Thus, when advancing and retreating states seek to cope with the changes in their relative power, war becomes especially likely.

As explained in Chapter 13, rapid disruptions in the global distribution of power have often preceded outbursts of aggression. Moreover, the propensity persists for transitions in states' relative capabilities to culminate in wars started by the weaker party. Equally persistent is the prediction of the power transition theory that advantages have shifted from the attacker to the defender. "In earlier centuries the aggressor seemed to have a 50-50 chance of winning the war, but this no longer holds. The chances of the starter being victorious are shrinking. In the 1980s only 18 percent of the starters were winners" (Sivard, 1991: 20).

Militarization

Many political leaders assume that a close association exists between a country's military strength and its likely use of force. For this reason they spend much time estimating their nation's military power relative to their rivals'.

The age-old question of whether military power is a correlate of war or peace has assumed renewed emphasis in the post–Cold War era. As we noted in Chapter 11, "the race for the most advanced military technology began in the highly industrialized countries, and for awhile it was confined there. It is now rapidly spreading to the Third World, largely with assistance both in equipment and technological aid of . . . the developed countries" (Sivard, 1991). Hence, at issue is whether this dispersion of weapons to the developing nations also will increase the probability of war.

As Third World countries accumulate the economic resources to equip their military establishments, many experts believe that the incidence of warfare will increase further before it recedes. The prediction stems from the historical pattern in Europe as that region developed.

During its transition from relative poverty to the apex of development, Europe was the location of the world's most frequent and deadly wars. The major European states fought about 65 percent of the time in the sixteenth and seventeenth centuries (Wright, 1942). Between 1816 and 1945, 59 percent of all international wars took place there, with one erupting on average every 1½ years (Singer, 1991: 58). Not coincidentally, this happened when the developing states of Europe were most energetically arming in competition with one another. Since then, however, interstate war has not occurred in Europe. As the European nations moved up the ladder of development in later centuries, they moved away from war.

In contrast, the developing countries now resemble Europe prior to 1945. If the Third World nations follow the European pattern, the future may well witness the specter of a peaceful, developed world surrounded by a violent, less-developed world.

Economic System

Recall the distinction drawn in Chapter 7 between open (market) economies, like those in Western Europe and North America, and closed (command) economies, like those in the former socialist systems of Eastern Europe and the Soviet Union, where governments actively regulated commercial transactions. At issue here is whether, as is often claimed, the difference influences the frequency of warfare.

The question has provoked controversy for centuries. Particularly since Marxism took root in Russia following the Bolshevik revolution in 1917, communist theoreticians claimed that capitalism *is* the primary cause of war—that capitalists practice imperialism and colonialism (see Chapter 5). According to this theory, capitalism produces surplus capital. The need to export it stimulates wars to protect foreign markets. Thus laissez-faire capitalism rationalized militarism for economic purposes. Citing the demonstrable frequency with which societies that practiced capitalism engaged in aggression, Marxists believed that the only way to end international war was to end capitalism.

Contrary to this theory is the neoliberal belief that free market systems promote peace, not war. Defenders of capitalism have long assumed that countries that practice free enterprise at home and free trade abroad are more pacific. The reasons are multiple, but they center on the premise that commercial enterprises are natural lobbyists for world peace because their profits depend on it. By extension, the reasoning continues, a world organized to minimize government regulation of internal markets will experience fewer external wars.

The evidence for these rival theories (like those surrounding all important controversies) is, not surprisingly, mixed. Conclusions depend in part on the mental maps used to organize perceptions about the influence of economics on international behavior, in part because alternative perspectives focus on different dimensions of the linkage. The controversy was at the heart of the ideological debate between East and West during the Cold War, when the relative virtues and vices of two radically different economic systems (communism and capitalism) were uppermost in peoples' minds. At the time, communists cited the previous record of wars initiated by capitalistic countries (Germany, Japan, and the United States in Vietnam, for example) to lend credence to the Marxist interpretation. The theory did not explain communist states' embarrassingly frequent use of force, however. The Soviet Union invaded Finland in 1939 and Afghanistan in 1979; North Korea attacked South Korea in 1950; Communist China attacked Tibet in 1959; Vietnam invaded Cambodia in 1975; and Cuba intervened militarily in Africa in the 1980s. Moreover, communist states repeatedly clashed with one another during the Cold War, as in the case of China and the Soviet Union in 1969, China and Vietnam in 1979 and again in 1987, the Soviet Union and Hungary in 1956, and the Soviet Union and Czechoslovakia in 1968. Thus the notion that socialist or communist states were inherently nonaggressive failed empirically.

More than this, communism's failure to produce economic growth hastened its rejection in Eastern Europe and in the very heartland of the communist experiment, the Soviet Union itself. With capitalism's triumph over communism, a phase of history "ended" (Fukuyama, 1992). By 1992 all but China, Cuba, and North Korea repudiated communism, preferring free market economies instead.

The revolutionary termination of the communist experiment does not end the historic debate about the link between economics and war, however. The issue of economic influences on international behavior remains. With the end of the Cold War, this basic theoretical question is even likely to command increasing interest, especially given the "shift in the relevance and usefulness of different power resources, with military power declining and economic power increasing in importance" (Huntington, 1991a).

Type of Government

The neoliberal institutionalist perspective on international politics predicts that not just free enterprise but also democracy will inhibit the frequency with which governments settle their disputes by force. Between 1987 and 1990, roughly a third of the countries on the planet converted their political systems to democratic rule. As a result, Freedom House, a private organization that monitors the progress toward democracy, estimated that a quarter of the world's people lived in free countries, two-fifths lived in partly free countries, and a third lived in not-free countries (*The Wall Street Journal*, December 30, 1991, p. A6). As we have noted in previous chapters, the march of democracy throughout the world in the recent past is a remarkable historical development (see Map 12.1, on page 448).

The recent "wave of democratization" (Huntington, 1991b) has provoked speculation that Western liberal democracy will become universal, "the final form of government" (Fukuyama, 1992) and that the growth of democracy will inaugurate a new era of peaceful world politics.

The belief that democratic policy-making institutions will produce peace follows the idealist conviction of eighteenth-century philosopher Immanuel Kant, in his book *Perpetual Peace*, namely that democracies are inherently less warlike than autocracies. He felt that public opinion restrains the freedom of rulers of democratic states to wage war, because in democratic governments the mass public would have to supply the soldiers and bear the human and financial costs of imperial policies.

History has been kind to Kant's views. "Although preventive war has been the preferred response of declining authoritarian leaders, no democracy has ever initiated such a war. Instead, depending on the regime type of the rising challenger, democratic states have chosen accommodation, defensive alliances, or internal balancing" (Schweller, 1992). Simply put, democracies have dealt with conflicts against other democracies by methods other than war (Doyle, 1986; Maoz and Abdolali, 1989; Manicas, 1989). This does not mean that democracies never experience war. "It appears that democracies fight as often as do other types of states" (Morgan and Schwebach, 1992; also Small and Singer, 1976) because democracies have been the targets of dictatorships' aggression. But democracies "seldom, if ever, fight one another" because the political culture of democratic states embraces norms against

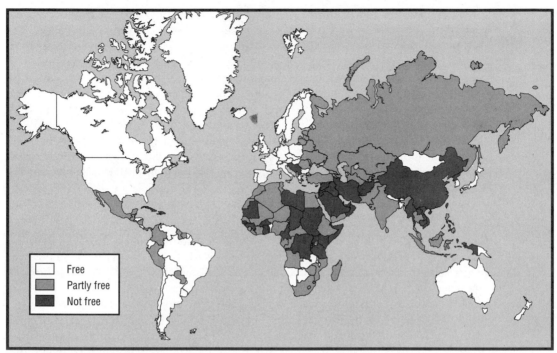

MAP 12.1 FREEDOM SPREADS: THE DIFFUSION OF DEMOCRATIC GOVERNANCE, DECEMBER 31, 1991
Source: Based on classifications of freedom in countries by Freedom House, as summarized in *The Wall Street Journal*, December 31, 1991, p. A6.

aggression as a method of conflict resolution and institutional procedures reinforce this constraint on leaders' policy choice (Morgan and Schwebach, 1992).

The experience of Western Europe since World War II is consistent with the view that democratic states are unlikely to engage in war with one another. Still, we must be careful not to assume too quickly that democracy is a force for peace.

> It was, after all, the democratization of conflict in the nineteenth century that restored a ferocity to warfare unknown since the seventeenth century; the bloodiest war in American history remains the one fought between two (by today's standards flawed) democracies—the Civil War. Concentration camps appeared during another conflict between two limited democracies, the Boer War. World War I was launched by two regimes—Wilhelmine Germany and Austria-Hungary—that had greater representation and more equitable legal systems than those of many important states today. And even when modern liberal democracies go to war they do not necessarily moderate the scope of the violence they apply; indeed, sensitivity to their own casualties sometimes leads to profligate uses of firepower or violent efforts to end wars quickly. Shaky democracies fight each other all the time. . . .We must remind ourselves just how peculiar the wealthy and secure democracies of the West are, how painful their evolution to stability and the horror of war with each other has been.

Perhaps other countries will find short-cuts to those conditions, but it would be foolish to assume they will. (Cohen, 1992: 37)

Thus, it would be premature and overly optimistic to assume that the growth of democratic governance (if it continues and is not reversed) assures a more peaceful world.

Nationalism

Nationalism—love of nation—is widely believed to be the cauldron from which wars often spring. "The tendency of the vast majority of people to center their supreme loyalties on the nation-state," political scientist Jack S. Levy explains, is a powerful catalyst to war. When people

> acquire an intense commitment to the power and prosperity of the state [and] this commitment is strengthened by national myths emphasizing the moral, physical, and political strength of the state and by individuals' feelings of powerlessness and their consequent tendency to seek their identity and fulfillment through the state, [then] assertive and nationalist policies are perceived as increasing state power and are at the same time psychologically satisfying for the individual and, in this way, nationalism contributes to war. (Levy, 1989a: 271)

The connection between nationalism and war enjoys a long history (see Box 12.2, page 450), but it has been especially pronounced in the twentieth century. The English novelist and essayist Aldous Huxley once termed nationalism "the religion of the twentieth century."[6] Today separatist nationalism is particularly virulent and intense: "In our modern age, nationalism is not resurgent; it never died. Neither did racism. They are the most powerful movements in our world today, cutting across many social systems. . . . We are witnessing a 'convulsive ingathering' of nations" (Gardels, 1991).

The potential magnitude of nationalistic-inspired war is great:

> More than 95 percent of the world's 168 states are multinational, that is, composed of many nations, some unconsenting. These 168 states assert sovereignty over the world's 3,000 to 5,000 nations and peoples. . . . State governments [are pitted] against guerrilla insurgencies and indigenous nations. Most of these wars are over territory, resources, and identity, not ideology. They are hidden from most people's view because the fighting is against peoples and countries that are not even on the map. (Nietschmann, 1991: 172–173).

This "binge of nationalism" is international and not just internal in its consequences (see Ryan, 1990). "Nationalism has often generated aggression abroad. Nationalism, including some of the more messianic variations of Zionism, has given us some three dozen costly wars in the Middle East since 1945. Most of them were inter-Arab wars; but all were painful" (Yoder, 1991). It was the threat of nationalism to world order that led former Soviet President Mikhail Gorbachev to warn in May 1992 that "the

---

[6] Kenneth Boulding has commented on the violence-provoking consequences of this disposition by noting that nationalism is "the only religion that still demands human sacrifice" (cited in Nelson, 1974).

Box 12.2
NATIONALISM, ETHNICITY, AND WAR

• • •

Nationalism is an attitude of mind, a pattern of attention and desires. It arises in response to a condition of society and to a particular stage in its development. It is a predisposition to pay far more attention to messages about one's own people, or to messages from its members, than to messages from or about any other people. At the same time, it is a desire to have one's own people get any and all values that are available. The extreme nationalist wants his people to have all the power, all the wealth, and all the well-being for which there is any competition. He wants his people to command all the respect and deference from others; he tends to claim all rectitude and virtue for it, as well as all enlightenment and skill; and he gives it a monopoly of his affection. In short, he totally identifies himself with his nation. Though he may be willing to sacrifice himself for it, his nationalism is a form of egotism written large. . . .

Even if most people are not extreme nationalists, nationalism has altered the world in many ways. Nationalism has not only increased the number of countries on the face of the earth, it has helped to diminish the number of its inhabitants. All major wars in the twentieth century have been fought in its name. . . .

Nationalism is in potential conflict with all philosophies or religions—such as Christianity—which teach universal standards of truth and of right and wrong, regardless of nation, race, or tribe. Early in the nineteenth century a gallant American naval officer, Stephen Decatur, proposed the toast, "Our country! In her intercourse with foreign nations, may she be always in the right, but our country, right or wrong." Nearly 150 years later the United States Third Army, marching into Germany following the collapse of the Nazi regime, liberated the huge concentration camp at Buchenwald. Over the main entrance to that place of torture and death, the Nazi elite guard had thoughtfully written, "My Country, Right or Wrong."

Source: Karl W. Deutsch, *Politics and Government* (Boston: Houghton Mifflin, 1974), pp. 124–125.

demons of nationalism are coming alive again, and they are putting the stability of the international system to the test. Even the United States itself is not immune from the dangers of nationalism."

This discussion of states' characteristics that influence their war proneness does not exhaust the subject. Many potential causes internal to the state exist. But however important domestic influences as a source of war might be, many believe that the nature of the international system is even more important.

Cycles of War and Peace

Classical political realism emphasizes that the roots of war inhere in human nature. In contrast, neorealism sees war springing from the decentralized character of the international system, as it requires that sovereign states rely on self-help for their security.

International anarchy may promote war's outbreak, but it fails to provide a complete explanation of its occurrence. To capture war's many structural determinants, we must consider how and why systems change. This requires an exploration of the impact of the distribution of military capabilities, balances (and imbalances) of power, the number of alliances and international organizations, the rules of international law, cultural and moral constraints, economic imperatives, and inequalities in the distribution of national and global wealth. At issue is how these systemic factors—the system's attributes and institutions—combine to influence changes in war's frequency. We will examine many of these factors in Chapters 13 and 14. Here we focus attention on cycles of war and peace at the international level.

Does Violence Breed Violence?

In 1935 U.S. President Franklin D. Roosevelt asserted that "war is a contagion." The adage "violence breeds violence" reflects that view and the corresponding notion that the seeds of future wars are found in past wars. From this perspective World War II was an outgrowth of World War I, and the successive wars in the Middle East are seemingly little more than one war with each battle stimulated by its predecessor. Because the frequency of past wars *is* correlated with the incidence of wars in later periods, war appears contagious and its future outbreak inevitable. If so, then something within the dynamics of world politics—its anarchical nature, its weak legal system, its uneven distribution of power, or some combination of structural attributes—makes the state system a war system.

Those subscribing to the belief in war's inevitability often take their ammunition from the historical fact that war has been so repetitive. We cannot safely infer that past wars have *caused* later wars, however. Hence, we should exercise care in drawing conclusions from chronological sequences, for the fact that a war precedes a later one does not establish that one caused the other to occur.

That history has been replete with war does not necessarily mean that we will always have it. War is not a universal institution (see Etzioni, 1968; Kluckhohn, 1944; Mead, 1968; Sumner, 1968). There are societies that have never known war, and, as noted, history has been immune to it for prolonged periods. Moreover, the outbreak of war since 1945 has stabilized and may even be declining, despite the large increase in the number of nations. This indicates that war is not necessarily inevitable and that historical forces do not control people's freedom of choice or experiences.

Cyclical Theories

If war is recurrent but not necessarily inevitable, how might we explain changes over time in its outbreak? The absence of a clear trend in the frequency of war, and the periodic outbreaks of war after intermittent stretches of peace, suggest that world history oscillates rhythmically between *long cycles* of war and peace.

Arnold J. Toynbee's *A Study of History* (1954) is a classical realist interpretation of history that sees it alternating rhythmically between periods of war and periods of peace. The more recent formal analysis of such cycles is known as *long-cycle theory*. As noted in Chapter 4, its proponents argue that cycles of world leadership and global war are operative over the past five centuries, with a "general war" erupting approximately once every century, although at irregular intervals (Modelski, 1987; Thompson, 1988; Rapkin, 1990).

Long-cycle theory seeks to explain how an all-powerful invisible hand built into the system's dynamics causes such peaks and valleys. Although the theory embraces many contending explanations (see Goldstein, 1988, for a comparison), they converge on the proposition that some combination of systemic properties (economic, military, and political) produces the frequency with which major wars have periodically erupted throughout modern history.

The long-cycle perspective is based on the fact that a great power has risen to a hegemonic (preponderant) position about every one hundred years. Portugal and the Netherlands rose at the beginning of the sixteenth and seventeenth centuries, respectively. Britain climbed to dominance at the beginning of both the eighteenth and nineteenth centuries. And the United States became a world leader at the end of World War II. During their reigns, these hegemonic powers monopolized military power and trade and determined the system's rules. Yet no hegemonic power has retained its position for more than three or four decades. In each cycle, overcommitments, the costs of empire, and ultimately the appearance of rivals led to the delegitimation of the hegemon's authority and to the deconcentration of power globally. As challengers to the hegemon's rule grew in strength, a "general war" erupted after a long period of peace in each century since 1400 (1494–1517, 1579–1609, 1688–1713, 1792–1815, and 1914–1945). At the conclusion of the general war a new world leader emerged dominant (Modelski, 1978, 1987), and the cyclical process began anew.

Such deterministic theories have intuitive appeal. It seems plausible, for example, that just as long-term downswings and recoveries in business cycles profoundly affect subsequent behaviors and conditions, so a war experience produces aftereffects that may last for generations. A nation at war will become exhausted and lose its enthusiasm for another war, but only for a time. This idea is labeled the *war weariness* hypothesis (Blainey, 1988). Italian historian Luigi da Porto expresses one version: "Peace brings riches; riches brings pride; pride brings anger; anger brings war; war brings poverty; poverty brings humanity; humanity brings peace; peace, as I have said, brings riches, and so the world's affairs go round." Because it takes time to move through these stages, alternations between periods of enthusiasm for war and weariness of war appear to be influenced by learning, forgetting, and aging.

Empirical tests of cyclical theories lead to conflicting results. Quincy Wright (1942) suggested that if cycles exist, intervals between major outbreaks of war last about fifty years. Lewis F. Richardson (1960a) and Pitirim Sorokin (1937) estimated that cycles extend over two hundred years from peak to peak (although both were somewhat skeptical and cautioned against attaching too much causal importance to their findings).

The validity of cyclical interpretations depends in part on the measures of war's frequency and magnitude that are used (see Goldstein, 1991). The evidence accumulated by the Correlates of War Research Project, for example, fails to establish the existence of a cycle in war's onset since 1815 (Singer, 1981). Moreover, "no cyclical patterns are apparent when we examine the military experiences of the individual nations which participated in several wars" (Small and Singer, 1972). We must therefore question assertions about recurrent cycles in international war.

A different picture emerges when the amount of war *under way* since 1815 rather than the number of wars begun is considered. Here, the evidence "suggests not so much that discrete wars come and go with some regularity, but that, with *some* level of such violence almost always present, there may be certain periodic fluctuations in the amount of that violence" (Small and Singer, 1982).

From several theoretical standpoints, therefore, we must question claims that the probability of warfare in the twenty-first century is predetermined. Although the historical record provides little basis for assuming that the war system is obsolete (see Majeed, 1991), it does suggest that peace is also possible. Both long periods of peace and long periods of warfare have existed in the past, and either could follow in the post–Cold War era.

If the disappearance of war is problematic over the long run, the character of conflict and violence may nevertheless fundamentally change. We now turn from our exploration of the multiple causes of interstate war to other uses of force on the world's stage.

OTHER MODES OF VIOLENCE IN WORLD POLITICS

Ours is an age of violence. This adage finds expression not only in wars between states but in other ways as well. We will consider four additional expressions of conflict and violence between and within states: crises, "low-intensity conflict," civil war, and terrorism.

Crisis, Coercive Diplomacy, and Intervention

"A crisis is a situation that (1) threatens the high-priority goals of the decision-making unit, (2) restricts the amount of time available for response before the decision is transformed, and (3) surprises the members of the decision-making unit by its occurrence" (Hermann, 1972). Most of the conspicuous crises of our age, such as the Cuban missile crisis, the Berlin blockade, the Sino-Soviet border clash and the Formosa Straits crisis, exhibited these attributes. Each contained the elements of surprise, threat, and time pressure, as well as the risk of war. In each, a sense of urgency provoked by others' unanticipated military maneuvers was involved. But none crossed the line into overt military hostilities.[7] Instead, all were managed successfully.

Crises result when one actor attempts to force an adversary to alter its behavior. The threat of warfare, or "the strategy of coercive diplomacy (or compellence, as some prefer to call it) employs threats or limited force to persuade an opponent to call off or undo an encroachment—for example, to halt an invasion or give up territory that has been occupied" (Craig and George, 1990). "Military power does not have to be used for it to be useful"; the threat of force may suffice by "coercing a country by demonstrating the quantity of force and highlighting the capability of, and intention to, use force" (Majeed, 1991). "Coercive diplomacy offers the possibility of achieving one's objective economically, with little bloodshed, fewer political and psychological costs, and often with much less risk of escalation than does traditional military strategy" (Craig and George, 1990).

The crises generated by coercive diplomacy thus perform the bargaining function that war often traditionally played, namely, "to resolve without violence, or with only minimal violence, those conflicts that are too severe to be settled by ordinary diplomacy and that in earlier times would have been settled by war" (Snyder and Diesing, 1977).

Figure 12.2 displays the distribution of 325 interstate crises between 1928 and 1985. It reveals a continuous stream of "higher-than-normal conflictual interactions" that destabilized "existing relationships and [posed] a challenge to the existing structure of an international system" (Brecher, Wilkenfeld, and Moser, 1988).[8]

Once they erupt, crises may escalate to war.[9] "The evidence of crisis-generated instability from 1945 to 1988 is overwhelming. . . . [19] of the 25 most destabilizing crises . . . were triggered by, or culminated in full-scale war. Moreover, the intensity of violence reached full-scale war in 50 of the 251 international crises during the four decades" (Brecher and Wilkenfeld, 1991: 103).

As noted, coercive diplomacy, which includes threats often associated with crisis, sometimes involves the limited use of force. International military interventions provide evidence of the application of force in conflict situations, which occurred more than 600 times throughout the world since World War II (see

---

[7] For crises to be managed successfully without escalating to war, policymakers, as rational actors, must be able to keep their quarrels within controllable bounds. Ole R. Holsti (1972) questions the validity of this assumption: "There is scant evidence that along with more lethal weapons we have evolved leaders more capable of coping with stress." Crises can easily escalate to war because of the time pressures, inadequate information, fear and anxiety, and impulsive risk-taking that normally accompany decision-making procedures during threatening situations (see Holsti, 1989a; also Rhodes, 1988).

[8] The frequency of international crises is sometimes measured by the incidence of *militarized disputes*, that is, "confrontations short of war characterized by the reciprocated threat, deployment, mobilization, or use of force" (Singer, 1991; also Gochman and Maoz, 1984).

[9] Examples of violence that were preceded by crisis include World War I (1914), Kashmir (1948), Suez (1956), Tibet (1959), the Bay of Pigs (1961), Goa (1961), and Kuwait (1990). Conversely, some situations popularly termed crises in fact do not meet these criteria. The global energy crisis during the 1970s is an example. Surely the situation involved "threat," but neither "surprise" nor "time pressure" describes it appropriately.

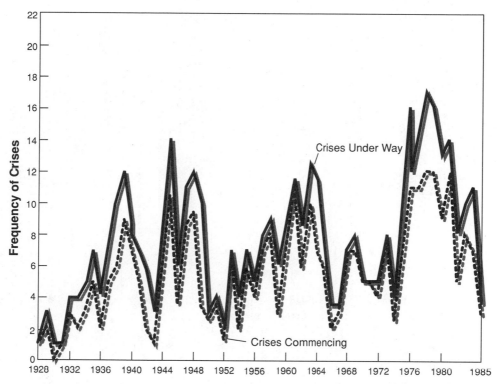

FIGURE 12.2 THE HISTORICAL DISTRIBUTION OF CRISES, 1928–1985
Source: Adapted from Michael Brecher, Jonathan Wilkenfeld, and Sheila Maser, *Crises in the Twentieth Century, Vol. I: Handbook of International Crises* (London: Pergamon Press, 1988), with data for 1979–1985 provided by Professor Wilkenfeld.

Figure 12.3, page 456). Included are 71 Cold War interventions by the United States and 25 by the Soviet Union (Pearson, Baumann, and Pickering, 1991: Table I).[10] A crisis atmosphere prevails in most interventions because "any foreign overt military intervention can precipitate or expand war [and] every instance . . . is an incipient war" (Tillema, 1989).

Crisis remains ubiquitous, but the correlation between the onset of crisis and war has declined, as all post–World War II crises between great powers have been managed without recourse to war. The great powers seem to have learned skills in crisis management and to have developed tacit rules for this purpose (George, 1986; also Tarr, 1991). Fear of the dire consequences should their management efforts fail doubtless contributed to the learning process (Gaddis, 1991a). In contrast, war-threatening disputes between unequals—those between powerful and weak states—continue unabated.

---

[10] Another inventory for the same period, using different criteria, counts 269 military interventions by 591 intervening states between 1945 and 1988, of which the great powers initiated one-fourth (Tillema, 1991).

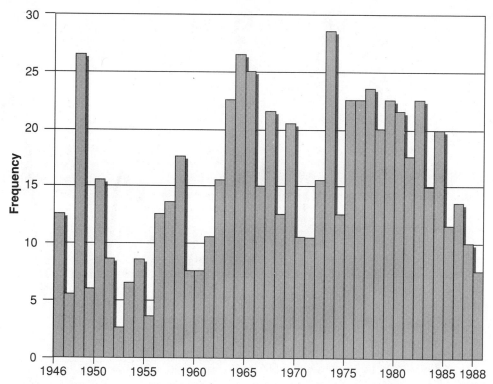

FIGURE 12.3   Annual Frequencies: Military Interventions, 1946–1988
Source: Adapted from Frederic S. Pearson, Robert A. Baumann, and Jeffrey Pickering,
"International Military Intervention: Global and Regional Redefinitions of Realpolitik," paper
presented at the Annual Meeting of the American Political Science Association, Washington,
D.C., August 29–September 1, 1991.

Low-Intensity Conflict

The destructiveness of modern weapons reduces the incentives for great and small
powers alike to resort to armed force and increases the propensity to substitute the
threat of force for its actual use. Still, violence has not ended, as states increasingly
engage in *low-intensity conflict* (LIC).

> [Low-intensity conflict] is warfare that falls below the threshold of full-scale military combat
> between modern armies (of the sort that occurred in the Korean War and at the onset of
> the Iran-Iraq War). Under U.S. doctrine, low-intensity conflict encompasses four particular
> types of operations: (1) *counterinsurgency* . . . combat against revolutionary guerrillas . . . ;
> (2) *pro-insurgency* . . . support for insurgents. . . ; (3) *peacetime contingency operations* [or]
> police-type actions . . . ; and (4) *military "shows of force,"* [which threaten] military maneu-
> vers. (Klare, 1988: 12)

These practices are not altogether new. They derive, for example, from the U.S.
experiment with counterinsurgency warfare in the Vietnam War and the prior practice

of "gunboat diplomacy." The United States used *shows of force* 286 times between 1946 and 1984, or an average of more than seven times a year (Blechman and Kaplan, 1978: 547–553; Zelikow, 1987: 34–36). Similarly, the Soviet Union prior to its fragmentation also engaged in such behavior over 150 times between the mid-1940s and late 1970s (Kaplan, 1981: 689–693).

As the concept is now used, low-intensity conflict is a symbol of warfare between the haves and have-nots. It refers primarily to methods for combating terrorism, insurgency, and guerrilla activities in the Third World to protect the interests of the powerful. Proxy wars, wars fought with mercenaries, psychological operations to terrorize the populace, death squads—these are part and parcel of the modern face of warfare below the level of overt military operations by the soldiers of a state's regular army. "What is crucial to recognize," notes political scientist Michael T. Klare (1988), "is that low-intensity conflict is a form of warfare in which *your* side suffers very little death or destruction, while the other side suffers as much damage as possible without producing undue hardship for your own society. . . . [Low-intensity conflict] doctrine . . . states that the privileged nations of the industrialized 'North' are vitally threatened by the starving, nonwhite masses of the underdeveloped 'South' and that this threat to the industrial West must be met by force short of war."

Low-intensity conflict thus describes the great powers' methods of combating "revolutionary strife, random violence, nuclear terrorism, and drug-running. . . . The strategy for conducting low-intensity war strikes at the heart of the development process, and that is its purpose. Physical attacks on roads, dams, and so forth, with the inevitable collateral damage to houses, schools, and hospitals, is accompanied by a psychological attack on those aspects of a revolutionary government's program that establish its legitimacy" (Barnet, 1990).

Three other characteristics are notable. Low-intensity conflict "is almost certain to be pervasive, is likely to be prolonged, and is often sufficiently unconventional as to defy being labeled as conflict in any traditional sense. It may be indistinguishable from police work; it can always be labeled police action" (Yarmolinsky, 1988). Despite its name, however, low-intensity conflict does not necessarily mean low levels of death or destruction. "The low-intensity conflict in Guatemala, for instance, . . . claimed well over 100,000 lives" (Klare, 1988: 12).

As noted in Chapter 11, great powers like the United States also now prepare for "mid-intensity" conflict (MIC), that is, for the kinds of disruptive localized wars of the sort fought against Saddam Hussein in 1991 (Klare, 1991). New threats are emerging beyond the traditional East-West antagonism of the last forty-five years, President George Bush declared in February 1990. "These contingencies must loom larger in [U.S.] defense planning," he said.

Civil War

Wars within nations—civil wars—have erupted far more frequently than have wars between states since World War II. It is thus internal wars and insurgencies, more than international wars, that tend to capture the headlines. Indeed, "most of the contemporary wars in the Third World have been waged by the developed world—either through direct participation or intervention through arms supply and covert operations" (Majeed, 1991).

Civil wars resulting in at least one thousand civilian and military deaths per year have erupted more than 120 times between 1816 and 1988 (Small and Singer, 1982; Singer, 1991: 66–75). The outbreak has been somewhat irregular. At least one civil war began in "only" 81, or less than half, of these years. However, over time civil war has become increasingly frequent (see Table 12.2). Nearly half of the civil wars since 1816 began after 1945 and "the frequency has doubled from 5.6 to 12.6 per decade" (Singer, 1991: 59). However, this apparent trend is in part a product of the increase in the number of independent states in the international system, which makes the incidence of civil war more probable statistically.

The amount of civil war *under way* provides a different picture of the worldwide spread of civil war. Civil wars have been under way internationally 82 percent of the time, or 142 years, between 1816 and 1988 (Small and Singer, 1982: 251–267; Singer, 1991: 22–25). "Of the approximately 120 ongoing wars [in the late 1980s], 72 percent (86) were state-nation [states fighting insurgencies] conflicts" (Nietschmann, 1991: 175).

The severity of civil wars is another of their troublesome attributes. The number of lives lost in civil violence has remained high since the Napoleonic Wars ended in 1815 (see Table 12.2), and casualty rates show an alarming growth, especially since World War II. One symptom is that ten of the fifteen most destructive civil wars between 1816 and 1980 occurred in the twentieth century; of those ten, seven occurred since World War II (Small and Singer, 1982: 241). Another characteristic is suggested by Ted Robert Gurr (1970: 3), who found that "ten of the world's thirteen most deadly conflicts [between 1815 and 1965] have been civil wars and rebellions."

TABLE 12.2 THE FREQUENCY AND SEVERITY OF 124 CIVIL WARS, 1816–1988

Period	No. of Civil Wars Begun	Total Months of Nations' Involvement in Civil War	Battle Deaths	No./% of Civil Wars Internationalized through Large-Scale Military Intervention
1816–1848	12	333.1	93,200	3 (25%)
1849–1881	20	625.4	2,891,600	1 (5%)
1882–1914	18	286.0	388,000	3 (17%)
1915–1945	14	486.3	1,631,460	4 (29%)
1946–1988	60	3,973.1	6,222,020	14 (23%)
Totals	124	5,703.9	11,226,280	25

Source: Data provided courtesy of the Correlates of War project at the University of Michigan under the direction of J. David Singer and Melvin Small, as retrieved and compiled by Ricardo Rodriguez.

Causes of Civil War

Civil war and revolution have been simultaneously defended as instruments of justice and condemned as the immoral acceptance of violent change. They contain ingredients of both. The revolutionaries who engineered the American, Russian, and Chinese revolutions claimed that violence was necessary to realize social change, political freedom, and independence, while the powers from whom they sought liberation berated the immorality of their methods.

Civil wars stem from a wide range of ideological, demographic, religious, ethnic, economic, social-structural, and political conditions. Internal violence is also a reaction to frustration and deprivation, especially when the distribution of wealth and opportunities is highly unequal (Gurr, 1970). These conditions partially account for the pervasiveness of civil war today in the developing countries. Note in this context that the seeds of civil strife are sown by national independence movements. "More than one-half (52 percent) of the wars in the post-1945 period were manifestations of the state-creation enterprise" (Holsti, 1991: 311). The potential growth of new nations in Europe and Asia in the aftermath of the Cold War and the breakup of the Soviet Union will likely increase the probability of local wars. Unrest and discontent, long held in check "at the point of a bayonet" (Brogan, 1990), have now been released. The civil war that splintered Yugoslavia in the early 1990s is a case in point.

The destabilization caused by rapid growth also helps to account for the ubiquity of internal war (see Olson, 1971). In contrast with what intuition might suggest, civil violence often erupts in countries in which conditions are improving, not deteriorating. "Economic modernization," former U.S. Secretary of State Henry Kissinger postulated, "leads to political instability rather than political stability." When modernization generates rising expectations that governments are unable to satisfy, civil war often follows (Gurr, 1970). This is the essence of *relative deprivation* as a cause of internal violence and war.

It is tempting to think of civil war as only an internal problem, stemming exclusively from conditions within countries. However, external factors often influence internal rebellions. "Every war has two faces. It is a conflict both between and within political systems; a conflict that is both external and internal. [It is undeniable that] internal wars affect the international system [and that] the international system affects internal wars" (Modelski, 1964).

We can distinguish several waves in the linkage between changes in the international system and the incidence of civil war. First, the effects of imperialism, industrialization, nationalism, mass communication, and ideology spawned the comparatively high levels of civil war between 1848 and 1870. Second, the frequent incidence of civil war between the end of World War II and the 1960s was caused by the breakup of the European colonial empires. And today in the post–Cold War era a third wave is evident, which can be termed *neonationalism*.

Neonationalism and the localized conflicts it spawns differ from the nationalism previously seen in the Third World.

> Earlier stages of Third World nationalism tended to revolve around the national liberation experience, the zeal engendered by the throwing off of colonial ties. . . . Neonationalism

is the product of more recent decades, going beyond classical nationalism and [includes] separatist subnationalism; that is, the expression of communal/ethnic aspirations of groups within the nation-state that are unhappy with their lot: Shiites in Iraq, Sikhs in India, Unighur Turks in Chinese Turkestan. It involves strong new drives toward separatism: the Moros in the Philippines, Georgians in the [former] Soviet Union, Catholics in Northern Ireland, Hungarians in Romania, Biafra in Nigeria, even Quebec in Canada. (Fuller, 1991–1992: 14–15)

Similarly, the civil strife that erupted in the Balkans and the Commonwealth of Independent States following the collapse of the Soviet internal empire in 1991 fit this pattern.

Civil War and Intervention

Because the great powers have global interests, they are apt to intervene militarily in civil wars to support friendly governments and to overthrow unfriendly ones. When they do, wars within states become internationalized.

It is often difficult to determine where an internal war ends and an international one begins. As Table 12.2 reveals, since 1816 one in five civil wars have become interstate wars through intervention by an external power. More than half of these large-scale military interventions have occurred since 1944, and three-fourths of them have appeared since that time.[11] Many U.S. and Soviet foreign entanglements during the Cold War were responses to internal instability (as in Lebanon, the Dominican Republic, Korea, Vietnam, Grenada, and Panama in the case of the United States, and Hungary, Czechoslovakia, Ethiopia, and Afghanistan in the case of the Soviet Union). Even today, the Third World remains the site of most violent conflicts in the world (see Map 12.2), nearly all of them internationalized in one way or another.

Civil Strife and External Aggression

If leaders assume that national cohesion will rise when an external threat exists, then when facing domestic unrest they may seek to manage it by initiating foreign adventures. At least since the ancient Greeks about whom Thucydides wrote, many have noted that leaders can wage war abroad to manage civil disturbance at home. Machiavelli, for instance, advised the Prince to undertake foreign wars whenever turmoil within the state became too great. Hermann Goering advocated the same idea in Nazi Germany, contending: "Voice or no voice, the people can always be brought to do the bidding of the leaders. That is easy. All you have to do is tell them they are being attacked and denounce the pacifists for lack of patriotism." John Foster Dulles (1939) expressed this idea also, noting that: "The easiest and quickest cure of internal dissension is to portray danger from abroad. Thus group authorities find it convenient

---

[11] A military intervention by one state into the civil war in another is said to occur if that participation is direct: One thousand troops or more must be committed to a battle zone, or one hundred casualties sustained. According to this measure, thirty-five cases of third party intervention were recorded between 1816 and 1988, resulting in the internationalization of twenty-five civil wars (see Small and Singer, 1982; Singer, 1991: 22–25).

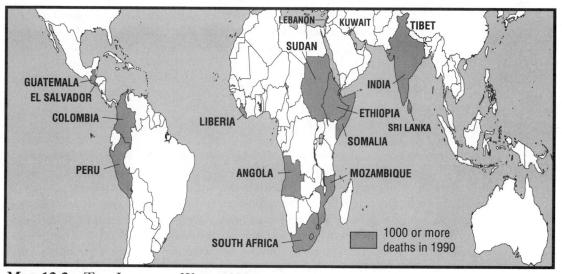

MAP 12.2 THE LOCUS OF WAR, 1990
Source: Adapted from Ruth Leger Sivard, *World Military and Social Expenditures 1991* (Washington, D.C., World Priorities, 1991), p. 20.

always to keep alive among the group members a feeling that their nation is in danger from one or another of the nation-villains with which it is surrounded."

The *diversionary theory of war* is predicated on the expectation that external war will result in increased domestic support for political leaders. "To put it cynically, one could say that nothing helps a leader like a good war. It gives him his only chance of being a tyrant and being loved for it at the same time. He can introduce the most ruthless forms of control and send thousands of his followers to their deaths and still be hailed as a great protector. Nothing ties tighter the in-group bonds than an out-group threat" (Morris, 1969).

Whether political leaders actually start wars to deal with domestic conflict is an empirical question. Many studies have examined the proposition, but few confirm it (see Levy, 1989b; Morgan and Bickers, 1992). It seems reasonable to assume that "war with the outside is sometimes the last chance for a state ridden with inner antagonisms to overcome these antagonisms" (Simmel, 1956), and that "statesmen may be driven to a policy of foreign conflict—if not open war—in order to defend themselves against the onslaught of domestic enemies" (Haas and Whiting, 1956), yet we cannot demonstrate that leaders frequently undertake these diversionary actions for this purpose. "The linkage depends," Levy (1989b) concludes, "on the kinds of internal conditions that commonly lead to hostile external actions for diversionary purposes." For example, "democratic states are particularly likely to use force externally during an election year, especially when the election occurs at a time of economic stagnation" (Ostrom and Job, 1986; also Russett, 1989). At other times, this linkage does not hold.

In general, then, the available evidence indicates that we must question this plausible, widespread theory of war. Perhaps the most compelling reason for the absence of a direct linkage is that "when domestic conflict becomes extremely intense it would seem more reasonable to argue that there is a greater likelihood that a state will retreat from its foreign engagements in order to handle the situation at home" (Zinnes and Wilkenfeld, 1971).

Terrorism

Transnational terrorism poses another alarming kind of violence in contemporary world politics. The instruments of terror are varied and the motivations of terrorists diverse, but "experts agree that terrorism is the use or threat of violence, a method of combat or a strategy to achieve certain goals, that its aim is to induce a state of fear in the victim, that it is ruthless and does not conform to humanitarian norms, and that publicity is an essential factor in terrorist strategy" (Laqueur, 1986).

Some terrorist activities begin and end in a single country. However, many transcend national borders. Thus terrorism today has a uniquely transnational character that afflicts many countries. In 1990 terrorists targeted the citizens and property of 73 countries in 533 separate attacks (U.S. Department of State, 1991b: 37).

Although terrorism dates to antiquity, it emerged as a significant international problem in the 1960s (Kidder, 1990) and grew to epidemic proportions in the 1970s and 1980s. Figure 12.4 shows the changing prevalence of terrorism in today's world. The general trend suggests an increasing level of transnational terrorist activity since 1968, followed by a decline since 1988.

Terrorism is a tactic of the powerless against the powerful. Thus it is not surprising that political or social minorities and ethnic movements perpetrate many acts of terrorism. Those seeking independence and sovereign statehood, like the Palestinians in the Middle East and the Basques in Spain, typify the kinds of aspirations that animate terrorist activity. In the industrialized world, terrorism often occurs where discrepancies in income are severe and where minority groups feel deprived of the political freedoms and privileges enjoyed by the majority. Guerrilla warfare normally associated with rural uprisings is not a viable route to self-assertion in the urbanized areas of the industrialized world, but terrorist tactics are.

Consideration of terrorists' motives underscores that terrorism is not perceived by all to be a disease. One person's terrorist may, to another, be a liberator. In fact, both governments and countergovernment movements claim to seek liberty, and both are labeled terrorists by those they oppose. The difference between nationalistic "freedom fighters," whose major complaint is that they lack a country, and the protectors of freedom, often lies in the eye of the beholder. This problem makes the definition of a terrorist group not altogether obvious or noncontroversial.

Seen from this angle, terrorism by ideologically motivated fanatics, extremists, and minorities at the periphery of society may not be very different from the kinds of terrorism conducted by the state governments that they oppose. This is especially true given the way in which modern (conventional) warfare is often conducted.

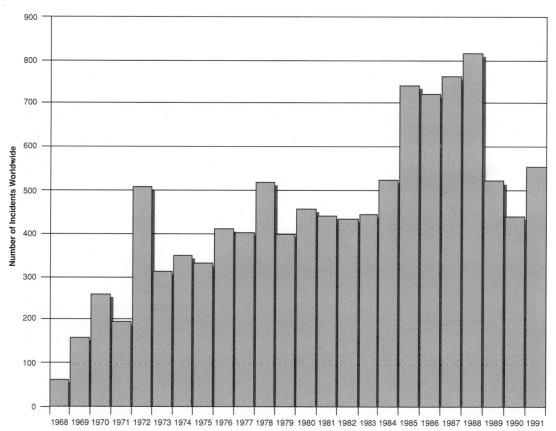

FIGURE 12.4   INTERNATIONAL TERRORIST INCIDENTS, 1968–1991
Source: Office of the Coordinator for Counterterrorism, U.S. Department of State, April, 1992.

Those who are described as terrorists, and who reject that title for themselves, make the uncomfortable point that national armed forces, fully supported by democratic opinion, have in fact employed violence and terror on a far vaster scale than what liberation movements have as yet been able to attain. The "freedom fighters" see themselves as fighting a just war. Why should they not be entitled to kill, burn and destroy as national armies, navies and air forces do, and why should the label "terrorist" be applied to them and not to the national militaries? (O'Brien, 1977: 56–57)

Although many terrorist groups today are undeniably groups without sovereignty that seek it, a broader definition of terrorism would acknowledge that many terrorist acts are state supported (see Bell, 1990; Crenshaw, 1990). Indeed, some states condone and support the terrorist activities of movements that espouse philosophies they embrace (or challenge the security of states they see as enemies). States have often financed, trained, equipped, and provided sanctuary for terrorists whose activities serve their foreign policy goals. This *state terrorism* is part of the claim that the United

States leveled in the 1980s at the behaviors of the Soviet Union, Syria, Iraq, and Libya, among others.[12] In a similar way, others accused the United States of sponsoring terrorist activities in Vietnam, Chile, Nicaragua, and elsewhere (Schlagheck, 1990).

Many terrorist sanctuaries have disappeared with the end of the Cold War. Still,

> it is unlikely that international terrorism is a passing and transitory phenomenon. The trend toward the weakening of central authority in governments, the rise in ethnic and subnational sentiments, and the increasing fractionalization of the global political process point toward its growth as a form of political protest and persuasion. Classic balance of power diplomacy is of little utility in dealing with it, for violent acts of small groups of people, or individuals, are difficult for governments to control. International terrorism is likely to continue and to expand because in the minds of many of its perpetrators it has proven to be "successful." (Pierre, 1984: 85)

THE HUMAN TRAGEDY OF VIOLENT CONFLICT . . . .

War exacts a terrible toll on human life. Its indelible mark is commemorated publicly by black flags of mourning that flutter from the homes of the war dead and memorials at grave sites. Monuments honor the courage displayed by the soldiers who gave their lives in their nations' wars, though in 1990 about 90 percent of the world's war victims were innocent civilians (Sivard, 1991: 20). Consider the grim statistics reported in UNICEF's *The State of the World's Children, 1992*. More than 1.5 million children were killed in wars during the 1980s, and more than 4 million were "physically disabled—limbs amputated, brains damaged, eyesight and hearing lost—through bombing, land-mines, firearms, torture. Five million children are in refugee camps because of war: a further 12 million have lost their homes" (in Raspberry, 1992: A31).

The tragic human consequences of violence are also revealed every day by the efforts of individuals and families seeking to escape its scourge. They can be observed fleeing from one country in hopes of finding refuge, and perhaps a better life, in another country. Religious preference, the color of one's skin, and the expression of political dissent are some of the factors that motivate refugees. Along with poverty, persecution, and the pain of hunger and starvation, war—whether intranational or international—remains a paramount cause.

The refugee asylum problem has assumed global dimensions. "United Nations estimates set the global number of refugees at about 17 million. Probably an equal number are displaced within national borders" (Meissner, 1992: 68). These "victims of protracted wars and civil strife" crossed national borders in the hope of escaping bloodshed and civil violence. They escape by air, they march by foot, and they travel

---

[12] The attack by Libyan embassy personnel on anti-Qaddafi demonstrators in London in April 1984 is an example of terrorist actions conducted by representatives of a state government. Those who retaliate against terrorist attacks become, in the eyes of the target, terrorist attackers. Thus the U.S. air strike against Libya in April 1986 provoked the charge that the United States itself practiced terrorism.

the oceans by boat. Whatever the means and the destination, their goal is the same: to find a place where survival is possible.

The ravages of war are not confined to its human victims. Some of the costs of war are economic, paid by survivors responsible for the debts and damages. This can take generations. Other costs are ecological. Consider here the 1991 Persian Gulf War (see Arkin, Durrant, and Cherni, 1991). The blackened skies have now cleared, but, as we noted in Chapter 9, the environmental damage may take decades to undo.

Could it be that a world so ingenious in perpetrating violence also will learn that war and violence are too costly, too destructive to continue? If so, can it discover viable paths to peace? In the subsequent chapters we will examine some solutions that policymakers and concerned citizens have proposed.

SUGGESTED READINGS

Brecher, Michael, Jonathan Wilkenfeld, and Sheila Moser. *Crises in the Twentieth Century: Vol. I: Handbook of International Crises.* Oxford, England: Pergamon Press, 1988.

Brogan, Patrick. *The Fighting Never Stopped: A Comprehensive Guide to World Conflict Since 1945.* New York: Vintage Books, 1990.

Gilad, Betty, ed. *Psychological Dimensions of War.* Newbury Park, Cal.: Sage Publications, 1990.

Gilpin, Robert. *War and Change in World Politics.* Cambridge, England: Cambridge University Press, 1981.

Holsti, Kalevi J. *Peace and War: Armed Conflicts and International Order 1648–1989.* New York: Cambridge Press, 1991.

Kegley, Charles W., Jr., ed. *International Terrorism: Characteristics, Causes, Controls.* New York: St. Martin's Press, 1990.

Lebow, Richard Ned. *Between Peace and War: The Nature of International Crisis.* Baltimore: Johns Hopkins University Press, 1981.

Levy, Jack S. "The Causes of War: A Review of Theories and Evidence," in Philip E. Tetlock, et al., eds., *Behavior, Society and Nuclear War, Vol. I.* New York: Oxford University Press, 1989, pp. 209–333.

Midlarsky, Manus I., ed. *Handbook of War Studies.* Boston: Unwin Hyman, 1989.

Reisman, W. Michael, and James E. Baker. *Regulating Covert Action: Practices, Contexts, and Policies of Covert Coercion Abroad in International and American Law.* New Haven, Conn.: Yale University Press, 1992.

Siverson, Randolph M., and Harvey Starr. *The Diffusion of War.* Ann Arbor: University of Michigan Press, 1991.

Thompson, Loren B., ed. *Low-Intensity Conflict: The Pattern of Warfare in the Modern World.* Lexington, Mass.: Lexington, 1989.

CHAPTER 13

• • •

MILITARY PATHS TO PEACE: ALLIANCES, THE BALANCE OF POWER, AND ARMS CONTROL

• • •

It is an unfortunate fact that we can only secure peace by preparing for war.

John F. Kennedy,
U. S. presidential candidate, 1960

I went into the British Army believing that if you want peace you must prepare for war. I now believe that if you prepare thoroughly for war you will get it.

Sir John Frederick Maurice,
British military officer, 1883

Many nations can inflict enormous destruction on their enemies. As a consequence, national security remains, as ever, elusive. Because of the escalating dangers of modern weapons, most states' sense of security has diminished, not increased, during this century.

To defend themselves, states have several options. They may (1) arm themselves; (2) form alliances to combine their armaments with those of other countries; (3) shift alliance partners to maintain a balance of power; or (4) negotiate arms control and disarmament agreements so as to reduce the threat of adversaries' weapons. In practice, most leaders usually simultaneously pursue various combinations of these approaches. Nonetheless, each represents a distinct military approach to security.

In Chapter 11 we covered the first defensive option by examining the search for national security through the acquisition of military capabilities and the practice of deterrence strategies. In this chapter we will explore the uses and consequences of the three other options.

ALLIANCES ·

Alliances are "formal associations of states for the use (or non-use) of military force, intended for either the security or the aggrandizement of their members, against specific other states" (Snyder, 1991). Alliances thus are coalitions that adhere to

• • •

realism's first rule of statecraft: to increase military capabilities. States can do this either by acquiring arms or by acquiring allies, and, as noted, throughout history states have vigorously pursued both methods. But of the two methods, alliances are more economical because they permit the defense burden to be shared.

This advantage might make alliances the preferred method for increasing military capabilities. Yet this solution has significant disadvantages, and making alliance choices has seldom been easy. It requires weighing the military strength, goals, and reliability of allies and of adversaries.

Alliances in World Politics: Rival Theories

Three contending schools of thought exist within the boundaries of classical political realism regarding these calculations.[1] The first image holds that alliances are basically advantageous. The second maintains that the costs of alliances usually outweigh the benefits, and that, because alliances are generally disadvantageous, states should eschew them except when absolutely necessary. The third holds alliances in contempt, arguing that they have proved so dangerous that prudent policymakers must avoid them altogether.

The Advantages of Alliance

Allies provide a means to counterbalance threats posed by potential aggressors in the anarchical international environment. Accordingly, "whenever in recorded history a system of multiple sovereignty has existed, some of the sovereign units when involved in conflicts with others have entered into alliances" (Wolfers, 1968), "even in advance, against [a] probable aggressor" (Morgenthau, 1959); alliances are "typically against, and only derivatively for, someone or something" (Liska, 1962).

Facing common dangers, states have several good reasons to ally.

> The primary benefit of alliance is obviously security. . . . Security benefits in a mutual defense alliance include chiefly a reduced probability of being attacked (deterrence), greater strength in case of attack (defense) and prevention of the ally's alliance with one's adversary (preclusion). (Snyder, 1991: 90)

Alliances have seldom been long-lasting, however, and have often dissolved when the common threat receded. For this reason, alliance formation usually is seen not as a goal in itself but as a strategy that includes both the recruitment of allies and the abandonment of them. Recognizing that "alignment and dealignment are the main short-term strategies for increasing security," the basic options consist of seeking "changes in foreign policy commitments, adding or expanding relations with nations that can provide immediate increases in one's security, and eliminating or curtailing relations with nations that are a drain on security" (Scarborough and Bueno de Mesquita, 1988). According to the logic of *realpolitik*, the only good alliance is one

---

[1] This synthesis of the rival images of alliances in *realpolitik* follows Kegley and Raymond (1990; also 1993).

that can be easily dissolved when the threat to the security of its members declines. As Britain's Lord Palmerston admonished in 1848, states "should have no eternal allies and no perpetual enemies"; their only duty is to follow their interests.

The Disadvantages of Alliance

The preeminent risk inherent in alliances with others is that they will bind one's state to a commitment that later may become disadvantageous. Throughout history policymakers have been ever mindful of the risk of entanglement. Entrusting their security to the pledges of others reduces their future freedom of action. Consequently, leaders usually adhere to warnings about the costs of commitments to allies, such as George F. Kennan's:

> The relations among nations, in this imperfect world, constitute a fluid substance, always in motion, changing subtly from day to day in ways that are difficult to detect from the myopia of the passing moment, and even difficult to discern from the perspective of the future one. The situation at one particular time is never quite the same as the situation of five years later—indeed it is sometimes very significantly different, even though the stages by which this change came about are seldom visible at the given moment. This is why wise and experienced statesmen usually shy away from commitments likely to constitute limitations on a government's behavior at unknown dates in the future in the face of unpredictable situations. (Kennan, 1984a: 238)

Hence, though alliances provide some measure of protection, binding a state to another reduces states' capacity to make accommodative realignments when conditions change. Indeed, the usefulness of any alliance is destined to diminish when the common external threat that brought the coalition into being recedes, as inevitably it will (Wolfers, 1962). Therefore policymakers are often advised not to take a fixed position on temporary convergences of national interests, and to forge alliances only to deal with immediate threats. The risks of entrapment and abandonment "tend to vary inversely: reducing one tends to increase the other" (Snyder, 1984). Hence many states' alliance policies are shaped by their acute awareness of the many risks of sharing their fate with allies (see Table 13.1).

The Dangers of Alliance

Many realists go further and counsel avoiding alliances altogether. They perceive alliance formation as dangerous for five basic reasons. First, alliances enable aggressive states to aggregate resources for offensive wars. Alliances simply do not deter war—they promote it because expansionist states can act more aggressively than they otherwise would when they can count on their allies' assistance. As Adolf Hitler said, "Any alliance whose purpose is not the intention to wage war is senseless and useless."

Second, alliances threaten enemies and provoke them to form counteralliances, with the result that the security of *both* coalitions is reduced.

> Peacetime alliances may occur in order to reduce the insecurity of anarchy or reduce armament costs. If they do they will tend to create relations of enmity as well as alignment.

> ## TABLE 13.1 ALLIANCES: SOME POSTULATED DANGERS
>
> Alliances . . .
> - Foreclose options
> - Reduce the capacity of states to adapt to changing circumstances
> - Weaken a state's influence capability by decreasing the number of additional partners with which it can align
> - Eliminate the advantages in bargaining that can be derived from deliberately fostering ambiguity about one's intentions
> - Provoke the fears of adversaries
> - Entangle states in disputes with their ally's enemies
> - Interfere with the negotiation of disputes involving an ally's enemy by precluding certain issues from being placed on the agenda for debate
> - Preserve existing rivalries
> - Stimulate envy and resentment on the part of friends who are outside the alliance and therefore are not beneficiaries of its advantages

Even if the initial alliance is not directed at a specific opponent, other states will perceive it as a threat and begin to behave as enemies, perhaps by forming a counteralliance. Not only will alliances identify friends and foes, they will create interests consistent with such relations. (Snyder, 1991: 88)

In a similar vein, "alliances both reveal any added support that a state may have, and the amount of support that a potential belligerent may need. . . . The reduction of uncertainty brought about by such information may be all that is needed to facilitate an aggressor's desire to attack another state" (Bueno de Mesquita, 1981).

Third, alliance formation may draw otherwise neutral parties into opposed coalitions. As Thomas Jefferson warned, alliances can be dangerously "entangling." They require members to come to one another's aid, so that alliances are likely to involve members in the wars of their partners.

Fourth, once states join forces, they must control the behavior of their own allies. Management of intra-alliance relations is necessary to deter each member from reckless aggression against its enemies that would threaten the security of the alliance's other members. Also, allies must work to deter defection from the alliance.

Fifth, the possibility always exists that today's ally might become tomorrow's enemy. Realists believe that all states are natural enemies, that there are no permanent friends or adversaries. The historical record is noteworthy in this respect. In the period between the Congress of Vienna in 1815 and the 1960s, wars between allies were commonplace. "More than 25 percent of coalition partners eventually [went] to war against each other" (Russett and Starr, 1989: 95). Thus, when alliances form they can increase the prospects for, and the scope of, war.

Alliances in the Realist and Idealist Images

In an address to the U.S. Senate on January 22, 1917, President Woodrow Wilson proposed that henceforth "all nations avoid entangling alliances which would draw them into . . . a net of intrigue and selfish rivalry." His advice reflected the belief that alliances and secret diplomacy transform limited conflicts into complex, global wars.

Like idealists such as Wilson, realists also stress the dangers and disadvantages of alliances. However, realists qualify their criticism by holding that alliances can be beneficial if policymakers remain flexible and if prevailing international norms support an elastic interpretation of alliance commitments and the rights of neutrals. Most policymakers schooled in the logic of *realpolitik* contend that entanglements occur only when alliance structures become rigid, when commitments are interpreted as irrevocable pledges, and when states operate from the belief that their commitments oblige them to take sides in their allies' serious disputes.

Let us examine these arguments more closely. Their veracity is best evaluated by observing the possible contribution of alliance formation to the maintenance of the balance of power, a controversial subject to which we now turn.

THE BALANCE OF POWER

International anarchy places responsibility for national security on each state, and, as the seventeenth-century English political philosopher Thomas Hobbes put it, states are engaged in a perpetual "war of all against all." To political realists and their neorealist colleagues (recall Chapter 2), reforming this self-help competitive system is not realistic because international anarchy is permanent.

Given the continuing popularity of these assumptions, how might policymakers effectively enhance their states' survival in such a disorderly system? To realists, survival and world order rest on the proper functioning of a system of military balances. What is the meaning of this approach, broadly captured in the phrase "balance of power"?

Assumptions of Balance-of-Power Theory

Balance of power is an ambiguous concept used in a variety of ways (see Claude, 1962; Haas, 1953). At the core of its many meanings is the idea that peace will result when military power is distributed so that no one state is strong enough to dominate the others. If one state, or a combination of states, gains enough power to threaten others, compelling incentives exist for those threatened to disregard their superficial differences and unite in a defensive alliance. The aggregation of power resulting from such collusion would, according to this conception, deter the would-be attacker from pursuing expansionism. Hence, from the laissez-faire competition of predatory and defensive rivals would emerge an equilibrium, a balance of contending factions, that would maintain the status quo.

Balance-of-power theory is also predicated on the premises that weakness invites attack and that countervailing power must be used to deter potential aggressors. If expansionist power drives guide every nation's actions, then all nations are potential adversaries, and each nation must strengthen its military capability to protect itself. Invariably, this reasoning rationalizes the quest for military superiority because others pursue it as well.

On the surface, these assumptions appear dubious because, self-fulfillingly, they could breed the very outcome most feared—a destructive globalized war. The European policymakers who fashioned balance-of-power theory in the decades following the Peace of Westphalia in 1648 were not irrational, however (see Gulick, 1955). They reasoned that a system founded on suspicion and competition in which all states were free to act in their perceived national interests would distribute power evenly through realignments, and this would curtail the temptation of any actor to seek to dominate others.

The Balance Process

In classic balance-of-power theory, fear of a third party would encourage alignments because those threatened would need help to offset the power of the mutual adversary. An alliance would add the ally's power to their own and deny the addition of that power to the enemy. As alliances combine power, the offsetting coalitions would give neither a clear advantage. Therefore, war would appear illogical and be averted.

To deter an aggressor, counteralliances were expected to form easily because states sitting on the sidelines could not risk nonalignment. If they refused to ally, their own vulnerability would encourage the expansionist state to attack them at a later time. In theory, the result of these individual calculations would be the formation of coalitions approximately equal in power.[2]

THE RULES OF THE BALANCE-OF-POWER GAME   To help maintain an even distribution of power, realists recommended rules of behavior that promoted fluid

---

[2] According to the so-called size principle, rational actors will tend to form coalitions sufficient in size to ensure victory and no larger; hence political coalitions tend to be roughly equal in size (see Riker, 1962). Morgenthau (1985) and Gulick (1955) also discuss the rationality of policies aimed at equalizing the power of competing coalitions, predicated on the willingness to recognize their interest in stopping aggression. As U.S. President Jimmy Carter expressed this premise in 1980, "History teaches perhaps few clear lessons. But surely one such lesson learned by the world at great cost is that aggression unopposed becomes a contagious disease."

and rapidly shifting alliances. They recognized that alliance competition would not automatically achieve equilibrium, and that a balance would develop only if states practiced certain behaviors. One requirement was that a great power not immediately threatened by the rise of another power or coalition would perform the role of "the balancer" by offsetting the new challenger's power. Great Britain often played this role in the eighteenth and nineteenth centuries, when it gave its support to one or another coalition to ensure that no one achieved preponderance. Winston Churchill (1948) described Britain's role in this process, declaring that "for 400 years the foreign policy of England has been to oppose the strongest, most aggressive, most dominating power on the continent, in joining the weaker states."

In addition to a balancer, all states had to behave according to the following "essential rules":

> (1) increase capabilities but negotiate rather than fight; (2) fight rather than fail to increase capabilities; (3) stop fighting rather than eliminate an essential actor; (4) oppose any coalition or single actor which tends to assume a position of predominance within the system; (5) constrain actors who subscribe to supranational organizational principles; and (6) permit defeated or constrained essential national actors to reenter the system as acceptable role partners. (Kaplan, 1957: 23)

According to these rules, competition is proper because it leads to the equalization of capabilities among the major competitors. The balance-of-power approach deals with the problem of war in a way that preserves the problem, for war is a way of measuring national power and a means for changing the distribution of power while perpetuating the essential features of the system itself.

Preconditions for Peace through Balance The successful operation of a balance-of-power system also presupposed that the prerequisites for its successful operation be present.[3] For example, to maintain a balance, states must possess accurate information about others' capabilities and motives. Moreover, the theory argues that there must also be (1) a sufficiently large number of independent states to make alliance formation and dissolution readily possible;[4] (2) a limited geographic area; (3) freedom of action for national leaders; (4) relative equality in states' capabilities; (5) a common political culture in which the rules of the system are recognized and respected; (6) a modicum of homogeneity across the system's members; (7) a weapons technology that inhibits quick mobilization for war, prevents preemptive first-strike attacks that defeat the enemy before it can organize a retaliatory response, and reduces the prospects of wars of annihilation; and (8) the absence of international or supranational institutions capable of interfering with states' alignments and realignments.

---

[3] The conditions believed necessary for the successful operation of the balance-of-power mechanisms remain somewhat controversial. Kenneth Waltz (1979) provides a useful review and critique of the conventional reasoning associated with this issue by advancing the neorealist thesis that "balance-of-power politics prevail whenever two, and only two, requirements are met: that the order be anarchic and that it be populated by units wishing to survive."

[4] Morton A. Kaplan (1957) postulates that a stable balance-of-power system requires at least five powerful states or blocs of states.

The preconditions characterize the environment of international politics during much of the period prior to World Wars I and II, but we can question whether they exist today. Are the assumptions underlying classic balance-of-power theory still warranted?

The Breakdown of Power Balances

Is international order truly a product of alliance formation and power balances, as many (Liska, 1968; Osgood, 1968) believe? Or, instead, when arms races and alliance formation combine power into polarized contending blocs, do the states so aligned find that their security actually diminishes?

If the assumptions of the balance-of-power theory are correct, then historical periods in which the basic preconditions for the operation of balance-of-power politics were in evidence should also have been periods in which war became less frequent. What does the historical record suggest?

The Eurocentric system that existed from the mid-seventeenth century until World War I is generally regarded as the "golden age" of balance-of-power politics. But even then the balance of power was always precarious at best (Dehio, 1962). Indeed, the regularity with which wars broke out in Europe between the mid-1600s and the early twentieth century, when the fundamental prerequisites for the mechanical "invisible hand" of the balance of power presumably existed, attests to the repeated failure of its mechanisms to preserve peace. Although the classical systems may at times have prolonged the length of peacetime between wars and possibly limited their duration and damage when they occurred, a balancing of power never kept the peace.[5] To be sure, several decades of peace existed during the balance of power in Europe (between the Congress of Vienna in 1815 and the outbreak of war across Europe in 1848, and after the Franco-Prussian War in 1871 until 1914).[6] But more striking is the destructiveness of the wars that erupted when the balance of power failed to prevent a general war.

It is noteworthy in this context that the pattern of recurrent general wars in Europe ended when the nuclear era began, after World War II. Since then, war among industrial societies has been virtually nonexistent—a "long peace" (Gaddis, 1986) took root. Could it be that nuclear weapons (the "balance of terror") deterred great-power belligerence since 1945 more than did the balance of power? Alliance formation and balance-of-power politics could not have caused this long peace because the rigid alliance blocs during the Cold War precluded the rapid realignments necessary for the equilibrium that balance-of-power theory envisions. Arguably, the destructiveness of

---

[5] Research shows that during the nineteenth century alliance formation was associated with the absence of war, but that throughout the first half of the twentieth century this linkage no longer held: As many nations became members of alliances, the international system was relatively more war prone (Singer and Small, 1968).

[6] It could be argued that the relative peace of nineteenth-century Europe was *not* the product of an equilibrium resulting from balance-of-power politics but, instead, was a result of the extraordinary preponderance of power possessed and used by Great Britain to keep peace among its European rivals (see Organski, 1968).

sophisticated weapons since the 1950s replaced the deterrent function that alliance formation and power balances performed in previous systems.

Equally questionable is the balance-of-power assumption that the relative strength of nations determines whether peace will result. Contrary evidence suggests that arming nations may actually invite attack upon themselves. In five of the nine wars involving the great powers in the 150 years following the Congress of Vienna, the nations attacked were stronger militarily than those initiating the war (Singer and Small, 1974). This empirical regularity does not speak well for the premise that seeking military advantages over others deters aggression.[7] Instead, the growth of a state's military power may so terrify its adversaries that they are motivated to initiate a preemptive strike in order to prevent their subjugation.

Collective Security versus Power Balances

The outbreak of World War I, perhaps more than any other event, discredited balance-of-power politics and promoted the search for alternatives to it. The catastrophic proportions of that war led many to view the balance-of-power mechanism as a *cause* of war instead of an instrument for its prevention. Indeed, many critics cited the arms races, secret treaties, and cross-cutting alliances surrounding balance-of-power politics before the outbreak of the war as its causes.

President Woodrow Wilson voiced the most vehement opposition to balance-of-power politics. He and other political idealists hoped to replace the balance of power with the principle of *collective security*.

The League of Nations embodied that principle, as it was built on the assumption that peace-loving nations could collectively deter—and, if necessary, counteract—aggression. Instead of accepting war as a legitimate instrument of national policy, collective security sought to inhibit war through the threat of collective action. The theory proposed (1) to retaliate against *any* aggression or attempt to establish hegemony—not just those acts that threatened particular countries; (2) to involve the participation of *all* member states—not just a sufficient number to stop the aggressor; and (3) to create an international organization to identify acts of aggression and to organize a military response to them—not just to let individual states decide for themselves whether to undertake self-help measures.

To the disappointment of its proponents, collective security also failed. Japan's aggression against Manchuria in 1931 (and China proper in 1937) and Italy's invasion of Ethiopia in 1935 were widely condemned, but collective resistance was not forthcoming. Furthermore, Germany's aggressive threats against Czechoslovakia and other European nations in the late 1930s elicited no collective response. Collective security did not prevent World War II and hence was discredited.

The Revival of Balance-of-Power Politics

Following World War II, realists maintained that national self-reliance was the only trustworthy safeguard of security, that peace would come through strength, and that

---

[7] Nor does the possession of superior firepower assure a state victory in warfare: "The chances of the starter of a war being victorious are shrinking. In the 1980s only 18 percent of the starters were winners" (Sivard, 1991: 20).

it was necessary to confront a potential aggressor with a preponderance of power to successfully deter its aggression. U.S. President Richard Nixon was one among many leaders who reaffirmed the balance-of-power approach when he opined, "We must remember the only time in the history of the world that we have had any extended period of peace is when there has been a balance of power. . . . It will be a safer world . . . if we have a strong, healthy United States, Europe, Soviet Union, China, Japan, each balancing the other."

To evaluate the validity of this proposition and of the balance-of-power theory in general, it is instructive to review the evolution of the international system's polarity structure since World War II during which a long, great power peace unfolded.

Post–World War II Models of the Balance of Power

Power can be distributed in different ways. Historically, these have ranged from highly concentrated distributions on one end of the continuum to highly dispersed distributions on the other. The former have included regional empires (such as the Roman Empire), while an example of the latter is the approximate equality of power held by the European nations at the conclusion of the Napoleonic Wars in 1815.

Following the conventional periodizations of analysts, we can identify three major configurations in the distribution of international power since 1945, with a possible fourth one emergent in the post–Cold War period.[8]

Unipolarity

Most nations were devastated by the global war that ended in 1945, but the United States was left in a clearly superordinate position, with its economy accounting for about half the combined GNP of the world's nations. The United States was also the only nation with the awesome new weapon, the atomic bomb. It had already demonstrated its willingness to use that weapon, which underscored to others that the United States was without rival and incapable of being counterbalanced. The United States was not just stronger than anybody—it was stronger than everybody. This immediate postwar power configuration was *unipolar* because power was concentrated in the hands of a single dominant hegemon. This period was short-lived, however.

Bipolarity

The recovery of the Soviet economy, the growth of its military capabilities, the maintenance of a large army, and growing Soviet animosity toward the United States soon gave rise to a new distribution of world power. The Soviets broke the U.S. monopoly of atomic weapons in 1949 and exploded a thermonuclear device in 1953, less than a year after the United States. This achievement symbolized creation of a

---

[8] Historians disagree as to the precise dates at which a particular distribution of power collapsed and a new one arose. For discussions of alternative periodizations, see Kaplan (1957); Oren (1984); Rosecrance (1963); and Thompson (1988).

bipolar distribution, as military capabilities became concentrated in the hands of two competitive *superpowers.*

The concentration of power (what scholars term *polarity*) into two dominant actors induced *polarization* as power combined through alliance formation to form two countervailing *blocs* or opposed coalitions.[9] The concept of polarization, which refers to the propensity of actors to cluster around the most powerful states, is especially apt in this context because a *pole* is a fit metaphor for a magnet—it both repels and attracts (Nogee, 1975). The formation of the North Atlantic Treaty Organization (NATO), linking the United States to the defense of Western Europe, and the Warsaw Pact, linking the Soviet Union in a formal alliance with its Eastern European clients, were manifestations of the polarization process through which states combined their military resources to reinforce a bipolar structure. The opposing alliance systems formed partly because the superpowers competed for allies and partly because the less powerful nations looked to one or the other of the superpowers for protection. Correspondingly, each superpower's allies gave it forward bases from which to carry on the competition. In addition, the involvement of most other states in the superpowers' struggle globalized the East-West conflict. Few states remained outside the superpowers' rival alliance networks as neutral or nonaligned actors.

By grouping the system's nation-states into two blocs, each led by a superpower, the Cold War's bipolar structure bred insecurity among all (Spanier, 1975). The balance was constantly at stake. Each bloc leader, fearing that its adversary would attain hegemony, viewed every move, however defensive, as the first step toward world conquest. The conflict became "zero-sum" because both sides viewed what one side gained as a loss for the other. Both therefore attached great importance to recruiting new allies, and fear that an old ally might desert the fold was ever present. Bipolarity left little room for compromise or maneuver and worked against the normalization of superpower relations (Waltz, 1990).

Bipolycentrism

The major Cold War coalitions associated with bipolarity began to disintegrate in the 1960s and early 1970s. As their internal cohesion eroded and new centers of power emerged, a bipolycentric system (Spanier, 1975) came into being. *Bipolycentrism* described the continued military superiority of the United States and the Soviet Union, and their allies' continued reliance on their respective superpower patrons for security. At the same time, increasing room for maneuver by the weaker alliance partners became possible. Hence the term *polycentrism*, indicating the emergence of diverse relationships among the nations subordinate to the superpowers at this second tier (such as the friendly relations that were nurtured between the United States and Romania, on the one hand, and those between France and the Soviet Union, on the other). The secondary powers also began to cultivate ties across alliance boundaries

---

[9] Note that these concepts are sometimes used interchangeably, but that they refer to distinct dimensions of the two primary ways military power is aggregated (or dispersed) at any point in time in the international system: by either independently building arms at home, or by states' aggregation of their arms through alliance formation.

(such as between Poland and West Germany) to enhance their bargaining position within their own alliance. The superpowers remained dominant militarily, but this less rigid system created new foreign policy roles, other than simply aligned or nonaligned.

Rapid technological innovation in the superpowers' major weapons systems was a principal catalyst of change. In particular, intercontinental ballistic missiles (ICBMs) eroded the necessity of forward-base areas for striking at the heart of the adversary and diminished the drive to create and maintain tight, cohesive alliance systems composed of reliable partners.

In addition, the narrowed differences in the superpowers' arsenals loosened the ties that had previously bound allies to one another. The European members of NATO in particular began to question whether the United States would indeed, as it had pledged, protect Paris or Bonn by sacrificing New York. Under what conditions might Washington or Moscow be willing to risk a nuclear holocaust? The uncertainty aroused by such questioning became pronounced as the pledge to extend deterrence to allies by retaliating against their attacker seemed increasingly insincere. As former CIA director Stansfield Turner acknowledged in 1986, "It's not conceivable that any president would risk the very existence of [the United States] in order to defend [our] European allies from a conventional assault."

In partial response to the dilemma this posed, other states, particularly France, decided to protect themselves by developing their own nuclear capabilities, with the result that the diffusion of power already under way gathered momentum.

As these changes unfolded in the 1970s and 1980s, Cold War categories used to classify "free world" (capitalist) and "socialist" (communist) countries' foreign policy alignments lost much of their relevance, as bipolycentrism implies. The revival of democratic capitalism in the late 1980s that led communist states to accept free market principles eroded further the adhesive bonds of ideology that had formerly helped these countries face their security problems from a common posture. Such fissures in both blocs widened, as disputes arose in the Western alliance over strategic doctrine, arms control, U.S. military bases on allies' territory, and "out-of-area conflicts" (those beyond the traditional geographical boundaries of NATO). Not only decomposing blocs, but also declining support in general for the sanctity of alliance commitments became evident. As fears of a new world war steadily lessened and the Cold War began to fade, leaders questioned whether defense alliances were still needed.

The events that began in 1989 with the tearing down of the Berlin Wall tore apart the post–World War II architecture of competing blocs. With the end of this division, and without a Soviet threat, the consistency of outlook and singularity of purpose that once bound NATO members together dissipated. To many critics, NATO and the Warsaw Pact had institutionalized antagonisms and perpetuated the Cold War—and were no longer needed.

Central to the unfolding debate was "the German question." According to Lord Ismay, the first secretary general of NATO, the original purpose of the Atlantic alliance was "to keep the Russians out, the Americans in, and the Germans down." In 1990, though the Soviet Union feared a "Fourth Reich"—a united, powerful, and potentially revisionist German state—the Soviet Union reversed its long-standing opposition to German unification and agreed to withdraw its military from Europe. It did not make that dramatic concession without conditions, however. It insisted that unification be orchestrated through the active management of *all* the major World War II allies, and that Germany reduce its armed forces and the United States keep a military presence in NATO on German soil.

Germany met all of these preconditions in 1990. In September the Four Powers (the United States, the Soviet Union, Great Britain, and France) and the two Germanys (the "Two plus Four") negotiated a treaty in Moscow that terminated the Four Powers' rights over Germany. German leaders declared they had no territorial claims to make in Europe, including the territories in Poland that were annexed during and after World War II. Moreover, they pledged never to obtain nuclear weapons, and to reduce their 670,000-person armed forces to 370,000 troops (in exchange for the removal of 370,000 Soviet soldiers from Germany by the end of 1994). And Germany and the Soviet Union signed a bilateral treaty under which the two powers promised never to attack each other.

The West greeted these agreements (and Soviet concessions) with enthusiasm because they symbolized at once the retreat of the Soviet Union from a region, East Europe, it had long regarded as central to its security, and the geostrategic shift of NATO influence into the heartland of the Warsaw Pact, which formally dissolved early in 1991.

Although in the early 1990s many perceived the need to replace NATO and the defunct Warsaw Pact with a new security arrangement, most leaders maintained that some configuration of collective defense pacts remained necessary to cement relationships and stabilize the rush of cascading events. President Bush, for example, was a vocal advocate of the continuing need to anchor security in alliances, pledging to keep U.S. troops in Europe and promising that the United States would remain the backbone of NATO, which he sought to preserve.

To others, a new Concert of Europe like that which the great powers created in the wake of the Napoleonic Wars in 1815 was needed. The Soviets and some Western analysts (Mueller, 1990; also Rosecrance, 1992) reasoned that it was useful to preserve NATO if it were restructured not to contain enemies but to control allies. For that, *all* the countries in Europe would be required to coordinate their defense policies. This would incorporate the East European and former Soviet republics pursuing democratization into a European-wide framework and possibly shift peacekeeping responsibilities from NATO to the larger Conference on Security and Cooperation in Europe (CSCE), which in 1992 expanded to fifty-two members when each of the former Soviet republics joined the organization.

An alternative scenario is the conversion of NATO from a military alliance to a larger community focused primarily on the political dimensions of security. The 1991 Rome Summit moved in this direction by drafting "The Alliance's New Strategic Concept." The Rome Declaration announced formation of a new North Atlantic Cooperation Council (NACC) "to build genuine partnership among the North Atlantic Alliance and the countries of Central and Eastern Europe." A later meeting witnessed the members of NATO sitting at the same table with the former Warsaw Pact states and newly independent Baltic republics, facing a request from Russia to become a member.

A united Europe would create a far more equal distribution of power than that which existed in the bipolycentric system of the 1970s and 1980s and the bipolar system that preceded it in the 1950s and 1960s. The wave of change could presage the beginning of a new multipolar system.

Multipolarity

U.S. Deputy Secretary of State Lawrence Eagleburger proclaimed in 1989 that "we are now moving into . . . a world in which power and influence is diffused among a multiplicity of states—[a] multipolar world." A *multipolar* system of relatively equal powers similar to the classical European balance-of-power system may indeed best describe the emerging distribution of power. Such a multipolar system might consist of the United States, Russia, Germany, Japan, and perhaps China. To these might be added the European Community, whose twelve members signed a (controversial) European Union treaty in February 1992 that called for the eventual amalgamation of Europe.

What will be the likely character of such a multipolar world? As we have seen, when power has been relatively evenly distributed in the past, each player has been assertive, independent, and competitive; diplomacy has displayed a nonideological, chesslike character; and conflict has been intense as each contender has nervously feared the power of its rivals.

In a new multipolar system, we can expect the major powers to align together against others on particular issues, as interests dictate. Behind the diplomatic smiles and handshakes, one-time friends and allies will grow apart, and formally "specialized" relationships will likely dissolve. Consider the U.S.-Japan-EC rivalry on the economic battlefield (Thurow, 1992).

Multipolarity also presages the potential alignment of former adversaries. The United States and the former Soviet republics, victors in World War II, now find themselves weary from the Cold War competition and apprehensive about an ascendant Germany and Japan. As a result, in the new multipolar world they could become "natural" allies, as Russian strategist Peter Gladkov put it in 1992. Hence, multipolarity opens the door to many fluid, cross-cutting alignments.

If the fundamental postwar trend toward the dispersion of global power continues, the prospects for peace will be affected. Which is the more probable consequence, war or peace?

Polarity and Peace?

In the wake of the Cold War and the disintegration of its bipolar structure, the long-standing debate has intensified about which type of power distribution—unipolar, bipolar, or multipolar—is the most stable. Let us compare the conflicting views in this controversy.[10]

---

[10] This discussion follows Kegley and Raymond (1992).

Unipolarity and Peace

One position, informed by the concentration of military power during the *pax Romana*, *pax Britannica*, and *pax Americana*, holds that "the periods of known preponderance are periods of peace":

> It is often claimed that a balance of power brings peace. . . . There were periods when an equal distribution of power between contenders actually existed . . . but these . . . were the exception rather than the rule. . . . Closer examination reveals that they were periods of war, not peace. (Organski, 1968: 293)

If this view is accurate, then peace will occur when one state acquires enough power to deter others' expansionist ambitions. The proposition springs from the arguments that "an unequal power distribution (or preponderance) promotes peace because the more powerful opponent has no need to go to war, while the weaker side would be foolish to do so," but that "an equal power distribution between opponents increases the likelihood of war because each opponent thinks it can win" (Simowitz, 1982).

If we think of the United States as the hegemonic power in the post–World War II system, these seemingly plausible conclusions about the stability of unipolar systems do not bode well for peace in the future. For if present trends continue, the so-called "unipolar moment" of unchallenged U.S. hegemony (Krauthammer, 1990–1991) will pass and the late 1990s will likely witness the continuing deconcentration of power. The new world order in this case would be increasingly disorderly (see also Chapter 7).

Bipolarity and Peace

In contrast, a second school of thought maintains that a bipolar world like the one that emerged in the 1950s is the most stable (for example, Waltz, 1964). Here the argument is that the heightened tension accompanying bipolarity compelled superpower caution and restrained their subordinate allies from provoking crises. According to this line of reasoning, stability, ironically, results from "the division of all nations into two camps [because it] raises the costs of war to such a high level that all but the most fundamental conflicts are resolved without resort to violence" (Bueno de Mesquita, 1975). Under such stark simplicities and balanced symmetries, the two leading rivals have incentives to manage crises to prevent them from escalating to war. It is also thought that the clarity surrounding bipolarity keeps leaders alert and promotes their caution.

Those who believe that a bipolar world is inherently more stable than a multipolar one draw support from the fact that in the bipolar environment of the 1950s, when the threat of war was endemic, major war did not occur. True, the superpowers went to the brink of war repeatedly, but they never went over the brink. Extrapolating, these observers (for example, Mearsheimer, 1990; also Saperstein, 1991) reason that because now a new multipolar distribution of global power makes it impossible to run the world from one or two centers, disorder will result:

> As the world becomes more multipolar—with economic leverage and even political-military power being more widely dispersed among nations—it isn't necessarily becoming a safer,

gentler globe. And as nations become more interdependent, they aren't necessarily becoming more cooperative.

[There] is every reason to believe that the world of the 1990s will be less predictable and in many ways more unstable than the world of the last several decades. . . .

It is rather basic. So long as there were only two great powers, like two big battleships clumsily and cautiously circling each other, confrontations—or accidents—were easier to avoid. Now, with the global lake more crowded with ships of varying sizes, fueled by different ambitions and piloted with different degrees of navigational skill, the odds of collisions become far greater. (House, 1989: A10)

Multipolarity and Peace

A third school of thought argues that multipolar systems, not unipolar or bipolar ones, are the least war prone. The reasons advanced differ, but there is a shared belief that polarized systems that either concentrate power as in a unipolar system, or that divide the globe into two antagonistic blocs, as in bipolarity, promote struggles for dominance. During the Cold War, for instance, "the leaders of each bloc [tried] to destroy and revolutionize their rivals [and sought] to wear down the other [by] using force to maintain and expand their blocs" (Pelz, 1991).

Moreover, this school perceives bipolarity as dangerously destabilizing because bipolarity by definition generates the fear that tempts each bloc to attain superior military capability. As Hans J. Morgenthau (1985) grimly described it, the Cold War's bipolar system reduced the international system "to the primitive spectacle of two giants eyeing each other with watchful suspicion. They [bent] every effort to increase their military potential to the utmost, since this is all they [had] to count on. Both [prepared] to strike the first decisive blow, for if one [did] not strike it the other might. Thus, contain or be contained, conquer or be conquered, destroy or be destroyed, [became] the watchwords of Cold War diplomacy." In contrast to bipolar competition, multipolar systems encompass a larger number of autonomous actors, giving rise to more potential alliance partners, which are essential to the operation of a balance to counterbalance a would-be aggressor, for shifting alliances can occur only when there are multiple power centers (Deutsch and Singer, 1964).

Note that this perspective portrays polarization[11] as hazardous because the structural rigidity it fosters significantly reduces interaction opportunities[12] and crosscutting allegiances that constrain conflict.[13] Under these circumstances, minor disagreements easily become magnified into larger tests of will. Lacking suppleness,

---

[11] A system with multiple power centers can be said to be moving toward a greater degree of polarization if its members form separate blocs whose external interactions are characterized by increasing levels of conflict while their internal interactions become more cooperative (Rapkin and Thompson with Christopherson, 1989). Conversely, polarization decreases when the number of alignments expands.

[12] The concept of *interaction opportunities* refers to the fact that as the number of autonomous actors increases, the probability that more actors will develop relationships with an expanding number of other actors also grows, thereby increasing the number of possible coalitions.

[13] Numerous studies provide evidence that polarized blocs (such as the European system on the eve of World War I) are war prone (for example, Wallace, 1973) whereas a moderate amount of flexibility in the structure of alliances has inhibited the onset of war. Historically, when tight, polarized alliances approximately equal in capability have emerged and alliance networks have tightened, the incidence of war has risen (Kim, 1989).

polarized configurations of power have historically deteriorated into struggles for preeminence between two armed hostile camps, and this means that "bipolarity can, at times, be just as destabilizing as multipolarity" (Thompson, 1988). Among the examples of unstable bipolar systems are the rivalries in antiquity between ancient Athens and Sparta and between the Greek confederations and the Persians, and, in more modern history, between Hapsburg and Valois in the sixteenth century, England and the Netherlands a century later, and England and France in the eighteenth century.

A Multipolar Future

A new, less polarized international system after the Cold War is likely. However, the probable consequences of a new multipolar system are not clear, as the three schools of thought on the relationship between polarity and global stability suggest.[14] Because "there is no real consensus on whether systems with a certain number of poles are more war prone than others" (Russett and Starr, 1989), it would be imprudent to jump to the conclusion that a new multipolar system necessarily spells another period of warfare. Different *types* of multipolar systems will emerge involving variant levels of commitment to alliances, and these combinations can produce very disparate outcomes. Because alternate scenarios are both possible and plausible, and the presence or absence of a particular polarity balance by itself will not dictate whether war will result, we have reasons to both celebrate and mourn the passing of the Cold War's competitive bipolar world.

To conclude, aggregation of power by states to balance power as a way to preserve peace has a rather checkered history. Often, the alliances formed and the distributions of power produced failed to avert a breakdown of world order. Yet history also suggests that outcomes depend on still other factors. One element finds expression in negotiated arms agreements designed to change the existing balance of power.

DISARMAMENT AND ARMS CONTROL . . . .

Some reformers have attacked the theory that power can be balanced with power to preserve world order, advocating instead the biblical prescription that nations should beat their swords into plowshares. The destructiveness and dispersion of today's weapons have inspired many people once again to take this idealist notion seriously.

Controlling Weapons Proliferation

Do the weapons of war contribute to its frequency? Several rationales suggest that they do (see Johansen, 1991). Countries build arms for use in conflict. A nation that

---

[14] Many investigations suggest that a direct relationship between multipolar systems and the probability of war cannot be safely drawn (see Bueno de Mesquita, 1981; Ostrom and Aldrich, 1978; Levy, 1985; Hopf, 1991).

arms itself signals to others its potentially aggressive designs. If others fear that the weapons are directed toward them, they often feel compelled to arm themselves. Furthermore, the possession of arms may tempt a threatened party to use them in a preemptive strike to defeat the stronger enemy before it can attack.

On the other hand, war cannot occur if the instruments of force are not available. Nor are nations without weapons always the most likely targets of aggression by their armed neighbors (although they are not freed from that fear). Instead, as the Bible suggests and as evidence supports, countries that have lived by the sword have died by the sword (see Midlarsky, 1975; Richardson, 1960a). The acquisition of arms may invite attack because weapons elicit fear and aggression in others. If enemies are most dangerous when provoked—and nothing is more provocative than a sophisticated system of delivering destruction—then the creation of intimidating weapons systems with which to threaten enemies may be counterproductive. This principle translates into the observation that each new increment of military power may give states that much *less* security.

The incentives for controlling arms have increased greatly since the horrors of Hiroshima and Nagasaki. The threat that nuclear weapons pose to stability and survival was expressed by President Kennedy in a 1961 address to the United Nations that still retains its relevance:

> Today, every inhabitant of this planet must contemplate the day when this planet may no longer be habitable. Every man, woman and child lives under a nuclear sword of Damocles, hanging by the slenderest of threads, capable of being cut at any moment by accident or miscalculation or by madness. The weapons of war must be abolished before they abolish us.
>
> Men no longer debate whether armaments are a symptom or a cause of tension. The mere existence of modern weapons—ten million times more powerful than any that the world has ever seen, and only minutes away from any target on earth—is a source of horror, and discord and distrust. Men no longer maintain that disarmament must await the settlement of all disputes—for disarmament must be a part of any permanent settlement. And men may no longer pretend that the quest for disarmament is a sign of weakness—for in a spiraling arms race, a nation's security may well be shrinking even as its arms increase.

These words conjure up Soviet Premier Nikita Khrushchev's prediction in 1962 that in the event of a nuclear exchange "the survivors would envy the dead." They call into question the conventional wisdom that arms produce security. Indeed, they question the very right to arm. When the destructiveness of weapons threatens the fate of the earth itself (see Sagan and Turco, 1990), abolishing the source of that threat ceases to appear to be a radical, utopian aspiration.

Before reviewing the historical record of efforts to change through negotiations the global distribution of weapons and the uses to which they can be put, and assessing its implications for peace, we need to recognize two distinctions, one between disarmament and arms control, a second between bilateral and multilateral agreements.

Although many people assume the terms are synonymous, *disarmament* is different from *arms control*. Arms control refers to agreements designed to regulate arms levels either by limiting their growth or by restricting how they might be used. This is a far less ambitious endeavor than disarmament, which seeks to reduce or eliminate weapons.

> In its most general conception, arms control is any type of restraint on the use of arms, any form of military cooperation between adversaries. Arms control can be implicit or explicit, formal or informal, and unilateral, bilateral, or multilateral. It is a process of jointly managing the weapons acquisition processes of the participant states in the hope of reducing the risk of war. . . . Arms control [refers] to formal agreements imposing significant restrictions or limitations on the weapons or security policies of the signatories.
>
> Disarmament rests on a fundamentally different philosophical premise than arms control. It envisions the drastic reduction or elimination of all weapons, looking toward the eradication of war itself. Disarmament is based on the notion that if there were no more weapons there would be no more war. This is a compelling proposition, with enough truth to give it a very long life in the history of thought about war and peace. Arms control, on the other hand, accepts the existence of weapons and the possibility of conflict. Contrary to popular impression, it is not necessarily about reducing arms levels. Arms control attempts to stabilize the status quo and to manage conflict, to encourage peaceful resolution of disputes and limit the resort to military force. Although many visceral opponents would be shocked at the thought, arms control is fundamentally a conservative enterprise. Disarmament, by contrast, is a radical one. Disarmament seeks to overturn the status quo; arms control works to perpetuate it. (Kruzel, 1991: 249)

Furthermore, as suggested, bilateral agreements should be differentiated from multilateral agreements. Because the former refer to agreements between only two countries, they are often easier to negotiate and to enforce than are the latter, which refer to agreements between three or more countries. Negotiating a multilateral agreement simultaneously binding on many states poses many obstacles, because states' security interests are very divergent, as are the domestic processes by which governments approve international agreements. As a result, the record of bilateral agreements differs from that of multilateral agreements with respect to both arms control and disarmament.

The Disarmament and Arms Control Record

It is hardly a novel idea that reducing the world's military arsenals is one way to control war. Yet until very recently one of the few constants in the changing international system has been the repetition with which states have advocated disarmament but failed to implement it. To be sure, in the past, some nations did succeed in reducing their armaments levels.[15] However, these achievements were rare, as many

---

[15] The Chinese states in 600 B.C. formed a disarmament league that produced a peaceful century for the league's members, and in the Rush-Bagot Agreement of 1818 Canada and the United States disarmed the Great Lakes. Disarmament proposals also figured prominently in the League of Nations' abortive World Disarmament Conference of 1932, and rather continuously in the United Nations since 1946 but especially in its "special sessions" on disarmament.

more nations raced to expand their arsenals than tried to cut them. Most disarmament was involuntary, the product of reductions imposed by coercion on the vanquished by the victors in the immediate aftermath of a war, as when the Allied powers after World War I attempted (unsuccessfully) to permanently disarm a defeated Germany. Instances of unilateral disarmament in the absence of coercion historically have been even less frequent. In short, to speak of disarmament is to speak of a phenomenon with few historical examples. With the end of the Cold War, this, as we will see, has begun to change.

In contrast with disarmament, there are many historical examples of arms control efforts. As early as the eleventh century the Second Lateran Council prohibited the use of crossbows in fighting. More recent examples include the 1899 and 1907 International Peace Conferences at the Hague that restricted the use of some weapons and prohibited others, and the agreement among the United States, Britain, Japan, France, and Italy at the Washington Naval Conferences (1921–1922) adjusting the relative tonnage of their fleets (followed and extended by the London Treaties of 1930 and 1936). Other examples include the 1919 St. Germain Convention on the export of arms, the 1925 Geneva Convention on arms trade, and the 1929 Geneva draft convention on arms manufacture. An unsuccessful example is found in the 1921 League of Nations effort to realize an arms production moratorium.

The post–World War II period saw a variety of new arms control proposals. The Baruch Plan (1946) called for the creation of a United Nations Atomic Development Authority that would have placed atomic energy under an international authority to ensure its use for only peaceful purposes, but the great powers never approved the proposal. (However, beginning in 1957 U.S. and Soviet scientists met informally at the so-called Pugwash Conferences to discuss processes for controlling nuclear weapons.) The Rapacki Plan of 1957, which would have prevented the deployment of nuclear weapons in Central Europe, also failed.

Nonetheless, leaders have made recurrent efforts to resolve differences so formal arms control agreements might be realized. Prominent among them are the arms control summit meetings of the United States and Soviet Union, the world's nuclear superpowers. Summit talks between the Cold War antagonists began in July 1955, when U.S. President Eisenhower and Soviet leader Nikita Khrushchev met in Geneva and Eisenhower made an "open skies" proposal for aerial reconnaissance to monitor military maneuvers. Among other things, these summits sought, and often resulted in, an improved atmosphere for serious arms control negotiations, and paved the way for the ambitious discussions under way to cement a new, post–Cold War world order based on a reduced and stable military power balance (see also Chapter 4).

In addition to bilateral summitry, multilateral negotiations on particular issues have sometimes taken on the character of institutionalized efforts to reach arms control agreements. Eight examples illustrate their range and breadth:

- The Mutual and Balanced Force Reductions Talks (MBFR) were conducted from 1973 to 1988 in an effort to realize force reductions between the blocs dividing Europe. These negotiations did not produce a treaty, but during the Cold War they sustained a "consensus that arms control negotiations are a necessary component of alliance defense strategy" and "were helpful in preparing for the Negotiations on Conventional Armed Forces in Europe (CFE)" (Hallenbeck and Shaver, 1991).

- The United Nations Committee on Disarmament, first convened in 1979, has conducted regular sessions to discuss ways to stabilize the balance of power at reduced levels.

- The Comprehensive Test Ban Negotiations have been held periodically since the late 1950s in an effort to reach agreement on a treaty banning all nuclear explosions. The Reagan administration broke off negotiations in 1982, citing verification obstacles and the need to test nuclear weapons as long as deterrence rested on them, but negotiations on verification protocols resumed in November 1987. New protocols were added to the existing Threshold Test Ban Treaty and the Peaceful Nuclear Explosions Treaty. They provide for three methods of cooperative verification: in-country seismic tests, on-site inspections, and a hydrodynamic system. Since then, negotiations have proceeded on further limits to nuclear testing.

- The Conventional Force Reductions in Europe negotiations, which began in March 1989, produced the Conventional Armed Forces in Europe (CFE) treaty signed by the twenty-three participating states in Paris in November 1990 and opened a new round of talks to negotiate new limits on military personnel, an aerial compliance system, and further conventional arms reductions.

- The Conference on Security and Cooperation in Europe (CSCE) begun in Helsinki in July 1973 has become the leading multilateral institution for managing the transformation of Europe from a system of counterpoised alliances (NATO and the Warsaw Pact) to one based on common principles stretching across the entire continent and North America. The Paris CSCE summit in November 1990, which followed on the heels of German unification and the CFE treaty reducing conventional forces in Europe, established a permanent CSCE secretariat and Conflict Prevention Center. In early 1992, the former republics of the Soviet Union joined the CSCE. The 1992 Helsinki CSCE meetings discussed the paths by which this enlarged community could apply the provisions of the 1975 Helsinki accords to the new European geopolitical environment. Discussion centered on the principles of the right of all peoples to self-determination, peaceful border changes, and prohibition of the use of force to settle disputes.

- The Nonproliferation Treaty (NPT) conferences, following the historic Treaty on Non-Proliferation of Nuclear Weapons signed by 138 non-nuclear weapons parties in 1968 (and 144 by 1991), have held Review Conferences at five-year intervals (1975, 1980, 1985, 1990) to discuss compliance and enforcement programs. The twenty-five-year review conference in 1995 will face the difficult task of renewing (extending) the NPT.

- The Conference on Disarmament (CD) emerged from the bilateral negotiations between the United States and the Soviet Union that began in 1976 to ban the production, stockpiling, and use of chemical weapons. In 1981 those closed negotiations moved to the multilateral Conference on Disarmament forum in Geneva, out of which the U.S.-Soviet Chemical Weapons Destruction Agreement of June 1990 was reached. The thirty-nine-nation Conference on Disarmament is conducting negotiations on a comprehensive and worldwide multilateral chemical weapons disarmament convention. The Persian Gulf War intensified interest in reaching an accord which laid the basis for a possible multilateral treaty to be signed in 1993.

• The Review Conferences of the Biological Weapons Convention have convened periodically since the 1972 Bacteriological (Biological) and Toxin Weapons Convention (TWC) was ratified. The 1972 convention was the first multilateral arms control agreement aimed at the complete elimination of an entire category of weapons of mass destruction. It banned the development, production, stockpiling, acquisition, or retention of biological and toxin weapons but did not specifically ban their use. That had already been done by the 1925 Geneva Protocol for the Prohibition of the Use in War of Asphyxiating, Poisonous, or Other Gases and of Bacteriological Methods of Warfare, and the two instruments were seen as complementing each other.

Table 13.2 on page 488 summarizes the major multilateral arms control agreements that have been reached since 1959. These agreements limit the range of permissible actions and weapons systems available to states, and have helped slow the global arms race and paved the way for more ambitious proposals in the new post–Cold War system. They also contribute important confidence-building measures that reduce the political tensions underlying the urge to arm.

Controlling Nuclear Arms: Superpower Agreements

Throughout the Cold War, Soviet and U.S. arms control efforts understandably focused on ways to lessen the threat of nuclear war. These efforts intensified with the disintegration of the Soviet Union into separate, independent republics. Table 13.3 on page 489 summarizes the results, listing the major *bilateral* arms control agreements between the two superpowers since 1960.

To these we might add an indeterminate number of tacit understandings about the level and use of weapons to which the two powers agreed; these are understandings that have not achieved the status of formal agreements but that the two superpowers observed nonetheless. They include occasional pledges to refrain from the offensive use of nuclear arsenals, as indicated by President Carter's and Soviet Foreign Minister Andrei Gromyko's promise that their states would never be the first to use nuclear weapons in any conflict. Such commitments were not legally binding (indeed, NATO based its *flexible response* strategy on the right to retaliate to an attack with nuclear weapons). Nonetheless, they took both superpowers in the direction of a no-first-use

TABLE 13.2 MAJOR MULTILATERAL ARMS CONTROL TREATIES AND AGREEMENTS

Date	Agreement	No. Signatories, 1991	Principal Objectives
1959	Antarctic Treaty	39	Prevents the military use of the Antarctic, including the testing of nuclear weapons
1967	Outer Space Treaty	93	Outlaws the use of outer space for testing or stationing any weapons, as well as for military maneuvers
1967	Treaty of Tlatelolco	23	Creates the Latin America Nuclear Free Zone by prohibiting the testing and possession of nuclear facilities for military purposes
1968	Limited Test Ban Treaty	119	Prohibits nuclear weapons in the atmosphere, outer space, and underwater
1968	Nuclear Nonproliferation Treaty	144	Prevents the transfer of nuclear weapons and nuclear weapons production technologies to non-nuclear weapon states
1971	Seabed Treaty	83	Prohibits the deployment of weapons of mass destruction and nuclear weapons on the seabed beyond a 12-mile coastal limit
1972	Biological Weapons Convention	112	Prohibits the production and storage of biological toxins; calls for the destruction of biological weapons stocks
1977	Environmental Modifications Convention	55	Bans the use of technologies that could alter the earth's weather patterns, ocean currents, ozone layer, or ecology
1981	Inhumane Weapons Convention	30	Prohibits the use of such weapons as fragmentation bombs, incendiary weapons, booby traps, and mines to which civilians could be exposed
1985	South Pacific Nuclear Free Zone (Roratonga) Treaty	9	Prohibits the testing, acquisition, or deployment of nuclear weapons in the South Pacific
1986	Confidence-Building and Security-Building Measures and Disarmament in Europe (CDE) Agreement (Stockholm Accord)	29	Requires prior notification and mandatory on-site inspection of conventional military exercises in Europe
1987	Missile Technology Control Regime (MTCR)	8	Restricts export of ballistic missiles and production facilities
1990	Conventional Armed Forces in Europe (CFE)	23	Places limits on five categories of weapons in Europe, and lowers balance of forces
1990	Confidence- and Security-Building Measures (CSBM) Agreement		Improves measures for exchanging detailed information on weapons, forces, and military exercises

TABLE 13.3 MAJOR BILATERAL ARMS CONTROL AGREEMENTS BETWEEN THE UNITED STATES AND THE SOVIET UNION

Date	Agreement	Principal Objectives
1963	Hot Line Agreement	Establishes a direct radio and telegraph communication system between the governments to be used in times of crisis
1971	Hot Line Modernization Agreement	Puts a hot line satellite communication system into operation
1971	Nuclear Accidents Agreement	Creates a process for notification of accidental or unauthorized detonation of a nuclear weapon; creates safeguards to prevent accidents
1972	Anti-ballistic Missile (ABM) Treaty (SALT I)	Restricts the deployment of antiballistic missile defense systems to one area, and prohibits the development of a space-based ABM system
1972	SALT I Interim Agreement on Offensive Strategic Arms	Freezes the superpowers' total number of ballistic missile launchers for a 5-year period
1972	Protocol to the Interim Agreement	Clarifies and strengthens prior limits on strategic arms
1973	Agreement on the Prevention of Nuclear War	Requires superpowers to consultation if a threat of nuclear war emerges
1974	Threshold Test Ban Treaty with Protocol	Restricts the underground testing of nuclear weapons above a yield of 150 kilotons
1974	Protocol to the ABM Treaty	Reduces permitted ABMs to one site
1976	Treaty on the Limitation of Underground Explosions for Peaceful Purposes	Broadens the ban on underground nuclear testing stipulated in the 1974 Threshold Test Ban Treaty; requires on-site observers of tests with yields exceeding 150 kilotons
1977	Convention on the Prohibition of Military or Any Other Hostile Use of Environmental Modification Techniques	Bans weapons that threaten to modify the planetary ecology
1979	SALT II Treaty (never ratified)	Places ceilings on the number of strategic delivery vehicles, MIRVed missiles, long-range bombers, cruise missiles, ICBMs, and other weapons; restrains testing
1987	Nuclear Risk Reduction Centers Agreement	Creates facilities in each national capital to manage a nuclear crisis
1987	Intermediate-range Nuclear Force (INF) Treaty	Eliminates U.S. and USSR ground-level intermediate- and shorter-range nuclear weapons in Europe and permits on-site inspection to verify compliance
1990	Chemical Weapons Destruction Agreement	Ends production of chemical weapons, commits cutting inventories of chemical weapons in half by the end of 1999 and to 5,000 metric tons by the end of 2002
1990	Nuclear Testing Talks	New protocol improves verification procedures of prior treaties
1991	START (Strategic Arms Reduction Treaty)	Reduces arsenals of strategic nuclear weapons by about 30 percent

doctrine. This paved the road to creation of greater institutional controls over the use of strategic weapons. Let us examine the major steps to these.

SALT

Of the superpowers' explicit, formal arms control agreements, the two so-called SALT (Strategic Arms Limitation Talks) agreements were precedent-setting. SALT I, signed in 1972, consisted of (1) a treaty that restricted the deployment of antiballistic missile defense systems to equal and very low levels and (2) a five-year interim accord on strategic offensive arms that restricted ICBM (intercontinental ballistic missile) and SLBM (submarine-launched ballistic missile) launchers. The SALT I agreement was essentially a confidence-building, "stopgap" step toward a longer-term, more comprehensive treaty. The 1979 SALT II agreement, then the most extensive arms control agreement ever negotiated, sought to realize that aim. The agreement called for placing an eventual overall ceiling of 2,250 on the number of ICBM launchers, SLBM launchers, heavy bombers, and ASBMs (air-to-surface ballistic missiles with ranges over six hundred kilometers) permitted each side. These limitations reduced by as many as 8,500 the total number of strategic nuclear weapons that the United States and the Soviet Union would have possessed by 1985 without the agreement.

The obstacles to arms control were illustrated by the problems that SALT II encountered, however, the U.S. Senate deferred ratification of the SALT II treaty indefinitely following the 1979 Soviet invasion of Afghanistan. Although both superpowers continued to abide by the basic terms of SALT II through the early 1980s, the "final result as embodied in SALT II was a clear disappointment to the hopes generated in the early 1970s. In essence, SALT II failed to achieve actual arms reductions. Its basic fault was that it would have permitted substantial growth in the strategic forces of both sides" (U.S. Department of State, 1983).

START

Against the background of what U.S. leaders labeled "the failed promise of SALT," they set the agenda for new approaches to strategic arms control.[16] In June 1982 the Reagan administration initiated a new round of arms talks aimed at significant reductions in the strategic arsenals of both superpowers. Termed START (Strategic Arms

---

[16] At this time, inspired by fear of the relentless arms race and frustration with the lack of progress in the arms control process, the idea of a "nuclear freeze" on the testing, production, and deployment of nuclear weapons gained momentum on both sides of the Atlantic. Freeze advocates were motivated by the view that it was a "delusion" to see "nuclear weapons as just one more weapon, like any other weapon, only more destructive" (Kennan, 1982). To help dispel this delusion, the American Catholic bishops composed a widely read pastoral letter that called for an immediate end to the arms race and asserted that the deliberate initiation of nuclear warfare, on however restricted a scale, could not be morally justified. As a policy proposal, a total freeze envisioned a path to disarmament that would first stop new weapons systems before starting to reduce the existing ones, built on the premise that both sides' deterrent capabilities were invulnerable and that a freeze would keep them that way. Once the arms race was curtailed, it was reasoned, arms reductions could then be considered. The nuclear freeze movement of the early 1980s helped set the stage for the progress that occurred in the early 1990s when the Cold War no longer constrained negotiations.

Reduction Talks), the initiative resumed the SALT process but expanded its agenda by seeking to remove asymmetries that had developed in the superpowers' weapons systems.

And, after nine years of bargaining, the negotiators overcame their differences and concluded the START treaty committing each side to *reduce* its strategic forces by one-third. Signed in June 1991, the treaty provided a baseline for future reductions and a verification regime to make transparent and predictable the two superpowers' capabilities and activities (see Chapter 11, Figure 11.5).

Or did it? The treaty was equally significant for what it did *not* regulate. The 600-page treaty, whose implementation would take seven years, only reduced the number of weapons of each side to the level they had when the START negotiations began in 1982. Moreover, the treaty did not achieve as much as many had once expected. As one analysis noted at the time it was concluded:

> The United States will be able to continue its strategic modernization program unencumbered by START and its existing force will be largely unaffected by START. The only modernization effort that may be curtailed is converting the B-1 bomber to carry ALCMs; the START bomber weapon counting rule would deter this conversion. . . .
>
> In other words, the United States will be able to have a modern, more accurate, and lethal force under START than today. In addition, the bomber weapon counting rules would allow the United States to deploy 3,000 to 6,000 weapons that are not counted. . . .
>
> The Soviet Union will for the most part be able to continue its modernization plans. . . . Under START, the Soviets will retain a highly lethal force of modern SS-18 missiles, which is sufficient to destroy with high confidence all U.S. ICBM silos and fixed launch facilities and hardened command posts. The Soviets will also retain a significant survivable mobile ICBM force of SS-24s and SS-25s. (Congressional Research Service, 1991: 53–54)

The Post–Cold War Disarmament Race

In September 1991, responding to widespread complaints that the START treaty barely started the kinds of arms reductions possible now that the threat of a Soviet attack had vanished, President Bush declared that the United States must seize "the historic opportunity now before us." He called long-range bombers off 24-hour alert, canceled plans to deploy the long-range MX on rail cars, and offered to negotiate with the Soviet Union sharp reductions in the most dangerous kinds of globe-spanning missiles. Bush also proposed to remove short-range nuclear weapons from U.S. bases in Europe and Asia and from U.S. Navy vessels around the world. Asking the Soviet Union, which Bush described as "no longer a realistic threat," to join the United States, the U.S. president warned that the proposed cuts might not be made if the Soviet Union did not respond in kind. This set the stage for a showdown on a new race to *dis*arm.

The fragmentation of the Soviet Union and the improved political relationship between Russia and the United States removed the major barriers to disarmament. Instructively, the disarmament process began first through unilateral proposals, and gained momentum only later through agreements painstakingly negotiated at the bargaining table. And it came about rapidly.

On January 25, 1992, new Russian President Boris Yeltsin, declaring that his country "no longer consider[ed] the United States our potential adversary," announced the decision to stop targeting U.S. cities with nuclear missiles. This cleared the way for another U.S. response. Four days later, in his State of the Union address, President Bush announced a series of unilateral arms cuts. Among them were the decision to suspend production of the B-2 bomber, halt development of the Midgetman mobile nuclear missile, and cease purchases of advanced cruise missiles. Bush also canceled production of warheads used aboard Trident submarine missiles.

Yeltsin did not wait for his scheduled summit meeting with Bush at Camp David to reply to this initiative. Within hours, Yeltsin recommended that the two powers reduce their nuclear arsenals to only 2,000 to 2,500 warheads each—far below the cuts called for in the START agreement and almost 50 percent greater than the reductions proposed by Bush. In other statements, Yeltsin announced his intention to reduce Russian military spending to less than one-seventh of the previous year's allocation and to trim the Russian army in half. And to emphasize the new climate of Russian-American friendship, Yeltsin proposed creating a joint U.S.-Russian global defense system and a new international agency to oversee the orderly reduction of nuclear weapons. He also proposed eliminating strategic nuclear weapons entirely by the year 2000.

Even in this hopeful climate of reciprocated reductions, during the spring of 1992 obstacles remained to dismantling the weapons with which each superpower had threatened the existence of the other. The differences centered on where the cuts should be made. Bush called for the elimination of all land-based strategic missiles with multiple warheads (MIRVs), the category in which Russia is strongest. But on submarine-launched missiles, where the United States had the advantage, Bush refused to accept reductions beyond a third and fought the Russian quest for across-the-board cuts.

In addition, efforts to modernize arsenals were scheduled to continue at this time. This meant that the former Cold War enemies could expect to be heavily armed after their cuts were complete. The lack of realistic targets and the technological breakthrough of miniaturization made most of the discarded weapons obsolete, so those deliberately scrapped did not mean that modernization plans had ended. The former adversaries were still militarily preparing to wage war, even with the planned cuts, and even with U.S. assistance to help the Russians destroy their weapons.

Yet, just when it appeared that the disarmament process might lose momentum, a new breakthrough was achieved. At the June 1992 Washington Summit, Presidents Yeltsin and Bush made the surprise announcement that Russia and the United States would make additional deep cuts in their strategic arsenals. The accord, which remained to be incorporated into a formal treaty, called for a reduction of the two powers' combined total nuclear arsenals from about 15,000 warheads to 6,527 by the year 2003 (see Table 13.4). But even more dramatically, what was termed the "Follow-on" treaty to START would reshape the strategic landscape not only by cutting the sheer number of warheads but also by altering drastically the kinds of weapons in each country's arsenal.

Under the proposed agreement, Russia and the United States would give up all

TABLE 13.4 AFTER START: PROJECTIONS OF U.S. AND RUSSIAN STRATEGIC NUCLEAR WARHEADS

	START		Follow-on Treaty (by the year 2003)	
	U.S.	Russia	U.S.	Russia
ICBM warheads	1,400	3,153	500	531
(heavy ICBM warheads)	(0)	(1,540)	(0)	(0)
SLBM warheads	3,456	1,744	1,728	1,744
Bomber Weapons	3,700	1,552	1,272	752
Total Warheads	8,556	6,449	3,500	3,027

Note: The numbers in this chart are estimates only. They are within treaty limits but, because of national force structuring choices, do not necessarily match them.
Source: The Arms Control Association, Fact Sheet, June 19, 1992.

of their land-based multiple warhead missiles. This would comprise a major concession on the part of Russia. As Jack Mendelsohn of the Arms Control Association observed, "On paper, it looks like the two forces will be reduced equally, but in fact the Russians will be giving up the backbone of their arsenal—land-based multiple warhead missiles—while [the United States] will be retaining the area of [its] greatest strength, sea-based ballistic missiles." In effect, the Russians would relinquish their most powerful missiles while the United States would only have to reduce the number of its most sophisticated missiles on its Trident submarines by 50 percent. The agreement would eliminate "the most threatening Russian nuclear weapons while allowing the United States to maintain its most advanced missiles" (Friedman, 1992).

If ratified and adhered to, the Follow-on START agreement could reduce the chances of war by banning the nuclear weapons that both powers would be most likely to use in a preemptive strike, while leaving them with only those weapons they would be likely to use in a retaliatory strike. By reducing the probability of a nuclear war, the agreement thus signaled the potential dawning of a new era. As President Bush put it, "With this agreement the nuclear nightmare recedes more and more for ourselves, for our children, and for our grandchildren." President Yeltsin concurred, noting that with the agreement, "we are departing from the ominous parity where each country was exerting every effort to keep up."

The Problematic Future of Arms Control

As promising as some of the great powers' recent arms control agreements might appear, the checkered history of their past negotiations testifies to the many obstacles that exist to arms control agreements, as well as the extent to which they are dependent on prior improvement in adversaries' political relations. That history raises questions about whether arms control agreements can restrain the arms race in the long run, as these obstacles could resurface in a new multipolar system characterized by great-power rivalry.

Until perhaps very recently, "the weapons prohibited had little, if any, military importance, and the outlawed activities [had] never been seriously contemplated as methods of war" (Goldblat, 1982). The international agreements reached controlled only those armaments that the parties to them had little incentive for developing in the first place or that had become obsolete. Do states purposely leave the most threatening problems outside negotiations and only seek to control the insignificant ones? Several indicators suggest that states do not take arms control seriously when they perceive their interests and survival to be at stake.

For example, consider first the disregard that some signatories to agreements demonstrate toward them. There were twelve alleged instances of the use of chemical and biological warfare between 1975 and 1981 that violated the 1972 Biological Weapons Convention (Goldblat, 1982: 100). Included among the allegations were the Vietnamese forces' use of poison gas against China (1979), the United States' use of chemical weapons in covert action in Cuba (1978–1981), the Iraqis' use of "chemical bombs" in occupied Iranian territory (1980), and the Soviet Union's use of lethal chemical weapons in Laos and Afghanistan over prolonged periods in such quantities as to produce a toxic "yellow rain."

Second, the continued testing of nuclear weapons also speaks to the propensity of states to make improvements in their weaponry a priority over their control. The six known nuclear states conducted 1,948 nuclear explosions between 1945 and 1992 (*The Defense Monitor*, Vol. 21, no. 3, 1992, p. 3). The pace did not slow as a result of the partial test ban treaty of 1963, which proscribed atmospheric and underwater testing but not underground explosions.[17] In fact, more explosions took place after 1963 than before.

Third, recall that the Nuclear Non-Proliferation Treaty (NPT) of 1968 obligated the non-nuclear nations not to manufacture or acquire nuclear weapons. Adherence to the agreement has been widespread. Yet the nuclear states' enthusiasm for ever more imposing arsenals showed no signs of abating until 1992. Given their historic appetite for expanded strategic inventories, it is understandable why members of the NPT question why they should remain restrained while the existing nuclear states continue to develop their nuclear capabilities (Spector and Smith, 1992).

Fourth, consider the sobering lessons suggested by the SALT agreements. SALT I did freeze the number of strategic launchers in operation or under construction but did not cover strategic bombers or prevent the kinds of qualitative improvements that would make quantitative thresholds meaningless. One such improvement was in the number of strategic warheads that a single missile could launch against an enemy. And in fact the number of multiple independently targetable warheads (MIRVs) deployed on missiles by the superpowers in 1977 was four times greater than when

---

[17] Testing continued even as the Cold War thawed, as witnessed by the fact that the United States conducted in September 1991 its sixth nuclear test of that year, and gave a cool reception to Mikhail Gorbachev's proposal at the Madrid Middle East peace conference in October 1991 to cease underground nuclear tests.

the SALT talks began, even though SALT I froze the number of delivery vehicles at the superpowers' disposal. Perhaps this troublesome outcome (experts now conclude that MIRVs were destabilizing and costly and reduced security) led Herbert Scoville, Jr., a former deputy director of the U.S. Central Intelligence Agency, to note at the time of the signing of SALT I that "arms control negotiations are rapidly becoming the best excuse for escalating rather than toning down the arms race." The pattern revealed in this and other developments prompted one former U.S. policymaker to conclude that "three decades of U.S.-Soviet negotiations to limit arms competition have done little more than to codify the arms race" (Gelb, 1979).

These Cold War experiences created doubt about the ability of agreements to control the size and dispersion of weapons. Why did states take decisions to arm that apparently imprisoned them in the grip of perpetual insecurity? On the surface, the incentives for meaningful arms control seem numerous. Significant controls would save money, reduce tension and hence the dangers of war, symbolize leaders' desire for peace, lessen health hazards, reduce the potential destructiveness of war, dampen the incentive for one state to seek a power advantage over others, diminish the possibility of being the target of a preemptive attack, and achieve a propaganda advantage for those advocating peace. To these we can add moral satisfaction and the opportunity to live in a global environment free of fear.

But states did not—and perhaps still do not—control significantly the growth of arms. Multiple reasons exist for reliance on military preparedness as a path to peace. They stem from the fear that is endemic to international anarchy. Most nations are reluctant to engage in arms limitations in a self-help system that requires each state to protect itself. Hence nations find themselves caught in a vicious circle of fear. This creates the "security dilemma"—a condition in no actor's interest but one that permits no easy escape. Its influence on behavior is potent and helps explain why throughout the Cold War military establishments subscribed to two basic principles: "(1) 'Don't negotiate when you are behind. Why accept a permanent position of number two?' and (2) 'Don't negotiate when you are ahead. Why accept a freeze in an area of military competition when the other side has not kept up with you?'" (Barnet, 1977). The result of this syndrome is clear: When fearful nations abide by the axiom that they should never negotiate from a position of weakness, then they are left with no option but to refuse to negotiate. Arms bargaining is a game of give and take, but all participants typically want to take much and give little. Given this posture, alongside the powerful restraining impact that domestic politics exert on the negotiation process (see Caldwell, 1991),[18] it is little wonder that meaningful agreements are so hard to achieve and that states develop weapons systems as bargaining chips for future negotiations.

---

[18] Many people benefit financially from the perpetuation of arms races and become lobbyists against arms agreements because they can lose their jobs by an abatement of military spending. Military-industrial complexes (see Rosen 1973; also Hooks, 1991) exist in nearly all societies whose influence is tied to the continuation of the arms race. The resistance of military planners and defense specialists to reductions in arsenals even in the wake of the Cold War attests to the continuing penchant of defense experts and arms manufacturers to insist that "prudence" dictates preparing for the worst contingency by retaining military preparedness at as high a level as possible.

Thus we should not expect too much of arms control, or exaggerate its potential. As one expert concludes,

> The history of the postwar era proves that arms control, if pursued wisely and properly, can reduce the threat; it can never eliminate the risk of war altogether. Arms control is not a substitute for weapons but a complement to them. Arms and arms control, one by creating the means to inflict unacceptable damage on a potential enemy and the other by protecting that capability from enemy attack, are both necessary for national security. A defense policy that fails to pursue the two together, that emphasizes one approach to the exclusion of the other, is dangerous and incomplete. . . .
>
> True international security depends not as much on arms or arms control as on reducing as much as possible the sources of conflict in international relations and on finding effective nonviolent means of resolving the conflicts that remain. (Kruzel, 1991: 268)

In Search of Peace

The obstacles to the control of arms are formidable. The idea that a disarmed world would be a more secure one does not have the force of history behind it, whereas the idea that military preparedness produces security does. As long as aggressive states exist, it would be imprudent to disarm. Arms control does not solve the basic problem of rivalry between states, because as long as states have and can use weapons, such agreements are little more than cooperative arrangements between adversaries. They define the competition and confine the potential destruction that can result in the event of war but do not remove the *source* of the conflict.

Alternatively, managing political conflicts without violence may be the key to arms control. For arms, after all, are less causes of war than they are symptoms of political tension: "Men do not fight because they have arms. They have arms because [they are afraid and] they deem it necessary to fight" (Morgenthau, 1985). From this perspective, controlling arms is contingent on removing the fears that underlie nations' political conflicts, for the quest for national security in an anarchical world springs from states' fear of one another. Yet, because one nation's security makes others insecure, nearly all nations prepare for war to defend themselves.

States, of course, pursue many paths to the realization of their national goals, of which security is the preeminent one. Thus they seek through deterrence to balance power with power while seeking simultaneously through arms control to remove the incentives for war that arms provide, because the weapons themselves may aggravate political tensions. In this sense the military paths to peace discussed in this chapter are intimately related to the quest for national security discussed in Chapter 11. Whether global security is served by nations' search for their own national security remains at issue, however. Perhaps the seeds of the world's destruction have been sown by the forces that propel the pursuit of peace and security through military might. Nothing makes the search for peace through political means more compelling. Hope may be inspired by the observations of former U.S. Secretary of Defense Robert McNamara: "We have reached the present dangerous and absurd confrontation by a long series of steps, many of which seemed rational in their time. Step-by-step we can undo much of the damage."

SUGGESTED READINGS

Bremer, Stuart A., and Barry B. Hughes. *Disarmament and Development: A Design for the Future.* Englewood Cliffs, N.J.: Prentice-Hall, 1990.

Bueno de Mesquita, Bruce. *The War Trap.* New Haven, Conn.: Yale University Press, 1981.

Claude, Inis L., Jr. *Power and International Relations.* New York: Random House, 1962.

Dunn, Lewis. "Arms Control: Looking Back, Looking Ahead," pp. 160–181 in Joseph Kruzel, ed., *American Defense Annual, 1991–1992.* New York: Lexington Books, 1992.

Gulick, Edward Vose. *Europe's Classical Balance of Power.* Ithaca, N.Y.: Cornell University Press, 1955.

Haas, Ernst B. "The Balance of Power: Prescription, Concept, or Propaganda?" *World Politics* 5 (July 1953): 442–477.

Kaplan, Morton. *System and Process in International Politics.* New York: Wiley, 1957.

Kapstein, Ethan B., ed. *Global Arms Production: Policy Dilemmas for the 1990s.* Washington, D.C.: University Press of America, 1992.

Kruzel, Joseph. "Arms Control, Disarmament, and the Stability of the Postwar Era," pp. 247–269 in Charles W. Kegley, Jr., ed., *The Long Postwar Peace.* New York: HarperCollins, 1991.

Rusi, Alpo M. *After the Cold War: Europe's New Political Architecture.* New York: St. Martin's Press, 1991.

Sabrosky, Alan Ned, ed. *Polarity and War: The Changing Structure of International Conflict.* Boulder, Colo.: Westview Press, 1985.

Walt, Stephen E. *The Origins of Alliances.* Ithaca, N.Y.: Cornell University Press, 1987.

CHAPTER 14

...

POLITICAL PATHS TO PEACE: INTERNATIONAL LAW, ORGANIZATION, AND INTEGRATION

...

Everything that is done in international affairs must be done from the viewpoint of whether it will advance or hinder the establishment of world government.

Albert Einstein, physicist, 1946

For the first time, it is clear that the United Nations is indispensable to us all.

Carlos Andres Perez, President of Venezuela, 1992

Since antiquity, the world has pursued two primary paths to peace. One emphasizes the use of *military* power, the other *political* solutions. This chapter examines three political approaches to world order embedded in the neoliberal tradition: international law, organization, and integration.

INTERNATIONAL LAW AND WORLD ORDER ....

In international affairs there is much disorder and recurrent warfare. This has led many critics to conclude that international law is "weak and defenseless" (Fried, 1971). Indeed, they ask, Is international law really law?

For many reasons, the answer to this question is yes. Although imperfect, transnational actors regularly rely on international law to redress grievances (see Joyner, 1992; Kim, 1991). They direct most of this activity to regulating routinized transnational intercourse in such areas as commerce, communications, and travel. Sometimes called *private* international law, this legal domain is largely invisible to the public because its accomplishments only infrequently command public attention. Yet private international law is the locus for all but a small fraction of international legal activities. It is here that the majority of transnational disputes are regularly settled, and in which the record of compliance compares favorably with that achieved in domestic legal systems (Brownlie, 1990).

In contrast, *public* international law, which addresses government-to-government relations, captures the headlines. It also captures most of the criticism, for here failures, when they occur, are very conspicuous. This is especially true with respect to the high politics of peace and security. When states use force, criticism intensifies. Consider, for example, former U.S. Secretary of State Dean Acheson's accusation that international law is "a crock" and Israeli Ambassador Abba Eban's lament that "international law is that law which the wicked do not obey and the righteous do not enforce."

Because this chapter examines the capacity of public international law to control war, our discussion will address only the laws and institutional machinery created to manage interstate conflict. That is, it explores that segment of public international law popularly regarded as most deficient.

Law at the International Level: Concepts and Principles

Public international law is usually defined as rules that govern the conduct of states in their relations with one another. The *corpus juris gentium* (the body of the law of nations) has grown considerably over the past three centuries, changing in response to transformations in international politics (Kaplan and Katzenbach, 1961). An inventory of the basic legal principles relevant to the control of war clarifies the international system's character.[1]

Principles of International Law

No principle of international law is more important than state *sovereignty*. Sovereignty means that no authority is legally above the state, except the authority that the state voluntarily confers on supranational organizations that it joins. Indeed, international law "permits a complete freedom of action" (Parry, 1968) to states to preserve their sovereign independence.

Nearly every legal tenet supports and elaborates the cardinal principle that nation-states are the primary subjects of international law. Although the Universal Declaration of Human Rights in 1948 expanded concern about states' treatment of individuals, states remain supreme. "Laws are made to protect the state from the individual and not the individual from the state" (in Gottlieb, 1982). Accordingly, the vast majority of rules address the rights and duties of states, not people. For instance, the principle of the sovereign *equality* of states entitles each state to full respect by other states and full protection of the system's legal rules. As a corollary, the right of independence guarantees states autonomy in their domestic affairs and external relations, under the logic that the independence of each presumes that of all. Similarly, the doctrine of *neutrality* permits states to avoid involvement in others' conflicts and coalitions. Furthermore, the *noninterference* principle forms the basis for *nonintervention*, that

---

[1] The rules of international law are multiple and difficult to summarize. For authoritative texts that describe the body of existing international legal principles, see von Glahn (1992), Akehurst (1987), and Brownlie (1990).

is, states' duty to refrain from uninvited involvement in another's internal affairs. This sometimes abused classic rule gives to governments the right to exercise jurisdiction over practically all things on, under, or above their bounded territory. (There are exceptions codified in international law, such as *diplomatic immunity* for nations' ambassadors while they represent their country abroad, and *extraterritoriality* that allows control of embassies on other states' terrain. But the precept of territorial integrity remains sacrosanct.)

In practice, domestic jurisdiction permits a state to enact and enforce whatever laws it wishes for its own citizens, including the rules for individuals to become citizens.[2] A state can create whatever form of government it desires without regard to its acceptability to other states. It also has freedom to regulate economic transactions within its boundaries and is empowered to conscript those living on its soil into its armed forces to fight—and die, if necessary—to defend the state.

The Montevideo Convention of 1933 on the Rights and Duties of States summarizes the major components of *statehood*. A state must possess a permanent population, a well-defined territory, and a government capable of ruling its citizens (claiming legitimacy) and managing formal diplomatic relations with other states. Other rules specify how and when these conditions are satisfied. Essentially, the acquisition of statehood is dependent on a political entity's recognition as such by other states. Whether or not a state exists thus rests in the hands of other states; that is, preexisting states are entitled to extend *diplomatic recognition* to another entity. *De facto* recognition is provisional and capable of being withdrawn in the event that the recognized government is superseded by another; it does not carry with it the exchange of diplomatic representatives or other legal benefits and responsibilities. The government that is recognized *de jure*, on the other hand, obtains full legal and diplomatic privileges from the granting state. The distinction emphasizes that recognition is a political tool of international law, implying approval or disapproval of a government.

Today, with the exception of Antarctica, which is administered jointly by several states and is outside the jurisdiction of any one of them, no significant land mass remains *terra nullius* (territory belonging legally to no one). Because nearly all of the earth's land surfaces are now within some state's sovereign control, the birth of a new state must necessarily be at the expense of an existing one. Hence, the recognition of a new state almost always means the recognition of a new government's control over a particular piece of territory. Because recognition is a voluntary political act, *nonrecognition* is a legally institutionalized form of public insult to a government aspiring to be accepted as legitimate by other governments, a form of sanction against an unwanted political regime.

States are free to enter into treaty arrangements with other states. Rules specify how treaties are to be activated, interpreted, and abrogated. International law holds that treaties voluntarily entered into are binding *(pacta sunt servanda)* but also reserves for states the right unilaterally to terminate treaties previously agreed to by reference

---

[2] Two basic principles govern the way nationality is conferred—*jus soli* (citizenship is determined by the state on whose territory the birth took place), and *jus sanguinis* (nationality is acquired by descent from a parent of a national), although some states recognize a combination of these conventions.

to the escape clause known as *rebus sic stantibus*—the principle that a treaty is binding only as long as no fundamental change occurs in the circumstances that existed when the treaty was concluded.

Procedures for Dispute Settlement

In addition to these general principles, international law provides a wide variety of legal methods for states to resolve their conflicts. The laws of *negotiation* do not obligate states to reach agreement or to settle their disputes peacefully, but they do provide rules for resolving conflicts. For example, international law advances explicit procedures for *mediation* (when a third party proposes a nonbinding solution to a controversy between two other states, as illustrated by President Carter's historic mediation at the 1978 Camp David meeting between Egypt and Israel); *good offices* (when a third party offers a location for discussions among disputants but does not participate in the actual negotiations, as Switzerland often does); and *conciliation* (when a third party assists both sides but does not offer any solution). In addition, rules for settling disputes also include *arbitration* (when a third party gives a binding decision through an ad hoc forum) and *adjudication* (when a third party offers a binding decision through an institutionalized tribunal, such as a court).

The Structural Limitations of the International Legal System

Sovereignty and the legal principles derived from it shape and reinforce international anarchy. The global condition is legally dependent on what governments choose to do with one another and the kinds of rules they voluntarily support. It is a legal system by and for them.

Many theorists consider the international legal system structurally defective because it depends so much on the attitudes and behaviors of those it governs. Because formal legal institutions (resembling those within states) do not exist at the international level, critics make the following points.

First, in world politics a legislative body capable of making laws does not exist. Rules are made only when states willingly observe them or embrace them in the treaties to which they voluntarily subscribe. There is no systematic method of amending or revoking them. Article 38 of the Statute of the International Court of Justice (or World Court), generally accepted as the authoritative statement on the sources of international law, affirms this. It states that international law derives from (1) custom, (2) international treaties and agreements, (3) national and international court decisions, (4) the writings of legal authorities and specialists, and (5) the "general principles" of law recognized since the Roman Empire as part of "natural law" and "right reason."

Second, in world politics no authoritative judicial body has power to identify the rules accepted by states, record the substantive precepts reached, intepret when and how the rules apply, and identify instances of violation. Instead, states are responsible for performing these tasks themselves. As we discuss below, the World Court does not have the power to perform these functions without states' consent.

Finally, in world politics there is no executive body capable of enforcing the rules. Rule enforcement usually occurs through the self-help actions of the victims of a transgression or with the assistance of their allies or other interested parties. No centralized enforcement procedures exist, and compliance is voluntary. The whole system rests, therefore, on states' willingness to abide by the rules to which they consent and on the ability of each to enforce through retaliatory measures the norms of behavior they value.

In sum, states are accountable to no one and abide by only those regulations they voluntarily subscribe to and enforce through self-help measures. The states themselves, not a higher authority, determine what the rules are, when they apply, and when and how they should be enforced. This raises the question, When everyone is above the law, is anyone ruled by it?

Still other weaknesses beyond the barriers to legal institutions posed by sovereignty warrant comment.

- *International law lacks universality.* An effective legal system must represent the norms shared by those it governs. According to the precept of Roman law *ubi societas, ibi jus* (where there is society, there is law), shared community values is a minimal precondition for the formation of a legal system. Yet the contemporary international order is culturally and ideologically pluralistic and lacks a common value consensus (McDougal and Lasswell, 1959). Some claim the Western-based international legal order approximates universality, yet state practice and the simultaneous operation of often incompatible legal traditions throughout the world contradict this claim (Bozeman, 1971).

- *International law justifies the competitive pursuit of national advantage without regard to morality or justice.* As in any legal system, in international politics the legal thing to do is not necessarily the moral thing to do (see Nardin, 1983). Indeed, international law legitimizes the drive for hegemony and contributes to conflict (Lissitzyn, 1963). Self-help does not control power; it is a concession to power. By worshiping the unbridled autonomy of sovereign independence, international law follows the realists' "iron law of politics"—that legal obligations must yield to the national interest (Morgenthau, 1985).

- *International law is an instrument of the powerful to oppress the weak.* In a voluntary consent system, the rules to which the powerful willingly agree are those that serve their interests. These rules therefore preserve the existing hierarchy (Friedheim, 1965). For this reason some claim that international law supports the so-called *structural violence* in world politics believed to benefit the strong at the expense of the weak (Galtung, 1969). Because enforcement is left "to the vicissitudes of the distribution of power between the violator of the law and the victim of the violation," political scientist Hans J. Morgenthau (1985) notes, "it makes it easy for the strong both to violate the law and to enforce it, and consequently puts the rights of the weak in jeopardy. A great power can violate the rights of a small nation without having to fear effective sanctions on the latter's part."

- *International law is little more than a justification of existing practices.* When a particular behavior pattern becomes widespread, it becomes legally obligatory, as rules *of* behavior become rules *for* behavior (Hoffmann, 1971). International law is a codification of custom. Hans Kelsen's contention that states ought to behave as they have customarily behaved (see Onuf, 1982), and E. Adamson Hoebel's (1961) dictum that "what the most do, others should do," reflect the positivist legal theory that when a type of behavior occurs frequently it becomes legal.[3] The dependence of rules on *custom* means that the policies of states shape law, not vice versa.

- *International law's ambiguity reduces law to a policy tool for propaganda purposes.* The vague, elastic wording of international law makes it easy for states to define and interpret almost any action as legitimate. "The problem here," observes Samuel S. Kim (1991), "is the lack of clarity and coherence [that enables] international law [to be] easily stretched, . . . to be a flexible fig leaf or a propaganda instrument." This ambivalence permits states to exploit international law to get what they can and to justify what they have obtained (Wright, 1953).

These deficiencies illustrate but do not exhaust the international legal order's alleged inadequacies. Critics note others. In combination, they suggest that international law is least developed in the realm of high politics where national security is at stake.

The Relevance of International Law

International law *is* fraught with deficiencies. Still, we can question the proposition that it is irrelevant to contemporary international politics.

States themselves do not deem public international law irrelevant. In fact, they attach much importance to it and expend considerable time and energy fighting over its interpretation and attempting to shape its evolution. All are decidedly interested in revising it in ways that serve their purposes and in maintaining those rules already in operation that advance their own interests. Indeed, if law were meaningless, we would not be able to point to the existence of a systematic code of rules repeatedly affirmed by states in multilateral agreements, resolutions, and declarations (Jones, 1991). These treaties, conventions, and formal declarations reflect state opinion and show there *are* basic principles that states formally recognize and agree to respect.

---

[3] Positivists stress states' customs as the most important source from which laws derive. In the absence of formal machinery for creating international rules, for evidence of what the law is, positivists observe leaders' foreign policy pronouncements, repeated usage in conventions voluntarily accepted by states, general practices (by an overwhelmingly large number of states), the judicial decisions of national and international tribunals, and legal principles stated in the resolutions of multinational assemblies such as the UN General Assembly.

An important reason states value international law and affirm their commitment to it is that they need a common understanding of the "rules of the game." International law is an "institutional device for communicating to the policy makers of various states a consensus on the nature of the international system" (Coplin, 1965). Law helps shape expectations, and rules reduce uncertainty and enhance predictability in international affairs. These communication functions serve every member of the international system, and the benefits they confer explain why states usually support international law and voluntarily accommodate their actions and policies to it. World politics would undoubtedly be more disorderly without this system, however imperfect and primitive it might be.

However, the system's members usually agree on certain general values at the same time that they often fail to recognize the implications of these values for their own behavior (Coplin, 1966). Thus it is tempting to agree with the critics that the lack of a centralized authority having supranational sanctioning powers makes international law useless for its most important function, the control of violence. This conclusion is questionable, however, as it stems from the misleading comparison critics often draw between the international legal order's primitive institutions and nation-states' highly centralized domestic legal systems. Comparison invites the specious conclusion that a formal legal structure (a centralized, vertical system of law) is automatically superior to a decentralized, self-help, horizontal system. The organizational differences between domestic (municipal) and international systems hide similarities and obscure the really important comparative question: Which type of legal order is more effective?

The absence of a reliable procedure of identifying a violation of international law and of an authority monopolizing enforcement instruments does not mean that states exercise their sovereign freedoms without restraint or routinely disobey existing customs and rules. A voluntary compliance system need not be normless. In fact, disobedience is rare. "The reality as demonstrated through their behavior," Christopher Joyner (1992) observes, "is that states do accept international law as law and, even more significant, in the vast majority of instances they usually obey it."

Why is this so? Self-restraint often works because even the most powerful states appreciate its benefits. International reputations are important. Those who play the game of international politics by recognized rules receive rewards. Those who ignore international law or who opportunistically break customary norms may pay costs for doing as they please; other nations thereafter may be reluctant to cooperate with them. Reprisals and retaliation by those victimized by a transgression are also to be feared, as is the loss of prestige. For this reason only the most ambitious or reckless state is apt flagrantly to disregard accepted standards of conduct.

Evidence shows that unorganized or primitive legal systems succeed in containing violence and ensuring compliance with rules (see Masters, 1969). Even in systems without the kinds of institutionalized procedures for punishing rule violation typically found in municipal legal systems (such as tribal societies without formal governments), sanctions often operate effectively (Barkun, 1968). Hence we should not be surprised to learn that "international law is not violated more often, or to a higher degree, than the law of other systems" (Joyner, 1992). The historical record demonstrates that states regularly have resolved their differences through legal procedures. Of 97 inter-state conflicts between 1919 and 1986, we observe no less than 168 attempts by the contending parties to negotiate, mediate, adjudicate, or otherwise settle their disputes through formal procedures of conflict resolution (note that one conflict may entail several types of settlement attempts). More impressively, 68 of these attempts were successful (Holsti, 1988: 420). In other words, since World War I states have been able to resolve their differences 70 percent of the time through use of one or more pacific settlement procedures.

It is also clear that formal institutions for rule enforcement do not guarantee rule compliance. No legal system can deter all of its members from breaking existing laws. Thus it is a mistake to expect a legal system to prevent all criminal behavior or to assert that any violation of the law proves the inadequacy of the legal structure. That asks too much of law. A single murder or burglary in a domestic system does not mean that all people disregard laws. Law is designed to deter crime, but it is unreasonable to expect it to prevent it.

Similarly, we should not view every breakdown of international law as confirming general lawlessness. Conditions of crisis strain all legal systems, and few, when tested severely, can contain all violence. Since 1500 more people have died from civil wars than have perished from wars between sovereign states (Sivard, 1991: 25). By this bloody criterion, the allegedly "deficient" international legal system performs its primary job—preventing violence—more effectively than the supposedly more so-phisticated domestic systems. Perhaps, therefore, the usual criteria by which critics assess legal systems are dubious. Should they be less concerned with structures and institutions, and more with performance?

Even the most skeptical of theorists who claim that leaders act without consider-ation of the rules must acknowledge that legal norms help order the process of bargaining and the formation of "security regimes" (Jervis, 1982). At the onset of militarized disputes, law "serves as a sort of signal to tell states which of these clashes are acceptable and which are deserving of retaliation" (D'Amato, 1982). Once a crisis erupts, rules eliminate the need to decide on a procedure for deciding—and this is no small service. It would be difficult to imagine a more peaceful world without these rules.

At another level, public international law makes possible the routinized transac-tions otherwise governed by private international law in such activities as international trade, foreign travel, mail flows, currency exchange, and debt obligations. Parties to the regimes in these areas regard them as binding and abide by their provisions (Kim, 1991; Soroos, 1986). Arguably, by removing disputes from possible resolution by armed force, international law reduces the sources of aggression. This helps make an anarchical world an orderly world nonetheless.

The Legal Control of Warfare

In the realm of behavior most resistant to legal control, the management of conflict, skeptics often claim that law clearly fails. If under international law states are "legally bound to respect each other's independence and other rights, and yet free to attack each other at will" (Brierly, 1944), international law may actually encourage war. To address this complaint, it is useful to examine the ethical and jurisprudential *just war* tradition from which the laws of war stem.

The Just War Doctrine

Many people are confused by international law because it both prohibits and justifies the use of force. This confusion derives from the *just war* tradition in Christian "realism" in which the rules of war are philosophically based. In the fourth century, St. Augustine questioned the strict view that those who take the life of another on behalf of the state's defense necessarily violate the commandment "Thou shalt not kill." He counseled that "it is the wrong-doing of the opposing party which compels the wise man to wage just wars." The Christian was obligated, he felt, to fight against evil and wickedness. To St. Augustine, the City of Man was sinful, in contrast to the City of God; in the secular world it was sometimes permissible to kill.

From this perspective evolved the modern just war doctrine as developed by such medieval secularists as Hugo Grotius, the "father" of international law. The just war doctrine consists of two categories of argumentation, *jus ad bellum* (the justice *of* a war) and *jus in bello* (justice *in* a war). The former sets the criteria by which a political leader may determine whether a war should be waged. The latter specifies restraints on the range of permissible tactics when a just war is fought.

These distinctions have been hotly debated since their inception. Drawing the line between murder and just war is a controversial task. Yet the just war theory encoded in international law for most of the twentieth century seeks to define these boundaries. According to this legal tradition, all "killing" is not "murder." International law recognizes limited circumstances in which lethal force may be justifiably used and provides guidelines for sanctioned methods.

At the core of the just war tradition is the conviction that the taking of human life may be sanctioned as the "lesser evil" when necessary to prevent life-threatening aggression. It was Sir Thomas More's contention that the assassination of an evil leader responsible for starting a war could be justified if the destruction of innocent lives would be prevented.[4] From this premise, a number of other precepts follow: (1) *last resort*—war is permissible only if all other means of resolution have been tried; (2) *legitimate authority*—the decision to go to war can be made only by a duly constituted

---

[4] Today, however, most states subscribe to the ban on killing leaders, no matter how evil, out of expedience—for to assassinate a war-mongering head of state would likely remove the person authorized to surrender and would justify plots of assassination against enemies worldwide—a freedom no leader wants. Perhaps this is why the Bush administration, in conformity with Executive Order 12333 that prohibits assassination of foreign leaders (thereby confirming the 1949 Geneva Conventions prohibiting the international targeting of noncombatants), did not authorize targeting Saddam Hussein during Operation Desert Storm in 1991, despite the fact that he was responsible for the naked aggression against Kuwait. Against this, however, is the counterargument more consistent with More's original view that "the 'proportionality' doctrine of international law supports a conclusion that it is wrong to allow the slaughter of [thousands of] relatively innocent soldiers and civilians if the underlying aggression can be brought to an end by the elimination of one guilty individual" (Turner, 1990).

authority; (3) *right intention*—war is justified only for the purpose of defense and not for revenge; (4) *probability of success*—there must be a reasonable chance that the war will succeed at a reasonable cost of life; (5) *appropriate goal*—a war can be initiated only to restore a peace that would be preferable to the conditions that were likely to materialize if the war had not been fought; and (6) *military purpose*—war is permitted to resist aggression but not to change an aggressor's type of government (Henkin, 1991).

The Evolving Laws of Warfare

Throughout history, international law has changed in response to changing global conditions. We will illustrate this by reviewing changes in the rules for war's initiation and the means by which it may be waged.

THE USE OF FORCE We can document a gradual but steady decline in the international community's tolerance of war (see Figure 14.1, page 508). Over time, the world community has voiced increasing disaffection with the absolute right of states to employ force to achieve their foreign policy objectives.[5]

The Hague conferences of 1899 and 1907 were early developments in shaping new attitudes toward war. It was World War I, however, that revealed more than any other factor the dangers springing from the fact that "under general international law, as it stood up to 1914, any state could at any time and for any reason go to war without committing an international delinquency" (Kunz, 1960).

In the aftermath of World War I, states began to revise their support of the legal right to use force. The Covenant of the League of Nations, which was incorporated as Part I of the Treaty of Versailles in 1919, implemented a new regime. Articles 11 to 17 stipulated that in no case could a state resort to war until three months after a judicial determination by the League had elapsed, and contained provisions subjecting any member "who committed an act of war against another member to sanctions." Another important step was taken in 1928 in the Treaty Providing for the Renunciation of War as an Instrument of National Policy, known as the Kellogg-Briand Pact. The prohibition was reaffirmed in the 1933 Anti-War Treaty of Rio de Janeiro and in the Nuremberg war crimes trials at the end of World War II. Both spoke of war as "the supreme international crime." The United Nations Charter (Article 2) expanded the prohibition by unequivocally outlawing both the threat and initiation of war. At the same time, Article 39 gave the international community the right to determine

[5] This is not to suggest that the right to use force to punish wrongdoers in just war theory has been repudiated. The "neo-just war doctrine . . . no longer seriously purports to accept the view that peace is unconditionally a higher view than justice. We have returned to the medieval view that it is permissible . . . to fight to promote justice, broadly conceived. Evil ought to be overturned, and good ought to be achieved, by force if necessary" (Claude, 1988). Indeed, some interpret just war theory to condone savage behavior to end a war quickly and coerce surrender. As the Prussian military theorist Karl von Clausewitz (1832) argued in *On War*, it is necessary to use "force unsparingly, without deference against the bloodshed involved. . . . To introduce into a philosophy of war a principle of moderation would be an absurdity. War is an act of violence pushed to its utmost bounds."

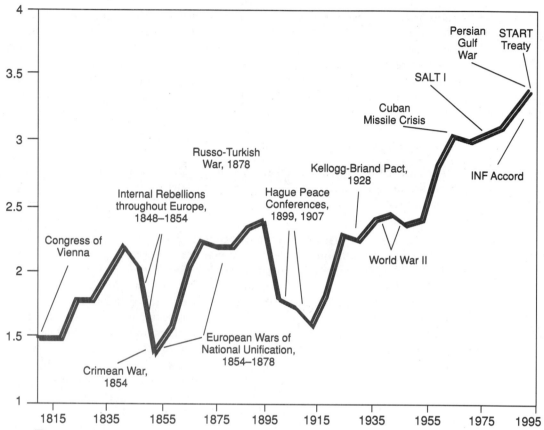

FIGURE 14.1 The Legal Prohibition of War, 1815–1992
Source: Transnational Rules Indicators Project (TRIP), as described by Charles W. Kegley, Jr., and Gregory A. Raymond, *When Trust Breaks Down* (Columbia: University of South Carolina Press, 1990).

"the existence of any threat to the peace, breach of the peace or act of aggression," and Article 42 authorized the Security Council "to take such action . . . as may be necessary to maintain or restore international peace and security."

Hence, over time legal injunctions have increasingly restricted states' right to resort to war. The doctrine of *military necessity* clarifies international law's position by justifying "protective" military measures taken to guard national interests but restricting the justification to threats in which the use of retaliatory force is absolutely necessary as a last recourse for defense (Claude, 1988). The modern conception of just war thus still embraces the traditional *jus ad bellum*, but now confines the right to wage a war to the purposes of punishing aggression, deterring attack, protecting innocents' human rights, and generally to defend "the system's rules" (Kelsen, 1945). This change modifies the political culture in which states compete: "The willingness of nations to subscribe, even in principle, to the renunciation of their rights to use force (except in self-defense) is a significant step, an expression of willingness to move in one direction rather than the other, and a disclosure of consensus on the most important aspect of political order in world affairs" (Falk, 1965).

Even though attitudes toward the use of force have changed, this has not necessarily caused a reduction in warfare or, even more optimistically, as some believe, its obsolescence. Although the major powers have avoided direct combat with one another since World War II, they have frequently used force against other states. Many of these actions were conducted in ways arguably prohibited by international law despite these states' professed respect for the nonintervention principle (Tillema and Van Wingen, 1982).

Still, because war is no longer licensed, *animus belligerandi* (the intention to make war) is a crime, and those who start a war are now criminals. That normative consensus may be an important psychological restraint on future policymakers' choices. (Political realists, however, would undoubtedly disagree, arguing that aggressive leaders will not be restrained by the mere delegitimization of violence.)

In addition to this prohibition, contemporary international law has sought to grapple with newer forms of conflict, although this has proven difficult. Consider two examples.

First, in response to the scourge of terrorism, international law advances guidelines for states' permissible military response. It restricts that response to cases where another state's responsibility for the act of terrorism is beyond all doubt. Moreover, "this right does not allow retaliation for past attacks. The response in self-defense to an armed [terrorist] attack must be necessary and proportional . . . and the victim of an act of terrorism will have to pursue other remedies against states it believes responsible and against the states that encourage, promote, condone, or tolerate terrorism or provide a haven to terrorists" (Henkin, 1991).

Second, consider the rise of military intervention and arms sales as policy instruments in world affairs, in the context of the concomitant decay since 1945 of the distinction between internal and international situations:

> International law does not forbid one state to sell arms to another state, and upon authentic invitation, a state may introduce military forces into the territory of another to assist the government for various purposes, including maintaining internal order. On the other hand, a state may not introduce arms or armed forces into a country without the consent of its government, surely not to support any groups hostile to the government. (Henkin, 1991: 63)

THE RULES FOR WAR'S CONDUCT   Laws regulating the methods that states may use in war—*jus in bello*—have also grown.[6] *In bello* restraints include the principles of

---

[6] The most dramatic evidence of this development was the 1977 Geneva Conference on Humanitarian Law. Two protocols were adopted; one added twenty-eight rules to the one principle governing internal wars since the 1949 Geneva Conventions; the other provided new instruments for "Red Cross law" stipulating regulations for the treatment of noncombatants and prisoners of war. Subsequently, the 1980 United Nations Conference on Prohibition or Restrictions of the Use of Certain Conventional Weapons Which May Be Deemed to Be Excessively Injurious or to Have Indiscriminate Effects adopted a convention and three protocol statements.

discrimination and *noncombatant immunity* that restrict military targets to soldiers and supplies in an effort to protect innocent civilians. *Lex talionis* (the laws of retaliation) specify conditions under which certain practices are legitimate. One category, *reprisals* (hostile and illegal acts permitted if taken in proportionate response to a prior hostile and illegal act) stipulate procedures for military occupations, blockades, shows of force, and bombardments. Another category, *retorsion* (hostile but legal retaliatory acts when taken in response to similar legal acts initiated by other states) provides rules for embargoes, boycotts, import quotas, tariffs, and travel restrictions to redress grievances.

The cynic may conclude that the laws of retaliation (particularly reprisals) are really instructions for killing. That conclusion is unwarranted, however. The restrictions on the weapons that can be used and the permissible methods of fighting, alongside the widening scope of acts regarded as war crimes, reduce killing in warfare. Consider the following examples (from von Glahn, 1992):

- No attacking of unarmed enemies
- No use of forbidden arms or munitions
- No firing on undefended localities without military significance
- No improper use or destruction of privileged (exempt, immune) buildings for military purposes
- No poisoning streams or wells
- No pillaging
- No killing or wounding military personnel who have surrendered or are disabled by wounds or sickness
- No assassinating and hiring assassins
- No ill-treating prisoners of war
- No compelling the inhabitants of occupied enemy territory to furnish information about the armed forces of the enemy or his means of defense
- No bombarding from the air to terrorize or attack civilian populations
- No attacking enemy vessels that have indicated their surrender by lowering their flag
- No destroying civilian cultural objects and places of worship

These illustrative objections to practices once condoned move warfare away from barbarism.

Law's Contribution to Peace

Cynics who contend that international law is irrelevant to the control of war overlook several dimensions of law's character. First, international law is not intended to prevent all warfare. Aggressive war is illegal, but defensive war is not. It is a mistake, therefore, to claim that international law has broken down whenever war has broken out.

Second, instead of doing away with war, international law preserves it as a sanction against the breaking of rules. Thus war is a device of last resort to punish aggressors and thereby maintain the system's legal framework.

Third, international law is an institutional substitute for war. Legal procedures exist to resolve conflicts before they erupt into open hostilities. Although they cannot deter war, they may make recourse to violence unnecessary by resolving disputes that otherwise might escalate to war.

To illustrate this latter proposition and evaluate the utility of judicial procedures, let us examine the impact of the World Court on states' behavior.

The World Court

The demonstrable capacity of pacific methods to reduce the frequency of war (see Holsti, 1988) does not mean that international adjudicative machinery is well developed or functionally effective. Nowhere is this more evident than with the International Court of Justice. Presumably created as the highest court on earth, in practice the World Court is a very inactive judicial institution. Between 1946 and 1988 it heard only fifty-five contentious cases, rendered judgments on only thirty of these, and handed down only nineteen advisory opinions (Bennett, 1991: 173–177).

Part of the reason behind the World Court's marginal impact is that most judicial conflict settlements take place in the domestic courts of one of the contestants or in other international tribunals. Here there is strong evidence of compliance with decisions that are reached (Falk, 1964; Lillich, 1972). Still other controversies are settled through ad hoc arbitration and adjudication proceedings before they are referred to a court for resolution.

The most important reason, however, is that the court's jurisdiction is not compulsory. Although all UN members are members of the court, less than a third have affirmed their willingness to accept automatically the court's limited compulsory jurisdiction in conflicts involving them, and all but a handful of these have stipulated reservations to their acceptance. The United States, for example, has weakened the Optional Clause in the so-called Connally amendment that reserves the U.S. right to determine the cases in which it will allow the court jurisdiction.

The World Court's weakness against powerful states was dramatized in 1984, when the United States announced that it would unilaterally withdraw from the World Court's jurisdiction its disputes with several Central American countries following Nicaragua's charge that the U.S. Central Intelligence Agency had illegally tried to "overthrow and destabilize" the elected Sandinista government. In particular, Nicaragua charged that the United States had illegally mined its ports and supplied money, military assistance, and training to the rebel *contra* forces. In denying the tribunal's authority, the United States was certainly not acting without precedent; others had done so previously. But some felt that by thumbing its nose at the court and the rule of law it represents, the United States had become an "international outlaw."[7] Others, however, felt that the United States was acting within its rights. The World Court supported the former view. In 1984, the court (by a vote of fifteen to one), without addressing the jurisdictional issue, ruled as follows:

> The right to sovereignty and to political independence possessed by the Republic of Nicaragua, like any other state of the region or of the world, should be fully respected and should not in any way be jeopardized by any military and paramilitary activities which are prohibited by the principles of international law, in particular the principle that states should refrain in their international relations from the threat or the use of force against the territorial integrity or the political independence of any state, and the principle concerning the duty not to intervene in matters within the domestic jurisdiction of a state. (*New York Times*, May 11, 1984, p. 8)

International Law after the Cold War

World order in the new post–Cold War system will depend to a considerable extent on the uses to which states put international law. Its alleged shortcomings lie not with the laws but with their creators—states. The intentions of states acting individually or in concert, and not the slow processes by which legal development grows, will be decisive. Whereas it seems likely that the capacity of international law to curtail aggression has improved now that Cold War competition has ceased to dominate world affairs, many barriers remain to creating, as John F. Kennedy expressed the hope, "a new world of law, where the strong are just and the weak secure and the peace preserved." That conclusion leads naturally to a consideration of the role that international organizations play in maintaining world peace.

INTERNATIONAL ORGANIZATION AND WORLD ORDER . . . .

Neoliberal institutionalists recommend, as a second political path to peace, the creation of international organizations.

> Prevention of war is clearly not the only, or in every case the primary, goal toward which international organizations are directed. There is, nevertheless, substantial justification for the popular expectation that international organizations will pursue that goal. The best known international institutions have been widely advertised as war-preventing agencies. (Claude, 1988: 70)

The growth of international organizations to deal with the problem of war has

---

[7] The American Society of International Law voted overwhelmingly on April 12, 1984, to urge the United States to reverse its decision. Harvard Law Professor Abram Chayes, who earlier in his career laid the legal foundations for the Kennedy administration's naval quarantine of Cuba during the 1962 missile crisis with the Soviet Union, elected to represent Nicaragua in its suit against the United States. Believing that the Nicaraguan leaders were acting "to uphold the rule of law in international affairs," Chayes stated that he thought it appropriate for the United States, which "purports to be bound by the rule of law," to be judged under "appropriate international procedures." He stated that "there is nothing wrong with holding the United States to its own best standards and best principles" (*New York Times*, April 11, 1983).

been persistent, particularly in the twentieth century. To understand this political approach, we must also understand its theoretical underpinnings. The expectations about and performance of the United Nations (UN) exemplify those theoretical premises.

The United Nations and the Preservation of Peace

Like its predecessor, the League of Nations, the UN's primary mission, as its charter states, is the "maintenance of international peace and security." The stipulation that membership is open to all "peace-loving" countries reaffirms this purpose. So does the charter's requirements that members "settle their international disputes by peaceful means."

Collective Security

Collective security is often viewed as an alternative to competitive alliances and the balance of power as a method for preserving peace. In a balance-of-power system, it is assumed that each nation acting in its own self-interest for its individual protection will form coalitions offsetting others, and that the resulting equilibrium will prevent war. In contrast, collective security asks each state to share responsibility for every other states' security. They are to take joint action against *any* transgressor, and *all* are to act in concert. This presumes that the superior power of the entire community will deter those contemplating aggression or, failing this, that collective action will defeat any violator of the peace.

In the aftermath of the League's failure to put collective security into practice, critics sadly noted the perhaps illusory expectations on which proponents had built the design. Many of the preconditions necessary for an effective system of collective security were lacking. The League's failures stemmed from the U.S. refusal to join the organization; the other great powers' fear that the League's collective strength might be used against them; disagreement over objectively defining an instance of aggression in which all concurred; states' pervasive dread of inequities in sharing the risks and costs of mounting an organized response to aggression; and states' general penchant for giving lip service to the value of general peace but their willingness to organize resistance only to threats to their own security. In the final analysis, the theory's central fallacy was that it expected a state's desire to see others protected to be as strong as its desire to protect itself. That assumption was not upheld in the interwar period. As a result, the League of Nations never implemented a true collective security system.

The architects of the United Nations were painfully aware of the League's disappointing experience. Thus while they voiced support for collective security, their design restored the balance of power to maintain peace. The United Nations Charter, signed June 26, 1945, permitted any of the Security Council's five permanent members (the United States, the Soviet Union, Great Britain, France, and China) to veto and thereby block any proposed enforcement action which any disapproved. Because the

Security Council could act in concert only when the permanent members fully agreed, the UN Charter was a concession to states' sovereign freedom:

> In the final analysis, the San Francisco Conference must be described as having repudiated the doctrine of collective security as the foundation for a general, universally applicable system for the management of power in international relations. The doctrine was given ideological lip service, and a scheme was contrived for making it effective in cases of relatively minor importance. But the new organization reflected the conviction that the concept of collective security had no realistic relevance to the problems posed by conflict among the major powers. (Claude, 1962: 164–165)

To further enhance the authority of the great powers relative to the United Nations, the charter severely restricted the capacity of the General Assembly to mount collective action. The charter authorized it only to initiate studies of conflict situations, bring perceived hostilities to the attention of the Security Council, and make recommendations for peacekeeping initiatives. Moreover, it restricted the role of the secretary general to that of chief administrative officer. Article 99 confined the secretary general and the working staff of the Secretariat created to aid him, to alerting the Security Council to peace-threatening situations and to providing administrative support for the peacekeeping operations that the Security Council authorized.

The UN's structure compromised the organization's security mission. Still, the United Nations is much more than a mere debating society. It is also more than an arena for the conduct of power politics. During the Cold War the United Nations fell short of many of the ideals its more ambitious founders originally envisioned, principally because its two most powerful members in the Security Council did not cooperate (see Chapter 6). Nevertheless, like any adaptive institution, the United Nations found ways to overcome the compromising legal restrictions that inhibited its capacity to preserve world order.

From Collective Security to Peacekeeping

The Korean police action in 1950 provided a glimmer of hope that the United Nations might overcome its institutional barriers to preserving world order. However, that episode was an intervention sponsored and fought by the United States under UN auspices and did not set a precedent for equally ambitious initiatives in later conflicts. The disillusioning Korean experience was the UN's last "enforcement" mission to defeat an aggressor until 1990, when, freed from the paralyzing grip of Cold War rivalry, the United Nations mounted a collective response to Iraq's invasion of Kuwait.

During the long interregnum between Korea and Kuwait, the UN adaptively sought to overcome the political obstacles posed by superpower discord. UN experiments with monitoring explosive situations began in its formative period. For example, in 1948 it created the United Nations Truce Supervision Organization (UNTSO) to monitor the ceasefire between Israel and neighboring countries and the United Nations Military Observer Group in India and Pakistan (UNMOGIP) for protecting a ceasefire zone in Kashmir. And, after the Korean War, these initiatives became precedents for a new approach. Acting in response to the Suez crisis under the Uniting for Peace resolution, in 1956 the General Assembly created the United Nations Emergency

Force (UNEF) and charged the secretary general with primary responsibility for managing the UN's first *peacekeeping* operation in the Sinai.

The assembly designed UNEF to forestall the superpowers' competitive intrusion into a potentially explosive situation and to overcome the Security Council's inaction. This innovative approach went beyond prior UN fact-finding commissions and observer forces. It was largely improvisational, since the charter had not made provisions for peacekeeping activities authorized by the General Assembly and managed by the secretary general. The principles underlying UNEF were different from collective security. The latter emphasized checking aggression through collective enforcement. UNEF, by contrast, emphasized noncoercive activities aimed at placing the UN's neutral "thin blue line" between the clashing armies to permit time for negotiations to resolve the conflict.

Success can be infectious. Following UNEF, the UN sprang into action to authorize other operations designed to forestall conflicts, which have since become closely identified with the process of peacekeeping. For example, in 1958 the UN Observer Group helped to defuse the crisis in Lebanon. And in 1960 the largest UN peacekeeping force ever entered the Congo to stabilize that newly independent country. Shortly thereafter, in 1964, the UN sent the UNFICYP peacekeeping force to Cyprus. Other increasingly diverse and ambitious UN peacekeeping operations followed from these precedents (see James, 1990). Table 14.1 on page 516 summarizes the most well-known operations, and Map 14.1 on page 519 displays their location throughout the globe.

Of these operations, it is reasonable to regard only UNYOM, in Yemen, as an outright failure, and UNIFIL, in Lebanon, as "limited" in success (Haas, 1986). But "in no case can the setback[s] be attributed to inadequacies of the operation[s]" (Skjelsbaek, 1989). UN missions thus have regularly succeeded in creating buffers between the warring disputants, providing time for negotiating cease-fires, and ensuring compliance with agreements. More impressively, on many occasions they have helped contain conflicts that threatened to escalate to large-scale wars with additional participants. "By keeping the situation quiet on the ground, they [have given] diplomats enough time to do their part of the job" (Skjelsbaek, 1989).

Over time, the roles associated with UN peacekeeping have moved from managing crises "during incipiency" to bolder security- and confidence-building measures, verification, legal assistance in civil wars, combating terrorism, humanitarian aid, drug interdiction, naval peacekeeping, and other operations beyond the activities originally envisioned for them (Rikhye, 1989).

The Changing Role of the Secretary General

Drawing on the UN's experience with UNEF, Secretary General Dag Hammarskjöld of Sweden articulated in his 1960 annual report to the world organization what he saw as the new United Nations role in managing peace and security. *Preventive diplomacy* describes Hammarskjöld's vision, a term that since has become virtually synonymous with United Nations peacekeeping:

> Preventive diplomacy . . . is of special significance in cases where the original conflict may
> be said either to be the result of, or to imply risks for, the creation of a power vacuum

Table 14.1 UN Peacekeeping Operations, Observer Missions, and Related Dispute Settlement Activities

Latin and Central America

IAPF. Inter-American Peace Force, 1965–1966: Dispatched by the Organization of American States, and authorized to act with it, UN representatives and military observers moderated civil unrest in the Dominican Republic.

ONUCA. UN Observer Group in Central America, 1989–present: Established to monitor the Guatemala (Esquipulas II) agreement that prohibited cross-border support for the *contra* rebels and, after March 1990, to help manage the voluntary demobilization of the Nicaraguan resistance.

ONUVEN. UN Mission for Verification of the Electoral Process in Nicaragua, 1988–present: Established to oversee elections following the truce and ensure continuing respect for democratic procedures.

ONUSAL. UN Observer Mission in El Salvador, May 1991–present: Created to implement the human rights agreement between the Government of El Salvador and the Farabundo Marti National Liberation Front (FMNL).

Africa

ONUC. French initials for the UN Operation in the Congo, 1960–1964: Authorized to maintain peace and order while preserving unity in the newly independent former Belgian colony.

UNTAG. United Nations Transition Assistance Group in Namibia, 1989–1990: Empowered administrators to supervise free elections in a democratic exercise of self-determination to convert Namibia from a South African colony to an independent nation in March 1990.

UNAVEM. UN Angola Verification Mission, May 1991: Verified the redeployment of South African troops southward and the withdrawal of Cuban troops from Angola.

UNAVEM II. UN Angola Verification Mission, June 1991–present: Established to monitor the implementation of the Angola Peace accords, agreed to by Angola and UNITA, and to monitor the Angolan police as set out in the Protocol of Estoni.

MINURSO. UN Mission for the Referendum in Western Sahara, April, 1991–present: To oversee elections to determine whether Western Sahara should become independent or integrated into Morocco.

Europe

UNMOG. UN Military Observers in Greece, 1952–1954: Created to restore order along borders separating Albania, Yugoslavia, and Bulgaria.

UNFICYP. UN Force in Cyprus, 1964–present: Established to prevent recurrence of fighting between contending Greek and Turkish communities and, since 1974, to supervise the cease-fire and maintain a buffer zone between the disputants.

TABLE 14.1 UN PEACEKEEPING OPERATIONS, OBSERVER MISSIONS, AND RELATED DISPUTE SETTLEMENT ACTIVITIES *(continued)*

Europe (continued)

UNPROFOR. UN Observer Mission in Yugoslavia, December 1991–present: Deployed to terminate fighting between Serbian federal army and Croatian forces in Yugoslavia and create a buffer zone while troops are withdrawn and demobilized.

Middle East

UNTSO. UN Truce Supervision Organization in Palestine, 1948–present: Created to supervise armistice among Israel, Jordan, Lebanon, and Syria, and cease-fire of 1967, it today operates with UNDOF and UNIFIL.

UNEF I and II. UN Emergency Force, 1956–1967, 1973–1979: Established to prevent Israel and Egypt from fighting in Sinai and Gaza Strip.

UNOGIL. UN Observer Group in Lebanon, June–December 1958: Established to police border dividing Lebanon and Syria.

UNDOF. UN Disengagement Observer Force, 1974–present: Created to monitor the buffer zone on the Golan Heights between Syrian and Israeli forces.

UNIFIL. UN Interim Force in Lebanon, 1978–present: Sent to police border dividing Lebanon and Israel, confirm withdrawal of Israeli troops, and establish effective authority in southern Lebanon.

UNYOM. UN Yemen Observation Mission, 1963–1964: Created to observe and monitor withdrawal of Saudi Arabian and Egyptian forces from Yemen.

UNIMOG. UN Iran-Iraq Military Observer Group, 1988–1991: Created to supervise cease-fire and police border between Iran and Iraq.

MFO. Multinational Force and Observers, 1981–present: To verify the level of forces in the zones created by the peace treaty between Israel and Egypt, and ensure freedom of navigation through the Strait of Tiran.

UNIKOM. UN Iraq-Kuwait Observation Mission, April 1991–present: Established to create a demilitarized zone between Iraq and Kuwait, deter violations of the boundary, restore Kuwait's independence, ensure Iraqi compliance with the UN's sanctions for Iraq's aggression, and observe hostile or potentially hostile actions.

Asia and the Pacific

UNMOGIP. UN Military Observer Group in India and Pakistan, 1948–present: Created to supervise cease-fire in Kashmir.

UNCFI. UN Commission for Indonesia, 1949–1951: Sent to settle disputes following Indonesian independence from the Netherlands.

> ### TABLE 14.1 UN PEACEKEEPING OPERATIONS, OBSERVER MISSIONS, AND RELATED DISPUTE SETTLEMENT ACTIVITIES *(continued)*
>
> *Asia and the Pacific*
>
> **NNSC.** Neutral Nations' Supervisory Commission for Korea, 1953–present: Established by the Armistice Agreement at the end of the Korean War, the Commission is to supervise, observe, inspect, and investigate the armistice and to report on these activities to the Military Armistice Commission. Today its main role is to maintain and improve relations between both sides and thus keep open a channel of communications.
>
> **UNGOMAP.** UN Good Offices Mission in Afghanistan and Pakistan, 1988–1990: Deployed military observers to monitor implementation of Geneva accords to assure withdrawal of Soviet troops, noninterference, and nonintervention.
>
> **OSGAP.** Office of the Secretary General in Afghanistan and Pakistan, 1989–present: To assist the Personal Representative of the Secretary General to oversee enforcement of General Assembly Resolution 44/15.
>
> **UNTEA/UNSF.** Temporary Executive Authority and UN Security Force in West New Guinea, 1962–1963: Engineered and monitored a cease-fire between Indonesian and Netherlands forces so peace negotiations could proceed without further incident.
>
> **UNIPOM.** UN India-Pakistan Observation Mission, 1965–1966: Established to oversee and supervise cease-fire in Rann of Kutch.
>
> **UNTAC.** UN Transitional Authority in Cambodia, March 1992–present: Force of 22,000 sent to disarm, demobilize, and disperse rebel factions and Vietnamese troops, organize and oversee free and fair elections.

between the main blocs. Preventive action in such cases must in the first place aim at filling the vacuum so that it will not provoke action from any of the major parties, the initiative for which might be taken for preventive purposes but might in turn lead to counter-action from the other side. The ways in which a vacuum can be filled by the United Nations so as to forestall such initiatives differ from case to case, but they all have this in common: temporarily . . . the United Nations enters the picture on the basis of its noncommitment to any power bloc . . . so as to provide to the extent possible a guarantee in relation to all parties against initiatives from others.

Hammarskjöld saw preventive diplomacy partly as a response to the need to take bolder conflict-avoidance measures by resolving conflicts before they reached the crisis stage (in contrast to ending wars once they erupt), but it also reflected his frustration with Security Council inaction.

More than his unobtrusive predecessor, Trygve Lie of Norway, who resigned in November 1952, Hammarskjöld saw the secretary general's role as that of an active crisis manager. He independently enlarged the defined responsibilities of the executive organ of the United Nations by using his "good offices" to mediate international disputes and by strengthening the UN's administrative support for peacekeeping operations.

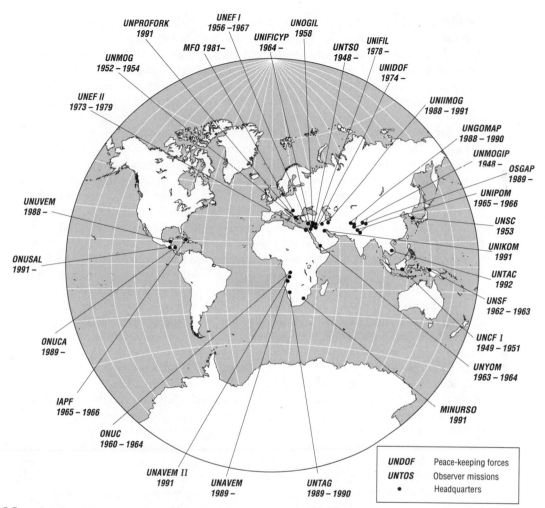

UNPROFORK
1991

UNEF I
1956–1967

UNOGIL
1958

MFO 1981–

UNIFICYP
1964 –

UNTSO
1948 –

UNIFIL
1978 –

UNMOG
1952 – 1954

UNIDOF
1974 –

UNEF II
1973 – 1979

UNIIMOG
1988 – 1991

UNGOMAP
1988 – 1990

UNMOGIP
1948 –

OSGAP
1989 –

UNUVEM
1988 –

UNIPOM
1965 – 1966

UNSC
1953

UNIKOM
1991

ONUSAL
1991 –

UNTAC
1992

UNSF
1962 – 1963

UNCF I
1949 – 1951

ONUCA
1989 –

UNYOM
1963 – 1964

IAPF
1965 – 1966

MINURSO
1991

ONUC
1960 – 1964

UNAVEM II
1991

UNAVEM
1989 –

UNTAG
1989 – 1990

UNDOF	Peace-keeping forces
UNTOS	Observer missions
•	Headquarters

MAP 14.1 UN PEACEKEEPING FORCES AND OBSERVER MISSIONS, 1948–1992

Source: Inventory based on an update of United Nations, *The Blue Helmets: A Review of United Nations Peacekeeping* (New York: United Nations, June, 1990), and modified to identify new UN operations since 1990.

Hammarskjöld met an untimely tragic death in the line of duty in September 1961. Afterward, his successor, U Thant of Burma, pursued a much less activist program through the two terms he held office until 1971. Constrained by increasing pressure from both the United States and the Soviet Union, U Thant concentrated on "quiet diplomacy" to manage crises that not he but the Security Council or the General Assembly identified. This approach was more akin to that which had prevailed in the early 1950s, stressing crisis response rather than crisis prevention.

Kurt Waldheim of Austria, who assumed the post of secretary general in 1972, shared U Thant's preference to avoid offending the great powers. Waldheim did seek to resolve some interstate disputes, as his efforts to obtain release of the U.S. hostages seized in Iran in 1979 illustrate. His initiatives were restrained, however. In his first public statement as secretary general, Waldheim stressed that "in this position one has to know the limits." This passivity endeared Waldheim to the superpowers, who rewarded his submissiveness by supporting his reappointment in 1976 to a second five-year term and by promoting his reelection to a third in 1981. But by this time China, insisting on the election of a candidate from the Third World and vowing to use its veto to prevent Waldheim's reelection, paved the way for the election of a more experienced diplomat with greater ambitions (Jakobson, 1991).

Waldheim's successor, Javier Pérez de Cuéllar of Peru, also held "quiet diplomacy" in respect. Yet Pérez de Cuéllar was outspokenly critical of the "alarming succession of international crises" in which "the United Nations is unable to play as effective and decisive a role as the Charter certainly envisaged for it." To rectify its impotence, he called for renewed use of the Security Council that "too often [finds] itself on the sidelines" because of alleged "partisanship, indecisiveness or incapacity arising from divisions among Member States." He felt the Security Council should "keep an active watch on dangerous situations and, if necessary, initiate discussions with the parties" to defuse them "at an early stage before they degenerate into violence." Lamenting the fact that "the power of exposure" was the secretary general's only authorized power under the charter, in May 1989 Pérez de Cuéllar declared that "I cannot accept that, in each and every case, we need agreement by the two great powers before we can advance." Acting on this principle, he aggressively pursued both *peacemaking* and *peacekeeping* initiatives. He explained his approach in these terms:

> I have tried to simplify the procedures for finding peaceful solutions to international conflicts. The sequence of events is always the same. First you have to get a truce—end the hostilities. That is what we call "peacemaking" in diplomatic parlance. Once that is achieved and approved by the UN Security Council, we set up operations to keep the peace. That is what we call "peacekeeping."

Cold War Obstacles to Conflict Prevention

This ambitious departure strengthened the UN's capacity to preserve world peace through efforts organized by the secretary general (see Skjelsbaek, 1991). Still, until the closing days of the Cold War, the UN's record of preventing and settling conflicts attested to the barriers that then existed, for "only about two out of five" of the UN's attempts to mediate conflicts succeeded (Holsti, 1988: 423). Another accounting recorded a total of 319 international disputes in which some fighting occurred between

1945 and 1984, of which only 137, or 43 percent, were referred to the UN for management; moreover, the United Nations failed to abate 47 percent of these disputes and failed to settle fully 75 percent of them (Haas, 1986: 17). Hence, the UN's *peacekeeping* record was more distinguished than its *peacemaking* achievements, for the world organization was more successful in ending wars than in preventing them.

Yet the successes that were recorded also demonstrate that the UN was to some extent able to transcend the substantial barriers symbolized by more than 220 vetoes in the Security Council, or on 35 percent of its 642 resolutions between 1946 and 1990 (Rourke, 1991: 464). This record of both success and incapacity suggests that the UN's efficacy as an instrument of conflict management in the Cold War's inauspicious climate was greatest when a conflict (1) did not involve the superpowers, (2) was outside the context of the East-West rivalry, (3) was opposed by both superpowers and other members of the Security Council, (4) was intense and in danger of spreading geographically, (5) entailed fighting (albeit at a limited level), (6) centered on a decolonization dispute, (7) involved "middle" and "small" states comparatively unprepared militarily, or (8) was identified as a threat to peace by the secretary general, who led efforts to organize the organization's resistance to its continuation. The record underscores the extent to which, as Trygve Lie noted in 1946, "the United Nations is no stronger than the collective will of the nations that support it. Of itself it can do nothing. It is a machinery through which nations can cooperate. It can be used and developed . . . or it can be discarded and broken."

Given this reality, it is understandable why, while the United Nations was a captive of Cold War competition, the UN directed its activities primarily toward addressing the deep-seated structural causes of war, where it could make a difference. This is seen in its "rear door" efforts to alleviate the conditions of poverty, inequality, frustration, and despair that provoke violence. In other words, for most of its existence the United Nations concentrated its efforts on *peacelessness* in the sphere of low politics, in response to an awareness that poverty causes more death, suffering, and human incapacity than does war (Alger, 1990) and because it is here rather than in the sphere of high politics that the UN's power is greatest.[8]

Despite its weaknesses, the United Nations in many respects is, as John F. Kennedy put it, "our last hope in an age where the instruments of war have far outpaced the instruments of peace." This promise gained new momentum on becoming fulfilled when the Cold War's end opened a new chapter on the UN's quest for world order.

The United Nations after the Cold War

The United Nations was a victim of superpower rivalry for more than four decades. Now, however, the Cold War no longer stands in the way of the organization's ability to fulfill its security-preserving mission.

---

[8] These programs include work on human rights, technical assistance, refugees, decolonization, world trade, drug trafficking, the law of the sea, protection of children, world food, social discrimination, the equality of women, agricultural development, religious discrimination, disaster relief, environmental protection, and a host of other world problems that influence the quality of life and prospects for conditions from which aggression springs.

U.S. President George Bush characterized Iraq's 1990 invasion of Kuwait as the first major test of the UN's ability to maintain peace in the new world order. Many people agreed. Their hopes were inspired by the UN's prior successes in the late 1980s. In 1988, Security Council Resolution 598 provided a framework for settling the eight-year Iraq-Iran war. A series of equally impressive achievements soon followed. The UN brokered the withdrawal of Soviet troops from Afghanistan, monitored elections in Nicaragua, helped orchestrate the peaceful independence of Namibia, negotiated cease-fires in Central America and the western Sahara, and negotiated a settlement of the long-drawn-out conflict in Cambodia. Bolstered by these accomplishments, the Security Council passed Resolution 678 authorizing "member states cooperating with the Government of Kuwait to use all necessary means" to coerce Iraq's withdrawal from Kuwait. Under the authority of this resolution, on January 16, 1991, President Bush ordered an air war against Iraq's military machine, the fourth largest in the world. Forty-three days later, Iraq agreed to a cease-fire and to a withdrawal from Kuwait.

The successful expulsion of Iraq from Kuwait was the first collective response to aggression under the auspices of the UN Security Council since the Korean war in 1950. Many felt it could become the springboard from which the United Nations might begin to perform a true collective security role. Although in some ways this achievement met Bush's so-called "test," the action was (like the Korean operation) a U.S.-dominated endeavor. The United States took the lead in drafting the UN resolutions and gaining acquiescence from the Security Council's permanent members for a military intervention, in place of the strategy of giving the UN-imposed economic blockade time to work. And the more than 500,000 troops deployed were almost exclusively American. To be sure, some coalition partners (especially France, Great Britain, and Saudi Arabia) also contributed forces and the Soviet Union also agreed to participate as well on condition that the military force operated under the United Nations flag, but that never happened. Hence the United States technically ran the war.

This left uncertain whether, as President Bush described it in his October 1990 address before the United Nations, "this is a new and different world. Not since 1945 have we seen the real possibility of using the United Nations as it was designed, as a center for international collective security." The issue remained, however, whether the United Nations might truly begin "to function in the way it was originally supposed to: as a center for organizing international actions to maintain or restore peace" (Jakobson, 1991). For this purpose, in 1990 Secretary General Pérez de Cuéllar established a planning and monitoring group within the United Nations and recommended that, as originally called for by Article 52 of the charter, the Security Council hereafter cooperate energetically with regional defense organizations to police emergent disputes.

That approach may, indeed, (re)gain acceptance now that the Cold War no longer remains an insurmountable obstacle to collective security. The new secretary general, Boutros Boutros-Ghali, could assert a commanding role to enable the organization to serve as a vehicle for maintaining world order.[9] In addition, the UN's capacity to take

---

[9] Boutros-Ghali, an urbane diplomat, announced his goal of making the United Nations a "reorganized, reinvigorated peacekeeper able to meet the challenges of the 21st century." Among his proposals was a call for member states to make available up to one thousand troops each for a UN peacekeeping force, that would be available on short notice for peacekeeping operations authorized by the Security Council.

the lead in peacekeeping may be strengthened by the shift of power from the General Assembly back to the Security Council where the five permanent members represent the major poles in an emerging multipolar system. The potential for that expanded role was suggested by the fact that, since 1988, the year the UN's blue helmets were awarded the Nobel Peace Prize, the United Nations launched more peacekeeping missions than it had in the previous forty-three years of its existence. Proposals to restructure the Security Council's membership (by giving, for example, the EC, Germany, Japan, and perhaps regional powers Brazil, India, and Nigeria status as permanent members) fit the goal of expanding the Security Council's ability to collectively police trouble spots around the globe.

Financial restraints work against the UN's managerial security role, however. Indeed, the United Nations cannot pay for its expanded list of new peacekeeping missions (such as its 14,000 peacekeeping troops sent in 1992 to Yugoslavia), let alone take on responsibility for the many new initiatives also under consideration. Consider the UN operations in Cambodia. Secretary General Boutros Boutros-Ghali's 22,000-member mission to monitor elections and administrate an interim government before elections would cost $2 billion. If the UN is to play a leading security role in the new world order, then huge sums of new money will have to be raised. The prospects are remote, however, unless the staggering arrearages owed the UN are paid (see Chapter 6).

Regional Security Organizations and Conflict Management

If the United Nations reflects the lack of shared values and a common purpose characteristic of a global community, perhaps geographically restricted regional organizations of states that already share some interests and cultural traditions offer better prospects.

During the Cold War, the North Atlantic Treaty Organization (NATO) and the Warsaw Pact (WTO) were the best-known examples of regional security organizations. Others included the ANZUS pact and the Southeast Asia Treaty Organization (SEATO). Regional organizations with somewhat broader political mandates beyond defense include the Organization of American States (OAS), the League of Arab States, the Organization of African Unity (OAU), the Nordic Council, the Association of Southeast Asian Nations (ASEAN), and the Gulf Cooperation Council.

Despite the fact that Article 51 of the United Nations Charter encouraged creation of regional organizations for collective self-defense, it would be misleading to describe NATO and the other Cold War regional organizations as a substitute collective security instrument for the United Nations. They were not. More accurately, they were regional alliance systems designed to deter a common external enemy. "Collective security properly refers to a global or regional system in which *all* member countries ensure each other against *every* member; no state is singled out in advance as the enemy, and each might be an aggressor in the future. Alliances, however, usually come into existence when the members are agreed on the identity of the enemy and wish to insure each other against him" (Haas, 1969).

For the United States, the external enemy was, of course, the Soviet Union. Although this was historically true for the other members of NATO as well, we can attribute the polycentrism that surfaced in the 1960s and intensified thereafter to members' declining perception of a common threat. Likewise, in other U.S.-sponsored mutual security systems (particularly the OAS and SEATO), controversies among the coalition partners about the identity of "the enemy" were endemic.

If the Soviet Union was the common threat that stimulated the creation of NATO, the United States was the perceived enemy of the Warsaw Pact. Thus the two principal Cold War alliance systems were created to enhance mutual security because each faced an external threat, and not to prevent interstate aggression generally. The opposing alliances may have contributed to the absence of war in Europe since 1945, but it is difficult to assign NATO and the Warsaw Pact exclusive credit for keeping the "long peace" in Europe. Their existence concurrent with the absence of interstate war during this period does not prove that the former caused the latter.

Similarly unresolved questions exist about whether other regional organizations have operated as effective peacekeeping mechanisms. Between 1945 and 1984, of 319 disputes, 86 (or only 27 percent) were referred to the Organization of American States (OAS), the Arab League, the Organization for African Unity (OAU), and the Council of Europe for management (Haas, 1986: 20), and the regional organizations failed to abate 44 percent and failed to settle 74 percent of these referrals (Haas, 1986: 17). These facts indicate that although regional organizations in some ways perhaps "seek to compensate for the deficiencies of global arrangements" (Haas, 1983) such as those that paralyzed the United Nations during the Cold War, more realistically they complemented the UN more than they acted as a substitute for it.

That role continues today. The crisis in Yugoslavia is a recent example. When the civil war broke out in June 1991 and Croatia declared its independence, neither NATO nor the EC was able to agree on action to preserve peace. After the EC, led by Germany, recognized the breakaway republics of Slovenia and Croatia as independent states, it turned to the UN to enforce a cease-fire and orchestrate the peace plan. This case and others suggest that regional organizations can bring conflict within their territory or in close proximity under control, but that they also lack the political will to control the most troublesome conflicts.

In the long run, regional organizations may help build security communities in which the expectation of peace exceeds the expectation of war. The processes through which such metamorphoses might occur are addressed by the functional and neofunctional approaches to peace.

POLITICAL INTEGRATION: THE FUNCTIONAL AND NEOFUNCTIONAL PATHS TO PEACE . . . .

Political integration refers either to the process or the product of efforts to build new political communities and supranational institutions that transcend the nation-state. Their purposes are to remove states' incentives for war and to outline a reform program to transform international institutions from instruments *of* states to structures *over* them.

World Federalism

Functionalism in its various manifestations does not represent a frontal attack on the nation-state by proposing to replace it with some central authority. That radical remedy is represented by *world federalism*. Federalists follow Albert Einstein's conviction that "there is no salvation for civilization, or even the human race, other than the creation of a world government." They recommend building a political union at the regional and global level like the U.S. federal structure that integrates the fifty states.

If people value survival more highly than relative national advantage, so federalists reason, they will willingly transfer their loyalty to a supranational authority to dismantle the multistate system that produces war and threatens to annihilate the human species. "World government," world federalists believe, "is not only possible, it is inevitable [because it appeals to] the patriotism of men who love their national heritages so deeply that they wish to preserve them in safety for the common good" (Ferencz and Keyes, 1991).

It is not surprising that ardent nationalists have vociferously attacked the revolutionary federalist "top-down" peace plan since it was first advocated. Because the plan seeks to subvert the nation-state system, it threatens many entrenched interests. More abstractly, other critics reject the world federalists' proposition that governments are bad but people are good, wise, and enlightened (see Claude, 1971). Likewise, they challenge the assumption that "necessity" will lead to global institutional innovation, for the need for something will not automatically bring it into existence.

Although still actively promoted by the United World Federalists (an international nongovernmental pressure group), aversion to war and raised consciousness of its dangers have not mobilized widespread grass-roots enthusiasm for a world government. Other approaches to reforming the world political system have attracted more adherents.

Functionalism

Classical functionalism is a rival but complementary reform movement also in the spirit of neoliberal institutionalism. In contrast to federalism, however, *functionalism* is directed not to the creation of a world federal structure with all its constitutional paraphernalia but, rather, to building "peace by pieces" through transnational organizations that emphasize the "sharing of sovereignty" instead of its surrender. Functionalism advocates a "bottom-up," evolutionary strategy for building cooperative ties among states.

Functionalists see technical experts, not professional diplomats, as the best agents for building collaborative ties bridging national borders, because the latter are overly protective of national interests at the expense of collective human interests. Rather than addressing the immediate sources of national insecurity, the functionalists' peace plan calls for transnational cooperation in technical (primarily social and economic) areas as a first step. Habits of cooperation learned in one technical area (such as physics or medicine), they assume, will *spill over* into others, especially if the experience is mutually beneficial and demonstrates the potential advantages of cooperative ventures in other related functional areas (such as transportation and communication).

To enhance the probability that cooperative endeavors will prove rewarding rather than frustrating, the functionalist plan recommends that less difficult tasks be tackled first. It assumes that successful mastering of one problem will then encourage attacking other problems collaboratively. If the process continues unabated, the bonds among nations will multiply, for no government would oppose the web of functional organizations that provide such clear-cut benefits to their citizens. Hence, "the mission of functionalism is to make peace possible by organizing particular layers of human social life in accordance with their particular requirements, breaking down the artificialities of the zoning arrangements associated with the principle of sovereignty" (Claude, 1971).

Many people found the functionalist approach to peace persuasive because, as its intellectual father David Mitrany (1966) argued in *A Working Peace System*, first published in 1943, it was based on self-interest.

> Functionalism proposes not to squelch but to utilize national selfishness; it asks governments not to give up sovereignty which belongs to their peoples but to acquire benefits for their peoples which were hitherto unavailable, not to reduce their power to defend their citizens but to expand their competence to serve them. It intimates that the basic requirement for peace is that states have the wit to cooperate in pursuit of national interests that coincide with those of other states rather than the will to compromise national interests that conflict with those of others. (Claude, 1971: 386)

The permanent problem-solving organizations created in the 1800s, such as the Rhine River Commission (1804), the Danube River Commission (1857), the International Telegraphic Union (1865), and the Universal Post Union (1874), suggested a process by which states might cooperate to enjoy mutual benefits and hence to launch the more ambitious experiments that functionalists anticipated. Their lessons informed the early organizational ideology that inspired the missions assigned to the UN's specialized agencies and the growth of international intergovernmental (IGO) and nongovernmental (INGO) organizations generally.

Functionalism as originally formulated did not pertain to multinational corporations (MNCs), but it is tempting to speculate that MNCs may facilitate the transformation of world politics in a manner consistent with functionalist logic. Individuals who manage global corporations often think and talk of themselves as a "revolutionary class" possessing a holistic, cosmopolitan vision of the earth that challenges traditional nationalism (Barnet and Müller, 1974). This ideology and the corresponding slogan "down with borders" are based on the assumptions that the world can be managed as an integrated unit, that global corporations can serve as agents of social change, that governments interfere unnecessarily with the free flow of capital and technology, and that the MNCs can promote compromise between contending states.

As a theory of peace and world order, however, functionalism does not take into account some important political realities. First, its assumption about the causes of war is questionable. Do poverty and despair cause war, or does war cause poverty and despair? Indeed, may not material deprivation sometimes breed—instead of aggression—apathy, anomie, and hostility without recourse to violence (see Gurr, 1970)? Why should we assume that the functionalist theory of war is more accurate than the many other explanations of global violence?

Second, functionalism assumes that political differences among nations will be dissolved by the habits of cooperation learned by experts organized transnationally to cope with technical problems. The reality is that technical cooperation is often more strongly influenced by politics than the other way around. The U.S. withdrawal from the International Labor Organization (ILO) and the United Nations Educational, Scientific, and Cultural Organization (UNESCO) because of their politicized nature dramatizes the primacy of politics.

Functionalists sometimes naively argue that technical (functional) undertakings and political affairs can be separated, but they cannot. If technical cooperation becomes as important to state welfare as the functionalists argue it will, states will not step aside. Welfare and power cannot be separated, because the solution of economic and social problems cannot be divorced from political considerations. Whether the authority and competency of transnational institutions can readily be expanded at the expense of national governments is, therefore, unlikely. Functionalism, in short, is an idea whose time has passed.

Neofunctionalism

A new, albeit derivative, theory arose in the 1950s to question the assumption that ever-expanding functional needs for joint action to address property rights, health, agriculture, and other shared problems would force the resolution of political disputes. Termed *neofunctionalism*, the reconstructed theory sought to address directly the political factors that obtrusively dominate the process of merging formerly independent states.

> *Neofunctionalism* holds that political institutions and policies should be crafted so that they lead to further integration through the process of . . . "the expansive logic of sector integration." For example, [the first] president of the ECSC [European Coal and Steel Community], [Jean] Monnet, sought to use the integration of the coal and steel markets of the six member countries as a lever to promote the integration of their social security and transport policies, arguing that such action was essential to eliminate distortions in coal and steel prices. [The] neofunctionalism of Monnet and others [had] as its ultimate goal . . . the creation of a federal state. (Jacobson, 1984: 66)

Neofunctionalism thus proposes to accelerate the processes leading to new supranational communities by purposely pushing for cooperation in areas that are politically controversial, rather than by avoiding them. Neofunctionalism advocates that the proponents of integration bring political pressure to bear at crucial decision points to persuade their opponents of the greater benefits of forming a larger community among its formerly independent national members.

The European Experience

Western Europe is the preeminent example of the application of neofunctionalist principles to the development of an integrated political community. As described in Chapter 6, within a single generation cooperation across European borders led to a single European economic market and, in the 1992 New Treaty of European Union, to the promise of a politically integrated European Community.

The opportunities (and problems) of launching a new chapter of European history were made evident at the Maastricht summit leading to the Union treaty. Alongside its agreement to complete the 1992 single-market program that is the most potent symbol of Europe's new dynamism, the treaty obliges the EC states to cooperate not just in finance and economics but in defense and foreign policy as well. However, even though, as British Foreign Secretary Douglas Hurd observed, "the Community is no longer fragile," obstacles to consolidation and unity remain, as some problems, including security policy, "at the heart of the functions of the nation state are better conducted directly between governments answerable to their national Parliaments." That sentiment punctuated the many points at which politics can impede the integrative process through which a "United States of Europe" might emerge. Given the chronic suspicion, selfishness, and tenacious national memories of the dark side of Europe's twentieth-century history—alongside the potential for interdependence to provoke competition and struggles for advantage—it is unclear whether the dream of true European unity will someday become a reality.

Yet, although many obstacles to political unification remain, the dream has gained believers and momentum. "We have reached the point of no return," Dutch Prime Minister Rudd Lubbers proclaimed on the eve of the signing ceremonies for the European Union treaty (to take effect January 1, 1993, contingent upon ratification by the twelve nations). And even if Europeans do not soon realize their aspiration of political union, Europe has already constructed a "security community" in which the expectation of war has vanished from one of the historically most violence-prone regions of the world (Deutsch and colleagues, 1957). German Chancellor Helmut Kohl expressed the sentiment that has swept Europe: "We have learned history's lesson, that violence is not a means of politics. European national states have no future. We need a European roof, and my goal . . . is the political unification of Europe."

Whereas the onset of armed hostility in the EC is very unlikely, the issue of how broad and geographically wide this integrative process will go is highly uncertain (see Chapter 6). And the number of members that ultimately join this "common European home" is likely to prove consequential for European security:

> It has been argued that a more unified western Europe will be better able to withstand the stresses of political upheaval in eastern Europe, and has thus become an imperative. Yet, it also can be argued that as the EC "deepens" it will become more of a closed club, unwilling to accommodate the legitimate demands of Poland, Czechoslovakia, Hungary, the Baltic States and other European states for trade and security. Thus, there is a danger that the

"one Europe" of the visionaries will in fact be two Europes, one rich and stable and the other poor and unstable. That could be a formula for future conflicts not unlike those of the past. (Melloan, 1991: A15)

The Preconditions for Regional Integration

The record of integrative experiments demonstrates that the factors promoting (or inhibiting) successful integration efforts are many and their mixture complex. It is not enough that two countries choose to interact cooperatively. Research indicates that the probability that such cooperative behavior will culminate in integration is remote in the absence of geographical proximity, steady economic growth, similar political systems, supportive public opinion led by enthusiastic leaders, cultural homogeneity, internal political stability, similar experiences in historical and internal social development, compatible forms of governmental and economic systems, similar levels of military preparedness and economic resources, a shared perception of a common external threat, bureaucratic compatibilities, and previous collaborative endeavors (Cobb and Elder, 1970; Deutsch, 1953). Although not all of these conditions must be present for integration to occur, the absence of more than a few considerably reduces the chances of success. The integration of two or more societies, let alone the entire world, is, in short, not easily accomplished.

European integration has served as a model for the application of the neofunctionalist approach to institution building and the pooling of sovereignty in other regions, including Africa, Asia, Latin America, and, until the demise of the Cold War, Eastern Europe. However, the evidence to date suggests that the integration of nation-states into larger political communities may be peculiarly relevant to the West's advanced industrial societies with democratic governance but of doubtful applicability to the Third World. The record, moreover, indicates that even where conditions are conducive, there is no guarantee that the sector integration will proceed automatically. Even in Europe, high hopes have alternated with periods of disillusionment. When momentum has occurred, *spillover*, involving either the deepening of ties in one sector or their expansion to another to ensure the members' satisfaction with the integrative process, has led to further integration. But there is no inherent expansive momentum in integration schemes. "Spillback" (when a regional integration scheme fails, as in the case of East African Community) and "spillaround" (when a regional integration scheme stagnates or its activities become encapsulated) are also possibilities.

Political Disintegration

The substantial difficulty that most regions have experienced in achieving the same level of institution building as has the European Community suggests the magnitude of existing barriers to the creation of new political communities out of previously divided ones. Furthermore, the paradox that "the planet is falling precipitantly apart *and* coming reluctantly together at the very same moment" (Barber, 1992) confounds predictions. Consider Europe, where important steps toward economic and political integration in the EC were taken in 1992 at the precise moment when

- the Soviet Union disintegrated into a loosely tied Commonwealth of Independent States threatening to splinter further;
- Czechoslovakia was formally reconstituted the Czech and Slovak Federal Republic; and
- civil war in Yugoslavia splintered the formerly United Slavic Federation of six republics, four of which sought recognition as independent states.

These counterintegrative and disintegrative developments transform the European political terrain. Indeed, in contrast to Western Europe, much of postcommunist Eastern Europe and the Balkans experienced the resumption of the historic ethnic quarrels and nationalistic passions that have bedeviled the region for centuries and helped cause two world wars. In 1991, fifteen new national flags were adopted to symbolize newly independent countries.

Equally sobering is the fact that other aspirant states are in line, as fifty regions worldwide declared themselves autonomous between 1989 and 1991 (*Harper's*, December 1991, p. 17). This wave of hypernationalism and quest for independence by minorities and sub-national grievance groups under the banner of self-determination threatens to *dismember* formerly integrated sovereign states, including such widely disparate states as Canada, South Africa, and the United Kingdom. Such developments are not new, of course, as the U.S. Civil War in 1861 exemplifies, but these counterintegrative tendencies remind us that nations may either amalgamate or fragment. There is little reason to expect integrative processes, once under way, to progress through the pull of their own momentum.

LAW, ORGANIZATION, AND WORLD ORDER ·

Neoliberal-institutionalist theories that focus on international law, organization, and political integration see war as deriving from the deficiencies built into the state system. Neoliberal reformers believe the system is the problem, not the solution, because existing arrangements make security dear and global welfare subservient to national welfare. To change this, they advocate legal and institutional methods to pool sovereignty. Seeing the international system as underdeveloped and unstructured, advocates of these reforms believe that a rebuilt state system can best extirpate the roots from which war has so often grown. Although the contributions of international law and institutions to this grand purpose have, to date, been rather modest, as long-term historical processes their impact should not be minimized. As Inis L. Claude avers,

> Particular *organizations* may be nothing more than playthings of power politics and handmaidens of national ambitions. But international *organization*, considered as an historical process, represents a secular trend toward the systematic development of an enterprising

quest for political means of making the world safe for human habitation. It may fail, and peter out ignominiously. But if it maintains the momentum that it has built up in the twentieth century, it may yet effect a transformation of human relationships on this planet which will at some indeterminate point justify the assertion that the world has come to be governed—that mankind has become a community capable of sustaining order, promoting justice, and establishing the conditions of that good life which Aristotle took to be the supreme aim of politics. (Claude, 1971: 447–448, emphasis added)

SUGGESTED READINGS

Bennett, A. Leroy. *International Organizations: Principles and Issues*, 5th ed. Englewood Cliffs, N.J.: Prentice Hall, 1991.

Claude, Inis L., Jr. *States and the Global System: Politics, Law and Organization*. New York: St. Martin's Press, 1988.

Falk, Richard A., Samuel S. Kim, and Saul H. Mendlovitz, eds. *The United Nations and a Just World Order*. Boulder, Colo.: Westview, 1991.

Haas, Ernst B. *When Knowledge Is Power: Three Models of Change in International Organizations*. Berkeley: University of California Press, 1990.

Henkin, Louis, et al. *Right v. Might: International Law and the Use of Force*, 2nd ed. New York: Council on Foreign Relations Press, 1991.

James, Alan. *Peacekeeping in International Politics*. New York: St. Martin's Press, 1990.

Jones, Dorothy V. *Code of Peace: Ethics and Security in the World of Warlord States*. Chicago: University of Chicago Press, 1991.

Joyner, Christopher C. "The Reality and Relevance of International Law," pp. 200–215 in Charles W. Kegley, Jr., and Eugene R. Wittkopf, eds., *The Global Agenda: Issues and Perspectives*, 3rd ed. New York: McGraw-Hill, 1991.

Nardin, Terry, and David R. Matel, eds. *Traditions of International Ethics*. Cambridge, England: Cambridge University Press, 1992.

Puchala, Donald J. "The Integration Theorists and the Study of International Relations," pp. 198–265 in Charles W. Kegley, Jr., and Eugene R. Wittkopf, eds., *The Global Agenda: Issues and Perspectives*, 2nd ed. New York: Random House, 1988.

Taylor, Paul, and A. J. R. Groom, eds. *International Institutions at Work*. New York: St. Martin's Press, 1988.

von Glahn, Gerhard. *Law Among Nations*, 6th ed. New York: Macmillan, 1992.

Part V

Toward the Twenty-first Century

. . .

The Global Predicament: Twelve Questions for a Transforming World

CHAPTER 15

• • •

THE GLOBAL PREDICAMENT: TWELVE QUESTIONS FOR A TRANSFORMING WORLD

• • •

Trend is not destiny.

René Dubos, French author, 1975

In the old world of the Cold War period, we knew what threatened us. In the new world, we will have to learn what threatens us.

Les Aspin, Representative,
U.S. Congress, 1992

The convergence of multiple world political trends in the twilight of the twentieth century points toward a new, transformed world order but one whose character has not yet developed sharp definition and vivid coloration. Thus U.S. President George Bush, commenting in late 1991 on the post–Cold War world, justifiably cautioned that "the enemy is uncertainty. The enemy is unpredictability."

What *is* certain is that the pace of change will challenge the wisdom of old beliefs and orthodox visions of the world. Because turmoil and turbulence govern contemporary international affairs, they require our asking unconventional questions about conventional ideas.

In this final chapter we pose twelve questions about the future based on our preceding analyses of contemporary world politics. How these questions are answered will significantly shape world politics during the remainder of this century and the next.

1. Are Nation-States Obsolete?

The changing environment of world politics challenges the traditional preeminence of the territorial nation-state, the primary actor in world politics for more than three centuries.

One of the hallmarks of human history in the late twentieth century is the increasing internationalization of the world: in production, trade, finance, technology, threats to security, communications, research, education, and culture. One major consequence of this is that the mutual penetration of economic, political, and social forces among the nations of the world is increasingly salient; and it may be the case that the governments of nation-states are progressively losing degrees of direct control over the global forces that affect them. (Smelser, 1986: 1)

Can the nation-state cope with the challenges it now faces? "A myth" is what John F. Kennedy called "the untouchability of national sovereignty." Henry Kissinger, a former U.S. secretary of state, labeled the nation-state "inadequate" and the emergence of a global community an "imperative." Zbigniew Brzezinski, a former U.S. presidential adviser, similarly asserted that "we are witnessing the end of the supremacy of the nation-state on the international scene" and noted that although "this process is far from consummated . . . the trend seems irreversible." These views question the nation-state's capacity to handle global challenges.

The nineteenth-century French sociologist Auguste Comte argued that societies create institutions to address problems and meet human needs, and that institutions disappear when they can no longer perform these functions. Today, the nation-state's managerial capabilities everywhere, irrespective of form of government, fail to inspire confidence. Lack of faith in governmental efficiency has reached epidemic proportions. No government is immune from attacks by its own citizens for its inability to protect its population or improve its life. Moreover, the existence of weapons of mass destruction erodes governments' claim to guarantee the common defense—a development that undermines the nation-state's primary *raison d'être*.

Other forces infuse the nation-state with vigor and encourage its persistence, however. "Obviously in some respects the nation-state is flourishing and in others it is dying," observes French political scientist Pierre Hassner (1968), adding, "it can no longer fulfill some of the most important traditional functions, yet it constantly assumes new ones which it alone seems able to fulfill." Thus, at the core of contemporary international politics lies a paradox: "At a time when the nation-state has appeared to be functionally obsolete, it has been reaffirmed by the same process which would call for its transcendence" (Morse, 1976).

2. Is Interdependence a Cure or a Curse?

Global interdependence lies at the heart of the internationalization of domestic politics. It poses a singular threat to the nation-state. Interdependence expands the range of global issues while making their management more difficult, as mutual vulnerabilities reduce states' autonomy and curtail their control of their own destinies.

From one perspective, global interdependence may draw the world's diverse components together in pursuit of mutual survival and welfare. Awareness of the common destiny of all, alongside the inability of sovereign nations to address many shared problems through unilateral national action, may energize efforts to put aside national competition. Conflict will recede, according to this reasoning, as few nations can disentangle themselves from the interdependent ties that bind them together in a common fate. From this perspective, then, we should welcome the continued tightening of interstate linkages, for they strengthen the seams that bind together the fragile tapestry of international relations.

From another, more pessimistic perspective, interdependence will not lead to transnational collaboration, regardless of how compelling the need may be. Instead, contact and mutual dependence will breed conflict. The absence of a community of nations remains, and nostalgia for the more autonomous nation-state abounds. Under conditions of competition and resurgent nationalism, the temptation to seek isolation from foreign economic involvement by creating barriers to trade and other economic transactions may be irresistible. So, too, may be the temptation to use force.

Thus, the tightening web of global interdependence foretells both opportunity and danger. If, on balance, the advantages of interdependence outweigh the disadvantages, then leaders must harness the means for accelerating its development. Conversely, if global interdependence undermines national and international welfare and security, they must try to contain and perhaps reverse its effects.

3. What Is the "National Interest"?

What goals should nation-states pursue? In earlier times, the answer was easy: the state should promote its internal welfare, protect itself from external attack, and preserve its values and way of life.

Leaders pursue the same goals today, but increasingly their domestic and foreign policy options are limited. We live in an age of trade-offs, as many problems can be resolved only at the risk of exacerbating others. Under such conditions, the quest for narrow self-advantage often carries prohibitively high costs. The historic tendency to define the national interest aggressively—my country, right or wrong—can be counterproductive domestically as well as internationally, as no country can long afford to pursue the quest for power in ways that reduce the security of its competitors.

Those who questioned orthodox definitions of the national interest in the past seldom found support, but this is changing. As the eminent anthropologist Margaret Mead mused, "Substantially we all share the same atmosphere today, and we can only save ourselves by saving other people also. There is no longer a contradiction between patriotism and concern for the world." Former U.S. Secretary of State Cyrus Vance voiced a similar idea, observing that "more than ever cooperative endeavors among nations are a matter not only of idealism but of direct self-interest."

E. H. Carr (1939), a pioneering political realist, was convinced of the realism of idealism, maintaining that opposition to the general interests of humankind does not serve one's self-interest. Nor is it served by a failure to recognize that the plight of others can ultimately threaten oneself—a view underscored by Martin Luther King, Jr., who urged that "injustice anywhere is a threat to justice everywhere."

4. Are Technological Innovations a Blessing or a Burden?

Technological innovations, like interdependence, offer solutions to some problems but cause others. As noted economist Wassily Leontief warned in 1987, "Technology is now, for better or worse, the principal driving force behind the ongoing rapid economic, social, and political change. Like any irrepressible force, the new technology can bestow on us undreamed of benefits but also inflict irreparable damage." They pave the way to new ways of preventing disease but also new ways of destroying others in war. Discoveries in microelectronics, information processing, transportation, energy, agriculture, communications, medicine, and biotechnology profoundly affect our lives and shape our future.

New technologies propel growth and alter behavior patterns. Still, "there appears to be a fundamental lag between the current rate of technological change and the rate of adjustment to these changes among decision-makers" (Blumenthal). The technological catalyst of change will promote progress only if it is properly and constructively managed and if the interconnectedness of technological innovation and economic, political, and military imperatives is recognized.

5. Of What Value Is Military Power?

Military might in the past enabled states to project power, exercise influence, and dominate others. Today the destructiveness of nuclear weapons and sophisticated conventional and unconventional weapons makes their use risky. Moreover, their threatened use is less convincing than ever. Yet continuing proliferation raises new questions alongside old ones. Security is a psychological phenomenon, but does the acquisition of more weapons augment it? Or are preparations for war and defense responsible for the security dilemma that all nations face?

To be sure, most national leaders agree with the ancient Greek philosopher Aristotle, who argued that "a people without walls is a people without choice." Hence most assume that preparing for war is necessary for peace. Yet, as Henry Kissinger explained, "the paradox of contemporary military strength is that the capacity to destroy is difficult to translate into a plausible threat even against countries with no capacity for retaliation." Today, the threat of force often lacks credibility. Military power has become impotent by its very strength.

Weapons may deter resort to force, but if military might no longer exacts compliance from others, then weapons have lost their role as a basis, or substitute, for diplomacy. And if military power is impotent, why pay the price of vigilance? Since no amount of military might can guarantee a nation invulnerability, preparations for war can be assessed only in terms of other consequences. Thresholds may exist beyond which the addition of greater destructive power is meaningless, and excessive preparations for war may leave a country heavily fortified with little left to defend, as U.S. President Eisenhower warned in 1961. U Thant, former secretary general of the United Nations, echoed this point when he noted that "the massive sums devoted to armaments . . . serve to feed the escalating arms race, to increase insecurity, and to multiply the risks to human survival."

The end of the Cold War will further erode justifications for the pursuit of military power as once implacable enemies proclaim a new friendship. The urge for military preparedness will nonetheless continue in a multipolar world. Hence the relative costs and benefits of preparations for war must be weighed against the kinds of threats to national security that still arise.

6. Is War Obsolete?

As noted, ideas and institutions wither away when they cease to serve their intended purpose, as the examples of slavery, dueling, and colonialism illustrate. Is war subject to this same phenomenon? Since World War II, legal prohibitions against the use of force have expanded, and war and interventions have been confined to battles among and in developing nations. The period since 1945 has been the longest span of great-power peace since the seventeenth century, thus raising expectations that the major powers have "retreated from doomsday" (Mueller, 1989). Hence the obsolescence of major war may be on the horizon.

Whether the seemingly unthinkable use of today's most destructive weapons has truly made war unthinkable is, of course, debatable. Instead, war may eventually disappear in another, far more frightening way—because resort to weapons of mass destruction will obliterate humankind. Thus the puzzle is when and by what means war will become obsolete. As Martin Luther King, Jr., put it, "The choice is either nonviolence or nonexistence."

7. The End of Empire?

Much of world history is written in terms of dreams of world conquest, the quest of rulers for world domination, and the efforts of others to prevent it. Some political leaders continue to think and act as though they believe others still actively plan territorial conquest. But the past five decades have witnessed the great powers' race to relinquish their overseas empires, not expand them. Even the Soviet Union, the last world empire of any size, has now disintegrated.

Why has the quest for empire seemingly ended? A plausible explanation is that empire did not benefit the imperial powers materially (Boulding, 1978). Political scientist William Langer, writing in the early 1960s, when the decolonization process was at its peak, argued similarly:

> It is highly unlikely that the modern world will revert to the imperialism of the past. History has shown that the nameless fears which in the late nineteenth century led to the most violent outburst of expansionism were largely unwarranted. The Scandinavian states and Germany since Versailles have demonstrated that economic prosperity and social well-being are not dependent on the exploitation of other peoples, while better distribution of wealth in the advanced countries has reduced if not obviated whatever need there may have been to seek abroad a safety-valve for the pressures building up at home. Even in the field of defense, the old need for overseas bases or for the control of adjacent territories is rapidly being outrun. (Langer, 1962: 129)

If imperialism, empire building, and territorial acquisition are no longer in a nation's self-interest, why should they continue to prepare for military defense against the imagined expansionist aims of others?

8. What Price Preeminence?

The quest for world conquest has waned, but national competition for status in the global pecking order continues. Prestige, respect, and wealth remain the core values of many states and the central goals for which they strive. To become or remain first in the international arena means competing for the political and economic means to bend others to one's will.

The potential long-term results of this competition are disquieting. The problems of primacy are numerous, the disadvantages of advantage many. With global leadership comes the burden of responsibility and the necessity of setting the pace and maintaining world order. Moreover, dominant nations are often the targets of other nations' resentment, envy, hostility, fear, and blame.

The quest for military superiority may lose much of its rationale in the aftermath of the Cold War and with the emergence of economics as the world's primary battlefield. Today, the increasingly high costs of military preeminence have quieted its appeal in national capitals. Military spending reduces industrial growth, weakens economic competitiveness, and, ultimately, undermines states' ability to pursue and preserve dominance:

> It has been a common dilemma facing previous "number-one" countries that even as their relative economic strength is ebbing, the growing foreign challenges to their position have compelled them to allocate more and more of their resources into the military sector, which in turn squeezes out productive investment and, over time, leads to the downward spiral of slower growth, heavier taxes, deepening domestic splits over spending priorities and a weakening capacity to bear the burdens of defense. (Kennedy, 1987: 533)

Many will not take this message seriously, however, as the one predicament that nearly every nation finds worse than being preeminent is being subject to another's dictates. Thus the pursuit of preeminence continues.

9. Is the World Preparing for the Wrong War?

To preserve peace, one must prepare for war. That remains the classical formula for national security. But would nations not be wiser to prepare to conquer the conditions that undermine prosperity, freedom, and welfare? "War for survival is the destiny of all species," observes philosopher Martin J. Siegel (1983). "In our case, we are courting suicide [by waging war against one another]. The world powers should declare war against their common enemy—the catastrophic and survival-of-the-fittest forces that destroyed most of the species of life that came before us."

Not all world leaders succumb to the single-mindedness of preparing to wage the wrong war. Voices that challenge the prevailing penchant are occasionally heard. President Miguel de la Madrid of Mexico in 1983 noted that "scarce resources are being used to sustain the arms race, thereby hindering the economic development of nations and international cooperation." Similarly, President François Mitterrand of France warned in the same year that "together we must urgently find the solutions to the real problems at hand—especially unemployment and underdevelopment. This is the battlefield where the outlines of the year 2000 will be drawn." And India's Prime Minister Indira Gandhi predicted that "either nuclear war will annihilate the human race and destroy the earth, thus disposing of any future, or men and women all over must raise their voices for peace and for an urgent attempt to combine the insights of different civilizations with contemporary knowledge. We can survive in peace and goodwill only by viewing the human race as one, and by looking at global problems in their totality."

Each of these rhetorical positions doubtless reflected the problems and self-interests the leaders faced at home and abroad, but they nonetheless reveal a minority viewpoint. The war of people against people goes on. Humankind may consequently plummet, not because it lacks opportunities, but because of its collective inability to see and to seize them. "Perhaps we will destroy ourselves. Perhaps the common enemy within us will be too strong for us to recognize and overcome," the eminent astronomer Carl Sagan (1988) lamented. "But," he continued, "I have hope. . . . Is it possible that we humans are at last coming to our senses and beginning to work together on behalf of the species and the planet?"

10. What Is Human Well-Being?

The once popular "limits to growth" proposition has been replaced by the maxim of sustainability, which emphasizes "the growth of limits." Thus sustainability means learning to live off the earth's interest, without encroaching on its capital.

Gross national product is the common measure of economic well-being throughout the world and "is closely bound up with human welfare. . . . Human welfare has dimensions other than the economic one. But it is rightly held that the economic element is *very* important, and that the stronger the economy the greater the contribution to human welfare" (Daly and Cobb, 1989).

A rise in a nation's economic output has different consequences for people currently living in poor societies compared with those in rich societies. For the inhabitants of most Third World countries, growth in GNP may mean more food, better housing, better education, and an increased standard of living. Because the affluent people living in the First World already have these basic amenities, additional increments to their income usually lead to the satisfaction of comparatively trivial needs.

The impact on the global commons of population growth and the continued striving for economic growth is critical nonetheless. "The incremental person in poor countries contributes negligibly to production, but makes few demands on world resources," explains economist Herman Daly (1973). By contrast, "the incremental person in the rich country contributes to his country's GNP, and to feed his high standard of living contributes greatly to depletion of the world's resources and pollution of its spaces." In both cases, then, continued population growth is detrimental—for poor societies, because it inhibits increases in per-capita income and welfare, and for rich societies, because it further burdens the earth's delicate ecological system.

An alternative to perpetual growth for the world's rich nations is a steady-state economy that seeks a constant stock of capital and population combined with as modest a rate of production and consumption of goods as possible. Because most advanced industrial nations have already approached zero population growth, or a steady state, realizing zero economic growth would require profoundly altered attitudes toward production and consumption. It would also require an alteration in attitudes toward cultural norms regarding leisure and satisfaction. Citizens would have to maximize the durability of goods and recycle more products. And they would have to restrain the profit motive that justifies the need for growth and the craving for unnecessary material goods. Similarly, policymakers would have to devise means of managing conflict other than by doling out increments of an ever-expanding pie—for in a steady-state economy the pie would no longer grow.

These ideas challenge the very foundations of Western civilization. Sustainability is a more realistic prospect, but even it will be hard to realize. Minimally, it requires rethinking the meaning of human welfare. Economic welfare remains critical to human welfare, but "the first question to ask is whether growth in the economy as measured by GNP actually contributes to the total well-being of people" (Daly and Cobb, 1989). Sustainable economic welfare, like sustainable development, requires sensitivity not only to economic growth but also to natural resource depletion, environmental damage, and the value of leisure (Daly and Cobb, 1989). But is there an alternative? Can growth in a finite world proceed infinitely? How long can finite energy sources sustain uncontrollable consumption before automobiles sputter to a stop, industries grind to a halt, and lights go out? How many pollutants can the atmosphere absorb before irreparable environmental damage is done? And how many people can a delicately balanced ecosystem support?

11. The End of History?

To many observers, the history of world affairs is the struggle between tyranny and liberty. The contest has taken various forms since antiquity: between kings and sovereign peoples; authoritarianism and republicanism; despotism and democracy; ideological principle and pragmatic governance. Labels are misleading and sometimes dangerous, but they form the vocabulary of diplomacy and the political theory of governance and statecraft. History, in this image, is a battle for the hearts and minds of civilizations, an ideological contest for the allegiance of humankind to a particular form of political, social, and economic organization.

Since the Bolshevik revolution in 1917 brought socialism to power in Russia and made Marxism a force in international affairs, the fight for allegiance in the twentieth century has been dominated by the contests between communism, fascism, and democratic capitalism. With the defeat of fascism in World War II and the collapse of the international communist movement a generation later, it has become fashionable to argue that we have witnessed the end of a historic contest of epic proportions—and hence "the end of history":

> The twentieth century saw the developed world descend into a paroxysm of ideological violence, as liberalism contended first with the remnants of absolutism, then bolshevism and fascism, and finally an updated Marxism that threatened to lead to the ultimate apocalypse of nuclear war. But the century that began full of self-confidence in the ultimate triumph of Western liberal democracy seems at its close to be returning full circle to where it started: not to an "end of ideology" of a convergence between capitalism and socialism, as earlier predicted, but to the unabashed victory of economic and political liberalism. (Fukuyama, 1989: 3)

The abrupt repudiation of communism in Moscow and Eastern Europe, and its probable demise in China, Cuba, and North Korea, raises expectations that history has indeed "ended" in the sense that democratic governments practicing free market capitalism at home and free trade abroad will become the rule throughout the world. To believers of the liberal faith, this is heart-warming. World order, they believe, can be created best by free governments practicing free trade. As Woodrow Wilson argued, making the world "safe for democracy" would make the world itself safe. From this perspective, the diffusion of democratic capitalism bodes well for the future of world politics in the next millennium.

Contrariwise, a less reassuring possibility is that history has not "ended" and that neither the battle between totalitarian and democratic governance nor the inclination of states to struggle among themselves for power is over. Instead, with the end of the ideological dimension to the Cold War, we may be witnessing not history's end but a watershed that, like previous turning points in history, signals history's resumption: the return to the ageless search for barriers against the resurgence of tyranny, nationalism, and war. Especially to followers of *realpolitik*, the most salient feature of world politics—the relentless competitive struggle for power—is permanent. The end of the Cold War does not assure us that the international community has moved beyond tyranny or interstate competition and war. As former Soviet President Mikhail Gorbachev noted in May 1992, "In the major centers of world politics, the choice, it would seem, has today been made in favor of peace, cooperation, interaction and overall security." However, he warned, "A major international effort will be needed to render irreversible the shift in favor of a democratic world—and democratic for the whole of humanity, not just half of it."

12. A Reordered Global Agenda?

The paradox of contemporary world politics is that a world liberated from the paralyzing grip of the Cold War must now face a series of challenges every bit as threatening and as potentially intractable. Global interdependence without the rigidity of Cold

War bipolarity has simultaneously enlarged the responsibilities and expanded the issues to be confronted.

Alongside the resurgence of nationalism, ethnic conflict, and separatist revolt, the sea changes in recent years have spawned a diffusion of new kinds of threats to world order: acid rain, AIDS, drug trafficking, ozone depletion, global warming, energy and food insecurity, desertification and deforestation, chronic debt, and neomercantilism and trade protectionism, among others.

The potential impact of these new threats is potent, but their importance does not necessarily mean that geo-economics or ecopolitics will replace geopolitics (Luttwak, 1990). Still, emerging trends suggest that, alongside the continuing threat of arms and ethnic and regional conflict, nonmilitary dangers will multiply. Accordingly, the distinction between high politics and low politics may disappear. "In the post–Cold War world low politics is becoming high politics" (Moran, 1991).

A NEW WORLD ORDER?

From our vantage point at the twilight of the twentieth century, the world has undergone a fundamental transformation. Previously established patterns and relationships have been obliterated. Something revolutionary, not simply new, has unfolded.

Juxtaposed against the revolutionary is the persistent—the durability of accepted rituals, existing rules, established institutions, and entrenched customs. These resist the pull of the momentous recent changes in world politics. Change and persistence coexist uneasily, and it is this intertwined mixture that makes the future so uncertain.

Two races govern the path between the world that is and the world that will be. The first is the race between knowledge and oblivion. Ignorance stands in the way of global progress and justice. Advances in science and technology far outpace resolution of the social and political problems they generate. Building the knowledge to confront these problems may therefore present the ultimate challenge. "The splitting of the atom," Albert Einstein warned, "has changed everything save our modes of thinking, and thus we drift toward unparalleled catastrophe. Unless there is a fundamental change in [our] attitudes toward one another as well as [our] concept of the future, the world will face unprecedented disaster."

"Knowledge is our destiny," the philosopher Jacob Bronowski declared. If the world is to forge a promising future, it must develop more sophisticated knowledge. Sophistication demands that we see the world as a whole as well as in terms of its individual parts. The temptation to picture others according to our images of ourselves and to project onto them our own aims and values must be overcome. We must discard the belief that there is a simple formula for a better tomorrow and resist single-issue approaches to reform. Toleration of ambiguity, even the pursuit of it, is essential.

The future of world politics also rests on a race between states' ability to act in concert and the forces militating against transnational collaboration. As U.S. Secretary of State James A. Baker urged in 1990, the international community must "use the end of the Cold War to get beyond the whole pattern of settling conflicts by force." Only concerted international cooperation can avert slipping "back into ever more savage regional conflicts in which might alone makes right." The world's capacity to summon the political will to implement the reforms necessary to meet global challenges is being tested.

The world's future is uncertain, but it is our future. The moving words of President Kennedy thus describe a posture we might well assume: "However close we sometimes seem to that dark and final abyss, let no man of peace and freedom despair. For he does not stand alone. . . . Together we shall save our planet or together we shall perish in its flames. Save it we can, and save it we must, and then shall we earn the eternal thanks of mankind."

SUGGESTED READINGS

Attali, Jacques. *Millennium: Winners and Losers in the Coming World Order*. New York: Random House, 1991.

Barber, Benjamin R. "Jihad vs. McWorld," *The Atlantic* 269 (March 1992): 53–63.

Daly, Herman, and John B. Cobb, Jr. *The Common Good*. Boston: Beacon Press, 1989.

Freedman, Lawrence. "Order and Disorder in the New World," *Foreign Affairs* 71 (No. 1, 1992): 20–37.

Fukuyama, Francis. *The End of History and the Last Man*. New York: Free Press, 1992.

Gaddis, John Lewis. "Toward the Post–Cold War World," *Foreign Affairs* 70 (Spring 1991): 102–122.

Heilbroner, Robert L. *An Inquiry into the Human Prospect: Looked at Again for the 1990s*. New York: W. W. Norton, 1992.

Miller, Lynn H. *Global Order: Values and Power in International Politics*, 2nd ed. Boulder, Colo.: Westview, 1990.

Nye, Joseph S., Jr. "What New World Order?," *Foreign Affairs* 71 (Spring 1992): 83–96.

Rosenau, James N., and Ernst-Otto Czempiel, eds. *Governance without Government: Order and Change in World Politics*. New York: Cambridge University Press, 1992.

Snow, Donald M. *The Shape of the Future: The Post–Cold War World*. Armonk, N.Y.: M. E. Sharpe, 1991.

Teich, Albert H., ed. *Technology and the Future*, 5th ed. New York: St. Martin's Press, 1990.

Toffler, Alvin. *Powershift: Knowledge, Wealth, and Violence at the Edge of the 21st Century*. New York: Bantam Books, 1991.

REFERENCES

• • •

ABRAHAMSSON, BERNHARD J. (1975) "The International Oil Industry," pp. 73–88 in Joseph S. Szyliowicz and Bard E. O'Neill (eds.), *The Energy Crisis and U.S. Foreign Policy*. New York: Praeger.

ADELMAN, KENNETH L., AND NORMAN R. AUGUSTINE. (1992) "Defense Conversion," *Foreign Affairs* 71 (Spring): 26–47.

"THE AGE OF AGING." (1982) *UN Chronicle* 19 (July): 82–84.

AHO, C. MICHAEL, AND MARC LEVINSON. (1988–1989) "The Economy After Reagan," *Foreign Affairs* 67 (Winter): 1–25.

AHO, C. MICHAEL, AND BRUCE STOKES. (1991) "The Year the World Economy Turned," *Foreign Affairs* 70 (No. 1): 160–178.

AKEHURST, MICHAEL. (1987) *A Modern Introduction to International Law*, 6th ed. London: Unwin Hyman.

ALGER, CHADWICK. (1990) "The U.N. in Historical Perspective." Paper presented to the International Research Conference on the Future of the United Nations, Ottawa, January 5–7.

———. (1965) "Personal Contact in Intergovernmental Organizations," pp. 523–547 in Herbert C. Kelman (ed.), *International Behavior*. New York: Holt, Rinehart & Winston.

ALLISON, GRAHAM T. (1971) *Essence of Decision: Explaining the Cuban Missile Crisis*. Boston: Little, Brown.

ALLISON, GRAHAM, AND ROBERT BLACKWILL. (1991) "America's Stake in the Soviet Future," *Foreign Affairs* 70 (Summer): 77–97.

ALLISON, GRAHAM, AND GREGORY F. TREVERTON. (eds.) (1992) *Rethinking America's Security: Beyond Cold War to New World Order*. New York: Norton.

ALLISON, GRAHAM, AND GRIGORY YAVLINSKY. (1991) "The Grand Bargain to Bring the Soviets to Market: Western Engagement Would Transform Its Economy," *Washington Post National Weekly Edition*, July 15–21, p. 24.

ALPEROVITZ, GAR. (1985) *Atomic Diplomacy: Hiroshima and Potsdam*. New York: Penguin.

ALPEROVITZ, GAR, AND ROBERT L. MESSER. (1991–1992) "Marshall, Truman, and the Decision to Drop the Bomb," *International Security* 16 (Winter): 204–214.

AMBROSE, STEPHEN E. (1985) *Rise to Globalism*, 4th rev. ed. New York: Penguin.

AMIN, SAMIR. (1987) "Democracy and National Strategy in the Periphery," *Third World Quarterly* 9 (October): 1129–1156.

———. (1974) *Accumulation on a World Scale: A Critique of the Theory of Underdevelopment*. New York: Monthly Review Press.

AMUZEGAR, JAHANGIR. (1990) "Oil and a Changing OPEC," *Finance and Development* 27 (September): 43–45.

———. (1987) "Dealing with Debt," *Foreign Policy* 68 (Fall): 140–158.

ANGELL, NORMAN. (1910) *The Great Illusion: A Study of the Relationship of Military Power in Nations to Their Economic and Social Advantage*. London: Weidenfeld and Nicholson.

APTER, DAVID E., AND LOUIS W. GOODMAN. (eds.) (1976) *The Multinational Corporation and Social Change*. New York: Praeger.

ARAD, RUTH W., AND UZI B. ARAD. (1979) "Scarce Natural Resources and Potential Conflict," pp. 23–85 in Ruth W. Arad, Uzi B. Arad, Rachel McCulloch, José Piñera, and Ann L. Hollick, *Sharing Global Resources*. New York: McGraw-Hill.

ARKIN, WILLIAM D., DAMIAN DURRANT, AND MARIANNE CHERNI. (1991) *On Impact: Modern Warfare and the Environment: A Case Study of the Gulf War*. Washington, D.C.: Greenpeace.

ART, ROBERT J. (1973) "Bureaucratic Politics and American Foreign Policy: A Critique," *Policy Sciences* 4 (December): 467–490.

ASHLEY, RICHARD K. (1984) "The Poverty of Neorealism," *International Organization* 38 (Spring): 255–286.

ASHLEY, RICHARD K., AND R. B. J. WALKER. (eds.) (1990) "Speaking the Language of Exile: Dissident Thought in International Studies," Special issue, *International Studies Quarterly* 34 (September): 259–417.

ASIMOV, ISAAC. (1979) *A Choice of Catastrophes*. New York: Simon & Schuster.

AUERBACH, STUART. (1991) "Made in America, Used by Iraq," *Washington Post National Weekly Edition*, March 18–24, p. 11.

• • •

AXELROD, ROBERT, AND ROBERT O. KEOHANE. (1985) "Achieving Cooperation Under Anarchy: Strategies and Institutions," *World Politics* 38 (October): 226–254.

BAER, M. DELAL. (1991) "North American Free Trade," *Foreign Affairs* 70 (Fall): 132–149.

BALASSA, BELA, AND MARCUS NOLAND. (1988) *Japan in the World Economy*. Washington, D.C.: Institute for International Economics.

BALDWIN, DAVID A. (1989) *Paradoxes of Power*. New York: Basil Blackwell.

———. (1985) *Economic Statecraft*. Princeton, N.J.: Princeton University Press.

———. (1971) "Cosmocorp: The Importance of Being Stateless," *Columbia Journal of World Business* 6 (November–December): 25–30.

BALL, NICOLE. (1991) *Briefing Book on Conventional Arms Transfers*. Boston: Council for a Livable World Education Fund.

BARAN, PAUL. (1968) *The Political Economy of Growth*. New York: Monthly Review Press.

BARBER, BENJAMIN R. (1992) "Jihad vs. McWorld," *Atlantic* 269 (March): 53–63.

BARKUN, MICHAEL. (1968) *Law Without Sanctions: Order in Primitive Societies and the World Community*. New Haven, Conn.: Yale University Press.

BARNABY, FRANK. (1991) "The Environmental Impact of the Gulf War," *Ecologist* 21 (July/August): 166–172.

BARNES, FRED. (1991) "Brilliant Pebble," *The New Republic*, April 1, pp. 10–11.

BARNET, RICHARD J. (1992) "The Disorders of Peace," *The New Yorker*, January 20, pp. 62–74.

———. (1990) "U.S. Intervention: Low-Intensity Thinking," *The Bulletin of the Atomic Scientists* 46 (May): 34–37.

———. (1980) *The Lean Years*. New York: Simon & Schuster.

———. (1979) "Challenging the Myths of National Security," *New York Times Magazine*, April 1, pp. 25, 56 passim.

———. (1977) *The Giants: Russia and America*. New York: Simon & Schuster.

BARNET, RICHARD J., AND RONALD E. MÜLLER. (1974) *Global Reach: The Power of the Multinational Corporations*. New York: Simon & Schuster.

BARON, SAMUEL H., AND CARL PLETSCH. (eds.) (1985) *Introspection in Biography: The Biographer's Quest for Self Awareness*. Hillsdale, N.J.: Analytic Press.

BEER, FRANCIS A. (1981) *Peace Against War: The Ecology of International Violence*. San Francisco: Freeman.

BELL, J. BOWYER. (1990) "Explaining International Terrorism: The Elusive Quest," pp. 178–184 in Charles W. Kegley, Jr. (ed.), *International Terrorism: Characteristics, Causes, Controls*. New York: St. Martin's Press.

BENEDICK, RICHARD ELLIOT. (1991) "Protecting the Ozone Layer: New Directions in Diplomacy," pp. 112–153 in Jessica Tuchman Mathews (ed.), *Preserving the Global Environment*. New York: Norton.

BENNETT, A. LEROY. (1991) *International Organizations: Principles and Issues*, 5th ed. Englewood Cliffs, N.J.: Prentice-Hall.

———. (1988) *International Organizations*, 4th ed. Englewood Cliffs, N.J.: Prentice-Hall.

BERGESEN, ALBERT. (1980) "From Utilitarianism to Globology: The Shift from the Individual to the World As a Whole As the Primordial Unit of Analysis," pp. 1–12 in Albert Bergesen (ed.), *Studies of the Modern World-System*. New York: Academic Press.

BERGESEN, ALBERT, AND RONALD SCHOENBERG. (1980) "Long Waves of Colonial Expansion and Contraction, 1415–1969," pp. 231–277 in Albert Bergesen (ed.), *Studies of the Modern World-System*. New York: Academic Press.

BERGSTEN, C. FRED. (1973) "The Threat from the Third World," *Foreign Policy* 11 (Summer): 102–124.

BERTELSEN, JUDY S. (ed.) (1977) *Nonstate Nations in International Politics*. New York: Praeger.

"Beyond Perestroyka: The Soviet Economy in Crisis." (1991) pp. 399–412 in Alexander Dallin and Gail W. Lapidus (eds.), *The Soviet System in Crisis*. Boulder, Colo.: Westview.

BHAGWATI, JAGDISH. (1991) *The World Trading System at Risk*. Princeton, N.J.: Princeton University Press.

BIERSTECKER, T. J. (1978) *Distortion or Development: Contending Perspectives on the Multinational Corporation*. Cambridge, Mass.: MIT Press.

BISSELL, RICHARD E. (1991) "After Foreign Aid—What?," *Washington Quarterly* 14 (Summer): 23–33.

———. (1990) "Who Killed the Third World?" *Washington Quarterly* 13 (Autumn): 23–32.

BLACK, JAN KNIPPERS. (1991) *Development in Theory and Practice*. Boulder, Colo.: Westview.

BLAINEY, GEOFFREY. (1988) *The Causes of War*, 3rd ed. New York: Free Press.

BLECHMAN, BARRY M., AND STEPHEN S. KAPLAN, WITH DAVID K. HALL, WILLIAM B. QUANDT, JEROME N. SLATER, ROBERT M. SLUSSER, AND PHILIP WINDSOR. (1978) *Force Without War*. Washington, D.C.: Brookings Institution.

BLIGHT, JAMES G., AND DAVID A. WELCH. (1989) *On the Brink: Americans and Soviets Re-examine the Cuban Missile Crisis*. New York: Hill & Wang.

BLOCK, FRED L. (1977) *The Origins of International Economic Disorder*. Berkeley: University of California Press.

BLOCK, HERBERT. (1981) *The Planetary Product in 1980: A Creative Pause?* Washington, D.C.: U.S. Department of State.

BLUMENTHAL, W. MICHAEL. (1988) "The World Economy and Technological Change," *Foreign Affairs* 66 (No. 3): 529–550.

BOONEKAMP, CLEMENS F. J. (1987) "Voluntary Export Restraints," *Finance and Development* 24 (December): 2–5.

BOSWELL, TERRY. (1989) "Colonial Empires and the Capitalist World-Economy: A Time Series Analysis of Colonization, 1640–1960," *American Sociological Review* 54 (April): 180–196.

BOULDING, KENNETH E. (1978) *Stable Peace*. Austin: University of Texas Press.

———. (1959) "National Images and International Systems," *Journal of Conflict Resolution* 3 (June): 120–131.

BOULDING, KENNETH E., AND TAPAN MUKERJEE. (eds.) (1972) *Economic Imperialism*. Ann Arbor: University of Michigan Press.

BOVARD, JAMES. (1991) "Fair Trade Is Unfair," *Newsweek*, December 9, p. 13.

BOZEMAN, ADDA B. (1971) *The Future of Law in a Multicultural World*. Princeton, N.J.: Princeton University Press.

BP Statistical Review of World Energy. (1991) London: British Petroleum Company.

BP Statistical Review of World Energy. (1987) London: British Petroleum Company.

BP Statistical Review of World Energy. (1984) London: British Petroleum Company.

BRAUDEL, FERNAND. (1984) *Civilization and Capitalism: 15th–18th Century*. Vol 3. New York: Harper & Row.

———. (1982) *Civilization and Capitalism: 15th–18th Century*. Vol 2. New York: Harper & Row.

———. (1981) *Civilization and Capitalism: 15th–18th Century*. Vol 1. New York: Harper & Row.

BRECHER, MICHAEL, AND JONATHAN WILKENFELD. (1991) "International Crises and Global Instability: The Myth of the 'Long Peace,' " pp. 85–104 in Charles W. Kegley, Jr. (ed.), *The Long Postwar Peace*. New York: HarperCollins.

BRECHER, MICHAEL, JONATHAN WILKENFELD, AND SHEILA MOSER. (1988) *Crises in the Twentieth Century. Vol I: Handbook of International Crises*. Oxford, England: Pergamon Press.

BRIERLY, JAMES L. (1944) *The Outlook for International Law*. Oxford, England: Clarendon Press.

BROAD, ROBIN, AND JOHN CAVANAGH. (1988) "No More NICs," *Foreign Policy* 72 (Fall): 81–103.

BROGAN, PATRICK. (1990) *The Fighting Never Stopped: A Comprehensive Guide to Conflict Since 1945*. New York: Vintage.

BRONFENBRENNER, URIE. (1971) "The Mirror Image in Soviet-American Relations," *Journal of Social Issues* 27 (No. 1): 46–51.

BROWN, HAROLD. (1983) *Thinking About National Security: Defense and Foreign Policy in a Dangerous World*. Boulder, Colo.: Westview.

BROWN, LESTER R. (1991) "The New World Order," pp. 3–20 in Lester R. Brown, Christopher Flavin, Sandra Postel, Linda Starke, Alan Durning, Hilary F. French, Jodi Jacobson, Marcia D. Lowe, Michael Renner, Nicholas Lenssen, John C. Ryan, and John E. Young, *State of the World 1991*. New York: Norton.

———. (1979) *Resource Trends and Population Policy: A Time for Reassessment*. Worldwatch Paper No. 29. Washington, D.C.: Worldwatch Institute.

———. (1978) *The Twenty-Ninth Day*. New York: Norton.

———. (1972) *World Without Borders*. New York: Vintage Books.

BROWN, LESTER R., EDWARD C. WOLF, LINDA STARKE, WILLIAM U. CHANDLER, CHRISTOPHER FLAVIN, CYNTHIA POLLOCK, SANDRA POSTEL, AND JODI JACOBSON. (1987) *State of the World 1987*. New York: Norton.

BROWNLIE, IAN. (1990) *Principles of Public International Law*, 4th ed. New York: Oxford University Press.

BUCHANAN, PATRICK. (1990) "America First—and Second, and Third," *National Interest* 19 (Spring): 77–82.

BUENO DE MESQUITA, BRUCE. (1981) *The War Trap*. New Haven, Conn.: Yale University Press.

———. (1975) "Measuring Systemic Polarity," *Journal of Conflict Resolution* 22 (June): 187–216.

BULL, HEDLEY. (1977) *The Anarchical Society: A Study of Order in World Politics*. New York: Columbia University Press.

BUNCE, VALERIE. (1991) "The Soviet Union Under Gorbachev: Ending Stalinism and Ending the Cold War," *International Journal* 46 (Spring): 220–241.

BUNDY, MCGEORGE. (1990) "From Cold War to Trusting Peace," *Foreign Affairs* 69 (No. 1): 197–212.

———. (1988) *Danger and Survival*. New York: Random House.

BUNGE, WILLIAM. (1988) *Nuclear War Atlas*. New York: Basil Blackwell.

BURGESS, JOHN, AND STUART AUERBACH. (1990) "Many Losers but Some Winners in the Gulf Crisis," *Washington Post National Weekly Edition*, August 20–26, p. 21.

BURKI, SHAHID JAVED. (1983) "UNCTAD VI: For Better or for Worse?" *Finance and Development* 20 (December): 16–19.

BYWATER, MARION. (1975) "The Lomé Convention," *European Community* 184 (March): 5–9.

CALDWELL, DAN. (1991) *The Dynamics of Domestic Politics and Arms Control.* Columbia, S.C.: University of South Carolina Press.

————. (1978) "A Research Note on the Quarantine of Cuba, October 1962," *International Studies Quarterly* 22 (December): 625–633.

————. (1977) "Bureaucratic Foreign Policy Making," *American Behavioral Scientist* 21 (September–October): 87–110.

CALVOCORESSI, PETER, GUY WINT, AND JOHN PRITCHARD. (1989) *Total War: The Causes and Courses of the Second World War,* 2nd ed. New York: Pantheon.

CAPORASO, JAMES A. (1980) "Dependency Theory: Continuities and Discontinuities in Development Studies," *International Organization* 34 (Autumn): 605–628.

————. (ed.) (1978) "Dependence and Dependency in the Global System," Special issue, *International Organization* 32 (Winter): 1–300.

CARR, E. II. (1939) *The Twenty-Years' Crisis, 1919–1939.* London: Macmillan.

CARTER, ASHTON B. (1990–1991) "Chairman's Note," *International Security* 15 (Winter): 3–4.

CARUS, W. SETH. (1990) *Ballistic Missiles in the Third World.* New York: Praeger.

CENTRE ON TRANSNATIONAL CORPORATIONS. (1991) *World Investment Report 1991: The Triad in Foreign Direct Investment.* New York: United Nations.

————. (1988) *Transnational Corporations in World Development: Trends and Prospects.* New York: United Nations.

————. (1985) *Transnational Corporations and International Trade.* New York: United Nations.

CHAN, STEVE. (1987) "Military Expenditures and Economic Performance," pp. 29–37 in U.S. Arms Control and Disarmament Agency, *World Military Expenditures and Arms Transfers 1986.* Washington, D.C.: U.S. Government Printing Office.

————. (1984) "Mirror, Mirror on the Wall . . .: Are the Free Countries More Pacific?" *Journal of Conflict Resolution* 28 (December): 617–648.

CHERNUS, IRA. (1987) *Dr. Strangegod: On the Symbolic Meaning of Nuclear Weapons.* Columbia: University of South Carolina Press.

CHILDE, V. GORDON. (1962) *Man Makes Himself.* New York: Mentor Books.

CHISWICK, BARRY R. (1990) "Reopening the Golden Door," *Washington Post National Weekly Edition,* October 15–21, p. 25.

CHOUCHRI, NAZLI. (1972) "Population, Resources, and Technology: Political Implications of the Environmental Crisis," *International Organization* 26 (Spring): 175–212.

CHOUCHRI, NAZLI, AND ROBERT C. NORTH. (1975) *Nations in Conflict.* San Francisco: Freeman.

————. (1972) "Dynamics of International Conflict: Some Policy Implications of Population, Resources, and Technology." pp. 80–122 in Raymond Tanter and Richard H. Ullman (eds.), *Theory and Policy in International Relations.* Princeton, N.J.: Princeton University Press.

CHURCHILL, WINSTON. (1948–1953) *The Second World War.* Boston: Houghton Mifflin.

————. (1948) *The Second World War: The Gathering Storm.* Boston: Houghton Mifflin.

CLAIBORNE, WILLIAM. (1990) "South Africa's Quiet Revolution," *Washington Post National Weekly Edition,* January 22–28, pp. 24–25.

CLAIRMONTE, FREDERICK, AND JOHN CAVANAGH. (1982) "Transnational Corporations and Global Markets: Changing Power Relations," *Trade and Development: An UNCTAD Review* 4 (Winter): 149–182.

CLANCY, TOM, AND RUSSELL SEITZ. (1991–1992) "Five Minutes Past Midnight—and Welcome to the New Age of Proliferation," *National Interest* 26 (Winter): 3–17.

CLAUDE, INIS L., JR. (1988) *States and the Global System: Politics, Law, and Organization.* New York: St. Martin's Press.

————. (1971) *Swords into Plowshares,* 4th ed. New York: Random House.

————. (1967) *The Changing United Nations.* New York: Random House.

————. (1962) *Power and International Relations.* New York: Random House.

CLAUSEN, PETER A. (1991) "Nuclear Proliferation in the 1980s and 1990s," pp. 144–169 in Michael T. Klare and Daniel C. Thomas (eds.), *World Security.* New York: St. Martin's Press.

VON CLAUSEWITZ, KARL. (1976 [1832]) *On War.* Princeton, N.J.: Princeton University Press.

COATE, ROGER A. (1988) *Unilateralism, Ideology, and U.S. Foreign Policy: The United States In and Out of UNESCO.* Boulder, Colo.: Lynne Rienner.

COBB, ROGER, AND CHARLES ELDER. (1970) *International Community.* New York: Harcourt, Brace & World.

COHEN, BENJAMIN J. (1989) "A Global Chapter 11," *Foreign Policy* 75 (Summer): 109–127.

———. (1983) "Trade and Unemployment: Global Bread-and-Butter Issues," *Worldview* 26 (January): 9–11.

———. (1973) *The Question of Imperialism*. New York: Basic Books.

COHEN, ELIOT A. (1992) "The Future of Military Power: The Continuing Utility of Force," pp. 33–40 in Charles W. Kegley, Jr., and Eugene R. Wittkopf (eds.), *The Global Agenda*, 3rd ed. New York: McGraw-Hill.

———. (1991) "After the Battle: A Defense Primer for the Next Century," *The New Republic*, April 1, pp. 19–26.

COLLINS, SUSAN M., AND DANI RODRIK. (1991) *Eastern Europe and the Soviet Union in the World Economy*. Washington, D.C.: Institute for International Economics.

COMMAGER, HENRY STEELE. (1983) "Misconceptions Governing American Foreign Policy," pp. 510–517 in Charles W. Kegley, Jr., and Eugene R. Wittkopf (eds.), *Perspectives on American Foreign Policy*. New York: St. Martin's Press.

COMMISSION ON INTEGRATED LONG-TERM STRATEGY. (1988) *Discriminate Deterrence*. Washington, D.C.: U.S. Government Printing Office.

COMMISSION ON TRANSNATIONAL CORPORATIONS. (1991) "Recent Developments Related to Transnational Corporations and International Economic Relations," U.N. Doc. E/E.10/1991/2, United Nations Economic and Social Council.

CONGRESSIONAL RESEARCH SERVICE. (1991) *Soviet-U.S. Relations*. Washington, D.C.: U.S. Congressional Research Service.

CONOVER, PAMELA J., AND STANLEY FELDMAN. (1984) "How People Organize the Political World: A Schematic Model," *American Journal of Political Science* 28 (February): 95–126.

COPLIN, WILLIAM D. (1971) *Introduction to International Politics*. Chicago: Markham.

———.(1966) *The Functions of International Law*. Chicago: Rand McNally.

———. (1965) "International Law and Assumptions About the State System," *World Politics* 17 (July): 615–634.

COSER, LEWIS. (1956) *The Functions of Social Conflict*. London: Routledge & Kegan Paul.

COX, MICHAEL. (1990) "From the Truman Doctrine to the Second Superpower Detente: The Rise and Fall of the Cold War," *Journal of Peace Research* 27 (February): 25–41.

CRAIG, GORDON A., AND ALEXANDER L. GEORGE. (1990) *Force and Statecraft*, 2nd ed. New York: Oxford University Press.

CRENSHAW, MARTHA. (1990) "Is International Terrorism Primarily State-Sponsored?," pp. 163–169 in Charles W. Kegley, Jr. (ed.), *International Terrorism: Characteristics, Causes, Controls*. New York: St. Martin's Press.

CUSACK, THOMAS R., AND RICHARD J. STOLL. (1990) *Exploring Realpolitik*. Boulder, Colo.: Lynne Rienner.

CUTLER, LLOYD N. (1978) *Global Interdependence and the Multinational Firm*. Headline Series No. 239 (April). New York: Foreign Policy Association.

D'AMATO, ANTHONY. (1982) "What 'Counts' As Law?," pp. 83–107 in Nicholas Greenwood Onuf (ed.), *Law-Making in the Global Community*. Durham, N.C.: Carolina Academic Press.

DALY, HERMAN E. (1973) "Introduction," pp. 1–29 in Herman E. Daly (ed.), *Toward a Steady-State Economy*. San Francisco: Freeman.

DALY, HERMAN E., AND JOHN B. COBB, JR. (1989) *For the Common Good*. Boston: Beacon Press.

DARMSTADTER, JOEL, AND HANS H. LANDSBERG. (1976) "The Economic Background," pp. 15–37 in Raymond Vernon (ed.), *The Oil Crisis*. New York: Norton.

DAVIDSON, KEAY. (1991) "Slashing U.S. Nuclear Arsenal Now Thinkable," *Sunday Advocate* (Baton Rouge, La.), November 10, p. E1.

DE CUÉLLAR, JAVIER PÉREZ. (1984) "The United Nations and World Politics," pp. 167–175 in Charles W. Kegley, Jr., and Eugene R. Wittkopf (eds.), *The Global Agenda*. New York: Random House.

DEGER, SAADET, AND RON SMITH. (1983) "Military Expansion and Growth in Less Developed Countries," *Journal of Conflict Resolution* 27 (June): 335–353.

DEHIO, LUDWIG. (1962) *The Precarious Balance*. New York: Knopf.

DER DERIAN, JAMES, AND MICHAEL J. SHAPIRO. (eds.) (1989) *International/Intertextual Relations: Postmodern Readings of World Politics*. Lexington, Mass.: D. C. Heath.

DERIVERA, JOSEPH H. (1968) *The Psychological Dimension of Foreign Policy*. Columbus, Ohio: Merrill.

DE RUYT, JEAN. (1989) *European Political Cooperation: Toward A Unified European Foreign Policy*. Washington, D.C.: Atlantic Council of the United States.

DESTLER, I. M., AND C. RANDALL HENNING. (1989) *Dollar Politics: Exchange Rate Policymaking in the United States*. Washington, D.C.: Institute for International Economics.

DE TOCQUEVILLE, ALEXIS. (1969 [1835]) *Democracy in America*. New York: Doubleday.

DEUDNEY, DANIEL, AND G. JOHN IKENBERRY. (1991–1992) "The International Sources of Soviet Change," *International Security* 16 (Winter): 74–118.

DEUTSCH, KARL W. (1953) "The Growth of Nations: Some Recurrent Patterns in Political and Social Integration," *World Politics* 5 (October): 168–195.

DEUTSCH, KARL W., SIDNEY A. BURRELL, ROBERT A. KANN, MAURICE LEE, JR., MARTIN LICHTERMAN, RAYMOND E. LINDGREN, FRANCIS L. LOEWENHEIM, AND RICHARD W. VAN WAGENEN. (1957) *Political Community and the North Atlantic Area*. Princeton, N.J.: Princeton University Press.

DEUTSCH, KARL W., AND RICHARD L. MERRITT. (1965) "Effects of Events on National and International Images," pp. 132–187 in Herbert C. Kelman (ed.), *International Behavior*. New York: Holt, Rinehart & Winston.

DEUTSCH, KARL W., AND J. DAVID SINGER. (1964) "Multipolar Power Systems and International Stability," *World Politics* 16 (April): 390–406.

Development Cooperation: 1991 Report. (1991) Paris: Organisation for Economic Co-operation and Development.

DE VITA, CAROL J. (1989) *America in the 21st Century: A Demographic Overview*. Washington, D.C.: Population Reference Bureau.

DIAZ-BRIQUETS, SERGIO. (1986) *Conflict in Central America: The Demographic Dimension*. Washington, D.C.: Population Reference Bureau.

DIETRICH, WILLIAM S. (1992) *In the Shadow of the Rising Sun: The Political Roots of American Economic Decline*. University Park: Penn State Press.

DIRENZO, GORDON J. (ed.) (1974) *Personality and Politics*. Garden City, N.Y.: Doubleday-Anchor.

DOBBS, MICHAEL. (1991) "Disaster, Nuclear and Bureaucratic," *Washington Post National Weekly Edition*, May 6–12, pp. 10–11.

DORAN, CHARLES F. (1991) *Systems in Crisis: New Imperatives of High Politics at Century's End*. Cambridge, England: Cambridge University Press.

DOXEY, MARGARET. (1990) "International Sanctions," pp. 242–261 in David G. Haglund and Michael K. Hawes (eds.), *World Politics: Power, Interdependence, and Dependence*. Toronto: Harcourt Brace Jovanovich.

DOYLE, MICHAEL W. (1986) "Liberalism and World Politics," *American Political Science Review* 80 (December): 1151–1169.

DRUCKER, PETER F. (1986) "The Changed World Economy," *Foreign Affairs* 64 (Spring): 768–791.

———. (1974) "Multinationals and Developing Countries: Myths and Realities," *Foreign Affairs* 53 (October): 121–134.

DULLES, JOHN FOSTER. (1939) *War, Peace, and Change*. New York: Harper.

DUNN, LEWIS A. (1989) "Chemical Weapons Arms Control," *Survival* 31 (May–June): 209–225.

DUNNE, PAUL, AND RON SMITH. (1990) "Military Expenditure and Unemployment in the OECD," *Defence Economics* 1 (No. 1): 57–73.

DURNING, ALAN. (1991) "Asking How Much Is Enough," pp. 153–169 in Lester R. Brown, Christopher Flavin, Sandra Postel, Linda Starke, Alan Durning, Hilary F. French, Jodi Jacobson, Marcia D. Lowe, Michael Renner, Nicholas Lenssen, John C. Ryan, and John E. Young, *State of the World 1991*. New York: Norton.

———. (1990) "Ending Poverty," pp. 135–153 in Lester R. Brown, Christopher Flavin, Sandra Postel, Linda Starke, Alan Durning, Jodi Jacobson, Michael Renner, Hilary F. French, Marcia D. Lowe, and John E. Young, *State of the World 1990*. New York: Norton.

———. (1989) *Poverty and the Environment: Reversing the Downward Spiral*. Worldwatch Paper No. 92. Washington, D.C.: Worldwatch Institute.

DYSON, FREEMAN. (1984) *Weapons and Hope*. New York: Harper & Row.

EAGLEBURGER, LAWRENCE S. (1989) "The 21st Century: American Foreign Policy Challenges," pp. 242–260 in Edward K. Hamilton (ed.), *America's Global Interests: A New Agenda*. New York: Norton.

EASTON, STEWART C. (1964) *The Rise and Fall of Western Colonialism*. New York: Praeger.

EBERSTADT, NICHOLAS. (1991) "Population Change and National Security," *Foreign Affairs* 70 (Summer): 115–131.

———. (1990) *U.S. Foreign Aid Policy—A Critique*. Headline Series No. 293 (Summer). New York: Foreign Policy Association.

EBINGER, CHARLES. (1985) "A 'Complacent' U.S. Courts New Oil Crisis," *U.S. News and World Report*, May 27, pp. 37–38.

ECKHARDT, WILLIAM. (1991) "War-Related Deaths Since 3000 BC," *Bulletin of Peace Proposals* 22 (December): 437–443.

———. (1990) "Civilization, Empires and Wars," *Journal of Peace Research* 27 (February): 9–24.

EHRLICH, PAUL R., AND ANNE H. EHRLICH. (1990) *The Population Explosion*. New York: Simon & Schuster.

EHRLICH, PAUL R., ANNE H. ERHLICH, AND JOHN P. HOLDREN. (1977) *Ecoscience*. San Francisco: Freeman.

EKINS, PAUL. (1991) *A New World Order: Grassroots Movements for Global Change*. London: Routledge.

EMMANUEL, ARGHIRI. (1972) *Unequal Exchange: An Essay on the Imperialism of Trade*. New York: Monthly Review Press.

ETZIONI, AMITAI. (1968) "Toward a Sociological Theory of Peace," pp. 403–428 in Leon Bramson and George W. Goethals (eds.), *War*. New York: Basic Books.

FALCOFF, MARK. (1990) "First World, Third World, Which World?" *The American Enterprise* 1 (July/August): 13–14.

FALK, RICHARD A. (1970) *The Status of Law in International Society*. Princeton, N.J.: Princeton University Press.

———. (1965) "World Law and Human Conflict," pp. 227–249 in Elton B. McNeil (ed.), *The Nature of Human Conflict*. Englewood Cliffs, N.J.: Prentice-Hall.

———. (1964) *The Role of Domestic Courts in the International Legal Order*. Syracuse, N.Y.: Syracuse University Press.

FALKENHEIM, PEGGY L. (1987) "Post-Afghanistan Sanctions," pp. 105–130 in David Leyton-Brown (ed.), *The Utility of International Economic Sanctions*. New York: St. Martin's Press.

FALLOWS, JAMES. (1983) "Immigration: How It's Affecting Us," *Atlantic* 252 (November): 45–52.

FEINBERG, RICHARD E., AND DELIA M. BOYLAN. (1992) "Modular Multilateralism: North-South Economic Relations in the 1990s," *Washington Quarterly* 15 (Winter): 187–199.

———. (1991) *Modular Multilateralism: North-South Economic Relations in the 1990s*. Washington, D.C.: Overseas Development Council.

FELD, WERNER J., AND ROBERT S. JORDAN, WITH LEON HURWITZ. (1988) *International Organizations: A Comparative Approach*, 2nd ed. New York: Praeger.

FELDSTEIN, MARTIN. (1985) "American Economic Policy and the World Economy," *Foreign Affairs* 63 (Summer): 995–1008.

FERENCZ, BENJAMIN B., AND KEN KEYES, JR. (1991) *PlanetHood*. Coos Bay, Ore.: Love Line Books.

FERGUSON, NIALL. (1991) "Funny Money," *New Republic*, July 1: 20–23.

FERGUSON, YALE H., AND RICHARD W. MANSBACH. (1988) *The Elusive Quest: Theory and International Politics*. Columbia, S.C.: University of South Carolina Press.

FESTINGER, LEON. (1957) *A Theory of Cognitive Dissonance*. Evanston, Ill.: Row, Peterson.

FETTER, STEVE. (1991) "Ballistic Missiles and Weapons of Mass Destruction: What Is the Threat? What Should Be Done?" *International Security* 16 (Summer): 5–42.

FIELDHOUSE, D. K. (1973) *Economics and Empire, 1830–1914*. Ithaca, N.Y.: Cornell University Press.

"FINANCING THE UNITED NATIONS." (n.d.) UNA-USA Fact Sheet. United Nations Association of the United States of America.

FISCHER, FRITZ. (1967) *Germany's Aims After the First World War*. New York: Norton.

FISCHER, STANLEY, AND ISHRAT HUSAIN. (1990) "Managing the Debt Crisis in the 1990s," *Finance and Development* 27 (June): 24–27.

FLAVIN, CHRISTOPHER. (1992) "Building a Bridge to Sustainable Energy," pp. 27–45 in Lester R. Brown, Christopher Flavin, Sandra Postel, Linda Starke, Alan Durning, Hilary F. French, Jodi Jacobson, Marcia D. Lowe, Michael Renner, Holly B. Brough, Nicholas Lenssen, John C. Ryan, and John E. Young, *State of the World 1992*. New York: Norton.

———. (1991–1992) "The Global Challenges of the Coming Energy Revolution," *Harvard International Review* 14 (Winter): 4–6, 60–61.

———. (1987) *Reassessing Nuclear Power: The Fallout from Chernobyl*. Worldwatch Paper No. 75. Washington, D.C.: Worldwatch Institute.

FLAVIN, CHRISTOPHER, AND NICHOLAS LENSSEN. (1991) "Designing a Sustainable Energy System," pp. 21–38 in Lester R. Brown, Christopher Flavin, Sandra Postel, Linda Starke, Alan Durning, Hilary F. French, Jodi Jacobson, Marcia D. Lowe, Michael Renner, Nicholas Lenssen, John C. Ryan, and John E. Young, *State of the World 1991*. New York: Norton.

"THE FORGOTTEN U.N.: AN INSIDE LOOK AT THE 45TH GENERAL ASSEMBLY." (n.d.) United Nations Association of the United States of America.

FOSTER, GREGORY D. (1989) "Global Demographic Trends to the Year 2010: Implications for U.S. Security," *Washington Quarterly* 12 (Spring): 5–24.

FRANK, ANDRE GUNDER. (1969) *Latin America: Underdevelopment or Revolution*. New York: Monthly Review Press.

FRANKEL, GLENN. (1987) "Weapons: The Global Commodity," *Washington Post National Weekly Edition*, January 12, p. 6–7.

FREEMAN, ORVILLE L. (1990) "Meeting the Needs of the Coming Decade: Agriculture vs. the Environment," *Futurist* 24 (November–December): 15–20.

FRENCH, HILARY F. (1991) "The EC: Environmental Proving Ground," *World Watch* 4 (December): 26–33.

———. (1990) *Green Revolutions: Environmental Reconstruction in Eastern Europe and the Soviet Union*. Worldwatch Paper No. 99. Washington, D.C.: Worldwatch Institute.

FREUD, SIGMUND. (1968) "Why War," pp. 71–80 in Leon Bramson and George W. Goethals (eds.), *War*. New York: Basic Books.

FRIED, JOHN H. E. (1971) "International Law—Neither Orphan nor Harlot, Neither Jailer nor Never-Never Land," pp. 124–176 in Karl W. Deutsch and Stanley Hoffmann (eds.), *The Relevance of International Law*. Garden City, N.Y.: Doubleday-Anchor.

FRIEDBERG, AARON. (1991) "The Changing Relationship between Economics and National Security," *Political Science Quarterly* 106 (Summer): 265–276.

FRIEDEN, JEFF. (1981) "Third World Indebted Industrialization: International Finance and State Capitalism in Mexico, Brazil, Algeria, and South Korea," *International Organization* 35 (Summer): 407–431.

FRIEDHEIM, ROBERT L. (1965) "The 'Satisfied' and 'Dissatisfied' States Negotiate International Law," *World Politics* 18 (October): 20–41.

FRIEDMAN, THOMAS L. (1992) "Reducing the Russian Arms Threat," *New York Times*, June 17, p. A7.

FUKUYAMA, FRANCIS. (1992) *The End of History and the Last Man*. New York: Free Press.

———. (1989) "The End of History?" The *National Interest* 16 (Summer): 3–18.

FULLER, GRAHAM E. (1991–1992) "The Breaking of Nations—and the Threat to Ours," *National Interest* 26 (Winter): 14–21.

GADDIS, JOHN LEWIS. (1992) *The United States and the End of the Cold War: Implications, Reconsiderations, Provocations*. New York: Oxford University Press.

———. (1991a) "Great Illusions, the Long Peace, and the Future of the International System," pp. 25–55 in Charles W. Kegley, Jr. (ed.), *The Long Postwar Peace*. New York: HarperCollins.

———. (1991b) "Toward the Post–Cold War World," *Foreign Affairs* 70 (Spring): 102–122.

———. (1990) "Coping With Victory," *Atlantic Monthly* 265 (May): 49–60.

———. (1986) "The Long Peace: Elements of Stability in the Postwar International System," *International Security* 10 (Spring): 99–142.

———. (1983) "Containment: Its Past and Future," pp. 16–31 in Charles W. Kegley, Jr., and Eugene R. Wittkopf (eds.), *Perspectives on American Foreign Policy*. New York: St. Martin's Press.

———. (1972) *The United States and the Origins of the Cold War*. New York: Columbia University Press.

GALTUNG, JOHAN. (1969) "Violence, Peace, and Peace Research," *Journal of Peace Research* 6 (No. 3): 167–191.

GARDELS, NATHAN. (1991) "Two Concepts of Nationalism" *New York Review of Books* 38 (November 21): 19–23.

GARDNER, LLOYD C. (1970) *Architects of Illusion*. Chicago: Quadrangle.

GATI, TOBY TRISTER. (ed.) (1983) *The US, The UN, and the Management of Global Change*. New York: New York University Press.

GELB, LESLIE H. (1983) "Oil = X in a Strategic Equation," *New York Times*, October 7, pp. 33, 36.

———. (1979) "The Future of Arms Control: A Glass Half Full," *Foreign Policy* 36 (Fall): 21–32.

GEORGE, ALEXANDER L. (1992) *Forceful Persuasion: Coercive Diplomacy as an Alternative to War*. Washington, D.C.: United States Institute of Peace.

———. (ed.) (1991) *Avoiding War: Problems of Crisis Management*. Boulder, Colo.: Westview.

———. (1986) "U.S.-Soviet Global Rivalry: Norms of Competition," *Journal of Peace Research* 23 (September): 247–262.

———. (1972) "The Case for Multiple Advocacy in Making Foreign Policy," *American Political Science Review* 66 (September): 751–785.

GERMAN, F. CLIFFORD. (1960) "A Tentative Evaluation of World Power," *Journal of Conflict Resolution* 4 (March): 138–144.

GILL, STEPHEN, AND DAVID LAW. (1988) *The Global Political Economy*. Baltimore: Johns Hopkins University Press.

GILPIN, ROBERT. (1987) *The Political Economy of International Relations*. Princeton, N.J.: Princeton University Press.

———. (1985) "The Politics of Transnational Economic Relations," pp. 171–194 in Ray Maghroori and Bennett Ramberg (eds.), *Globalism Versus Realism: International Relations' Third Debate*. Boulder, Colo.: Westview.

———. (1984) "The Richness of the Tradition of Political Realism," *International Organization* 38 (Spring): 287–304.

———. (1981) *War and Change in World Politics*. Cambridge, England: Cambridge University Press.

———. (1975) *U.S. Power and the Multinational Corporation*. New York: Basic Books.

The Global 2000 Report to the President. (1980a) Vol. I: Entering the Twenty-first Century. Washington, D.C.: U.S. Government Printing Office.

The Global 2000 Report to the President. (1980b) Vol. II: The Technical Report. Washington, D.C.: U.S. Government Printing Office.

GOCHMAN, CHARLES S., AND ZEEV MAOZ. (1984) "Militarized Interstate Disputes, 1816–1976: Procedures, Patterns, and Insights," *Journal of Conflict Resolution* 28 (December): 585–616.

GOLDBLAT, JOZEF. (1982) *Agreements for Arms Control: A Critical Survey*. London: Taylor & Francis.

GOLDSTEIN, JOSHUA S. (1991) "The Possibility of Cycles in International Relations," *International Studies Quarterly* 35 (December): 477–480.

———. (1988) *Long Cycles: Prosperity and War in the Modern Age*. New Haven, Conn.: Yale University Press.

GOLDSTEIN, JOSHUA S., AND JOHN R. FREEMAN. (1990) *Three-Way Street: Strategic Reciprocity in World Politics*. Chicago: University of Chicago Press.

GOTTLIEB, GIDON. (1982) "Global Bargaining: The Legal and Diplomatic Framework," pp. 109–130 in Nicholas Greenwood Onuf (ed.), *Law-Making in the Global Community*. Durham, N.C.: Carolina Academic Press.

GRAHAM, THOMAS R. (1979) "Revolution in Trade Politics," *Foreign Policy* 26 (Fall): 49–63.

GRAVES, ERNEST. (1991) "The Future of U.S. Security Assistance and Arms Sales," *Washington Quarterly* 14 (Summer): 47–56.

GREENBERGER, ROBERT S. (1991) "U.N. Could Soon Find Itself Stretched Too Thin as Peacekeeping Role Grows," *Wall Street Journal*, September 30, p. A10.

———. (1989) "Baker is Pressing 'Linkage' with Soviets, Even Though Policy Has Limitations," *Wall Street Journal*, March 6, p. A8.

GREENHOUSE, STEVEN. (1992) "Ecology, the Economy and Bush," *New York Times*, June 14, pp. 1, 6.

GREENSTEIN, FRED I. (1987) *Personality and Politics*. Princeton, N.J.: Princeton University Press.

GREGG, ROBERT W. (1977) "The Apportioning of Political Power," pp. 69–80 in David A. Kay (ed.), *The Changing United Nations*. New York: Academy of Political Science.

GREY, EDWARD. (1925) *Twenty-five Years, 1892–1916*. New York: Frederick Stokes.

GRIECO, JOSEPH M. (1990) *Cooperation Among Nations: Europe, America, and Non-Tariff Barriers to Trade*. Ithaca, N.Y.: Cornell University Press.

———. (1988a) "Anarchy and the Limits of Cooperation: A Realist Critique of the Newest Liberal Institutionalism," *International Organization* 42 (Summer): 485–507.

———. (1988b) "Realist Theory and the Problem of International Cooperation: Analysis with an Amended Prisoner's Dilemma Model," *Journal of Politics* 50 (August): 600–624.

GRUBB, MICHAEL. (1990) "The Greenhouse Effect: Negotiating Targets," *International Affairs* 66 (January): 67–89.

GRUHN, ISEBILL V. (1976) "The Lomé Convention: Inching Toward Interdependence," *International Organization* 30 (Spring): 241–262.

GULICK, EDWARD VOSE. (1955) *Europe's Classical Balance of Power*. Ithaca, N.Y.: Cornell University Press.

GURR, TED ROBERT. (1970) *Why Men Rebel*. Princeton, N.J.: Princeton University Press.

HAAS, ERNST B. (1986) *Why We Still Need the United Nations: The Collective Management of International Conflict, 1945–1984*. Berkeley, Calif.: Institute of International Studies, University of California.

———. (1983) "Regime Decay: Conflict Management and International Organizations, 1945–1981," *International Organization* 37 (Spring): 189–256.

———. (1969) *Tangle of Hopes*. Englewood Cliffs, N.J.: Prentice-Hall.

———. (1953) "The Balance of Power: Prescription, Concept, or Propaganda?" *World Politics* 5 (July): 442–477.

HAAS, ERNST B., AND ALLEN S. WHITING. (1956) *Dynamics of International Relations*. New York: McGraw-Hill.

HAGAN, JOE D. (1992) *Political Opposition and Foreign Policy in Comparative Perspective*. Boulder, Colo.: Lynne Rienner, forthcoming.

HAGGARD, STEPHAN, AND BETH A. SIMMONS. (1987) "Theories of International Regimes," *International Organization* 41 (Summer): 491–517.

HALLENBECK, RALPH A., AND DAVID E. SHAVER. (eds.) (1991) *On Disarmament*. New York: Praeger.

HALLIDAY, FRED. (1987) "Gorbachev and the 'Arab Syndrome': Soviet Policy in the Middle East," *World Policy Journal* 4 (Summer): 415–442.

HANRIEDER, WOLFRAM F. (1978) "Dissolving International Politics: Reflections on the Nation-State," *American Political Science Review* 72 (December): 1276–1287.

HANSEN, ROGER D. (1980) "North-South Policy—What's the Problem?" *Foreign Affairs* 58 (Summer): 1104–1128.

———. (1979) *The North-South Stalemate*. New York: McGraw-Hill.

HANSON, PHILIP. (1991) "Soviet Economic Reform: Perestroika or 'Catastroika'?" *World Policy Journal* 8 (Spring): 289–318.

HARDEN, BLAINE. (1987) "AIDS May Replace Famine As the Continent's Worst Blight," *Washington Post National Weekly Edition*, June 15, pp. 16–17.

HARDIN, GARRETT. "The Tragedy of the Commons." *Science* 162 (December): 1243–1248.

HARRIS, NIGEL. (1987) *The End of the Third World*. Vol. 1. Harmondsworth, England: Pelican.

HART, JEFFREY A. (1978) "The New International Economic Order Negotiations: From the Sixth Special Session to the End of the North-South Dialogue." Paper presented at the Meeting of the Peace Science Society, Boca Raton, Fla., April 6–7.

HASSNER, PIERRE. (1968) "The Nation-State in the Nuclear Age," *Survey* 67 (April): 3–27.

HAYTER, TERESA. (1971) *Aid as Imperialism*. Baltimore: Penguin.

HEAD, IVAN L. (1989) "South-North Dangers," *Foreign Affairs* 68 (Summer): 71–86.

HECHT, JAMES L. (1991) "The Grand Bargain to Bring the Soviets to Market: Are We Prepared to Undo 70 Years of Communism?" *Washington Post National Weekly Edition*, July 15–21, pp. 24–25.

HEILBRONER, ROBERT L. (1991) *An Inquiry into the Human Prospect: Looked At Again for the 1990s*. New York: Norton.

———. (1977) "The Multinational Corporation and the Nation-State," pp. 338–352 in Steven L. Spiegel (ed.), *At Issue: Politics in the World Arena*. New York: St. Martin's Press.

HEILIG, GERHARD, THOMAS BÜTTNER, AND WOLFGANG LUTZ. (1990) "Germany's Population: Turbulent Past, Uncertain Future," *Population Bulletin* 45 (No. 4). Washingtin, D.C.: Population Reference Bureau.

HELMAN, UDI. (1990) "Environment and the National Interest: An Analytical Survey of the Literature," *Washington Quarterly* 13 (Autumn): 193–206.

HENKIN, LOUIS. (1991) "The Use of Force: Law and U.S. Policy," pp. 37–69 in Stanley Hoffmann, et al. (eds.), *Right v. Might: International Law and the Use of Force*, 2nd ed. New York: Council on Foreign Relations.

HENRY, JAMES S. (1987) "Brazil Says: Nuts," *New Republic*, October 12, pp. 25, 28–29.

HERKEN, GREGG. (1982) *The Winning Weapon: The Atomic Bomb in the Cold War, 1945–1950*. New York: Vintage.

HERMANN, CHARLES F. (1988) "New Foreign Policy Problems and Old Bureaucratic Organizations," pp. 248–265 in Charles W. Kegley, Jr., and Eugene R. Wittkopf (eds.), *The Domestic Sources of American Foreign Policy*. New York: St. Martin's Press.

———. (1972) "Some Issues in the Study of International Crisis," pp. 3–17 in Charles F. Hermann (ed.), *International Crises*. New York: Free Press.

HERMANN, CHARLES F., CHARLES W. KEGLEY, JR., AND JAMES N. ROSENAU. (eds.) (1987) *New Directions in the Study of Foreign Policy*. Boston: Allen & Unwin.

HERMANN, MARGARET G. (1987) "Role Theory and Foreign Policy Dynamics: The African Arena," pp. 161–198 in Stephen G. Walker (ed.), *Role Theory and Foreign Policy Analysis*. Durham, N.C.: Duke University Press.

———. (1976) "When Leader Personality Will Affect Foreign Policy: Some Propositions," pp. 326–333 in James N. Rosenau (ed.), *In Search of Global Patterns*. New York: Free Press.

HERMANN, MARGARET G., AND CHARLES F. HERMANN. (1989) "Who Makes Foreign Policy Choices and How: An Empirical Inquiry," *International Studies Quarterly* 33 (December): 361–387.

HERSH, SEYMOUR. (1991) *The Sampson Option: Israel's Nuclear Arsenal and American Foreign Policy*. New York: Norton.

HERZ, JOHN H. (1951) *Political Realism and Political Idealism*. Chicago: University of Chicago Press.

HIGGINS, BENJAMIN, AND JEAN DOWNING HIGGINS. (1979) *Economic Development of a Small Planet*. New York: Norton.

HIGGS, ROBERT. (ed.) (1991) *Arms, Politics, and the Economy: Historical and Contemporary Perspectives*. Oakland, Calif.: The Independent Institute.

HILSMAN, ROGER. (1967) *To Move a Nation*. New York: Doubleday.

HOEBEL, E. ADAMSON. (1961) *The Law of Primitive Man*. Cambridge, Mass.: Harvard University Press.

HOFFMANN, STANLEY. (1971) "International Law and the Control of Force," pp. 34–36 in Karl W. Deutsch and Stanley Hoffmann (eds.), *The Relevance of International Law*. Garden City, N.Y.: Doubleday-Anchor.

———. (1961) "International Systems and International Law," pp. 205–237 in Klaus Knorr and Sidney Verba (eds.), *The International System*. Princeton, N.J.: Princeton University Press.

———. (1960) *Contemporary Theory in International Politics*. Englewood Cliffs, N.J.: Prentice-Hall.

HOLLOWAY, DAVID. (1983) *The Soviet Union and the Arms Race*. New Haven, Conn.: Yale University Press.

HOLMES, JOHN W. (1977) "A Non-American Perspective," pp. 30–43 in David A. Kay (ed.), *The Changing United Nations*. New York: Academy of Political Science.

HOLSTI, KALEVI J. (1991) *Peace and War: Armed Conflicts and International Order, 1648–1989.* Cambridge, England: Cambridge University Press.

———. (1988) *International Politics: A Framework for Analysis,* 5th ed. Englewood Cliffs, N.J.: Prentice-Hall.

———. (1970) "National Role Conceptions in the Study of Foreign Policy," *International Studies Quarterly* 14 (September): 233–309.

HOLSTI, OLE R. (1989a) "Crisis Decision Making," pp. 8–84 in Philip E. Tetlock, Jo L. Husbands, Robert Jervis, Paul C. Stern, and Charles Tilly (eds.), *Behavior, Society, and Nuclear War.* New York: Oxford University Press.

———. (1989b) "Models of International Relations and Foreign Policy," *Diplomatic History* 13 (Winter): 15–43.

———. (1972) *Crisis Escalation War.* Montreal: McGill-Queen's University Press.

———. (1962) "The Belief System and National Images: A Case Study," *Journal of Conflict Resolution* 6 (September): 244–252.

HOLSTI, OLE R., AND JAMES N. ROSENAU. (1984) *American Leadership in World Affairs.* Boston: Allen & Unwin.

HOMER-DIXON, THOMAS F. (1991) "On the Threshold: Environmental Changes as Causes of Acute Conflict," *International Security* 16 (Fall): 76–116.

HOOKS, GREGORY. (1991) *Forging the Military-Industrial Complex.* Urbana, Ill.: University of Illinois Press.

HOPF, TED. (1991) "Polarity, the Offense-Defense Balance, and War," *American Political Science Review* 85 (June): 475–493.

HOPKINS, RAYMOND F., ROBERT L. PAARLBERG, AND MITCHEL B. WALLERSTEIN. (1982) *Food in the Global Arena.* New York: Holt, Rinehart & Winston.

HOUSE, KAREN ELLIOT. (1989) "As Power Is Dispersed Among Nations, Need for Leadership Grows," *Wall Street Journal,* February 21, p. A10.

HOWARD, MICHAEL E. (1983) *The Causes of War.* Cambridge, Mass.: Harvard University Press.

HUFBAUER, GARY CLYDE. (ed.) (1990) *Europe 1992: An American Perspective.* Washington, D.C.: The Brookings Institution.

———. (1989–1990) "Beyond GATT," *Foreign Policy* 77 (Winter): 64–76.

HUFBAUER, GARY CLYDE, JEFFREY J. SCHOTT, AND KIMBERLY ANN ELLIOTT. (1990) *Economic Sanctions Reconsidered: History and Current Policy,* 2nd ed. Washington, D.C.: Institute for International Economics.

HUGHES, THOMAS L. (1985–1986) "The Twilight of Internationalism," *Foreign Policy* 61 (Winter): 25–48.

Human Development Report 1991. (1991) New York: Oxford University Press.

Human Development Report 1992. (1992) New York: Oxford University Press.

HUNTER, ROBERT E. (1988) "Changing Roles for Military Power," *Los Angeles Times,* January 5, p.7.

HUNTINGTON, SAMUEL P. (1991a) "America's Changing Strategic Interests," *Survival* 33 (January/February): 3–17.

———. (1991b) *The Third Wave: Democratization in the Late Twentieth Century.* Norman, Okla.: University of Oklahoma Press.

———. (1989) "No Exit: The Errors of Declinism," *National Interest* 17 (Fall): 3–10.

———. (1973) "Transnational Organizations in World Politics," *World Politics* 25 (April): 333–368.

HURWITZ, JON, AND MARK PEFFLEY. (1990) "Public Images of the Soviet Union: The Impact of Foreign Policy Attitudes," *Journal of Politics* 52 (February): 3–28.

———. (1987) "How Are Foreign Policy Attitudes Structured? A Hierarchical Model," *American Political Science Review* 81 (December): 1099–1120.

HUTH, PAUL. (1988) *Extended Deterrence and the Prevention of War.* New Haven, Conn.: Yale University Press.

HYLAND, WILLIAM G. (1990) "America's New Course," *Foreign Affairs* 69 (Spring): 1–12.

———. (1987) "Reagan-Gorbachev III," *Foreign Affairs* 66 (Fall): 7–21.

IGNATIUS, DAVID. (1987) "We've Learned to Stop Worrying and Love Arms Control—And in the Process, the U.S. and the Soviets Reversed Roles," *Washington Post National Weekly Edition,* September 14, p. 25.

IKLÉ, FRED CHARLES. (1991–1992) "Comrades in Arms," *The National Interest* 26 (Winter): 22–32.

INTERNATIONAL ENERGY AGENCY. (1982) *World Energy Outlook.* Paris: Organisation for Economic Co-operation and Development.

International Financial Statistics Yearbook. (1991) Washington, D.C.: International Monetary Fund.

INTERNATIONAL MONETARY FUND. (1987) *World Economic Outlook.* Washington, D.C.: International Monetary Fund.

INTERNATIONAL MONETARY FUND, THE WORLD BANK, ORGANISATION FOR ECONOMIC CO-OPERATION AND DEVELOPMENT, AND EUROPEAN BANK FOR RECONSTRUCTION AND DEVELOPMENT. (1990) *The Economy of the USSR.* Washington, D.C.: World Bank.

ISAAK, ROBERT A. (1991) *International Political Economy: Managing World Economic Change.* Englewood Cliffs, N.J.: Prentice-Hall.

ISLAM, SHADA. (1982) "Stabex Sour Note As Brussels Rings Changes," *South* 24 (October): 71–72.

JACOBSEN, KURT. (1978) *The General Assembly of the United Nations.* New York: Columbia University Press.

———. (1969) "Sponsorships in the United Nations: A System Analysis," *Journal of Peace Research* 6 (No. 3): 235–256.

JACOBSON, HAROLD K. (1984) *Networks of Interdependence: International Organizations and the Global Political System.* New York: Knopf.

JACOBSON, HAROLD K., WILLIAM M. REISINGER, AND TODD MATHERS. (1986) "National Entanglements in International Governmental Organizations," *American Political Science Review* 80 (March): 141–159.

JACOBSON, JODI. (1989) "Abandoning Homelands," pp. 59–76 in Lester R. Brown, Christopher Flavin, Sandra Postel, Linda Starke, Alan Durning, Lori Heise, Jodi Jacobson, Michael Renner, and Cynthia Pollock Shea, *State of the World 1989.* New York: Norton.

JAKOBSON, MAX. (1991) "Filling the World's Most Impossible Job," *World Monitor* 4 (August): 25–33.

JAMES, ALAN. (1990) *Peacekeeping in International Politics.* New York: St. Martin's Press.

JANIS, IRVING. (1982) *Groupthink: Psychological Studies of Policy Decisions and Fiascoes,* 2nd ed. Boston: Houghton Mifflin.

JENSEN, LLOYD. (1982) *Explaining Foreign Policy.* Englewood Cliffs, N.J.: Prentice-Hall.

JERVIS, ROBERT. (1991–1992) "The Future of World Politics: Will It Resemble the Past?" *International Security* 16 (Winter): 39–73.

———. (1991) "Will the New World Be Better?" pp. 7–19 in Robert Jervis and Seweryn Bialer (eds.), *Soviet-American Relations After the Cold War.* Durham, N.C.: Duke University Press.

———. (1982) "Security Regimes," *International Organization* 16 (Spring): 357–378.

———. (1976) *Perception and Misperception in World Politics.* Princeton, N.J.: Princeton University Press.

JOFFE, JOSEF. (1990) "Entangled Forever," *National Interest* 21 (Fall): 35–40.

———. (1985) "The Foreign Policy of the Federal Republic of Germany," pp. 72–113 in Roy C. Macridis (ed.), *Foreign Policy in World Politics,* 6th ed. Englewood Cliffs, N.J.: Prentice-Hall.

JOHANSEN, ROBERT C. (1991) "Do Preparations for War Increase or Decrease National Security?" pp. 224–244 in Charles W. Kegley, Jr. (ed.), *The Long Postwar Peace.* New York: HarperCollins.

JOHNSON, JAMES TURNER. (1991) "Can Contemporary War Be Just? Elements in the Moral Debate," pp. 177–192 in Charles W. Kegley, Jr., and Kenneth L. Schwab (eds.), *After the Cold War: Questioning the Morality of Nuclear Deterrence.* Boulder, Colo.: Westview.

———. (1987) *The Quest for Peace: Three Moral Traditions in Western Cultural History.* Princeton, N.J.: Princeton University Press.

JONAH, JAMES O. C. (1991) "Critical Commentary: A Third World View of the Implications of Superpower Collaboration," in Thomas G. Weiss and Meryl A. Kessler (eds.), *Third World Security in the Post–Cold War Era.* Boulder, Colo.: Lynne Rienner.

JONES, DOROTHY V. (1991) *Code of Peace: Ethics and Security in the World of Warlord States.* Chicago: University of Chicago Press.

JÖNSSON, CHRISTER. (1982) "The Ideology of Foreign Policy," pp. 91–110 in Charles W. Kegley, Jr., and Pat McGowan (eds.), *Foreign Policy: USA/USSR.* Beverly Hills, Calif.: Sage.

JOYNER, CHRISTOPHER C. (1992) "The Reality and Relevance of International Law," pp. 202–215 in Charles W. Kegley, Jr., and Eugene R. Wittkopf (eds.), *The Global Agenda,* 3rd ed. New York: McGraw-Hill.

KAISER, DAVID. (1990) *Politics and War: European Conflict from Philip II to Hitler.* Cambridge, Mass.: Harvard University Press.

KANT, IMMANUEL. (1969 [1795]) *Perpetual Peace.* New York: Columbia University Press.

KAPLAN, MORTON A. (1957) *System and Process in International Politics.* New York: Wiley.

KAPLAN, MORTON A., AND NICHOLAS DEB. KATZENBACH. (1961) *The Political Foundations of International Law.* New York: Wiley.

KAPLAN, STEPHEN S. (1981) *Diplomacy of Power.* Washington, D.C.: The Brookings Institution.

KAPSTEIN, ETHAN BARNABY. (1992) *The Political Economy of National Security: A Global Perspective.* New York: McGraw-Hill.

———. (1991–1992) "We Are Us: The Myth of the Multinational," *National Interest* 26 (Winter): 55–62.

KARP, REGINA. (ed.) (1991) *Security with Nuclear Weapons? Different Perspectives on National Security.* New York: Oxford University Press.

KEENY, SPURGEON M., JR., AND WOLFGANG K. H. PANOFSKY. (1981) "MAD vs. NUTS: Can Doctrine or Weaponry Remedy the Mutual Hostage Relationship of the Superpowers?" *Foreign Affairs* 60 (Winter): 287–304.

KEGLEY, CHARLES W., JR. (1992) "The New Global Order: The Power of Principle in a Pluralistic World," *Ethics and International Affairs* 6: 21–42.

———. (ed.) (1991) *The Long Postwar Peace: Contending Explanations and Projections.* New York: HarperCollins.

———. (1988) "Neoidealism: A Practical Matter," *Ethics and International Affairs* 2: 173–197.

KEGLEY, CHARLES W., JR., AND STEVEN W. HOOK. (1991) "U.S. Foreign Aid and U.N. Voting: Did Reagan's Linkage Strategy Buy Deference or Defiance?" *International Studies Quarterly* 35 (September): 295–312.

KEGLEY, CHARLES W., JR., AND GREGORY A. RAYMOND. (1993) "Networks of Intrigue? Realpolitik, Alliances, and International Security," forthcoming in Frank Wayman and Paul F. Diehl (eds.), *Reconstructing Realpolitik.* Ann Arbor: University of Michigan Press.

———. (1992) "Must We Fear a Post–Cold War Multipolar World?" *Journal of Conflict Resolution* 36 (September): 573–582.

———. (1990) *When Trust Breaks Down: Alliance Norms and World Politics.* Columbia, S.C.: University of South Carolina Press.

KEGLEY, CHARLES W., JR., AND EUGENE R. WITTKOPF. (1991) *American Foreign Policy: Pattern and Process*, 4th ed. New York: St. Martin's Press.

KELMAN, HERBERT C. (ed.) (1965) *International Behavior: A Social-Psychological Analysis.* New York: Holt, Rinehart & Winston.

———. (1970) "The Role of the Individual in International Relations," *Journal of International Affairs* 24 (No. 1): 1–17.

KELSEN, HANS. (1945) *General Theory of Law and State.* Cambridge, Mass.: Harvard University Press.

KEMP, GEOFFREY. (1990) "Regional Security, Arms Control, and the End of the Cold War," *Washington Quarterly* 13 (Autumn): 33–51.

KENNAN, GEORGE F. (1984a) *The Fateful Alliance: France, Russia, and the Coming of the First World War.* New York: Pantheon.

———. (1984b) "Soviet-American Relations: The Politics of Discord and Collaboration," pp. 107–120 in Charles W. Kegley, Jr., and Eugene R. Wittkopf (eds.), *The Global Agenda.* New York: Random House.

———. (1982) *The Nuclear Delusion.* New York: Pantheon.

———. (1976) "The United States and the Soviet Union, 1917–1976," *Foreign Affairs* 54 (July): 670–690.

———. (1967) *Memoirs.* Boston: Little, Brown.

———. (1951) *American Diplomacy, 1900–1950.* New York: New American Library.

———. ["X"] (1947) "The Sources of Soviet Conduct," *Foreign Affairs* 25 (July): 566–582.

KENNEDY, PAUL. (1992) "A Declining Empire Goes to War," pp. 344–346 in Charles W. Kegley, Jr., and Eugene R. Wittkopf (eds.), *The Future of American Foreign Policy.* New York: St. Martin's Press.

———. (1987) *The Rise and Fall of the Great Powers.* New York: Random House.

KEOHANE, ROBERT O. (ed.) (1986a) *Neorealism and Its Critics.* New York: Columbia University Press.

———. (1986b) "Realism, Neorealism and the Study of World Politics," pp. 1–26 in Robert O. Keohane (ed.), *Neorealism and Its Critics.* New York: Columbia University Press.

———. (1984) *After Hegemony: Cooperation and Discord in the World Political Economy.* Princeton, N.J.: Princeton University Press.

———. (1983) "Theory of World Politics: Structural Realism and Beyond," pp. 503–540 in Ada Finifter (ed.), *Political Science: The State of the Discipline.* Washington, D.C.: American Political Science Association.

KEOHANE, ROBERT O., AND STANLEY HOFFMANN. (eds.) (1991a) "Institutional Change in Europe in the 1980s," pp. 1–39 in Robert O. Keohane and Stanley Hoffmann (eds.), *The New European Community: Decisionmaking and Institutional Change.* Boulder, Colo.: Westview.

———. (eds.) (1991b) *The New European Community: Decisionmaking and Institutional Change.* Boulder, Colo.: Westview.

KEOHANE, ROBERT O., AND JOSEPH S. NYE, JR. (1989) *Power and Interdependence*, 2nd ed. Glenview, Ill.: Scott, Foresman/ Little, Brown.

———. (1988) "Complex Interdependence, Transnational Relations, and Realism: Alternative Perspectives on World Politics," pp. 257–271 in Charles W. Kegley, Jr., and Eugene R. Wittkopf (eds.), *The Global Agenda*, 2nd ed. New York: Random House.

———. (1985) "Two Cheers for Multilateralism," *Foreign Policy* 60 (Fall): 148–167.

———. (1977) *Power and Interdependence.* Boston: Little, Brown.

———. (1975) "International Interdependence and Integration," pp. 363–414 in Fred I. Greenstein and Nelson W. Polsby (eds.), *International Politics: Handbook of Political Science.* Vol. 8. Reading, Mass.: Addison-Wesley.

KEYFITZ, NATHAN. (1991) "Population Growth Can Prevent the Development That Would Slow Population Growth," pp. 37–77 in Jessica Tuchman Mathews (ed.), *Preserving the Global Environment.* New York: Norton.

KIDDER, RUSHWORTH M. (1990) "Why Modern Terrorism?" pp. 135–138 in Charles W. Kegley, Jr. (ed.), *International Terrorism: Characteristics, Causes, Controls*. New York: St. Martin's Press.

KIDRON, MICHAEL, AND DAN SMITH. (1991) *The New State of War and Peace: An International Atlas*. New York: Simon & Schuster.

KIM, SAMUEL S. (1991) "The United Nations, Lawmaking and World Order," pp. 109–124 in Richard A. Falk, Samuel S. Kim, and Saul H. Mendlovitz (eds.), *The United Nations and a Just World Order*. Boulder, Colo.: Westview.

KIM, WOOSANG. (1989) "Power, Alliance, and Major Wars, 1816–1975," *Journal of Conflict Resolution* 33 (June): 255–273.

KINDLEBERGER, CHARLES P. (1973) *The World in Depression, 1929–1939*. Berkeley: University of California Press.

———. (1969) *American Business Abroad*. New Haven, Conn.: Yale University Press.

KISSINGER, HENRY A. (1982) *Years of Upheaval*. Boston: Little, Brown.

———. (1979) *White House Years*. Boston: Little, Brown.

———. (1973) "Secretary Kissinger at Pacem in Terris," news release of the Bureau of Public Affairs, U.S. Department of State (October 10).

———. (1969) "Domestic Structure and Foreign Policy," pp. 261–275 in James N. Rosenau (ed.), *International Politics and Foreign Policy*. New York: Free Press.

KLARE, MICHAEL T. (1991) "Behind Desert Storm: The New Military Paradigm," *Technology Review* 94 (May–June): 28–36.

———. (1990a) "Wars in the 1990s: Growing Firepower in the Third World," *The Bulletin of the Atomic Scientists* 46 (May): 9–13.

———. (1990b) "Who's Arming Who? The Arms Trade in the 1990s," *Technology Review* 93 (May–June): 45–50.

———. (1988) "Low-Intensity Conflict," *Christianity and Crisis*, February 1, pp. 11–14.

———. (1987) "The Arms Trade: Changing Patterns in the 1980s," *Third World Quarterly* 9 (October): 1257–1281.

———. (1985) "Leaping the Firebreak," pp. 168–173 in Charles W. Kegley, Jr., and Eugene R. Wittkopf (eds.), *The Nuclear Reader: Strategy, Weapons, War*. New York: St. Martin's Press.

KLUCKHOHN, CLYDE. (1944) "Anthropological Research and World Peace," pp. 143–152 in L. Bryson, Laurence Finkelstein, and Robert M. MacIver (eds.), *Approaches to World Peace*. New York: Conference on Science, Philosophy, and Religion.

KNORR, KLAUS. (1977) "International Economic Leverage and Its Uses," pp. 99–126 in Klaus Knorr and Frank N. Trager (eds.), *Economic Issues and National Security*. Lawrence: Regents Press of Kansas.

———. (1975) *The Power of Nations*. New York: Basic Books.

KNORR, KLAUS, AND JAMES N. ROSENAU. (eds.) (1969) *Contending Approaches to International Politics*. Princeton, N.J.: Princeton University Press.

KNORR, KLAUS, AND SIDNEY VERBA. (eds.) (1961) *The International System*. Princeton, N.J.: Princeton University Press.

KNUDSEN, BAARD BREDRUP. (1984) *Europe Versus America: Foreign Policy in the 1980s*. Paris: Atlantic Institute for International Affairs.

KOBER, STANLEY. (1990) "Idealpolitik," *Foreign Policy* 79 (Summer): 3–24.

KOHN, HANS. (1944) *The Meaning of Nationalism*. New York: Macmillan.

KOKOSHIN, ANDREY. (1992) "U.S.-Soviet Security Cooperation in the Post–Cold War Era," pp. 203–211 in Joseph Kruzel (ed.), *American Defense Annual, 1991–1992*. New York: Lexington Books.

KORANY, BAHGAT. (1986) *How Foreign Policy Decisions Are Made in the Third World*. Boulder, Colo.: Westview.

KOZYREV, ANDREI V. (1990) "The New Soviet Attitude Toward the United Nations," *Washington Quarterly* 13 (Summer): 41–53.

KRAMER, MARK. (1991a) "Soviet Foreign Policy After the Cold War," *Current History* 90 (October): 317–322.

———. (1991b) "Warheads and Chaos," *National Interest* 25 (Fall): 94–97.

KRASNER, STEPHEN D. (1985) *Structural Conflict: The Third World Against Global Liberalism*. Berkeley: University of California Press.

———. (1983) *International Regimes*. Ithaca, N.Y.: Cornell University Press.

———. (1982) "Structural Causes and Regime Consequences," *International Organization* 36 (Spring): 185–206.

———. (1981) "Transforming International Regimes: What the Third World Wants and Why," *International Studies Quarterly* 25 (March): 119–148.

———. (1979) "Tokyo Round: Particularistic Interests and Prospects for Stability in the Global Trading System," *International Studies Quarterly* 23 (December): 491–531.

————. (1978) *Defending the National Interest.* Princeton, N.J.: Princeton University Press.

————. (1974) "Oil is the Exception," *Foreign Policy* 14 (Spring): 68–84.

————. (1972) "Are Bureaucracies Important? (Or Allison Wonderland)," *Foreign Policy* 7 (Summer): 159–179.

KRATOCHWIL, FRIEDRICH, AND JOHN GERARD RUGGIE. (1986) "International Organization: A State of the Art on the Art of the State," *International Organization* 40 (Autumn): 753–775.

KRAUTHAMMER, CHARLES. (1991a) "The Lonely Superpower," *The New Republic* July 29: pp. 23–27.

————. (1991b) "The Unipolar Moment," *Foreign Affairs* 70 (No. 1): 23–33.

KRUGMAN, PAUL. (1990) *The Age of Diminished Expectations: U.S. Economic Policy in the 1990s.* Cambridge, Mass.: MIT Press.

KRUZEL, JOSEPH. (1991) "Arms Control, Disarmament, and the Stability of the Postwar Era," pp. 247–269 in Charles W. Kegley, Jr. (ed.), *The Long Postwar Peace.* New York: HarperCollins.

KUCZYNSKI, PEDRO-PABLO. (1987) "The Outlook for Latin American Debt," *Foreign Affairs* 66 (Fall): 129–149.

KUDRLE, ROBERT T. (1987) "The Several Faces of the Multinational Corporation: Political Reaction and Policy Response," pp. 230–241 in Jeffry A. Frieden and David A. Lake (eds.), *International Political Economy.* New York: St. Martin's Press.

KUHN, THOMAS S. (1970) *The Structure of Scientific Revolutions.* Chicago: University of Chicago Press.

KUKLINSKI, JAMES H., ROBERT C. LUSKIN, AND JOHN BOLLAND. (1991) "Where Is the Schema? Going Beyond the 'S' Word in Political Psychology." *American Political Science Review* 85 (December): 1341–1355.

KUNZ, JOSEF L. (1960) "Sanctions in International Law," *American Journal of International Law* 54 (April): 324–347.

KUTTNER, ROBERT. (1991a) "Another Great Victory of Ideology Over Prosperity," *Atlantic Monthly* 283 (October): 32 et passim.

————. (1991b) *The End of Laissez-Faire: National Purpose and the Global Economy After the Cold War.* New York: Knopf.

LANGER, WILLIAM L. (1962) "Farewell to Empire," *Foreign Affairs* 41 (October): 115–130.

LAQUEUR, WALTER. (1986) "Reflections on Terrorism," *Foreign Affairs* 65 (Fall): 86–100.

LASKSHMANAN, T. R., AND AKE ANDERSSON. (1991–1992) "Western European Energy Policy in Turmoil and Transition," *Harvard International Review* 14 (Winter): 17–20.

LASZLO, ERVIN, JORGE LOZOYA, A. K. BHATTACHARYA, JAIME ESTEVEZ, ROSARIO GREEN, AND VENKATA RAMAN. (1980) *The Obstacles to the New International Economic Order.* Elmsford, N.Y.: Pergamon Press.

LAYNE, CHRISTOPHER. (1990–1991) "America's Stake in Soviet Stability," *World Policy Journal* 8 (Winter): 61–88.

LEBOW, RICHARD NED. (1981) *Between Peace and War: The Nature of International Crisis.* Baltimore: Johns Hopkins University Press.

LEVENTHAL, PAUL L. (1992) "Plugging the Leaks in Nuclear Export Controls: Why Bother?" *Orbis* 36 (Spring): 167–180.

LEVI, ISAAC. (1990) *Hard Choices: Decision Making Under Unresolved Conflict.* New York: Cambridge University Press.

LEVI, WERNER. (1981) *The Coming End of War.* Beverly Hills, Calif.: Sage.

LEVY, JACK S. (1992) "The Causes of War: Contending Theories," pp. 61–71 in Charles W. Kegley, Jr., and Eugene R. Wittkopf (eds.), *The Global Agenda*, 3rd ed. New York: McGraw-Hill.

————. (1991) "Long Cycles, Hegemonic Transitions, and the Long Peace," pp. 147–176 in Charles W. Kegley, Jr. (ed.), *The Long Postwar Peace.* New York: HarperCollins.

————. (1989a) "The Causes of War: A Review of Theories and Evidence," pp. 209–333 in Philip E. Tetlock, Jo L. Husbands, Robert Jervis, Paul C. Stern, and Charles Tilly (eds.), *Behavior, Society, and Nuclear War.* New York: Oxford University Press.

————. (1989b) "The Diversionary Theory of War: A Critique," pp. 259–288 in Manus I. Midlarsky (ed.), *Handbook of War Studies.* Boston: Unwin Hyman.

————. (1985) "The Polarity of the System and International Stability: An Empirical Analysis," pp. 41–66 in Alan Ned Sabrosky (ed.), *Polarity and War.* Boulder, Colo.: Westview.

LEWIS, MAUREEN A., ET AL. (1992) *AIDS in Developing Countries: Cost Issues and Policy Tradeoffs.* Washington, D.C.: Urban Institute Press.

LEWIS, PAUL. (1992) "U.N.'s Fund Crisis Worsens as Role in Security Rises," *New York Times*, January 27, pp. A1, A5.

LEWIS, W. ARTHUR. (1978) *The Evolution of the International Economic Order.* Princeton, N.J.: Princeton University Press.

LEWONTIN, R. C., STEVEN ROSE, AND LEON J. KAMIN. (1984) *Not in Our Genes: Biology, Ideology, and Human Nature.* New York: Pantheon.

LEYTON-BROWN, DAVID. (1990) "The Roles of the Multinational Enterprise in International Relations," pp. 224–241 in

David G. Haglud and Michael K. Hawes (eds.), *World Politics: Power, Interdependence, and Dependence*. Toronto: Harcourt Brace Jovanovich.

―――. (1987) "Introduction," pp. 1–4 in David Leyton-Brown (ed.), *The Utility of Economic Sanctions*. New York: St. Martin's Press.

LIFTON, ROBERT JAY, AND RICHARD FALK. (1982) *Indefensible Weapons: The Political and Psychological Case Against Nuclearism*. New York: Basic Books.

LIJPHART, AREND. (1974) "The Structure of the Theoretical Revolution in International Relations," *International Studies Quarterly* 18 (March): 42–49.

LILLICH, RICHARD B. (1972) "Domestic Institutions," pp. 384–424 in Cyril E. Black and Richard A. Falk (eds.), *The Future of the International Legal Order*. Princeton, N.J.: Princeton University Press.

LINDBLOM, CHARLES E. (1977) *Politics and Markets.* New York: Basic Books.

LINDSAY, JAMES M. (1986) "Trade Sanctions As Policy Instruments: A Re-examination," *International Studies Quarterly* 30 (June): 153–173.

LIPOW, JONATHAN. (1990) "Defense, Growth, and Disarmament: A Further Look," *Jerusalem Journal of International Relations* 12 (June): 49–59.

LISKA, GEORGE. (1968) *Alliances and the Third World*. Baltimore: Johns Hopkins University Press.

―――. (1962) *Nations in Alliance: The Limits of Interdependence*. Baltimore: Johns Hopkins University Press.

LISSITZYN, OLIVER J. (1963) "International Law in a Divided World," *International Conciliation* 542 (March): 3–69.

LISTER, FREDERICK K. (1986) *Fairness and Accountability in U.N. Financial Decision-Making*. United Nations Management and Decision-making Project. New York: United Nations Association of the United States of America.

LORENZ, KONRAD. (1963) *On Aggression*. New York: Harcourt, Brace & World.

LOVELL, JOHN P. (1970) *Foreign Policy in Perspective*. New York: Holt, Rinehart & Winston.

LUCKHAM, ROBIN. (1984) "Militarisation and the New International Anarchy," *Third World Quarterly* 6 (April): 351–373.

LUDLOW, PETER. (1991) "The European Commission," pp. 85–132 in Robert O. Keohane and Stanley Hoffmann (eds.), *The New European Community: Decisionmaking and Institutional Change*. Boulder, Colo.: Westview.

LUTTWAK, EDWARD N. (1990) "From Geo-Politics to Geoeconomics," *National Interest* 20 (Summer): 17–23.

MACFARQUHAR, RODERICK. (1991) "The Anatomy of Collapse," *New York Review of Books* 35 (September 26): 5–9.

MACHIAVELLI, NICCOLÓ. (1950 [1513]) *The Prince and The Discourses*. New York: Random House.

MACKINDER, SIR HALFORD. (1919) *Democratic Ideals and Reality*. New York: Henry A. Holt.

MACNEILL, JIM. (1992) "Sustainable Development: What Is It?" pp. 379–387 in Charles W. Kegley, Jr., and Eugene R. Wittkopf (eds.), *The Global Agenda*, 3rd ed. New York: McGraw-Hill.

―――. (1989–1990) "The Greening of International Relations," *International Journal* 45 (Winter): 1–35.

MACRIDIS, ROY C. (ed.) (1989) *Foreign Policy in World Politics*, 8th ed. Englewood Cliffs, N.J.: Prentice-Hall.

MAHAN, ALRED THAYER. (1890) *The Influence of Sea Power in History*. Boston: Little, Brown.

MAJEED, AKHTAR. (1991) "Has the War System Really Become Obsolete?" *Bulletin of Peace Proposals* 22 (December): 419–425.

MANICAS, PETER. (1989) *War and Democracy*. Oxford, England: Basil Blackwell.

MAOZ, ZEEV, AND NASRIN ABDOLALI. (1989) "Regime Types and International Conflict," *Journal of Conflict Resolution* 33 (March): 3–36.

MARANTZ, PAUL. (1987) "Economic Sanctions in the Polish Crisis," pp. 131–146 in David Leyton-Brown (ed.), *The Utility of International Economic Sanctions*. New York: St. Martin's Press.

MARKUSEN, ANN, PETER HALL, SCOTT CAMPBELL, AND SABINA DIETRICK. (1991) *The Rise of the Gunbelt: The Military Remapping of America*. New York: Oxford University Press.

MARTIN, LINDA G. (1989) "The Graying of Japan," *Population Bulletin* 44 (No. 2). Washington, D.C.: Population Reference Bureau.

MASSING, MICHAEL. (1990–1991) " 'Structural Adjustment' in the Third World Has Been a Bust," *Washington Post National Weekly Edition*, December 31–January 6, p. 24.

MASSON, PAUL R. (1990) "Long-term Macroeconomic Effects of Aging Populations," *Finance and Development* 27 (June): 6–9.

MASTANDUNO, MICHAEL. (1991) "Do Relative Gains Matter? America's Response to Japanese Industrial Policy," *International Security* 16 (Summer): 73–113.

MASTANDUNO, MICHAEL, DAVID A. LAKE, AND G. JOHN IKENBERRY. (1989) "Toward a Realist Theory of State Action," *International Studies Quarterly* 33 (December): 457–474.

MASTERS, ROGER D. (1969) "World Politics As a Primitive Political System," pp. 104–118 in James N. Rosenau (ed.), *International Politics and Foreign Policy*. New York: Free Press.

MATHEWS, JESSICA T. (1992) "Coping with the Uncertainties of the Greenhouse Effect," pp. 366–372 in Charles W. Kegley, Jr., and Eugene R. Wittkopf (eds.), *The Global Agenda*, 3rd ed. New York: McGraw-Hill.

———. (1991) "Iraq's Nuclear Warning," *Washington Post National Weekly Edition*, July 22–28, p. 19.

———. (1990) "The Greenhouse Effect: Apparently It's for Others to Worry About," *Washington Post National Weekly Edition*, July 9–15, p. 29.

MAYUR, RASHMI. (1984) "The Third World and Tomorrow," *The Futurist* 18 (April): 21–23.

McCGWIRE, MICHAEL. (1991) *Perestroika and Soviet National Security*. Washington, D.C.: The Brookings Institution.

McCLELLAND, CHARLES A. (1966) *Theory and the International System*. New York: Macmillan.

McCULLY, PATRICK. (1991) "Discord in the Greenhouse: How WRI is Attempting to Shift the Blame for Global Warming," *Ecologist* 21 (July/August): 157–165.

McDOUGAL, MYRES S., AND HAROLD D. LASSWELL. (1959) "The Identification and Appraisal of Diverse Systems of Public Order," *American Journal of International Law* 53 (January): 1–29.

McGOWAN, PATRICK J., WITH THE ASSISTANCE OF BOHDAN KORDAN. (1981) "Imperialism in World-System Perspective," *International Studies Quarterly* 25 (March): 43–68.

McKIBBEN, BILL. (1989) "Reflections: The End of Nature," *New Yorker*, September 11, pp. 47–48 passim.

McNAMARA, ROBERT S. (1991) "Alternative Views of a Post–Cold War World," *Wingspread* 13 (Summer): 1–12.

———. (1984) "Time Bomb or Myth: The Population Problem," *Foreign Affairs* 62 (Summer): 1107–1131.

McNAUGHER, THOMAS L. (1990) "Ballistic Missiles and Chemical Weapons: The Legacy of the Iran-Iraq War," *International Security* 15 (Fall): 5–34.

MEAD, MARGARET. (1968) "Warfare Is Only an Invention—Not a Biological Necessity," pp. 270–274 in Leon Bramson and George W. Goethals (eds.), *War*. New York: Basic Books.

MEAD, WALTER RUSSELL. (1990) "On the Road to Ruin: Winning the Cold War, Losing Economic Peace," *Harper's* 280 (March): 59–64.

———. (1989) "American Economic Policy in the Antemillenial Era," *World Policy Journal* 6 (Summer): 385–468.

———. (1988–1989) "The United States and the World Economy," *World Policy Journal* 6 (Winter): 11–45.

MEADOWS, DONELLA H., DENNIS L. MEADOWS, JØRGEN RANDERS, AND WILLIAM W. BEHRENS III. (1974) *The Limits to Growth*. New York: New American Library.

MEARSHEIMER, JOHN J. (1990) "Back to the Future: Instability in Europe After the Cold War," *International Security* 15 (Summer): 5–56.

———. (1983) *Conventional Deterrence*. Ithaca, N.Y.: Cornell University Press.

MEISSNER, DORIS. (1992) "Managing Migrations," *Foreign Policy* 86 (Spring): 66–83.

MELANSON, RICHARD A. (1983) *Writing History and Making Policy: The Cold War, Vietnam, and Revisionism*. Lanham, Md.: University Press of America.

MELLOAN, GEORGE. (1991) "Maastricht's Ghost of Europes Past, and Future," *Wall Street Journal*, December 9, p. A15.

MERRICK, THOMAS W. (1989) *America in the 21st Century: A Global Perspective*. Washington, D.C.: Population Reference Bureau.

———. (1986) "World Population in Transition," in *Population Bulletin* 41 (No. 2). Washington, D.C.: Population Reference Bureau.

THE MIDDLE EAST. (1991) 7th ed. Washington, D.C.: Congressional Quarterly, Inc.

MIDLARSKY, MANUS I. (1988) *The Onset of World War*. Boston: Unwin Hyman.

———. (1975) *On War*. New York: Free Press.

MILLS, C. WRIGHT. (1956) *The Power Elite*. New York: Oxford University Press.

MINTER, WILLIAM. (1986–1987) "South Africa: Straight Talk on Sanctions," *Foreign Policy* 65 (Winter): 43–63.

MITRANY, DAVID. (1966) *A Working Peace System*. Chicago: Quadrangle.

MODELSKI, GEORGE. (ed.) (1987) *Exploring Long Cycles*. Boulder, Colo.: Lynne Reinner.

———. (1978) "The Long Cycle of Global Politics and the Nation-State," *Comparative Studies in Society and History* 20 (April): 214–235.

———. (1964) "The International Relations of Internal War," pp. 14–44 in James N. Rosenau (ed.), *International Aspects of Civil Strife*. Princeton, N.J.: Princeton University Press.

MODELSKI, GEORGE, AND WILLIAM R. THOMPSON. (1989) "Long Cycles and Global War," pp. 23–54 in Manus I. Midlarsky (ed.), *Handbook of War Studies*. Boston: Unwin Hyman.

MØLLER, BJØRN. (1992) *Common Security and Nonoffensive Defense: A Neorealist Perspective*. Boulder, Colo.: Lynne Reinner.

MOON, BRUCE E., AND WILLIAM J. DIXON. (1985) "Politics, the State, and Basic Human Needs: A Cross-National Study," *American Journal of Political Science* 29 (November): 661–694.

MORAN, THEODORE H. (1991) "International Economics and U.S. Security," *Foreign Affairs* 69 (Winter): 74–90.

MORAWETZ, DAVID. (1977) *Twenty-five Years of Economic Development, 1950 to 1975*. Washington, D.C.: World Bank.

MORGAN, T. CLIFTON, AND KENNETH N. BICKERS. (1992) "Domestic Discontent and the External Use of Force," *The Journal of Conflict Resolution* 36 (March): 25–52.

MORGAN, T. CLIFTON, AND SALLY HOWARD CAMPBELL. (1991) "Domestic Structure, Decisional Constraints and War," *Journal of Conflict Resolution* 35 (June): 187–211.

MORGAN, T. CLIFTON, AND VALERIE L. SCHWEBACH. (1992) "Take Two Democracies and Call Me in the Morning: A Prescription for Peace?" *International Interactions* 17 (No. 4): 305–320.

MORGENTHAU, HANS J. (1985) *Politics Among Nations*, 6th ed. Revised by Kenneth W. Thompson. New York: Knopf.

———. (1983) "Defining the National Interest—Again," pp. 32–39 in Charles W. Kegley, Jr., and Eugene R. Wittkopf (eds.), *Perspectives on American Foreign Policy*. New York: St. Martin's Press.

———. (1969) "Historical Justice and the Cold War," *New York Review of Books* 16 (July 10): 10–17.

———. (1959) "Alliances in Theory and Practice," pp. 184–212 in Arnold Wolfers (ed.), *Alliance Policy in the Cold War*. Baltimore: The Johns Hopkins University Press.

———. (1948) *Politics Among Nations*. New York: Knopf.

MORRIS, DESMOND. (1969) *The Human Zoo*. New York: Dell.

MORSE, EDWARD L. (1990–1991) "The Coming Oil Revolution," *Foreign Affairs* 69 (Winter): 36–56.

———. (1986) "After the Fall: The Politics of Oil," *Foreign Affairs* 64 (Spring): 792–811.

———. (1976) *Modernization and the Transformation of International Relations*. New York: Free Press.

MORSE, RONALD D. (1991–1992) "Japan: Crafting an Energy Strategy for Competitiveness in the World Market," *Harvard International Review* 14 (Winter): 14–16.

MOSER, PAUL K. (ed.) (1990) *Rationality in Action: Contemporary Approaches*. New York: Cambridge University Press.

MOSSAVAR-RAHMANI, BIJAN. (1983) "The OPEC Multiplier," *Foreign Policy* 52 (Fall): 136–148.

MOWLANA, HAMID. (1983) "Needed: A New World Information Order," *USA Today* 112 (September): 42–44.

MOYNIHAN, DANIEL PATRICK. (1975) "The United States in Opposition," *Commentary* 59 (March): 31–44.

MOYNIHAN, DANIEL P., WITH SUZANNE WEAVER. (1978) *A Dangerous Place*. Boston: Little, Brown.

MUELLER, JOHN. (1992) "The Obsolescence of Major War," pp. 41–50 in Charles W. Kegley, Jr., and Eugene R. Wittkopf (eds.), *The Global Agenda*, 3rd ed. New York: McGraw Hill.

———. (1991) "Deterrence, Nuclear Weapons, Morality, and War," pp. 69–97 in Charles W. Kegley, Jr., and Kenneth L. Schwab (eds.), *After the Cold War: Questioning the Morality of Nuclear Deterrence*. Boulder, Colo.: Westview.

———. (1990) "A New Concert of Europe," *Foreign Policy* 77 (Winter): 3–16.

———. (1989) *Retreat from Doomsday: The Obsolescence of Major War*. New York: Basic Books.

MÜLLER, RONALD. (1973–1974) "Poverty Is the Product," *Foreign Policy* 13 (Winter): 71–103.

MUNASINGHE, HOHAN. (1991–1992) "Energy Policies for Sustainable Growth in Developing Countries," *Harvard International Review* 14 (Winter): 25–28, 63.

MURPHY, CARLYE. (1990) "The Rich Get Richer and the Poor Get Resentful," *Washington Post National Weekly Edition*, November 19–25, p. 18.

MURPHY, CRAIG N. (1983) "What the Third World Wants: An Interpretation of the Development and Meaning of the New International Economic Order Ideology," *International Studies Quarterly* 27 (March): 55–76.

NARDIN, TERRY. (1983) *Law, Morality, and the Relations of States*. Princeton, N.J.: Princeton University Press.

NAU, HENRY R. (1990) *The Myth of America's Decline*. New York: Oxford University Press.

NELSON, STEPHAN D. (1974) "Nature/Nurture Revisited: A Review of the Biological Bases of Conflict," *Journal of Conflict Resolution* 18 (June): 285–335.

The New Population Debate: Two Views on Population Growth and Economic Development. (1985) Washington, D.C.: Population Reference Bureau.

NIEBUHR, REINHOLD. (1947). *Moral Man and Immoral Society*. New York: Scribner's.

NIETSCHMANN, BERNARD. (1991) "Third World War: The Global Conflict Over the Rights of Indigenous Nations," pp. 172–176 in Robert M. Jackson (ed.), *Global Issues 91/92*. Guilford, Conn.: Dushkin.

NINCIC, MIROSLAV. (1989) *Anatomy of Hostility: The U.S.-Soviet Rivalry in Perspective*. Chicago: Harcourt Brace Jovanovich.

———. (1982) *The Arms Race: The Political Economy of Military Growth.* New York: Praeger.

NITZE, PAUL. (1991) "After Iraq, Nukes Can Be Junked," *Wall Street Journal*, December 24, p. A6.

NOGEE, JOSEPH L. (1975) "Polarity: An Ambiguous Concept," *Orbis* 28 (Winter): 1193–1224.

NOLAN, JEANNE E., AND ALBERT D. WHEELON. (1990) "Third World Ballistic Missiles," *Scientific American* 263 (August): 16–27.

NORMAN, COLIN. (1979) *Knowledge and Power: The Global Research and Development Budget.* Worldwatch Paper No. 31. Washington, D.C. Worldwatch Institute.

NOWZAD, BAHRAM. (1990) "Lessons of the Debt Decade," *Finance and Development* 27 (March): 9–13.

NYE, JOSEPH S., JR. (1990) *Bound to Lead: The Changing Nature of American Power.* New York: Basic Books.

———. (1989–1990) "Arms Control After the Cold War," *Foreign Affairs* 68 (Winter): 42–64.

———. (1987) "Nuclear Learning and U.S.-Soviet Security Regimes," *International Organization* 41 (Summer): 371–402.

———. (1971) *Peace in Parts.* Boston: Little, Brown.

NYE, JOSEPH S., JR., AND ROBERT O. KEOHANE. (1971) "Transnational Relations and World Politics: An Introduction," *International Organization* 25 (Summer): 329–349.

OBERDORFER, DON. (1991) *The Turn: From the Cold War to a New Era.* New York: Poseidon.

O'BRIEN, CONOR CRUISE. (1977) "Liberty and Terrorism," *International Security* 2 (Fall): 56–67.

O'BRIEN, PATRICK M. (1988) "Agricultural Productivity and the Global Food Market," pp. 394–408 in Charles W. Kegley, Jr., and Eugene R. Wittkopf (eds.), *The Global Agenda*, 2nd ed. New York: Random House.

OLSON, MANCUR. (1982) *The Rise and Decline of Nations.* New Haven, Conn.: Yale University Press.

———. (1971) "Rapid Growth As a Destabilizing Force," pp. 215–227 in James C. Davies (ed.), *When Men Revolt and Why.* New York: Free Press.

ONUF, NICHOLAS GREENWOOD. (1989) *World of Our Making.* Columbia, S.C.: University of South Carolina Press.

———. (1982) "Global Law-Making and Legal Thought," pp. 1–82 in Nicholas Greenwood Onuf (ed.), *Law-Making in the Global Community.* Durham, N.C.: Carolina Academic Press.

OREN, NISSAN. (ed.) (1984) *When Patterns Change: Turning Points in International Politics.* New York: St. Martin's Press.

ORGANSKI, A. F. K. (1968). *World Politics.* New York: Knopf.

ORGANSKI, A. F. K., AND JACEK KUGLER. (1980) *The War Ledger.* Chicago: University of Chicago Press.

OSGOOD, ROBERT E. (1968) *Alliances and American Foreign Policy.* Baltimore: Johns Hopkins University Press.

OSTROM, CHARLES W., JR., AND JOHN H. ALDRICH. (1978) "The Relationship Between Size and Stability in the Major Power International System," *American Journal of Political Science* 22 (November): 743–771.

OSTROM, CHARLES W., AND BRIAN L. JOB. (1986) "The President and the Use of Force," *American Political Science Review* 80 (June): 554–566.

OVERSEAS DEVELOPMENT COUNCIL. (1991) "The Gulf Crisis: Impact on Developing Countries," *Policy Focus*, No. 6. Washington, D.C.: Overseas Development Council.

OWEN, OLIVER S. (1989) "The Heat Is On: The Greenhouse Effect and the Earth's Future," *Futurist* 23 (September–October): 34–40.

PAARLBERG, ROBERT L. (1980) "Lessons of the Grain Embargo," *Foreign Affairs* 59 (Fall): 144–162.

PAPP, DANIEL S. (1986) *Soviet Policies Toward the Developing World During the 1980s.* Maxwell Air Force Base, Ala.: Air University Press.

PARENTI, MICHAEL. (1969) *The Anti-Communist Impulse.* New York: Random House.

PARRY, CLIVE. (1968) "The Function of Law in the International Community," pp. 1–54 in Max Sørensen (ed.), *Manual of Public International Law.* New York: St. Martin's Press.

PEARLSTEIN, STEVEN. (1991) "A Wholesale Change in the Arms Bazaar," *Washington Post National Weekly Edition*, April 15–21, pp. 8–9.

PEARSON, FREDERIC S., ROBERT A. BAUMANN, AND JEFFREY J. PICKERING. (1991) "International Military Intervention: Global and Regional Redefinitions of Realpolitik." Paper presented at the Annual Meeting of the American Political Science Association, Washington, D.C., August 29–September 1.

PELZ, STEPHEN. (1991) "Changing International Systems, the World Balance of Power, and the United States, 1776–1976," *Diplomatic History* 15 (Winter): 47–81.

PERLE, RICHARD. (1991) "Military Power and the Passing Cold War," pp. 33–38 in Charles W. Kegley, Jr., and Kenneth L. Schwab (eds.), *After the Cold War: Questioning the Morality of Nuclear Deterrence.* Boulder, Colo.: Westview.

PHILIPS, ROSEMARIE, AND STUART K. TUCKER. (1991) *U.S. Foreign Policy and Developing Countries: Discourse and Data 1991.* Washington, D.C.: Overseas Development Council.

PIERRE, ANDREW J. (1984) "The Politics of International Terrorism," pp. 84–92 in Charles W. Kegley, Jr., and Eugene R. Wittkopf (eds.), *The Global Agenda*. New York: Random House.

PIPES, RICHARD. (1977) "Why the Soviet Union Thinks It Could Fight and Win a Nuclear War," *Commentary* 26 (July): 21–34.

PIRAGES, DENNIS. (1986) "World Energy Crisis 1995," *Futures Research Quarterly* 2 (Fall): 31–47.

———. (1978). *The New Context for International Relations: Global Ecopolitics*. North Scituate, Mass.: Duxbury Press.

Population in Perspective. (1986) Washington, D.C.: Population Reference Bureau.

POPULATION REFERENCE BUREAU. (1981) *World Population: Toward the Next Century*. Washington, D.C.: Population Reference Bureau.

POTTER, WILLIAM C. (1992) "The New Nuclear Suppliers," *Orbis* 6 (Spring): 199–210.

POTTS, MARK. (1991) "Going Hunting for the Biggest Game in Town," *Washington Post National Weekly Edition*, February 18–24, pp. 18–19.

POURGERAMI, ABBAS. (1991) *Development and Democracy in the Third World*. Boulder, Colo.: Westview.

PREEG, ERNEST H. (1989) "The GATT Trading System in Transition: An Analytic Survey of Recent Literature," *Washington Quarterly* 12 (Autumn): 201–213.

PUCHALA, DONALD J. (1988) "The Integration Theorists and the Study of International Relations," pp. 198–265 in Charles W. Kegley, Jr., and Eugene R. Wittkopf (eds.), *The Global Agenda*, 2nd ed. New York: Random House.

———. (ed.) (1983) *Issues Before the 38th General Assembly of the United Nations, 1983 and 1984*. New York: United Nations Association of the United States of America.

———. (1982–1983) "American Interests and the United Nations," *Political Science Quarterly* 97 (Winter): 571–588.

PUCHALA, DONALD T., AND ROGER A. COATE. (1989) *The Challenge of Relevance: The United Nations in a Changing Environment*. Hanover, N.H.: The Academic Council of the United Nations System.

PUTNAM, ROBERT. (1988) "Diplomacy and Domestic Politics: The Logic of Two-Level Games," *International Organization* 42 (Summer): 427–460.

QUANDT, WILLIAM B. (1991) "The Middle East in 1990," *Foreign Affairs* 70 (No. 1): 49–69.

RAPHAEL, THERESE. (1991) "The Yeltsin Military Strategy," *Wall Street Journal*, August 30, p. A6.

RAPKIN, DAVID P. (ed.) (1990) *World Leadership and Hegemony*. Boulder, Colo.: Lynne Rienner.

RAPKIN, DAVID, AND WILLIAM THOMPSON, WITH JON A. CHRISTOPHERSON. (1989) "Bipolarity and Bipolarization in the Cold War Era," *Journal of Conflict Resolution* 23 (June): 261–295.

RASPBERRY, WILLIAM. (1992) "Seeing Past the Children," *Washington Post*, January 1, p. A31.

RAVENHILL, JOHN. (1984). "What Is to Be Done for Third World Commodity Exporters? An Evaluation of the STABEX Scheme," *International Organization* 38 (Summer): 537–574.

REICH, ROBERT B. (1990) "Who Is Us?" *Harvard Business Review* 68 (January–February): 53–64.

———. (1983) "Why Democracy Makes Economic Sense," *New Republic*, December 19, pp. 25–32.

RENNER, MICHAEL. (1991) "Assessing the Military's War on the Environment," pp. 132–152 in Lester R. Brown, Christopher Flavin, Sandra Postel, Linda Starke, Alan Durning, Hilary F. French, Jodi Jacobson, Marcia D. Lowe, Michael Renner, Nicholas Lenssen, John C. Ryan, and John E. Young, *State of the World 1991*. New York: Norton.

———. (1990a) "Ending Poverty," pp. 135–153 in Lester R. Brown, Christopher Flavin, Sandra Postel, Linda Starke, Alan Durning, Jodi Jacobson, Michael Renner, Hilary F. French, Marcia D. Lowe, and John E. Young, *State of the World 1990*. New York: Norton.

———. (1990b) *Swords Into Plowshares: Converting to a Peace Economy*. Worldwatch Paper No. 96. Washington, D.C.: Worldwatch Institute.

———. (1989) "Forging Environmental Alliances," *World Watch* 2 (November–December): 8–15.

———. (1987) "Shaping America's Energy Future," *World Policy Journal* 4 (Summer): 383–414.

REPETTO, ROBERT. (1987) "Population, Resources, Environment: An Uncertain Future," *Population Bulletin* 42 (No. 2). Washington, D.C.: Population Reference Bureau.

REUTLINGER, SHLOMO. (1985) "Food Security and Poverty in LDCs," *Finance and Development* 22 (December): 7–11.

RHODES, EDWARD. (1988) "Nuclear Weapons and Credibility: Deterrence Theory Beyond Rationality," *Review of International Studies* 14 (January): 45–62.

RICHARDSON, LEWIS F. (1960a) *Arms and Insecurity*. Pittsburgh: Boxwood Press.

———. (1960b) *Statistics of Deadly Quarrels*. Chicago: Quadrangle.

RICHBURG, KEITH B. (1990) "Going from Famine to Feast—Literally," *Washington Post National Weekly Edition*, May 21–27, p. 18.

RIGGS, ROBERT E. (1977) "One Small Step for Functionalism: UN Participation and Congressional Attitude Change," *International Organization* 31 (Summer): 515–539.

RIGGS, ROBERT E., AND JACK C. PLANO. (1988) *The United Nations: International Organization and World Politics*. Chicago: Dorsey Press.

RIKER, WILLIAM H. (1962) *The Theory of Political Coalitions*. New Haven, Conn.: Yale University Press.

RIKHYE, INDAR JIT. (1989) *The Future of Peacekeeping*. New York: International Peace Academy.

RISSE-KAPPEN, THOMAS. (1991) "Public Opinion, Domestic Structure, and Foreign Policy in Liberal Democracies," *World Politics* 43 (July): 479–512.

ROCA, SERGIO. (1987) "Economic Sanctions Against Cuba," pp. 87–104 in David Leyton-Brown (ed.), *The Utility of International Economic Sanctions*. New York: St. Martin's Press.

ROSECRANCE, RICHARD. (1992) "A New Concert of Powers," *Foreign Affairs* 71 (Spring): 64–82.

———. (1990) *America's Economic Resurgence: A Bold New Strategy*. New York: Harper & Row.

———. (1986) *The Rise of the Trading State: Commerce and Conquest in the Modern World*. New York: Basic Books.

———. (1963) *Action and Reaction in World Politics*. Boston: Little, Brown.

ROSEN, STEVEN J. (ed.) (1973) *Testing the Theory of the Military-Industrial Complex*. Lexington, Mass.: Heath.

ROSENAU, JAMES N. (1990) *Turbulence in World Politics: A Theory of Change and Continuity*. Princeton, N.J.: Princeton University Press.

———. (1980) *The Scientific Study of Foreign Policy*. New York: Nichols.

ROSENAU, PAULINE MARIE. (1992) *Post-Modernism and the Social Sciences*. Princeton, N.J.: Princeton University Press.

ROSENTHAL, JOEL H. (1991) *Righteous Realists*. Baton Rouge: Louisiana State University Press.

ROSTOW, W. W. (1960) *The Stages of Economic Growth*. Cambridge, England: Cambridge University Press.

ROTHSTEIN, RICHARD. (1988) "Give Them a Break: Third World Debtors and a Cure for Reaganomics," *New Republic*, February 1, pp. 20–24.

ROTHSTEIN, ROBERT L. (1988) "Epitaph for a Monument to a Failed Protest? A North-South Retrospective," *International Organization* 42 (Autumn): 725–748.

———. (1979) *Global Bargaining: UNCTAD and the Quest for a New International Economic Order*. Princeton, N.J.: Princeton University Press.

ROURKE, JOHN T. (1991) *International Politics on the World Stage*, 3rd ed. Guilford, Conn.: Dushkin.

RUGGIE, JOHN GERARD. (1985) "The United States and the United Nations: Toward a New Realism," *International Organization* 39 (Spring): 343–356.

———. (1983) "Continuity and Transformation in the World Polity: Toward a Neorealist Synthesis," *World Politics* 35 (January): 261–285.

RUMMEL, RUDOLPH. (1983) "Libertarianism and International Violence," *Journal of Conflict Resolution* 27 (March): 27–71.

RUSSETT, BRUCE M. (1990) *Controlling the Sword: The Democratic Governance of National Security*. Cambridge, Mass.: Harvard University Press.

———. (1989) "Economic Decline, Electoral Pressure, and the Initiation of Interstate Conflict," pp. 123–140 in Charles Gochman and Allen Ned Sabrosky (eds.), *Prisoners of War? Nation-States in the Modern Era*. Lexington, Mass.: D. C. Heath.

———. (1984) "Dimensions of Resource Dependence: Some Elements of Rigor in Concept and Policy Analysis," *International Organization* 38 (Summer): 481–499.

———. (1982) "Defense Expenditures and National Well-Being," *American Political Science Review* 76 (December): 767–777.

RUSSETT, BRUCE, AND HARVEY STARR. (1989) *World Politics: The Menu for Choice*, 3rd ed. New York: W. H. Freeman and Company.

RUSSETT, BRUCE, AND JAMES S. SUTTERLIN. (1991) "The U.N. in a New World Order," *Foreign Affairs* 70 (Spring): 69–83.

RYAN, STEPHEN. (1990) *Ethnic Conflict and International Relations*. Brookfield, Vt.: Gower.

SACHS, JEFFREY. (1989) "Making the Brady Plan Work," *Foreign Affairs* 68 (Summer): 87–104.

SAGAN, CARL. (1988) "The Common Enemy," *Parade*, February 7, pp. 4–7.

SAGAN, CARL, AND RICHARD TURCO. (1990) *A Path Where No Man Thought: Nuclear Winter and the End of the Arms Race*. New York: Random House.

SAND, PETER H. (1991) "International Cooperation: The Environmental Experience," pp. 236–279 in Jessica Tuchman Mathews (ed.), *Preserving the Global Environment*. New York: Norton.

SANDERSON, STEVEN E. (ed.) (1984) *The Americas in the New International Division of Labor*. New York: Holmes & Meier.

SAPERSTEIN, ALVIN M. (1991) "The 'Long Peace'—Result of a Bipolar Competitive World?" *The Journal of Conflict Resolution* 35 (March): 68–79.

SCARBOROUGH, GRACE E. IUSI, AND BRUCE BUENO DE MESQUITA. (1988) "Threat and Alignment," *International Interactions* 14 (No. 1): 85–93.

SCHECHTER, MICHAEL G. (1979) "The Common Fund: A Test Case for the New International Economic Order." Paper presented at the Annual Meeting of the International Studies Association/South, Athens, Ga., October 4–6.

SCHELL, JONATHAN. (1984) *The Abolition*. New York: Knopf.

SCHELLING, THOMAS C. (1978) *Micromotives and Macrobehavior*. New York: Norton.

———. (1966) *Arms and Influence*. New Haven, Conn.: Yale University Press.

SCHLAGHECK, DONNA M. (1990) "The Superpowers, Foreign Policy, and Terrorism," pp. 170–177 in Charles W. Kegley, Jr. (ed.), *International Terrorism: Characteristics, Causes, Controls*. New York: St. Martin's Press.

SCHLESINGER, ARTHUR, JR. (1986) *The Cycles of American History*. Boston: Houghton Mifflin.

———. (1983) "Pretension in the Presidential Pulpit," *Wall Street Journal*, March 17, p. 26.

———. (1967). "Origins of the Cold War," *Foreign Affairs* 46 (October): 22–52.

SCHNEIDER, STEPHEN H. (1989) "The Changing Climate," *Scientific American* 261 (September): 70–79.

SCHOETTLE, ENID C. B. (1992) "U.N. Dues: The Price of Peace," *The Bulletin of the Atomic Scientists* 48 (June): 14–16.

SCHREIBER, ANNA P. (1973) "Economic Coercion As an Instrument of Foreign Policy: U.S. Economic Measures Against Cuba and the Dominican Republic," *World Politics* 25 (April): 387–413.

SCHROEDER, GERTRUDE E. (1991) "A Critical Time for Perestroika," *Current History* 90 (October): 323–327.

SCHWELLER, RANDALL. L. (1992) "Domestic Structure and Preventive War," *World Politics* 44 (January): 235–269.

SEBENIUS, JAMES K. (1991) "Designing Negotiations Toward a New Regime: The Case of Global Warming," *International Security* 15 (Spring): 110–148.

SEWELL, JOHN W. (1992) "The Metamorphosis of the Third World: U.S. Interests in the 1990s," pp. 222–238 in Charles W. Kegley, Jr., and Eugene R. Wittkopf (eds.), *The Future of American Foreign Policy*. New York: St. Martin's Press.

———. (1991) "Foreign Aid for a New World Order," *Washington Quarterly* 14 (Summer): 35–45.

SEWELL, JOHN W., AND CHRISTINE E. CONTEE. (1987) "Foreign Aid and Gramm-Rudman," *Foreign Affairs* 65 (Summer): 1015–1036.

SHANNON, THOMAS RICHARD. (1989) *An Introduction to the World-System Perspective*. Boulder, Colo.: Westview.

SHAW, R. PAUL, AND YUWA WONG. (1989). *Genetic Seeds of Warfare: Evolution, Nationalism and Patriotism*. Boston: Unwin Hyman.

SHEPHERD, GEORGE W., JR. (ed.) (1991) *Effective Sanctions on South Africa*. New York: Praeger.

SHERRY, MICHAEL. (1977). *Preparing for the Next War*. New Haven, Conn.: Yale University Press.

SHEVARDNADZE, EDUARD. (1991) *The Future Belongs to Freedom*. New York: Free Press.

SHIVA, VANDANA. (1991) "The Green Revolution in the Punjab," *Ecologist* 21 (March/April): 57–60.

SHONFIELD, ANDREW. (1980) "The World Economy 1979," *Foreign Affairs* 58 (No. 3): 596–621.

SHULMAN, MARSHALL D. (ed.) (1986) *East-West Tensions in the Third World*. New York: Norton.

SIEGEL, MARTIN J. (1983) "Survival," *USA Today* 112 (August): 1–2.

SIMMEL, GEORG. (1956) *Conflict*. Glencoe, Ill.: Free Press.

SIMON, HERBERT A. (1985) "Human Nature in Politics: The Dialogue of Psychology with Political Science," *American Political Science Review* 79 (June): 293–304.

———. (1957) *Models of Man*. New York: Wiley.

SIMON, JULIAN L. (1981) *The Ultimate Resource*. Princeton, N.J.: Princeton University Press.

SIMON, JULIAN L., AND HERMAN KAHN. (eds.) (1984) *The Resourceful Earth: A Response to Global 2000*. Oxford, England: Blackwell.

SIMOWITZ, ROSLYN. (1982) *The Logical Consistency and Soundness of the Balance of Power Theory*. Denver: Graduate School of International Studies, University of Denver.

SINGER, HANS W., AND JAVED A. ANSARI. (1988) *Rich and Poor Countries*, 4th ed. London: Unwin Hyman.

SINGER, J. DAVID. (1991) "Peace in the Global System: Displacement, Interregnum, or Transformation?" pp. 56–84 in Charles W. Kegley, Jr. (ed.), *The Long Postwar Peace*. New York: HarperCollins.

———. (1981) "Accounting for International War: The State of the Discipline," *Journal of Peace Research* 18 (No. 1): 1–18.

———. (ed.) (1968) *Quantitative International Politics*. New York: Free Press.

———. (1961) "The Level-of-Analysis Problem in International Relations," pp. 77–92 in Klaus Knorr and Sidney Verba (eds.), *The International System*. Princeton, N.J.: Princeton University Press.

————. (1960) "Theorizing About Theory in International Politics," *Journal of Conflict Resolution* 4 (December): 431–442.

SINGER, J. DAVID, AND MELVIN SMALL. (1974) "Foreign Policy Indicators: Predictors of War in History and in the State of the World Message," *Policy Sciences* 5 (September): 271–296.

————. (1968). "Alliance Aggregation and the Onset of War, 1815–1945," pp. 247–285 in J. David Singer (ed.), *Quantitative International Politics*. New York: Free Press.

SIVARD, RUTH LEGER. (1991) *World Military and Social Expenditures 1991*. Washington, D.C.: World Priorities.

————. (1982) *World Military and Social Expenditures 1982*. Leesburg, Va.: World Priorities.

————. (1981) *World Energy Survey*. Leesburg, Va.: World Priorities.

————. (1979a) *World Energy Survey*. Leesburg, Va.: World Priorities.

————. (1979b) *World Military and Social Expenditures 1979*. Leesburg, Va.: World Priorities.

SIVERSON, RANDOLPH M., AND JULIAN EMMONS. (1991) "Democratic Political Systems and Alliance Choices," *Journal of Conflict Resolution* 35 (June): 285–306.

SKJELSBAEK, KJELL. (1991) "The U.N. Secretary-General and the Mediation of International Disputes," *Journal of Peace Research* 28 (February): 99–115.

————. (1989) "United Nations Peacekeeping and the Facilitation of Withdrawals," *Bulletin of Peace Proposals* 20 (September): 253–264.

SKLAIR, LESLIE. (1991) *Sociology of the Global System*. Baltimore: Johns Hopkins University Press.

SKOLNIKOFF, EUGENE R. (1990) "The Policy Gridlock on Global Warming," *Foreign Policy* 79 (Summer): 77–93.

SLATER, JEROME, AND DAVID GOLDFISCHER. (1988) "Can SDI Provide a Defense?" pp. 74–86 in Charles W. Kegley, Jr., and Eugene R. Wittkopf (eds.), *The Global Agenda*, 2nd ed. New York: Random House.

SMALL, MELVIN, AND J. DAVID SINGER. (1982) *Resort to Arms: International and Civil Wars, 1816–1980*. Beverly Hills, Calif.: Sage.

————. (1979) "Conflict in the International System, 1816–1977: Historical Trends and Policy Futures," pp. 89–115 in Charles W. Kegley, Jr., and Patrick J. McGowan (eds.), *Challenges to America*. Beverly Hills, Calif.: Sage.

————. (1976) "The War-Proneness of Democratic Regimes, 1816–1965," *Jerusalem Journal of International Relations* 1 (March): 50–69.

————. (1972). "Patterns in International Warfare, 1816–1965," pp. 121–131 in James F. Short, Jr., and Marvin E. Wolfgang (eds.), *Collective Violence*. Chicago: Aldine-Atherton.

SMART, IAN. (1976) "Uniqueness and Generality," pp. 259–281 in Raymond Vernon (ed.), *The Oil Crisis*. New York: Norton.

SMELSER, NEIL J. (1986) "External and Internal Factors in Theories of Social Change." Paper presented to the German-American Conference on Social Change and Modernization. Berkeley, Calif., August 26–28.

SMITH, MICHAEL JOSEPH. (1986) *Realist Thought from Weber to Kissinger*. Baton Rouge: Louisiana State University Press.

SMITH, ROGER K. (1987) "Explaining the Non-Proliferation Regime: Anomalies for Contemporary International Relations Theory," *International Organization* 41 (Spring): 251–281.

SMITH, RON P., AND GEORGE GEORGIOU. (1983) "Assessing the Effect of Military Expenditures on OECD Economies: A Survey," *Arms Control* 4 (May): 3–15.

SMITH, STEVE, AND MICHAEL CLARKE. (1985) *Foreign Policy Implementation*. London: Allen & Unwin.

SMITH, TONY. (1981) "The Logic of Dependency Theory Revisited," *International Organization* 35 (Autumn): 755–776.

————. (1979) "The Underdevelopment of Development Literature: The Case of Dependency Theory," *World Politics* 31 (January): 247–288.

SNIDAL, DUNCAN. (1991a) "International Cooperation Among Relative Gains Maximizers," *International Studies Quarterly* 35 (December): 387–402.

————. (1991b) "Relative Gains and the Pattern of International Cooperation," *American Political Science Review* 85 (September): 701–726.

————. (1985). "The Limits of Hegemonic Stability Theory," *International Organization* 49 (Autumn): 579–614.

SNIDER, LEWIS W. (1991) "Guns, Debt, and Politics: New Variations on an Old Theme," *Armed Forces and Society* 17 (Winter): 167–190.

SNOW, DONALD M. (1991) *The Shape of the Future*. Armonk, N.Y.: M. E. Sharpe.

SNYDER, GLENN H. (1991) "Alliance Threats: A Neorealist First Cut," pp. 83–103 in Robert L. Rothstein (ed.), *The Evolution of Theory in International Relations*. Columbia: University of South Carolina Press.

————. (1984) "The Security Dilemma in Alliance Politics," *World Politics* 36 (July): 461–495.

SNYDER, GLENN H., AND PAUL DIESING. (1977) *Conflict Among Nations: Bargaining, Decision-Making, and System Structure in International Crisis*. Princeton, N.J.: Princeton University Press.

SOMIT, ALBERT. (1990) "Humans, Chimps, and Bonobos: The Biological Bases of Aggression, War, and Peacemaking," *Journal of Conflict Resolution* 34 (September): 553–582.

SORENSEN, THEODORE C. (1990) "Rethinking National Security," *Foreign Affairs* 69 (Summer): 1–18.

———. (1963) *Decision Making in the White House*. New York: Columbia University Press.

SOROKIN, PITIRIM A. (1937) *Social and Cultural Dynamics*. New York: American Book.

SOROOS, MARVIN S. (1992) "The Tragedy of the Commons in Global Perspective," pp. 388–401 in Charles W. Kegley, Jr., and Eugene R. Wittkopf (eds.), *The Global Agenda*, 3rd ed. New York: McGraw-Hill.

———. (1986) *Beyond Sovereignty: The Challenge of Global Policy*. Columbia: University of South Carolina Press.

SPANIER, JOHN. (1975) *Games Nations Play*, 2nd ed. New York: Praeger.

SPECTOR, LEONARD S., AND JACQUELINE R. SMITH. (1992) *Nuclear Threshold: The Spread of Nuclear Weapons 1990–1991*. Boulder, Colo.: Westview.

SPERO, JOAN EDELMAN. (1990) *The Politics of International Economic Relations*, 4th ed. New York: St. Martin's Press.

SPIEGEL, STEVEN L. (1985) *The Other Arab-Israeli Conflict*. Chicago: University of Chicago Press.

SPIVACK, NEAL, AND ANN FLORINI. (1986) *Food on the Table: Seeking Global Solutions to Chronic Hunger*. New York: United Nations Association of the United States of America.

SPROUT, HAROLD, AND MARGARET SPROUT. (1971) *Toward a Politics of the Planet Earth*. New York: Van Nostrand.

SPYKMAN, NICHOLAS. (1944) *Geography of Peace*. New York: Harcourt Brace.

STERN, ERNEST, AND WOUTER TIMS. (1976) "The Relative Bargaining Strength of the Developing Countries," pp. 6–50 in Ronald G. Ridker (ed.), *Changing Resource Problems of the Fourth World*. Washington, D.C.: Resources for the Future.

STERNER, MICHAEL. (1990–1991) "Navigating the Gulf," *Foreign Policy* 81 (Winter): 39–52.

STETSON, MARNIE. (1991) "People Who Live in Green Houses . . . ," *World Watch* 4 (September–October): 22–29.

STEWART, MICHAEL. (1984) *The Age of Interdependence: Economic Policy in a Shrinking World*. Cambridge, Mass.: MIT Press.

STOBAUGH, ROBERT. (1982) "World Energy to the Year 2000," pp. 29–57 in Daniel Yergin and Martin Hillenbrand (eds.), *Global Insecurity*. New York: Penguin.

STOBAUGH, ROBERT, AND DANIEL YERGIN. (1979) "After the Second Shock: Pragmatic Energy Strategies," *Foreign Affairs* 57 (Spring): 836–871.

STOESSINGER, JOHN G. (1977) *The United Nations and the Superpowers: China, Russia, and America*. New York: Random House.

STRANG, DAVID. (1991) "Global Patterns of Decolonization, 1500–1987," *International Studies Quarterly* 35 (December): 429–545.

———. (1990) "From Dependence to Sovereignty: An Event History Analysis of Decolonization 1870–1987," *American Sociological Review* 55 (December): 846–860.

STRANGE, SUSAN. (1985) "Protectionism and World Politics," *International Organization* 39 (Spring): 233–259.

———. (1982) "*Cave! Hic Dragones*: A Critique of Regime Analysis," *International Organization* 36 (Spring): 479–496.

SUMNER, WILLIAM GRAHAM. (1968) "War," pp. 205–228 in Leon Bramson and George W. Goethals (eds.), *War*. New York: Basic Books.

TALBOTT, STROBE. (1990) "Rethinking the Red Menace," *Time*, January 1, pp. 66–72.

TANTER, RAYMOND, AND RICHARD ULLMAN. (eds.) (1972) *Theory and Policy in International Relations*. Princeton, N.J.: Princeton University Press.

TAPLIN, GRANT B. (1992) "Revitalizing UNCTAD," *Finance and Development* 29 (June): 37–38.

TARR, DAVID W. (1991) *Nuclear Deterrence and International Security: Alternative Security Regimes*. New York: Longman.

TAYLOR, PHILLIP. (1984) *Nonstate Actors in International Politics*. Boulder, Colo.: Westview.

THOMPSON, WILLIAM R. (1988) *On Global War: Historical-Structural Approaches to World Politics*. Columbia, S.C.: University of South Carolina Press.

THUROW, LESTER C. (1992) *Head to Head: Coming Economic Battles Among Japan, Europe, and America*. New York: William Morrow.

———. (1985) "America, Europe, and Japan: A Time to Dismantle the World Economy," *The Economist* 297 (November 9): 21–26.

TILLEMA, HERBERT K. (1991) *International Armed Conflict Since 1945: A Bibliographic Handbook of Wars and Military Interventions*. Boulder, Colo.: Westview.

——. (1989) "Foreign Overt Military Intervention in the Nuclear Age," *Journal of Peace Research* 26 (May): 179–195.

TILLEMA, HERBERT K., AND JOHN R. VAN WINGEN. (1982) "Law and Power in Military Intervention: Major States After World War II," *International Studies Quarterly* 26 (June): 220–250.

TIMMERMAN, KENNETH. (1991) *The Death Lobby: How the West Armed Iraq.* Boston: Houghton Mifflin.

TODARO, MICHAEL P. (1989) *Economic Development in the Third World*, 4th ed. New York: Longman.

TONELSON, ALAN. (1991) "What Is the National Interest?" *Atlantic Monthly* 268 (July): 35–52.

TOPPING, JOHN C., JR. (1990) "Global Warming: Impact on Developing Countries," *Policy Focus*, No. 6. Washington, D.C.: Overseas Development Council.

TOWNSEND, JOYCE CAROL. (1982) *Bureaucratic Politics in American Decision Making.* Washington, D.C.: University Press of America.

TOYNBEE, ARNOLD J. (1954) *A Study of History.* London: Oxford University Press.

TRACHTENBERG, MARC. (1990–1991) "The Meaning of Mobilization in 1914," *International Security* 15 (Winter): 120–150.

TRIFFIN, ROBERT. (1978–1979) "The International Role and Fate of the Dollar," *Foreign Affairs* 57 (Winter): 269–286.

TUCHMAN, BARBARA. (1962) *The Guns of August.* New York: Dell.

TUCKER, ROBERT W. (1990) "1989 and All That," *Foreign Affairs* 69 (Fall): 93–114.

——. (1980) "America in Decline: The Foreign Policy of 'Maturity'," *Foreign Affairs* 58 (No. 3): 449–484.

TUNANDER, OLA. (1991) "Bush's Brave New World: A New World Order—A New Military Strategy," *Bulletin of Peace Proposals* 22 (December): 355–368.

TURNER, ROBERT F. (1990) "What's Wrong with Killing Saddam Hussein?," *Washington Post National Weekly Edition*, October 15–21, p. 24.

TYLER, PATRICK E. (1992) "Pentagon Drops Goal of Blocking New Superpowers," *New York Times*, May 24, pp. 1, 14.

UNITED NATIONS. (1991a) *World Economic Survey 1991.* New York: United Nations.

——. (1991b) *The World's Women 1970–1990: Trends and Statistics.* New York: United Nations.

UNITED NATIONS CONFERENCE ON TRADE AND DEVELOPMENT. (1991) *The Least Developed Countries: A Statistical Profile—1990.* New York: United Nations.

UNITED NATIONS FUND FOR POPULATION ACTIVITIES. (1991) *State of World Population 1991.* New York: United Nations Fund for Population Activities.

U.S. ARMS CONTROL AND DISARMAMENT AGENCY. (1992) *World Military Expenditures and Arms Transfers, 1990.* Washington, D.C.: U.S. Government Printing Office.

——. (1990) *World Military Expenditures and Arms Transfers, 1989.* Washington, D.C.: U.S. Government Printing Office.

——. (1989) *World Military Expenditures and Arms Transfers 1988.* Washington, D.C.: U.S. Government Printing Office.

——. (1979) *Arms Control 1978.* Washington, D.C.: U.S. Government Printing Office.

U.S. CENTRAL INTELLIGENCE AGENCY. (1988) *Handbook of Economic Statistics.* Washington, D.C.: U.S. Government Printing Office.

——. (1977) *The International Energy Situation: Outlook to 1985.* Washington, D.C.: U.S. Central Intelligence Agency.

U.S. DEPARTMENT OF ENERGY. (1987a) Energy Information Administration. *Monthly Energy Review* (October).

——. (1987b) *Energy Security.* Washington, D.C.: U.S. Department of Energy.

U.S. DEPARTMENT OF STATE. (1991a) *Report to Congress on Voting Practices in the United Nations 1990.* Washington, D.C.: U.S. Department of State.

——. (1991b) *Patterns of Global Terrorism: 1990.* Washington, D.C.: U.S. State Department.

——. (1990) *Report to Congress on Voting Practices in the United Nations 1989.* Washington, D.C.: U.S. Department of State.

——. (1983) *Security and Arms Control: The Search for a More Stable Peace.* Washington, D.C.: U.S. Government Printing Office.

——. (1978) "World Population: The Silent Explosion—Part 1," *Department of State Bulletin* 78 (October): 45–54.

U.S. OFFICE OF TECHNOLOGY ASSESSMENT. (1991a) *Energy in Developing Countries.* Washington, D.C.: U.S. Government Printing Office.

——. (1991b) *U.S. Oil Import Vulnerability.* Washington, D.C.: U.S. Government Printing Office.

VAN DE KAA, DIRK J. (1987) "Europe's Second Demographic Transition," *Population Bulletin* 42 (No. 1). Washington, D.C.: Population Reference Bureau.

VAN EVERA, STEPHEN. (1990–1991) "Primed for Peace: Europe After the Cold War," *International Security* 15 (Winter): 7–57.

VARON, BENSION, AND KENJI TAKEUCHI. (1974) "Developing Countries and Non-Fuel Minerals," *Foreign Affairs* 52 (April): 497–510.

VASQUEZ, JOHN. (1993) *The War Puzzle*. Cambridge, England: Cambridge University Press, forthcoming.

———. (1991) "The Deterrence Myth: Nuclear Weapons and the Prevention of Nuclear War," pp. 205–223 in Charles W. Kegley, Jr. (ed.), *The Long Postwar Peace*. New York: HarperCollins.

VERBA, SIDNEY. (1969) "Assumptions of Rationality and Non-Rationality in Models of the International System," pp. 217–231 in James N. Rosenau (ed.), *International Politics and Foreign Policy*. New York: Free Press.

VERNON, RAYMOND. (1982) "International Trade Policy in the 1980s: Prospects and Problems," *International Studies Quarterly* 26 (December): 483–510.

———. (1979) "The Fragile Foundations of East-West Trade," *Foreign Affairs* 57 (Summer): 1045–1051.

———. (1976) "An Introduction," pp. 1–14 in Raymond Vernon (ed.), *The Oil Crisis*. New York: Norton.

———. (1975) "Foreign Operations," pp. 275–298 in James W. McKie (ed.), *Social Responsibility and the Business Predicament*. Washington, D.C.: The Brookings Institution.

———. (1971) *Sovereignty at Bay*. New York: Basic Books.

VOLGY, THOMAS J., AND JON E. QUISTGARD. (1974) "Correlates of Organizational Rewards in the United Nations: An Analysis of Environmental and Legislative Variables," *International Organization* 28 (Spring): 179–205.

VON GLAHN, GERHARD. (1992) *Law Among Nations*, 6th ed. New York: Macmillan.

WALDHEIM, KURT. (1984) "The United Nations: The Tarnished Image," *Foreign Affairs* 63 (Fall): 93–107.

WALKER, R. J. B. (1987) "Realism, Change, and International Political Theory," *International Studies Quarterly* 31 (March): 65–86.

WALKER, WILLIAM O. (1991) "Decision-making Theory and Narcotic Foreign Policy: Implications for Historical Analysis," *Diplomatic History* 15 (Winter): 31–45.

WALLACE, MICHAEL D. (1973) "Alliance Polarization, Cross-cutting, and International War, 1815–1964," *Journal of Conflict Resolution* 17 (December): 575–604.

WALLACE, MICHAEL, AND J. DAVID SINGER. (1970) "Intergovernmental Organization in the Global System, 1815–1964: A Quantitative Description," *International Organization* 24 (Spring): 239–287.

WALLERSTEIN, IMMANUEL. (1988) *The Modern World-System III: The Second Era of Great Expansion of the Capitalist World-System, 1730–1840*. San Diego: Academic Press.

———. (1980) *The Modern World-System II*. New York: Academic Press.

———. (1974a) *The Modern World-System: Capitalist Agriculture and the Origins of the European World-Economy in the Sixteenth Century*. New York: Academic Press.

———. (1974b) "The Rise and Future Demise of the World Capitalist System: Concepts for Comparative Analysis," *Comparative Studies in Society and History* 16 (September): 387–415.

WALLIS, ALLEN. (1986) "U.S.-EC Relations and the International Trading System." Address before the Luxembourg Society for International Affairs, October 8. U.S. Department of State, Bureau of Public Affairs, Current Policy No. 889.

———. (1983) "A Collective Approach to East-West Economic Relations." Address before the American Society of Business Press Editors, Chicago, June 20, U.S. Department of State, Bureau of Public Affairs, Current Policy No. 495.

WALTERS, ROBERT S. (1983) "America's Declining Industrial Competitiveness: Protectionism, the Marketplace and the State," *PS* 16 (Winter): 25–33.

WALTERS, ROBERT S., AND DAVID H. BLAKE. (1992) *The Politics of Global Economic Relations*, 4th ed. Englewood Cliffs, N.J.: Prentice-Hall.

WALTZ, KENNETH N. (1991) "Realist Thought and Neorealist Theory," pp. 21–38 in Robert L. Rothstein (ed.), *The Evolution of Theory in International Relations*. Columbia, S.C.: University of South Carolina Press.

———. (1990) "The Emerging Structure of International Relations." Paper presented at the Annual Meetings of the American Political Science Association, San Francisco, August 28–31.

———. (1979) *Theory of International Politics*. Reading, Mass.: Addison-Wesley.

———. (1975) "Theory of International Relations," pp. 1–85 in Fred I. Greenstein and Nelson W. Polsby (ed.), *International Politics: Handbook of Political Science*. Vol. 8. Reading, Mass.: Addison-Wesley.

———. (1970) "The Myth of National Interdependence," pp. 205–223 in Charles P. Kindleberger (ed.), *The International Corporation*. Cambridge: MIT Press.

———. (1964) "The Stability of a Bipolar World," *Daedalus* 93 (Summer): 881–909.

———. (1954) *Man, the State, and War*. New York: Columbia University Press.

WATKINS, JAMES D. (1991–1992) "Balance in US Energy Policy for the 1990s and Beyond," *Harvard International Review* 14 (Winter): 7–10.

WATTENBERG, BEN J. (1989) *The Birth Dearth*. New York: Pharos Books.

WAYDA, MARK. (1992) "The DOD Annual Report to Congress, FY92," pp. 213–220 in Joseph Kruzel (ed.), *American Defense Annual, 1991–1992*. New York: Lexington Books.

WAYMAN, FRANK, AND PAUL F. DIEHL. (eds.) (1993) *Reconstructing Realpolitik*. Ann Arbor: University of Michigan Press, forthcoming.

WEIDENBAUM, MURRAY. (1992) *Small Wars, Big Defense: Paying for the Military After the Cold War*. New York: Oxford University Press.

WEISSKOPF, MICHAEL. (1991) "Paying the Overheating Bill," *Washington Post National Weekly Edition*, February 11–17, p. 33.

WELLER, ROBERT H., AND LEON F. BOUVIER. (1981) *Population: Demography and Policy*. New York: St. Martin's Press.

WELTMAN, JOHN J. (1974) "On the Obsolescence of War," *International Studies Quarterly* 18 (December): 395–416.

WENDZEL, ROBERT L. (1980) *International Relations: A Policymaker Focus*. New York: Wiley.

WHELAN, JOSEPH G., AND MICHAEL J. DIXON. (1986) *The Soviet Union in the Third World: Threat to World Peace?* Washington, D.C.: Pergamon-Brassey's.

WHITE, RALPH K. (1990) "Why Aggressors Lose," *Political Psychology* 11 (June): 227–242.

WILLIAMS, SHIRLEY. (1991) "Sovereignty and Accountability in the European Community," pp. 155–176 in Robert O. Keohane and Stanley Hoffmann (eds.), *The New European Community: Decisionmaking and Institutional Change*. Boulder, Colo.: Westview.

WINIECKI, JAN. (1989) "CPEs' Structural Change and World Market Performance: A Permanently Developing Country (PDC) Status," *Soviet Studies* 41 (July): 365–381.

WIRTH, TIMOTHY E. (1991–1992) "The Need for a More Responsible Energy Policy," *Harvard International Review* 14 (Winter): 11–13.

WITTKOPF, EUGENE R. (1990) *Faces of Internationalism: Public Opinion and American Foreign Policy*. Durham, N.C.: Duke University Press.

WOLF, EDWARD C. (1986) *Beyond the Green Revolution: New Approaches for Third World Agriculture*. Worldwatch Paper No. 73. Washington, D.C.: Worldwatch Institute.

WOLFERS, ARNOLD. (1968) "Alliances," pp. 268–271 in David L. Sills (ed.), *International Encyclopedia of the Social Sciences*. New York: Macmillan.

———. (1962) *Discord and Collaboration*. Baltimore, Md.: Johns Hopkins University Press.

———. (1952) "National Security As an Ambiguous Symbol," *Political Science Quarterly* 67 (December): 481–502.

WOLF-PHILLIPS, LESLIE. (1987) "Why 'Third World'?: Origin, Definitions and Usage," *Third World Quarterly* 9 (October): 1311–1327.

WOLPIN, MILES. (1983) "Comparative Perspectives on Militarization, Repression, and Social Welfare," *Journal of Peace Research* 20 (No. 2): 129–156.

WOODS, ALAN. (1989) *Development and the National Interest: U.S. Economic Assistance into the 21st Century*. Washington, D.C.: Agency for International Development.

WOODWARD, BOB. (1991) *The Commanders*. New York: Simon & Schuster.

WOODWARD, BOB, AND RICK ATKINSON. (1990) "Launching Operation Desert Shield," *Washington Post National Weekly Edition*, September 3–9, pp. 8–9.

WOODWELL, GEORGE M. (1990) "The Effects of Global Warming," pp. 116–132 in Jeremy Leggett (ed.), *Global Warming: The Greenpeace Report*. New York: Oxford University Press.

WORLD COMMISSION ON ENVIRONMENT AND DEVELOPMENT. (1987) *Our Common Future*. New York: Oxford University Press.

World Development Report 1991. (1991) New York: Oxford University Press.

World Development Report 1990. (1990) New York: Oxford University Press.

World Development Report 1987. (1987) New York: Oxford University Press.

World Development Report 1986. (1986) New York: Oxford University Press.

World Development Report 1984. (1984) New York: Oxford University Press.

World Development Report 1983. (1983) New York: Oxford University Press.

WORLD RESOURCES INSTITUTE. (1992) *World Resources 1992–93*. New York: Oxford University Press.

————. (1990) *World Resources 1990–91*. New York: Oxford University Press.

WRIGGINS, W. HOWARD. (1978) "Third World Strategies for Change: The Political Context of North-South Interdependence," pp. 19–117 in W. Howard Wriggins and Gunnar Adler-Karlsson, *Reducing Global Inequalities*. New York: McGraw-Hill.

WRIGHT, QUINCY. (1955) *The Study of International Relations*. New York: Appleton-Century-Crofts.

————. (1953) "The Outlawry of War and the Law of War," *American Journal of International Law* 47 (July): 365–376.

————. (1942) *A Study of War*. Chicago: University of Chicago Press.

WYMAN, RICHARD L. (ed.) (1991) *Global Climate Change and Life on Earth*. New York: Routledge, Chapman and Hall.

YARMOLINSKY, ADAM. (1988) "Low-Intensity Conflict: Causes, Consequences, and Questionable Cures," pp. 96–101 in Charles W. Kegley, Jr., and Eugene R. Wittkopf (eds.), *The Global Agenda*, 2nd ed. New York: Random House.

Yearbook of International Organizations, 1991/92. (1991) Vol. 1. Munich: K. G. Sauer.

Yearbook of International Organizations, 1991/92. (1991) Vol. 2. Munich: K. G. Sauer.

Yearbook of International Organizations, 1983. (1984) Vol. 1: Organization Descriptions and Index. Munich: K. G. Sauer.

YODER, EDWIN M., JR. (1991) "Isolationists Would Put America on a Dangerous Course," *The State* (Columbia, S.C.), December 14, p. A10.

YOUNG, JOHN E. (1991) "Reducing Waste, Saving Materials," pp. 39–55 in Lester R. Brown, Christopher Flavin, Sandra Postel, Linda Starke, Alan Durning, Hilary F. French, Jodi Jacobson, Marcia D. Lowe, Michael Renner, Nicholas Lenssen, John C. Ryan, and John E. Young, *State of the World 1991*. New York: Norton.

YOUNG, ORAN. (1986) "International Regimes: Toward a New Theory of Institutions," *World Politics* 39 (October): 104–122.

————. (1980) "International Regimes: Problems of Concept Formation," *World Politics* 32 (April): 331–356.

ZACHER, MARK W. (1991) "Toward a Theory of International Regimes," pp. 119–137 in Robert L. Rothstein (ed.), *The Evolution of Theory in International Relations*. Columbia, S.C.: University of South Carolina Press.

ZAGARE, FRANK C. (1990) "Rationality and Deterrence," *World Politics* 42 (January): 238–260.

ZELIKOW, PHILIP. (1987) "The United States and the Use of Force: A Historical Summary," pp. 31–81 in George K. Osburn, Asa A. Clark IV, Daniel J. Kaufman, and Douglas E. Lute (eds.), *Democracy, Strategy, and Vietnam*. Lexington, Mass.: Lexington Books.

ZINNES, DINA A. (1980) "Prerequisites for the Study of System Transformation," pp. 3–21 in Ole R. Holsti, Randolph M. Siverson, and Alexander L. George (eds.), *Change in the International System*. Boulder, Colo.: Westview.

ZINNES, DINA A., AND JONATHAN WILKENFELD. (1971) "An Analysis of Foreign Conflict Behavior of Nations," pp. 167–213 in Wolfram F. Handieder (ed.), *Comparative Foreign Policy*. New York: McKay.

GLOSSARY

Acid rain: precipitation that has been made acidic through contact with sulfur dioxide and nitrogen oxides.

ACP nations: African, Caribbean, and Pacific developing nations linked to the European Community through treaties of cooperation.

Adjudication: a conflict resolution procedure where a third party makes a binding decision through an institutionalized tribunal.

Aid burden: the ratio between foreign aid expenditures and a donor's income as measured by gross national product.

Algiers summit conference (1973): the international meeting that resulted in the Group of 77 joining forces with the non-aligned movement.

Alliance: a formal agreement among states for the purpose of coordinating their behavior in the event of certain specified military contingencies.

Anarchy: an absence of governmental authority.

Apartheid: the South African policy of racial separation.

Appeasement: a policy that attempts to buy off a potential aggressor with concessions that may conflict with the country's principles.

Arbitration: a conflict resolution procedure where a third party makes a binding decision through an ad hoc forum.

Arms control: agreements designed to regulate arms levels.

ASAT weapon: antisatellite weapon.

Asian Tigers: the four Asian NICs (Hong Kong, South Korea, Singapore, and Taiwan) that experienced rates of economic growth during the 1980s far greater than the more advanced industrial societies of the First World.

Atlantic Charter: a declaration issued in 1941 by U.S. President Franklin D. Roosevelt and British Prime Minister Winston Churchill outlining the principles that would guide the construction of a postwar general security system.

Baker initiative: a proposal to resolve the Third World debt problem by encouraging domestic economic reforms and seeking new loans from private banks.

Balance of payments: a summary statement of a state's financial transactions with the rest of the world, including such items as foreign aid transfers and the income of citizens employed abroad who send their paychecks home.

Balance-of-power theory: a body of thought that contends peace will result when military power is distributed in such a way that no one state can dominate the others.

Balance of trade: a state's net trade surplus or deficit, based on the difference in the value of its imports and exports.

Balancer: a role played by a state that gives its support to one or another side of a dispute to ensure that no one achieves preponderance.

Bandung Conference (1955): a meeting of twenty-nine African and Asian nations that was held in Bandung, Indonesia, to devise a strategy to combat colonialism.

Baruch Plan (1946): a call for the creation of a United Nations Atomic Development Authority that would place atomic energy under international authority.

Beggar-thy-neighbor policy: efforts to promote domestic welfare by promoting trade surpluses that can be realized only at other countries' expense.

Behavioralism: an approach to the study of international relations that emphasizes the application of scientific methods.

Bilateral aid: foreign aid that flows directly from one country to another.

Billiard ball model: a metaphor that compares world politics to a game in which billiard balls (states) continuously clash and collide with one another. The actions of each are determined by their interactions with the others, not by what occurs within them.

Biological Weapons Convention (1972): an agreement prohibiting the development, production, and stockpiling of biological weapons.

Bipolar: an international system containing two dominant power centers.

Bipolarization: the clustering of smaller states in alliances around two dominant power centers.

Bipolycentrism: the existence of military bipolarity between the United States and Soviet Union coupled with multiple political centers of independent foreign policy decisions.

Bloc: a rigid, highly cohesive alliance among a group of states.

Brady initiative: an approach to resolving the Third World debt crisis by reducing the debt of all debtor nations.

Bretton Woods system: the rules, institutions, and decision-making procedures devised during World War II to govern international economic relations in the postwar era.

Brezhnev Doctrine: the assertion by Soviet President Leonid Brezhnev following the 1968 Soviet invasion of Czechoslovakia that the USSR had the right to intervene to preserve communist party rule in any state within the Soviet bloc.

Brinkmanship: the threat of nuclear escalation in a confrontation to compel submission.

Brundtland Commission: the 1987 World Commission on Environment and Development that called for sustainable development.

Bureaucratic politics model: an interpretation of policy making that stresses the bargaining and compromises among contending governmental organizations and agency heads that exert influence on the foreign policy choices of political leaders.

Camp David Declaration on New Relations (1992): a joint statement by Russian President Boris Yeltsin and U.S. President George Bush that asserts the relationship between Russia and the United States will be characterized by friendship and partnership.

Carrying capacity: the maximum biomass that can be supported by a given territory.

Cartel: an organization of the producers of a commodity that seeks to regulate the pricing and production of the commodity.

Carter Doctrine: a statement by President Jimmy Carter declaring U.S. willingness to use military force to protect its interests in the Persian Gulf.

Chernobyl nuclear accident: a nuclear catastrophe that occurred at a power plant in the Ukraine during 1986.

Classical imperialism: the first wave of European empire building that began during the fifteenth century, as the Dutch, English, French, Portuguese, and Spanish used their military power to achieve commercial advantages overseas.

Closed economic system: a system based

on a centrally planned or command economy.

Club of Rome: a private group that has popularized a neo-Malthusian interpretation of the consequences of growth.

Coercive diplomacy: the use of threats or limited force to persuade an adversary to call off or undo an encroachment.

Collective good: goods that are jointly supplied and from which it is not possible to exclude beneficiaries on a selective basis.

Collective security: a system of world order in which aggression by any state will be met by a collective response.

Colonialism: the rule of a region by an external sovereign power.

Commonwealth of Independent States (CIS): the political entity that replaced the Soviet Union on January 1, 1992.

Comparative advantage: the principle according to which any two nations will benefit if each specializes in those goods it produces comparatively cheaply and acquires, through trade, goods that it can only produce at a higher cost.

Compellence: the use of nuclear weapons as instruments of coercive diplomacy.

Complex interdependence: an approach to the study of international relations that challenges the realist assumptions that nation-states are the only important actors in world politics, that national security issues dominate decision-making agendas, and that military force is the only means of exercising influence in international politics.

Concert of Europe: a system of great-power conference diplomacy organized in Europe after the Napoleonic Wars.

Conciliation: a conflict resolution procedure where a third party assists both sides but offers no solution.

Conventional (liberal) theory of economic development: a theory that emphasized indigenous impediments to Third World development. Based on the assumption that growth meant increasing increments of per-capita GNP, the task was to identify and remove obstacles to growth and supply missing components, such as investment capital.

Coordinating Committee (Cocom): a multilateral mechanism designed to induce U.S. allies to join a unified effort to restrict the export of strategic and high-technology goods from West to East.

Cornucopians: optimists who question limits-to-growth analyses and contend that markets effectively maintain a balance between population, resources, and the environment.

Council for Mutual Economic Assistance (CMEA): an international economic organization created in 1949 containing the Soviet Union and the countries of Eastern Europe.

Counterforce targeting: targeting an opponent's military forces and weapons.

Counterinsurgency: combat against revolutionary guerrillas.

Countervalue targeting: targeting an opponent's industrial and population centers.

Crisis: a situation that threatens high-priority goals, restricts the time available for response, and surprises decision makers.

Cultural imperialism: imposing one country's value system on another people who do not welcome such foreign influence.

Current history: an approach to understanding international relations that focuses on the description of historical events, not theoretical explanation.

Debt decade: a prolonged financial crisis that began in 1982 when it appeared that Third World debtor nations might default on their loans.

Debtor's cartel: a proposal that Third World debtor nations confront the creditor nations with a coalition to press for a solution to the debt crisis.

Declaration on the Granting of Independence to Colonial Countries and Peoples (1960): a declaration passed by the UN General Assembly that proclaimed the subjection of any people to colonial domination was a denial of human rights.

Demographic transition theory: an explanation of population changes over time that highlights the causes of declines in birthrates and deathrates.

Dependence theory: a theory that claims the relationship between advanced capitalist societies and those at the periphery of the world economy is exploitative. According to this view, capitalism's need for external sources of demand and profitable investment outlets led to the penetration of virtually every part of the Third World and the establishment of a dominance-dependence relationship between North and South.

Dependent development: the industrialization of peripheral areas within the confines of the dominance-dependence relationship between North and South.

Détente: the relaxation of tensions between adversaries.

Deterrence: a preventive strategy designed to dissuade an adversary from doing what it would otherwise do.

Disarmament: agreements designed to reduce or eliminate weapons.

Diversionary theory of war: the contention that leaders initiate conflict abroad as a way of increasing national cohesion at home.

Dollar convertibility: a commitment by the U.S. government to exchange dollars for gold.

Domino theory: a metaphor that predicts the fall to communism in one country will cause the fall of its neighbors, and in turn still others.

Dualism: the existence of a rural, impoverished, and neglected sector of society operating alongside an urban, developing, or modernizing sector, where there is little interaction between the two sectors.

Dual use technology: technology that has both commercial and military uses.

Ecological transition: a process in situations of high population growth where human demands come to exceed sustainable yield.

Economic sanctions: governmental actions aimed at inflicting deprivation on a target state through the limitation or termination of economic relations.

Elitist decision making: a model of the policy-making process that ascribes disproportionate control over foreign policy making to a small ruling group.

Engel's law: poorer families spend a greater percentage of their budget on food than do higher-income groups.

Entente Cordiale: an alliance between Britain and France established in 1902.

Eurocrat: a member of the professional staff who assist the Executive Commission of the European Community.

European Community (EC): a regional organization composed of the European Coal and Steel Community, the European Atomic Energy Community, and the European Economic Community.

European Free Trade Association (EFTA): an organization created in 1960 as a counterpoint to the European Economic Community.

European Monetary System (EMS): an arrangement designed to stabilize the currency values of European Community members against one another and against the dollar.

Export-led industrialization: a strategy that involves developing domestic export industries capable of competing in overseas markets.

Export quota: a barrier to free trade imposed pursuant to negotiated agreements between producers and consumers.

Extended deterrence: a strategy that seeks to deter an adversary from attacking one's allies.

Fertility rate (total): the average number of children born to a woman (or a group of women) during her lifetime.

Financial veto: withholding payment selectively from certain UN programs as a way to register dissatisfaction with the organization's activities and to change them.

Firebreak: the psychological barrier between conventional and nuclear war.

First World: countries that share a commitment to varying forms of democratic political institutions and developed market economies, including Australia, Canada, Israel, Japan, Malta, New Zealand, South Africa, and the countries of Western Europe.

Fixed exchange rates: a system under which states establish the parity of their currencies and commit themselves to keeping fluctuations in their exchange rates within very narrow limits.

Food ladder: a conceptualization based on the biological food chain. As personal income increases, individuals move up the ladder, consuming grains indirectly as meat rather than directly.

Food security: access by all people at all times to enough food for an active, healthy life.

Fossil fuels: fuels such as coal, petroleum, and natural gas that are formed from organic remains.

Fourteen Points speech (1918): a speech delivered by U.S. President Woodrow Wilson that called for open diplomacy, self-determination, free trade, freedom of the seas, disarmament, and collective security.

Fourth World: the "least developed" of the less-developed countries.

Free-floating exchange rates: a system in which market forces determine currency values.

Free riders: those who enjoy the benefits of collective goods but pay little or nothing for them.

Functionalism: a bottom-up approach to fostering political integration through transnational organizations that emphasize sharing sovereignty.

General Agreement on Tariffs and Trade (GATT): an international organization that seeks to promote and protect the most-favored-nation principle as the basis for international trade.

General Assembly: one of six principal organs established by the United Nations Charter. It is the only body representing all the member states. Decision making follows the principle of majority rule, with no state given a veto.

Generalized System of Preferences (GSP): a scheme that permits First World nations to grant preferences to developing nations without violating GATT's nondiscrimination principle.

Glasnost: the Russian word for Soviet President Mikhail Gorbachev's policy of openness.

Global warming: a suspected consequence of greenhouse gases that trap heat remitted from earth which would otherwise escape into outer space.

Good offices: the third-party offering of a location for discussions among disputants.

Green revolution: the introduction of new high-yield grains to Third World countries.

Group of Seven (G-7): Britain, Canada, France, Germany, Italy, Japan, and the United States. Leaders from these industrialized nations meet in regular economic summit conferences.

Group of 77 (G-77): a coalition of the world's poor countries formed during the 1964 United Nations Conference on Trade and Development (UNCTAD) in Geneva. Originally composed of 77 states, the coalition now numbers over 120 developing countries and continues to press for concessions from the wealthy nations.

Groupthink: the propensity of cohesive, insulated groups to suffer from a deterioration of mental efficiency, reality testing, and moral judgment.

Gunboat diplomacy: a show of military force, historically called naval force.

Hague Peace Conferences (1899, 1907): international meetings that restricted the use of certain weapons and sought to promote peaceful methods of dispute resolution.

Hegemon: a dominant military and economic state that uses its unrivaled power to create and enforce rules aimed at preserving the existing world order and its own position in that order.

Hegemonic stability theory: a theory that draws attention to the impact of preeminent states (hegemons) on international cooperation and the maintenance of stability.

Helsinki Accord (1975): an agreement signed by NATO, the Warsaw Pact, and thirteen neutral and nonaligned European countries that sought to establish peace in Europe by calling for the implementation of confidence-building measures, economic, environmental, and scientific cooperation, and the free flow of people, ideas, and information.

Hero-in-history model: an interpretation of the foreign policy-making process that equates national action with the preferences and initiatives of the highest officials in national governments.

Hidden veto: the ability of the United States during the formative period of the United Nations to persuade a sufficient majority of other UN Security Council members to vote negatively on an issue so as to avoid the stigma of having to cast the single blocking vote.

High politics: geostrategic issues of national and international security that pertain to matters of war and peace.

Horizontal nuclear proliferation: an increase in the number of states that possess nuclear weapons.

Horizontal system of law: a decentralized, self-help system of law.

Hot line: a communications link between Moscow and Washington that permits national leaders to communicate directly during a crisis.

Human Development Index (HDI): an index that uses life expectancy, literacy, the average number of years of schooling, and income to assess a country's human development performance.

ICBM: intercontinental ballistic missile.

Imperial overstretch: a condition where a state's external commitments exceed its ability to fulfill them.

Import quotas: a nontariff barrier to free trade that involves limits on the quantity of a particular product that can be imported from abroad.

Import-substitution industrialization: a strategy that involves encouraging domestic entrepreneurs to manufacture products otherwise imported from abroad.

Inadvertent war: a war that is not the result of anyone's master plan; rather it occurs due to uncertainty, confusion, and circumstances beyond the control of those involved.

Independents (oil companies): competitors of the major oil companies who historically stood outside of the international oil regime controlled by the majors.

Instrumental rationality: a conceptualization of decision making asserting that individuals have preferences, and when faced with two or more alternatives, they will choose the one that yields the preferred outcome.

Interdependence: a situation of mutual dependence defined as mutual sensitivity and mutual vulnerability.

Intergovernmental international organization (IGO): an international organization whose members are nation-states.

Intermediate-range Nuclear Force (INF) Treaty (1987): an agreement between the United States and Soviet Union to remove intermediate range nuclear forces from Europe.

International Court of Justice (ICJ): the primary judicial organ of the United Nations; also known as World Court.

International Labor Organization: a UN specialized agency responsible for improving working conditions in member countries.

International Monetary Fund (IMF): a specialized agency of the United Nations that seeks to maintain monetary stability and assist member states in funding balance-of-payments deficits.

International nongovernmental organization (INGO): an international organization whose members are private individuals and groups.

International regime: the set of rules, norms, and decision-making procedures that governs state behavior within a given area of activity.

Irredentism: the desire by one nation to annex territory held by another that is historically or ethnically related to the first nation.

Irreversible conservation measures: permanent steps taken toward conserving a resource.

Just war: a doctrine that pertains to the moral considerations by which war may be undertaken and how it should be fought once it begins.

Kellogg-Briand Pact (Pact of Paris, 1928): a treaty that sought to outlaw war as an instrument of national policy.

League of Nations mandate system: the placement of colonies previously held by the Central Powers of World War I under the administration of certain Allied nations. Implicit in the system was the idea that colonies were a trust rather than a territory to be exploited.

League of Nations: a global intergovernmental organization established after World War I.

Levels of analysis: alternative perspectives on world politics that may focus on the personal characteristics of decision makers, the attributes of states, or the structure of the international system.

Liberal International Economic Order (LIEO): the set of regimes created after World War II designed to promote monetary stability and reduce barriers to the free flow of trade and capital.

Linkage theory: a set of assertions that claims leaders should take into account another country's overall behavior when deciding whether to reach agreement on any one specific issue.

Lomé Convention (1975): an agreement between the European Community and the ACP nations that granted the latter trade preferences and established STABEX.

Long-cycle theory: a theory that focuses on the rise and fall of the leading global powers as the central political process of the modern world system.

Long peace: the period of great-power relations extending from the end of World War II until the present. It is the longest period of great-power peace in modern history.

Low-intensity conflict: fighting that falls below the threshold of full-scale military combat between modern armies.

Low politics: socioeconomic and welfare issues that pertain to matters of material well-being.

Maastricht summit (1991): a meeting of European Community members in the Netherlands that set forth a framework for achieving greater European unity.

Macropolitical perspective: an approach to the study of international affairs that looks at world politics as a system, with general global patterns of interaction among parts.

Majors (oil companies): British Petroleum, Compagnie Francaise des Petroles, Exxon, Gulf, Mobil, Royal Dutch Shell, Standard Oil of California, and Texaco.

Malthusian projection: the prediction that population when unchecked increases in a geometric ratio, whereas subsistence increases in only an arithmetic ratio.

Marshall Plan: a program of grants and loans established by the United States to assist the recovery of Western Europe after World War II.

Massive retaliation: the strategic posture of the United States during the Eisenhower administration.

Mechanical majority: a complaint voiced by the Soviet Union during the early history of the United Nations that the United States enjoyed a commanding position in the General Assembly due to the fact that its allies constituted a majority of the UN membership on whose support the United States could always depend.

Mediation: a conflict resolution procedure where a third party offers a nonbinding solution to the disputants.

Mercantilism: the economic philosophy advocating government regulation of economic life to increase state power and security. Under this philosophy, state power was assumed to flow from the possession of national wealth measured in terms of gold and silver. Exporting more than is imported constitutes one way to accumulate the desired bullion.

Mirror images: the propensity of each member of a conflict to see the other as the other sees it.

MIRV: multiple independently targetable reentry vehicle.

Montevideo Convention (1933): an agreement that summarizes the major components of statehood and the rights and duties of states.

Mortality rate: the crude deathrate is the most common measure of mortality. The age-adjusted deathrate is often used in its place because the age-adjusted deathrate is free of distortions due to differences in age composition.

Most-favored-nation (MFN) principle: tariff preferences granted to one nation must be granted to all others exporting the same product.

Multilateral aid: aid that is channeled through international institutions.

Multinational corporation (MNC): a business enterprise organized in one society with activities in another growing out of direct investment abroad.

Multipolar: an international system containing more than two dominant power centers.

Munich Conference (1938): the conference at which Britain and France accepted Adolf Hitler's demand to annex the German-populated area of Sudetenland in Czechoslovakia.

Mutual assured destruction (MAD): a system of mutual deterrence where both sides possess the ability to survive a first strike and launch a devastating retaliatory attack.

Mutual security: a belief that a diminution in the national security of one's adversary reduces one's own security.

Mutual sensitivity: liability of states to costs imposed by external events before policies are changed to deal with the situation.

Mutual vulnerability: liability of states to

costs imposed by external events even after policies have been changed to deal with the situation.

Nation: a collection of people who, on the basis of ethnic, linguistic, or cultural affinity, perceive themselves to be members of the same group.

National attributes: characteristics of nation-states (such as level of economic development or extent of military capability) that may influence foreign policy behavior.

Nationalism: loyalty to a nation.

Nation-state: a polity (system of government) controlled by members of some nationality recognizing no higher authority.

Neocolonialism (neo-imperialism): unequal exchanges that permit wealthy First World countries to exploit others through the institutionalized processes of the contemporary world political economy.

Neofunctionalism: a reconstitution of the functionalist theory of integration that directly addresses political factors.

Neoliberal institutionalism: a perspective on world politics that concentrates on the ways international organizations and other nonstate actors promote international cooperation.

Neo-Malthusians: pessimists who warn of the global ecopolitical implications of uncontrolled growth.

Neomercantilism: a trade policy whereby a state seeks to maintain a balance-of-trade surplus by reducing imports, stimulating domestic production, and promoting exports.

Neorealism: a variant of realism that emphasizes the anarchic structure of the international system rather than human nature in its explanation of international political foreign policy behavior.

New Imperialism: the second wave of European empire building that began in the 1870s and extended until the outbreak of World War I in which colonies became an important symbol of national power and prestige.

New international division of labor: a projection that developing nations will provide the First World with manufactured and processed goods, while the latter will provide developing nations with raw materials and agricultural products.

New International Economic Order (NIEO): a demand by the Third World to replace the U.S.-sponsored Liberal International Economic Order (LIEO) with an international economic regime that is more favorable to the interests of developing countries.

Newly Industrialized Countries (NICs): a group of upper-middle–income countries that have become important exporters of manufactured goods, as well as important markets for the major industrialized countries that export capital goods. Included within this group are Brazil, Hong Kong, Mexico, Singapore, South Korea, Taiwan, and Yugoslavia.

New World Information and Communication Order (NWICO): a demand by the Third World for a new regime covering the flow of information between North and South due to dissatisfaction with the media coverage provided by news agencies from the developed countries.

Nixon Doctrine: the position taken by President Richard Nixon that U.S. allies should bear a greater share of the burden for their own defense.

Nomothetic generalization: lawlike statement about relationships between variables that is presumed to hold across time and space.

Nonalignment: a foreign policy posture in which states do not participate in military alliances with either the East or West because of a fear that one form of domination might simply be replaced by another.

Noninterference principle: the duty of states to refrain from uninvited involvement in another's internal affairs.

Nontariff barriers: an inhibition against the free flow of goods and services across national boundaries that does not involve an import tax or duty.

Nuclear Nonproliferation Treaty (1968): an international agreement that seeks to prevent horizontal proliferation.

Nuclear utilization theory: a body of strategic thought that claims deterrent threats could be more credible if nuclear weapons are made more usable.

Oil shocks: the rapid increases in oil prices in the aftermath of the Yom Kippur War, the revolution in Iran, and the invasion of Kuwait.

OPEC: Organization of Petroleum Exporting Countries.

OPEC decade: the period between October 1973 and March 1983, which saw the rise and decline of OPEC's power in the world political economy.

Open economic system: a system based on a market economy.

Open skies proposal (1955): a call for allowing aerial reconnaissance to monitor military maneuvers.

Operations Plan 90-1002: a plan devised in the early 1980s that called for a massive air- and sea-lift of U.S. military personnel and equipment in the event of conflict in the Middle East where the United States had no military bases.

Orderly Market Arrangements (OMAs): voluntary export restrictions that involves a government-to-government agreement and often specific rules of management.

Ozone depletion: the thinning of the ozone layer in the upper atmosphere due to the release of chlorofluorocarbons.

Pacta sunt servanda: the international legal norm that treaties are binding.

Paradigm: a theoretical perspective that gives direction to research by indicating what problems in a field of inquiry are more important than others and what criteria should govern their investigation.

Parallel currency: the universal acceptance of the dollar in the immediate postwar period as the currency against which every other country sold or redeemed its own national currency in the exchange markets.

Peacekeeping: the use of a UN military force to function as a buffer between disputants in order to prevent fighting.

Perestroika: the Russian word for Soviet President Mikhail Gorbachev's policy of economic restructuring.

Physical Quality of Life Index (PQLI): an index that uses life expectancy, infant mortality, and literacy rates to assess progress in meeting basic human needs.

Plaza Agreement (1985): an agreement by the major industrialized nations to coordinate efforts at managing exchange rates internationally and interest rates domestically.

Pluralist decision making: a model of the policy-making process that highlights the role of competitive domestic groups in pressuring a government for policies responsive to their interests and needs.

Political idealism: an approach to international relations that assumes people are not by nature sinful or wicked, and that harmful behavior is the result of structural arrangements that motivate people to act selfishly.

Political integration: the process or the product of efforts to build new political communities and supranational institutions that transcend the nation-state.

Political realism: an approach to international relations that assumes people by nature are sinful or wicked, and that the purpose of statecraft is to acquire the power needed to survive in a hostile environment.

Pooled sovereignty: the sharing of decision-making responsibility among several governments and between them and international institutions.

Population momentum: the concept that population growth will continue for several decades after replacement-level fertility is achieved.

Postbehavioralism: an approach to the study of international relations that calls for increased attention to the policy relevance of research.

Post-Positivism: an approach to the study of international relations that calls for an emphasis on the subjective nature of images of world politics.

Power transition theory: the contention that war is most likely to occur when the differentials between the capabilities of rival states narrow.

Preferential trade: the granting of special trade treatment to certain states.

Price inelasticity of demand: a condition where price increases have little impact on the amount of a commodity that is consumed.

Price inelasticity of supply: a condition where new producers of a commodity cannot enter a market to take advantage of higher rates of return.

Primary products: raw materials and agricultural products.

Private international law: law pertaining to routinized transnational intercourse between or among nongovernmental actors.

Procedural rationality: a conceptualization of rationality that is based on perfect information and a careful weighing of all possible courses of action.

Pronatalist policy: a conscious governmental attempt to increase fertility.

Protectionism: the use of tariff and nontariff barriers to restrict imports.

Public international law: law pertaining to government-to-government relations.

Rapacki Plan (1957): a call for the denuclearization of Central Europe.

Rational decision-making model: an idealized portrayal of decision making according to which the individual uses the best information available to choose from the set of possible responses that alternative most likely to maximize his or her goals.

Reagan Doctrine: a pledge by President Ronald Reagan of U.S. support for anti-communist insurgents seeking to overthrow Soviet-supported governments.

Rebus sic stantibus: the international legal norm that reserves the right of states to terminate treaties unilaterally if conditions at the time of the signing have since changed.

Relative burden of military spending: the ratio of defense spending to gross national product.

Reparations: compensation paid by a defeated state for damages or expenditures sustained by the victor during hostilities.

Reprisal: hostile and illegal retaliatory acts.

Retorsion: hostile but legal retaliatory acts.

Reversible conservation measures: nonpermanent conservation measures that often derive from behavioral changes.

SALT (Strategic Arms Limitations Talks): two sets of agreements reached during the 1970s between the United States and the Soviet Union that established limits on strategic nuclear delivery systems.

Satisficing behavior: the propensity of decision makers to select the choice that meets minimally acceptable standards.

Schematic reasoning: the processing of new information according to a memory structure that contains a network of genetic scripts, metaphors, and stereotypical characters.

Second-strike capability: the capacity of a state to retaliate militarily after absorbing a first-strike attack.

Second World: a group of countries that possessed centrally-planned economies. It consisted of the Soviet Union and its allies in Eastern Europe during the Cold War.

Secretary-General: the chief administrative officer of the United Nations and head of the Secretariat, one of the six principal organs established by the United Nations Charter.

Security Council: one of six principal organs established by the United Nations Charter. Its primary responsibility is the maintenance of international peace and security.

Security dilemma: the propensity of armaments undertaken by one state for ostensibly defensive purposes to be perceived by others as threatening.

Self-determination: the doctrine that asserts nationalities have the right to determine what political authority will represent and rule them.

SLBM: submarine-launched ballistic missile.

Sovereignty: the principle that no authority is above the state.

Special drawing rights (SDRs): reserves created and held by the International Monetary Fund (IMF) that member states can draw on to help manage the values of their currencies.

Sphere of influence: a region dominated by the power of a foreign state.

Spiral model: a metaphor used to describe the tendency of efforts to enhance defense to result in escalating arms races.

STABEX: a compensatory financing scheme operated by the European Community for the benefit of the ACP nations.

Standard operating procedures (SOPs): established methods to be followed for the performance of designated tasks.

START (Strategic Arms Reduction Talks): a series of negotiations that led to a 1991 treaty to reduce U.S. and Soviet strategic forces.

State: a legal entity that possesses a permanent population, a well-defined territory, and a government capable of exercising sovereignty.

State terrorism: the support of terrorist groups by governmental authorities.

Strategic Defense Initiative (SDI): a ballistic missile defense system using space-based laser technology.

Summit conference: personal diplomatic negotiations between national leaders.

Supranational authority: the power of an international institution to make decisions binding on its national members without being subject to their individual approval.

System transformation: profound changes in the units that make up the international system, the predominant foreign policy goals that the units seek, or what the units can do to each other with their military and economic capabilities.

Terms of trade: the ratio of export prices to import prices. Developing nations believe that the prices they receive for their exports fall in the long run, while the prices of the manufactured goods they import increase steadily.

Theory: a set of interrelated propositions that purports to explain or predict.

Third World: a term commonly used to refer to the world's poorer, economically less-developed countries. It includes all of Asia, the Middle East, and Oceania except Israel, Japan, Turkey, Australia, and New Zealand, all of Africa except South Africa, and all of the Western Hemisphere except Canada and the United States.

Three Mile Island nuclear accident: an accident in a Pennsylvania nuclear power plant during 1979 that resulted in the largest-ever level of radioactive contamination by the U.S. commercial nuclear industry.

Tied aid: the existence of conditions or "strings" attached to foreign aid.

Tokyo Round of GATT: multilateral trade negotiations held between 1973 and 1979.

Tragedy of the commons: a metaphor widely used to explain the impact of human behavior on ecological systems. Rational self-interested behavior by individuals may have a destructive collective impact.

Transfer-pricing mechanism: the trading of commodities between a parent company's subsidiaries in different countries in order to record profits in jurisdictions where taxes are low.

Treaty of Rome (1957): the agreement that created the European Economic Community, popularly known for many years as the European Common Market.

Truman Doctrine: the declaration by U.S. President Harry S Truman that the policy of the United States must support "free peoples who are resisting attempted subjugation by armed minorities or by outside pressures."

Unipolar: an international system containing a single dominant power center.

Unitary actor: a conceptualization of the policy-making process that assumes all states and individuals responsible for their foreign policies will confront the problem of national survival in similar ways.

United Nations Conference on Trade and Development (UNCTAD): a special trade conference held in Geneva in 1964 and now a United Nations organization whose primary mission has been the promotion of Third World trade and development.

United Nations Educational, Scientific and Cultural Organization (UNESCO): the UN specialized agency responsible for promoting cooperation in the fields of education, science, and culture.

United Nations Emergency Force (UNEF): authorized by the General Assembly in 1956 under the Uniting for Peace procedures to attempt to restore peace in the Middle East following the outbreak of war between Egypt and a coalition of Britain, France, and Israel.

Uniting for Peace Resolution: a device which empowered the United Nations General Assembly to meet in emergency sessions to deal with threats to peace and acts of aggression.

Uruguay Round of GATT: multilateral trade negotiations begun in 1986 and extended indefinitely in 1990. Principal issues considered include nontariff barriers, intellectual property rights, and trade in agricultural products.

Vertical nuclear proliferation: an increase in the capabilities of existing nuclear powers.

Vertical system of law: a centralized, hierarchical system of law.

Voluntary Export Restrictions (VERs): a generic term for all bilaterally agreed restraints on trade.

War contagion: a metaphor that likens the diffusion of war to the spread of disease.

War weariness hypothesis: the contention that a nation at war will become exhausted and lose its enthusiasm for another war, but only for a time.

Washington Naval Conferences (1921–1922): arms control meetings that resulted in an agreement among Britain, France, Italy, Japan, and the United States to adjust relative tonnage of their fleets.

Weighted voting: a system in which votes are distributed among states in proportion to their financial contribution to an organization.

World federalism: an approach to integration based on the merger of previously sovereign states into a single federal union.

World-system theory: a theory that views the world as a single capitalist world-system. It is characterized by an international division of labor in which core states specialize in the capital-intensive production of sophisticated manufactured goods and peripheral states concentrate on the labor-intensive production of raw materials and agricultural commodities.

Yalta Conference (1945): a meeting of Winston Churchill, Franklin D. Roosevelt, and Joseph Stalin in the Russian Crimea to design a new, post–World War II order.

Zero-sum: the perception that a gain for one side in a rivalry is a loss for the other side.

ACKNOWLEDGMENTS

Box 5.1: "The Chronology of Decolonization" Peter J. Taylor, ed. *World Government* (New York, Oxford University Press, 1990), pp. 16–17, 40, 112. Reprinted by permission of Oxford University Press, Inc.

Box 6.1: *A Guide to the European Community* (Washington, D.C.: E.C. Delegation to the United States, 1991), n.p. Courtesy of the Delegation of the E.C. Commission to the United States, 1991.

Box 6.3: "Transnational Investment Highlights of the 1990's" *Transnationals* 3 (March 1991): 2, 3. Reprinted by permission of the United Nations.

Box 7.1: "The Bretton Woods Conference and Its Twin Institutions" *World Development Report 1985* (New York: Oxford University Press, 1985), p. 15. Reprinted by permission of Oxford University Press, Inc.

Box 7.3: "Comparative Advantage and the Gains from Trade" Daniel Rosen, *The Basics of Foreign Trade and Exchange* (New York: Federal Reserve Bank of New York, 1987). Reprinted by permission.

Box 7.4: "The Costs of Trade Conflict" Paul Krugman, *The Age of Diminished Expectations: U.S. Economic Policy in the 1990s* (Cambridge, MA: MIT Press, 1990), p. 105. Reprinted by permission.

Box 7.6: "From a Centrally Planned to a Market Economy" *World Development Report 1991* (New York: Oxford University Press, 1991), pp. 145–146. Reprinted by permission of Oxford University Press, Inc.

Box 8.1: From *World Development Report, 1991*. Copyright © 1991 by The International Bank for Reconstruction and Development/The World Bank. Reprinted by permission of Oxford University Press, Inc.

Box 8.2: "The Evolving Stages of UNCTAD" summary description of UNCTAD I through UNCTAD V from Mahmud A. Burney, "A Recognition of Interdependence: UNCTAD V," *Finance and Development* 16 (September 1979): 18; summary description of UNCTAD VI and UNCTAD VII adapted from Shahid Javed Burki, "UNCTAD VI: For Better or for Worse?" *Finance and Development* 20 (December 1983): 18–19; and Carlston B. Boucher and Wolfgang E. Siebeck, "UNCTAD VII: New Spirit in North-South Relations?" *Finance and Development* 24 (December 1987): 14–16. Reprinted by permission of the International Monetary Fund.

Box 9.1: "The Secret of the Persian Chessboard," Carl Sagan, *Parade*, February 14, 1989, p. 14. Reprinted by permission of the author.

Box 11.1: "Military and Other Social Expenditures" Ruth Leger Sivard, *World Priorities and Social Expenditures 1991* (Washington, D.C.): World Priorities, 1991. Reprinted by permission.

Box 11.2: "Convergence in the Superpowers' Weapons Systems: A Chronology of Reciprocal Developments" Ruth Leger Sivard, *World Military and Social Expenditures 1987–1988* (Washington, D.C.: World Priorities, 1987), p. 14. Reprinted by permission.

Box 11.3: "National Security in the 1990's: Defining a New Basis for U.S. Military Forces," *The Changing Security Environment*, Rep. Les Aspin, address before the Atlantic Council of the United States, January 6, 1992, p. 21. Reprinted by permission.

Box 11.5: "Redefining 'Security' in the 'New World Order' " from *World Security: Trends and Challenges at Century's End* by Michael T. Klare and Daniel C. Thomas (New York: St. Martin's Press, 1991), p. 3. Reprinted with permission of St. Martin's Press, Inc.

Box 12.2: Deutsch, Karl W., *Politics and Government*. Copyright © 1974 by Houghton Mifflin Company. Used by permission.

INDEX

Abortion, U.S. delegation opposition to at
    World Population Council, 316
Absolute poverty, 327
Acheson, Dean, 95
Acid rain, 333
    and coal production, 369
Adjudication, 501
Afghanistan, Soviet invasion of, 101, 167, 257,
    362–363
Africa
    death rates from AIDS in, 309–310
    food production in, 326
    imperialism in, 121
    life expectancy in, 310
African, Caribbean, and Pacific (ACP)
    countries, 183n
    and preferential trade, 279
Agricultural subsidies
    in the European Community, 248
    in the U.S., 248
Agriculture
    tariff barriers on products, 244
    trends in production, 323–324
    world trade in, 247–248
Agriculture, U.S. Department of, role of, in
    foreign policy making, 50

Alaskan oil
    and completion of pipeline, 353
    and oil production, 357
Albania, government in, 68
Algeria, 126
    government in, 69
Alliances, 148, 523. *See also* Balance of power
    advantages of, 467–468
    dangers of, 468–470
    definition of, 466–467
    disadvantages of, 468
    in the realist and idealist images, 470
    rival theories on, 467–470
Andropov, Yuri, 101, 109
Angola, government in, 68
Animus belligerandi, 509
Anschluss, 80
Anticommunism, 87
Antisatellite (ASAT) weapons, 403
Anti-War Treaty of Rio de Janeiro (1933), 507
ANZUS pact, 523
Apartheid, and economic sanctions against
    South Africa, 380–381
Appeasement, 80–81
Arab-Israeli War (1967), 364
Arab League, 524

Arabs, peace talks with Israel (1991), 260
Arbatov, Georgy, 102, 109
Arbitration, 501
Argentina
  government in, 68
  and Third World debt, 289
  use of borrowed money by, 290
Aristide, Jean-Bertrand, 68
Arms control
  and the Cold War, 100–101
  and control of weapons proliferation,
      482–484
  and disarmament, 482–487
  historical examples of, 485–487
  of nuclear arms, 487–496
  problematic future for, 493–496
  SALT agreements on, 100–101, 422, 490,
      494, 495
Arms exporters, 398, 400
Arms importers, 398
Arms trade
  motives for, 400–402
  trends in the, 397–400
Asian Tigers, income level in, 131
Aspin, Les, 535
Association of South East Asian Nations
      (ASEAN), 183n, 188, 523
Atlantic Charter, 159
Atomic bomb, power of, 402
Australia, imperialism of, 125
Austria, interest in European Community
      membership, 183
Automobile industry, U.S. position in, 232n,
      237

Bacteriological (Biological) and Toxin
      Weapons Convention (TWC) (1972),
      407, 487, 494
Baker, James A., 71, 262
Baker initiative, 291–292
Balance of payments, 212
  correcting deficiency in, 221
  financing of deficits, 212–213
Balance of power, 29, 470. *See also* Alliances
  breakdown of, 473–474
  collective security versus, 474
  game rules, 471–472
  post–World War II models of the, 475
    bipolarity, 475–476
    bipolycentrism, 476–479
    unipolarity, 475
  preconditions for peace through, 472–473
  revival of, 474–475

Balance-of-Power theory, assumptions of,
      470–475
Balance of trade, 212
  trying to maintain favorable, 120–121
Ballistic missiles
  proliferation of, 406–407
  psychological effects of, 405
Bangladesh, 126
  government in, 68
Barnet, Richard J., 341
Baruch Plan (1946), 485
Beggar-thy-neighbor policies, 233
Behavioral approach, to study of international
      relations, 25–28
Behavioralism, 35
Belgium, and end of empire, 126
Berlin blockade, 161, 453
Berlin Wall, fall of, 68
Bilateral arms control agreements
  differentiation between multilateral
      agreements and, 484
  major, 489
Biological weapons, trends in, 405
Biosphere, 3
Bipolarity
  and balance of power, 475–476
  of the Cold War, 111, 113
Bipolycentrism, and balance of power,
      476–479
Birthrates, uncertainty of, and world
      population growth, 310–311
Bissell, Richard, 152
Bolivia, government in, 68
Bolshevik revolution, 87
Bonaparte, Napoleon, 59
Boutros-Ghali, Boutros, 170n, 522
Brady initiative, 293
Brazil
  debt payment by, 292
  financial support of United Nations by,
      170
  government in, 68
  and Third World debt, 289
  use of borrowed money by, 290
Bretton Woods system, 218
  institutions developed in, 218, 220
  participation of Soviet Union in, 256
  U.S. role in the, 219, 221–225, 243–244
Brezhnev, Leonid, 96, 97, 109, 421–422
Brezhnev Doctrine, 96
Brinkmanship, 420
British Petroleum, as nonstate actor, 154
Bulgaria, government in, 68

Bureaucracy, and efficiency and
    rationality, 50
Bureaucratic behavior, attributes of, 53
Bureaucratic management of foreign
    relations, 50
Bureaucratic organization, limits of, 50–53
Bureaucratic policy making, consequences of,
    54–56
Bureaucratic politics, of foreign policy
    decision-making, 49–56
Bureaucratic politics model, 51–52
Bureaucratic recalcitrance, 54–56
Burkina Faso, government in, 68
Bush, George, 3, 71, 341, 436
    on collapse of communism, 106, 109
    and creation of New World Order, 367, 430
    and end of Cold War, 5, 103
    meeting with Boris Yeltsin, 492–493
    and Persian Gulf War, 46–47, 52–53, 360,
        363, 522
    on threat of global nuclear war, 441
    trade policies under, 250
Byelorussia, as United Nations member,
    156n
Byrnes, James, 87, 94–95

Cambodia, government in, 68–69
Cameroon, government in, 68
Camp David Declaration on New Relations
    (1992), 5, 107, 425–426
Camp David meeting (1978), 362, 501
Canada, and conclusion of free trade
            agreements with U.S., 248
Capitalism
    movement from socialism to, 251–254,
        256–261
    special responsibilities of, 214–215
Caribbean Community (CARICOM), 188
Carnegie, Andrew, 19–20
Carpenter, Ted Galen, 110
Carter, Jimmy
    on arms sales, 400
    and nuclear technology, 409
    and trade relations with Soviet Union, 257,
        258
Carter Doctrine, 101, 362–363
Central Commission for the Navigation of the
    Rhine, 155
Central Intelligence Agency, role of, in foreign
    policy making, 50
Centrally planned economies, 116, 211–213
    transformation of, to market economy, 255

Centre on Transnational Corporations, 189
Chamberlain, Neville, 80
Chemical weapons, 494
    trends in, 405
Cheney, Dick, 52
Chernenko, Konstantin, 101
Chernobyl, 371–372
Child deathrates, in Third World, 304
Chile, government in, 68
China
    foreign policy process in, 54
    imperialism in, 121
    role of geopolitics in shaping foreign policy
        of, 61
    and United Nations membership, 164
Chlorofluorocarbons, link of, to ozone
        depletion, 336
Churchill, Winston, 4, 59, 83, 159, 441
Civil strife, and external aggression, 460–462
Civil war, 457–458
    causes of, 459–460
    frequency and severity of, 458
    human costs of, 458
    and intervention, 460
Classical imperialism, 120–121
Classical international trade theory, 238–239
Classical realism, 23
    continuing relevance of, 25
Closed economic systems, 212–213
Closed political system, 64.
Coal, as energy source, 344–345, 369
Coercive diplomacy, 419–420
    and crises, 454–456
Coexistence, 96–97
Cold War
    arms negotiations and SALT, 100
    bipolar power distribution in, 111, 113
    causes of, 85–90
    coexistence, 96–97
    Containment Doctrine, 93–94
    détente, 97, 99–100, 223
        demise of, 101–102
    from détente to renewed hostility, 256–258
    deterrence after the, 428–433
    end of, 4, 5, 33, 72, 103–108, 253
        great-power relations after the, 112
        impact of, on developing countries, 263
        implication of, for arms trade, 400–402
        and the "Long Peace," 108–110
        and nuclear disarmament, 410–411
        opportunities created by, 295
        as signal for end of nonalignment, 149
    First World in, 116

international law after the, 512
obstacles to conflict prevention, 520–521
phases and character of, 90–111
renewed dialogue, 102
role of United Nations in, 161, 176
spheres of influence and the formation of blocs, 94–96
strategic doctrine during, 419–428
United Nations post, 521–523
and use of economic sanctions, 378–380
Collective good, 215
Collective security, 523
versus power balance, 474
and preservation of peace, 513–514
Colonialism
end of the acceptability of, 115
in the interwar period, 125–126
and rise and fall of European empires, 117–127
Cominform, 96
Command economics, 211–213
Commerce, U.S. Department of, role of, in foreign policy making, 50
Commodities
recycling, 376
stockpiling of, 376
substitution, 376
and terms of trade, 275–279
Commodity power, and resource dependence, 374–377
Common Agricultural Policy (CAP), institution of, by European Community, 244
Commons, freedom of the, 339
Commons arrangement, toward managed, 334–339
Commonwealth of Independent States (CIS)
economy of, 116
future of the, 106
impact of demographic trends on national security, 318
Communism
collapse of, 109–110
and use of force, 446–447
Comparative advantage, 232–233, 234
Comparative foreign policy, 36–37
Complex interdependence, as a world view, 31–32
Comprehensive Test Ban Negotiations, 486
Concert of Europe, 113
Conciliation, 501
Conference on Disarmament (CD), 486–487

Conference on Security and Cooperation in Europe (CSCE) (1992), 478, 486
Conflict, comparison with war, 436n
Conflict management, and regional security organizations, 523–524
Conflict of interests, as cause of Cold War, 86
Conflict prevention, Cold War obstacles to, 520–521
Congo. *See* Zaire.
government in, 68
Congress of Vienna, 113
Connally Amendment, 511, 512
Containment Doctrine, 93–94
Conventional Armed Forces in Europe (CFE) (1990), Treaty on, 106, 401, 424, 486
Conventional theory, of economic development, 142
Conventional weapons and delivery systems, trends in, 403–404
Coordinating Committee (Cocom), U.S. sponsorship of, 256
Core-periphery concept, 144–145
Core states, 144–145
Corpus juris gentium, 499
Correlates of War Research Project, 453
Cosmocorp, 189
Côte d'Ivoire, government in, 68
Council for Mutual Economic Assistance (CMEA), 252, 253
Council of Arab Economic Unity, 188
Council of Europe, 524
Counterforce strategy, 420
Countervalue posture, 420
Cox, Michael, 110
Crisis
and coercive diplomacy, 454–456
definition of, 453
escalation to war, 454
Critical social theory, 28
Cuba
Soviet Union aid to, 254
U.S. sanctions against, 378–379
Cuban missile crisis (1962)
challenge of, to peace, 96
and coercive diplomacy, 420, 453
and rational decision-making, 46
role of bureaucratic organization in, 51, 54
Currency
Bretton Woods system of, 218–225, 243–244, 255
determining rates of exchange for, 218
devaluation of, 218

fixed exchange rates for, 219
free-floating exchange rates, 224
impact of Plaza agreement on, 229–230
parallel, 219
reasons for fluctuation of currency rates, 226–227
Current history approach to the study of international relations, 19–20
Cyclical theories of war, 451–453
Czechoslovakia
  and arms export, 401
  government in, 68
  interest in European Community membership, 183*n*
  origin of, post–world War I, 77
  1948 coup in, 161
  and World War II, 81

Damage limitation, 422
Danube River Commission (1857), 526
Deathrates, uncertainty of, and world population growths, 309–310
Debtor nations, massive capital flight from, 290–291
Declaration on the Granting of Independence to Colonial Countries and Peoples (1960), 126
Deconstructionism, 28
Defacto recognition, 500
Defense, U.S. Department of, role of, in foreign policy making, 50
Deforestation
  as cause of global warming, 332–333
  in Third World, 328
Delors, Jacques, 179, 186
Democracies
  consequences of the spread of, 66–67, 69
  foreign policy performance of, 65–66
  and involvement in war, 447–449
Demographic changes
  correlates of, 317–322
    impact of demographic trends
      on economic development, 318–322
      on global commons, 328–334
      on global food security, 323–327
      on national security, 317–318
Demographic transition theory, 307–309
  lessons of the, 316
  phases of, 310–311
Dependency theory, 36
  core arguments of, 286
  of economic development, 142–144

Dependentistas, 143
Desertification, in Third World, 328
Détente, 97, 99–100
  demise of, 101–102
Deterrence, after the Cold War, 428–433
Developed countries. *See* First World
Developing countries. *See* Third World
Development Assistance Committee (DAC), of the Organization for Economic Cooperation and Development (OECD), as foreign aid donor, 282
Diplomatic immunity, 500
Diplomatic recognition, 500
Disarmament. *See also* Arms control
  and arms control, 482–487
  post–Cold War, 491–493
Dispute settlement, procedures for, 501
Diversionary theory of war, 461–462
Division of Labor, development of new international, 271
Dollar. *See* U.S. dollar
Dollar convertibility, 219
Dollar overhang, 229
Domestic jurisdiction, 500
Domino theory, 87
Donovan, "Wild Bill," 71
Dresser Industries controversy, 202
Dualism
  dependency theory rejection of, 143–144
  in developing societies, 140–141
Dubos, René, 535
Dulles, John Foster, 86, 96
Duration of independence, and involvement in war, 444
Durning, Alan, 297
Dutch, imperialism of, 120

Earth, carrying capacity of, 297–298
Earth Summit, 335
  U.S. position at, 337
East. *See also* Second World
  historical perspective of commercial ties with West, 256–258
  isolation of, from West, 256
East Germany, immigrant workers in, 315*n*
East Pakistan, 126
Ecological perspective, on world politics, 297
Economic and Monetary Union, 185
Economic capacity, as source of power, 392, 394
Economic Community of West African States (ECOWAS), 188

Economic development
  conventional theory of, 142
  dependency theory of, 142–144
  impact of demographic trends on,
    318–322
  measuring, 132, 134–138
  role of, in shaping foreign policy, 63–64
  Third World aim in, 174–175
  world-system theory of, 144–145
Economic factors, and commodity power,
  375–376
Economic growth, and military spending,
  415–419
Economics
  laissez-faire, 124
  mercantilism, 120, 124
  stagnation in post–World War I period,
    124–125
Economic sanctions
  as instruments of foreign policy, 378–384
  reasons for, 382–384
Economic system, and involvement in war,
  446–447
Economies, open versus closed, 211–213
Ecosphere, 3
Effective demand, 327
Einstein, Albert, 498
Eisenhower, Dwight D.
  on Cold War, 87, 96
  and defense spending, 416
  on foreign policy, 58
  on military power, 538
  and military spending, 415
  and security dilemma, 433
  and use of nuclear weapons, 420
Elitism, 65
El Salvador, Soccer War between Honduras
  and, 151
Emigration, global patterns of, 311–315
Empire, end of, 539–540
Energy consumption
  global patterns of, 342–344
  and gross national product (GNP), 343
Energy security, methods of ensuring,
  364–366
Energy sources. See also Oil
  alternative, 367–368
    coal, 344–345, 369
    hydropower, 370
    natural gas, 369–370
    and reduced reliance on OPEC oil,
      353
Entente Cordiale, in World War I, 74

Enterprise, 169
Environmental refugees, 312
Environmental terrorism, 330
Estonia
  origin of, post–world War I, 77
  post–World War II, 83
  United Nations admission of, 156
Ethnocentrism, as cause of World War I, 76
Eurocentric system, of power balances,
  473–474
Eurocurrencies, 222
Europe
  fertility rate in, 310
  immigrants to, 314
  political unification of, 528–529
European Atomic Energy Community, 177
European Coal and Steel Community (ECSC),
  177
European Community (EC), 282. See also
    European Economic Community
  and agricultural subsidies, 248
  chronology of events, 180–181
  communities making up, 177
  creation of, 191
  and development of currency system, 231
  Executive Commission
    Court of Justice, 178
    European Parliament, 178
  extension of preferential trade to Third
    World, 244
  functions of, 181, 183
  historical development of, 183
  impact of, on multinational corporations,
    191–193
  and institution of Common Agricultural
    policy, 244
  legislative process in, 182
  and Maastricht Summit (1992), 185, 528
  membership of, 177
  and operation of STABEX, 278–279
  organizational components and decision-
    making procedures, 177–178
  pooled sovereignty in, 179, 181
  powers of, 179
  prospect of an enlarged, 183–185
  as threat to open, liberal regime, 250
European currency unit (ECU), 231
European Economic Community, 177. See also
    European Community (EC)
European empires, rise and fall of, 117–127
European Free Trade Association (EFTA)
  creation of, 183
  membership of, 183

European imperialism
    first wave of, 120–121
    second wave of, 121–126
European Monetary System (EMS),
        launching of, 231
European Political Cooperation (EPC),
        185–186
European Recovery Program,
        U.S.-sponsored, 256
European System of Central Banks (ESCB),
        231
Eurosclerosis, 184
Exchange rates. *See* Currency
Exponential increase, 302–303
Export controls, of technology transfer,
        409–410
Export-led industrialization (ELI), 273
Export quotas, 236
Extended deterrence, 420–421
External aggression, civil strife and, 460–462
Extraterritoriality, 500

Fair trade, versus free trade, 246–247
Falkland Islands (Malvinas) War, 290, 401
Family planning, and population growth, 316
Federalism, world, 525
Ferdinand, Archduke, 75
    assassination of, 73–74
Fertility rates, and population growth,
        303–304
Finland
    interest in European Community
        membership, 183
    origin of, post–World War I, 77
    role of geopolitics in shaping foreign policy
        of, 61–62
First World, 116
    consumption in, 329–330
    country make-up of, 116
    demographic transition in, 308
    and dependence on commodities, 377
    energy consumption in, 344
    impact of demographic trends on economic
        development in, 321–322
    impact of demographic trends on the global
        commons in, 329
    military spending by, 396
    move toward zero population growth in,
        305–306
    and production of greenhouse gases, 331
    and transformation of world political
        economy from perspective of,
        209–261

Fixed exchange rates, 219
Follow-on START agreement, 492–493
Food ladder concept, consumption patterns
        described by, 327
Food security, 324–327
Force, use of, in war, 507–509
Ford, Gerald, 55
Ford Motor, as nonstate actor, 154
Foreign affairs, democracies in, 66
Foreign aid
    conditionality, 284–285
    form and purposes of, 280, 281
    volume and value of, 280, 282–284
Foreign exchange markets, appreciation of the
        dollar in, 291
Foreign policy
    actors in, 43, 44–49
    definition of, 43, 44
    economic sanctions as instruments of,
        378–384
    primary goals of, 44
Foreign policy behavior, 60
    economic development, 63–64
    geopolitics as factor in, 61–62
    military capabilities, 62–63
    types of government, 64–69
Foreign policy decision-making, 43
    bureaucratic politics of, 49–56
    nation-states in, 43–44
    role of leaders in, 56–60
    unitary actor and rational decision–making,
        44–49
    impediments to rational choice, 47–49
Foreign policy goals, of Third World nations,
        145–151
Foreign policy making
    constraints on, in a transforming world,
        69–70
    impact of images on, 17n
Foreign relations, bureaucratic management
        of, 50
Foreign workers, migration of, 314n
Formosa Straits crisis, 453
Fossil fuels
    burning of as cause of global warming, 333
    dependence on, 344–347
Fourteen Points speech, 22
France
    foreign policy in, as cause of World
        War I, 76
    imperialism of, 120, 121
Franco, Francisco, 81
Frank, Andre Gunder, 142–143

Freedom of communications issue, 173
Free-floating exchange rates, 224
Free market system and involvement in war, 446
Free riders, 215
Free trade
   versus fair trade, 246–247
   and hegemonic decline, 239, 241
Friedberg, Aaron L., 112
Functionalism, 525–527
Future, predicting, 7

Gaidar, Yegor, 107*n*
Gasohol, as alternative fuel, 353
General Agreement on Tariffs and Trade (GATT), 33, 220, 243–244
   generalized system of preferences, 274
   granting of observer status to Soviet Union, 259
   inabilities of, 245
   and the most-favored-nation principle, 243
   nondiscrimination principle, 274
   and promotion of nondiscrimination, 231–232
   rules on nondiscrimination in trade, 250–251
   Third World attitudes toward, 264, 275
   trade negotiations
      Kennedy Round, 244
      Tokyo Round, 245–246, 274
      Uruguay Round, 236–237, 243–244, 246–250, 274
Geneva Conference on Humanitarian Law (1977), 509
Geneva conventions, 485, 506*n* (1949), 506*n*
Geneva Protocol for the Prohibition of the Use in War of Asphyxiating, Poisonous, or Other Gases and of Bacteriological Methods of Warfare (1925), 406, 487
Geneva summit (1955), 96, 97
Geopolitics, as factor in foreign policy behavior, 61–62
Germain Convention (1919), 485
German Democratic Republic, government in, 68
German people, political unification of, 311–312
Germany
   and causes of World War II, 79–80
   emergence of, as industrial state, 124
   foreign policy in, as cause of World War I, 74–75, 76
   impact of demographic trends on national security, 317–318
   imperialism of, 121
   role of geopolitics in shaping foreign policy of, 61
   undervalued currency in, 224
   unification of, and European Community expansion, 186*n*
Ghana, government in, 68
Gladkov, Peter, 109
Glasnost, 106
Glassboro summit (1967), 97
Global 2000 Report of the President, 316
Global agenda, reordered, 543–544
Global commons
   impact of demographic trends on, 328–334
   impact of population growth on, 541–542
Global demographic patterns and trends, 299–301
   factors affecting national and regional variations in population growth, 301, 303
      demographic transition theory, 307–309
      fertility rates, 303–304
      population momentum, 304–306
   global patterns of emigration and immigration, 311–312
      causes of migration, 312
      consequences of migration, 312, 314–315
   population projections
      uncertain birthrates, 310–311
      uncertain deathrates, 309–310
Global disparities, in income and wealth, 127–145
Global food security, impact of demographic trends on, 323–327
Global patterns, of energy consumption, 342–344
Global predicament, twelve questions for a transforming world, 535–545
Global problématique, 34
Global warming, 330–332
   causes of, 332–333
   consequences of, 333–334
   coping with, 337–339
   as transnational policy problem, 339
Good offices, 501
Goods, distinguishing between public and collective, 215
Gorbachev, Mikhail
   assumption of power, 253, 424
   and disintegration of Soviet Union, 37, 254

and ending of Cold War, 102–106, 543
failed conservative coup against, 106, 260
importance of, in shaping Soviet state, 59
and military expenditures, 109
resignation of, 113
on threat of nationalism, 449–450
Government
effect of type of, on foreign policy, 64–69
type of, and involvement in war, 447–449
Governmental politics, 51
Great Britain
and balance of power, 472
as European core state, 124
foreign policy in, as cause of World War I, 74–75
hegemonic decline of, 216
imperialism of, 120, 121
and India, 126
laissez-faire in, 124
leadership role of, 215
preference for open economy, 214
role of geopolitics in shaping foreign policy of, 61
Great Depression, as cause of World War II, 82
Greater East Asian Co-Prosperity Sphere, 81
Great man, versus zeitgeist debate, 60
Great-power rivalry, 71–114
in Cold War, 85–110
in post–Cold War world, 111–114
quest for hegemony, 72–73
in World War I, 73–79
in World War II, 79–85
Greece, foreign policy of ancient, 65
Greenhouse gases, 331
Green Revolution, 323
Grenada, 102
Gross national product (GNP), and energy consumption, 343
Gross world product, U.S. share of, 216
Group of Five, 229–230
and Louvre meeting (1987), 229–230
and Plaza Agreement (1985), 229
Group of Seven (G-7), 179n, 230
Group of 77
and adoption of Integrated Programme for Commodities, 277–279
cohesive power of, 175, 267
and drive for New International Economic Order, 173, 174
formation of, 146, 267–268
Growth optimists, 316–317, 323
Growth pessimists, 316, 318–319, 323–324

Guerrilla warfare, 462
Guest workers, 314–315
migration of, 314n
Gulf Cooperation Council, 523
Gulf War. See Persian Gulf War

Hague conferences (1899 and 1907), 507
Haiti, government in, 68
Hammarskjöld, Dag, 515, 518, 520
Havana Charter, 243
Health rate, death due to inadequate, 309–310
Hegemonic decline
and free trade, 239, 241
and international stability, 216–218
Hegemonic stability, 34
Hegemonic stability theory, 33–34, 214, 215, 216
Hegemony
in decline, 224–225
definition of, 34, 214
and hegemonic stability, 214–218
"malign" view of, 215–216
movement to multilateral management, 225, 227–230
negative connotations of, 215
under stress, 222–224
Heilbroner, Robert, 115
Heisbourg, François, 154
Helsinki Accords (1975), 100
Hero-in-history model, 56–57, 63
limits to, 59–60
History, end of, 542–543
Hitler, Adolf, 56, 61, 80, 81, 82–83
Hobbes, Thomas, 22n
Honduras, Soccer War between El Salvador and, 151
Hong Kong, 131
government in, 68
Horizontal proliferation, 407–411
Host country, 189
Hughes, Emmet John, 58
Human development index (HDI), 134–136
Human nature
rule of, in political theory, 20n
and war, 442–443
Human tragedy, of violent conflict, 464–465
Human well-being, defining, 541–542
Hungary
government in, 68
interest in European Community membership, 183n
1956 revolution in, 167
transformation to market economy, 255

Hunter, Robert, 209
Hussein, Saddam, 103. *See also* Persian Gulf
     War
   and military capabilities, 63
   and oil production, 360–361
Hydropower, as alternative energy source,
     370

Iacocca, Lee, 246
Idealism, 35, 79
Idealist reform program, 21–22
Idealist world view, 20–21
Ideological incompatibilities, as cause of Cold
     War, 86–88
Iklé, Fred Charles, 389
Images of reality, 16
   nature of, 16–17
   role of, in international politics, 17
   sources of, 16
   sources of change, 18
Immigration, global patterns of, 311–315
Imperialism
   classical, 120–121
   new, 121–126
Imperial overstretch, thesis of, 418
Import quotas, 236
Import-substitution industrialization (ISI),
     273
Income levels
   in developing countries, 139
   global disparities in, 127–145
India, and Great Britain, 126
Indonesia, income level in, 130
Infant industries, 238
Inflation, and fluctuation of currency rates,
     226
INGOs, definition of, 155*n*
Institutionalism, neoliberal, 30–33
Instrumental rationality, distinguishing
     between procedural rationality and,
     56–57
Interaction opportunities, 481*n*
Inter-American, Asian, and African
     Development banks, as foreign aid
     donor, 282
Interdependence
   benefits of, 210
   as cure or curse, 536–537
   Third World debt and management of,
     289–295
Interdependent world, trade strategies in,
     231–241

Interest rates, in U.S., 227, 229
Intermediate-Range Nuclear Force (INF)
     Treaty (1987), 103, 403, 424
International Bank for Reconstruction and
     Development (IBRD). *See* World
     Bank
International commerce, evolution of rules
     governing, 213–214
International cooperation
   and political realism, 213
   prospects for, 334–335
International Court of Justice. *See* World
     Court
International economic relations, dominance
     and dependence in, 141–145
International Energy Agency, creation of, 364
International governmental organization,
     definition of, 155*n*
International intergovernmental organization
     (IGO), 155–158
International Labor Organization (ILO), 172
   U.S. withdrawal from, 527
International law
   contributions of, to peace, 510–512
   post–Cold War, 512
   principles of, 499–501
   private, 498
   public, 498–499
   relevance of, 503–505
   structural limitations of the, 501–503
   on use of unconventional weapons, 406
   and world order, 498–512
International Monetary Fund (IMF)
   creation of, 218–219, 220
   and creation of Special Drawing Rights
     (SDRs), 222
   debt relief role of, 291
   maintenance of Compensatory Contingency
     Financing Facility by, 277
   role of, in Liberal International Economic
     Order, 33
   as source of funds, 212–213
   Soviet interest in membership in, 259
   Third World belief in bias of, 264
International monetary regime,
     transformation of the, 218–231
International nongovernmental organizations
     (INGOs), 155
   growth of, 155–156
International nongovernment organizations,
     158
International Olympic Committee, as
     nonstate actor, 154

International organizations, 512
  growth of, 155–159, 512–513
  and the politics of peace and security,
    158–159
International Peace Conferences at the Hague
    (1899 , 1907), 485
International politics. *See* World politics
International regimes, 32–33
  influence of, on world political economy,
    217–218
  sovereign states in, 203–204
International relations
  behavioral approach to, 25–28
  current history approach to, 19–20
  neorealist structural approach to, 28–30
International Seabed Authority, 169
International stability, and hegemonic
    decline, 216–218
International Telegraphic Union (1865), 526
International Telephone and Telegraph
    (ITT), and politics, 200
International Trade Organization (ITO), 220
  need for U.S. support for, 243
Intervention, and civil war, 460
Interwar period
  colonialism and self-determination in the,
    125–126
  economic stagnation in, 125
Iran
  as emerging security threat, 362
  nuclear interests of, 410
Iran, Shah of, 59
Iran-Contra affair, 53
Iran-Iraq war
  and arms sales, 401
  and oil production, 360
  threat of spread, 362, 364
Iraq. *See also* Persian Gulf War
  and acquisition of nuclear weapons,
    409–410
  economic sanctions against over Kuwait
    crisis, 381–382
  mandate of, 125
  use of chemical weapons by, 406, 494
Irredentism, as cause of World War II, 79–80
Isolation, 148
Israel
  creation of mandate leading to, 125
  impact of demographic trends on national
    security, 317–318
  peace talks with Arab countries (1991), 26(
  U.S. conclusion of free trade agreements
    with, 248
Italy, and World War II, 81

Jackson-Vanik Amendment to the Trade Act
    of 1974, 257*n*
Japan
  aging of society in, 321–322
  economic strategy of, 249–250
  emergence of, as partner in international
    monetary management, 229
  energy efficiency of, 344, 345
  energy policy in, 337
  export-oriented economy of, 321–322
  exports-to-GNP ratio, 241, 243
  and global investments, 193, 196–197
  imperialism of, 121, 125
  neomercantilism in, 235
  protectionist trade policies, 244
  trade negotiations between U.S. and,
    249–250
  undervalued currency in, 224
  U.S. exports to, 246*n*
  U.S. imports from, 246*n*
  and World War II, 81
Jervis, Robert, 111
Jihad, 87
Johnson, Lyndon B.
  inflation under, 224
  U.S. trade policy under, 244
Jonah, James O. C., 115
Jordan, government in, 69
Jus ad bellum, 508
Jus Sanguinis, 500*n*
Jus soli, 500*n*
Just War Doctrine, 506–507

Kant, Immanuel, on democracy, 67
Kashmir, 126
Kassebaum Amendment, 170–171
Kellogg-Briand Pact (1928), 21, 79, 507
Kennan, George F., 22*n*, 89
  and Containment Doctrine, 93–94, 108
Kennedy, John F., 436, 466
  and Cuban missile crisis, 51–52, 54
  on future of world, 545
  on international law, 512
  on national sovereignty, 536
  and rational decision making, 46, 47
  on tension reduction, 97
  on threat of nuclear weapons, 483
  on total war, 391
Kennedy, Robert, 52
Kennedy Round, 244
Kenya, government in, 68
Khrushchev, Nikita, 96, 420, 483

Kindleberger, Charles, 209, 215
Kissinger, Henry A., 43
  on bureaucratic recalcitrance, 54–55
  on détente, 97, 99
  linkage theory of, 99
  on political realism, 22n
  and rational decision making, 48
  on Soviet-American relations, 57
Korean Airlines flight 007, 102
Korean police action (1950), 514
Korean War, 95
Krauthammer, Charles, 112
Kuwait. See also Persian Gulf War
  income level in, 130
  limits of bureaucratic organization in, 52–53

Laissez-faire, 124
Latin America
  import-substitution industrialization
    strategy in, 273
  independence of countries in, 117
  role of geopolitics in shaping foreign policy
    in, 62
Latin American Integration Association
    (ALADI), 187
Latvia
  origin of, post–world War I, 77
  post–World War II, 83
  United Nations admission of, 156
Law of the Sea Treaty, 169
Leaders
  factors affecting capacity to lead, 57–59
  role of, in foreign policy decision making,
    56–60
  self-image of, 58
League of Arab States, 523
League of Nations
  and collective security, 21, 159, 474
  covenant of, 507
  creation of, 22, 79
  expulsion of Soviet Union from, 82
  failure of, 82
  and German membership, 80
  mandates under, 125
  membership of, 81–82
Least developed countries, disparity of income
    and wealth in, 130
Legal control of war, 505–510
Lenin, Vladimir I., 77, 123
Less developed countries (LLDCs), 270
Leubsdorf, Carl P., 110
Levels-of-analysis issue, in study of world
    politics, 37–38

Lewis, Anthony, 110
Lex talionis, 510
Liberal International Economic Order
    (LIEO), 33, 146, 201, 264
  interdependence as key to transformation
    of, 297
  political bases of, 211
Libya, as catalyst for first oil shock, 348
Lie, Trygve, 518
Limits to Growth (1974), 316
Lincoln, Abraham, on foreign policy, 58
Linkage theory, 99
Lithuania
  origin of, post–World War I, 77
  post–World War II, 83
  United Nations admission of, 156
Lomé Convention, 183n, 278–279
London Naval Conference, 21
Long-cycle theory, 36, 72–73, 452
Louvre meeting (1987), 230
Low-intensity conflict (LIC), 456

Maastricht summit (1992), 185, 528
Machiavelli, Niccolò, 22–23, 22n
Machtpolitik, 80
Mackinder, Sir Halford, 20n, 62n
Macroeconomic policy coordination, 229–230
Macrosociological theory of economic
    change, 36
Madagascar, government in, 68
Madrid Middle East Peace Conference
    (October 1991), 494n
Mahan, Alfred Thayer, 20n, 62n
Malthus, Thomas, 299–301, 323
Mandate system, 125–126
Manufactured goods, Third World export of,
    271–275
Marcos, Ferdinand, 59, 68
Market economics, 211–213
  transformation of centrally planned
    economy to, 255
Market incentives, and increase in food
    production, 325–326
Marshall Plan, 89–90, 219, 221, 256
Marx, Karl, 87
Marxists, on imperialism, 123
Massive retaliation, 420
Maurice, John Frederick, 466
McKinley tariff, 233
McNamara, Robert, 52
Mearsheimer, John J., 112
Mediation, 501
Meline tariff, 233

Mental maps, 14
Mercantilism, 120–121
    waning of, 121
Mercator, Gerardus, 11
Mercator projection, 11, 13
Mexico
    oil production in, 350n, 353
    and Third World debt, 289
Middle East. *See also* Organization of
            Petroleum Exporting Countries
    increase in arms imports by, 398
    in the New World Order, 366–367
    migrant-related tensions in, 315
    oil reserves in, 355
    oil supply/production in, 347–349
Mid–intensity conflict (MIC), 457
Migration
    causes of, 312
    consequences of, 312, 314–315
    transnational, 312
Militarization, and involvement in war,
            445–446
Militarized disputes, incidence of, 454n
Military capabilities
    as goal in Third World, 149–151
    inferring power from, 393–394
    quest for, 395–411
    role of, in shaping foreign policy, 62–63
    trends in, 396–405
Military Necessity Doctrine, 508
Military power, value of, 538–539
Military preparedness and war, adverse
            environmental consequences of,
            330
Military spending
    and economic growth, 415–419
    relative burden of, 411
    and social priorities, 411–415
    trends in, 395–396
Military strength, as source of power, 392,
            394–395
MINEX, 279n
Minuteman III missile, warheads carried by,
            403
Mirror images, 17
MIRVs (multiple independently targetable
            reentry vehicles), 403
Misperceptions, as cause of Cold War, 88–90
Missile Technology Control Regime (MTCR),
            406, 494–495
Modelski, George, 43
Modern state system, emergence of the, 117,
            120

Monetary arrangement, development of
            regionalized, 230–231
Mongolia, government in, 68
Monopoly power, market conditions
            necessary for, 375
Montevideo Convention on the rights and
            duties of states (1933), 500
Montreal Protocol on Substances That
            Deplete the Ozone Layer (1987), 336
Moralism, 23
Morgenthau, Hans J., 22n
Most-favored-nation trade status, 232
    U.S. granting to Soviet Union, 257
Multifiber Arrangement (1986), 237n
Multilateral agreements
    differentiation between bilateral agreements
            and, 484
    major, 488
Multilateral aid, 280
Multilateralism
    movement to regionalism, 250–251
    U.S. retreat from, 169
Multilateral trade negotiations
    Kennedy Round of, 244
    Tokyo Round of, 245–246, 274
    Uruguay Round of, 236–237, 243–244,
            246–250, 274
Multinational corporations (MNCs)
    benefits of, 189, 190–191, 286–287
    controlling, 201–203
    costs of, 189, 190–191, 287–289
    and dependency theory, 143
    and functionalism, 526
    global reach and economic power, 189,
            191–198
    growth of, 188–189
    impact of European Economic Community
            on, 191–193
    impact on home and host nations, 198–200
    as nonstate actor, 154
    patterns of foreign direct investment, 193,
            196–198
    and politics, 200–201
    proliferation and tremendous size of,
            189
    role of, in energy production, 347
    and technological development, 139
Multinational oil companies, and control of oil
            production, 354
Multiple independently targetable warheads
            (MIRVs), 403, 494–495
Multipolarity
    and balance of power, 479

and peace, 481–482
in post–Cold War world, 113–114
reemergence of, as factor in World War II, 81–82
Munich Conference (1938), 80
Mutual and Balanced Force Reductions Talks (MBFR), 485–486
Mutual Assured Destruction (MAD), 421–422, 425
Mutual deterrence, 420–423
Mutual sensitivity, 210
Mutual vulnerability, 210

Namibia, 125
Nation, 44. *See also* Nation state
National character, expression of, in war, 443
National decision making, and unitary actor(s), 44–49
National interest, defining, 537
Nationalism
    as cause of World War I, 76
    as cause of World War II, 79–80
    and involvement in war, 449–450
    neo-, and civil war, 459–460
National poverty, and involvement in war, 444
National security
    definition of, 389
    impact of demographic trends on, 317–318
    and oil, 360–367
    power in international politics, 391–392
        changing nature of world power, 394–395
        elements of national power, 392–393
        inferring power from capabilities, 393–394
    as public good, 215
    quest for military capabilities, 395
        proliferation problem, 406–411
        trends in military capabilities, 396–405
        trends in military spending, 395–396
    and security dilemma, 390–391
    Third World quest for, 149
Nation state
    alliances between, 466–470
    and arms control, 482–496
    and the balance of power, 470–482
    concern for relative gains, 213–214
    in foreign policy decision making, 43–44
    internal characteristics of, and involvement in war, 443–450
    national interests of, 537

obsolescence of, 535–536
realism on, 23
relative power potential of, 392
responding to economic challenges, 213
security dilemma of, 390–391
NATO. *See* North Atlantic Treaty Organization (NATO)
Natural gas, as alternative fuel, 353, 369–370
Negotiation, 501
Neocolonialism, 117, 148
Neofunctionalism, 527–529
Neoimperialism, 117, 148
Neoliberal institutionalism, 30–33, 35
    intellectual roots of, 31
Neoliberalism, 31
Neo–Malthusians, 316
Neomercantilism, 232, 233, 235–238
    and costs of protectionism, 238
    and export quotas, 236
    and import quotas, 236
    and infant industries, 238
    and nontariff barriers, 237–238
Neonationalism, and civil war, 459 460
Neorealism, 25
    and study of international relations, 28–30
    theory of, 29–30
Nepal, government in, 68
Neutrality, Doctrine of, 499
New imperialism, 121–123
    economic explanations of the, 123–124
    political explanations of the, 124–125
New International Economic Order (NIEO), 173
    demise of, 267–270
    developing nations demand for, 262–264
    in Third World nations, 145–147
Newly industrialized countries (NICs), 247, 270
    dependency theory, explanation of phenomenon, 145
    disparity in income and wealth in, 131–132
    and export-led industrialization, 273
    and export quotas, 237
New Treaty of European Union (1992), 528
New World Information and Communication Order (NWICO), 173, 174
New World Order
    development of, 544–545
    oil and the Middle East in the, 366–367
    redefining "security" in the, 434
    Russian (Republic) strategy in, 431–433
    U.S. strategy in the, 430–431

New Zealand, imperialism of, 125
Niebuhr, Reinhold, 22n
Nietzsche, Friedrich, 22n
Niger, government in, 68
Nigeria
  government in, 68
  income level in, 130
Nixon, Richard M., 389
  on balance of power, 475
  and Cold War, 97
  economic policy under, 224
  linkage theory of, 99
  U.S. trade policy under, 244
  on Vietnam War, 441
Nixon Doctrine, 100
Nonaligned movement, origin of, 148
Nonalignment, as goal in Third World,
    148–149
Nondiscrimination, and most-favored-nation
    principle, 231–232
Noninterference principle, 499–500
Nonintervention, 499–500
Non–Proliferation Treaty (NPT), 407, 486
Nonrecognition, 500
Nonstate actors, in world politics, 154–205
Nonstate nations, 44n
Nontariff barriers, 237–238, 240
Nordic Council, 157, 523
North. See also First World; North–South
    conflict
  population growth in, 301
North, Oliver, 53
North American Free Trade Agreement
    (NAFTA), 250
North Atlantic Cooperation Council (NACC),
    478
North Atlantic Treaty Alliance, 392
North Atlantic Treaty Organization
    (NATO), 95
  and bipolarity, 476
  and bipolycentrism, 477–478
  commitment of members to, 187
  flexible response strategy of, 487
  and polycentrism, 524
  and regional security, 157, 523
North Korea, United Nations admission of,
    156
North Sea, and oil production, 353, 357
North–South conflict, 115–153. See also
    North; South
  and achievement of food security, 324–327
  noninvolvement of Second World countries
    in, 263

  political economy of, 270–289
    commodity exports and terms of trade,
      275–279
    development finance, 279–285
    engines of growth, 286–289
    exporters of primary products and
      manufactured goods, 271–275
    in the 1990s, 295
Nuclear age, realism in, 23–24
Nuclear attack, views of the aftermath of, 440
Nuclear deterrence, 425
Nuclear disarmament, 410–411
Nuclear energy, as alternative energy source,
    370–373
Nuclear know-how, proliferation of, as
    international concern, 151
Nuclear Nonproliferation Treaty (NPT)
    (1968), 97, 409–410, 494
Nuclear power, as alternative fuel, 353
Nuclear Utilization Theory, 422–423
Nuclear weapons
  destructiveness of, 439
  proliferation of, 407
  superpower agreements for controlling,
    487–496
  trends in, 402–403
Nuclear winter, 309

Oil
  and alternative energy sources, 367–373
  demand and conservation of, 351–353
  development and impact of inexpensive,
    344–347
  on disutility of resource power, 373–378
  and economic sanctions, 378–384
  making of OPEC decade, 342, 347–349
    development of fossil fuel dependence,
      344–347
    global patterns of energy consumption,
      342–344
    rise of OPEC, 347–349
    U.S. role in, 349–350
  and national security, 360–367
    emerging security threat, 362–364
    ensuring energy security, 364–366
    oil and the Middle East in New World
      Order, 366–367
  in the New World Order, 366–367
  and the Persian Gulf War, 360–361
  reserves in, 355
  role of OPEC in controlling prices of, 225,
    227–230

shape of the future, 354
  oil supply and demand, 355–359
  OPEC's changing fortunes, 354–355
  U.S. oil import vulnerability and
    dependence, 359–360
supply and demand
  non-OPEC production, 357–358
  oil reserves, 355
  Soviet energy production, 358–359
  Third World demand for, 355–357
toward the future, 384–385
unmaking of OPEC decade, 350–351
  consumption, 351–353
  production, 353–354
Oil-exporting countries, disparity of income
    and wealth in, 130–131
Oil shock
  impact of, on foreign debt, 290
  in 1973–1974, 341, 342, 347, 348–349
  in 1979–1980, 341, 350, 362
  in 1990, 341–342, 361
Olympic boycott, 102
Omnibus Trade and Competitiveness Act
    (1988), 247, 248
  Super 301 provision of, 248–249
OPEC. *See* Organization of Petroleum
    Exporting Countries (OPEC)
Open economic systems, 211–213
Open political system, 64. *See also* Democratic
    system
Operation Desert Shield, 53, 103. *See also*
    Persian Gulf War
Operations Plan 90-1002, 53
Orderly market arrangements (OMAs),
    236–237
Organizational process, 51
Organization for African Unity (OAU), 523,
    524
Organization for Economic Cooperation and
    Development (OECD) as foreign aid
    donor, 282
Organization of American States (OAS), 523,
    524
Organization of Petroleum Exporting
    Countries (OPEC)
  changing fortunes in, 354–355
  as foreign aid donor, 282–283
  income level in, 130
  and international monetary system, 225,
    227–230
  making of, 342, 347–349
    development of fossil fuel dependence,
      344–347

global patterns of energy consumption,
    342–344
  rise of OPEC, 347–349
  U.S. role in, 349–350
members of, 130*n*
and oil production, 353–354
and reducing dependence on foreign oil,
    350–354
success of, as a political force, 377
unmaking of, 350–351
  consumption, 351–353
  production, 353–354
and use of multinational oil companies, 201
Outer Space Treaty (1967), 97
Overseas Development Council (ODC), 132,
    134*n*
Ozone depletion, coping with, 335–337

Pacta sunt servanda, 500–501
Pact of Paris, 79
Pakistan, government in, 68
Palestine, mandate of, 125
Palestine Liberation Organization (PLO), as
    nonstate actor, 154
Paradigm, 18*n*
Paraguay, government in, 68
Partial Test Ban Treaty (1963), 97
Peace
  and bipolarity, 480–481
  contributions of international law to,
    510–512
  and multipolarity, 481–482
  and political integration, 524–530
  role of United Nations in preservation of,
    513–523
Peaceful Nuclear Explosions Treaty, 486
Peacekeeper missile, warheads carried by, 403
Peace of Paris, as cause of World War II, 80
Peace of Westphalia (1648), 117, 120
Perestroika, 106
Perez, Carlos Andres, 498
Pérez de Cuéllar, Javier, 154, 170*n*, 172, 520,
    522
Perle, Richard, 109
Permanent Court of International Justice,
    creation of, 21
Persian Gulf War
  and arms trade, 400, 401, 406
  and creation of New World Order, 430–433
  death rate in, 309
  and economic sanctions against Iraq,
    381–382
  environmental costs of, 465

and environmental terrorism, 330
European Community's response to, 186
impact on oil prices, 356
and national decision making, 46
and oil crisis, 350–351, 360–361
and Operation Desert Shield, 53, 103
payment of costs in, 366n
and price of oil, 341–342
and trends in weaponry, 404
unconventional weapons used in, 405
United Nations involvement in, 176, 522
and U.S. budget concerns, 230
Peru
    debt payment by, 293
    government in, 68
Peters, Arno, 11
Peters projection, 11, 14
Petrodollars, 227
Physical Quality of Life Index (PQLI), 132,
        134, 135–136, 137
Pipes, Richard, 102
Pipeline issue, differences between the United
        States and its NATO allies on, 258
Plaza agreement (1985), 229
Pluralism, 65
Plutonium, in nuclear energy production,
        372n
Poitiers effect, 240–241
Poland
    interest of, in European Community
        membership, 183n
    origin of, post–World War I, 77
    and start of World War II, 81
    and Third World debt, 289
    U.S. sanctions against on imposition of
        martial law in, 379–380
    post–World War II, 83
Polar projection, 13, 15
Policy making, as rational choice, 45–47
Political autonomy, as goal in Third World, 147
Political disintegration, 529–530
Political economy, 209–210
    historical overview of North-South
        dialogue, 264–270
        evolving stages of UNCTAD, 268–269
        New International Economic Order,
            264–265
            and demise of, 267–270
    integrating socialist economies into,
        258–260
    new climate for economic development,
        263–267
    in the 1990s, 295

of North-South relations, 270–289
    commodity exports and terms of trade,
        275–279
    development finance, 279–285
    engines of growth, 286–289
    exporters of primary products and
        manufactured goods, 271–275
    and Third World debt and the
        management of interdependence,
        289–295
and trade strategies in an interdependent
        world, 231–241
and transformation of international
        monetary regime, 218–231
and transformation of international trade
        regime, 241, 243–251
and transformation of socialism to
        capitalism, 251–254, 256–261
Political factors, and commodity power,
        376–377
Political idealism, 20–22
    and inevitability of war, 159
Political integration, 524–530
Political psychology, 16
Political realism, 22–25, 44–45
    and international cooperation, 213
Politics
    distinction between high and low, 11n
    and multinational corporations, 200–201
Polycentrism, 476
Pooled sovereignty, 179, 181
Population growth
    debate between optimists and pessimists,
        315–317
    exponential increases in, 302–303
    factors affecting national and regional
        variations in, 301, 303–309
    high, in developing countries, 138–139
    impact of, on economic prospects of
        developing societies, 131
    impact of, on global commons, 541–542
    rapid growth of world, 299–301
Portugal, imperialism of, 120, 121
Positivism, 28
Postbehavioralism, 27–28
Post–Cold War World, great-power rivalry
        in, 111–114
Postmodernism, 28
Postpositivism, 28
Poststructuralism, 28
Potsdam Agreement, 83
Poverty
    human dimensions of, 132, 133

national, and involvement in war, 444
and unequal access to food, 326–327
Powell, Colin, 52
Power
    changing nature of world, 394–395
    as concept in structural realism, 29
    concern for relative, 390
    definition of, 391
    elements of national, 392–393
    inferring, from military capabilities, 393–394
    in international politics, 391–392
    as relational, 393–394
    security as function of, 391
    soft versus hard, 395
Power transition theory, and involvement in war, 444–445
Prebisch, Raúl, 36, 146
Preeminence, price of, 540
Preferential trade, for Third World countries, 273–275
Preventive diplomacy, 515, 518
Primary products, Third World export of, 271, 272
Private international law, 498
Procedural rationality, distinguishing between instrumental rationality and, 56–57
Product-cycle theory, on multinational corporations, 192n
Pronatalist policies, wisdom of pursuing, 322
Protectionism, costs of, 238
Public international law, 498–499
Public preferences, impact on democratic foreign policy, 65
Pueblo crisis, 394
Pugwash Conferences, 485

Qaddafi, Muammar, 57
    and military capabilities, 63

Radioactive nuclear wastes, issue of disposal of, 371–372
Rapacki Plan (1957), 485
Rational choice
    impediments to, 47–49
    policy making as, 45–47
    World War I as, 75–76
Rationality
    definition of, 46n
    distinguishing between procedural and instrumental, 56–57

Reagan, Ronald, 55
    and demise of détente, 101–102
    and end of Cold War, 103
    and Libya, 57
    and Star Wars, 423–424
    trade policies under, 247
    and trade relations with Soviet Union, 258
Reagan Doctrine, 102
Realism, 22–25, 35
    continuing relevance, 25
    extension of, 28–30
    limitations of, 24–25
    in nuclear age, 23–24
    structural, 28–30
Realpolitik, 24, 85, 467–468, 543
Rebus sic stantibus, 501
Recycling, of commodities, 376
Red Cross law, 509
Refugee asylum problem, global dimensions of, 464–465
Regime change, 264
Regional integration, preconditions for, 529
Regional security organizations, and conflict management, 523–524
Replacement-level fertility, as goal, 306
Research and development expenditures, 140n
Resource dependence, and commodity power, 374–377
Resource power, disutility of, 373–377
Revolutionary liberator, role of, 148
Rhine River Commission (1804), 526
Robinson, Arthur, 11
Robinson projection, 11, 12
Roman Catholic Church, as nonstate actor, 154
Romania, government in, 68
Rome, Treaty of, 179
Rome Summit (1991), 478
Roosevelt, Franklin D., 55, 59, 83, 159, 451
Rosicrucian Order, 155
Rush-Bagot Agreement (1818), 484n
Russia. *See also* Soviet Union
    foreign policy in, as cause of World War I, 75, 76
Russian Republic, strategy of, in the New World Order, 431–433

Salas, Rafael M., 297
SALT Agreements. *See* Strategic Arms Limitation Talks (SALT)
Samoa, government in, 68
San Francisco Charter, 176
Santayana, George, 4

Saudi Arabia
    and arms purchases, 400
    financial support of United Nations by, 170
    foreign policy of, 64–65
    in New World Order, 367
    oil production in, 350, 357*n*
    U.S. protection of, 362, 363
Scapegoat phenomenon, 65*n*
Science, versus traditionalism, 25–26
Scientific approach, 25–26
Scowcroft, Brent, 52
SCUD-B missile, 405
Second Lateran Council, 485
Second-strike capability, 421
Second World. *See also* East
    country make-up of, 116
    noninvolvement of, in North-South debate,
        263
Security
    as function of power, 391
    redefining, in the New World Order,
        434
Security dilemma, 390–391
    escaping the, 433
Self-determination, in the interwar period,
        125–126
Seville Statement (1986), 442–443
Shultz, George, 115
Siberian pipeline, building of, 364–366
Singapore, 131
Single European Act (1987), 179, 184, 185
Sino-Soviet border clash, 453
Size principle, and coalition formation, 471*n*
Smith, Adam, 121
Smith, W. Y., 112
Smoot-Hawley Act (1930), 233
Soccer War (1969), 151
Social cognition theory, 16
Social Democrats, as nonstate actor, 154
Socialism, movement from, to capitalism,
        251–252, 256–261
Socialist economies, integrating into the world
        political economy, 258–260
Social priorities, and military spending,
        411–415
Sociosphere, 3
Soil erosion, in Third World, 328
South. *See also* North-South conflict; Third
        World
    population growth in, 301
South Africa
    and economic sanctions over Apartheid,
        380–381

impact of demographic trends on national
    security, 318
South Asian Association for Regional
    Cooperation (SAARC), 188
Southeast Asia Treaty Organization
    (SEATO), 523, 524
Southern African Development Coordination
    Conference (SADCC), 188
South Korea, 131
    United Nations admission of, 156
South-West Africa, 125
Sovereign states, in international regimes,
    203–204
Sovereignty, concept of, 120
Soviet Union. *See also* Cold War
    aid to Cuba, 254
    breakup of, and spread of nuclear weapons,
        410
    and building of Siberian pipeline, 364–366
    Chernobyl explosion in, 371–372
    commercial relations with U.S., 254
    energy development in former, 358–359
    expulsion of, from League of Nations, 82
    fragmentation of, 6
    under Gorbachev, 59, 102–106, 254, 259,
        260
    granting of observer status in GATT to,
        259
    invasion of Afghanistan, 101, 167, 257,
        362–363
    key events in disintegration of, 104–105
    under Khrushchev, 96, 420, 483
    as natural gas market, 370
    nuclear arsenal of, 403, 410
    role of geopolitics in shaping foreign policy,
        61–62
    spheres of influence and formation of blocs,
        94–96
    as superpower, 63
    transformation of socialism to capitalism,
        251–254
    United States granting of most-favored-
        nation trade status, 257
    United States misperceptions of, as cause of
        Cold War, 88–90
    use of veto in United Nations, 161–162
    withholding of United Nations payments
        by, 168
Spain, imperialism of, 120, 121
Spanish Civil War, 81
Special Drawing Rights (SDRs), 222
Speculation, and fluctuation of currency rates,
    226–227

Spiral model, 390
Spykman, Nicholas, 62*n*
STABEX, 278–279
Stages of growth theory, 143
Stalin, Joseph, 81, 83, 93, 96
Standard operating procedures (SOPs), 51
Standards of living, measuring, 134–138
START. *See* Strategic Arms Reduction Treaty (START)
Star Wars ballistic missile defense (BMD) system, 423
State, 44. *See also* Nation state
  as unitary actors, 44–45
State, U.S. Department, role of, in foreign policy making, 50
State sovereignty, 23
State terrorism, 463–464
Steel, Ronald, 112
Steel industry, U.S. position in, 232*n*, 234
Stock market crash in 1987, 229, 230
Stockpiling commodities, 376
Strategic Arms Limitation Talks (SALT), 100–101
  SALT I (1972), 100, 422, 490, 494–495
  SALT II (1979), 100–101, 422, 490
Strategic Arms Reduction Treaty (START), 106, 424–425, 490–491
Strategic Defense Initiative (SDI), 423–424
Strategic Doctrine, during Cold War, 419–428
Strategic trade, 238–239
Structural Impediments Initiative (SII), 249
Structuralism, as cause of World War I, 74–75
Structural realism, 25, 28–30
Substitution of commodities, 376
Suez Canal, and oil transport, 364
Summit meetings, 98–99, 257
Sweden, interest in European Community membership, 183
Switzerland
  foreign policy of, 65
  role of geopolitics in shaping foreign policy of, 61
Syria, mandate of, 125
Systems theory of international politics, 28–29

Taiwan, 131
Taiwan Straits crises, 95
Tanzania, government in, 68
Technological dependence, 287
  in developing countries, 139–140

Technological innovations, as solutions, 537–538
Technology transfer, export controls of, 409–410
Terms of trade, commodity exports and the, 275–279
Terra nullius, 500
Territorial conquest, as foreign policy, 6
Terrorism, 462–464
  and international law, 509
Terrorist sanctuaries, disappearance of, 464
Thant, U, 520, 538
Third World
  ability to wield commodity power, 373, 374
  and advocation of balanced flow of communications, 174
  and arms sales, 401–402
  arms trafficking in, 398
  attempt to create New World Information and Communication Order (NWICO), 173
  climate for economic development, 263–264, 265–266
  and commodity exports and terms of trade, 275–279
  country make-up of, 116
  debt burden of, 227, 229
  demographic transition in, 308
  dependency ratios in, 320–321
  dependent children in, 319
  and destructiveness of war, 439
  and development finance, 279–285
  and development of new international division of labor, 271
  diversity in income and wealth in, 127, 130–132
  dualism in, 140–141
  emergence of industrial powers in, 273
  and energy consumption, 331, 343–344
  export of manufactured goods by, 271–275
  export of primary products by, 271, 272
  fertility rates in, 304
  foreign policy goals of, 145–151
  and global warming, 338–339
  growing militarization of, 396–405
  growth strategies in, 273
  impact of demographic trends on economic development in, 319–321
  impact of demographic trends on the global commons in, 328
  impact of oil shocks on, 227

impediments to growth in a typical, 138–141
low-intensity conflict in, 457
militarization of, and involvement in war, 445–446
and military spending, 396, 416
multinational corporations in, 286–289
new international economic order in, 145–147
oil supply and demand in, 355–357
pervasiveness of civil war in, 459
population growth in, 301
and preferential trade, 273–275
and price stabilization, 277–279
superpower intervention into civil war in, 460
total labor force in, 319–330
transformation of world economy from perspective of, 262–295
and Uniting for Peace process, 167
use of United Nations as forum, 164, 174–176
Third World debt and the management of interdependence, 289–295
Third worldism, end of, 152–153
Thirty Years' War, 120
Thompson, Kenneth W., 22n
Three Mile Island, 371, 372
Threshold Test Ban Treaty, 486
Thucydides, 22, 65
Tocqueville, Alexis de, 65, 85
Tokyo Round, of GATT trade negotiations, 245–246, 274
Toynbee, Arnold J., 71
Trade, preferential, 273–275
Trade Act (1974), Jackson-Vanik Amendment of, 257n
Trade conflict, costs of, 242
Trade Expansion Act (1962), 244
Trade strategies, in an interdependent world, 231–241
Traditionalism, versus science, 25–26
Tragedy of the commons, 298–299
Transfer-pricing mechanism, 288
Transjordan, mandate of, 125
Transnational bank (TNB), as force in world political economy, 189
Treasury, U.S. Department of, role of, in foreign policy making, 50
Treaty Providing for the Renunciation of War as an Instrument of National Policy (1928), 507

Trickle down theory, 142
Triple Alliance, in World War I, 74
Triple Entente, 76
Truman, Harry S, 55, 83, 94
Truman Doctrine, 94, 96
Turkey, interest in European Community membership, 183n
Turning points, wars as, 437

U-2 spy plane, 96
Ukraine
interest in European Community membership, 183n
as United Nations member, 156n
Unconventional weapons
proliferation of, 406–407
trends in, 405
UNCTAD. See United Nations Conference of Trade and Development
Underutilization, 139
Union of International Associations, 158
Unipolarity
and balance of power, 475
and peace, 480
Unitary actors
and national decision making, 44–49
states as, 44–45
United Arab Emirates, income level in, 130
United Nations (UN)
anti-Western bias of, 166
budget of, 169n, 170n
changing role of the secretary general, 515, 518, 520
characteristics of, 156–157
charter of, 156–157, 160, 166, 169n, 169, 507–508, 513–514, 522, 523
and Cold War, 176
Conference on Environment and Development (1992), 335, 338
Conference on the Human Environment (1972), 335
determination of assessments, 169n
Disarmament Conference, 407
and East-West relations, 159–176
Economic and Social Council, 160
economic sanctions against Iraq, 341–342
Environment Programme, 336
financial restraints of, 523
General Assembly, 160
and majority rule, 162–166
High Commission for Refugees, 312
International Court of Justice, 160

Korean police action, 514
membership of, 156
as nonstate actor, 154
and obstacles to conflict prevention,
520–521
peacekeeping actions of, 513–523
and Persian Gulf War, 176, 522
post–Cold War, 521–523
power of, 6
relationship between budget assessments
and voting strength, 171
role of, in delegitimization of colonialism,
126–127
role of Third World in, 174–176
role of United States in
control of purse strings in, 168–172
membership in affiliated agencies, 172–174
in peacekeeping operations, 166–167
Secretariat, 160
Security Council, 86, 159–160
and the unanimity rule, 161–162
shift of power in, 522–523
sponsorship of World Population
Conferences, 315–316
structure of, 514, 521
study on *The World's Women 1970–1990*, 311
Third World use of, as forum, 164, 174–176
Trusteeship Council, 160
trusteeship system of, 126
and Yugoslavia crisis, 524
United Nations Atomic Development
Authority, 485
United Nations Children's Fund (UNICEF),
158
United Nations Committee on Disarmament,
486
United Nations Commission on Transnational
Corporations, 202–203
United Nations Conference on Prohibition or
Restrictions of the Use of Certain
Conventional Weapons Which May
Be Deemed to Be Excessively
Injurious or to Have Indiscriminate
Effects (1977), 509n
United Nations Conference of Trade and
Development (UNCTAD),
(Geneva, 1964), 130, 146, 264
evolving stages of, 268–269
first conference of, 274
as forum for North–South dialogue,
265–266
and price stabilization, 277–279

United Nations Development Program
(UNDP), 134, 138, 282
United Nations Educations, Scientific and
Cultural Organization (UNESCO),
173, 527
United Nations Emergency Force (UNEF),
167, 168, 514–515
United Nations Fund for Population activities
(UNFPA), 158
United Nations Interim Force in Lebanon
(UNIFIL), 168
United Nations Law of the Sea Conference,
265
United Nations Military Observer Group in
India and Pakistan (UNMOGIP),
514
United Nations Operation in the Congo
(UNOC), 167, 168
United Nations Truce Supervision
Organization (UNTSO), 514
United States. *See also* Cold War
aging of, 322
and Baker initiative, 291–292
balance-of-payments deficits in, 224
balance of trade in, 224
bilateral and unilateral initiatives in,
248–250
and Brady initiative, 293
budget deficit of, 229
challenge to leadership of and liberal trade
regime, 245–250
commercial relations with Soviet Union,
254
and control of United Nations purse strings,
168–172
and crisis over Kuwait, 381–382
as debtor nation, 229
decline in productivity, 249
dependence of, on foreign energy sources,
230
development of oil–based technologies in,
345–346
and development of strategic petroleum
reserves, 364
economic sanctions against Poland and
Soviet Union in 1981, 379–380
economic sanctions against South Africa
over *Apartheid*, 380–381
economic sanctions against Soviet Union
over Afghanistan intervention, 379
exports to Japan, 246n
food exports of, 246–247

energy efficiency of, 344, 345
energy policy in, 337
farm support program in, 248
granting of most-favored-nation trade status
    to Soviet Union, 257
hegemonic leadership role of, 216
immigration into, 314, 315
impact of oil shocks on, 225, 227–230
imperialism of, 121
imports from Japan, 246n
interest rate in, 227, 229
leadership role of, 215, 224–225
    in creating liberal trade regime, 241,
        243–245
and membership in affiliated agencies,
        172–174
motives for arms trade, 400–401
move toward zero-population growth, 321
as natural gas market, 370
nuclear arsenal of, 403
oil consumption in, 346–347, 349–350,
    352–353
oil import vulnerability and dependence,
    359–360
oil production in, 349–350, 353
population growth of, 300–301, 303
position in steel and automobile industries,
    232n
position of, in United Nations, 162–166
post–World War II leadership role of, 221
preference for open economy, 214
problem of illegal aliens, 314
and redefining the post–Cold War security
    environment, 429
role of
    in Bretton Woods Regime, 219, 221–225,
        243–244
    in shaping OPEC, 349–350
    in United Nations peacekeeping
        operations, 166–167
    in world political economy, 216–218
role of geopolitics in shaping foreign policy
    of, 61
share of gross world product, 216
Soviet misperceptions of, as cause of Cold
    War, 88–90
and sponsorship of Coordinating
    Committee (Cocom), 256
strategy of, in the New World Order,
    430–431
as superpower, 63
support for SDI, 424

trade negotiations between Japan and,
    249–250
and tying of foreign aid to purchases,
    283–284
use of economic sanctions by, 378–382
use of show of force by, 457
and use of veto in United Nations, 162
vulnerability of economy to foreign financial
    stocks, 221
U.S. Agency for International Development,
    152
U.S. Arms Control and Disarmament
    Agency, 151
U.S. bilateral and unilateral initiatives,
    248–250
U.S.-Canada Free Trade Agreement (1988),
    250
U.S. Commission on Long-Term Strategy, 425
U.S. dollar
    appreciation of, 227, 229
    economic role of, 219
    exchange rate of, and the trade deficit, 249
    and Marshall Plan, 219, 221
    and the Plaza agreement, 229–230
    value of, 228, 229
U.S.-Russian alliance, prospect of, 425, 428
U.S.-Soviet Chemical Weapons Destruction
    Agreement (June 1990), 487
U.S.-Soviet Convention Arms Transfer Talks
    (CATT), 406
Uniting for Peace, 167
    resolution, 514
Universal Declaration of Human Rights
    (1948), 499
Universal Post Union (1874), 526
Uranium, in nuclear energy production, 372n
Urbanization, as global phenomenon, 320
Uruguay, government in, 68
Uruguay Round, 237n, 243, 246–250, 274
    fair trade, 246–247
    free trade, 246–247
    U.S. bilateral and unilateral initiatives,
        248–250
    and voluntary export restrictions, 236–237,
        240, 247–248

Venezuela, debt payment by, 293
Versailles, Treaty of (1919), 77, 79, 80, 125,
    507
Vertical proliferation, 407–411
Vienna Convention on Protection of the
    Ozone Layer (1985), 336

Vietnam War, impact of, on handling of
    Kuwait crisis, 52
Violence, breeding of, by violence, 451
Violent conflict, human tragedy in, 464–465
Voluntary export restraints (VERs), 236–237,
    240, 247

Waldheim, Kurt, 520
Wallace, Henry A., 89n
Wallerstein, Immanuel, 36, 144
War
    causes of, 442–453
    comparison with conflict, 436n
    cycles of, 451–453
    definition of, 436
    destructiveness of, 439–442
    diversionary theory of, 461–462
    evolving laws of, 507–510
    frequency of, 436–438
    geographical confinement of, 439–440
    and human nature, 442–443
    impact of military capabilities on nature of,
        404
    internal characteristics and involvement,
        443–450
    legal control of, 505–510
    nature of, 438–442
    obsolescence of, 539
    preparation for wrong, 540–541
    refugees as byproducts of, 312
    rules for conduct of, 509–510
    as turning points in international politics, 5,
        19, 437
    weapons and the obsolescence of Great-
        power, 440–442
    and weapons proliferation, 482–484
Warsaw Pact, 103, 253, 392, 476, 523
Warsaw Treaty Organization (WTO), 95
War weariness hypothesis, 452
Washington Naval Conferences (1921–1922),
    21, 79, 485
Washington Summit (1992), 492–493
Wealth, global disparities in, 127–145
Weapons. See also Arms control
    advances in, 6
    controlling proliferation of, 482–484
    destructiveness of modern, 439
    trends in, 402–405
West
    historical perspective of commercial ties
        with East, 256–258
    isolation of, East from, 256

Western European Union (WEU), 187
West Germany, integration of East Germany
    into economy of, 259
West Pakistan, 126
Wilhelm II, 58, 61, 75
Wilson, Woodrow, 22, 125
    Fourteen Points speech of, 22, 79
Women, status of, and family size, 311
World Bank, 218–219, 220
    as foreign aid donor, 280, 282
    Soviet interest in membership in, 259
World Commission on Environment and
        Development, and the Brundtland
        Commission, 335
World Court, 512
    jurisdiction of, 512
    weaknesses of, 512–513
World Disarmament Conference (1932), 484n
World economy, rate of expansion, 344
World federalism, 525
World order, and international law, 498–512
World political economy
    effects of OPEC oil shocks on, 225, 227–230
    national economies, 210–218
    role of U.S. in, 216–218, 224
World politics
    analytical challenge in, 38
    continuity and change in, 4–6
    ecological perspective on, 297
    future of, 544–545
    hierarchies in, 6
    image and reality in, 11–15
    images of reality in, 16–17
    levels-of-analysis issue in study of,
        37–38
    nonstate actors in, 154–205
    power in, 391–395
    quest for theory, 18–34
    role of images in, 17
    science of, 26–27
    sources of image change, 18
    in world of change, 34–38
World system theory, 28–29, 36
    of economic development, 144–145
    on new imperialism, 123–124
World trade
    correlation between global welfare and,
        232–233
    importance of United States in, 241, 243
    transformation of the, 241, 243–251
World view
    complex interdependence as a, 31–32

idealist, 20–21
realist, 22–25
World violence, other modes of, 453–465
World War I, 73–74
causes of, 74–77
consequences of, 77–79
as inadvertent war, 74
as rational choice, 75–76
use of chemical weapons in, 405
World War II, 79
causes of, 79–83
consequences of, 83–85
losses in, 17
use of unconventional weapons in, 405
Worldwatch Institute, 140*n*

Yalta, 83

Yeltsin, Boris, 107
meeting with George Bush, 492–493
Yemen, government in, 69
Yom Kippur War (1973), 341, 362, 375
and use of oil as weapon, 348
Yugoslavia
civil war in, 186–187, 524
origin of, post–World War I, 77

Zaire, 126
government in, 68
Zeitgeist debate, versus great man, 60
Zero population growth
move toward in First World, 305–306
U.S. move toward, 321
Zionism, 449
United Nations position on, 165–166
Zubok, Vladislav, 109